Characteristics of Behavior Disorders of Children and Youth

Fourth Edition

James M. Kauffman
UNIVERSITY OF VIRGINIA

MERRILL PUBLISHING COMPANY
A Bell & Howell Information Company
Columbus ☐ London ☐ Toronto ☐ Melbourne

Cover Art: Michael Linley

Published by Merrill Publishing Company
A Bell & Howell Information Company
Columbus, Ohio 43216

This book was set in Garamond.

Administrative Editor: Vicki Knight
Production Coordinator: Molly Kyle
Art Coordinator: Vincent Smith
Cover Design Coordinator: Cathy Watterson

Chapter opening photos: chapters 1, 4, 16, 18, Bruce Johnson/Merrill; chapters 3, 13, Gail Meese/Merrill; chapter 5, Kevin Fitzsimons/Merrill; chapter 6, Jean Greenwald/Merrill; chapter 7, Courtesy Pro-Ed Inc.; chapter 8, Lloyd Lemmerman/ Merrill; chapters 9, 14, Gale Zucker; chapter 10, Mike Penney; chapters 11, 12, David Strickler; chapter 15, Michael Siluk; chapter 17, Mark Freado; chapter 19, Susan Hartley.
Part opening photos: Part One — *top,* Andy Brunk/Merrill; *middle,* David Strickler; *bottom,* Jo Hall/Merrill; Part Two — *top, middle,* Kevin Fitzsimons/Merrill; *bottom,* Bruce Johnson/Merrill; Part Three — *top,* Gail Meese/Merrill; *middle,* Tom Hubbard/Merrill; *bottom,* Gale Zucker; Part Four — *top,* Mike Penney; *middle,* Paul Conklin; *bottom,* Bruce Johnson/Merrill; Part Five — *top,* Susan Hartley; *middle,* Kevin Fitzsimons/Merrill; *bottom,* Bruce Johnson/Merrill.

Library of Congress Catalog Card Number: 88-61925
International Standard Book Number: 0-675-21032-1
Printed in the United States of America
3 4 5 6 7 8 9 — 93 92 91 90

For my children, Tim and Missy

Preface

This book, like the earlier editions, is intended primarily as an introductory text in special education for children and youth with behavior disorders (those called "seriously emotionally disturbed" in federal regulations). Because behavior disorders are commonly observed in children and youth receiving special education regardless of their categorical designations, the book will also be of value in courses dealing with characteristics of mental retardation, learning disabilities, and other handicapping conditions. Students in school psychology, educational psychology, or abnormal child psychology may also find the book useful.

Users of previous editions will notice several new features in the fourth edition. Study questions at the beginning of each chapter help students read for a more specific purpose and with better understanding. Chapter summaries give more complete recapitulations of basic concepts. Vignettes and essays heighten interest and amplify concepts. In addition to extensive updating throughout, the book is newly organized and has several new chapters. The fourth edition's new and expanded coverage includes chapters on prevalence, conceptual models, screening, evaluation, classification, cultural causal factors, and covert antisocial behavior, and sections have been added to the topics of substance abuse, depression, and suicide.

The organization of this book differs noticeably from that of most alternative texts. The emphasis is on clear description of disordered behavior and research of factors implicated in its development. Unlike other texts in this discipline, this book is not organized around theoretical models or psychiatric classifications but around basic concepts related to disordered behavior: the nature, extent, and history of the problem and conceptual approaches to it; assessment of the problem; major causal factors; the many facets of disordered behavior; and a personal statement about teaching pupils whose behavior is disordered. This organization, I hope, encourages students to become critical thinkers and problem solvers.

Part One introduces major concepts and historical antecedents of contemporary special education for students with behavioral disorders. Chapter 1 begins with a series of vignettes to orient the reader to the characteristics of children and youth with behavioral disorders and the ways they disturb others. We then discuss problems in defining behavior disorders, with emphasis on the special difficulties of educational definitions. In Chapter 2, prevalence of behavior disorders is discussed from a conceptual problem-solving perspective rather than as an exercise in memory of facts and figures. Chapter 3 traces the growth of the field—how it grew out of the disciplines of psychology, psychiatry, and public education—and summarizes major current trends. Chapter 4 summarizes major conceptual models that guide thinking about educating youngsters who have behavior disorders and provides a sketch of the conceptual model underlying the orientation of the book.

Part Two deals with procedures and problems in assessing disordered behavior. Chapter 5 reviews screening procedures and the problems in effectively and efficiently screening student populations. Chapter 6 takes up the topics of evaluation for eligibility and intervention, with attention to social validation and the IEP. In Chapter 7, approaches to classification of disorders are discussed, with major emphasis on behavioral dimensions derived from factor analytic studies.

Part Three concerns the origins of disordered behavior, with attention to the implications of causal factors for special educators. Chapter 8 discusses biological factors; Chapter 9 summarizes research on the role of the family; Chapter 10, the influence of the school; and Chapter 11, cultural factors. Each chapter integrates current research findings that may help us understand why children and youth become disturbed and what preventive actions might be taken.

Specific types of disorders are discussed in Part Four. The chapters are organized around major behavioral dimensions derived from factor analyses of behavioral ratings by teachers and parents. While no categorical scheme suggests an unambiguous way to group all types of behavior disorders, I have tried to devote chapters to behavioral dimensions that have emerged most consistently from empirical work. Each chapter is organized into discussions of definition and prevalence, causal factors and prevention, assessment, and intervention and education for specific types of problems, and each emphasizes issues germane to special education.

Part Five contains only one chapter, my synthesis of the preceding material from a teacher's perspective. This is a personal statement, and it is intended only to suggest some basic assumptions about teaching students who exhibit troublesome behavior.

Several comments are necessary to clarify my intent in writing this book. First, developmental processes are an important concern. I have tried to integrate the most relevant parts of the vast and scattered literature on child development and relate these to behavior disorders of children and youth. In struggling with this task, I have attempted not only to summarize what is known about why disordered behavior develops but also to suggest how behavioral development can be influenced for the better. Second, in concentrating primarily on research and theory grounded in replicable experimental data, I have revealed a bias toward a social learning viewpoint. I believe that when we examine the literature with a willingness to be swayed by empirical evidence rather than by devotion to humanistic ideology alone, then a social learning bias is understandable. Third, this book is not a comprehensive treatment of the subject of behavior disorders. An introductory book must leave much unsaid · and many loose ends that need tying up. Unquestionably, the easiest thing about writing this book was to let it fall short of saying it all and hope that readers will pursue the information in the works cited in the references.

I have tried to address the interests and concerns of teachers and of students preparing to become teachers. Consequently, I have described many interventions briefly, particularly in the chapters in Part Four. I emphasize, however, that this text does not provide the details of educational methods and behavioral interventions that are necessary for implementation by teachers. This is not a methods or how-to-do-it book.

Any shortcomings of this book are my responsibility alone. I am grateful to the reviewers of the third edition, who offered advance suggestions for the fourth, and to the reviewers of the manuscript of the fourth edition for their careful reading and many helpful comments. The perceptive suggestions of Jane Nowacek and Kathy McGee, University of Virginia; Jeanne M. Bauwens, Boise State University; David L. Gast, University of Kentucky; James Krouse, Clarion University; Joy Rogers, Loyola University of Chicago; Qaisar Sultana, Eastern Kentucky University; and Philip Swicegood, Sam Houston State University, resulted in significant improvements in every chapter. I am particularly grateful to Kathy McGee for her assistance in searching for and copying references and requesting permission to reprint material from other sources.

J. M. K.
Charlottesville, VA

Contents

PART ONE

The Problem
and Its History

Definition: The Nature of the Problem

As you read this chapter, keep these guiding questions in mind:

☐ Why should a behavior disorder be considered a handicap?

☐ What is the difference between behavior disorder and serious emotional disturbance?

☐ What criteria should one use in deciding that behavior is disordered or abnormal?

☐ Why is defining behavior disorders so difficult?

☐ How is the current federal definition inconsistent with Bower's research and his intention in writing a definition?

☐ Why is the judgment of teachers or a multidisciplinary team a necessary part of any school-based definition of behavior disorder?

This book is about children and youth who arouse negative feelings and induce negative behavior in others. They are not often popular or leaders among their peers. Typically, they experience academic failure in addition to social rejection or alienation. Most adults choose to avoid them as much as possible. Their behavior is so persistently irritating to authority figures that they seem to be asking for punishment or rebuke. Even in their own eyes, these children and youth are usually failures; they obtain little gratification from life and repeatedly fall short of their aspirations. They are handicapped; compared to nonhandicapped individuals, their options in important aspects of daily living are highly restricted. Their handicaps are the result of their behavior, which is discordant with their social-interpersonal environments; their behavior costs them many opportunities for gratifying social interaction and self-fulfillment.

VARIETY OF LABELS

This book is about children and youth who are usually called *emotionally disturbed* or *behaviorally disordered*. We use the terms *emotionally disturbed* (or simply *disturbed*) and *behaviorally disordered* interchangeably throughout this book because the terminology of the field is in a period of transition. "Seriously emotionally disturbed" is the label currently used in federal legislation and regulations regarding special education. "Behaviorally disordered" is the term preferred by many professionals in the field of special education, however, because it is a more accurate descriptor of the socialization difficulties of children and youth (Huntze, 1985; Lloyd, Kauffman, & Gansneder, 1987; Walker, 1982; Wood, 1987a). "Behaviorally disordered" also seems to be a less stigmatizing label than "emotionally disturbed" (Feldman, Kinnison, Jay, & Harth, 1983; Smith, Wood, & Grimes, in press). Yet in the professional literature and in the laws and regulations of various states, many additional terms refer to the same population. For the most part, these terms are combinations of one of the terms from column A and another from column B in Table 1.1. Thus, in a given state, the label may be *emotionally handicapped* or *emotionally impaired,* while in another it may be *behaviorally impaired.* Occasionally combinations of two words from column A appear with one from column B—*socially and emotionally maladjusted, socially and emotionally disturbed, personally and socially maladjusted,* and so on. The point is that the terminology of the field is confused—sometimes, it seems as confused as the children and youth to whom we apply the labels (Kauffman, 1986a).

TABLE 1.1
Combinations of Terms

Column A	Column B
Emotionally	Disturbed
Behaviorally	Disordered
Socially	Maladjusted
Personally	Handicapped
	Conflicted
	Impaired

DEVELOPMENTAL NORMS VERSUS SOCIOCULTURAL EXPECTATIONS

Some of the behaviors that handicapped children and youth exhibit are recognized as abnormal in nearly every cultural group and social stratum. Muteness, serious self-injury, the eating of feces, and murder are examples of disorders that are seldom or never considered culture-specific. These disordered behaviors represent discrepancies from universally accepted developmental norms. On the other hand, children and youth are often handicapped simply because their behavior violates standards peculiar to their culture or the social institutions in their environment, such as their school. Academic achievement, various types of aggression, sexual behavior, language patterns, and so on will be judged deviant or normal depending on the prevailing attitudes in the individual's ethnic and religious group, family, and school. Failing to read, hitting others, taking others' belongings, masturbating, and swearing, for example, are evaluated according to the standards of the child's community. Thus a given act or pattern of behavior may be considered disordered or deviant in one situation or context, but not in another—simply because of differences in the expectations of the people with whom the child or youth lives. The majority of behavioral disorders are defined by such sociocultural expectations, not by universal developmental norms. Research now indicates, however, that behaviors violating some sociocultural expectations may also signify developmental difficulties. Hyperaggression and covert antisocial behavior, for example, are disorders of conduct that not only violate social expectations but also create developmental risk (Kazdin, 1987; Walker, Shinn, O'Neill, & Ramsey, 1987).

BEHAVIOR SHAPED BY ITS SOCIAL CONTEXT (ECOLOGY)

Many behavior disorders, though not all, originate or are made worse by the child's or youth's social interactions. The disorders are learned through modeling, reinforcement, extinction, and punishment—learning processes that shape and maintain much of everyone's behavior, both normal and deviant (Bandura, 1986). Adults and youngsters in the child's or youth's environment may accidentally arrange conditions that cause and support undesirable, inappropriate behavior. Ironically, the same adults who unwittingly shape inappropriate behavior may then initiate action to have the child or youth labeled "disturbed," "disordered," or "maladjusted." The child or youth might behave quite differently if these adults changed their own behavior in relation to the youngster's, or if he or she were placed in a different social environment. The problem in these cases is partly, and sometimes mostly, in the caretakers' or peers' behavior.

One might be tempted to conclude that the disturbed child or youth is not "to blame" for the way others react. But youngsters' behavior influences the actions of their parents, their teachers, their peers, and others who interact with them. Children "teach" their parents, teachers, and peers how to behave toward them as surely as they are taught by these others (Bell & Harper, 1977; Emery, Binkoff, Houts, & Carr, 1983). It is not appropriate to ascribe "fault" exclusively to either the youngster with a behavioral disorder or to others in the environment. Teaching and learning are interactive processes in which teacher and learner frequently, and often subtly, ex-

5

change roles. When a youngster has difficulty with teachers, peers, or parents, it is as important to consider their responses to the behavior as it is to evaluate the youngster's reactions to others. It is not surprising, therefore, that an ecological perspective on the problem of disordered behavior has become popular.

An ecological perspective takes into account the interrelationships between the child or youth and various aspects of the environment. The problem of disturbed behavior is not viewed simply as a youngster's inappropriate actions but, rather, as undesirable *interactions* and *transactions* between the youngster and other people. For example, a child's temper tantrums in school could indeed be a problem. An ecological perspective demands that the behavior of the child's teachers, peers, and parents—their expectations, demands, and reactions to the child's tantrums and other behavior—be taken into consideration to explain and deal with the problem.

TYPES OF DISORDERS AND CAUSES

The environmental conditions under which children and youth display disordered behavior vary widely. Some youngsters endure extremely adverse circumstances, including abuse, neglect, and pervasive disadvantage, without becoming disturbed; others succumb to adverse circumstances; and some become disturbed in environments that are clearly conducive to normal development.

Although environmental conditions affect how children and youth behave, biological factors also exert a strong influence. Why some children are relatively vulnerable and others invulnerable to environmental conditions is not known (Rutter, 1985). A wide variety of causal factors may give rise to a wide variety of behavior disorders, and the relationships among causes and disorders is exceedingly complex, as will become apparent in subsequent chapters. We can seldom determine the cause of the disorder in individual cases.

EXAMPLES OF DISORDERED BEHAVIOR

There are many specific ways that children and youth can cause negative feelings and reactions in others. As we will see in following chapters, disordered behavior may be described according to two primary dimensions: *externalizing* (aggressive, acting-out behavior) and *internalizing* (social withdrawal). The following cases illustrate the range in types of behavioral disorders and the variety of factors that can cause children and youth to become disturbed. We have chosen these examples to show that disordered behavior has been reported in the literature of earlier centuries as well as in current writings; it appears in young children as well as adolescents; it is exhibited by individuals who have grown up in privileged homes of caring parents as well as by those who have been reared in poverty or under abusive conditions; it is often accompanied by lower than average intelligence but sometimes by intellectual brilliance; it may be characterized by externalizing (acting out) or internalizing (withdrawn) behavior or alternation between the two; and it may be described from the perspective of an observer or of the self. Note too that behavior disorders of every type can be found in both males and females and in all racial and ethnic groups.

Nevertheless, as we shall see in other chapters, behavior disorders are not equally prevalent among all categories of individuals; some groups are more prone than others to some disorders.

In the case of Tony, notice that the youth's disordered behavior obviously is disturbing to the community, is of long standing, has been resistant to intervention by a variety of individuals (including teachers), and seems related to adverse environmental conditions.

Tony

When he was 8, Tony Singleton [not his real name] was getting high on dope and booze he says he stole from his mother.

At 14, he was incarcerated after being convicted of breaking and entering, and petit larceny.

When, as a 17-year-old, he attacked two women near the University of Virginia, authorities decided juvenile court was no longer appropriate. And, in February, a Charlottesville Circuit judge sentenced 18-year-old Singleton to 11 years behind bars.

Court documents based on statements by Singleton and interviews with people who have tried to help him produce a picture of a troubled youth who throughout his short life has received services from an assortment of psychologists, social workers, probation officers and teachers. . . .

A psychiatric evaluation of Singleton prepared this year by Park E. Dietz of the Forensic Psychiatry Clinic at the University of Virginia paints a portrait of a confused and desperate young man. Singleton told Dietz he was neglected by his mother, a local plant worker who was often away from home. She never married Singleton's father but lived with a succession of boyfriends, one of whom would regularly beat Singleton.

Singleton said his mother had "reefer," or marijuana, and at a very young age he began to steal both "reefer" and money from her.

He said he sometimes smoked the dope. Other times he sold it to kids on the streets of Charlottesville.

Between 1974 and 1976, the Charlottesville Social Services Department, which investigates complaints of abused and neglected children, received reports that Singleton, between 5 and 7 years old at the time, was not properly cared for.

A worker from the department observed that Singleton's mother left him free to roam. While unsupervised, he would break into cars and houses. Singleton was not properly dressed and occasionally slept outdoors.

Social workers arranged to have Singleton taken from his mother and placed with his paternal grandmother.

The grandmother lived in a three-bedroom house with 11 other people, including a mentally retarded daughter.

A probation officer who visited the home in 1983 described it:

"There was no front doorknob on the inside of the front door. She (the grandmother) has a rug pushed up against the door to prevent cold air from coming inside as the door does not meet the base of the frame tightly.

"The blue walls have a few holes in them and the drapes are falling down. (Her) clothes hang on a clothesline which extends along the wall of her living room. . . . A foul odor permeates the air. . . . She sleeps in the den on a sofa."

When Singleton entered school, a psychologist found the youngster was functioning below average. Almost a decade later, Singleton, 15 at the time, was reading and doing arithmetic at the fifth grade level.

Singleton was placed in special education classes at Burnley-Moran Elementary and Buford Middle schools.

A Buford teacher described him as "desperate for friends but . . . has difficulty establishing relationships."

Schoolmates teased him about his unpleasant odor, caused by bedwetting.

To avoid the taunts, Singleton built a partition around his desk.

Early in 1983, Singleton was convicted of burglary and theft and placed on probation.

While on probation, he violated curfew and exhibited behavior problems, and was placed in the Boys Attention Home, a house in Charlottesville for juveniles whose next step into the juvenile justice system would place them in a more restrictive state learning center.

His probation officer said that while Singleton was there he "refused to follow rules or complete chores and on several occasions left the program without permission."

He was transferred that summer to the Barrett Learning Center, a state juvenile detention facility in Hanover.

Authorities there initially noticed gradual improvement in Singleton's behavior. But eventually, he started cursing the staff and breaking the rules daily. . . . (McHugh, 1987, pp. A1, A6)

The news story goes on to describe Tony's medical problems—surgery to correct an undescended testicle and a low level of the sex hormone testosterone—as well as his involvement in robbery and attempted rape. In Tony's case we see obvious factors contributing to his troublesome behavior. At first glance, at least, his behavior seems less puzzling than Mark's (whose story follows) because we understand how an unfavorable environment and physical problems can make a child want to strike out at others. It is harder to understand the hostility or nastiness of a youth who has been reared in an economically privileged environment. We find fewer ready explanations for a "chip on the shoulder" attitude, particularly when the youth is blessed with intellectual superiority in addition to economic advantage.

Mark

The nervous, anxious, and seemingly hostile adolescent sat on the far side of the 6-foot classroom table. He fingered a pack of Marlboros, turning them over and over. His concentration was intense, unrelenting, compulsive, almost as if he hoped, by concentrating on the cigarettes, to direct the thoughts of the alternative school's staff away from him.

At first glance, he looked more like a candidate for admission to one of the better prep schools than for a slot in an alternative program. He was wearing a blue, oxford-cloth shirt, cream-colored cords, and docksiders. He hadn't bothered to tuck the shirt in and one button too many had been left open. His fine blond hair was just a little too long. (It would become a badge of honor during the year and an excuse for not seeking employment.) . . .

He arrived at school early enough on the first day to claim the coveted last desk in the last row. He systematically walled in his space. The back of his chair was always against the classroom wall. Books, papers, pencils, pens; anything he owned was strewn, like a fortress, on the floor around his desk. . . .

Mark was maniacal about keeping his space for himself. He wanted no one near him and would become verbally abusive if anyone touched him. He was struggling for attention, and at the same time refusing to accept it.

Mark's verbal contortions ranged from sophisticated wit to murderous descriptions of the ways he would eliminate his prime adversary in the classroom (me) to new and unheard of vulgarities.

When a very slow student in the class was awed on learning that Mark lived in the best section of town, he explained that the only difference was that Perrier® came out of the Matthews' faucets.

At least once a day he would consider himself victimized, and me the victimizer. Requests for classwork were considered irrational. Requests for a halt to a variety of obscenities were considered unfounded. Any request that required some form of cooperation was considered untimely. After refusing to participate, Mark would offer vivid details on his latest plan for my elimination. These would often come after I would reach out to him and especially after I would try to touch him.

Mark created many new vulgarities and embellished old ones with disarmingly picturesque terms. The adults associated with the program were well over 30 and none of us had heard many of Mark's vulgarities. One staff member began compiling a working dictionary of Mark's barbarisms. . . .

He was often sent to the solitary confinement of "the cubicle" to stop his disruption of the class and permit other students to work. I spent hours there with him looking at and talking to the hurt, intelligent eyes of a superior being. Repeatedly, he rejected verbal or physical contact.

As the school year drew to a close, his nervous, compulsive, repetitive behavior intensified. Even while sitting still, he seemed to be pacing the walls in the parameters of his being. His concentrated mental isometrics were increasingly painful, trying, and irrational. . . . (Maruskin-Mott, 1986, p. 53)

We are tempted to see students like Mark as products of our time. They appear to be victims of the hidden stresses of modern life or products of economically privileged but emotionally destructive families (which confuse the child with conflicting and inconsistent messages). But similar cases and identical explanations (the heightened levels of stress in contemporary life) were being presented in the literature many years ago (see Kauffman, 1976). Consider the case of N. B., presented a century and a half ago.

N. B.

N. B., aged 16, was described to me by his father, who came to consult me, in regard to his management, as a boy of singularly unruly and intractable character; selfish, wayward, violent without ground or motive, and liable under the paroxysm of his moodiness to do personal mischief to others; not, however, of a physically bold character. He is of a fair understanding, and exhibits considerable acuteness in sophisticated apologies for his wayward conduct. He has made little progress in any kind of study. His fancy is vivid, supplying him profusely with sarcastic imagery. He has been subjected at different times, and equally without effect, to a firmly mild and to a rigid discipline. In the course of these measures, solitary confinement has been tried; but to this he was impassive. It produced no effect.

He was last in a very good seminary in a town in —, where he drew a knife upon one of the officers of the establishment, while admonishing him; and produced a deep feeling of aversion in the minds of his companions, by the undisguised pleasure which he showed at some bloodshed which took place in this town during the disturbance of 18– –.

He has not appeared to be sensually disposed, and he is careful of property. His bodily health is good, and he has never had any cerebral affection. This boy was further described to me as progressively becoming worse in his conduct, and more savagely violent to his relatives. Still I easily discovered that he was unfavourably situated; for his relations appeared to be at once irritable and affectionate; and the total failure of various plans of education was throwing him entirely upon their hands.

As an instance of the miserable pleasure which he took in exciting disgust and pain, I was told, that when 13 years old, he stripped himself naked and exposed himself to his sisters. (Mayo, 1839, pp. 68–69)

Behavior disorders typically call to mind the externalizing behavior of boys, and indeed the most typical child or youth with a behavior disorder is an acting-out male. Professionals and the public are becoming increasingly aware, however, that behavior disorders occur among girls and that internalizing behavior can be extremely serious in its consequences. Eating disorders (particularly **anorexia** and **bulimia**), which are most common among adolescent girls, have received much attention in the professional literature and the popular press in recent years. The case of Lynn is rather typical.

Lynn

Lynn was 12¼ years old when she was admitted to the Children's Hospital Medical Center in Cincinnati with *marasmus,* shock, and a weight of 16.6 kg [about 36.5 lb]. Through dieting, she had lost 44 percent of her premorbid weight, down to 36¾ pounds, which represented 55 percent of her ideal body weight for height and age. She was admitted to the Intensive Care Unit, where she was incoherent, confused, hypothermic, drowsy, and depressed. She shunned all oral intake, and denied she had a medical or psychiatric problem. She admitted feeling fat, despite everyone's telling her she was emaciated. (Maloney, Pettigrew, & Farrell, 1983, p. 54)

By the time a youngster reaches adolescence, his or her disordered behavior is often of long standing, although this is not always the case. Children may begin exhibiting disordered behavior at a very early age. When the onset of troublesome behavior occurs during the preschool years, the child is often found to have a serious disorder such as **autism** or **schizophrenia**. Brady is typical of children diagnosed as **autistic**.

Brady

At first sight, Brady looks like he should be selling corn flakes on television commercials. He is a beautiful 4-year-old with huge brown eyes, curly brown hair, and delicate bone structure. Yet, one only needs to observe him for a few minutes until the bizarre behavior so characteristic of autism becomes evident.

Brady was adopted at the age of 6 weeks by his present parents. He has always enjoyed very good health although he is a poor eater and remains quite thin. His physical development has been unremarkable except for a delay in standing and walking. While walking was delayed, his mother reports that at 19 months he just "stood up and walked." He never went through the toddler stage. Once walking, Brady could run, jump, and balance himself with apparent ease. He is now very agile and can, according to his mother, "run full speed on the top of a narrow fence."

Brady's mother first became concerned when the boy actively resisted affection. Typically, he would not allow anyone to hold or cuddle him and, when people made such overtures toward him, he stiffened, pushed away, and screamed. On those rare occasions when he would allow his mother to hold him, he did so passively, not holding her in return. He was like a limp rag doll. As might be expected, Brady was a very "good" baby. He never demanded attention, did not cry for his mother, and was most content when left alone. Even now he will wander off by himself, away from the family, and remain isolated for as long as possible. He does not interact with peers and actively withdraws from social initiations of other children. . . .

Brady did not speak until the age of 3. At first he used words such as "ma ma" and "da da" but he used them indiscriminately, apparently unable to tie them to the correct referents. As his speech increased, it was entirely **echolalic**. He presently engages in a great deal of immediate and delayed **echolalia**, all with minimal communicative intent. He can label objects and pictures, but does so in an echolalic fashion. For example, when presented with a picture of a truck, he may say "What is this, Brady? It's a truck. That's good, Brady." The truck picture triggers a delayed echolalic response. His receptive language is somewhat more advanced than his expressive language. Although he typically echoes questions and commands, he can comply with simple requests, such as to answer his name or sit in a chair. . . .

Brady's affect is typical of many autistic children in that it seems unrelated to the environmental context. He swings from laughter to tearful sobs almost instantaneously and without apparent reason. He laughs quite frequently while staring into space and also laughs when punished. He also seems unable to understand or respond to the emotional behavior of others. Thus, he seems truly isolated from the social environment. (From "Infantile Autism" by L. Schreibman & J. I. Mills, in T. H. Ollendick & M. Hersen (Eds.), *Handbook of Child Psychopathology*. Copyright © 1983 by Plenum. Reprinted with permission.)

In addition to the characteristics already noted, Schreibman and Mills (1983) describe Brady's excessive concern for maintaining sameness in his environment, his **self-stimulation**, and his inconsistent and uneven pattern of abilities and performances on tests. While Brady's behavior is characteristic of children with autism, it is not the pattern of behavior we see in all young children with disordered behavior. Consider the case of Frankie, who exhibited disordered behavior of a very different sort at the age of 4 years.

Frankie

At age four, Frankie was referred to a therapeutic preschool program by his day care center. He had been expelled from the center for severe behavior problems, disobedience, tantrums, hurting other children, and disrupting the program. At the home he shared with his 18-year-old mother and alcoholic grandmother, Frankie deliberately drank charcoal starter fluid. At first his mother denied that Frankie had problems. Gradually, she responded to the staff and parents at the therapeutic preschool, and Frankie began to change his behavior. (Knitzer, 1982, pp. 3–4)

Disturbed children and youth usually present problems to many of the people with whom they have contact. Most relevant to the focus of this book are the difficulties they cause teachers and peers at school. All veteran teachers of students with behavior disorders recall incidents in which the pupils defeated their best efforts to instruct or maintain order. In many cases, teachers marvel at the wild antics of their students or the seemingly unsolvable puzzle their behavior presents. And, in retrospect, many leading experts are amused by their naiveté—which sometimes served them well and sometimes was disastrous—in dealing with students who are difficult to manage and teach (see Foster, 1986; Kauffman & Lewis, 1974; Patton, Payne, Kauffman, Brown, & Payne, 1987). Pearl Berkowitz, an important figure in the development of special education for students with behavior disorders, relates some of her early experiences as follows.

Pearl Berkowitz

If you could look back and focus on my most vivid memory, you might see me, now the teacher in Mrs. Wright's former classroom, futilely hovering over two hyperactive twelve-year-old girls who are fighting about which one should use the free half of an easel, while on the other side of this easel, a big, burly, belligerent boy is calmly painting, secure in the knowledge that no one would dare question his right to do so. Standing near the window is a small, thin-faced, pale, remote-looking boy who is staring at the fish tank, apparently just watching the fish swim around. Next to him, another boy is sitting on the rocker tickling himself under the chin with the mink tails he has just cut off the collar of the school secretary's new spring coat. Two children, a boy and a girl, perched on the old dining table, are playing a loud game of checkers, while another boy is silently resting, stretched out atop an old upright piano which I had inveigled into my room. Sporadically, in the midst of this magnificent atmosphere for learning, some child says to another, "Your mother," and the entire class seems to leap together and land in a football pile-up on the floor, while I stand helplessly by.

Of course I made many mistakes, but I hope I also learned something from each. Let me share just one of these early mistakes with you. I was doing my weekly planning when a brilliant idea occurred to me. I decided that the greatest contribution I could make that week would be to bring some culture into the lives of those poor, deprived, disturbed children at Bellevue. To start on this enriching experience, I elected to read to them a favorite poem from my own elementary school days, "The Owl and the Pussycat." Imagine my consternation at the chaos I caused when I reached the lines, "What a beautiful pussy you are, you are. What a beautiful pussy you are." The children actually tumbled out of my room with noisy screaming and guffawing. Within minutes, I was left alone in the classroom, bewildered and unaware of what had caused the difficulty. I had a lot to learn. (Berkowitz, 1974, pp. 30–31)

Surprises are part of teaching disturbed children, even after one has been at it many years and become highly skilled; mistakes and disappointments, as well as successes and gratification, are part of the territory. Patricia L. Pullen describes an unexpected response to good teaching procedure with Barry, a 9-year-old youngster who exhibited a variety of problem behaviors.

Patricia L. Pullen

Perhaps my most frustrating and surprising experience with Barry involved an attempt to reinforce him with praise for appropriate behavior. One day as I was working with another group of children across the room I observed him playing quietly and appropriately with a classmate. Because this was something he seldom did that I wanted to encourage, I decided to do what I'd been taught will "reinforce" good behavior. I walked over to Barry, knelt beside him, gave him a hug, and commented, "Barry, I really like the way you're playing quietly with the blocks and having fun with Susie." He looked at me strangely, jumped to his feet, and screamed at me, "Well, fuck you, shitload!" (Patton et al., 1987, p. 30)

When a teacher has success with a student whose disordered behavior has presented major problems, the gratification is enormous. Winfield L. Chadwick, a teacher with experience in both special and general education, provides one such example.

Winfield L. Chadwick

During my second year of teaching emotionally handicapped students, I was assigned an 8th grader whose problem could be best described as "math phobia." He had violent reactions (tantrums, vomiting, etc.) to any and all math assignments. After much counseling and a variety of other interventions, he was turned over to me to "cure." We began at rock bottom; we discussed the problem and possible solutions. But we were getting nowhere. The plan I decided to employ involved implementation of successive approximations of the final goal—to complete a 35-problem math assignment without any complications in the regular classroom. By beginning with just writing numbers, then doing one problem, then two problems, then three, and so on, he eventually was able to complete a 35-problem worksheet in my classroom. But he was still unable to complete an assignment of even 1 or 2 problems in a regular class, so the entire process had to be replicated in the "new" environment as well. All the while, through good and bad times, he was given the support and reinforcement he needed to reach the goal. It took us 3½ months to finally reach our goal, but we did it! The day Robert sat in that 8th grade math class and successfully completed his assignment was a great day for both of us. It seemed like such a small step to most people, but Robert and I knew what a giant step it actually was for him. (Hallahan & Kauffman, 1988, p. 195)

Finally, it is important to consider how disordered behavior looks and feels from the perspective of the child or youth. As Bower (1980, p. 201) notes, "Of all the afflictions to which human beings are heir, none is more difficult to understand, conceptualize, or assess than that called 'emotional.'" Our conceptualizations cannot be complete until we have been able to set aside the analysis of "problem" or "disorder" from the adult's perspective and see it through the child's eyes. We can find many examples of the child's perspective in contemporary literature. Let us consider two examples of the youngster's view of school-related problems taken from the personal retrospectives of two noted special educators, Esther P. Rothman and Sheldon R. Rappaport.

Esther P. Rothman

From the start, I hated school, deeply, irrevocably, and silently. Kindergarten was anathema. Rather than take me to the doctor every other day with sore throats and stomachaches that were strictly school-induced, my mother finally capitulated and let me stay at home. First grade was no better, however, and as my sore "threats" would no longer work, and as the compulsory school laws prevented my mother from withdrawing me, I had no alternative but to start off for school daily and then divert myself to the rocks and crevices that then underlay the Hellsgate Bridge in the new and growing suburb of Queens, twenty minutes away by subway from the lower East Side where I was born.

I wonder if teachers really appreciate how overwhelmingly frightening it is to be a truant. Fear possessed me completely—fear of ridicule by school-loving seatmates, each of whom was smarter than ten of me put together; fear of God, who was certainly going to punish me by striking my parents dead; but, most of all, fear of tongue-lashings by arm-twisting teachers, who were going to debase me by "leaving me back." Which indeed they did. I was a "holdover." My teacher didn't bother to explain to my mother why I was left back, but she clearly told everyone else. I couldn't read. And I couldn't read because I played hooky—or so she said. The fact that I was already reading Hebrew and the exotic adventures of Dickie Dare in my friend Lilly's third-grade reader was totally unknown to my teacher, yet I am certain, even now, that if she had known it, she would not have altered her decision.

My teacher was what I knew she was—anti-Semitic—because my mother told me so. This was a word I learned very early in life, and I accepted it casually as I accepted being an alien, one of only four Jewish children in the entire school. I felt special—not a bad feeling, but not completely good either.

I was never permitted to hold the American flag in front of the class for our morning class salute—a sacrosanct ceremony in every classroom in the entire school. My shoes were never clean enough. Once I was told I had lice. Or sometimes I did not have a handkerchief safety-pinned to the lower shoulder of my dress; this handkerchief always had to be in that exact same spot—never elsewhere. I never figured out how it was that we were supposed to blow our noses, and I never asked. I settled it myself. I had a handkerchief for showing and a handkerchief for blowing. And usually I forgot one or the other or both deliberately because I firmly believed that good little girls should never need to blow their noses at all. It was too crass. Instead, I stuffed pencil tip erasers up my nostrils. As for boys, I never even wondered what they did. Handkerchiefs were not within their generic classification.

These memories come flooding over me as I write—the hurt of being labeled a liar by a seventh-grade teacher who did not believe I had written a composition using

the word *chaos* because I could not give him a definition of it. Did he never understand that I knew the word chaos down to my very toes because I felt it deeply every
day of my life in school? Then there was the day my fifth-grade teacher threw into the
garbage can the chocolate cake my mother had baked for a class party and which the
children had voted to give to the teacher because it was the prettiest cake of all. And
going farther back, I remember staring at the school map that hung—large, frightening, and overwhelming—from the border of the chalkboard and trying desperately to
find New York State while not another child spoke—every eye, especially the teacher's, was glued to me. But worst of all was the indignity, fear, and humiliation of having to cheat on a test because I could not remember whether four-fifths equalled 80
percent. (Rothman, 1974, pp. 221–222)

Sheldon R. Rappaport

That school day had been like all others—bright with the joy of being with children
and blurred in a kaleidoscope of activity. But in late afternoon, there was something
different in the way Miss Joseph asked us to take our seats. Her customary calm and
warmth were missing. On top of that, she announced that the principal had come to
talk to us. My stomach squinched "danger."

The principal, small, grayed, and austere, spoke in her usual clipped fashion
about the importance of working hard in school. As her train of thought thundered
by, I was aware only of its ominous roar. The meaning of her words did not come
into focus until she made the pronouncement: "Those boys and girls who have frit-
tered away their time, and as a consequence will not be promoted to second grade,
will stand when I call their names." Then she called my name.

The shock and mortification staggered me, making it difficult to struggle out of
my seat and stand beside my desk. Who stood when she called the other names, the
faces of those who remained seated, and what further remarks she intoned all blurred
into a macabre dance that encircled my shame. Breathing was painful and had, I was
sure, a ridiculously loud rasp which was heard by everyone. My legs rebelled at supporting my weight, so my fingers, aching tripods of ice, shared the burden. In contrast
to the cold of my numbed face were the hot tears that welled in my eyes and threatened to spill down my cheeks to complete my degradation.

The principal left. Class was over. Amid joyous shouts, children milled through
the door that for them was the entrance to summer fun and freedom. Some may have
spoken to me, to tease or to console, but I could not hear them. The warm and pretty
Miss Joseph was there, speaking to me, but I could neither hear nor respond. The
borders of my mind had constricted like a hand clutching my pain.

Daily I sat staring at a book that would not surrender to me its meaning. In my
war with the book, now and again I was victorious over an isolated word, but the
endless legion of pages ultimately defeated me. Repeatedly, I looked back over the
unfriendly, unyielding rows of print to find a word that I could recognize. In doing so,
my failures amassed by the minute, like a swelling mob jeering at me. Finally, the fury
rising within me burst from my fists, while from between clenched teeth I silently
cursed the head I was pounding. To me, the immutable reality was that my head was
bad. It caused my frustration. It sponsored my shame. I knew no alternative but to
beat it into becoming a smarter head. That failed, too, adding daily to my feelings of
frustration and worthlessness.

Daily terrors were walking the eight blocks to and from school and going into
the school yard for recess. Being all flab and clumsiness and wearing thick glasses
made me a ready target for any kid who needed to prove his prowess by beating me
up. And the number who needed that were legion. Consequently, a rainy day became

a reprieve. To awaken to a rainy morning was like an eleventh-hour stay of execution. It meant no recess outdoors. And nobody who wanted to fight. But even better than a rainy morning was being ill. Only then, in my bed, in my room, did I feel really secure. In the fall of third grade I missed twenty-two days of school. I was confined to bed with rheumatic fever, as I learned from the family doctor when I didn't have the desired wind for distance running while in college. Despite pains which I can still vividly recall, that confinement is the most peaceful of all my childhood memories.

The only outdoor activities I enjoyed were pretend ones. (The woman who lived in the next row house must have been sainted.) To get me out of the house, my mother put on the open porch the piano stool I played with. It became the steering wheel of a huge, powerful truck (you know how loud they are), which I guided flawlessly along endless highways, gaining the admiration of all whom I passed. At other times, I ventured across the street where the vacant lot became a battlefield on which I, clothed in my father's army tunic and overseas cap, performed feats of heroism and distinction for which I received countless medals and accolades. Those fantasized moments of glory apparently nourished my thin strand of self-respect enough to enable it to withstand the daily siege on my pride.

At night, when the cannonade of derision was still and my imperiled pride temporarily safe, I implored God and the Christ, Jesus, to see to it that tomorrow would not hold for me the tortures of today. I offered all possible concessions and deals, but relentlessly the tomorrows of Monday to Friday were no better. (Rappaport, 1976, pp. 347–350)

Other descriptions of disordered behavior and its treatment are scattered throughout this book. In each case it is important to consider not only the unpleasant or disturbing features of the youngster's behavior, but also the circumstances that may have contributed to the problem and the reactions of others (both peers and adults). Disturbed children and youth should not be viewed merely as youngsters who cause others to experience anger, grief, anxiety, or other unpleasantness. They are troubled as well as troubling, and they must often live in situations that are not conducive to satisfactory interpersonal relations. Teachers must be sensitive to the students' pain, even while they themselves are being pained by the youngsters' misbehavior, puzzling responses, or failures in their classrooms.

PROBLEMS OF DEFINITION

The cases you have read about so far may clearly illustrate what disturbed children and youth can be like; nevertheless, descriptions are not a definition. These youngsters' problems may seem obvious, but the way they should be defined as a group is not obvious. In fact, neither the field of child psychology nor the field of special education has an adequate definition of behavioral disorder (CCBD Executive Committee, 1987; Smith et al., in press).

The children and youth who are the topic of this book etch pictures in one's memory that are not easy to erase. The foregoing discussion and descriptions provide the basis for an intuitive grasp of what a behavior disorder is, but the definition of such a disorder—the construction of guidelines that will foster valid and reliable judgments about who is and who is not disturbed—is anything but simple. One reason it is so difficult to arrive at a reliable definition is that behavioral disorder is not a thing that exists outside a social context, but a label assigned according to cultural rules (Burbach, 1981). Perhaps a science of behavior exists, but the objective methods of natural science play a relatively minor role in designating someone as deviant. Disordered behavior is whatever behavior a culture's chosen authority figures designate as intolerable. Typically, it is behavior that is perceived to threaten the stability, security, or values of that society (Rhodes & Paul, 1978).

Defining "behavioral disorder" or "emotional disturbance" is unavoidably subjective, at least in part. One can be objective and precise in measuring specific responses of individuals, and one can be painstakingly explicit in stating social norms, cultural rules, or community expectations for behavior. But one must ultimately realize that norms, rules, and expectations, and the appraisal of the extent to which particular individuals deviate from them, require subjective judgment. As Rhodes and Paul (1978) state:

> The epiphenomenal problem of deviance is complex and the definitions that exist are many. Each time a group of special children gain social and professional attention, a plethora of definitions of the problems of these children follow. The inconsistency is not, as is typically thought, simply in the definitions, but rather in the primary view of the world from which the definition is derived. (p. 137)

Differences in world views or conceptual models are but one factor in the problem of definition. In addition, problems are created by the differing purposes of definition, by difficulties in measuring behavior, by the range and variability of normal and deviant behavior, by the relationships among behavior disorders and other exceptionalities, by the transience of many behavior problems during human development, and by the disadvantages inherent in labeling deviance.

Differences in Conceptual Models

Before 1950, virtually all interventions with disturbed children and youth were derived from Freudian theory or variations of a psychodynamic model. Within the past four decades, however, a variety of alternative approaches, each associated with a distinctly different conceptual model, have been developed. In addition to the psychodynamic model, biological, sociological, behavioral, ecological, psychoeducational, educational, and phenomenological models have been described (see Bandura, 1986; McDowell, Adamson, & Wood, 1982; Smith et al., in press). Each of these conceptual models includes a set of assumptions about why children behave as they do and what must be done to correct disorders. Among proponents of divergent models, the nature of the problem presented by disordered behavior is at the heart of the controversy. It is not surprising, then, that a definition derived from the tenets of one conceptual model does little but baffle or disappoint those who hold the assumptions of a different model. Writing a definition to which all can subscribe, regardless of conceptual persuasion, may be impossible. An additional problem derives from the fact that many concepts about the disorders of children and youth are merely adaptations of conceptual models of adult psychopathology and do not consider the developmental differences of youngsters at various ages (Achenbach, 1985; Gelfand & Peterson, 1985).

We will discuss conceptual models more fully in Chapter 4; it suffices to say here that people who disagree about what emotional disturbance is at a theoretical or philosophical level are unlikely to agree on a practical definition. Proponents of a psychodynamic conceptual model, for example, start with the assumption that observable behavior is only symptomatic of an underlying problem of personality integration. To a behaviorist, the real problem is nothing more than the observable behavior itself. The basic assumptions of psychoanalysts and behaviorists are irreconcilable differences that simply preclude agreement about how to correctly define behavior disorders.

Differing Purposes of Definitions

Definitions should serve the purposes of the social agents who use them. Within the social structure, courts, schools, clinics, and families rely on different criteria to define behavior disorders. Courts give greatest attention to law-violating behavior, schools primarily to academic failure, clinics to reasons for referral, and families to behavior that violates their rules or strains their tolerance. Perhaps formulating a single definition that is useful to all the social agents who are responsible for youngsters' conduct is impossible. In this book we are primarily concerned with definitions that serve the purposes of public education. Consequently, the focus is on school-related issues, and the children and youth in question are often referred to as "students."

Others point out that a definition can be useful for at least these purposes: to guide delivery of services to children and youth through administrative channels; to reflect a particular theoretical position or structure a discussion; or to describe populations of individuals for research (Cullinan & Epstein, 1979). No authoritative definition used to structure discussion or to give apparent substance to theory has been generally accepted as correct by most professionals who work with disturbed children and youth. These definitions have had little or no influence beyond the covers of the books in which they appear. And, as Wood and Lakin (1979) found, definitions used in research studies vary so widely from study to study that they have added to the confusion about the nature of disordered behavior.

Administrative definitions used by various state departments of education include statements indicating that a disturbed child or youth exhibits characteristics such as these:

Disorders of emotions and/or behavior

Interpersonal problems

Inability to learn or achieve at school

Behavior that differs from a norm or age-appropriate expectations

Problems of long standing

Problems that are severe

A need for special education

Surveys also reveal that the definitions of state education agencies often include statements regarding the supposed causes of disordered behavior (often citing biological or family factors), requirements for certification of the youngster (often specifying who may legitimately decide to classify the child or youth as disturbed), and exclusions (for example, a statement that the behavior disorders of an individual included in the disturbed category cannot be caused by mental retardation or serious health impairments) (Cullinan & Epstein, 1979).

School administrative definitions vary so much that a student might be classified as disturbed in one state but not in another. Clearly, definitions are seriously problematic if a student can change from "normal" to "disturbed" merely by moving across a state line. States may be moving slowly toward aligning their definitions with that used in federal regulations under the Education for All Handicapped Children Act (Public Law 94-142); nevertheless, great variability remains in terminology and definition from state to state. Moreover, the current federal definition itself presents serious problems, as we will see (see also CCBD Executive Committee, 1987; Smith et al., in press).

Difficulties in Measuring Behavior

No tests measure personality, adjustment, anxiety, or other relevant psychological constructs precisely enough to provide a sound basis for defining behavioral disorder. Psychometric tests may contribute to understanding a youngster's behavior, but the tests' reliability and validity are simply inadequate for purposes of dividing the disturbed from the nondisturbed. While the problems of reliability and validity are especially great for projective tests, which purportedly measure unconscious mental processes, these problems also occur in personality inventories, behavior rating scales, and screening tests designed to sift out students who may have a behavior disorder.

Some of the difficulty in measurement is a result of attempts to assess supposed internal states or personality constructs that cannot be observed directly. Direct observation and measurement of behavior have begun to reduce reliance on indirect measurement, but these newer assessment techniques have not resolved the problem of definition. While it may be more useful to a teacher to know how frequently a student hits classmates or sasses an adult than to know the student's responses to psychometric tests, there is no consensus among teachers or psychologists as to what frequency of a given behavior or behaviors indicates emotional disturbance. Local norms for given behavior problems may be useful in screening (Walker, Severson, Stiller, Williams, Haring, Shinn, & Todis, 1988), but they do not provide a general definition.

To compare students for purposes of classification as disturbed or nondisturbed, behavior must be measured under specified environmental conditions. This standard is required because behavior is typically quite sensitive to its social context: students behave differently under different circumstances. Even if environmental conditions are specified and students' behaviors are measured directly and reliably under those conditions, however, we are still not likely to derive a satisfactory definition. The reason is that, given a single set of environmental circumstances, disordered and adaptive behavior are defined by more than behavioral frequencies. Adaptive and disordered behavior are defined by the student's ability or inability to modulate his or her behavior in everyday environments to avoid the censure of others and obtain their approval. The problem of measurement here is analogous to that in the fields of vision and hearing. Central visual acuity and pure tone auditory thresholds can be measured rather precisely under carefully controlled conditions, but these measures do not indicate how efficiently one will see or hear in one's everyday environment (except within very broad limits). Two people with the same auditory acuity, for example, may function quite differently, one as hearing (using oral language almost exclusively) and the other as deaf (relying mostly on manual communication). Visual and auditory efficiency must be assessed by observing how the individual adapts to the changing demands of the environment for seeing and hearing. Behavioral adaptation must also be judged by observation and according to how well one meets environmental demands that often subtly change. This judgment calls for experienced "clinical" appraisal, which includes precise measurement of behavior but goes beyond quantitative assessment.

Range and Variability of Normal and Deviant Behavior

A wide range of behavior may be considered normal; the difference between normal and disordered behavior is usually one of degree rather than kind, and there is no sharp line between the two. Nondisturbed children and youth do nearly everything that those who are disturbed do, but they perform these acts under different conditions, at a different age, or at a different rate. Crying, throwing temper tantrums, fighting, whining, spitting, urinating, screaming, and so on are all behaviors that can be expected of nondisturbed as well as disturbed youngsters. Only the situations in which disturbed children and youth perform these acts or the intensity and rate at which they do them sets them apart. Longitudinal studies and surveys of youngsters' and parents' perceptions of problem behavior show clearly that a large number of children and youth who are considered "normal" show disturbed behaviors, such as tantrums, destructiveness, fearfulness, and hyperactivity to some degree and at some time during their development (see, for example, Achenbach & Edelbrock, 1981). Most students are considered at some time by one of their teachers to be a behavior problem in school (Campbell, 1983; Rubin & Balow, 1978). The problem of definition, then, involves comparison against a nebulous and constantly changing standard—for most behaviors, there are no quantitative norms to measure a disturbed youngster's behavior against.

There is also great variability in deviant behavior. Deviant acts can range from physical assault on others to extreme withdrawal. An individual may exhibit behavior that alternates between these extremes, and the degree of deviance may change markedly over time or with changes in the environment. It is thus inappropriate to consider most classifications of human behavior as mutually exclusive, such that one must be considered either aggressive or nonaggressive, psychotic or nonpsychotic, and so on (see Quay, 1986a). Writing a definition that deals adequately with the many types and degrees of disorder is extremely difficult.

Relationships Among Behavioral Disorders and Other Exceptionalities

As Hallahan and Kauffman (1977) point out, there are more similarities than differences among mildly mentally retarded, learning disabled, and emotionally disturbed students. Severely retarded and severely disturbed students also share many common characteristics. There is considerable literature regarding behavior disorders in mentally retarded individuals (Barrett, 1986; Epstein, Cullinan, & Polloway, 1986). Not only is it often difficult to distinguish among students with psychosis, autism, or mental retardation, but in some cases it is also difficult to distinguish young severely/profoundly disturbed students from those who are deaf, blind, or brain damaged (Keogel, Rincover, & Egel, 1982). Of course, a student may have more than one type of disability. Disordered behavior may occur in combination with any other type of exceptionality; indeed, behavior disorders probably occur more frequently in combination with other disabilities than alone. Defining behavior disorders in a way that excludes other handicapping conditions, therefore, is unrealistic. A behavior disorder should be defined specifically enough to be of value in working with children and youth whose single or primary disability is maladaptive behavior, but broadly enough to admit its coexistence with other disabilities. This is no easy matter.

Transience of Many Behavior Problems

Available evidence indicates that behavior problems are often transitory. Behavior problems exhibited by young children seem likely to disappear within a few years unless they are severe or include high levels of hostile aggression and destructiveness. Thus definitions of behavior disorders must take into account age-specific and developmentally normal problems that do not persist over a long period of time (Campbell, 1983; Gelfand & Peterson, 1985). For this reason, among others, it seems prudent to some to define *behavior,* rather than children or youth, as disturbed or disordered (Quay, 1986a).

Disadvantages in Labeling Deviance

A problem associated with the issue of definition is the practice of labeling—attaching a diagnostic or classifying label to the student or behavior. Assigning any label is dangerous in that the label is likely to stigmatize and can significantly alter the youngster's opportunities for education, employment, and socialization (Burbach, 1981; Hallahan & Kauffman, 1988). This seems to be true regardless of the conceptual foundation of the definition with which the label is associated or the semantics of the label. As Hobbs (1975a) observed in his classic study of the labeling process, the labels employed in special education are often unrelated to the student's behavioral characteristics. Factors that affect placement into a diagnostic category are social class, the professional group choosing the label, and official policies and legal restrictions. Furthermore, once a student is labeled, changing the label may be difficult or impossible. Thus the terminology as well as the conceptual bases of definitions is at issue (Smith et al., in press; Wood, 1987a). Definitions should be couched in language that will minimize damage to students when they are identified as members of a deviant group.

IMPORTANCE OF DEFINITION

The issue of definitions may not at first appear serious. If a student is disturbed when adult authorities say so, then why not concern ourselves with the more important issue of effective intervention and leave the question of definition to those who enjoy arguments about words? Serious reflection leads us ultimately to conclude that definition is too important to leave to chance or whim.

The definition one accepts will reflect how one conceptualizes the problem of disordered behavior and, therefore, what intervention strategies one considers appropriate. A definition communicates succinctly a conceptual framework that has direct implications for practitioners. Medical definitions imply the need for medical interventions, educational definitions imply the need for educational solutions, and so on. Furthermore, a definition specifies the population to be served and thereby has a profound effect on who receives intervention as well as how they will be served. It follows that if a definition specifies population, then it will provide the basis for estimates of prevalence. Finally, decisions of legislative bodies, government executives, and school administrators concerning allocation of funds and training and employment of personnel will be guided by the implications of working definitions. Vague and inappropriate definitions will contribute to confused and inadequate legislation, foggy administrative policies, nonfunctional teacher training, and ineffective intervention. Definition of behavior disorders is, then, a crucial as well as a difficult problem, and it behooves special educators to construct the soundest possible definition.

A case in point—definitional problems affecting services to disturbed students—is the current federal definition, which has been widely criticized as inadequate or inappropriate for a variety of reasons. The definition seems to indicate that a student must be failing academically to be classified as emotionally disturbed for special education purposes. This feature of the definition may result in denial of services to a large number of students whose behavior is seriously disordered but whose academic skills are judged adequate for their grade placement (Kauffman, 1986a; Morse, 1985; Smith et al., in press).

THE CURRENT FEDERAL DEFINITION: ITS DERIVATION AND STATUS

During the past 25 years, numerous definitions of emotional disturbance have been constructed. Each has served the particular purposes of the writer, but none has resolved the problems of terminology, specificity, clarity, and usefulness that we have discussed. Only one has had a significant influence on public policy at the national level—that of Bower (1981). The current federal definition derives from Bower's research involving thousands of students in California in the 1950s. Although Bower's definition is a logical interpretation of his findings, the version that was adopted by the U.S. Department of Education has been widely criticized as illogical (see Bower, 1982; CCBD Executive Committee, 1987; Kauffman, 1986a; Raiser & Van Nagel, 1980). To understand the issues, one must first understand Bower's definition and then compare it to the federal version, point by point.

Bower, in what has become a classic treatise on definition and identification of disturbed youngsters, defined emotionally handicapped students as those exhibiting one or more of five characteristics to a marked extent and over a period of time:

1. An inability to learn which cannot be explained by intellectual, sensory, or health factors . . .

2. An inability to build or maintain satisfactory interpersonal relationships with peers and teachers . . .
3. Inappropriate types of behavior or feelings under normal conditions . . .
4. A general, pervasive mood of unhappiness or depression . . .
5. A tendency to develop physical symptoms, pains, or fears associated with personal or school problems (Bower, 1981, pp. 115–116).

According to Bower, the first of these characteristics, problems in learning, is possibly the most significant school-related aspect of disturbed youngsters' behavior. Another important feature of his definition is the inclusion of degrees or levels of severity.

> Emotional handicaps may be displayed in transient, temporary, pervasive, or in-tensive types of behavior. To complete the definition, it would be necessary to establish a continuum in which the degree of handicap can be perceived and perhaps estimated, especially as it relates to possible action by the school. One could begin such a continuum with (1) children who experience and demonstrate the normal problems of everyday living, growing, exploration, and reality testing. There are some, however, who can be observed as (2) children who develop a greater number and degree of symptoms of emotional problems as a result of normal crises or stressful experiences, such as death of father, birth of sibling, divorce of parents, brain or body injury, school entrance, junior high school en-trance, or puberty. Some children move beyond this level of adjustment and may be described as (3) children in whom moderate symptoms of emotional malad-justment persist to some extent beyond normal expectations but who are able to manage an adequate school adjustment. The next group would include (4) children with fixed and recurring symptoms of emotional maladjustment who can with help profit by school attendance and maintain some positive relationships in the school setting. Beyond this are (5) children with fixed and recurring symptoms of emo-tional difficulties who are perhaps best educated in a residential school setting or temporarily in a home setting. (Bower, 1981, p. 119)

Bower's definition has many good points, particularly its specification of five characteristic types of behavior shown by disturbed students. Still, it does not easily enable one to determine if a particular child or youth is or is not emotionally hand-icapped. There is much latitude in terms like *to a marked extent* and *over a period of time*. There is also a need for subjective judgment about each of the five charac-teristics. Consider the problems in answering these questions:

> Just what is an inability to learn? Is it evidenced by a one-year lag in achievement, or six months, or two years? Does it include inability to learn appropriate social behavior, or only academic skills?

> How do you establish that an apparent inability to learn is not explainable by intellectual factors or health factors? Do health factors include mental health factors?

> Exactly what are satisfactory interpersonal relationships with peers?

> What behavior is inappropriate, and what are normal conditions?

> When is unhappiness pervasive?

Even though Bower's definition is widely cited and may be the best available, it obviously lacks the precision necessary to take much of the subjectivity out of decision making. This may not be a fault of his definition—it may be the nature of the problem of definition. The definition Bower offers has had a tremendous impact on public policy not because of its accuracy, but primarily because it is included, with few significant changes, in the rules and regulations governing implementation of the Education of the Handicapped Act (EHA). Section 121a.5 of the rules and regulations, with the most significant differences between it and Bower's definition indicated by italics, reads as follows:

> "Seriously emotionally disturbed" is defined as follows:
>
> (i) The term means a condition exhibiting one or more of the following characteristics over a long period of time and to a marked degree, *which adversely affects educational performance*:
>
> (A) An inability to learn which cannot be explained by intellectual, sensory, or health factors;
>
> (B) An inability to build or maintain satisfactory interpersonal relationships with peers and teachers;
>
> (C) Inappropriate types of behavior or feelings under normal circumstances;
>
> (D) A general, pervasive mood of unhappiness or depression; or
>
> (E) A tendency to develop physical symptoms or fears associated with personal or school problems.
>
> (ii) *The term includes children who are schizophrenic* [or autistic].[1] *The term does not include children who are socially maladjusted, unless it is determined that they are seriously emotionally disturbed.* (45 C.F.R. 121a.5[b][8] [1978])

As noted by our use of italics, the federal rules and regulations contain three statements not found in Bower's original definition. These added statements do not make the definition clearer; in fact, they come close to making nonsense of it. The additional clause "which adversely affects educational performance" is particularly puzzling. One might speculate that it is a pro forma statement (that is, set up in advance) that PL 94-142 is concerned only with educational matters. The clause is redundant, however, with characteristic (A), "An inability to learn," if educational performance is considered to mean academic achievement. Moreover, a student is extremely unlikely to exhibit one or more of the characteristics listed to a marked degree and for a long time without adverse effects on academic progress. But what should one conclude about a student who exhibits, for example, characteristic (D), "A general, pervasive mood of unhappiness or depression," and is academically advanced for his or her age and grade? If educational performance is interpreted to mean academic achievement, then the student would seem to be excluded from the category of seriously emotionally disturbed; however, if educational performance is interpreted to include personal and social satisfaction in the school setting, then the clause is superfluous. Even greater

---

1. The federal definition was revised to exclude autistic students. Autism was made a subcategory under "Other Health Impaired" because of the belief that it is a condition having biological causes. Bower (1982) notes the logical problems inherent in excluding autistic and socially maladjusted students from his definition and from the federal version.

confusion is created by part (ii) regarding schizophrenia and autism (that is, childhood psychoses) and social maladjustment. Any psychotic youngster would clearly be included under the original definition; that is, any such child or youth will exhibit one or more of the five characteristics listed (especially B and/or C) to a marked degree and over a long period of time. Therefore, the addendum is unnecessary. If a student is labeled schizophrenic but does not exhibit one or more of the five characteristics, then the label has been applied inappropriately and should not result in his or her being labeled seriously emotionally disturbed. The final addendum regarding social maladjustment is incomprehensible. A youngster cannot be socially maladjusted by any credible interpretation of the term without exhibiting one or more of the five characteristics (especially B and/or C) to a marked degree and over a long period of time (Bower, 1982).

PERSPECTIVES ON DEFINITION

In the early part of the twentieth century, psychiatric perspectives on definition tended to be accepted with little question by school personnel. Bower's work in California public schools in the 1950s and 1960s and the growth of special education programs for disturbed students led to definitions' becoming more closely related to students' behavior in the classroom. Today most professionals recognize that a given definition is never adequate for all purposes. As Knitzer (1982) commented, "It is hard to talk about children and adolescents who need mental health services. Terms like 'mentally ill,' 'behaviorally disordered,' or 'psychotic' take away their uniqueness and pain" (p.

So, Who's Crazy?

In an address given in 1981 when he was president of the Council for Children with Behavioral Disorders, Dr. C. Michael Nelson discussed the complex issues involved in deciding who "owns" the problems of troubled and troubling children and youth. In a paper delivered several years later, he made the following thought-provoking comments.

"I intentionally chose [the term *crazy*] over the jargon preferred in our profession, such as psychotic, emotionally disturbed, or behaviorally disordered, because it more accurately conveys my impression that such labels are readily applied to anything or anybody we don't understand or with whom we disagree. The judgment that someone or something is crazy is relative and situational. It depends upon who is doing the judging, the standards against which they are judging, and the limits of the context in which the judgment is applied. . . .

"So, who's crazy? The way I see it, there are several candidates for the title. You might think of this as a multiple choice test. Is it (a) children and youth—our traditional choice; (b) ourselves—by which I mean teachers, teacher trainers, and other professional caretakers; (c) the 'system'—which includes schools, agencies of state and federal government, as well as professional organizations; (d) society itself; or (e) all of the above?" (Nelson, 1985, p. 9)

3). The most useful definition is one that clearly focuses on the behavior problems of students in schools. Bower's definition is admirably suited for use in educational settings.

Ironically, the current federal definition may be contributing to underservice of behaviorally disordered students. The addenda to Bower's definition allow so many interpretations that students who need services may be excluded relatively easily. Some can be excluded because they are not academically retarded; others because they are judged to be socially maladjusted but not emotionally disturbed (see Center & Obringer, 1987; Kauffman, 1986a; Kauffman, Cullinan, & Epstein, 1987; Knitzer, 1982). Legal arguments continue over such issues as whether a student must be academically retarded under the definition and whether adjudication as delinquent qualifies a juvenile as "seriously emotionally disturbed."

The definition of behavior disorder or emotional disturbance remains partly subjective, even though several relevant characteristics of a disturbed or behaviorally disordered student's behavior can be described clearly (Smith et al., in press). The definition of disturbance or disorder eludes complete objectivity for the same reasons that happiness and depression defy completely objective definition. This does not mean that the effort to devise more objective means of identifying disturbed students must be abandoned (as we will discuss further in Part Two [see Walker et al., 1988]). Nor does it mean that it is impossible to improve the definition. For the definition to be most useful to educators, however, the subjective judgments that go into identifying students must include those of the teachers who work with them. In decisions made by groups of professionals, the *teacher,* not the psychologist, social worker, or psychiatrist, should be viewed as the most important "imperfect test" in determining that a student needs help (Gerber & Semmel, 1984). Reliance on teachers' judgments puts great responsibility on teachers for moral and ethical conduct in decision making (Kauffman, 1984), but it is a responsibility they cannot avoid.

SUMMARY

Children and youth with behavior disorders are handicapped by behaviors that are discordant with their social-interpersonal environments. The definition of behavior disorders is a difficult matter complicated by differences in conceptual models, differences in the purposes of various social agencies, problems in measuring social-interpersonal behavior, variability in normal behavior, confusing relationships among behavior disorders and other exceptionalities, the transience of many childhood behavior disorders, and the effects of pejorative labels. No definition can be made completely objective. No definition has been universally accepted. The most common definition used in educational contexts is that proposed originally by Bower and incorporated in the rules and regulations for PL 94-142. This definition specifies marked and persistent characteristics having to do with:

1. School learning problems
2. Unsatisfactory interpersonal relationships
3. Inappropriate behavior and feelings

4. Pervasive unhappiness or depression
5. Physical symptoms or fears associated with school or personal problems.

Inclusion and exclusion clauses of questionable meaning have been appended to these characteristics in the federal definition. Although improvements in definition are possible, and more objective criteria for identification are being developed, teachers' responsibility for judging students' behavior cannot be avoided.

2

Prevalence: The Extent of the Problem

As you read this chapter, keep these guiding questions in mind:

☐ In what sense does identification of behavior disordered students require arbitrary decisions?

☐ What is the difference between prevalence and incidence?

☐ Why have special educators been more concerned with prevalence than with incidence?

☐ Why is it so difficult to arrive at precise prevalence figures?

☐ How can we use false positive and false negative scores on a behavior rating scale to estimate prevalence?

☐ What arguments can one use to defend the position that two percent of the student population is a conservative estimate of prevalence of behavior disorders?

☐ Approximately what percentage of the public school population is now served by special education under the *seriously emotionally disturbed* category?

☐ Why does it seem unlikely that two percent of the school-age population will be served by special education (under the category of *seriously emotionally disturbed*) in the foreseeable future?

I t could probably be said of nearly all children and youth at some time and in some social context that they were disturbed or exhibited a behavior disorder. But to classify nearly all children and youth as handicapped by these isolated, transitory, or minor problems would be silly. Indeed, suggestions that 20 percent or more of children and youth have serious psychological problems are met with public disbelief and professional skepticism (cf. Smith et al., in press). A typical reaction is that "bleeding hearts" are making much ado about the normal pains of growing up, bemoaning the usual slings and arrows that people must suffer as part of their daily lives. Another reaction occurs when teachers' reports are the basis for estimating the numbers of problems. Teachers tend to mistake their own ineptitude in managing behavior for the behavior disorders of students. Because of their shortcomings in understanding and teaching children, they misperceive problems as students' rather than their own. For advocates of handicapped students to argue convincingly for special services, they must be able to present a strong case for the assertion that the students' problems are highly unusual and debilitating.

The question to consider here is "How frequently does a student's disordered behavior clearly stand out from the usual difficulties of childhood and youth and seriously limit that individual's options for social and personal development?" Obviously, the answer to this question cannot be entirely objective. The question requires establishment of arbitrary criteria, which may be quite objective; however, choosing the criteria requires subjective judgment. Consider similar questions; "How heavy (or thin or tall or short) must a person of given age be to qualify as exceptional for medical purposes?" "How little income must a person have to be considered poor for purposes of public assistance?" "How different from the average in intelligence and social adaptation must a student be to qualify as mentally retarded (or gifted) for special education purposes?" In each case, we can "make" more people deviant— obese, poor, retarded, or disturbed, for example—simply by changing an arbitrary definition. Physicians, economists, social workers, psychologists, or educators may make their case for a given criterion, and their arguments may be convincing to legislators or others who make public policy or establish standards for judgment. The standards and policy are merely a matter of consensus, and they can be changed at will. For example, the American Association on Mental Deficiency "literally revolutionized the incidence, prevalence, and concept of mental retardation, all with the simple stroke of [the] pen" (Blatt, 1975, p. 414) when the IQ criterion for mental retardation was lowered from one standard deviation to two standard deviations below the mean (that is, the IQ cutoff score was lowered from about 85 to about 70).

The number or percentage of children and youth who are judged to have disordered behavior, then, is a matter of choice. Disordered behavior is not a "thing," an objective entity that can be detached from the observer. Behavior disorder, like poverty, is a social reality that we construct on the basis of our judgment as to what is tolerable and what is desirable (Kauffman, Gerber, & Semmel, 1988). Our task as professionals is to struggle with issues of prevalence, to make the most intelligent and caring choices we can about the lives of children and youth. We must seek to identify those students—and only those—for whom the risks associated with identification (such as social stigma) are outweighed by the advantages (effective intervention). This is no easy task. While we can and must make difficult judgments about the

30

risks and advantages entailed in identification, we can seldom be absolutely certain that our judgment of the individual case is correct (Kauffman, 1984). Try to decide which of the students in the following descriptions has a behavior disorder. The descriptions are very brief, and you probably believe you should have more information before making judgments about whether these students are disturbed. You should, in fact, have more information; *anyone* should, and anyone would probably be unprofessional in making a judgment based solely on this information.

Who Has a Behavior Disorder?

These descriptions are based on actual case histories. Some of the children and youth were labeled behavior disordered or emotionally disturbed; others were not. Some were placed in regular classrooms; others in special classes or institutions. These brief case descriptions illustrate the difficulties even experts face in deciding who is and who is not disturbed.

Barry

Barry has five older siblings, the youngest of whom is 10 years older than he. He has always been the "baby of the family" in everyone's eyes, especially his mother's. He is now a rotund third-grader whose torpor is remarkable. His obesity, sluggishness, and infantile behavior (e.g., he prefers to play with small stuffed animals) make him a constant and easy target for teasing by his classmates. Since he entered kindergarten, Barry's mother has brought him to school daily, sat in her car in the parking lot during the entire school day in case he should "need" her at any time, brought his lunch to him and fed him in the hall or in her car, and whisked him home after school. Her life seems absurdly devoted to his safety and comfort, yet ironically calculated to impair his psychological and physical growth and development. School officials suspect that Barry was bottle-fed until he was in the second grade, and they know that his diet now consists primarily of junk foods. He has no friends his age, and he will not participate in age-appropriate play in the classroom or on the playground. He is constantly teased by other children because of his weight and infantile behavior.

Darlene

Darlene's mother conceived her when she was a 12-year-old sixth-grader. Recently graduated from high school, the mother is now pregnant with her third child. Darlene is a first-grader who frequently gets into trouble because she hits or pokes other children, fails to do her work, and disobeys the teacher. Other children are beginning to shy away from her in fear. She is bright-eyed and gregarious with adults, and the casual observer may not suspect that the teacher sees her as a significant problem.

Nathan

Nathan is an eighth-grader with an IQ in the gifted range. Although he is highly intelligent and creative and scores high on standardized achievement tests, his report cards contain only Ds and Fs. All his teachers and the school principal are exasperated with his constant clowning in class, his refusal to complete assignments (and his insistence that sloppy, incomplete work is sufficient), and his frequent "macho" behavior that gets him into fights with other students. His mother, a divorced former teacher, is at her wit's end with him at home; he is slovenly, refuses to do chores, threatens her and his older sister with physical violence, and was recently caught shoplifting.

Claudia

Claudia is the wispy 16-year-old daughter of a wealthy attorney. Her favorite book is the Bible; she is preoccupied with remaining slender in this life and earning the right to ecstatic happiness forever in the next. Her schoolwork is always perfect, or nearly so. She has only one close friend, a woman in her early 20s who has a history of suicide attempts. Claudia complains constantly of being tired, of being unable to sleep, and of being too fat. She is forever dieting and exercising, and she frequently vomits immediately after she eats a normal meal. She offers profuse apologies for any imperfection anyone points out in her behavior or academic performance.

Now let us look at a somewhat more detailed description. See if you think T. J. has a behavior disorder.

T. J.

T. J. is an 11-year-old fifth-grader. His IQ is 115. He has no significant physical anomalies and no history of developmental delay in motor development or language. He had no particular difficulties academically until fourth grade. His academic performance was about average until last year, when his grades suddenly began to deteriorate. This year he is earning mostly Ds and Fs.

T. J. was not known as a problem child in school until last year. But every teacher who has dealt with him in the past 18 months has commented on his frequent misbehavior. He is difficult to manage because of his high rates of out-of-seat behavior, talking out, teasing, and temper outbursts. He is usually defiant of teachers and argumentative with his peers. These problems are, in the opinion of his current teachers, increasing. His belligerence recently resulted in several fights in and around school, including one in which another child was injured and required medical attention. Two weeks ago he was caught shoplifting a bag of candy from the local drugstore. Ratings by his teachers on a problem checklist indicate that his behavior is a problem more often than that of 90 percent of his schoolmates.

T. J. has no close friends, although he is sometimes tolerated briefly in school situations by other boys who exhibit similar behavior patterns. He and his two older brothers live with his mother and stepfather, who provide little supervision or control. His parents have never shown any interest in his school progress or lack of it, and they have refused to recognize that any of his behavior, including the fights and shoplifting, is a problem.

T. J.'s current teachers are quite concerned about him for several reasons. He does not complete most of his academic work and is failing in most subjects. He disrupts the class frequently by hitting or taunting other students or mumbling complaints about the teacher and assignments. He spends a lot of his time in class drawing "tattoos" on his arms with felt-tip pens. None of his three experienced teachers, who manage 63 fifth graders as a team, has been able to establish a close relationship with T. J. or produce significant improvement in his behavior. (Kauffman, 1984, p. 62)

For special education purposes, should one consider T. J. disturbed? On the basis of the information presented, experts may disagree. Of course, one may argue that additional information is necessary to justify a decision. But regardless of how much additional information one might amass, the decision would probably remain questionable. Some would argue that T. J. is a problem, but not emotionally disturbed. Perhaps he needs help, but not in the form of special education. Some might suggest that his home life and his teachers' lack of expertise are responsible for his behavior. T. J. and everyone else involved would have more to lose than to gain by his being identified as a student with behavior disorders. His problems can best be addressed through consultation with his regular class teachers on how to manage his behavior in the classroom and by providing social workers to help his parents do a better job at home.

Others would argue that T. J. shows all the classic signs of a student in trouble, one who is unlikely to improve without direct intervention. He is certainly headed for more social and academic trouble unless something is done, probably through provision of special education and related services. Special educators are the most appropriate professionals to deal with the situation, and the benefits of identifying him for special education would clearly outweigh the risks. He can be taught academic and social skills most effectively through placement in a special program for part of the school day with a smaller group of students and a teacher specially trained to manage such problems. After weighing all the outcomes—for T. J., his classmates, his teachers, and his parents—the greatest benefits and least damage will be done by placing him in special education.

Understandably, heated arguments about prevalence will continue into the foreseeable future. After all, the issues are both complex and emotional; they include economics, statistics, law, public policy, and concern for the welfare of children.

MEANING OF PREVALENCE AND INCIDENCE

Prevalence refers to the total number of individuals with X disorder in a given population. The prevalence of a disorder is calculated for a given period or for a point in time. Thus federal reports typically include the number of students with behavior disorders counted at a particular time during the school year. Prevalence is often expressed as a percentage of the population; the total number of cases is divided by the total number of individuals in the population. Thus, if 40 students out of a total student population of 2,000 in a school or school district are identified as having behavior disorders, then the prevalence rate is two percent.

Incidence refers to the rate of *inception*—the number of *new* cases of X disorder in a given population. *Cases* can refer to *individuals* or to *episodes* of the disorder (that is, an individual might be counted more than once during the incidence period if he or she exhibits the disorder, subsequently does not exhibit the disorder or goes into remission, and then again exhibits the disorder). Incidence, like prevalence, may be expressed as a percentage of the population, but this can be misleading when episodes rather than individuals are counted. Incidence addresses the question "How often does this disorder occur?" whereas prevalence addresses the question "How many individuals are affected?"

For special education purposes, prevalence has usually had more meaning than incidence. Prevalence has been the statistic of interest because most exceptionalities with which special educators deal have been assumed to be developmental, life-long characteristics. Consequently, teachers and school administrators have most often been concerned about knowing or estimating the number of students who have behavior disorders or mental retardation or some other disability in any given school year. Incidence of certain disorders or problems is often also important, however, particularly when making judgments regarding trends in the school population. The incidence of pregnancy, suicidal behavior, or drug and alcohol use among public school students, for example, may be critical for planning and evaluating intervention programs. Moreover, special educators are becoming increasingly aware that exceptionalities can be episodic. A student may function quite differently in one grade than in another, or even change rather drastically over a period of weeks or months. Behavior disorders, as well as giftedness, mental retardation, and learning disabilities, are not necessarily immutable characteristics. To the extent that disorders are transient or episodic, incidence becomes equally as important as prevalence.

IMPORTANCE OF PREVALENCE AND INCIDENCE ESTIMATES

Prevalence and incidence estimates have little meaning for the classroom teacher of disturbed children. When your responsibility is to teach a class of difficult children and you know that there are many more such pupils whose teachers or parents are waiting anxiously for the day when their child can enter your class, what difference does it make whether two percent or five percent or ten percent of the school's students have behavior disorders?

For those who plan and administer special education programs at a districtwide or statewide or nationwide level, however, prevalence and incidence are extremely important. Prevalence estimates and incidence rates are the basis for requesting budgets, hiring staff, planning inservice programs, and so on. Frequently, school boards or school administrators decide to cut budgets or allocate additional funds because the percentage of children served under a categorical program is more than or less than that of neighboring school districts or state or national averages. Thus, although prevalence issues may seem irrelevant or purely academic to classroom teachers, these issues can ultimately affect their working conditions.

PROBLEMS OF ESTIMATION

Estimates of the prevalence of behavior disorders vary from about 0.5 percent of the school population to 20 percent or more. It is easy to see why estimates are varied and confused. First, since the definition of disordered behavior is unsettled, the number of disturbed students cannot be determined accurately or reliably. It is difficult, if not impossible, to count the instances of a phenomenon that has no precise definition. Second, there are numerous ways to estimate the number of students with behavior disorders, and differences in methodology can produce drastically different results. Third, the number of students counted by any definition and methodology can be influenced more by powerful social policy and economic factors than by professional training or clinical judgment (Kauffman, 1986a; Magliocca & Stephens, 1980). Judgments about who is and who is not disturbed or otherwise handicapped for special education purposes are surely influenced by social consequences and their economic implications (Kauffman et al., 1988). We will discuss each of these problems—definition, methodology, and policy and economic factors.

Lack of Standard Definition

The effect of differences in definitions on estimates of prevalence needs no more elaboration. But even when the same definition is used, estimates of prevalence differ. Consider that a survey of state directors of special education (Schultz, Hirshoren, Manton, & Henderson, 1971) found prevalence estimates ranging from 0.5 percent to 15 percent in various states. Even using a standard written definition, people seem to carry their own private definitions in their heads; they differ greatly in how they match the written definition to students' behavior.

The Methodology of Estimation

Prevalence and incidence are usually estimated from a sample of the population in question; that is, it is usually not feasible to count every case in an entire state or nation, or even in an extremely large school district. (Exceptions are the annual counts of the number of handicapped children served by special education under federal and state laws and reported to state and federal agencies.) The estimate must be generated from standard screening procedures applied to a carefully selected sample. The methodological problems are similar to those of conducting a poll or making a projection during an election. Different numbers will likely be obtained, depending on how the sample is selected and what questions are asked.

The methodology of estimating behavior disorders has not been well developed. How data are gathered and from whom they are taken make a difference in the number of cases or episodes counted. Should teachers, parents, psychologists, students, or some combination of these be consulted? That is, what should be the criteria, and who should serve as judges? Should one rely on mailed questionnaires, personal interviews, referrals to social agencies, behavior ratings, or direct observation of behavior? And how should the survey sample be selected? For reasons of economy, most prevalence surveys have relied on questionnaires or behavior ratings. For purposes of identifying disordered behavior in the schools, teacher judgment is obviously relevant and has been shown to be effective and reliable as well.

Because no standard methodology has been developed, and perhaps for other reasons as well, estimates of prevalence and incidence of behavior disorders among child populations have varied wildly. Moreover, most studies of prevalence and incidence are open to criticism on methodological grounds. Methodological problems notwithstanding, we can make reasonable estimates of prevalence. One way to make a rough estimate is to compare behavior ratings of students who are already identified and receiving services to the ratings of nonidentified students. False negatives (students who should be but have not been identified) and false positives (students who have been identified but should not have been) can be estimated by establishing cutoff scores for behavior ratings, noting the extent to which distributions of scores for referred and nonreferred (or identified and nonidentified) individuals are overlapping. Achenbach and Edelbrock (1981) provide a rationale for this approach using parents' ratings of children who were referred and of children who were not referred for mental health services:

> In the absence of any litmus test for either mental health or disorder in children, it appears that actual referral for mental health services is an appropriate morbidity criterion against which to validate discrimination procedures, at least where mental health services are available regardless of family income. The value of actual referral is that it typically reflects persisting problems on the part of the child in one or more important life areas. Thus, even when parents do not perceive problems, pressure from school personnel and others seeing the child's behavior in natural settings often compels parents to seek help. Although false positives can certainly result from parental intolerance of normal child behavior or from parents' seeking help for themselves, and false negatives can result from parental intransigence despite pressure to seek help, actual referral is probably as good a criterion as any other currently available. It may often be better than direct psychiatric assessments and mental health workers' ratings of parents' reports. (pp. 56–57)

Into Achenbach and Edelbrock's paragraph, we could substitute school-related phrases (for example, "actual identification of students for special education") for those related to mental health (for example, "actual referral for mental health services"). That is, one could argue that actual identification of students for special education is an appropriate criterion against which to judge the definition of behavior disorder and procedures intended to discriminate behavior disordered from nondisordered students. A score on a behavior rating scale cannot be taken as an indication that a student is disturbed; it is only one indication that the student may need special education or mental health services. Given these assumptions, the question then becomes, "What percentage of the nonidentified group is similar enough to students in the already identified sample that they could reasonably be considered candidates for the same treatment?" This methodology is a comparison of two frequency distributions, such that areas of overlap in the distributions are of concern, as illustrated in Figure 2.1.

As shown by the hypothetical distributions in Figure 2.1, some nonidentified students will score as high or higher than some identified students; conversely, some identified students will score lower than some who have not been identified. If an arbitrary cutoff score is chosen as the criterion, then false negatives and false positives can be identified. False negatives can be considered candidates for identification or as potentially in need of services; false positives can be considered candidates for reclassification as "nonhandicapped" (perhaps as a result of misclassification, perhaps as a result of therapeutic intervention). Table 2.1 shows the results of one study involving teachers' behavior ratings on the *Behavior Problem Checklist* (Quay & Peterson, 1975) for 727 behaviorally disordered and 1,116 nonidentified students (Cullinan, Epstein, & Kauffman, 1984). Note that the percentage of false positives increased and the percentage of false negatives decreased with a higher cutoff score.

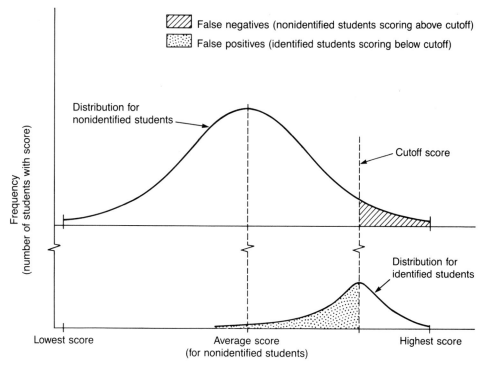

FIGURE 2.1

Hypothetical Frequency Distributions of Behavior Rating Scores for Nonidentified and Identified Students Showing Cutoff Score as Criterion for False Negatives and False Positives

TABLE 2.1

False Negatives and False Positives for 90 and 95 Percentile Cutoff Scores Based on Nonhandicapped Students on Total-Problems BPC Score, by Age-by-Sex Subgroups

	90 Percentile Criterion			95 Percentile Criterion		
Subgroups	Cutoff Score	% False Negative[a]	% False Positive[b]	Cutoff Score	% False Negative[b]	% False Positive[b]
Male						
elementary	21	10.6	22.4	28	5.5	57.8
middle	26	9.0	45.2	34	4.9	73.5
senior high	28	9.9	59.9	32	4.5	73.8
Female						
elementary	16	9.5	25.0	21	5.1	41.7
middle	20	8.8	27.3	25	5.3	34.1
senior high	25	10.1	66.2	37	4.0	90.9

[a]NH students with a BPC total score > cutoff score

[b]BD students with a BPC total-problem score < cutoff score

Source: From "Teachers' Ratings of Students' Behaviors: What Constitutes Behavior Disorder in Schools?" by D. Cullinan, M.H. Epstein, and J.M. Kauffman, 1984, *Behavioral Disorders, 10,* p. 17. Copyright 1984 by The Council for Exceptional Children. Reprinted with permission.

Using a similar methodology with parents' ratings, Achenbach and Edelbrock (1981) found that about nine percent of a group of nonreferred children scored outside the normal range (that is, were false negatives) and about 26 percent of referred children scored within the normal range (that is, were false positives) when the cutoff score was the 90th percentile for the nonreferred group. These results are strikingly similar to those of Cullinan et al. (1984), except for senior high school students in the Cullinan et al. sample.

Could one reasonably conclude on the basis of the Achenbach and Edelbrock (1981) and Cullinan et al. (1984) studies that about nine percent of the nonidentified population is behavior disordered? Probably not. The behavior rating scores alone are not convincing, and a substantial percentage of the identified students were false positives. Allowing for a considerable margin of error in the classifications that would result from the behavior ratings, is it a reasonable guess that three percent to six percent of the population is behavior disordered? Probably so. To illustrate, let us assume that two percent of the school population is now classified as behavior disordered (a high estimate). Let us also assume that half of these students are misclassified, such that only one percent are "truly" disordered or "actually" belong in special education. Let us also assume that only one-fourth of the false negatives (or one-fourth of nine percent) in the Achenbach and Edelbrock and Cullinan et al. studies are "actually" behavior disordered (a conservative estimate). The percentage of the population "actually" behavior disordered would thus be estimated at 3.25 percent.

Social Policy and Economic Factors

At any given time, two percent is a modest estimate of the school population whose behavior disorders are deserving of special education. Because PL 94-142 requires that *all* handicapped children, including the seriously emotionally disturbed, be identified and provided special education appropriate for their individual needs, it could be expected that at least two percent of the school population has been identified and is being served. Recent reports from the U.S. Department of Education, however, indicate that only about half that prevalence estimate (about one percent) is receiving services (cf. Hallahan & Kauffman, 1988; Kauffman, 1986a). Social policy (as embodied in PL 94-142) and economic factors are probably responsible, in part, for the discrepancy between reasonable prevalence estimates and the number of students served. It seems highly probable that future prevalence estimates will be lowered to reflect the percentage of students actually served by special education; it seems unlikely that services will be expanded to approximate reasonable prevalence estimates. The reason is simple: the law *requires* that *all* seriously emotionally disturbed students be identified *and that all identified students be provided special education and related services to meet their needs.* Furthermore, the threatened penalty for a state's noncompliance with these requirements is a cutoff of all federal education funds. As we have seen, the definition of emotional disturbance is sufficiently vague and subjective that just about any student can be included or excluded, so long as inclusion or exclusion can be said to serve a useful purpose. School systems and states find it useful to stay within their budgets and maintain federal support. Official nonrecognition of the needs of students whose deviant behavior can be ignored is a convenient way for many school officials to avoid the hassles, risks, and costs of expanded services. In addition, many professionals find it easy to rationalize nonidentification of students whose behavior is not disordered in the extreme (Kauffman, 1984, 1988).

REASONABLE ESTIMATES OF PREVALENCE

The question most relevant to discussion here is, "What is a reasonable estimate of the percentage of students whose behavior is so persistently troublesome that special education is desirable?" The best available evidence indicates that the estimate of two percent is too conservative, although it was used for over two decades (approximately 1955–1980) by the U.S. Department of Education. The Department of Education revised its prevalence estimate downward to a range of 1.2 percent to 2.0 percent for several years during the mid-1980s, but since then has not published an estimate.

More reasonable estimates based on population surveys appear to be in the range of three to six percent of the student population (see Achenbach & Edelbrock, 1981; Cullinan et al., 1984; Graham, 1979; Juul, 1986). Bower (1981), using his own definition and data from ratings by teachers, peers, and students themselves, estimated that about ten percent of school age children and youth are emotionally handicapped. His study can be criticized, however, for using a methodology that forced about ten percent of the students surveyed into the emotionally handicapped category. An important estimate of prevalence for educators is a longitudinal study by Rubin and Balow (1978). Each year they asked teachers to report via questionnaire whether the children in their study sample had shown behavior problems. The decision as to what constituted a problem was left to the individual teacher. Over half of the 1,586 children Rubin and Balow studied were at *some* time during their school years considered by at least *one* of their teachers to show a behavior problem. In any given year, about 20 to 30 percent of the children were considered by at least one teacher to be a problem. Most importantly, 7.4 percent of the children (11.3 percent of the boys and 3.5 percent of the girls) were considered a problem by *every* teacher who rated them over a period of three years. As we have noted, an estimate derived from the Achenbach and Edelbrock study (1981) indicated the prevalence of behavior disorder as judged by parents to be well above two percent; and teachers' ratings of students identified as disturbed and those not identified also suggested that considerably more than two percent of the school population could reasonably be considered to have behavior disorders (Cullinan et al., 1984).

Several findings are consistent across a variety of studies that span more than a quarter of a century (Achenbach & Edelbrock, 1981; Bower, 1981; Cullinan et al., 1984; Glidewell & Swallow, 1968; Griffiths, 1952; Rubin & Balow, 1978; Rutter, Tizard, Yule, Graham, & Whitmore, 1976; see also Graham, 1979; Juul, 1986). First, *most* children and youth exhibit seriously troublesome behavior at some time during their development. Second, more than two percent of school-age youngsters are considered by teachers and other adults—consistently and over a period of years—to exhibit disordered behavior and to fit the federal definition of "seriously emotionally disturbed." For example, the 7.4 percent of the child population that Rubin and Balow (1978) found to be consistently identified as behavior problems over a period of three years appears to fit the federal definition: when compared to other children, they scored significantly lower on achievement tests in language, reading, spelling, and arithmetic in addition to their persistently and pervasively troublesome behavior in school. These children also scored significantly lower on tests of intelligence, were classified by significantly lower socioeconomic levels, totaled significantly higher numbers of grade retentions, and required more special services (remedial reading, speech therapy, psychological evaluation, and so on), all of which are characteristics associated with behavior disorders. The picture emerging from studies of the characteristics of students now in programs for behavior disordered students, and of those not identified but who show similar characteristics, is one of serious academic and social difficulties (Cullinan et al., 1984; Kauffman et al., 1987) that are not likely to be overcome without intervention.

TRENDS IN PREVALENCE ESTIMATES AND PERCENTAGE OF STUDENTS SERVED BY SPECIAL EDUCATION

During the decade of the mid-1970s to the mid-1980s, the percentage of the public school population receiving special education services grew from about 0.5 percent to about 1.0 percent; however, since 1986, growth in services for disturbed students has been negligible. Recent government statistics indicate that about 350,000 to 400,000 students are now being served by special education programs under the "seriously emotionally disturbed" category. It is also important to recognize, however, that the percentage of students receiving services is based on the number of children and youth enrolled in public schools, not the number in the U.S. population (Kauffman, 1986a). Census statistics indicate that about 40 percent of the U.S. population between the ages of three and 21 are not enrolled in public schools and were excluded from calculation of the percentage of the population served (U.S. Department of Education, 1984). One must grant that some children and youth between the ages of three and 21 are not enrolled in public schools for legitimate reasons (because they are younger or older than the ages for which attendance is required or are enrolled in a private school, for example). Yet it is a safe assumption that a significant proportion of the 40 percent of the population not enrolled in public schools (about 30 million of the 70 million children and youth in the relevant age bracket) are handicapped and in need of special education. Although some argue that nearly all students who need special education are receiving it today, prevalence and service data lead to a very different conclusion (Kauffman, 1984, 1986a, 1988; Morse, 1985).

The percentage of students served varies drastically from state to state and among school districts (Smith et al., in press). Hallahan, Keller, and Ball (1986) have shown that *seriously emotionally disturbed* is one of the most variable categories of special education in terms of differences among states. This variability is probably attributable, at least partly, to confusion regarding the definition of serious emotional disturbance.

As noted, the federal government used a prevalence estimate of 2.0 percent for about 25 years before suggesting a range of 1.2 to 2.0 percent in the mid-1980s and then dropping the estimate entirely. The government obviously prefers not to allow wide discrepancies between prevalence estimates and the actual number of students served. It is easier to cut prevalence estimates than to serve more students. Moreover, if an appearance of compliance is to be maintained, it is best to work from the assumption that the number of students served is the number who need service.

Social policy and economic realities have effectively precluded the public schools' identification of two percent or more of the school age population as seriously emotionally disturbed. Consideration of the economic realities alone illustrates the difficulty in increasing services to match a two-percent prevalence estimate. A decade ago, calculations indicated that nearly one billion dollars more per year would be needed from the federal government, plus nearly 1.4 billion dollars from state and local sources, to serve two percent of the students in public schools (Grosenick & Huntze, 1979). These figures did not include funds for training personnel or allowances for inflation. Today, services for two percent of the public school population would require several billions more from federal sources alone than is currently budgeted. It is highly unlikely that federal or state legislatures or local schools will make the required amounts of money available for training personnel and operating programs for two percent of the public school population.

Faced with a shortage of adequately trained personnel and insurmountable budget problems, what can we expect of school officials? They cannot risk litigation and loss of federal funds by identifying disturbed students they cannot serve. It is reasonable to expect that they will identify as many disturbed students as they can find resources to serve. The tragedy is that social policy (PL 94-142) mandates the impossible and that the public—and a growing number of professionals—are likely to change their perceptions to match economic realities. The social policy mandate changes the question, at least for those who manage budgets, from "How many disturbed students are there in our schools?" to "How many disturbed students can we afford to serve?" And to save face and try to abide by the law, it is tempting to conclude that there are, indeed, just as many disturbed students as one is able to serve.

Pressures *not* to identify students as having behavior disorders have become powerful (Kauffman, 1986b, 1988). Distaste for identifying students as exceptional and for providing special programs outside the regular class, even on a part-time basis, has led to efforts to merge or restructure special and general education, usually referred to as the *regular education initiative* (REI) (see Hallahan, Kauffman, Lloyd, & McKinney, 1988). Proponents argue that most students now considered handicapped are not handicapped at all, or are so mildly disabled that we can expect regular classroom teachers, with little additional training or assistance, to deal with them effectively. This viewpoint, however well intentioned, has a strong negative effect on the recognition of behavior disorders as disabilities or handicapping conditions for which special education and related services are appropriate (Braaten, Kauffman, Braaten, Polsgrove, & Nelson, in press; Kauffman, 1988). The trend appears to be toward identification of only those students whose behavior offends or disturbs others most egregiously—those with the most severe disorders. We do not seem to be nearing the day when special education and related services will be provided even for most of the three percent that Morse (1985) considers "very seriously impaired" (p. ix).

In 1986 a meeting of education and mental health experts resulted in the following conclusions regarding underservice of disturbed students by special education (National Mental Health Association, 1986).

A majority of SED [seriously emotionally disturbed] children are never identified as such and consequently do not receive the services they need. The reasons for this underidentification are many:

There is concern about the stigma of labeling a child as "severely emotionally disturbed."

No clear definition of SED eligibility exists in the law; therefore, states have had to operationalize a definition, resulting in a tremendous disparity among states.

A lack of uniformity in identification procedures exists in states and localities.

Because of funding constraints, states may set limits on the number of SED children they will identify.

Children may not be identified, not only because of limited funding, but also because few or no appropriate services may be available in their community or because communities lack confidence in their ability to develop appropriate services due to lack of funding or because this is a difficult population to serve.

A lack of clarity among clinicians in the mental health field on definitions and diagnoses compounds the difficulty educators have in making an assessment that a child is severely emotionally disturbed.

The law explicitly excludes children who are "socially maladjusted," yet the distinctions between socially maladjusted and severely emotionally disturbed are confusing and meaningless. This confusion in labeling can result in some children not being identified or served.

There is a tendency to identify children who present significant behavioral problems, and to overlook those who do not act out. In some communities, this, in part, results in an over-representation of black males identified as SED and an under-identification of females of all races, who may not be labeled as troublesome.

There are limited outreach efforts by schools and education systems to parents and professionals in the community to identify SED youth.

There are also differences for SED children, compared to other populations with handicaps, in the degree of their handicap. SED children tend to be more disturbed before they are identified; those with mild or moderate disturbances may never be identified. (p. 5)

PREVALENCE AND INCIDENCE OF SPECIFIC DISORDERS

So far we have considered behavior disorders in the general case. But because there are many types of disordered behavior, it is possible to estimate the prevalence of some specific problems. Unfortunately, many of the same difficulties of estimation we have discussed for the general case also arise when considering more specific disorders. The classification of behavior disorders is almost as problematic as the general definition. In addition, the methodology of estimation is at least as varied for many specific disorders as for the general case. Consequently, estimates of prevalence and incidence of specific disorders vary and are confusing. Whenever possible, we will provide prevalence data in chapters dealing with specific disorders.

SUMMARY

Nearly all children and youth exhibit, at some time during their development, behavior that could be considered disordered. Labeling 20 percent or more of the child population "disturbed," however, results in disbelief by the general public and alternative explanations by educators. Prevalence figures must be accompanied by convincing arguments that the identified population is in need of special services because their problems are highly unusual and debilitating. Establishing criteria for identification, however, requires arbitrary judgment regarding what degree of behavioral difference is tolerable as well as a judgment as to the relative risks of identification and nonidentification.

Prevalence refers to the number or percentage of individuals exhibiting a disorder at or during a given time. Incidence refers to the number of new cases of a disorder occurring during a given interval. Prevalence has been of greatest interest to special educators because most disabilities have been assumed to be developmental and to entail life-long characteristics. However, special educators are increasingly aware that types of disability, particularly some disorders of learning and behavior, are episodic. Consequently, incidence is becoming of greater interest. Prevalence and incidence may seem irrelevant to the everyday work of the teacher, but they are important issues for those who plan and administer programs, with consequent implications for the teacher's working conditions.

Estimates of prevalence and incidence are made difficult by the lack of a standard definition of emotional disturbance, by methodological problems, and by social policy and economic factors. If no standard definition is accepted, then it is difficult to count cases of disordered behavior. Because the methodology of estimation in behavior disorders is not well developed, we can expect arguments about the meaning of existing studies and difficulties in designing adequate studies. One way to estimate prevalence is to compare behavior ratings of identified populations to the ratings of students who have not been identified. Nonidentified students whose scores are above a cutoff score (for example, the 90th percentile) may be false negatives or candidates for services (that is, *possibly* in need of services). Identified students whose scores fall below the same cutoff may be false positives (perhaps not in need of services). Finally, social policy as embodied in PL 94-142, which requires special education and related services for all handicapped children, plus lack of sufficient funds to provide needed services and teacher training, appear to force prevalence estimates below the levels indicated by research.

The U.S. Department of Education for many years used a prevalence estimate of two percent, although the federal government now publishes no estimate. Reasonable estimates based on the best available research are that three to six percent of the school-age population are in need of special education and related services because of their disordered behavior. Although the percentage of students served increased from about 0.5 percent to about 1.0 percent from the mid-1970s to the mid-1980s, it does not seem likely that dramatic increases in the percentage will occur in the foreseeable future. Economic factors and other pressures, such as the regular education initiative and other moves toward nonidentification, appear likely to limit future estimates of prevalence.

3

The History of the Problem: Development of the Field

As you read this chapter, keep these guiding questions in mind:

☐ What factors make it difficult to trace the history of special education for students with behavior disorders?

☐ What events in the late 1700s set the stage for more humane and effective treatment of children and youth with behavior disorders?

☐ What was moral therapy, and why was it abandoned in the nineteenth century?

☐ What events and trends in the late nineteenth century led to a decline in effective treatment for youngsters with behavior disorders and mental retardation?

☐ What were the predominant emphases in programs for disturbed children and youth in the first half of the twentieth century?

☐ What were the theoretical roots and social forces behind the conceptual models that emerged after 1960?

☐ What are recent trends in the field?

We have seen that the issues of definition and prevalence are difficult matters to resolve. Has this always been the case, or is the difficulty peculiar to the present era of rapid technological development, social change, and the tendency to take conflicts to court? We are tempted to believe that in an earlier era, when life was simpler, the issues were less difficult. Perhaps life was simpler long ago, but much of the historical literature suggests that questions of how to identify social deviance and what to do about it once it is recognized have always been perplexing.

The connectedness of current issues to past problems is an important concept. Today's difficulties cannot be well understood if we assume they emerge from present circumstances alone. While knowledge of history is no guarantee that mistakes will not be repeated, ignorance of history virtually ensures that no real progress will be made. Thus consideration of the historical background of current issues and contemporary practices will serve us well.

Teachers in every era have faced the problem of disorderly and disturbing student behavior (Braaten, 1985). Throughout history one can find examples of youngsters' behavior that angered and disappointed their parents or other adults and violated established codes of conduct. The historical roots of special education for students with behavior disorders are not easy to identify, however. Although behavior disorders of children and youth have long been recognized, it is only relatively recently that systematic special educational provisions for these students have been devised. As Lewis (1974) states:

> When charting the growth of this field, one must make an arbitrary decision concerning a starting point. No matter where one begins, examples of earlier programs or treatments probably can be identified. Tracing the history of the field presents great difficulty because these children have been subsumed under so many different labels and because labeling itself frequently has been determined by the sociological and scientific conditions of the moment. Thus, the beginning of the field of education for the disturbed child is difficult to find; it is lost not only in the confusions of sociological history but also in the myriad of disciplines that criss-cross its development. (p. 5)

To the extent possible, this chapter focuses on the history of *education* for disturbed students and other interventions directly relevant to educational concerns. A purely educational emphasis is not possible, for the conceptual foundations of special education lie for the most part in the disciplines of psychology and psychiatry; its historical origins are thus intertwined inseparably with the histories of other fields of study and practice. Over the years education has come to play a prominent role in the treatment of youngsters' behavior disorders. As this historical sketch unfolds, therefore, it will become increasingly educational in focus.

LATE 1700S: DISPELLING IGNORANCE, NEGLECT, AND ABUSE

Before 1800, handicapped children and youth of any description were at best protected from abuse, and we know of few systematic attempts to teach them. Behavior disorders were believed to be evidence of Satan's power, and children and adolescents were often punished under the law as adults (Bremner, 1970; Despert, 1965). Abuse, neglect, cruel medical treatment (for example, bleeding), and excessive punishment were common and often accepted matter-of-factly for children as well as adults who showed undesirable behavior. Not until the period following the American and French Revolutions in the closing years of the eighteenth century did kind and effective treatment of the "insane" and "idiots" (terms then used to designate mentally ill and mentally retarded individuals, adults and children alike) begin to appear. In that era of political and social revolution, emphasis on individual freedom, human dignity, philanthropy, and public education set the stage for humane treatment and education of handicapped people.

Immediately after the French Revolution, Phillipe Pinel, a distinguished French physician and one of the earliest psychiatrists, unchained several chronic mental patients who had been confined and brutalized for years in the Bicetre Hospital in Paris. When treated with kindness and respect and with the expectation that they would behave appropriately, these formerly deranged and regressed patients showed dramatic improvement in behavior. Pinel's revolutionary and humane methods were widely known and used in Europe and the United States during the first half of the nineteenth century. His approach, which was elaborated upon by his students and admirers, became known as **moral treatment**.

One of Pinel's students was Jean Marc Gaspard Itard, another French physician, who in the late 1700s and early 1800s attempted to teach the "wild boy of Aveyron" (Itard, 1962). This boy, named Victor, was found in the forest where he had apparently been abandoned at an early age. Pinel believed him to be profoundly retarded ("idiotic"), but it is clear from Itard's description that he exhibited many of the behaviors characteristic of severely and profoundly disturbed children. Itard was convinced that the boy could be taught practical skills, including speech, and he was remarkably successful, although Victor never uttered more than a few words. Itard's work with the boy provided the basis for the teaching methods of Edward Seguin and other educators of "idiots" later in the nineteenth century. His book remains a fascinating and moving classic in the education of the handicapped. Contemporary educational methods for retarded and disturbed students are grounded in many of the principles expounded by Itard almost two centuries ago (Lane, 1976).

Besides the work of Pinel and Itard in Europe, developments in America in the late 1700s were also a prelude to education for disturbed children and youth. Most important was the influential writing of Dr. Benjamin Rush of Philadelphia, often considered the father of American psychiatry. Following the American Revolution, Dr. Rush became a strong proponent of public education and public support for schools for poor children.[1] His writings argue vehemently and eloquently against corporal punishment and cruel discipline and for kind and prudent methods of behavior control. His words, first published in 1790 in *The Universal Asylum and Columbian Magazine,* have the ring of present-day child advocacy and appeals for more caring relationships with children:

---

[1] For excerpts from the writings of Benjamin Rush, see Bremner (1970), pp. 218–223, 249–251.

I conceive corporal punishments, inflicted in an arbitrary manner, to be contrary to the spirit of liberty, and that they should not be tolerated in a free government. Why should not children be protected from violence and injuries, as well as white and black servants? Had I influence enough in our legislature to obtain only a single law, it should be to make the punishment for striking a schoolboy, the same as for assaulting and beating an adult member of society.

The world was created in love. It is sustained by love. Nations and families that are happy, are made so only by love. Let us extend this divine principle, to those little communities which we call schools. Children are capable of loving in a high degree. They may therefore be governed by love. (Bremner, 1970, pp. 222–223)

Rush does not advocate the abandonment of discipline. He suggests mild forms of punishment in school: private admonition, confinement after school hours, and requiring the child to hold a small sign of disgrace of any kind in the presence of the other children. If the child does not respond to these methods, Rush recommends dismissing the child from school and turning the business of discipline over to the parents. His emphasis on education and love-oriented methods of control had a profound influence on the early years of American psychiatry and the moral therapy employed in many American lunatic asylums during the first half of the nineteenth century.

THE 1800S: THE RISE AND FALL OF MORAL THERAPY[2]

Twentieth-century descriptions of nineteenth-century treatment of youngsters with behavior disorders are usually brief and negative (Despert, 1965; Kanner, 1957, 1962; Lewis, 1974; Rubenstein, 1948). Only relatively recently has the history of public education for such children and youth been traced (Berkowitz & Rothman, 1967a; Hoffman, 1974, 1975). The literature of the nineteenth century is meager by current standards; children in this literature are often looked upon and treated psychologically as miniature adults; and bizarre ideas (such as the notions that insanity could be caused by masturbation, by studying too hard, or by watching someone have an epileptic seizure) are persistent. However, most histories of childhood behavior disorders consistently contain certain inaccuracies and distortions that lead to under-estimating the value of the nineteenth-century literature in approaching present-day problems (Kauffman, 1976).

The nineteenth-century literature on "insanity" and "idiocy," in which we find most of the literature on youngsters' behavior disorders, leads one to conclude that nearly every current important issue has been an issue for well over a century. Whether these issues persist because of the intractability of the sociopsychological problems they represent or because of the ineptness with which potential solutions have been implemented is moot; the study of historical contributions is crucial in assessing current problems: "History is the basic science. From history flows more than knowl-

[2]Section adapted from J.M. Kauffman, "Nineteenth-Century Views of Children's Behavior Disorders: Historical Contributions and Continuing Issues," *Journal of Special Education* (1976) *10*, 335–349. Used with permission.

edge, more than prescription, more than how it was—how we might try to make it become" (Blatt, 1975, p. 402).

Mental Retardation and Behavior Disorder

One reason the nineteenth century is not often considered an important era in the field of behavior disorders is that the relationship between behavior disorders and mental retardation is overlooked. It is clear to many writers that mentally retarded and emotionally disturbed students are not as different in their characteristics as was assumed several decades ago, regardless of whether one considers mildly and moderately retarded and disturbed or severely and profoundly handicapped students (Balthazar & Stevens, 1975; Barrett, 1986; Crissy, 1975; DeMyer et al., 1974; Hallahan & Kauffman, 1977; Kanner, 1960; Menolascino, 1972). Nineteenth-century writers also recognized the great similarity between "idiocy" (retardation) and "insanity" or "madness" (disturbance). Not until 1886 was there a legal separation between "insanity" and "feeblemindedness" in England (Hayman, 1939).

Some nineteenth-century descriptions of "idiocy" and its varieties present a picture of youngsters who today might well be labeled *psychotic* or *autistic*. Itard's (1962) description of Victor, written at the end of the eighteenth century, is important as a study of behavior disorder as well as a treatise on mental retardation. Esquirol (1845), a French physician, describes in considerable detail the physical and behavioral features of an 11-year-old "imbecile" admitted to the Salpetriere hospital:

> R. usually sits with her knees crossed, her hands beneath her apron, and is almost constantly raising or depressing her shoulders. Her physical health is good, and she has a good appetite. She is a gourmand, worrying herself much about what she shall have to eat at her meals; and if she sees one of her companions eating, cries and calls for something for herself. Whilst with her parents, she was accustomed to escape and run to the shop of a pastrycook who lived near, and devour the first pie that she saw. She was also in the habit of entering a grocer's shop, seizing upon the bottles of liquor, and if they attempted to prevent her from drinking, dashed them upon the ground. . . . She is cunning and conceited. On wetting the bed, as she sometimes does, she defends herself, and accuses the servant girl of it. She detests her roommate, who is mute, and poorly clad. She has been caught thrusting needles into the blistered surface, which had been made upon the person of her wretched companion. (p. 450)

The description of Charles Emile, a 15-year-old "idiot" at the Bicetre, also contains reference to severely disordered behavior. Brigham (1845) summarized the observations of Voisin, a physician at the Bicetre, who said of Charles:

> He was wholly an animal. He was without attachment; overturned everything in his way, but without courage or intent; possessed no tact, intelligence, power of dissimulation, or sense of propriety; and was awkward to excess. His *moral sentiments* are described as *null,* except the love of approbation, and a noisy instinctive gaiety, independent of the external world. . . . Devouring everything, however disgusting, brutally sensual, passionate—breaking, tearing, and burning whatever he could lay his hand upon; and if prevented from doing so, pinching, biting, scratching, and tearing himself, until he was covered with blood. He had the particularity

of being so attracted by the eyes of his brothers, sisters, and playfellows, as to make the most persevering efforts to push them out with his fingers. . . . When any attempt was made to associate him with the other patients, he would start away with a sharp cry, and then come back to them hastily. (p. 336)

Dorothea Dix reported in 1844 the shock of finding in an asylum "a little girl, about nine or ten years of age, who suffered the fourfold calamity of being blind, deaf, dumb, and insane. I can conceive of no condition so pitiable as that of this unfortunate little creature, the chief movements of whose broken mind, were exhibited in restlessness, and violent efforts to escape, and unnatural screams of terror" (Bremner, 1970, p. 777). Dix recognized that behavior disorders could occur in combination with other handicaps. Institutions for deaf and blind individuals, as well as those with mental retardation, served children and youth who would fall into the contemporary categories of autistic or disturbed.

The eminent American educator of the handicapped, Samuel Gridley Howe, understood the difficulty in separating mildly disturbed from mildly retarded students. He uses the term "simulative idiocy" (Howe, 1852) to describe the problem that today would be termed **pseudoretardation**—the *appearance* of mental retardation presented by a nonretarded person. In short, the close relationship between mental retardation and emotional disturbance in children (and in adults) was known in the nineteenth century, and the observations of many nineteenth-century writers are surprisingly consonant with today's emphasis on the similarities and overlapping characteristics, etiologies, and interventions for these two handicapped groups.

As far as treatment is concerned, the historical reviews of Hoffman (1974, 1975) show that public schools of the late nineteenth century made provisions for inept and unruly students who today would comprise groups labeled *emotionally disturbed, learning disabled,* or *educable mentally retarded.* "Incorrigible," "defective," and non-English-speaking students were typically lumped together in special ungraded classes with little or no regard for their specific educational needs. Thus, early public education for students with behavior disorders must be viewed in the context of attempts to deal with the problem of mental retardation as well.

Theories of Etiology

By the end of the eighteenth century, believing that behavior disorders should be treated by religious means because they were caused by demon possession was no longer in vogue among the experts of the day. Nineteenth-century writers were, however, undeniably preoccupied with the relationship between masturbation and insanity, particularly insanity in children and youth. The prevailing belief was that masturbation caused (or at least aggravated) insanity (Hare, 1962; Rie, 1971).[3] Nevertheless, some did question the causal relationship between masturbation and insanity long before the beginning of the twentieth century. Stribling (1842), who refers to

---

[3]The idea that masturbation was an intolerably horrible and debasing practice had not been laid to rest by the end of the nineteenth century. Castration and ovariotomy were still used in the 1890s and early 1900s in attempts to stop masturbation in and sexual interests of "idiotic," "imbecile," "feebleminded," and "epileptic" children and youth, many of whom exhibited other disturbing behaviors (Bremner, 1971, pp. 885–857).

masturbation as a "detestable vice" and a "degrading habit," comments eloquently on associative and causal relationships:

> There is no subject connected with insanity of more interest than the causes from which it proceeds; and there is none certainly in regard to which the enquirer has more difficulty to ascertain the truth. The ignorance of some, and the aversion of others to disclosing the circumstances (which are often of a delicate character) connected with the origin of the patient's malady, are obstacles frequently to be encountered in such investigations—whilst even with the intelligent and communicative, it too often occurs that cause and effect are so confounded, as that the one is improperly made to take the place of the other. . . .
>
> Masturbation . . . as a cause of insanity, we are induced to think is often much exaggerated. Intellect is the great regulator of the human passions and propensities; and as we possess the latter in common with and to as great a degree as other animals, it is only by the former that we are distinguished from and elevated above them. When therefore the mind is thrown into chaos, and man is no longer a rational creature, his animal nature acquires the ascendancy and directs his actions. In this state, too, he is almost invariably cut off from intercourse with his kind, and hence this detestable vice in too many instances becomes his daily habit. When, therefore, in this condition it is first observed, the beholder, forgetting the circumstances which preceded, at once imagines that as no other cause for the mental disorder had ever been assigned, he has made the important discovery; and thus, what in most cases was merely the result of reason dethroned, is chronicled as the monster which expelled her from her empire. (pp. 22–23)

Many of the "causes" of mental illness listed by nineteenth-century writers are laughable indeed: "idleness and ennui," "pecuniary embarrassment," "sedentary and studious habits," "inhaling tobacco fumes," "gold fever," "indulgence of temper" (Stribling, 1842); "suppression of hemorrhoids," "kick on the stomach," "bathing in cold water," "sleeping in a barn filled with new hay," "study of metaphysics," "reading vile books," "license question," "preaching sixteen days and nights," "celibacy," "sudden joy," "ecstatic admiration of works of art," "mortified pride," "Mormonism," "duel," "struggle between the religious principle and power of passion" (Jarvis, 1852); ad infinitum. Nevertheless, writers of the day did question supposed cause-effect relationships, as we see in the quotation from Stribling and in Jarvis's comment that masturbation could not be evaluated as a factor in any increase of insanity because "we have no means of knowing whether masturbation increases or diminishes" (Jarvis, 1852, p. 354).

Some psychiatrists of the early nineteenth century identified etiological factors in youngsters' behavior disorders that are today given serious consideration. For example, Parkinson in 1807 and West in 1848 (in Hunter & Macalpine, 1963) pointed to the interaction of temperament and child rearing, overprotection, overindulgence, and inconsistency of discipline as factors in the development of troublesome behavior. In Parkinson's words:

> That children are born with various dispositions is undoubtedly true; but it is also true, that by due management, these may be so changed and meliorated by the attention of a parent, that not only little blemishes may be smoothed away, but even those circumstances which more offensively distinguish the child, may, by proper management become the characteristic ornaments of the man. . . . On the

treatment the child receives from his parents, during the infantile stage of his life, will, perhaps, depend much of the misery or happiness he may experience, not only in his passage through this, but through the other stages of his existence. (Hunter & Macalpine, 1963, p. 616)

These observations of Parkinson, published in 1807, are consistent with the more recent findings of Thomas, Chess, and Birch (1968), and his comments on inconsistency in child rearing and discipline are much like those of Haring and Phillips (1962). Note Parkinson's modern ideas:

> If, on the one hand, every little sally of passion and impatience is immediately controlled; if those things which are admissible are regularly permitted, and those which are improper are as regularly withheld, the wily little creature will soon learn to distinguish that which is allowed of, from that which is prohibited. He will, indeed, urge his claim, for that to which he has been taught he has a right, with manly boldness; but will not harass himself and his attendants, with ceaseless whinings or ravings, to obtain that which uniform prohibition has placed beyond his expectance. But a melancholy reverse appears, if, on the other hand, no consistency is observed in his management; if, at one time, the slightest indulgence is refused, and at another the most extravagant, and even injurious cravings, are satisfied, just as the caprice of the parent may induce him to gratify his ill humor, by thwarting another; or to amuse his moments of *ennui,* by playing with his child as a monkey, and exciting it to those acts of mischief and audacity for which, in the next moment, it may suffer a severe correction. Continually undergoing either disappointment or punishment; or engaged in extorting gratifications, which he often triumphs at having gained by an artful display of passion; his time passes on, until at last the poor child frequently manifests ill nature sufficient to render him odious to all around him, and acquires pride and meanness sufficient to render him the little hated tyrant of his playfellows and inferiors. (reprinted in Hunter & Macalpine, 1963, pp. 616–617)

Summary of Theories

While biological causes of retardation and behavior disorders were recognized during the first half of the nineteenth century, the emphasis was on environmental factors, especially early discipline and training. It is not surprising, then, that interventions in that period center on environmental control—providing the proper sensory stimulation, discipline, and instruction.

As Hoffman (1974, 1975) notes, the impact of Darwinist thought in the late nineteenth century was profound. The British philosopher, Herbert Spencer, and the American spokesman for social Darwinism in the United States, William Graham Sumner, saw the seeds of social decay and destruction in the unchecked propagation of the lower classes and defective individuals, as did Dr. Walter E. Fernald (1893), the distinguished medical superintendent of the Massachusetts School for the Feeble-minded. The ideas of social evolution, survival of the fittest, and **eugenics** were to lead inevitably to the writing and influence of Henry H. Goddard, an early twentieth-century progenitor of special education (Balthazaar & Stevens, 1975; Smith, 1962). The favored position in the late nineteenth and early twentieth centuries was that undesirable behavioral traits represented inherited flaws and that intervention should be limited to selective breeding.

Intervention

One cannot deny that many children and youth, including those with behavior disorders and limited intellect, were neglected and abused in the nineteenth century. Bremner (1970, 1971), Hoffman (1974, 1975) and Rothman (1971) amply document the cruel discipline, forced labor, and other inhumanities suffered by children and youth in the 1800s. Although many nineteenth-century attempts at education and treatment of handicapped youngsters were primitive compared to the best that can be offered today, some behavior disordered youngsters in the nineteenth century received considerably better care than many such children receive today. If one were to concentrate on the neglect and abuse of youngsters in institutions, schools, detention centers, and homes in the twentieth century, one might justifiably conclude that the plight of children and youth has not improved much in the last hundred years (Blatt & Kaplan, 1966; Deutsch, 1948; Knitzer, 1982; Rothman, 1971). Contrasting the best contemporary thinking and treatment to the worst of the nineteenth century creates a dark and distorted vision of the last century, with its references to imprisonment, cruelty, punishment, neglect, ignorance, bizarre ideas (masturbatory insanity), and absence of effective education and treatment for youngsters with behavior disorders (Despert, 1965; Kanner, 1962; Rie, 1971; Rubenstein, 1948). As it happens, many nineteenth-century leaders in the treatment of children with behavior disorders were more enlightened than their critics have assumed. Unfortunately, some of their brightest successes, such as moral treatment, have usually been ignored.

Seldom has moral treatment been mentioned in connection with children and youth. "Moral treatment, in modern technical jargon, is what we mean by resocialization by means of a growing list of therapies with prefaces such as recreational, occupational, industrial, music—with physical education thrown in for good measure" (Bockoven, 1956, p. 303). Bockoven points out that these therapies do not add up to moral treatment, which implies an integrated total treatment program (see Brigham, 1847, for a succinct description of moral treatment).[4] Rie (1971) discusses moral treatment of the 1800s but largely discounts its relevance for child psychopathology because youngsters were not admitted to institutions in great numbers. Yet children and youth did find their way into institutions and were treated by moral therapists during the first half of the nineteenth century (*Annual Reports of the Court of Directors of the Western Lunatic Asylum,* 1836–1850, 1870; *American Journal of Insanity,* Vols. I–VI, 1844–1850; Esquirol, 1845; Hunter & Macalpine, 1974; Mayo, 1839). For example, Francis Stribling, a prominent moral therapist of the early 1800s, reports that of 122 patients in Western Lunatic Asylum during 1841, nine were under the age of 20 and two under the age of 15 (Stribling, 1842). Thus, we need to include moral treatment in the types of care offered to children and youth in that era.

Moral therapists emphasized constructive activity, kindness, minimum restraint, structure, routine, and consistency in treatment. Furthermore, obedience to authority

---

[4]The term *moral treatment* did not, as some have surmised, connote religious training. Originally, as translated from Pinel's work, moral treatment meant *psychological* as opposed to *medical* treatment of insanity and included every therapeutic endeavor other than medication or surgery. For further discussion of moral treatment, see Bockoven (1972), Caplan (1969), Carlson and Dain (1960), Dain and Carlson (1960), Grob (1962), Menninger (1963), Rees (1957), and Ullmann and Krasner (1969).

and conformity to rules were primary features of child-care institutions and child-rearing dogma in mid-nineteenth century America (Rothman, 1971). Rothman indicates that the emphasis on obedience and conformity was sometimes carried to a ridiculous or even harmful extreme, that some youngsters languished in jails or poorhouses, and that the concepts of structure, consistency, and reeducation were sometimes distorted to include cruel and excessive punishment. Still, it is evident from the writing of moral therapists that humane, nonpunitive care was the goal. Mayo (1839) provides an example of the type of treatment afforded behavior disordered children and youth by moral therapists. (The following is a continuation of his report on the case of the adolescent boy described in Chapter 1.)

Moral Therapy

When I saw him (December 8th, 18– –), he received me courteously but suspiciously; his demeanor was soft, but there was a bad expression about his mouth; I believe his eyes gave him the appearance of softness; they were large and dark; his skin was smooth; he was small for his age, not having grown for some years. On my addressing him in regard to his peculiarities, he equivocated and became irritable; and he asserted that he was under impulses which he could not resist. He spoke unkindly of his father, and tried to snatch out of my hand a very wicked letter written by himself to one of his relatives, which I produced as an evidence of his misconduct. This peculiarity seemed to pervade his views of his own conduct,—that he contemplated past offenses, not only as what could not be recalled, but also, as what ought not to be remembered to his disadvantage.

Having satisfied my mind by careful observation, that the accounts given by his relatives were substantially correct, and that the ordinary principles of education, however skillfully applied, would here lead to no salutary result, I suggested the following line of treatment, as calculated to give him his best chance of moral improvement. Let him reside in the neighborhood, or, if possible, in the family of some person competent to undertake this charge, under the attendance of two trustworthy men, who should be subject to the authority of the superior above alluded to; one of these persons should be in constant attendance upon him; but if coercion should be required in order to induce him to comply with reasonable requests, both should be employed so as not to make such violence necessary as should produce the slightest bodily pain. The object of this plan would be to accustom him to obedience, and by keeping him in a constant state of the exercise of this quality, for such a length of time as might form a habit, to adapt him to live in society afterwards, on terms of acquiescence in its rules.

Now the principle of management suggested here, is that ordinarily applied to insane patients alone; but this young man could not be considered insane in any accredited use of the term. He was totally free from false perception, or inconsequential thoughts; he was neat in his person, agreeable in his address, and of an intellect above rather than below par. Yet, education in its appeal to the moral principle had been tried on him in many various forms with total unsuccess: youth was advancing into manhood; and his chances of attaining a state, in which he might be a safe member of society, were becoming slender according to any of the usual methods of moral education.

The case seemed to warrant the application of the principle recommended; and after much thought, I determined to try it in the only way in which it was practicable to me, namely, in the walls of an establishment, a few miles from the place in which I resided, the proprietor of which was well known to me for excellent judgment and an amiable character.

I took him to this establishment, accompanied by his father and another relative, showed him at once into his apartment; and briefly told him why he was placed there; and how inflexible he would find his restraint there, until he should have gained habits of self-control. At the same time I pointed out to him the beautiful and wide grounds of the establishment, and the many comforts and enjoyments which he might command by strict obedience. This I stated to him in the presence of his two relatives, whom I then at once removed from the room. When I saw him about an hour afterwards, the nearest approach to surprise and annoyance which he made, was the expression, "that he never was in such a lurch before." He wished to see his father again before he left the house, not however, apparently from motives of feeling, but in order to address some persuasives to him against the scheme. I refused this interview.

For about a fortnight he behaved extremely well. He then lost his self-command, kicked his attendant, and struck him with a bottle of medicine. On this, I went over to see him; he vindicated himself with his usual ingenuity; but looked grave and somewhat frightened,—when I told him, that if he repeated this offence, he would be placed in a strait waistcoat, not indeed as a punishment, but as a means of supplying his deficiency of self-control. He expresses no kindly feeling towards his relatives; but confesses the fitness of his treatment and confinement. It appears to me, that he is tranquilized by his utter inability to resist.

January 16th, 18– –. Visiting N.B. today, I told him, that he might write letters to his father or uncle, but that he would at present receive none from them. To have refused him permission to write letters would have been tyrannical; besides, they would afford insight into his character; to have allowed him to receive letters, would have been an interference with that principle of entire separation from his family, which I wished to maintain, until he should have learned the value of those ties to which he has been indifferent. He made complaints in very unimportant matters against his servant, to which I paid attention, but gave no credence. Great unfairness in these remarks. I have endeavoured to make him understand, that in dealing with Mr. N____, the proprietor of the establishment, and myself he can neither enjoy the pleasure of making us angry, nor hope for advantage from sophistry. But that strict justice will be done him, upon the terms originally stated to him.

In a letter to his father about this time, I observe—"the plan evidently works well. He is practicing self-restraint successfully; not indeed from conviction of its moral fitness, but from having ascertained its necessity. He is aware of the state of entire subjection in which he is placed; and yet his spirits do not flag, neither does his health suffer. It is curious, that he has ceased to use his old argument in conversation with me, that past conduct ought not to be taken into the account in regard to present proceedings." From the time above alluded to, during his stay at the establishment, which I continued for fourteen months, no further outbreak against authority took place. He ceased to be violent, because the indulgence of violence would imply risk of inconvenience to himself, without the comfort which he had formerly derived from it in exciting the anger of his friends or giving them pain. (Mayo, 1839, pp. 69–70)

By the middle of the nineteenth century, educators were providing programs for intellectually limited and behaviorally disordered students. Schools in asylums for "insane" and "idiotic" students flourished for a time under the leadership of humanistic teachers who developed explicit teaching methods (Brigham, 1845, 1847, 1848; Howe, 1851, 1852; Ray, 1846). As Bockoven (1956) notes, education was a prominent part of moral treatment. Teaching and learning were considered conducive to mental health—a concept that can hardly be considered bizarre or antiquated.

Most of the education for severely and profoundly behavior disordered children and youth, aside from the academic instruction offered in asylums for "the insane," was provided under the rubric of education for "idiots." The teaching techniques employed by leading educators of retarded students were amazingly modern in many respects—based on individual assessment, highly structured, systematic, directive, and multisensory, with emphasis on training in self-help and daily living skills for those with severe disabilities, frequent use of games and songs, and suffusion with positive reinforcement (Brigham, 1848; Itard, 1962; Ray, 1846; Seguin, 1866). Despite the overenthusiasm and excessive claims of success by moral therapists and early educators of retarded students (Howe, Itard, and Seguin), the basic soundness of their work and the changes they were able to produce in disturbed and retarded children and youth remain impressive (Balthazar & Stevens, 1975). At midcentury the prevailing attitude was one of hope and belief that every handicapped student could be helped. As Brigham (1845) states:

> The interesting question is, to what extent can careful and skillful instruction make up for these natural deficiencies [of idiotic children]; and, as already done for the deaf, the dumb, and the blind, reclaim for these unfinished creatures the powers and privileges of life. The exertions of future philanthropists will answer this question. Improvement must not be looked for beyond what is strictly relative to the imperfect individual in each case; but it would seem to be true of idiots, as of the insane in general, that there is no case incapable of some amendment; that every case may be improved or cured, up to a certain point—a principle of great general importance in reference to treatment. (pp. 334-335)

In the nineteenth century, considerable concern was shown for children and youth who were delinquent, vagrant, aggressive, disobedient, or disadvantaged (poor or orphaned), but not considered "insane" or "idiotic" (Bremner, 1970, 1971; Eggleston, 1987; Rothman, 1971). Many of these youngsters, who today might be categorized as mildly or moderately handicapped (behavior disordered or retarded), found their way into jails and almshouses. There was, however, a strong movement to establish child-care institutions (orphan asylums, reformatories, houses of refuge, and so on) for the purpose of reforming and rehabilitating children and youth. The intent was to protect wayward, handicapped, and poor youngsters and to provide for their education and training in a humane, familial atmosphere. Concern for the futures of those exhibiting acting-out behavior was not entirely misguided. Contemporary longitudinal studies tend to confirm what nineteenth-century writers suspected— aggressive, acting-out, delinquent behavior in youngsters predicts misfortune for their later adjustment (Robins, 1966, 1979).

Intervention in the public schools became a reality only after the enactment of compulsory attendance laws in the closing decades of the century. One reason for enacting compulsory attendance laws, in fact, was the large number of non-English-speaking immigrant youngsters who poured into the United States during this period. Immigrant children and youth, authorities felt, should be compelled to be socialized and Americanized by the schools. Once the attendance laws were enacted and enforced, many students obviously interfered with the education of the majority and benefited little from the regular class themselves. Before these youngsters had been compelled to go to school, they had merely dropped out, causing no problems except by roaming the streets and committing delinquent acts. Partly out of concern for such problems, the public schools established ungraded classes. In 1871, authorities in New Haven, Connecticut, opened an ungraded class for truant, disobedient, and insubordinate children. Soon afterward, other cities followed suit, and classes for the socially maladjusted and "backward" (that is, mentally retarded) students grew rapidly (Berkowitz & Rothman, 1967a; Hoffman, 1974). These special classes, as well as corporate schools and similar institutions, became little more than dumping grounds for all manner of misfits. Whether the students or the public school administrators were the misfits was as pertinent a question for that era as it is for the present (Cruickshank, Paul, & Junkala, 1969).

Changes within the 1800s

The nineteenth century cannot be viewed as a unitary or homogeneous historical period. In the years between 1850 and 1900, important changes took place in attitudes toward severe and profound behavior disorders and mental deficiency, and rather dramatic differences appeared in the type of care afforded in institutions. Optimism, pragmatism, inventiveness, and humane care, associated with moral treatment and model social programs in the first half of the century, gave way to pessimism, theorizing, rigidity, and dehumanizing institutionalization after the Civil War. The failure of private philanthropy and public programs to solve the problems of "idiocy," "insanity," and delinquency and to rectify the situations of the poor led to cynicism and disillusionment. More and larger asylums and houses of refuge were not the answers. The many complex reasons for the retrogression after 1850 include economic, political, social, and professional factors analyzed by Bockoven (1956, 1972), Caplan (1969), Deutsch (1948), Grob (1973), Kanner (1964), Menninger (1963), Rothman (1971), and Ullmann and Krasner (1969).

Ironically, most historical comment on children's behavior disorders seems to favor the last decades of the century as more auspicious in the development of child psychiatry (Alexander & Selsnick, 1966; Harms, 1967; Kanner, 1973c; Rie, 1971; Walk, 1964). MacMillan's (1960) review of the literature suggests that the earlier decades provided a richer body of information, at least for the severely and profoundly disturbed:

> Examination of the 19th century literature relating to psychosis in childhood shows that the psychotic child was an object of study in the first part of the century, and that a substantial body of knowledge on the subject was accumulated in that period. Toward the latter part of the century, not only did the level of knowledge decline, but the psychotic child even seems to have ceased to have been an object of study. (p. 1091)

These observations seem to be borne out by examination of some of the literature published during the last decades of the century. Certainly, there is little or nothing to be found in the writings of Hammond (1891), Maudsley (1880), or Savage

(1891) that improves upon earlier works insofar as treatment is concerned. The valuable and insightful work of the late nineteenth-century psychiatrists (such as Griesinger) reviewed by Harms (1967) is concerned with the theory and diagnosis of psychological disturbances in children and youth. After the demise of moral treatment about midcentury, psychiatry became increasingly engrossed in varieties of psychodynamic theory, and therapeutic action on behalf of patients often gave way to interest in diagnosis and classification. Educational and reform efforts with problem children and delinquents increased in number and size, but not in quality or effectiveness. Hoffman (1974) notes that "in each case, what began as sincere, humanistic efforts toward change were turned into near caricatures of their original purposes" (p.71). Before 1900 it was clear that institutionalization did not mean treatment and that special class placement meant marred identity.

Late 1800s

By the end of the nineteenth century, several textbooks had been published about the psychiatric disorders of children and youth. These books deal primarily with etiology and classification and, as Kanner (1960) notes, tend toward fatalism. Psychiatric disorders were assumed to be the irreversible results of such widely varied causes as masturbation, overwork, hard study, religious preoccupation, heredity, degeneracy, or disease. The problems of obstreperous children and juvenile delinquents had not been solved, but new efforts were being made: Lightner Witmer established a psychoeducational clinic at the University of Pennsylvania in 1896; Chicago and Denver established the country's first juvenile courts in 1899. Events and trends during the first decades of the twentieth century represented a gradual increase in concern for the child with disordered behavior.

1900 TO 1960: ESTABLISHMENT OF INTERVENTION PROGRAMS

1900 to 1910

Several important events in the first years of the twentieth century gave direction and impetus to concern for children and youth for many years to come. Ellen Key, the Swedish sociologist, awakened great interest with her prophecy that the twentieth century would be "the century of the child" (Key, 1909). Clifford W. Beers, a bright young man who experienced a nervous breakdown in 1900 and later recovered, recorded his experiences in a mental hospital. His autobiography, *A Mind that Found Itself* (Beers, 1908), had a profound influence on public opinion. Along with the psychiatrist Adolph Meyer and the philosopher and psychologist William James, Beers founded the National Committee for Mental Hygiene in 1909. The mental hygiene movement resulted in efforts at early detection and prevention, including the establishment of mental hygiene programs in schools and the opening of child guidance clinics.[5] Dr. William Healy founded the Juvenile Psychopathic Institute for the psy-

---

[5]For descriptions of mental hygiene programs and special school provisions for maladjusted children during this era, see the historical account of Berkowitz & Rothman (1967a).

chological and sociological study of juvenile delinquents in 1909. Healy and his second wife, Augusta Bronner, along with Grace M. Fernald, Julia Lathrop, and others in Chicago began their systematic study of repeated juvenile offenders that influenced research and theory for many years.[6] Also during these years, Alfred Binet introduced an intelligence scale to measure children's performance and to predict their success at school. Sigmund Freud and his contemporaries began writing widely on the topics of infant sexuality and human mental development. The work of Freud and other psychoanalysts was to have a profound effect on the way children's behavior was viewed and, eventually, on attempts to educate disturbed children and youth. Finally, during these years Drs. Henry Goddard and Walter Fernald forwarded the notion that mental retardation is inseparably linked to criminality and degeneracy (Doll, 1967; Hoffman, 1974; Smith, 1962).

1911 to 1930

Concern for the mental and physical health of children expanded greatly after 1910 (Ollendick & Hersen, 1983). In 1911, Dr. Arnold Gesell founded the Clinic for Child Development at Yale, and in 1912, Congress created the U.S. Children's Bureau "to investigate and report upon all matters pertaining to the welfare of children and child life among all classes of our people." The first teacher training program in special education began in Michigan in 1914. By 1918, all states had compulsory education laws, and in 1919, Ohio passed a law for statewide care of handicapped children. By 1930, sixteen states had enacted laws allowing local school districts to recover the excess costs of educating exceptional children and youth (Henry, 1950). Educational and psychological testing were becoming widely used and school psychology, guidance, and counseling were emerging. Mental hygiene and child guidance clinics became relatively common by 1930, and by this time child psychiatry was a new discipline (Kanner, 1973c). According to Kanner, child guidance clinics of this era made three major innovations: (1) interdisciplinary collaboration; (2) treatment of any child whose behavior was annoying to parents and teachers, not just the severe cases; and (3) attention to the effects of interpersonal relationships and adult attitudes on child behavior (Kanner, 1973c, pp. 194–195).

In the 1920s, demand arose for mental hygiene programs in the schools, and some school systems established such programs. Thomas Haines, director of the Division of Mental Deficiency of the National Committee for Mental Hygiene, called for statutes governing the study and training of *all* exceptional children in the public schools, including the "psychopathic, the psychoneurotic, and those who exhibit behavior problems" (Haines, 1925). In an article in the *New Republic,* Dr. Smiley Blanton (1925), director of the Minneapolis Child Guidance Clinic and a practicing child psychiatrist, describes the operation of mental hygiene clinics in the public schools of Minneapolis.[7] The staff consisted of a psychologist, three psychiatric social workers (who had been teachers before they became social workers), 20 visiting teachers, and 10 corrective speech teachers. One of the functions of the clinic was to

---

[6]See Healy (1915a, b; 1931) and Healy and Bronner (1926); also Eggleston, 1987.
[7]See Bremner (1971), pp. 947–957, 1040–1057.

organize a course in mental hygiene for high school juniors and seniors. Another objective was to establish behavior clinics in kindergartens. The clinic took referrals from teachers and parents and also served preschool and juvenile court cases. After referral to the clinic, a child was studied carefully and a staff meeting was held to determine a course of action. Typically, the staff talked things over with the parents and teacher and tried to change their attitudes toward the child. Specific instructions were given on behavior management, and a social worker would then go to the home or classroom to help carry out the program.

Two professional organizations that are particularly important to the education of disturbed children were founded in the 1920s. The Council of Exceptional Children, organized in 1922, was then made up primarily of educators but included other professionals and parents. The group became a powerful force for the appropriation of monies and the passage of legislation concerning the education of all handicapped children. The American Orthopsychiatric Association (AOA), dominated by the professions of child psychiatry, clinical psychology, and social work but including education and other disciplines as well, was founded in 1924. The AOA did much to encourage research and dissemination of information regarding therapeutic and educational endeavors with behavior disordered children.

1931 to 1945

The Depression and World War II necessarily diverted attention and funds from education of handicapped students. There were, however, more handicapped students in special education in 1940 than in 1930, and by 1948, 41 of the 48 states had enacted laws authorizing or requiring local school districts to make special educational provisions for at least one category of exceptional children (Henry, 1950). The vast majority of special classes were for the educable mentally retarded. Programs for students with behavior disorders were relatively few and were designed primarily for acting-out and delinquent children and youth in large cities.

Hitler's rise to power in Europe provided several unanticipated benefits for the education of handicapped children in this country. Several people who were later to influence special education fled to the United States, including Bruno Bettelheim, Marianne Frostig, Alfred Strauss, and Heinz Werner.[8] (We will touch on some of their contributions later.)

Several significant developments in child psychiatry occurred during this period. The first psychiatric hospital for children in the United States, the Bradley Home, was established in Rhode Island in 1931 (Davids, 1975). Leo Kanner of Johns Hopkins University contributed immeasurably to the field with the first edition of his textbook *Child Psychiatry* in 1935 and with his initial descriptions of early infantile autism (Kanner, 1943, 1973a, b, c). Here is his description of his first experience with children who would later be said to have "Kanner's syndrome."

> In October 1938, a 5-year-old boy was brought to my clinic from Forest, Mississippi.
> I was struck by the uniqueness of the peculiarities which Donald exhibited. He

---

[8]See Frostig (1976), Hallahan and Cruickshank (1973), and Hallahan and Kauffman (1976, 1977).

could, since the age of 2½ years, tell the names of all the presidents and vice-presidents, recite the letters of the alphabet forwards and backwards, and flawlessly, with good enunciation, rattle off the Twenty-Third Psalm. Yet he was unable to carry on an ordinary conversation. He was out of contact with people, while he could handle objects skillfully. His memory was phenomenal. The few times when he addressed someone—largely to satisfy his wants—he referred to himself as "You" and to the person as "I." He did not respond to any intelligence tests but manipulated intricate formboards adroitly. (Kanner, 1973a, p. 93)

During the 1930s, Despert (a 1968 collection of her papers) and Potter (1933), with Kanner and others, tried to clarify the characteristics of various categories of severely and profoundly disturbed youngsters. Dr. Lauretta Bender, also writing on the topic of childhood schizophrenia, pioneered the development of education for these children in the 1930s. Having organized the children's ward at Bellevue Psychiatric Hospital in New York City in 1934, she appealed in 1935 to the New York City Board of Education for teachers to staff special classrooms for severely disturbed children at Bellevue. The Board responded by assigning two substitute teachers to teach ungraded classes (the category used for mentally retarded children) at Bellevue under the administration of the school for the physically handicapped. Despite inadequate facilities and a complete lack of instructional materials in the beginning, the program succeeded (Wright, 1967). The Bellevue school was to become a fertile training ground for future leaders, most notably Pearl Berkowitz and Esther Rothman (Berkowitz, 1974; Rothman, 1974).

By the end of the 1930s, the literature on children's behavior disorders had grown to sizable proportions (Baker & Stullken, 1938). Attempts had been made to define emotional disturbance and to delineate several subclassifications. Surveys of children's behavior problems and teachers' attitudes toward misbehavior (Wickman, 1929) had been completed, and there had been efforts to estimate the prevalence of behavior disorders. Various plans of special education for disturbed children, such as special rooms, schools, classes, and consultative help, had been tried.

The Post-War Years and the 1950s

Following the Second World War, additional varieties of severely disturbed children were described by the psychiatric profession.[9] Mahler (1952) delineates a form she calls *symbiotic infantile psychosis* (overattachment to the mother); Rank (1949) introduces the term *atypical child* (any severe disturbance of early development resulting from problems of relationship between mother and child); Bergman and Escalona (1949) describe children with unusual sensitivity to sensory stimulation; and Robinson and Vitale (1954) write about children with circumscribed interest patterns. All of these children with severe disorders fit under the general category of childhood psychosis.

The 1940s and 1950s saw a rising wave of interest in the education of disturbed children. In 1944, Bruno Bettelheim began his work with severely disturbed children

---

[9]For succinct summaries of the contributions of numerous individuals working in this era, see Haring and Phillips (1962).

at the Sonja Shankman Orthogenic School at the University of Chicago. His concept of a "therapeutic milieu" (Bettelheim, 1950; Bettelheim & Sylvester, 1948) continues to be used in educational methods based on psychoanalytic thought (Bettelheim, 1961, 1970; Redl, 1959a, 1966; Trieschman, Whittaker, & Brendtro, 1969). During the 1940s, Fritz Redl and David Wineman began their work with hyperaggressive youngsters in Detroit. Basing their strategies on the ideas of Bettleheim and others who were psychoanalytic in their thinking regarding delinquency (Aichorn, 1935; Eissler, 1949; Freud, 1946), Redl and Wineman describe their use of a therapeutic milieu and a technique called the **life space interview** at Pioneer House, a residential setting for young aggressive and delinquent boys (Redl & Wineman, 1951, 1952). The efforts and thoughts of Redl and Wineman influenced an entire generation of educators of the disturbed (Long, 1974; Morse, 1974).

The New York City Board of Education organized its 600 schools in 1946.[10] These schools, arbitrarily numbered from 600 to 699, were established specifically for the purpose of educating disturbed and maladjusted youngsters. Some were day schools located in regular school buildings; others were located in residential diagnostic and treatment settings (Berkowitz & Rothman, 1967a).

One of the most important publications of the 1940s was a book by Alfred A. Strauss and Laura E. Lehtinen, *Psychopathology and Education of the Brain-Injured Child* (1947). This book summarizes the work of Strauss and his colleagues (especially Heinz Werner) and students at the Wayne County Training School in Northville, Michigan, and the Cove Schools in Racine, Wisconsin. Although much of the work of Werner and Strauss was with the exogenous (postnatally brain-damaged) mentally retarded child, Strauss and Lehtinen recognized that learning problems exist in some children of normal intelligence. They attributed these learning difficulties to brain injury; however, they recognized that emotional maladjustment is characteristic of such children:

> The response of the brain-injured child to the school situation is frequently inadequate, conspicuously disturbing, and persistently troublesome. The following excerpts from teacher's reports are illustrative.
>
> J.M., 7 years old: "... doesn't pay attention to any directions. He is unaware of anything said, yet at times he surprises me by noticing things that others don't."
>
> D.J., 7 years old: "... attention hard to hold. Asks constantly: "When can I go? Can I go now?" etc. No initiative. Little self-control. Seems high strung and nervous. ..."
>
> D.H., 8 years old: "... has proven quite a serious problem in behavior. Has acquired the habit of throwing himself into tantrums at the slightest provocation. ..."
>
> J.K., 8 years old: "... has made scarcely any social adjustments in relationships with other children, he loses all self-control, becoming wild and uncontrollable; he is extremely nervous and excitable; his attention span is very short and he is unable to concentrate for more than a few minutes. During work periods he jumps from one activity to another. ..." (Strauss & Lehtinen, 1947, p. 127)[11]

---

[10]The designation "600" has now been dropped in favor of a random numbering system. This decision was made in 1965, after it became apparent that 600 was stigmatizing. For additional description of education in schools of this type, see Tobin (1971).

[11]From *Psychopathology and Education of the Brain-Injured Child* by A. A. Strauss and L. L. Lehtinen, 1947, pp. 127, 129–130. Copyright 1947 by Grune & Stratton. Reprinted by permission.

For such children, Strauss and Lehtinen recommended a highly structured educational approach and a highly consistent, distraction-free environment. Besides general educational principles, they describe special methods for teaching arithmetic, reading, and writing. Their work is particularly important because it provided the foundation for the later efforts of Cruickshank (Cruickshank, Bentzen, Ratzeburg, & Tannhauser, 1961) and Haring and Phillips (1962).

By the early 1950s, interest in special education for students with behavior disorders gained considerable momentum. In fact, one could say that this area of special education came of age by the end of the 1950s, for one no longer had to be content with examining developments in psychiatry or with citing references in mental retardation. Education of disturbed students had become a field of specialization in its own right. One early indication of mental health professionals' recognition of the importance of education in dealing with the behavior disordered student was publication of a symposium on the education of emotionally disturbed children (Krugman, 1953). This issue was one of the first attempts by the *American Journal of Orthopsychiatry* to devote an appreciable number of pages specifically to a collection of papers on the importance of schools and education. Among the papers of the symposium are those of Louis Hay (1953), detailing the Junior Guidance Class Program in New York City, and Dr. J. Cotter Hirschberg (1953), explaining the important roles of education in residential treatment of the severely disturbed child. It is worthy of note that the second part of the *Forty-ninth Yearbook of the National Society for the Study of Education* on the education of exceptional children (the first in its history, published in 1950) includes a chapter on the education of socially maladjusted children and youth (Stullken, 1950). Another landmark event of the early 1950s was the founding of the League School by Carl Fenichel in 1953 (Fenichel, 1974; Fenichel, Freedman, & Klapper, 1960). The League School was the first private day school for seriously emotionally disturbed children in the United States. Fenichel, who had training in psychoanalysis, began the school using a permissive, psychoanalytic orientation, but soon gave this up in favor of a more directive, psychoeducational approach (Fenichel, 1966, 1974).

In 1955, the first book describing classroom teaching of disturbed children appeared.[12] In it, Leonard Kornberg (1955) recounts his experiences in teaching 15 disturbed boys at Hawthorn-Cedar Knolls, a residential school near New York City. His teaching approach was based primarily on psychoanalytic thought and drew heavily on the interpersonal therapeutic process—"dialogue" and responding to "I" and "otherness." As he puts it, "The essential classroom event is the transaction of meaning among more than two persons, as contrasted with the two-person contact of a therapy situation" (Kornberg, 1955, p. 132). This emphasis on interpersonal relationship and psychiatric-dynamic ideas is predominant in the literature of the 1950s.

---

[12]The books that appeared before 1955 are not primarily descriptions of classroom teaching, although Redl and Wattenberg discuss mental health in teaching and others (e.g., Bettelheim, 1950; Hymes, 1949; Pearson, 1954; Prescott, 1954; Redl & Wineman, 1951, 1952; Slavson, 1954) examine the relationship between psychoanalysis, psychotherapy, other forms of treatment, and mental health efforts and education. Also Axline (1947) and Moustakas (1953) describe play therapy with children. Until the early 1960s, the most explicit teaching methods for children with behavior disorders were probably found in the classic books by Strauss and Lehtinen (1947) and Strauss and Kephart (1955).

By the mid-1950s, it was recognized that systematic procedures were needed to identify disturbed students in the public schools. Eli Bower and others began research in California that culminated in publication of the screening instrument devised by Bower and Lambert (1962) and other writings of Bower (1960, 1975). Concern for teaching disturbed children and youth had grown by the late 1950s to the extent that an initial study of teacher preparation was reported by Mackie, Kvaraceus, and Williams (1957). The last years of the decade were auspicious for the field because numerous individuals were attaining new vantage points on the education of disturbed children: Pearl H. Berkowitz and Esther P. Rothman were collaborating in New York City; William C. Morse and Nicholas J. Long were working at the University of Michigan's Fresh Air Camp for disturbed children; Frank M. Hewett was beginning his studies with severely disturbed children at the University of California at Los Angeles; Nicholas Hobbs and William C. Rhodes began conceptualizing new strategies at George Peabody College in Nashville, Tennessee; William M. Cruickshank and Norris G. Haring were conducting research projects in the public schools of Maryland and Virginia; and Richard J. Whelan was developing a directive, structured approach to teaching disturbed children and youth at the Menninger Clinic in Topeka, Kansas. These activities resulted in a wave of publications and research that burst upon the field in the 1960s and 1970s.

1960 TO 1985: THE EMERGENCE OF CONCEPTUAL MODELS

A steady stream of events after 1960 led to the current diversity of theory and practice in the education of disturbed students. While much of the groundwork was laid prior to 1960, only after that point were specific classroom practices articulated. Then, special classes for disturbed students in the public schools proliferated to such a degree that planning guidelines were published (Hollister & Goldston, 1962) and a nationwide survey of special classes was conducted (Morse, Cutler, & Fink, 1964). Professionals banded together in 1964 to form a new division of the Council for Exceptional Children, the Council for Children with Behavioral Disorders. Various curriculum designs for behavior disordered students were outlined (Kauffman, 1974a; Rhodes, 1963), and curricula to teach specific social-interpersonal skills were developed (Fagen, Long, & Stevens, 1975; Walker, Hops, & Greenwood, 1981). A series of three annual conferences on the education of emotionally disturbed children was held at Syracuse University, bringing together educators and psychologists of divergent viewpoints (Knoblock, 1965, 1966; Knoblock & Johnson, 1967). Preparation of personnel to work with disturbed children received federal support in 1963 with the enactment of Public Law 88-164 (amending PL 85-926 of 1958). The National Society for Children and Adults with Autism (initially called the National Society for Autistic Children) was founded in 1965, and the Association for Persons with Severe Handicaps (initially called the Association for the Severely Handicapped) was organized in 1974, reflecting increased interest in the field.

To review all the important events and trends of the years between 1960 and 1985 would be impossible, but we will summarize several of the more critical developments. These events are organized around conceptual models, because it was during this era that distinctly different and competing concepts of emotional disturbance and intervention clearly emerged. (We will discuss the implications of various conceptual models more thoroughly in Chapter 4.)

Psychoanalytic View

In 1960, Berkowitz and Rothman published their now classic book, *The Disturbed Child: Recognition and Psychoeducational Therapy in the Classroom*. After describing various classifications of disturbed children, they devote four chapters to the teacher's role and classroom procedures. The underlying theory is psychoanalytic, and their suggested approach is quite permissive. In a later book, Berkowitz and Rothman (1967b) pulled together descriptions by several individuals of a variety of programs for disturbed children in New York City. Together they further delineated their concept of clinical teaching (Rothman & Berkowitz, 1967b), proposed a paradigm for a clinical school (Rothman & Berkowitz, 1967a), and described methods of teaching reading to emotionally disturbed students (Rothman & Berkowitz, 1967c). In other works Berkowitz (1974) reported the status of public schools in treatment centers and described her continued work in institutional schools in New York City; Rothman (1970, 1974) wrote more about her involvement with the Livingston School.

Psychoeducational Approach

Just as Berkowitz and Rothman's later publications reflected movement from a strictly psychoanalytic perspective toward a more pragmatic stance, the work of Morse and others at the University of Michigan in the 1960s showed a tendency to emphasize practical considerations and ego development. Morse and Long, in collaboration with Ruth G. Newman, published the first edition of a landmark volume, *Conflict in the Classroom* (Long, Morse, & Newman, 1965). This book brought together the ideas of Redl and Morse regarding the life space interview, but included several disparate viewpoints, ranging from the psychoanalytic (Freud, 1965) to the behavioral (Haring & Whelan, 1965). The life space interview (LSI) grew out of Redl's work at Pioneer House in Detroit in the 1940s and 1950s (see Heuchert & Long, 1980). At or shortly after a behavioral crisis, the teacher (or other child worker) conducts an LSI to strengthen the youngster's ego and help the youngster understand and interpret correctly the problems he or she has just encountered (Long & Newman, 1965; Morse, 1953, 1965b; Morse & Wineman, 1965; Redl, 1959b). Also in the 1960s, Morse explained his idea of the crisis teacher—a teacher skilled in LSI techniques and remedial teaching who would be prepared to take over the management and teaching of a difficult student for a short period of time (during a behavioral crisis), and to obviate the need for full-time special class placement (Morse, 1965a, 1971a, b). More recently, Fagen et al. (1975) presented a psychoeducational self-control curriculum, and Fagen (1979) described psychoeducational methods for adolescents (see also Dembinski, Schultz, & Walton, 1982; Rezmierski, Knoblock, & Bloom, 1982; Rich, Beck, & Coleman, 1982).

Humanistic Education

As Martin (1972) noted, individualism and humanism were the forces shaping special education in the 1960s and 1970s. There was concern for the particular educational needs of black and other minority group youngsters, especially those from inner-city areas and poverty backgrounds (Dennison, 1969; Dokecki, Strain, Bernal, Brown, & Robinson, 1975; Johnson, 1969, 1971; Rothman, 1970, 1974). For emotionally disturbed students it was suggested that radical departures from past educational practices were needed. **Countertheorists**, who depart markedly from tradition and are not accepted as fellow professionals by established authorities in their fields, became a strong force in the mid-1960s. Many who were part of this countertheory group considered themselves humanists and subscribers to the freedom and openness called for by Carl Rogers (1969) and others (Kohl, 1970; Kozol, 1972; Leonard, 1968; Neill, 1960).

> Countertheory is what countertheorists say and do. Usually it begins with the school or the child and works back to the theory from there. It means a bent toward the humanistic ideas of writers like Abraham Maslow (1962, 1968). It is a tendency toward freer education, more in the hands of the student and less determined from above than in most models. Often it means a spirit of rebelliousness and innovation. And it is not so much a body of theory as it is a praxic. (Burke, 1972, p. 577)

In special education for disturbed students, pleas for freedom, openness, and humanism were made by Dennison (1969), Grossman (1972), Knoblock (1970, 1973, 1979), Knoblock and Goldstein (1971), and Trippe (1970). Humanistic education tends to emphasize the affective side of learning and teaching (see Morse, Ardizzone, MacDonald, & Pasick, 1980; Schultz, Heuchert, & Stampf, 1973).

Ecological Approach

The 1960s also saw the rise of the ecological approach to disturbed children. Based primarily on the writing of Hobbs (1965, 1966, 1974) and Rhodes (1965, 1967, 1970), this approach calls for intervention not only with the disturbed child or youth, but also with his home, school, and community.[13] The most important project associated with the ecological approach was Project Re-ED. After having worked extensively in the mental health field in this country and having observed the European **educateur** programs,[14] Hobbs, along with Rhodes, Matthew J. Trippe, Wilbert W. Lewis, Lloyd M. Dunn, and others, began Re-ED programs in Tennessee and North Carolina in the early 1960s. Re-ED schools focused on health rather than illness, teaching rather than treatment, learning rather than fundamental personality change, the present and future rather than the past, and on the child's total social system rather than his or her intrapsychic processes exclusively (Hobbs, 1965). In the initial Re-ED schools, youngsters were served in a residential setting during the week but returned home on

---

[13]Hobbs, Rhodes, and others draw upon the theoretical formulations and field work of ecological psychologists such as Roger C. Barker and Herbert F. Wright (Barker & Wright, 1949, 1954; Barker, 1968; see also Gump, 1975).

[14]See Linton (1969, 1970) as well as Hobbs (1974) for descriptions of the educateur programs.

weekends. A central aspect of Project Re-ED was the selection and training of the teacher-counselors, who carried out the moment-to-moment and day-to-day work with youngsters, and the liaison teachers, who maintained communication and coordination with the home and regular school class (Hobbs, 1966, 1974). Work with the Re-ED and educateur models continues, and most evaluations appear to support the efficacy of an ecological approach (Daly, 1985; Lee, 1971; Lewis, 1982; Votel, 1985; Weinstein, 1969). Furthermore, the initial work of Hobbs and Rhodes apparently gave impetus to the research and writing of others who emphasize ecological concepts (Apter & Conoley, 1984; Graubard, 1976; Graubard, Rosenburg, & Miller, 1971; Rosenburg & Graubard, 1975; Swap, 1974, 1978; Swap, Prieto, & Harth, 1982).

Behavioral Approach

In the late 1950s and early 1960s, some special educators began to make explicit use of basic behavior principles and behavior modification techniques (cf. Forness & MacMillan, 1970; Kazdin, 1978; Cullinan, Epstein, & Kauffman, 1982). The behavior modification frame of reference was derived primarily from B.F. Skinner's (1953) basic research and writing; however, its initial application to the education of disturbed students was the work of many individuals, a number of whom were influenced by the work of Heinz Werner, Alfred Strauss, Laura Lehtinen, Newell Kephart, and others who devised methods of teaching brain-injured children at the Wayne County Training School in the 1940s.

William M. Cruickshank and his colleagues conducted an experimental public school program for brain-injured and hyperactive children (many of whom had emotional difficulties) in Montgomery County, Maryland, in the late 1950s. The report of this project (Cruickshank et al., 1961) described a highly structured program similar in many ways to that outlined earlier by Strauss and Lehtinen (1947). The report emphasized control of extraneous stimuli and use of a consistent routine and consistent consequences for behavior. Shortly after the Montgomery County Project, Norris G. Haring and E. Lakin Phillips extended the concept of structure to work with emotionally disturbed students in the public schools of Arlington, Virginia (Haring & Phillips, 1962; Phillips, 1967; Phillips & Haring, 1959). Their major hypothesis is that disturbed youngsters lack order, predictability, and consistency in their environment and need the stability and consistent demands of Cruickshank's program. They particularly emphasized the use of consistent consequences for behavior (a basic behavior modification principle). A structured approach as defined by Haring and Phillips consists of three primary elements: clear directions; firm expectations that the child would perform as directed; and consistent follow-through in applying consequences for behavior. Later in the '60s, Haring collaborated with Richard J. Whelan at the University of Kansas Medical Center to refine and extend the concept of structure (Haring & Whelan, 1965; Whelan & Haring, 1966), which was extended even further in the late 1960s and into the 1970s by Haring and Phillips to include the behavior modification technology of direct daily measurement of behavioral rates (Haring, 1968, 1974b; Haring & Phillips, 1972). Whelan, Haring's collaborator at Kansas University, had previously developed a structured approach to teaching at the Southard School of the Menninger Clinic in Topeka, Kansas (Whelan, 1963, 1966). Whelan has expanded and refined the concept of structure and the use of behavior principles with disturbed students (Whelan, 1974; Whelan & Gallagher, 1972).

Others were also pioneering the behavioral approach to disturbed children and youth. Herbert C. Quay and his associates contributed immeasurably to the classification of disordered behavior (Quay, 1975). Gerald R. Patterson and his colleagues studied the families of aggressive children and contributed many insights into the coercive processes that operate in such families, as well as effective techniques for managing aggression (Patterson, 1982; Patterson, Reid, Jones, & Conger, 1975). The report of Zimmerman and Zimmerman (1962) was a prelude to an outpouring of behavior modification research with disturbed students in the latter part of the decade. Their simple anecdotal reports of how they resolved two behavior problems—temper tantrums and refusal to write spelling words—by systematic use of consequences was followed by a spate of technically sophisticated reports in the behavior modification literature. Many behavioral psychologists, including those interested in special education and emotionally disturbed children, made tremendous strides in therapeutic endeavors in the 1960s and 1970s (Goodall, 1972).

One behavioral psychologist interested in special education was Frank Hewett. Two of his areas of activity are particularly noteworthy. First, in the middle 1960s, he designed an *engineered classroom* that employed a token (point) system as well as special curricula and centers of activity. The Santa Monica Project, an early trial of his program, has become a frequently cited and widely emulated behavioral approach (Hewett, 1967, 1968). As part of his research and training activities, Hewett also proposed a hierarchy of educational tasks for disturbed children (Hewett, 1964a) and a hierarchy of competencies for their teachers (Hewett, 1966). He continued to write of his research and training using behavioral methods (Hewett, 1970, 1971, 1974). His second area of interest was the teaching of severely and profoundly disturbed children. Through systematic use of operant conditioning (reinforcement) techniques, he was able to teach speech and reading skills to an autistic boy (Hewett, 1964b, 1965).

Finally, during the 1960s and 1970s, there was a dramatic increase in interest and effort to educate children and youth with severe handicaps, including those with severe behavior disorders.[15] The formation of The Association for Persons with Severe Handicaps and the National Society for Children and Adults with Autism has already been mentioned. The intervention techniques that gained widest acceptance in this era and proved to be most effective with psychotic students were behavior modification methods. Although the professionals who made contributions in this area are too numerous to name, the work of O. Ivar Lovaas is particularly notable. First at the University of Washington and later at the University of California at Los Angeles, Lovaas and his colleagues researched the teaching of language and daily living skills to autistic and schizophrenic children (Lovaas, 1966, 1967, 1982; Lovaas & Koegel, 1973; Lovaas, Koegel, Simmons, & Long, 1973; Lovaas, Young, & Newsom, 1978; Devany, Rincover,

---

[15]Part of the reason for this growing interest and effort was the litigation in which the parents of exceptional children were plaintiffs. Court decisions that all children, including those with the most severe handicaps, have a right to public education gave impetus to local schools to make provisions for such children and to the Office of Special Education Programs (U.S. Department of Education) to support training programs for teachers of such students.

& Lovaas, 1981). His work, along with that of others who employed operant conditioning techniques, demonstrates that severely disturbed students can learn when appropriate conditions are arranged and that one need not wait for this learning to occur spontaneously.

PROJECTS IN THE 1970S

Many special projects with long-range implications for disturbed children and youth were conducted in the 1970s, most under the sponsorship of federal agencies. We will briefly describe three projects that illustrate the scope and diversity of efforts to improve the education of disturbed youngsters: a project on conceptual models, one involving labeling, and another focused on analysis of needs.

To delineate clearly and to synthesize the diverse ideologies and practices in the field, William C. Rhodes and others at the University of Michigan began the Conceptual Project in Emotional Disturbance in the early 1970s. Recognizing the fragmentation and conflict in the field, but also the commonalities and the mood of ecumenicalism among various factions, Rhodes set about to clarify the conceptual models and their associated methods of intervention (Rhodes & Head, 1974; Rhodes & Tracy, 1972a, 1972b), and his work has become a standard reference in the field.

The Project on Classification of Exceptional Children was directed by Nicholas Hobbs in the early 1970s. This project was conducted (at the request of the Secretary of Health, Education and Welfare) to examine the consequences of labeling exceptional children of all categories, including the behaviorally disordered. The results (Hobbs, 1975a, 1975b) reflect the stigmatizing and damaging effects of an inadequate classification and labeling process, an issue of intense concern in the first half of the 1970s. Beginning in the late 1970s, a federally funded project on national needs analysis and leadership training in behavior disorders was launched at the University of Missouri. The work of Judith Grosenick and Sharon Huntze documented the unmet needs of emotionally disturbed children in the nation's schools and outlined many unanswered questions regarding educational programs (Grosenick & Huntze, 1979, 1983).

CURRENT ISSUES AND TRENDS

Still a current issue is whether most behavior disordered children and youth are receiving an appropriate education as required under Public Law 94-142, which went into effect in 1978. PL 94-142 is a complex and prescriptive piece of legislation (see Bateman & Herr, 1981; Hallahan & Kauffman, 1988; Turnbull & Turnbull, 1986). Its central feature is the requirement that every handicapped child, including those categorized as seriously emotionally disturbed, receive a free, appropriate education. The intention of the law certainly cannot be faulted, and some of its effects have undoubtedly been salutary. Because they are defined under the law as handicapped, troubled students who are identified as emotionally disturbed cannot now legally be excluded from school or denied an appropriate education. The promise of the law to ensure appropriate education for every handicapped child and youth, however, remains unfulfilled (Coffey, 1987; Knitzer, 1982). By 1985, only about one-half of a very conservative estimate of the number of disturbed students were being provided special education, or about one percent of students enrolled in public schools (U.S. Department of Education, 1986). The prospect that all such students will be served within the near future is not good. Limited economic resources, shortage of trained personnel, unreliable classification systems, technical requirements of the law, and lack of pressure for services from parents of nonpsychotic disturbed children and youth are factors working against dramatic increases in the number of disturbed students that will receive special education (Kauffman, 1986a, 1988).

Another persistent issue is the definition and terminology used in federal legislation and regulations. Reauthorization of many of the provisions of PL 94-142 were included in the Education of All Handicapped Act Amendments of 1983 (PL 98-199). The amendments also authorized a study of replacing the term *seriously emotionally disturbed* with *behaviorally disordered*. Unfortunately, the recommendation (Tallmadge, Gamel, Munson, & Hanley, 1985) was that the term not be changed. Despite research evidence and professional opinion to the contrary (Huntze, 1985; Lloyd et al., 1987; Smith et al., in press), it appears that the federal government will not soon alter the definition and terminology it uses in legislation and regulations.

An increasingly important issue is the settings in which youngsters with behavior disorders are served. This issue has several identifiable subquestions: (1) How can we achieve better integration of disturbed youngsters into general education? (2) Should *any* students be pulled out of general education for special services? (3) To what extent are special education programs at the secondary level a special case in which greater integration or mainstreaming is not feasible? (4) What is the role of special education in rehabilitating incarcerated youth?

In 1987, the U. S. Department of Education (Special Education Programs) began funding large-scale research efforts to find more effective ways of integrating behaviorally disordered adolescent and preadolescent students into general education. Funding was prompted by the observation in federal reports that students with behavior disorders tend to spend a lower percentage of their school day in general education classes than do handicapped students in other special education categories. The Department of Education wants to find the most effective possible procedures for increasing the proportion of the school day that behavior disordered students spend with their nonhandicapped peers. Research findings from these projects should become available to practitioners in the 1990s (Epstein & Repp, 1987; Lloyd, Kauffman, & Kupersmidt, 1987).

During the late 1980s calls were made for greater integration of special and regular education for *all* handicapped students. In fact, some proposed a merger of regular and special education or called for abandonment of all "pull-out" programs in which students are taught in any setting other than the regular class. These calls for radically integrating or merging became known as the *regular education initiative* (REI) (see Hallahan & Kauffman, 1988; Hallahan et al., 1988). The probable effects of the REI on teachers, behavior disordered students, and nonhandicapped students are matters of considerable controversy, and many special educators appear to be skeptical of the outcome (Braaten et al., in press; Hallahan et al., 1988; Kauffman, 1987). Although mainstreaming, or at least increased integration, may indeed be desirable and feasible for many or most students, there are questions about the limits to which the concept of integration can be pushed without becoming counterproductive. The problems of handicapped students in secondary schools present particularly difficult questions.

By the late 1980s, programs at the secondary level, particularly the transition from school to work, had become a national priority in special education (Rusch & Phelps, 1987). Many mildly handicapped students, particularly those with behavior disorders and learning disabilities, were known to drop out or be "elbowed out" of high schools (Edgar, 1987). Most of these youth, in addition to being mildly handicapped, are poor, minority, male students. Should we make greater efforts to integrate them into high school academic programs that do not meet their needs and in which their continued presence or success are highly improbable? Or should they be offered a special curriculum, a separate educational track? Edgar (1987) states the difficult choices succinctly: "What a dilemma—two *equally* appalling alternatives: integrated mainstreaming in a nonfunctional curriculum which results in horrendous outcomes (few jobs, high dropout rate) or separate, segregated programs for an already devalued group, a repugnant thought in our democratic society" (p. 560). The complex issues will persist, and, as Edgar points out, the answer to the issue of integration may differ somewhat for many handicapped students at the secondary level (see also Schumaker & Deshler, 1988).

Because the federal definition of "seriously emotionally disturbed" excludes those who are socially maladjusted but not emotionally disturbed, providing services to incarcerated youth has been particularly problematic (Mesinger, 1986; Murphy, 1986a, 1986b). Incarcerated youth obviously exhibit disordered behavior, since they have been identified as social deviants. But arguments about their classification as emotionally disturbed and their need for special education continue. A central issue is whether a youth's placement in a detention setting is, in itself, a sufficient reason to provide special education. Federal grants to study the special education needs of incarcerated youth were funded in the 1980s (see Rutherford, Nelson, & Wolford, 1985, 1986), and efforts to define appropriate education for youths in prisons and detention centers continue. In 1987 the first book devoted to special education in the criminal justice system was published (Nelson, Rutherford, & Wolford, 1987).

The issue of special education's service to very young children with behavior disorders is just emerging. In 1986 Congress passed PL 99-457, which extends (beginning with the 1990–91 school year) the requirements of PL 94-142 to all handicapped children three to five years of age. PL 99-457 applies even in states that do not provide free public education to nonhandicapped children three to five years of age. The law also includes incentives for states to develop early intervention programs for handicapped infants and infants at risk, from birth to age 36 months. Thus school officials must begin dealing with issues of appropriate education—including identification and intervention—for behavior disordered children who have been considered preschoolers. The young children served under PL 99-457 will include those whose disabilities are multiple and severe; their handicapping conditions cannot be easily ignored, and advocates for services to them and their families are relatively easy to find. Much more difficult, however, is the task of advocating for and identifying young children at risk for behavior disorders, including those whose problems are not yet severe at age three years. Early intervention with handicapped and at-risk children hold promise for prevention. As Gelfand and Peterson (1985) note, "At this [preschool] age range many types of learning are taking place rapidly and simultaneously, which may potentiate the effects of intervention programs" (p. 110). Because language, motor, cognitive, and social learning are so closely linked in infancy and early childhood, effective intervention will necessarily involve more than concern for children's social-emotional responses.

Finally, the conceptual models that emerged during the past quarter century are evolving into more sophisticated, integrative approaches. Based on a melding of behavioral and cognitive research, many leaders in the field are embracing intervention strategies variously called *cognitive-behavior modification* (see Bandura, 1986; Mahoney, 1974; Meichenbaum, 1977, 1979, 1980) and *individual psychology* (see Morse, 1985). These strategies take into consideration how individuals think and feel about their behavior as well as how people's social environments influence the way they behave. In short, many of the simplistic notions of the past—that behavior can always be modified effectively merely by manipulating its consequences, or that behavior cannot be changed until the student gets insight into the nature of the problem—have been put to rest. Today's best practices ignore neither the realities of human affective and cognitive experiences nor the reality that people's behavior is powerfully influenced by its consequences.

SUMMARY

Children and youth with behavior disorders have been recognized throughout history. Before 1800, most of them were thought to be possessed, wicked, or idiotic. Efforts to educate disturbed students began in the nineteenth century, first in "lunatic" asylums and institutions for "idiots" and later in houses of refuge, detention centers, and public school classes for truants, troublemakers, and "backward" pupils. The mental hygiene and child study movements of the early twentieth century highlighted the problems of behavior disorders in children and youth and led to efforts to deal more effectively with disturbed youngsters in homes and schools. In the 1940s, several syndromes of severely disturbed behavior were clearly described. Several psychoanalytically-oriented educational programs began in the late 1940s and the 1950s. The 1960s and early 1970s were periods of rapid growth in educational interventions for disturbed children. Diverse theories ranging from psychoanalytic to behavioral led to divergent educational practices. Besides the forces of psychoanalysis and behaviorism, the field was influenced by the growth of ecological and humanistic psychology. The history of the field cannot be captured merely by reviewing a chronology of events, but a chronology can help one grasp the development of ideas and trends. Some of the important events in the history of the field are listed in Table 3.1.

Definition, prevalence, and terminology remain current issues of great importance to special educators. Issues of increasing importance revolve around the settings in which behavior disordered students should be taught. The federal government has funded research projects to find more effective ways of integrating adolescents and preadolescents with behavior disorders into general education. Proposals to merge or radically integrate regular and special education have, however, met with consid-

TABLE 3.1

Chronology of Important Events Relating to Children with Behavior Disorders, 1799–1987

Year	Event
1799	Itard publishes his report of the wild boy of Aveyron
1825	House of Refuge, first institution for juvenile delinquents in the U.S., founded in New York; similar institutions founded in Boston (1826) and Philadelphia (1828)
1841	Dorothea Dix begins crusade for better care of the insane
1847	State Reform School for Boys, the first state institution for juvenile delinquents, established in Westborough, Massachusetts
1850	Massachusetts incorporates school for idiotic and feebleminded youth at urging of Samuel Gridley Howe; Edward Seguin moves to the United States
1866	Edward Sequin publishes *Idiocy and Its Treatment by the Physiological Method*
1871	Ungraded class for truant, disobedient, and insubordinate children opens in New Haven, Connecticut
1898	New York City Board of Education assumes responsibility for two schools for truant children
1899	First U.S. juvenile court established in Chicago
1908	Clifford Beers publishes *A Mind that Found Itself*
1909	National Committee for Mental Hygiene founded; Ellen Key publishes *The Century of the Child*; William Healy founds the Juvenile Psychopathic Institute in Chicago
1911	Arnold Gesell founds the Clinic for Child Development at Yale University
1912	Congress creates the U.S. Children's Bureau
1919	Ohio passes law for statewide education of the handicapped
1922	Council for Exceptional Children founded
1924	American Orthopsychiatric Association founded
1931	First psychiatric hospital for children in the U.S. founded in Rhode Island
1935	Leo Kanner publishes *Child Psychiatry*; Loretta Bender and others begin school for psychotic children at Bellevue Psychiatric Hospital in New York City
1943	Leo Kanner describes early infantile autism
1944	Bruno Bettelheim opens the Orthogenic School at the University of Chicago
1946	New York City Board of Education designates 600 schools for disturbed and maladjusted pupils; Fritz Redl and David Wineman open Pioneer House in Detroit
1947	Alfred Strauss and Laura Lehtinen publish *Psychopathology and Education of the Brain-Injured Child* based on work at Wayne County Training School in Northville, Michigan
1950	Bruno Bettelheim publishes *Love is Not Enough*
1953	Carl Fenichel founds the League School, first private day school for severely emotionally disturbed children, in Brooklyn
1955	Leonard Kornberg publishes *A Class for Disturbed Children,* first book describing classroom teaching of disturbed children
1960	Pearl Berkowitz & Esther Rothman publish *The Disturbed Child,* describing permissive, psychoanalytic educational approach
1961	William Cruickshank et al. publish *A Teaching Method for Brain-Injured and Hyperactive Children,* reporting results of a structured educational program in Montgomery County, Maryland; Nicholas Hobbs and associates begin Project Re-ED in Tennessee and North Carolina
1962	Norris Haring and Lakin Phillips publish *Educating Emotionally Disturbed Children,* reporting results of a structured program in Arlington, Virginia; Eli Bower and Nadine Lambert publish *An In-School Process for Screening Emotionally Handicapped Children* based on research in California

TABLE 3.1
continued

Year	Event
1963	PL 88-164 provides federal money for support of personnel preparation in the area of emotionally disturbed
1964	William Morse, Richard Cutler, and Albert Fink publish *Public School Classes for the Emotionally Handicapped: A Research Analysis*; Council for Children with Behavioral Disorders established as a division of Council for Exceptional Children
1965	Nicholas Long, William Morse, and Ruth Newman publish *Conflict in the Classroom*; National Society for Children and Adults with Autism founded; First Annual Conference on the Education of Emotionally Disturbed Children held at Syracuse University
1968	Frank Hewett publishes *The Emotionally Disturbed Child in the Classroom,* reporting use of an engineered classroom in Santa Monica, California
1970	William Rhodes begins Conceptual Project in Emotional Disturbance, summarizing theory, research, and intervention
1974	Association for Persons with Severe Handicaps founded
1975	Nicholas Hobbs publishes *Issues in the Classification of Children* and *The Futures of Children,* reporting the work of the Project on the Classification of Exceptional Children
1978	PL 94-142 (enacted in 1975) requires free, appropriate education for all handicapped children, including the seriously emotionally disturbed; federal funding for National Needs Analysis studies at University of Missouri
1986	PL 99-457 enacted, extending provisions of PL 94-142 to all handicapped children three to five years of age by school year 1990-91; statistics show that about one percent of students enrolled in public schools are receiving special education services as seriously emotionally disturbed, only about one-half a conservative estimate of prevalence
1987	U.S. Department of Education, Special Education Programs, begins funding of major research projects on integration of adolescent and preadolescent students; C. Michael Nelson, Robert B. Rutherford, and Bruce I. Wolford publish *Special Education in the Criminal Justice System.*

erable skepticism, particularly as such integration might be applied at the secondary level. Extension of special education to incarcerated youth and provision of special services to very young children with behavior disorders are emerging trends. Conceptual models are evolving into more sophisticated and integrated approaches that address students' behavior and cognitions in social systems.

4

Conceptual Models: Approaches to the Problem

As you read this chapter, keep these guiding questions in mind:

- ☐ How are beliefs about human nature linked to one's choice of intervention strategies?
- ☐ Under what circumstances might someone use nonbiological interventions even though a behavior problem is known to be caused by a physiological disorder?
- ☐ What assumptions might prevent someone who accepts a psychodynamic model from trying to change disordered behavior immediately?
- ☐ What are the major goals of the life-space interview, an intervention strategy associated with the psychoeducational approach?
- ☐ What role does the teacher play in a humanistic approach?
- ☐ In what ways is an ecological approach compatible with behavioral and social cognitive theory?
- ☐ From the perspective of a behavioral model, what is the most important strategy in changing maladaptive behavior?
- ☐ What is the most important concept underlying social cognitive theory, and what implication does it have for understanding the disordered behavior of children and youth?

P eople in every culture have sought to conceptualize unusual or disturbing human behavior in terms of causal factors and to trace back to those same factors ways to eliminate, control, and prevent deviant acts. From the innumerable causes and remedies that have been suggested over the centuries, we can identify several conceptual themes. These themes have remained remarkably consistent for thousands of years, and contemporary versions are merely elaborations and extensions of their ancient counterparts (Kauffman, 1974b). For purposes of explanation and control of behavior, humans have been variously conceptualized, for example, as spiritual beings, biological organisms, rational and feeling persons, and products of their environments.

Educators have always struggled with how human behavior—both troublesome and desirable—should be conceptualized. What one believes people to be determines what explanations one seeks for behavior. If people are thought to be spiritual beings, then mystical or religious approaches to changing their behavior will be adopted. If people are conceptualized as biological organisms, then medical, surgical, or dietary treatments will be prescribed. If people are said to be rational and feeling persons, then cognitive and affective interventions will be attempted. And if people are analyzed as products of environmental events, then antecedent and consequent events will be controlled in efforts to modify behavior. How one responds to disordered behavior is linked to what one believes about the nature and causes of human conduct.

Today we recognize so many possible causes of troublesome behavior that sorting through them has become a troubling task. One does not need professional training to see how nearly every aspect of young people's lives is fraught with potential for psychological problems. Adults are beginning to recognize that children and youth feel stress in everyday life, and that school experiences can be particularly stressful (Schultz & Heuchert, 1983). Recognizing that children and youth face stress, however, does not bring understanding of the causes of disordered behavior or its remedy. It is one thing to recognize stress; it is quite another to articulate a coherent view of how stress affects human development and determine what kinds are most significant. The accompanying box illustrates the popular and somewhat naive view that causes of disordered behavior are everywhere, lurking amid all a youngster's experiences. Whether this is so is moot; one needs a set of principles, a conceptual model or framework, to organize and make sense of the vast array of ideas and information about the causes and cures of disordered behavior.

Nearly every reader of this book will know that there are alternative theories of behavior (or schools of psychology). Each conceptual model offers an explanation of human behavior and suggests how to change it. The problem is not the number of models, however; rather, it is choosing or constructing a theory or philosophy of behavior and evaluating conceptual models accordingly. More simply, the most difficult problem is deciding what is believable and what is not believable about the causes of human behavior.

Besides believability, there is also the matter of deciding how to group and analyze ideas in the construction of concepts. We will talk about three different levels of analysis or grouping. First we will examine a traditional exposition of models. Since the early 1970s, when Rhodes and his colleagues published summaries of the Conceptual Models Project, teacher educators and researchers have provided this now traditional grouping of concepts: biogenic, psychodynamic, psychoeducational, hu-

Why Do Children and Youth Have Behavior Disorders?

Stress has always been with young people. Why suddenly have they gone wild, spewing terrifying statistics on us?

First of all, young people are more alone than they have ever been before . . . and stress increases without the touch of the calming hand. The family that used to be their mainstay has crumbled: aunts and uncles live in distant cities; cousins pass briefly at weddings and funerals; and for every two marriages in the United States, there is one divorce. It is hardly a joke that the nursery school story of Goldilocks today deals with Baby Bear, Mama Bear, and Stepfather Bear.

More married women are working today than are staying at home. More husbands are battering their wives; more parents are abusing their children. More husbands and wives have extramarital sex. A suburban housewife said the other day, "My child came home from school crying—he was the only one in his class living with both parents."

With the family shifting, where does the young person go for support? Not to church—he has not been raised as an attender. Not to school—the old teacher who cared has retired. Not to the community—the family has been transplanted so often in father's upward mobility that the child has no community.

No, today's youth finds support in his peer group. And these young people, like him, are scared and stress-burdened and themselves unsupported. They lean against one another like a house of cards.

Secondly, today's young people are pushed into greater competition than ever before. There are more of them in sheer numbers struggling for first place: to get the best mark, the most money, the highest football score, the most dates. They are rated by judges who set up the criteria for success, often arbitrarily. They are intelligent or slow according to the Stanford-Binet's definition of IQ. They are popular according to the head cheerleader's or football captain's model. They get into college if their talents match those that Educational Testing Service holds up as important. So the struggle becomes one, not only for success, but also for conformity. The loner is doomed to the stress of failure. The group is doomed to the stress of competition.

Society, which is merely a conglomerate of parents, teachers and community members, teaches young people to measure self- worth against success. So they dare not to be less than best. Some are lucky and learn to accept second-best.

Finally, never before have children been so indulged, so prized, so placated as today. The cause may be parental guilt or that old chestnut, "I want her to have more than I had." No matter—the result is the same: a generation of young people who cannot cope with the negatives the rest of us had to grow accustomed to. They get what they want—at no little expense to their parents—from birth through adolescence. They get what they see on television. They get what their friends have. Parents seem afraid to say "No."

The easy life leaves children with little sense of accountability. Parents team up to help them switch the blame. A child does poorly in school—Mother says the teacher is no good. A sixteen-year-old wants liquor at this party—Dad winks at the law. One mother boasted, "I will never let Rachel be upset if I can possibly prevent it." She prevented it, and Rachel is now at a psychiatrist's. She is six years old.

Now we find ourselves in the 1980s, in a world where the myth of childhood is being torn to bits . . . where children are beset with stress they are ill-equipped to handle . . . in a world where, unable to *scream* out, they *act* out their hurt. . . in a world where we adults, unable to interpret their screams, react only to their behavior. For we are deaf to our own cries of fear.

Excerpts from CHILDSTRESS! Understanding and Answering Stress Signals of Infants, Children and Teenagers by M. S. Miller, Copyright 1982 by M. S. Miller. Reprinted by permission of Doubleday, a division of Bantam, Doubleday, Dell Publishing Group, Inc.

manistic, ecological, and behavioral. Second, we will discuss a conceptual model derived primarily from social learning principles. Third, we will describe an integrated model applied to the classification of disordered behavior, analysis of causal factors, methodology of assessment, and intervention.

TRADITIONAL EXPOSITION OF CONCEPTUAL MODELS

Biogenic Approach

Human behavior involves neurophysiological mechanisms; that is, a person cannot perceive, think, or act without the involvement of his or her anatomy and physiology. One set of conceptual models begins with one or both of two hypotheses: (1) that disordered behavior represents a physiological flaw, or (2) that behavior can be brought under control through physiological processes. Some writers, for example, suggest that disorders such as autism, hyperactivity, depression, or hyperaggression are manifestations of genetic factors, brain dysfunction, food additives, biochemical imbalance, or are simply disorders most responsive to or most easily ameliorated by surgery or chemicals. According to these models, recognition of the underlying biological problem is critical; successful treatment may or may not, however, be aimed at resolving the physiological flaw. In many cases we know of no way to repair or ameliorate the brain damage, genetic process, or metabolic disorder. Consequently, one must be satisfied with understanding the physiological cause of the disorder and making appropriate adaptations to it. Some behavior management strategies are based on hypotheses about physiological processes but do not address known physiological disorders. Students may be given stimulant drugs to help control hyperactivity, or may be taught biofeedback techniques to help them gain self-control, even though no illness or brain injury has been identified. Interventions associated with the biogenic approach are drug therapy, dietary control, exercise, surgery, biofeedback, and alteration of environmental factors that exacerbate the physiological problem. (See Cossairt, Marlowe, Stellern, & Jacobs, 1985; deCatanzaro, 1978; DesLauriers & Carlson, 1969; Feingold, 1975, 1976; Rimland, 1964; and Werry, 1986a, for examples and discussion.)

Psychodynamic Approach

Dynamic psychiatry is concerned with hypothetical mental mechanisms and their interplay in the developmental process. Psychodynamic models, sometimes called *psychoanalytic* models because psychoanalytic theory provides so many of their tenets, rest on the assumption that the essence of behavior disorders is *not* the behavior itself but a "pathological" imbalance among the dynamic parts of one's personality (the id, ego, and superego). A disturbed youngster's behavior is merely symptomatic of an underlying "mental illness"; the cause of mental illness is usually attributed to excessive restriction or excessive gratification of the individual's instincts at a critical stage of development or to early traumatic experiences. Interventions based on a psychodynamic model stress the importance of individual psychotherapy for the child (and often for the parents as well) and the necessity of a permissive, accepting classroom teacher. Problems in relating to youngsters, whether as teacher or therapist, are often interpreted in terms of the adult's own unconscious conflicts. Extreme importance is placed on understanding the unconscious motivation for behavior, on the assumption that once it is understood (and not until), the problem will be resolved. Another assumption is that if the underlying, unconscious conflict is not understood and resolved, then any improvement in the "symptomatic" behavior is trivial or even harmful, and the symptom will be replaced by another. (See Axline, 1947; Berkowitz & Rothman, 1960; Bettelheim, 1970; Freud, 1965; Gartner, 1985; Kornberg, 1955; Scharfman, 1978; Tuma & Sobotka, 1983; and Watkins & Schatman, 1986, for examples and discussion.)

Psychoeducational Approach

The psychoeducational model shows concern for unconscious motivations and underlying conflicts (hallmarks of psychodynamic models), yet also stresses the realistic demands of everyday functioning in school, home, and community. This model assumes that academic failure and misbehavior can be dealt with directly and therapeutically without focusing efforts on resolution of unconscious motivations. There is great reliance on **ego psychology**, an offshoot of psychodynamic theory. Proponents attempt to focus on tasks of the **ego**—one's conscious self—and to help the student acquire self-control through self-understanding. Intervention based on a psychoeducational model may include therapeutic discussions or *life-space interviews* to get youngsters to understand that what they are doing is a problem, recognize their motivations, observe the consequences of their actions, and plan alternative responses to use in similar future circumstances. Emphasis is on the youngster's gaining insight that will result in behavioral change, not on changing behavior directly. (See Dembinski et al., 1982; Fagen, 1979; Fenichel, 1974; Heuchert & Long, 1980; Long, 1974; Long & Newman, 1965; Morse, 1974; Redl, 1966; Rezmierski et al., 1982; and Rich et al., 1982, for examples and discussion.)

Humanistic Approach

Humanistic education draws heavily from humanistic psychology, the sociopolitical movement of the late 1960s and early 1970s known as the counterculture or countertheory movement, and the free school, open education, alternative school, and deschooling ideas of the same era. A humanistic approach emphasizes self-direction, self-fulfillment, self-evaluation, and free choice of educational activities and goals, but the theoretical underpinnings of humanistic models are hard to identify. A teacher who devises an education for disturbed students based on a humanistic model will be more a resource and catalyst for learning than a director of activities. The teacher is unauthoritarian and promotes a classroom atmosphere best described as open, free, nontraditional, affectively charged, and personal. An assumption underlying most humanistic approaches is that youngsters will find their own solutions to their problems if they are merely freed to do so in a loving and supportive environment. (See Burke, 1972; Dennison, 1969; Knoblock, 1970, 1973, 1979; Neill, 1960; and Rogers, 1969, for examples and discussion.) Some of the elements of affective education

(Morse et al., 1980) and some characteristics of alternative schools, sometimes called "schools of choice" (Fizzell, 1987) fit the model of humanistic education.

Ecological Approach

An ecological model is based on concepts in ecological psychology, community psychology, and the work of European *educateurs* who work with youngsters in their homes and communities as well as their schools. The student is considered an individual enmeshed in a complex social system, both a giver and a receiver (excitor and responder) in social transactions with other students and adults in a variety of roles and settings. Emphasis is on study of the child's entire social system, and intervention is directed, ideally, toward all facets of the student's milieu. Interventions used in ecological programs have tended to emphasize behavioral and social learning concepts. (See Daly, 1985; Hobbs, 1966, 1974; Lewis, 1982; Rhodes, 1965, 1967, 1970; Swap, 1974, 1978; Swap et al., 1982; and Votel, 1985, for examples and discussion.)

Behavioral Approach

Two major assumptions underlie a behavioral model: the essence of the problem is the behavior itself, and behavior is a function of environmental events. Maladaptive behavior is viewed as inappropriate learned responses; therefore, intervention should consist of rearranging antecedent events and consequences to teach more adaptive behavior. A behavioral model derives from the work of behavioral psychologists. With its emphasis on precise definition and reliable measurement, careful control of the variables thought to maintain or change behavior, and establishment of replicable cause-effect relationships, it represents a natural science approach. Interventions based on a behavioral model consist of choosing target responses, measuring their current level, analyzing probable controlling environmental events, and changing antecedent or consequent events until reliable changes are produced in the target behaviors. (See Cooper, Heron, & Heward, 1987; Cullinan et al., 1982; Kerr & Nelson, 1983; Kerr, Nelson, & Lambert, 1987; Morris, 1985; Nelson, 1981; Walker, Reavis, Rhode, & Jenson, 1985, for examples and discussion.)

DEVELOPING AN INTEGRATED MODEL

In practice, few professionals adhere rigidly to a single conceptual model. Most realize that multiple perspectives are needed for competent practice. Yet there is a limit to the degree to which one can be eclectic, picking and choosing concepts and strategies from various models, without being simple-minded and self-contradictory. Some conceptual models are not complementary; they suggest radically different and incompatible approaches to a problem. (The box illustrates contrasting conceptualizations of similar behavior problems and intervention strategies that are diametrically opposed.) Clearly, acceptance of one set of assumptions about human behavior sometimes implies rejection of another.

Contrasting Conceptual Models

Different conceptual models can lead to extremely different ways of dealing with similar behavior problems, as these two cases illustrate.

Bettelheim (1970) presented the case of a four-year-old girl who had been diagnosed as psychotic and unmanageable. She frequently attempted to smash people's eyeglasses. If she was prevented from doing this, her behavior became extremely wild. Bettelheim suggested that if this girl were ever to be helped, he would have to understand why she engaged in this behavior; and she would have to be helped to understand her own behavior as well. To achieve this understanding, it would be necessary to simply accept the breaking of glasses. Consequently, breaking glasses was accepted for three years, until the child was able to reveal the hidden, unconscious meaning of her behavior. Through listening to the girl talk about her past and observing her behavior, Bettelheim arrived at this interpretation. The girl's mother had been a chronic schizophrenic, a person extremely difficult to understand. The girl decided that since her mother wore glasses, which helped her see better and therefore understand things, she would try to understand her mother by putting on her glasses. But when she put on the glasses, she saw worse instead of better. This infuriated the girl—the injustice that her mother could see better but she saw worse with the glasses and still could not understand her mother's behavior. She was so infuriated that she felt compelled to break all reminders or symbols of this injustice. Bettelheim relied totally on unraveling an interpretation of the unconscious motivation of the girl's misbehavior, not on any procedures designed to control it directly.

Wolf, Risley, and Mees (1964) reported the case of a three-year-old boy diagnosed as schizophrenic. The boy threw severe temper tantrums, frequently injured himself purposely, and was tyrannical with his parents. He had developed cataracts at nine months of age, and both lenses had been removed from his eyes. His rages had begun at about the time his cataracts were discovered, and his parents were not able to get him to wear his glasses. Wearing his glasses was important to prevent further loss of vision, but his glasses were often thrown or broken. Wolf and his associates decided on a direct approach to the problem that involved altering the conditions and consequences for wearing glasses. One strategy was using a negative consequence for tantrums. They placed the boy in his room for ten minutes (or longer, if he were still having a tantrum at the end of the "time out") every time he had a tantrum or threw off his glasses. Another strategy was rewarding approximations of the desired behavior, wearing the glasses. The boy was given frequent small rewards (bites of food) for positive behavior—first for holding the empty frames, then for putting them up to his eyes, then for doing the same with plain lenses, then for looking through prescription lenses, and so on. Wolf et al. also modified the frames of the glasses so that putting them on and wearing them appropriately was more likely. In short, they modified the environment to encourage desirable behavior and reduce misbehavior without delving into the unconscious motivation or hidden meanings of the child's conduct.

Although certain features of the two cases differ (such as the children's genders and physical health), they are similar in that the problem behavior involves persistent attempts to break eyeglasses. Although one might argue that the children's problems actually differed in several significant respects, the psychologists who treated the cases have distinctive conceptual orientations that guide their approaches to whatever problems they attack. That is, Bruno Bettelheim would have probably approached the second case by trying to determine the unconscious significance of the boy's behavior, and Montrose Wolf probably would have analyzed the contingencies operating in the case of the young girl.

Selection and Use of Conceptual Models

One has several distinct options in treating the issue of conceptual models. First, one can adopt a single model as an unvarying theme, a template by which to judge all hypotheses and research findings. Although this option has the advantages of consistency and clarity, it is disconcerting to many careful thinkers because it rests on the questionable assumption that reality is sufficiently encompassed by one set of hypotheses about human behavior.

Second, one can take a nonevaluative stance, a posture that treats all concepts equally, deserving the same attention and respect. This option has immediate appeal in its acknowledgement that every model has limitations, and allows the reader to choose from an unbiased treatment of all contestants. There are, however, many drawbacks; under the guise of eclecticism, this option rests on the implicit assumption that we have no sound reasons for discriminating among ideas. It fosters the attitude that behavior management and education, like religion and political ideology, are better left to personal belief than to scientific scrutiny. And, it leads inevitably to witless self-contradiction.

A third option, and the one chosen for this book, is to focus on hypotheses that can be supported or refuted by replicable and public empirical data—ideas that lend themselves to investigation by the methods of natural science. The result of this choice is that most of the discussion is consistent with a social cognitive model, and useful concepts from other models are discussed as they are related to social learning. The psychodynamic approach is ignored, for the most part, and psychoeducational and humanistic approaches are given limited coverage because relatively little reliable evidence (from a natural science point of view) is available to support them. Biogenic models are discussed because they are open to empirical investigation, but these models are not treated extensively because of their limited implications for the work of educators.

My choice for this book does not mean I believe there is only one "way of knowing"; I do believe, however, that some ways of knowing are better than others for certain purposes. For educators who work with troubled children and youth, I believe the natural science tradition provides the firmest foundation for competent professional practice. The most useful knowledge is derived from experiments that can be repeated and that consistently produce similar results—in short, information obtained from investigations conducted according to well established rules of scientific inquiry. Not every problem can be approached through scientific experiment, and in such cases one must rely on other sources of wisdom—clinical experience, intuition, expert opinion, logical analysis, and so forth. But to the extent that reliable, quantitative, experimental evidence is available or can be obtained, I believe educators should make it the basis for their practice (see Kauffman, 1987, for further discussion). Furthermore, the most useful scientific information for teachers is that derived from controlled experiments that reveal how the social environment can be arranged to modify behavior and how individuals can be taught self-control. Biological experiments have relatively few implications for the work of teachers. Teachers do not choose students' genes, perform surgery, prescribe drugs, control diet, or do physical therapy. Teachers do, however, have enormous power over the social environment of the classroom, as well as a significant measure of control over how they think about behavior problems and how they act. Therefore, our emphasis is on social learning.

A Social Cognitive Approach

Social cognitive theory is an attempt to explain human behavior from a natural science perspective by integrating what is known about the effects of the environment (the behaviorist position) and what is known about the role of cognition (cognitive psychology). Scientific research indicates indisputably that the consequences of our behavior—environmental responses created by our actions—affect the way we are likely to behave in the future. But behavioral research alone cannot explain the subtleties and complexities of human conduct. Social cognitive theory emphasizes *personal agency*: the ability of humans to use symbols for communication, to anticipate future events, to learn from observation or vicarious experience, to evaluate and regulate themselves, and to be reflectively self-conscious. Personal agency adds a needed dimension to a behavioral analysis and provides a more complete explanation of human behavior.

Social cognitive theory is *not,* however, merely a combination of behavioral and cognitive psychology. It is also a reconceptualization of the direction, interaction, and reciprocality of effects. It suggests that people are not merely products of their environments, as described by radical behaviorists; nor are they simply driven to behave as they do by internal forces, the view of radical psychodynamic theorists. But it suggests in addition that behavior results from reciprocal influences among the environment (both social and physical), personal factors (thoughts, feelings, perceptions), and the individual's behavior itself. This "triadic reciprocality," described by Bandura (1977, 1978, 1986), is depicted in the center of Figure 4.1, showing that behavior (*B*), person variables (*P*), and environment (*E*) constantly influence one another.

Under some conditions, one of the three factors shown in Figure 4.1 may play a more influential role than another, but usually all three elements are involved. As Bandura (1986) notes, "Reciprocality does not mean symmetry in the strength of bidirectional influences. Nor is the patterning and strength of mutual influences fixed in reciprocal causation. The relative influence exerted by the three sets of interacting factors will vary for different activities, different individuals, and different circumstances" (p. 24). Thus the three sets of interacting factors might be depicted as in the outer portions of Figure 4.1. Under many circumstances, all three factors exert reciprocal influence, as shown by the central part of the figure in which the three circles (representing sets of factors) intersect. Under other circumstances, the intersections of and interactions between two of the sets of factors, or the effects of only one set, are of primary concern.

An example of strong reciprocal causal connections between two factors, with only weak connection to the third, is the extremely fearful child who will not make any approach to dogs. In this case, environment and person variables intersect and are closely tied, as shown in the upper right section of Figure 4.1. Environment, *E,* and person variables, *P,* interact reciprocally, as shown by the solid line connecting

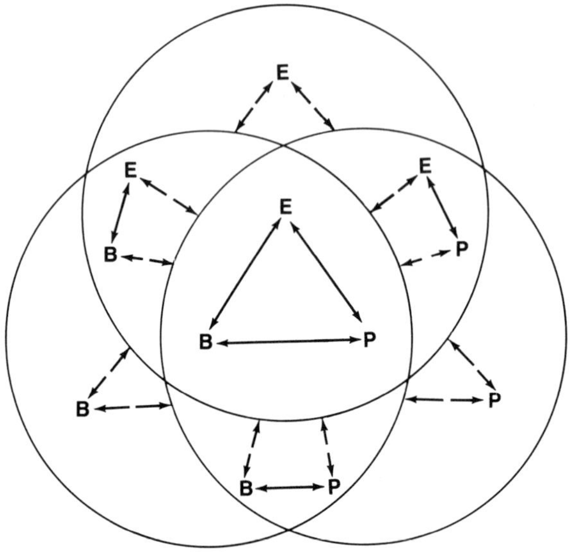

FIGURE 4.1

Triadic Reciprocality in Social Cognitive Theory. Environment (*E*), behavior (*B*), and person variables (*P*) influence each other reciprocally. Solid lines connecting *B, P,* and *E* represent strong reciprocal effects; dashed lines represent weaker influence. Circles represent environment, behavior, and person variables and their shared (intersecting) reciprocal effects.

them; but the connection to behavior is weaker, as indicated by the broken lines connecting them to behavior, *B*. Dogs may arouse great fear in the child, and the fear may lead the child to avoid environments that include dogs and seek dog-free environments, which effectively reduce anxiety. But the child's behavior involving dogs may be extremely limited, consisting almost entirely of stereotyped avoidance rather than varied and adaptive responses (see Kauffman, 1979; Kauffman & Kneedler, 1981).

An example of person variables affecting each other reciprocally but having only weak connections to behavior and environment is an individual who becomes more and more anxious on the basis of thoughts and affective states. "In the personal realm of affect and thought, there exist reciprocal escalating processes, as when frightening thoughts arouse internal turmoil that, in turn, breeds even more frightening thoughts" (Bandura, 1986, p. 25). Such processes are represented in the lower right section of Figure 4.1, in which an isolated subset of person variables, *P,* is connected to behavior and environment by dashed lines, indicating weaker causal connections.

A detailed exposition of social cognitive theory is far beyond the scope of this book. Full understanding of the theory demands study of the work of its foremost proponent, Albert Bandura (see, for example, Bandura, 1977, 1978, 1986). We have sketched the theory here merely to provide a framework for later discussion. The primary concept to keep in mind is Bandura's notion of *triadic reciprocality*. An important implication of this concept is that behavior disorders are comprehensible only in the contexts, both personal and social, in which they occur. For example, studies of how teachers control their students' behavior must be extended to include students' effects on teachers; that is, *transactions,* or mutual influences. The emphasis of social cognitive theory on reciprocality of effects in human transactions is entirely consistent with an ecological approach.

A STRUCTURE FOR DISCUSSION

Given a social cognitive model for conceptualizing human behavior, what is the best way to structure a coherent discussion of the characteristics of the behavior disorders of children and youth? As Bandura (1986) notes, it is impossible to study all possible reciprocal actions at once; trying to examine all causal factors simultaneously paralyzes scientific study because the task is overwhelmingly complex. We must study behavior, its assessment, its causes, and its effects in simpler, more manageable segments. This is true whether one is conducting research or summarizing and interpreting it.

Figure 4.2 indicates that assessment and intervention are overlapping activities. It also indicates that types of disorders and causal factors are interconnected. We might choose to analyze a particular "slice" of the model, such as the assessment of genetic factors in depression, but we can never completely separate the particular problem we are analyzing from all other problems. If we are studying the assessment of genetic factors in depression, then we cannot totally ignore the assessment of temperament as a causal factor and the design of interventions involving peers and parents. The point is that, while we focus on a particular topic, we must be aware of its connectedness to others. Our focus in the following chapters will first be on assessment (Part

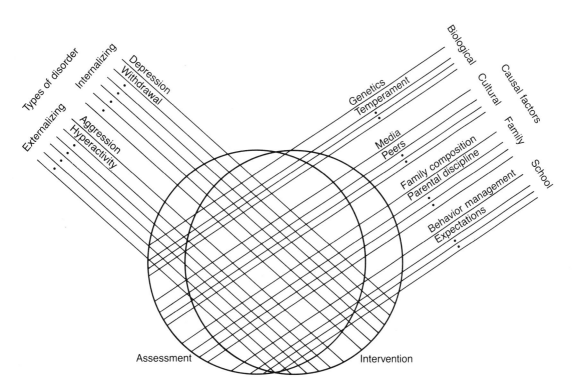

FIGURE 4.2
Structure for Analysis of Disordered Behavior

Two), then on causal factors (Part Three), then on types of disorders (Part Four), and finally on intervention (Part Five).

SUMMARY

Beliefs about the nature of human beings determine what explanations one seeks for behavior and the strategies one uses in approaching behavior disorders. Throughout history, people have been conceptualized as spiritual beings, as biological organisms, as rational and feeling individuals, and as products of their environments. Each conceptualization has led to intervention approaches. Conceptual models, which help organize and interpret information, are necessary for making sense of the vast array of ideas and information about the causes and cures of disordered behavior. Traditional expositions of conceptual models in behavior disorders include descriptions of biogenic, psychodynamic, psychoeducational, humanistic, ecological, and behavioral models. Although practitioners and scholars seldom employ one model exclusively, they must have a rational basis for choosing among models; some are logically incompatible and suggest opposite courses of action. A model derived from scientific experiments in social learning and self-control provides the most defensible basis for professional practice. A social cognitive approach, which emphasizes triadic reciprocity among behavior, person variables, and environment provides a consistent theme for this book.

PART TWO

Assessment of Disordered Behavior

5

Screening: Narrowing the Field

As you read this chapter, keep these guiding questions in mind:

☐ What is the primary purpose of any screening procedure?

☐ Why do few school systems use systematic screening procedures for behavior disorders?

☐ Why does early detection of behavior disorders usually involve secondary rather than primary prevention?

☐ What factors make screening for infants' and preschoolers' behavior disorders particularly difficult?

☐ What criteria should we use in devising and selecting screening procedures?

☐ How should prereferral strategies function as an intermediate step between screening and evaluation for special education?

☐ In what ways should screening represent convergence and confirmation of concerns?

S evere behavior disorders of children and youth are easy to detect. Rational people have no difficulty arriving at a consensus that certain behavior is deviant and calls for intervention. But the majority of behavior disorders are not so severe nor so readily identified. Indeed, *mildly disordered* fades into *normal* in a haze of conjecture. In decisions regarding identification of specific individuals, divided opinions are common even among experts (Kauffman, 1984). Consequently, it is often desirable to reduce the size of the population being considered during the identification process, screening out those who are almost certainly *not* disturbed and screening in for further study those who probably *are* disturbed. Further assessment is then necessary to determine whether a youngster should be identified as disturbed and, if so, how to manage and classify the problem behavior.

ISSUES IN SCREENING PROCEDURES

Effective screening means becoming a good "suspectition" (Bower, 1981). It means being able to pick out cases that are not immediately obvious and identify incipient problems (those that are just beginning) with a high degree of accuracy. The reason for screening youngsters with behavior disorders (or any other disability, for that matter) is based on the assumption that early identification and treatment are more effective, efficient, and humane than letting problems fester until they arouse the concern of even hardened observers. Furthermore, PL 94-142 requires efforts to identify *all* handicapped children and youth. Still, few school systems carry out systematic and effective screening for disturbed students. One reason for failure to screen systematically is that many more students than could be served by special education would likely be referred. Students who are referred must be carefully evaluated, and evaluation is a costly and potentially stigmatizing, anxiety-provoking process for both student and parents. Students who are identified must, by law, be provided with appropriate special education and related services, which is even more costly and stigmatizing. So it is not really surprising that many school systems rely primarily on teacher-initiated referral; only students who trouble their teachers to the breaking point become targets for evaluation (see National Mental Health Association, 1986).

Early Identification and Prevention

Screening is often justified by the argument that early identification will lead to prevention. Although this argument is both rational and supported by various research findings, translating concern for prevention into effective screening procedures is difficult (see Gelfand, Ficula, & Zarbatany, 1986; Gelfand & Peterson, 1985; Nietzel & Himelein, 1986; Weissberg & Allen, 1986). Chief among the difficulties are defining the disorders to be prevented and separating serious from trivial behavior problems. Effective screening must eliminate common behavior problems that do not carry serious consequences or that are virtually certain to resolve themselves without intervention. As Achenbach and Edelbrock (1981) comment,

> Largely as a legacy of the success of early detection and treatment of organic diseases, it has been assumed that mass screening of children could identify incipient behavioral and developmental disorders that could then be ameliorated

through prompt intervention. Enthusiasm for this view has inspired legislative mandates for early screening, despite a lack of clarity concerning the nature of the disorders to be detected, the procedures for detecting them, the means of ameliorating them, and their typical outcomes without intervention. (p. 56)

Problems in screening for prevention differ with developmental level and purpose for screening. Efforts to prevent behavior problems demand a developmental perspective that takes into account developmental milestones associated with chronological age, life events, different environments, and intervention strategies (Gelfand et al., 1986; Gelfand & Peterson, 1985). The purpose of screening for behavior disorders is usually *secondary prevention,* as opposed to *primary prevention*. "Primary prevention is the prevention of the occurrence, or at least the expression, of the disability; secondary prevention is something less ambitious" (Ornitz, 1986, p. 75). Secondary prevention is the prevention of side effects and exacerbation of an existing disorder; thus prevention of behavior disorders is intended to minimize the stress experienced by the family, teachers, and peers of a youngster who exhibits disordered behavior and to minimize the complications or worsening of the disorder itself.

Screening for behavior disorders among infants and preschool children is particularly problematic. Severely disabled children who are considered autistic have often been perceived by their parents as "different" from birth or from a very early age. Pediatricians often identify these and other cases in which extremely troublesome behavior is part of a **pervasive developmental disorder**. But trying to select infants and preschoolers who need special education and related services because of relatively *mild* behavior disorders is quite another matter (Gelfand et al., 1986). No one has yet figured out how to do that reliably, for several reasons. First, large and rapid changes occur during development from infancy to middle childhood. Infants and preschoolers have not yet acquired the language skills that are the basis for much of the older child's social interaction. Second, a child's behavioral style or temperament in infancy interacts with parenting behavior to determine later behavior patterns. For example, "difficult" behavior x at the age of ten months is not predictive of inappropriate behavior y at six years. Behavior management techniques that parents and teachers use from ten months to six years need to be taken into account (Thomas & Chess, 1984; Thomas et al., 1968). Third, parents vary markedly in their tolerance of behavioral differences in children. Because a problem *is* a problem primarily by parental definition in the preschool years, it is difficult to decide on a standard set of behaviors that are deviant (Achenbach & Edelbrock, 1981; Campbell, 1983). (Exceptions, as we have said, are obvious developmental lags.) Finally, the school itself is a potential source of behavior problems—its structure, demands for performance of new skills, and emphasis on uniformity may set the stage for disorders that simply do not appear until the child enters school. PL 99-457 may facilitate development of procedures for screening young children for behavior disorders, as it extended the provisions of PL 94-142 to children three to five years of age.

Selecting and Devising Screening Procedures

Some screening procedures are more effective and efficient than others. The following criteria should be considered before selecting a procedure (Hobbs, 1975a).

1. Who should do the screening: general classroom teachers, special educators, psychologists, parents, or some combination of these?
2. What is known about the reliability and validity of the screening instruments? Are they appropriate for specific developmental levels and fair to various cultural and ethnic groups?
3. Does screening identify cases that are not obvious? Is anything actually gained beyond providing services to students already known to be disturbed?
4. Are "false positives" and "false negatives" obtained during screening, and what happens as a result? Are students often misidentified as disturbed or are truly disturbed students often overlooked? When they are, how prompt and effective is the corrective action?
5. When students are identified as needing further study or special services as a result of screening, do they actually get what they need?
6. Is screening more cost-effective than periodic, comprehensive assessment of students already receiving services?

These are critical questions for evaluating screening programs, but for the foreseeable future, they are moot questions in most schools and communities. Economic realities and social policy severely limit the responses of most schools and communities to effective screening (see Chapters 1 and 2).

Prereferral Strategies

Effective screening results in further evaluation of some students. Before a student is evaluated for special education services, however, teachers must try to accommodate his or her needs in regular classes. These efforts must be documented and must show that the student is not responding well to reasonable adaptations of the curriculum and behavior management techniques used in the regular classroom (see Smith et al., in press; Wood, Smith, & Grimes, 1985). Prereferral strategies are an intermediate step between screening and evaluation; they aim to reduce the number of "false positives," to prevent misidentification, and to avoid wasting effort on unnecessary formal evaluations.

Prereferral strategies will sometimes result in successful management of the student in a regular classroom without the need for special education. Early detection of problems increases the likelihood of finding effective solutions without removing the student from the problem situation. Even with the best available prereferral strategies and flawless teamwork of general and special educators, however, some students' needs will not be met in regular classes (Braaten et al., in press; Lloyd et al., 1988). Screening should result in prompt attempts to find solutions to the problems of selected students in regular classes without evaluating them for special education. Failure to find solutions within a reasonable time should, however, result in prompt referral for evaluation; eternal hope should not spring from failure. (The accompanying box discusses referral following prereferral strategies.)

What Do I Do Before Referral?

Before making a referral, you will be expected to document the strategies that you have used in your class to meet the student's educational needs. Regardless of whether the student is later found to have a handicapping condition, your documentation will be useful in the following ways: (1) you will have evidence that will be helpful to or required by the committee of professionals who will evaluate the student; (2) you will be better able to help the student's parents understand that methods used for other students in the class are not adequate for their child; and (3) you will have records of successful and/or unsuccessful methods of working with the student that will be useful to you and any other teacher who works with the student in the future.

Your documentation of what you have done may appear to require a lot of paperwork, but careful record keeping will pay off. If the student is causing you serious concern, then you will be wise to demonstrate your concern by keeping written records. Your notes should include items such as the following:

☐ Exactly what you are concerned about
☐ Why you are concerned about it
☐ Dates, places, and times you have observed the problem
☐ Precisely what you have done to try to resolve the problem
☐ Who, if anyone, helped you devise the plans or strategies you have used
☐ Evidence that the strategies have been successful or unsuccessful

P. L. Pullen & J. M. Kauffman, *What should I know about special education? Answers for classroom teachers.* Austin, TX: Pro-Ed, 1987, pp. 6-7.

SCREENING INSTRUMENTS

Hundreds of behavioral rating scales are available, nearly all of which are potentially useful as screening instruments (McMahon, 1984). Many other procedures, including self-reports, sociometrics, direct observation, and interviewing are used in assessing children's social-emotional behavior (Brown, 1987; Ollendick & Hersen, 1984). Thus we cannot cover the range of instruments that might be used for screening behavior disorders, but will concentrate on several representative instruments. The *Revised Behavior Problem Checklist* (Quay & Peterson, 1987), which can also be used as a screening instrument, is described in Chapter 7. Use and interpretation of these instruments requires careful study of the test materials and manuals.

Behavior Rating Profile (Brown & Hammill, 1983)

The *Behavior Rating Profile* (BRP) is a battery of six subtests or components: Teacher Rating Scale, Parent Rating Scale, Student Rating Scales (Home, School, and Peer), and Sociogram. Because separate norms are available for each part, each component can be used independently or in combination with any of the other parts. The entire instrument can be used to derive an "ecological profile." The ecological profile in-

When Has A Referral Been Justified?

Nearly all professionals agree that a referral is not justified just because a teacher observes that a student misbehaves or has an academic problem in the classroom. Nevertheless, professionals often disagree about how much effort to expend on accommodating the student's needs before the teacher requests an evaluation for special education.

School systems are increasingly likely to require teachers to complete referral forms on which they describe behavioral characteristics and prereferral strategies. Consider Don and Bill, and imagine that you had to make decisions based solely on the information provided here. Are the referrals justifiable? If so, why? If not, what additional information or level of detail or specificity would make them justifiable?

Don

Don is a second grader whose teacher provides the following reasons for referral. "His behavior is continually disruptive. He is verbally abusive and physically aggressive. He will not follow instructions (such as to get proper book out, put candy away, ask for permission to leave the room, etc.). He uses vulgar, offensive words. He is untruthful." The teacher judges his academic performance to be average in spelling, handwriting, social studies, and physical education; below average (but not failing) in reading, language, arithmetic, science, and music. No recent test scores are reported.

Don's mother was contacted about a month ago—when she was asked to come to school following Don's suspension. She is aware of Don's behavior problems and is cooperative with school personnel. She is aware of Don's referral and is in agreement with it.

Don was retained in first grade. He has so far attended three different schools. His current teacher reports that she contacted Don's previous teachers, who reported similar problems but had no suggestions for his management. The resource teacher has suggested and tried several different behavior management strategies, none of which has been successful. Don's current teacher has tried behavioral contracting, preferential seating, and peer tutoring, as well as reasoning with him, trying to help him see the consequences of unacceptable behavior, isolating him from peers, withholding all or part of his recess, sending him to the principal, and changing his placement to a classroom with fewer troublesome students. These strategies have been tried for a period of about two months; none has been successful.

Bill

Bill is a fourteen-year-old eighth grader with a history of fighting, defiance, disruption, and lewd conduct. His present placement is in a special education resource room, with participation in as many regular classes as possible. School staff, including a behavioral consultant, have been devising special behavior management plans for him

---

dicates how different respondents (self, teachers, parents, and peers) perceive the student in different settings (home, school, and social life). Norms for ages six through eighteen allow classification of the student's behavior as within the "normal" range or within a "deviant" range.

The three self-rating scales that students complete require "true" or "false" responses to a variety of statements. The three scales consist of 20 items each, inter-

during the past year. He is now being referred for possible placement in a more re-strictive, residential setting.

At the beginning of the school year, Bill was harrassing certain female staff members. This was dealt with by teaching Bill alternatives to staring (such as glancing) and by informing him of the severe consequences that would result from his staring, making slurping noises, and vocalizing or mouthing lewd remarks. He has responded well to this program and has been penalized only once for lewd behavior.

The program in effect at the beginning of the school year included a general behavior checklist on which Bill's behavior was rated each period on each of five be-haviors: followed directions, participated, paid attention, classwork completed, and homework turned in. Teachers rated each behavior on the following scale: 3 = Great!, 2 = OK, 1 = Not Acceptable, ? = Not Applicable. Points could be earned for scoring threes and lost for scoring ones. Earned points could be exchanged in homeroom and during seventh period for activities and free time. Instruction in desirable classroom behavior was provided in homeroom. This plan was in effect from the beginning of school to mid-October. Bill could exhibit the desired behaviors, but he performed them sporadically.

In mid-October a set of consequences for resource and regular class settings was added for Bill's disruptive behavior. Regular classroom teachers were given the option of a quick ejection from their class (ignore, warn, eject); resource teachers were given the option of keeping him after school and having him walk home.

Because Bill was ending up in the office too much to suit the principal, even with the added consequences, additional interventions were tried. Direct observations were made to determine the extent to which Bill was following directions, including obeying classroom rules. He was found to be compliant with directions and rules about 60 to 75 percent of the time on the average; he was engaging in a high level of disruptive and defiant behavior, and his compliance tended to fluctuate wildly (for ex-ample, from zero to 86 percent compliance on one day). More explicit systems of penalties and rewards were devised; a "levels" plan was implemented, in which Bill could earn greater freedom and independence in school, plus food rewards, for im-proved behavior. Bill earned edible rewards on two occasions, then stated that he was no longer interested in "behaving for burgers."

In addition to the contingencies devised for Bill, the behavioral consultant has been providing instruction in social skills. These skills include asking for help from staff and responding appropriately to confusing and/or contradictory instructions or queries from staff.

Bill's behavior has been extremely variable from day to day since the beginning of school. Although he has reached several specific goals (has not being ejected from more than four classes in ten days), there has been no general trend toward improve-ment. In fact, Bill was recently suspended from school for one day.

I am grateful to Betty Hallenbeck, Charlottesville Public Schools, Charlottesville, VA, for providing the information about Don, and to Lee Jones, Oakridge School District, Oakridge, OR, for the information about Bill.

mingled into one 60-item list. These are representative items for the *Student Rating Scale: Home*:

1. My parents "bug" me a lot.
33. I have lots of nightmares and bad dreams.
47. I often break rules set by my parents.

These are items for the *Student Rating Scale: School*:

14. I sometimes stammer or stutter when the teacher calls on me.
29. My teachers give me work that I cannot do.
59. The things I learn in school are not as important or helpful as the things I learn outside school.

These are items for the *Student Rating Scale: Peer*:

6. Some of my friends think it is fun to cheat, skip school, etc.
10. Other kids don't seem to like me very much.
31. I seem to get into a lot of fights.

The *Teacher Rating Scale* requires teachers to rate each of 30 items as "Very Much Like the Student," "Like the Student," "Not Much Like the Student," or "Not At All Like the Student." These are representative items:

4. Tattles on classmates
17. Is an academic underachiever
30. Doesn't follow class rules

The *Parent Rating Scale* requires parents to rate each of 30 items as "Very Much Like My Child," "Like My Child," "Not Very Much Like My Child," or "Not At All Like My Child," using items like these:

1. Is verbally aggressive to parents
10. Is shy; clings to parents
27. Won't share belongings willingly

The *Sociogram* is a peer-nominating technique in which teachers ask students questions such as "Which of the girls and boys in your class would you most like to work with (or least like to work with) on a school project?" Each student in the class is asked to name three of his or her classmates for each question.

Test of Early Socioemotional Development (Hresko & Brown, 1984)

The *Test of Early Socioemotional Development* (TOSED) is an extension of the BRP for younger children, ages three through seven. It has four components: Student Rating Scale, Teacher Rating Scale, Parent Rating Scale, and Sociogram. Like the BRP, the scales can be used individually or in combination. Unlike the BRP, however, the TOSED questions for children are administered orally.

Social-Emotional Dimension Scale (Hutton & Roberts, 1986)

The *Social-Emotional Dimension Scale* (SEDS) is a school-based rating scale with items written to represent the five characteristics of emotionally handicapped students listed in Bower's (1981) definition, which is essentially also the current federal definition. The 32-item scale can be used by teachers of students five years, six months through eighteen years, five months of age. The total SEDS score can be compared to norms for typical students to identify those who are "average," "at risk," "high risk," or "very high risk" for behavior problems. Subscale scores can be used to identify risk related to one of six types of problem behavior: avoidance of peer interaction, aggressive interaction, avoidance of teacher interaction, inappropriate behavior, depressive reaction, and physical/fear reaction. Teachers rate the student on a three-point scale ("never or rarely," "occasionally," "frequently") for each item; these are representative:

4. Student looks directly at other students when appropriate.
10. Student fights physically with other students.
13. Student initiates conversation with the teacher.
18. Student does things that fit inappropriately with what others are doing.
23. Student says derogatory things about self.
27. Student complains of headaches or stomachaches.

Child Behavior Checklist (Achenbach & Edelbrock, 1981, 1984)

The *Child Behavior Checklist* (CBCL) is available in both parent's report and teacher's report forms. It is one of the most thoroughly researched rating scales available (McMahon, 1984). The teacher's report, adapted from the parent version, includes items for rating problem behavior as well as school performance and adaptive behavior. The teacher rates each of the 112 behavior problems on the checklist on a three-point scale, "Not True (as far as you know)," "Somewhat or Sometimes True," or "Very True or Often True." Representative items are as follows.

2. Hums or makes other odd noises in class
9. Can't get his/her mind off certain thoughts; obsessions (describe)
10. Can't sit still, restless, or hyperactive
11. Clings to adults or too dependent
12. Complains of loneliness
13. Confused or seems to be in a fog
14. Cries a lot
15. Fidgets
16. Cruelty, bullying, or meanness to others
47. Overconforms to rules
48. Not liked by other pupils
57. Physically attacks people
58. Picks nose, skin, or other parts of body (describe)
74. Showing off or clowning
82. Steals
84. Strange behavior (describe)
86. Stubborn, sullen, or irritable
96. Seems preoccupied with sex
101. Truancy or unexplained absence
105. Uses alcohol or drugs (describe)
107. Dislikes school

The teacher's report form of the CBCL can be used with students ages six through sixteen. Scores can be plotted on a Child Behavior Profile form that relates specific items to problem factors such as these (specific factors depend on the age and sex group): social withdrawal, anxious, unpopular, obsessive-compulsive, immature, self-destructive, hyperactive, and aggressive. Items describing adaptive functioning are related to factors such as working hard, behaving appropriately, learning, and being happy.

Systematic Screening for Behavior Disorders (Walker, Severson, & Haring, 1985; Walker, Severson, Stiller, Williams, Haring, Shinn, & Todis, 1988)

Walker et al. have devised a screening procedure for use in elementary schools based on the assumption that teacher judgment is a valid and cost-effective (though greatly underused) method of identifying behavior disordered students. Teachers tend to overrefer students who exhibit externalizing behavior problems—those who act out or exhibit **conduct disorder**. Teachers tend to underrefer students with internalizing problems—those who are characterized by anxiety and social withdrawal. To make certain that students are not overlooked in screening, and to minimize time and effort, a three-step or "multiple gating" process is used.

In the first step, or "gate," the teacher lists and rank-orders students with externalizing and internalizing problems, listing those who best fit descriptions of externalized problems and internalized problems and ranking them from most like to least like the descriptions. The second step requires that the teacher complete two checklists for the three highest-ranked students on each list—those who have passed through the first "gate." One checklist asks the teacher to indicate whether the pupil exhibited specific behaviors during the past month ("steals," "has tantrums," "uses obscene language or swears"); the other requires that the teacher judge how often ("never," "sometimes," "frequently") each student shows certain characteristics ("follows established classroom rules," "cooperates with peers in group activities or situations"). The third step requires observation of students whose scores on the checklists exceed established norms—those who have passed through the second "gate." Students are observed in the classroom and on the playground by a school professional other than the usual classroom teacher (a school psychologist, counselor, or resource teacher). Classroom observations indicate the extent to which the student meets academic expectations; playground observations assess the quality and nature of social behavior. These direct observations, in addition to teacher ratings, are then used to decide whether the student has problems that warrant full evaluation for special education. The procedures that Walker and his colleagues devised are the most fully developed screening system currently available for use in school settings.

SCREENING AS CONVERGENCE AND CONFIRMATION OF CONCERNS

One person's opinion or a single score on a rating scale or other instrument should never be considered adequate for screening. A student should be selected for evaluation only when several observers share the suspicion that he or she may have a behavior disorder and their shared suspicion is confirmed by data obtained from structured observations or ratings. Otherwise, the risk is too high that the student will be unnecessarily labeled and stigmatized, that his or her privacy rights will be violated, and that resources will be wasted on fruitless evaluations.

The goal of screening should be to obtain information from a variety of sources and to use instruments that facilitate hypotheses regarding the reciprocal influence of the behavior, the environments in which it occurs, and the student's personal perspectives. This goal is consistent with an ecological approach and with a social-cognitive conceptual model.

SUMMARY

Screening means narrowing the field to those students most likely to have behavior disorders. It involves becoming a good "suspectition," so that incipient cases and those that are not immediately obvious are reliably identified. Although PL 94-142 requires identification of all handicapped children, few school systems use systematic screening procedures to identify students with behavior disorders. If schools were to use such screening procedures, they would be likely to identify more students than could be served by special education.

One rationale for screening is that early identification will result in effective early intervention. Although this rationale is supportable, translating concern into screening procedures is difficult. Screening for behavior disorders involves, for the most part, secondary prevention—preventing complications and exacerbation of existing problems. Effective screening of infants and young children with mild behavior disorders is particularly difficult for educators because young children's behavior is sensitive to parental management, and parents, not teachers, define preschoolers' problem behavior. Criteria for selecting screening instruments include who will be the respondents, the psychometric characteristics of the instruments, and the anticipated outcomes of screening. Prereferral strategies are a necessary intermediate step between screening and referral for evaluation. Before formal evaluation for special education, school personnel must make documented efforts to resolve the student's problems and provide appropriate education in the regular classroom. When prereferral strategies fail, the teacher should not delay in referring the student for evaluation.

Many rating scales and other instruments can be used for screening. Screening should never consist of a single individual's judgment or be based on data from a single instrument. Convergence of judgments based on confirmation from a variety of sources should be the basis for screening decisions.

6

Evaluation: Measurement and Planning for Instruction

As you read this chapter, keep these guiding questions in mind:

☐ How has evaluation of exceptional children changed during the past two decades?

☐ How is evaluation for eligibility different from and similar to evaluation for intervention?

☐ What are the implications of the fact that youngsters seldom refer themselves for evaluation?

☐ How can professionals work to overcome unpredictability, unreliability, and bias in evaluation for eligibility?

☐ What types of procedures should be used to evaluate a student referred because of disordered behavior?

☐ How does curriculum-based evaluation differ from the more traditional approach?

☐ What is involved in social validation, and why is it important?

☐ How do direct observation, curriculum-based evaluation, and social validation relate to writing individualized education programs (IEPs)?

S ignificant changes in the evaluation of exceptional children and youth have occurred during the past two decades. One change is a shift in terminology. Psychologists and educators still occasionally use the term *diagnosis* with reference to
behavior disorders. Diagnosis has largely been replaced by *evaluation* and *assessment,*
however, because diagnosis connotes the classification of disease. In the vast majority
of cases, there is no evidence that disordered behavior is a disease in any usual sense
of the term. The terms *assessment* and *evaluation* are more appropriate for educational
purposes because they connote measurement of nonmedical as well as physiological
factors related to social learning and adaptation.

Another change is a substantial increase in the availability of assessment devices
and information about the assessment process. Evaluation of learning and behavior
is now recognized as a task of considerable complexity, with entire books devoted
to behavioral assessment and educational evaluation (Hammill, 1987; Hargrove &
Poteet, 1984; Howell & Morehead, 1987; Mash & Terdal, 1981; Ollendick & Hersen,
1984; Salvia & Ysseldyke, 1985). Most books on behavioral intervention or instructional
methods devote chapters or special sections to these topics (Bornstein & Kazdin,
1985; Kerr et al., 1987; O'Leary & Johnson, 1986). Several journals devoted entirely
to assessment issues, such as *Behavioral Assessment* and *Diagnostique,* are available
in most university libraries, and the Council for Exceptional Children has a division
devoted to assessment (Council for Educational Diagnostic Services [CEDS]). Many
universities offer specific courses in psychoeducational assessment as part of teacher
training. If you are preparing to teach students with behavior disorders, you will need
to study evaluation procedures in greater detail than this chapter offers.

Finally, legal issues have taken a prominent place in assessment. A student who
is referred for special education must first be evaluated to determine whether he or
she is eligible for services under PL 94-142 and related state legislation (see Pullen
& Kauffman, 1987; Turnbull & Turnbull, 1986). Federal regulations require that this
assessment be completed by an interdisciplinary team of qualified specialists, as
described in the accompanying box. If the initial assessment is properly conducted,
the results will be useful not only for determining eligibility for special education,
but for planning instruction regardless of the student's placement in special or general
classes. If the student receives special education, then the evaluation data must be
used in writing an individualized education program (IEP). The law requires a new
IEP for each year the student receives special education; it demands a full-scale
reevaluation of eligibility for special education at least every three years. Evaluation
is thus a central issue in the legal aspects of special education.

When a youngster exhibits behavior troublesome enough to result in referral
and evaluation, it is important to assess his or her behavior and its context so as to
plan an appropriate intervention. Determining precisely the nature and extent of the
problem, finding its possible causes and exacerbating factors, designing methods for
changing it, and monitoring the outcome are necessary components of evaluation for
educational purposes. This type of evaluation is an ongoing process that is an integral
part of teaching and intervention in disordered behavior.

Evaluation thus serves two major purposes: first, determining whether the student should be identified or classified for special education or other purposes; second,
providing information relevant to intervention. These purposes are not mutually

What General Rules Apply to Evaluation for Special Education?

An evaluation entails individualized assessment of the student's educational needs. It typically includes four components: medical, psychological, social, and educational. All evaluation procedures must be completed before the student's eligibility for special education can be determined. The assessment must be completed by a group of professionals qualified to evaluate the student's problems, at least one of whom must be a teacher or specialist qualified to teach students with disabilities like the one the child is suspected of having.

The student must be assessed in each area of known or suspected disability. Evaluation must be done using methods or tests that are not racially or culturally discriminatory, and it must be done in the student's native language or usual mode of communication. The tests must be reliable and valid for the purposes for which they are used. Furthermore, no single test or method of evaluation can be used as the sole criterion for determining the student's eligibility for special education. After parental permission for evaluation is obtained, the school must complete all components within 65 days. (Note: 65 days is a federal requirement; some state laws set a limit of less than 65 days.)

The test results and other records about the student must be kept confidential. No one but teachers and other professionals who work with the student is allowed to review the records without parental permission. It is unprofessional and illegal to share information from the evaluation with professionals who are not directly involved with the student's education. However, parents must, by law, be informed of the results of the evaluation in language they can understand, and the school must allow parents to see their child's records if they so request.

If parents disagree with the school's evaluation data, they have a right to have their child evaluated somewhere else and present the results to the school. Then, if parents and the school cannot reach an agreement about an accurate evaluation, by law either party may request a hearing.

After a student is placed in special education, his or her progress is assessed each year by the teacher. However, a full reevaluation involving an interdisciplinary team must be completed at least every 3 years. This is called a *triennial* evaluation and is done to decide whether the student's placement is still appropriate.

P. L. Pullen & J. M. Kauffman, *What Should I Know About Special Education? Answers for Classroom Teachers*. Austin, TX: Pro-Ed, 1987.

exclusive; information gained during initial evaluation for purposes of classification should obviously be helpful in designing initial teaching and management strategies. The same evaluation procedures are, in large measure, appropriate for both eligibility and intervention. Nevertheless, the focus of initial evaluation is clearly a yes/no decision for special education and related services, whereas the primary concerns of ongoing evaluation are designing the intervention and measuring progress. Furthermore, evaluation for eligibility must be multidisciplinary, with emphasis on ruling out as many causes of the problem as possible. Evaluation for intervention, on the other hand, focuses more on classroom performance and what can be done to improve the student's behavior.

Whether evaluation is for eligibility or intervention, two considerations are important: the source of referral and the initial appearance of a problem. Young children almost never refer themselves for evaluation; even youths seldom do. Children and youth are usually brought to the attention of mental health workers or special educators by their parents, teachers, or other adults. The evaluation is thus almost always prompted by adults' judgments of youngsters' behavior rather than by the children's opinions about themselves. Adult referral of children and youth has two immediate implications. First, the evaluation must involve appraisal of at least one referring adult as well as the youngster. Appraisal of the adult who refers the youngster is necessary to validate the concern about the disturbing behavior and discover how the adult's responses to the youngster might be contributing to the problem. Second, attempts must be made to determine the youngster's own view of the situation. No humane and ethical approach to the disordered behavior can disregard or trivialize the youngster's opinions of his or her problems and treatment. Some youngsters' opinions are not accessible because of their lack of communication skills, and some youngsters' opinions must be overruled because they are clearly not in their own best interests. Still, the rights of children and youth must be protected, and their opinions, when they can be determined, should be weighed seriously in decisions about identification and treatment.

Behavior problems are not always what they seem at first. Sometimes an explanation is difficult to find, not because the disordered behavior is buried deep in someone's psyche, but simply because some of the most relevant facts are hard to extract from the situation. Consider the case of Ray.

Ray

Throughout elementary school, Ray's teachers described him as a bright, cooperative, and sociable student. His work habits and general attitude toward school were very good. He achieved at or above grade level in all subjects and was popular among his peers. During the first few months of junior high school, all of Ray's teachers gave a similar general description. By the middle of seventh grade, however, Ray's behavior had changed dramatically.

Ray was absent from school with increasing frequency. He dropped out of all the extracurricular activities in which he had formerly participated. His teachers reported that he did not often complete assignments, frequently daydreamed in class, and was generally uninvolved in class activities. His grades dropped below passing.

Ray's teachers attempted to alter his behavior by a variety of means. They gave verbal praise, additional privileges, and points exchangeable for tangible rewards contingent upon appropriate behavior, but these techniques did not produce the desired behavior changes. Curricular modifications were made repeatedly, but Ray remained uninvolved in classroom activities. In fact, he was absent from school more and more frequently as time went on. He was unwilling to discuss the problem with his teachers or the guidance counselor. Phone calls and letters to his parents went unanswered. Only after being warned of a potential fine for truancy did Ray's parents agree to discuss the situation with school personnel. A conference was arranged with Ray, his parents, teachers, and the guidance counselor.

During the conference, Ray's parents stated that he remained at home during his absences from school. The relationship between Ray and his mother appeared to be overly solicitous (they greeted each other with a kiss and held hands during most of the discussion). Ray's father was attentive, but generally silent throughout the conference. Both parents agreed to make certain that Ray would attend school regularly.

Over the next few weeks Ray's attendance improved only slightly. The case was then referred to the school mental health team, which was comprised of the teachers, guidance counselor, social worker, school psychologist, and a psychiatrist. Reviewing the case, the psychiatrist emphasized that Ray had unmet dependency needs and was experiencing separation anxiety. The teachers initiated activities the psychiatrist recommended to enhance Ray's self-concept, increase his independence, and develop his sense of autonomy and control. Demonstrable results, in terms of improved attendance rates, were not evident after a month of such efforts.

As the final effort before taking legal action against Ray's parents, the social worker made a home visit one day when Ray was absent. Upon her arrival, the social worker found Ray comforting his obviously battered mother. His mother then revealed that her husband, an alcoholic, had been fired from his job a few months earlier. During this period of unemployment, he frequently drank excessively and became physically abusive toward her. When Ray was home, however, his father was usually not abusive or beat Ray's mother less severely. (This case was contributed by James Krouse.)

Ray's case illustrates the point that evaluation may need to involve more than assessing only the student's problem. A student can hardly be expected to attend school and be interested in school activities when he knows that his attendance will probably result in his mother's being beaten. This reasonable explanation for Ray's behavior was not immediately obvious. Appropriate intervention in this case would have focused on resolving the abuse of Ray's mother as well as increasing his school attendance.

Sometimes evaluation focuses too much on the student's behavior and does not tap some critical item of information, which is often difficult to obtain. If the student's behavior is understood as a reasonable response to the circumstances of his or her life, then decisions regarding eligibility and intervention can be made with greater confidence.

EVALUATION FOR ELIGIBILITY

As already mentioned, federal regulations require that evaluation for eligibility involve multiple sources of data and assessment by a multidisciplinary team (MDT). Evaluation of academic performance is critical because most students identified as behaviorally disordered have serious academic problems as well as problems of social adjustment (Kauffman et al., 1987). Evaluation of physical status, cognitive development, and language skills is also important because problems in any one of these areas can contribute to disordered behavior. Evaluation of the social environment of the home and the student's emotional responses to parents, teachers, and peers are essential for understanding the social influences that may be contributing to the problem. Ideally, the MDT carefully weighs information obtained from evaluations in all these areas before deciding the student's eligibility for special education.

Unfortunately the MDT seldom functions with ideal care and reliability. In practice, decisions are often made with information from limited sources, and the decision-making process tends to be unreliable—not predictable on the basis of objective data from tests and observations alone (Smith et al., in press). One reason for the lack of predictability is the absence of guidelines regarding just how the MDT must function. Another reason is the lack of clear criteria for defining behavior disorder. Still another reason is the tendency of some evaluation procedures to turn up irrelevant or unhelpful information; for example, physiological or psychological tests may have little value for educational decisions. Decision making might become more objective along some dimensions by tightening the criteria for definition and by using expert systems, in which computer programs use multiple sources of data to establish complex and entirely objective criteria. Such efforts to objectify the decision- making process do not, unfortunately, take into consideration the fact that the definition of disordered behavior is necessarily subjective, as we saw in Chapter 1. More objective and reliable instruments and computer programs may *help* people make better decisions, but they cannot become the sole bases for decision making.

A major problem in evaluation for eligibility is that the decisions of those who declare a student behavior disordered for special education purposes tend to be unreliable (unpredictable or inconsistent) when judged against criteria such as standardized test scores and objective behavioral observations. Different groups and different individuals may evaluate according to different criteria; they may use different criteria for students who differ in sex, race, socioeconomic status, and so forth. Inconsistency is a serious concern because it can indicate bias or inappropriate discrimination in evaluation (Smith et al., in press). The solution, however, is not to make the judgments conform to objective psychometric criteria alone (such as test scores or quantitative values in computer programs), nor is it to abandon the goal of more reliable, predictable, or consistent decisions. The most desirable response is to stress professional responsibility in decision making (see Kauffman, 1984; Smith, 1985; Smith et al., in press). These are key actions in discharging that responsibility:

- ☐ Obtaining inservice training in appropriate evaluation procedures
- ☐ Refusing to use evaluation procedures that you are not qualified to use and refusing to accept evaluation data from unqualified personnel
- ☐ Functioning as a member of an MDT to ensure that a single individual does not make the eligibility decision
- ☐ Insisting that multiple sources of data be made available to the MDT and that the eligibility decision be made on the basis of all relevant data
- ☐ Requiring implementation of documented prereferral strategies prior to evaluation for eligibility
- ☐ Involving the parents and, if appropriate, the student in the eligibility decision to be sure they are informed of the nature of the problem and the implications of identification
- ☐ Documenting the presence of disordered behavior, its adverse effect on the student's assessment, and the need for special education and related services
- ☐ Considering the interests of all parties affected by the eligibility decision— student, peers, parents, and teachers
- ☐ Estimating the probable risks and benefits of identifying and not identifying the student for special education
- ☐ Remaining sensitive to the possibility of bias in the use of procedures and interpretation of data

EVALUATION FOR INTERVENTION

Adequate evaluation for the purpose of intervention requires careful attention to a wide range of factors that may be important in the origin and modification of problem behavior. Thus, whenever possible, information must be obtained from parents, teachers, peers, the student, and impartial observers. Evaluation for special education interventions also requires focusing on the student's problems as they are manifested in school. Procedures for evaluating students referred for behavior disorders should include at least standardized tests of intelligence and achievement, behavior ratings, assessment of peer relations, interviews, self-reports, and direct observations. An emerging approach to evaluation, particularly of academic achievement, is curriculum-based assessment (CBA). In some cases involving **psychosomatic disorders**, psychophysiological measures such as heart rate are obtained (O'Leary & Johnson, 1986).

Standardized Tests of Intelligence and Achievement

Standardized tests can be used to estimate what a student has learned and to compare his or her performance to the norms of age mates. They can provide a description of current abilities and point to areas in need of instruction. A test of intelligence provides evidence of a student's learning in general skill areas; a test of academic achievement taps more specific skills. Neither type of test, however, provides much information about just what a student should be taught.

There are good reasons for using standardized intelligence and achievement tests; it is helpful, for example, to know how a student's progress in learning skills compares to other students' progress in a national sample. One must, however, avoid serious pitfalls, which include possible bias in favor of certain cultural, ethnic, or socioeconomic groups (bias in terms of a disproportionate number of students from one of these groups who score within a certain range on a given test). Other pitfalls are a margin of error in the scores students achieve at a given testing, changes in scores over time or after instruction, and failure of the scores to predict important outcomes. An IQ derived from a standardized test is not a measure of intellectual potential, nor is it static or immutable; it is merely a measure of general learning in certain areas compared to the learning of other students of the same age who comprised the normative sample. An IQ is only a *moderately* accurate predictor of what a student is likely to learn in the future *if no special intervention is provided*. Remember that a student's performance on a given test on a given day can be influenced by many factors, and even under the best conditions, the score is an *estimate* of a range in which the student's true score is likely to fall.

Considering the pitfalls in standardized testing is particularly important in evaluating students with behavior disorders. Disordered behavior tends to interfere with learning and academic performance, during both instruction and testing. Consequently, students with behavior disorders are likely to perform below their true abilities on standardized tests. Students with behavior disorders, as a group, tend to score lower than average on intelligence and achievement tests. Careful evaluation of their abilities is warranted, therefore, to avoid mistakes in setting expectations for their performance.

Many standardized tests are normative—a student's score is compared to the scores of a large, presumably similar, sample of individuals on which the test was normed. Some standardized tests are criterion-referenced; that is, they do not explicitly compare a student's performance to that of a normative group but, rather, indicate whether the student has or has not achieved a specific skill (criterion). Ultimately, a criterion-referenced test is a standardized test with a single yes-no score or criterion rather than an aggregate score. The criterion was probably chosen because most students of the same age in a comparison group have reached it. Thus a criterion-referenced test presents many of the same problems as norm-referenced tests—possible bias because of the criteria chosen, invalidity of the criteria as measures of true ability to perform, variability of the student's performance, and so on.

Objections to well-known intelligence and achievement tests, as well as to other standardized measures, are often based on criticism of the inappropriate use and interpretation of test scores—unintelligent or unprofessional psychometric procedures that can ruin the value of any evaluation procedure. The value and limitations of standardized and normative testing have been discussed in detail (Bateman & Herr, 1981; Hammill, 1987; Salvia & Ysseldyke, 1985). Despite their limitations, standardized tests of intelligence and achievement, used with appropriate caution, can be helpful in assessing important areas of strength, weakness, and progress.

Behavior Ratings

Besides the several behavior rating scales described in Chapter 5, other scales commonly used in evaluation of behavior disorders are the *Revised Behavior Problem Checklist* (Quay & Peterson, 1987), and the *Louisville School Behavior Checklist* (Miller, 1972). For assessment of hyperactivity, the *Conners Teacher Rating Scale* (Conners, 1969) is often used. Sometimes several individuals (parents and teachers, for instance) complete rating scales, then the ratings are compared to assess the level of agreement about the student's behavior. Besides the usefulness of rating scales for indicating types of problems a student tends to exhibit (see Chapter 7), they can be used repeatedly to evaluate progress in reaching intervention goals.

Rating scales are subject to the same dangers of misuse and misinterpretation as any other standardized assessment instrument regarding reliability, validity, inappropriate application, and bias. Another possible misuse is to ask teachers who are not sufficiently acquainted with a student to complete a behavior rating scale.

Assessment of Peer Relations

Interaction with and acceptance by the peer group are necessary for normal social development. Students with behavior disorders often do not develop normal peer relations (Fox, 1987; Hollinger, 1987; Sabornie, 1985; Sabornie & Kauffman, 1985). Some are socially withdrawn, and maintain a low profile with their classmates by avoiding peer interaction. Others are aggressive toward peers. A disruptive influence in any group activity, they maintain a high profile with their classmates, although their peers actively reject them. In either case, the disturbed student ends up alone because he or she does not have the necessary social skills for the positive reciprocal exchanges that characterize friendships. Research increasingly indicates that problems in social interaction with peers are a prominent feature of a variety of behavior disorders, a highly significant problem of exceptional children and youth that demands evaluation and intervention in its own right (Farrington, 1986a; Shores, 1987; Simpson, 1987).

There are various ways to evaluate peer relations. Some screening instruments include rating scales that are completed by peers; some include sociometric questions for assessing acceptance or rejection among peers (see Chapter 5). Sociometric techniques are not necessarily part of a screening procedure, but are often used in research and evaluation in which peer relations are a central concern. Direct observation is sometimes used to measure how often the student makes social initiations or responds appropriately to peers' initiations.

Interviews

Interviews vary widely in structure and purpose. They can be freewheeling conversations or can follow a prescribed line of questioning for obtaining information about specific behaviors or developmental milestones. They can be conducted with verbal children as well as with adults.

Skillful interviewing is no simple matter. When troublesome behavior is in question, it is not easy to keep the interviewee(s) from becoming defensive. And an interview in which answers represent half-truths, misleading information, or avoidance will not be much help in evaluation. (Consider the difficulty in obtaining helpful information from Ray and his parents in the case we discussed earlier.) Furthermore, one must maintain a healthy skepticism about the accuracy of interview responses that require memory of long-past events. It is also important to weigh carefully the interviewees' subjective opinions, especially when their responses are emotionally charged or seriously discrepant from other subjective reports or objective evidence. Finally, extracting and accurately recording the most relevant information from an interview requires keen judgment and excellent communication skills.

Interviews should help the evaluator get an impression of how the student and significant others interact and feel about each other. They should also help members of the evaluation team decide what additional types of information they need. But interviews can accomplish these ends only to the extent that the interviewer has great interpersonal skills, the experience and sensitivity to make sound clinical judgments, and the ability to focus on information about the relevant behavior and its social contexts.

Kanfer and Grimm (1977) suggest five categories in which interviewers may want to pursue questions:

1. *Behavioral deficits,* such as the student's lack of information about how to behave; lack of specific social skills; lack of skill in self-monitoring and self-control; lack of access to or responsiveness to important reinforcers; lack of daily living skills.
2. *Behavioral excesses,* such as debilitating anxiety or preoccupation with self.
3. *Inappropriate environmental control,* such as deviant sexual responses or insensitivity to violence; unavailability of opportunity to practice desirable behavior; inefficient organization of activities.

4. *Inappropriate responses to self,* such as misperception of one's abilities; unrealistic evaluations or predictions; inaccuracy in describing one's internal states.

5. *Inappropriate contingencies,* such as lack of reinforcement for appropriate behavior; reinforcement of inadequate or undesirable behavior; excessive reward for desirable responses; random reinforcement (or reward that is not dependent on any particular kind of behavior).

Descriptions of behavior, competencies, environmental conditions, and consequences obtained from interviews may be helpful, but are often inaccurate and cannot be relied upon without verification from other sources (Kanfer & Grimm, 1977). It is important to note discrepancies between reports given to interviewers and information obtained from direct observation, as they can sometimes be crucial in designing interventions. If, for example, teachers or parents report that they frequently praise appropriate behavior and ignore misconduct but direct observation shows the opposite, then the adults' misperceptions must be taken into account in designing an intervention plan.

Self-Reports

Self-reports require students to respond to behavior rating scales or interviews. Students may be asked to complete checklists, rate themselves, or describe their behavior or feelings. How students perceive themselves and how they respond emotionally to various circumstances is an important part of the assessment of *person variables,* the cognitive processes and affective states that are part of Bandura's (1986) social cognitive model (see Chapter 4). Self-reports are particularly important when evaluating anxiety, fears, and depression—disorders that are highly affective (see O'Leary & Johnson, 1986). They can be useful in identifying the points of stress a student feels most acutely. Self-reports are also critical in evaluating covert self-verbalizations that are part of cognitive-behavioral interventions (see Harris, Wong, & Keogh, 1985). Self-reports are of limited value, however, for youngsters who are nonverbal or unable to organize their responses coherently.

Direct Observations

A large body of behavioral research supports the commonsense practice of observing students in the environments in which problems are reported (Ollendick & Hersen, 1984). An extensive technology of direct observation and recording has been developed, much of which is directly applicable to teaching (Kerr & Nelson, 1983; Kerr et al., 1987; Morris, 1985). Direct observation is a particularly important approach to evaluating disorders that involve externalized problems, those in which the student strikes out at and disturbs others.

Direct behavioral observation can address questions like these:

In what settings (home, school, math class, or playground) is the problem behavior or behavioral deficit exhibited?

With what frequency, duration, or force does the behavior occur in various settings?

What happens immediately before the behavior occurs—what seems to set the occasion for it?

What happens immediately after the behavior occurs that may serve to strengthen or weaken it?

What other inappropriate responses are observed?

What appropriate behavior could be taught or strengthened to lessen the problem?

What does the student's behavior communicate to others?

Direct observation requires careful definition of observable target behaviors and frequent, usually daily, recording of occurrence. Some interventions and evaluation procedures depend on this methodology. A behavioral approach to teaching disturbed students makes direct observation a central feature of intervention, and curriculum-based assessment depends upon direct observation and recording of academic and social behavior. Direct observation is also an important aspect of many interventions derived from a social cognitive model.

Curriculum-Based Evaluation

An evaluation methodology involving frequent, direct measurement of students' performance using their typical curriculum materials began to emerge in the mid-1980s (Deno, 1985; Shinn & Marston, 1985). In the literature, it has been called curriculum-based measurement (Deno, 1985), curriculum-based assessment (Germann & Tindal, 1985), and curriculum-based evaluation (Howell & Morehead, 1987). This methodology contrasts sharply to more traditional approaches to evaluation, in which students are given tests that include many items they have never seen before. The assumption underlying the traditional approach is that the test items are representative of a pool of similar items on which the student has been or should have been instructed. The assumption of curriculum-based methodology is that it is more accurate and useful to measure student performance with the curriculum materials used in the students' daily instruction.

Proponents of curriculum-based evaluation stress that the most important information for planning intervention and evaluating instruction is obtained from students' responses to daily instruction, not from standardized normative tests on which items may be only obliquely related to what the students have actually been taught. Students are therefore tested frequently—often daily—by being asked to complete brief tasks taken from their current instructional materials. Individual students' performances are compared to those of others in the same school using the same curriculum. For example, students might be asked to read aloud for one minute from a passage in their usual reader, perhaps three times per week. Their reading rates (words read correctly per minute and/or errors per minute) are then recorded. To evaluate written language, students might be asked to provide a three-minute sample of their writing in response to a topic sentence. Math performance might be evaluated by asking students to complete as many computation problems as they can in two minutes, with the problems taken from their basal text. Students who are having difficulty, and who might be considered exceptional for special education purposes, are thus identified on the basis of their usual educational performance compared to that of their classroom peers.

Curriculum-based evaluation is important because most students who receive special education because of behavior disorders have academic deficits (Kauffman et al., 1987). Furthermore, proponents of curriculum-based methods include social skills among measurable performances (Germann & Tindal, 1985; Howell, 1985; Howell & Morehead, 1987). A student's and his or her classmates' specific behavioral problems or social skills, such as hitting classmates, making derogatory comments about self, making positive social initiations, and taking turns can be recorded systematically for comparison. If the student's behavior is significantly different from that of other students, then he or she may be identified as needing a special teaching procedure to change the targeted behavior and the results can be evaluated by noting changes in the student's behavior compared to the peer group. The significant difference between this kind of curriculum-based evaluation and direct observation is this: a curriculum-based approach assumes that the school is using a coherent social skills curriculum, that is, that social skills are being taught systematically. Unfortunately, social skills curricula are not yet well developed, and many schools have not implemented existing curricula (Hollinger, 1987; Howell & Morehead, 1987).

Physical and Psychophysiological Measures

We know that physical disorders and diseases can affect the way people behave, so if there is reason to suspect that a referred student may have a physical ailment, a thorough physical exam should be obtained from a physician. Sometimes the search for causes of disordered behavior includes special neurological or physiological tests. These may include an **electroencephalogram** or measures of heart rate or electrical conductivity of the skin under different conditions. Such procedures are usually used in evaluating disorders in which a physiological problem is suspected as the primary cause or in which both physiological and psychological factors are involved. Information from these types of evaluations seldom has direct implications for planning educational interventions.

EVALUATION AND SOCIAL VALIDATION

Those who are responsible for assessing students must be concerned with the scientific or technical quality of their work as well as the social validity of the outcomes. *Social validity* means that the clients (parents, teachers, and students) who are ostensibly being helped, as well as those who intervene, are convinced that (1) a significant problem is being addressed, (2) the intervention procedures are acceptable, and (3) the outcome of intervention is satisfactory (cf. Wolf, 1978). Social validation is the process of evaluating the clinical importance and personal/social meaningfulness of intervention. As Kazdin (1977) pointed out, social validation involves social comparison and subjective evaluation (that is, comparison to peers who do not exhibit the disorder). It requires subjective judgments of specially trained and/or nonprofessional persons about the client's behavior. To the extent that a student's behavior is markedly different from that of a valid comparison group before intervention but indistinguishable from the comparison group's behavior after intervention, social validity is established by social comparison. (Note that this is consistent with curriculum-based methodology.) And, to the extent that clients and trained observers perceive that the quality of the student's behavior is unacceptable before intervention but markedly improved or desirable after intervention, social validity is indicated by subjective evaluation. Social validation is a particularly important issue for special educators when radical reform or merging of general and special education are proposed (see Braaten et al., in press; Hallahan et al. 1988).

USE OF EVALUATION DATA IN WRITING INDIVIDUALIZED EDUCATION PROGRAMS

Evaluation for special education carries legal as well as professional implications. Ultimately, evaluation data must be used to legitimize decisions about the student's identification, placement, and instruction. The outcomes of these decisions must be summarized in the student's IEP.

Notes on the IEP

What Is an IEP?

An IEP is a written agreement between the parents and the school about what the child needs and what will be done to address those needs. It is, in effect, a contract about services to be provided for the student. By law an IEP must include the following: (1) the student's present levels of academic performance; (2) annual goals for the student; (3) short-term instructional objectives related to the annual goals; (4) the special education and related services that will be provided and the extent to which the child will participate in regular education programs; (5) plans for starting the services and the anticipated duration of the services; and (6) appropriate plans for evaluating, at least annually, whether the goals and objectives are being achieved.

Are Teachers Legally Liable for Reaching IEP Goals?

No. Federal law does not require that the stated goals be met. However, teachers and other school personnel are responsible for seeing that the IEP is written to include the six components listed above, that the parents have an opportunity to review and participate in developing the IEP, that the IEP is approved by the parents before placement, and that the services called for in the IEP are actually provided. Teachers and other school personnel are responsible for making a good-faith effort to achieve the goals and objectives of the IEP.

P. L. Pullen & J. M. Kauffman, *What Should I Know About Special Education? Answers for Classroom Teachers*. Austin, TX: Pro-Ed, 1987.

All types of evaluation procedures may yield relevant information about a student's education. Several procedures are particularly important, however, for the IEPs of students with behavior disorders. Although not every acceptable IEP includes them, direct observation, curriculum-based evaluation, and social validation procedures offer rich sources of information that should be the basis for instructional planning. Direct observational data allows the teacher to choose specific behavioral targets for intervention and to set quantitative goals and objectives for behavioral change. Curriculum-based procedures allow the teacher to be precise about academic goals and objectives in the student's everyday curriculum. A curriculum-based approach also encourages the teacher to select or devise a social skills curriculum, an essential area of learning for students with behavior disorders. Both direct behavioral observation and curriculum-based evaluation encourage appropriate social comparisons and provide the basis for social validation. The legal mandates for involving a multidisciplinary team in the eligibility decision and encouraging parents to participate in development of the IEP require at least a minimal level of social validation.

IEPs differ greatly in format, level of detail, and conceptual orientation. This is understandable, given the freedom of schools to choose their formats, the range of conceptual models in the field of behavior disorders, and the differences in individual students' needs as well as their parents' wishes and demands. The accompanying box shows sample statements from an actual IEP, along with comments about IEP preparation. Although an IEP must include academic goals and objectives, we are discussing only the items directly related to behavior. For further discussion of writing IEPs, see Kerr et al., (1987), Larsen and Poplin (1980), Lovitt (1980), Turnbull, Strickland, and Brantley (1982), and Turnbull and Turnbull (1986).

SUMMARY

Significant changes have occurred in evaluation of exceptional students during the past two decades: terminology has shifted from diagnosis to assessment and evaluation; available information has increased dramatically, and legal mandates have influenced the evaluation process. Evaluation should produce helpful information for deciding eligibility for special education and planning for intervention. Youngsters seldom refer themselves for evaluation, and problems are often not what they first appear. Thus evaluation must include the adult(s) who referred the student, as well as the student's own perceptions of the problem, and one must seek out all relevant information.

Evaluation for eligibility must be handled by a multidisciplinary team. Ideally, the MDT considers all relevant information and makes unbiased, reliable decisions. In practice, MDTs do not always make predictable, unbiased decisions. Although better evaluation instruments and expert systems may help to improve the reliability of eligibility decisions, improving reliability and reducing bias will also depend on individuals' commitment to higher professional standards of conduct.

Evaluation for intervention should typically include standardized tests of intelligence and achievement, behavior ratings, assessment of peer relations, interviews, self-reports, and direct behavioral observations. An emerging approach is curriculum-based evaluation, in which students' performance is measured frequently (often daily)

Performance, Goals, Objectives, Evaluation: How Should IEPs Be Written for Behavior?

Fred is a second grader placed in a special class for students with behavior disorders. The following items are taken from his IEP.

Present Level of Educational Performance: Behavioral

Can now work independently for extended periods of time and is quite motivated academically. However, he still needs to learn to get along with other children and to respect adults in authority.

Area of Instruction: Social Competency

Annual Goal: Will demonstrate increased time working on assignments independently. Short-Term Objectives

1. Increase in-seat behavior
2. Increase time on task
3. Increase time working independently on selected assignments

Annual Goal: Will demonstrate improved social skills. Short-Term Objectives

1. Demonstrate appropriate ways of requesting help for academic or social needs
2. Demonstrate socially approved interactions with peers
3. Demonstrate increased acceptance of authority figures

Most teachers and administrators would probably judge these to be acceptable IEP components. Certainly, anyone reading these components would get a general idea of Fred's behavioral problems and what the teacher intends to accomplish, but they could be more precise and specific. Questions that might arise about Fred's present level of educational performance include these: What is the average amount of time Fred works independently? What specific social skills does Fred demonstrate toward peers, and what skills does he lack? How does Fred show lack of respect for authority? Additional questions could be asked about annual goals and short-term objectives: How much (to what criterion) should in- seat behavior, time on task, and working independently be increased? What is an appropriate request for help? How are socially approved interactions with peers and acceptance of authority defined? What percentage of the time and under what conditions should Fred be expected to demonstrate appropriate requests for help, socially approved interactions, or acceptance of authority?

Suggestions for greater precision or specificity imply the need to define and measure behavior more carefully. Many behavioral psychologists and special educators believe that it is highly desirable, perhaps critical, for teachers to measure behavior and behavioral change; most behavioral research includes such measurement. Behavioral objectives include a description of behavior in measurable terms, the conditions under which the behavior will be performed, and the criterion for judging its performance. Thus the objective for Fred should read something like this: "During seatwork activities, Fred will remain in his seat at least 80 percent of the time for at least four days in any five-day period, as indicated by direct observation using a ten-second interval recording system." This level of precision and specificity may be desirable; whether it is realistic to expect it from classroom teachers is another issue. If you are preparing to teach or to work with teachers, you will have to carefully weigh the arguments for precision in measurement against the realities of the classroom.

I am grateful to Betty Hallenbeck, Charlottesville, Virginia Public Schools, for providing information about Fred's IEP.

using the curriculum materials in which they are working. Curriculum-based methods can be applied to social skills as well as to the traditional academic curriculum.

Social validation is an evaluation strategy involving comparisons between behavior disordered students and their peers, as well as comparisons between the target student's behavior before and after intervention. It emphasizes obtaining objective evidence and consensus among the principal parties that (1) the problem is important, (2) the intervention is appropriate, and (3) the outcome is satisfactory.

Evaluation data should be useful in writing the IEP for a student who is placed in special education. Direct observation, curriculum-based evaluation, and social validation are procedures with special relevance for the IEPs of students with behavior disorders.

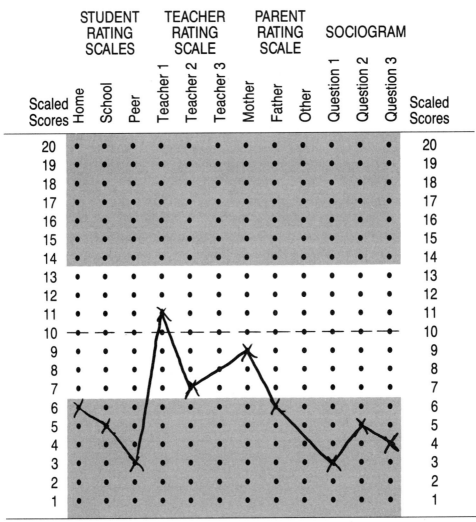

(Scaled Scores: Mean = 10, Standard deviation = 3)

7

Classification: Terminology and Behavioral Clusters

As you read this chapter, keep these guiding questions in mind:

☐ Why is classification of disordered behavior important?

☐ What are the greatest drawbacks of using psychiatric classifications in special education?

☐ What sections of DSM-III can be used to classify children's and adolescents' disorders?

☐ How do dimensional systems of classification come closer to the ideal than do psychiatric systems?

☐ What assumption prevents *individuals* from being classified using a dimensional approach?

☐ In what ways can we differentiate infantile autism and childhood schizophrenia?

The variety of youngsters' perplexing behavior dazzles even sage observers of youthful conduct. The diversity of behavior problems requires grouping disorders with similar critical features; it is not possible to treat every individual in every respect as a unique case. Even though no two individuals are entirely alike, constructing effective assessment and intervention procedures requires identification of common features of behavior. When it comes to planning for education or therapy, it is perhaps more important to know how youngsters are alike than how they are different.

Classifying youngsters as disturbed or behaviorally disordered, however, is not highly informative. The general label gives no indication of what kind of behavior to expect from a particular student, except that some behavior will be aberrant. For clearer communication, and because classification is basic to scientific investigation, those who study disturbed youngsters have tried to devise ways to classify disordered behavior more precisely. Behaviors with common attributes are clustered under various labels. Many of the children whose behavior is described in this book, for example, are representative of conduct disorder. This label denotes a specific type of behavioral difficulty and leads to the prediction that the youngster will exhibit hyperaggressive or "acting out" behavior rather than shyness, passivity, and social withdrawal (Kazdin, 1987).

Classification should be based on reliably observed phenomena. The classification of a given disorder should have a clear relationship to its nature, origin, or course. Psychiatry, mimicking the empirical classification of diseases in physical medicine, has devised systems of classification of *mental disease* that have an intriguing mystique but little substance. That is, the psychiatric classification of behavior disorders has typically been based on subjective criteria and unverifiable assumptions. Classifications in a medical (psychiatric) model include presumed diseases of personality structures. They are often based on conjecture about disorders of hypothetical parts of the psyche that are not open to direct measurement.

Understandably, therefore, the usual psychiatric systems of classification have been quite unreliable. A given classification has had little or no implications for treatment, particularly educational treatment, of most disorders (Achenbach, 1985; Achenbach & Edelbrock, 1983; Sinclair, Forness, & Alexson, 1985). Newer classification systems, especially behavioral or dimensional systems, have tended to be more reliable and valid because they are based, to a greater extent than psychiatric categories, on direct observation of specific behaviors. Nevertheless, psychiatric classifications are widely used, and educators will encounter psychiatric labels in working with behavior disordered students.

PSYCHIATRIC CLASSIFICATION

The most widely accepted *psychiatric* system of classification that psychiatrists and psychologists use is the most recent edition of the American Psychiatric Association's *Diagnostic and Statistical Manual of Mental Disorders*; the third edition is referred to as DSM-III (American Psychiatric Association, 1980). The American Psychiatric Association revised the manual in 1987, but did not designate it as a new edition; thus

122

it is called DSM-III-R (American Psychiatric Association, 1987). Most of the changes in the revised edition are relatively minor adjustments of terminology; for example, "attention deficit disorder with hyperactivity" was changed to "attention- deficit hyperactivity disorder," "stereotyped movement disorders" was changed to "tic disorders," and "tobacco withdrawal" was changed to "nicotine withdrawal" (Dumont, 1987). DSM-III-R contains a section on disorders usually first evident in infancy, childhood, or adolescence. In diagnosing an infant, child, or adolescent, the clinician first considers the diagnostic categories listed in this section of the manual; if no appropriate diagnosis can be found in this section, then the clinician considers diagnoses listed in other, adult sections of the manual. Diagnoses from the adult sections that are most often applicable to children or adolescents are listed as follows (brief definitions of these terms appear in the Glossary):

- [ ] Organic mental disorders
- [ ] Psychoactive substance use disorders
- [ ] Schizophrenia
- [ ] Mood disorders
- [ ] Schizophreniform disorder
- [ ] Somatoform disorders
- [ ] Sexual disorders
- [ ] Adjustment disorder
- [ ] Psychological factors affecting physical condition
- [ ] Personality disorders

Diagnoses from the childhood or adolescence section of DSM-III-R may apply to adults if, as children or adolescents, they manifested any of these conditions, and if the condition has persisted and no adult category is appropriate (American Psychiatric Association, 1987, p. 27). The categories that apply primarily to infants, children, and adolescents are listed in Table 7.1.

Educators should be familiar with the terminology of psychiatric classification because they may see it in psychological and psychiatric evaluations. Educators may not, however, decide how youngsters' disorders should be categorized in psychiatric classification systems. Moreover, psychiatric classification has little relevance for behavior management or instruction. Some writers have noted that DSM-III does not result in reliable classification of children's disorders (Achenbach & Edelbrock, 1983; Klerman, Vaillant, Spitzer, & Michels, 1984). The same has been noted for DSM-III-R (Dumont, 1987). DSM-III-R is controversial, even among psychiatrists and psychologists. Some mental health professionals and educators feel that many of its minor changes in terminology and categories are more cosmetic and confusing than helpful. Some believe that the frequent use of "other" or "not otherwise specified" categories, such as "Specific developmental disorder not otherwise specified," indicate that the classification system is overly specific, failing to account for many cases. Some see certain categories as inappropriate for inclusion in a diagnostic manual of mental disorders—academic skills disorders, stuttering, and gender identity disorder, for example. For these reasons we do not use DSM-III-R as the primary basis for organizing our discussion of behavior disorders, but because of their prominence in psychiatry and psychology, we will occasionally refer to DSM-III and DSM-III-R diagnostic categories.

123

TABLE 7.1

Diagnostic Categories of DSM-III-R for Disorders Usually First Evident in Infancy, Childhood, or Adolescence

I. DEVELOPMENTAL DISORDERS
  A. Mental Retardation
    1. Mild mental retardation
    2. Moderate mental retardation
    3. Severe mental retardation
    4. Profound mental retardation
    5. Unspecified mental retardation
  B. Pervasive Developmental Disorders
    1. Autistic disorder
    2. Pervasive developmental disorder not otherwise specified
  C. Specific Developmental Disorders
    1. Academic skills disorders
      a. Developmental arithmetic disorder
      b. Developmental expressive writing disorder
      c. Developmental reading disorder
    2. Language and speech disorders
      a. Developmental articulation disorder
      b. Developmental expressive language disorder
      c. Developmental receptive language disorder
    3. Motor skills disorder
      a. Developmental coordination disorder
    4. Specific developmental disorder not otherwise specified
  D. Other Developmental Disorders
    1. Developmental disorder not otherwise specified
II. DISRUPTIVE BEHAVIOR DISORDERS
  A. Attention-Deficit Hyperactivity Disorder (ADHD)
  B. Conduct Disorder
    1. Group type
    2. Solitary aggressive type
    3. Undifferentiated type
  C. Oppositional Defiant Disorder

BEHAVIORAL DIMENSIONS

Achenbach (1985) and Quay (1986a) discuss the features of existing classification systems in detail, as well as the characteristics of ideal systems. Ideally, a classification system should include *operationally defined categories*; that is, categories defined in such a way that the behaviors comprising them can be measured. The system should also be *reliable*: an individual should be classified consistently by different observers, and the assignment of someone to a category should be consistent over a reasonable period of time. The categories should be *valid*: assignment to a category should be determinable in a variety of ways (that is, by a variety of observational systems or

TABLE 7.1
continued

III. ANXIETY DISORDERS OF CHILDHOOD OR ADOLESCENCE
    A. Separation Anxiety Disorder
    B. Avoidant Disorder of Childhood or Adolescence
    C. Overanxious Disorder
IV. EATING DISORDERS
    A. Anorexia Nervosa
    B. Bulimia Nervosa
    C. Pica
    D. Rumination Disorder of Infancy
    E. Eating Disorder Not Otherwise Specified
V. GENDER IDENTITY DISORDERS
    A. Gender Identity Disorder of Childhood
    B. Transsexualism
    C. Gender Identity Disorder of Adolescence or Adulthood, Nontranssexual Type (GIDAANT)
    D. Gender Identity Disorder Not Otherwise Specified
VI. TIC DISORDERS
    A. Tourette's Disorder
    B. Chronic Motor or Vocal Tic Disorder
    C. Transient Tic Disorder
    D. Tic Disorder Not Otherwise Specified
VII. ELIMINATION DISORDERS
    A. Functional Encopresis
    B. Functional Enuresis
VIII. SPEECH DISORDERS NOT CLASSIFIED ELSEWHERE
    A. Cluttering
    B. Stuttering
IX. OTHER DISORDERS OF INFANCY, CHILDHOOD, OR ADOLESCENCE
    A. Elective Mutism
    B. Identity Disorder
    C. Reactive Attachment Disorder of Infancy or Early Childhood
    D. Stereotype/Habit Disorder
    E. Undifferentiated Attention-Deficit Disorder

rating scales), and it should be highly predictive of particular behaviors. An ideal system of classification should also have clear implications for treatment and prognosis. Of the alternative systems available, dimensional systems most closely approximate the ideal.

Dimensional classifications are descriptions of behavioral clusters (highly intercorrelated behaviors). Complex statistical procedures, such as factor analysis, are used to find behavioral dimensions based on behavior ratings. The statistical analyses reveal which behavior problems tend to occur together to form a syndrome or dimension. In early studies (e.g., Ackerson, 1942; Hewitt & Jenkins, 1946), behavior

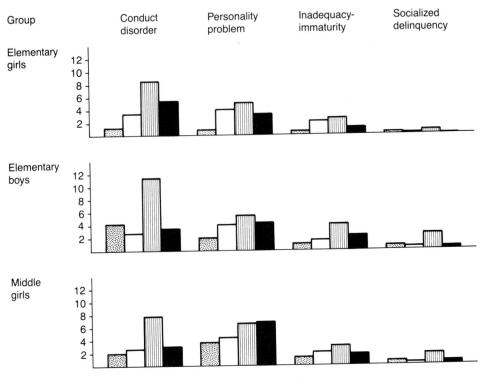

FIGURE 7.1.

Means of Four Behavior Problem Checklist Factor Scores (for nonhandicapped [NL], educable mentally retarded [MR], behaviorally disordered [BD], and learning disabled [LD] groups of boys and girls at each of three age levels [elementary = 8−10, middle = 11−13, senior = 14−16])

traits were obtained from reports in children's case histories. The behaviors were listed and then clustered by visual inspection of the data. Current statistical analyses are much more precise. Two behavior rating scales from which dimensional classifications are commonly extracted are the *Revised Behavior Problem Checklist* (RBPC) (Quay & Peterson, 1987) and the *Child Behavior Checklist* (CBCL) (Achenbach & Edelbrock, 1981, 1984). (The teacher report form of the CBCL was briefly described in Chapter 5.)

Revised Behavior Problem Checklist

During many years of research with a previous version of the BPC, Quay and others identified four pervasive patterns in youngsters' problem behavior (Quay, 1975, 1977; Von Isser, Quay, & Love, 1980). These are generally described as follows:

> Conduct disorder—characterized by verbal and overt physical aggression, disruptiveness, negativism, irresponsibility, and defiance of authority

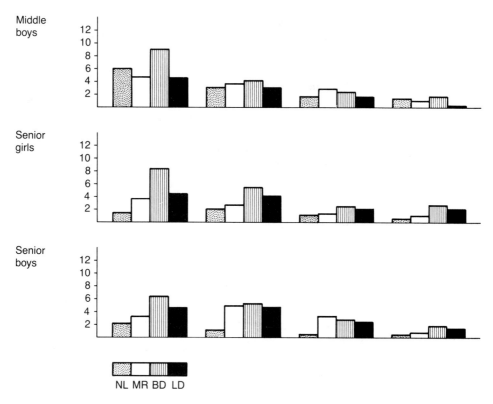

FIGURE 7.1 (*continued*)

Data from "Adjustment Problems of Mildly Handicapped and Nonhandicapped Students" by D. Cullinan and M.H. Epstein, 1985, *Remedial and Special Education, 6*(2), pp. 5–11.

Anxiety-withdrawal (also called Personality problem)—characterized by over-anxiety, social withdrawal, seclusiveness, shyness, sensitivity, and other indications of retreat from the environment

Immaturity (also sometimes referred to as Inadequacy-immaturity)—characterized by preoccupation, short attention span, passivity, daydreaming, sluggishness, and other failures to meet developmental expectations

Socialized aggression—typically involving gang activities, group stealing, truancy, and identification with a delinquent subculture

Research over many years has consistently found several or all of these dimensions of disordered behavior among samples of handicapped and nonhandicapped youngsters (Cullinan et al., 1984; McCarthy & Paraskevopoulos, 1969; Quay, Morse, & Cutler, 1966). Behavior disordered youngsters are nearly always rated higher than any other identified group on all dimensions of problem behavior, and the differences tend to be greatest on the conduct disorder dimension. Boys usually have higher problem scores than girls. The results of a large-scale study (Cullinan & Epstein, 1985) are displayed in Figure 7.1. In this study the behavior problem scores of the BD group were significantly higher than those of the other groups, compared across all behavioral dimensions, age levels, and both sexes. Boys' problem scores were significantly higher than girls' scores on the conduct disorder dimension, but not on the others.

Factor analyses of the RBPC indicate six dimensions or scales, some of which are essentially the same as the four usually found in studies with the earlier version of the rating scale (Quay & Peterson, 1987). Table 7.2 shows the six scales and representative items from them. Further research will be necessary to determine whether the newer scales (psychotic behavior and motor excess) are reliable and whether they appear as frequently as the other dimensions among students with behavior disorders. Note that these scales are also defined by fewer items than the other four scales.

Child Behavior Checklist

Achenbach and his colleagues have researched the behavior ratings of behavior disordered and nonidentified youngsters using both parent and teacher forms of the

TABLE 7.2
Representative Items from the Six Scales of the RBPC

Scale	Item No.	Item
I. Conduct Disorder	2	Seeks attention; "shows-off"
(CD)	5	Disruptive; annoys and bothers others
(22 items)	17	Fights
	19	Has temper tantrums
II. Socialized	7	Steals in company with others
Aggression (SA)	18	Loyal to delinquent friends
(17 items)	20	Truant from school, usually in company with others
	24	Has "bad" companions, ones who are always in some kind of trouble
	54	Freely admits disrespect for moral values and laws
III. Attention	13	Short attention span; poor concentration
Problems —	31	Distractible; easily diverted from the task at hand
Immaturity (AP)	35	Sluggish, slow moving, lethargic
(16 items)	44	Answers without stopping to think
IV. Anxiety-	4	Self-conscious; easily embarrassed
Withdrawal (AW)	21	Hypersensitive; feelings are easily hurt
(11 items)	22	Generally fearful; anxious
	27	Depressed; always sad
V. Psychotic	12	Repetitive speech; says same thing over and over
Behavior (PB)	39	Expresses strange, far-fetched ideas
(6 items)		
VI. Motor Excess	1	Restless; unable to sit still
(ME)	25	Tense; unable to relax
(5 items)		

Source: From *Manual for the Revised Behavior Problem Checklist* (pp. 20–22) by H.C. Quay and D.R. Peterson, 1987, Coral Gables, FL: Auhor.

CBCL (Achenbach, 1985; Achenbach & Edelbrock, 1981, 1984, 1989). They have identified several *broad band* factors or syndromes, the most common being *overcon-
trolled* and *undercontrolled*. Similar broad-band or general factors have also been
called *internalizing* and *externalizing*. More specific or *narrow-band* syndromes
identified through statistical analyses of behavioral ratings are shown in Table 7.3.
Note that the most commonly identified narrow-band syndromes are aggressive, hyperactive, delinquent, schizoid, depressed, and social withdrawal.

The different labels used for syndromes is somewhat confusing. Achenbach and
Edelbrock's undercontrolled (or externalizing) is a rough approximation of Quay and
Peterson's conduct disorder and socialized aggression dimensions; their overcon-
trolled (or internalizing) syndrome approximates Quay and Peterson's anxiety-withdrawal and immaturity dimensions.

A PERSPECTIVE ON DIMENSIONAL CLASSIFICATION

An important concept underlying the classification of behavioral dimensions is that
all individuals exhibit the characteristics of all the dimensions, but to varying degrees

TABLE 7.3
Number of Studies That Have Identified Syndromes Through Multivariate Analyses

Syndrome	Case Histories	Mental Health Workers	Teachers	Parents	Total
Broad Band					
Overcontrolled	2	1	7	7	17
Undercontrolled	3	3	7	8	21
Pathological Detachment	3	—	1	—	4
Learning Problems	—	—	1	1	2
Narrow Band					
Academic Disability	—	1	—	3	4
Aggressive	3	4	3	10	20
Anxious	1	2	3	2	8
Delinquent	3	1	2	8	14
Depressed	2	1	2	7	12
Hyperactive	3	2	3	8	16
Immature	—	1	2	3	6
Obsessive-Compulsive	1	—	2	2	5
Schizoid	3	4	—	6	13
Sexual Problems	1	2	—	3	6
Sleep Problems	—	—	—	4	4
Social Withdrawal	1	1	3	7	12
Somatic Complaints	1	—	—	9	10
Uncommunicative	—	1	—	3	4

Source: From "Diagnostic, taxonomic, and assessment issues" by T.M. Achenbach & C. Edelbrock, 1989. In T.H. Ollendick
& M. Hersen (Eds.), *Handbook of child psychopathology* (2nd ed.). New York: Plenum. Copyright 1989 by Plenum. Reprinted
by permission.

(Quay, 1986a). Thus it is erroneous to assume that an individual may be rated high on only one dimension. Many students with behavior disorders have multiple problems, and they may receive high ratings on several dimensions. Students' behavior is classified according to certain statistical clusters of items on the rating scale; individuals are not classified. While the same perspective is taken in DSM-III-R (that is, disorders are classified, not people), dimensional classification has the advantage of being based on more reliable, empirically derived categories.

These observations bring us back to a foundational concept related to the definition of disordered behavior: behavior disorder is not an all-or-nothing phenomenon. How different an individual's behavior must be from that of others before we invoke the label *disordered* is a matter of judgment, an arbitrary decision based on an explicit or implicit value system. The same concept applies to the subclassification of disorders within the general category. How high an individual's rating must be on a particular factor or dimension before his or her behavior is said to be problematic is a matter of judgment. That judgment may be guided by statistical analyses, but the statistics themselves are not sufficient.

CLASSIFICATION OF SEVERE BEHAVIORAL DISORDERS

Behavior along the different dimensions can vary from minor, even trivial, to extremely serious problems; however, some youngsters' behavior is characterized by differences that appear to be qualitatively as well as quantitatively different (Wenar, Ruttenberg, Kalish-Weiss, & Wolf, 1986). These children are frequently described as inaccessible to others, as unreachable or out of touch with reality, or as mentally retarded. They are often unresponsive to other people, have bizarre language and speech patterns or no functional language at all, exhibit grossly inappropriate behavior, lack everyday living skills, or perform stereotypical, ritualistic behavior. There is not much debate about whether children with such severe disabilities, often referred to in the general case as *psychotic,* are identifiable as a special group. Prior and Werry (1986) provide a nontechnical definition of psychotic behavior: "The interpretation of oneself, of the world, and of one's place in it, is so seriously at variance with the actual facts of the matter as to interfere with everyday adaptation and to strike the impartial observer as incomprehensible" (p. 156).

There is considerable debate, however, about how to subdivide such severe disorders in a reliable and helpful way. The most common distinction between the two major groups is made on the basis of age of onset. If the onset occurs before the child is 30 months old, the label *infantile autism* is typically applied; if after 30 months, the youngster is usually said to have *childhood schizophrenia*. Although we can see much overlap in the behavioral characteristics of these two groups, the reason for the distinction by age of onset is easy to understand. One need only examine the age distribution of first-observed pervasive developmental problems. Figure 7.2 shows that onset is more frequent before the age of 30 months and after the age of 12 years than between those ages. Parents describe many autistic children as seeming odd or obviously different from birth—aloof, cold, and unresponsive. According to the data in Figure 7.2, the onset of psychotic behavior during middle childhood is quite

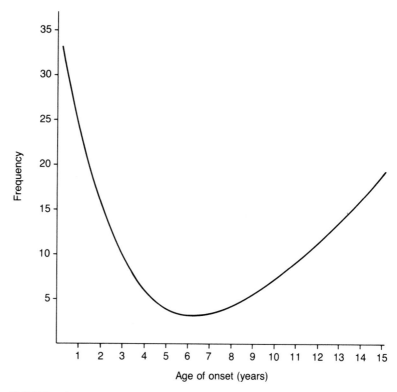

FIGURE 7.2

Approximate Distribution of Cases of Childhood Psychotic Behavior by
Age of Onset

Note: Curve sketched from data presented in "The Development of Infantile Autism" by M. Rutter,
1974, *Psychological Medicine, 4,* p. 148.

unusual. Thus infantile autism (onset of psychotic behavior before the age of two-
and-a-half years) and childhood schizophrenia (onset of psychotic behavior in later
childhood or adolescence) are typically differentiated primarily on the basis of first
appearance of symptoms. Rutter and Schopler (1987) note several other important
distinctions between autism and schizophrenia: schizophrenia tends to run in families,
autism rarely does; delusions and hallucinations are characteristic of schizophrenia
but rare in autism; schizophrenia is often episodic—periods of normal or near normal
functioning interspersed with psychotic behavior—but autism is characterized by
persistent symptoms; and epileptic seizures are seen in about 25 percent of children
with autism, whereas schizophrenic children rarely have seizures. Nevertheless, some
children diagnosed as autistic are later diagnosed as schizophrenic (Petty, Ornitz,
Michelman, & Zimmerman, 1984).

Confusion and disagreement regarding diagnostic classification persist. Debate
about just what is necessary and sufficient to distinguish psychotic from retarded
youngsters goes back more than a century and continues today (Rutter & Schopler,
1987). Infantile autism is considered a *pervasive developmental disorder* because the

characteristics are present from birth or from a very early age and affect all or nearly all areas of functioning. But uncertainty about exactly what symptoms distinguish autism from other pervasive developmental disorders and psychosis of early childhood is common (Prior & Werry, 1986). Aside from an apparent consensus that someone can be both mentally retarded and autistic or psychotic and that autism is distinguished from childhood schizophrenia primarily by age of onset, there is little agreement.

According to DSM-III, the diagnostic criteria for infantile autism are (in addition to onset prior to 30 months)

Pervasive lack of responsiveness to other people ("autism")

Gross deficits in language development

Peculiar speech patterns (for example, echolalia, metaphorical language, reversal of pronouns) if speech is present

Bizarre responses (for example, resistance to change, peculiar interest in or attachments to objects)

Absence of delusions or hallucinations characteristic of schizophrenia

DSM-III-R (1987) provides more detailed criteria for diagnosis of autistic disorder, "a severe form of Pervasive Developmental Disorder, with onset in infancy or childhood" (p. 38). Childhood onset is defined as after 36 months of age. Diagnosis depends on the presence of at least eight of sixteen specific behavioral characteristics. Characteristics are listed under three main headings: (A) "Qualitative impairment in reciprocal social interaction. . ."; (B) "Qualitative impairment in verbal and nonverbal communication, and in imaginative activity. . ."; and (C) "Markedly restricted repertoire of activities and interests. . ." (pp. 38–39).

The description of 4-year-old Brady in Chapter 1 illustrated the characteristics of autism. More information about Brady further illustrates the typical manifestations of autism (see Kanner, 1973a; Kanner, Rodriguez, & Ashenden, 1972; and Kanner's original 1943 articles [reprinted in Howells, 1971] for further descriptions of children and adults with autism).

Brady

The extent of Brady's social withdrawal is. . .illustrated by his almost nonexistent eye contact and his failure to notice other people in his immediate environment. During the diagnostic evaluation interview with one of the authors, he at no time gave any indication that he was aware of the examiner's presence in the room. Indeed, despite numerous attempts to gain his attention (calling his name, offering toys, etc.) he never established eye contact or responded in any manner. On one occasion, when the examiner reached out and touched him, he pulled abruptly away and said "NO!" This was his only acknowledgment of the examiner in almost 2 hours.

Perhaps most disturbing to Brady's parents is his lack of any attachment to them. Not only does the child resist affection but he does not seem to "need" them. He is not upset when his mother leaves him (e.g., at preschool), nor is he happy when she returns. He frequently does not seem to even notice their presence. He does not spontaneously come to them for comfort when hurt nor at any other time. His mother sums it up by saying that she feels Brady "uses" her for the attainment of his needs and that he is not really attached to her. "If it wasn't me filling his needs," she says, "it could just as well be a stranger. . . ."

Brady's parents suspected a hearing impairment might be the reason for some of his unusual behaviors. He did not speak until age 3, which might be attributed to deafness. Similarly, he neither responded to his name, loud noises, nor the voices of others. However, a hearing evaluation and the appearance of echolalia dispelled concerns about a hearing impairment. Brady's apparent sensory deficit was typically autistic in nature.

Like many other autistic children, Brady is very concerned with maintaining sameness in his environment. He notices even the most minute changes in furniture arrangements or if anything in a room is out of its usual place. On such occasions he will become quite agitated and will attempt to restore the situation to its previous state. He also remembers specific routes to places (even if he has been there only once) and resists any attempt to deviate from the route on future occasions. This resistance typically takes the form of a tantrum. As part of Brady's demand for order and sameness, he has established a number of rituals that must be performed a certain way. These include certain sequences of behavior for toileting, eating, and dressing. Again, any interruption of the ritual is met with a tantrum. Perhaps related to his attention to his environment are Brady's unusual and intense fears. His mother reports that these fears are irrational, intense, and frequently changing. For example, at the time of evaluation Brady was terrified of bread (he would eat it but not touch it), tortillas, yellow ducks, and pictures of five dogs. His reaction to these last three items took the form of screaming, crying, and violent shaking.

Brady exhibits several self- stimulatory behaviors including foot-to-foot rocking, rocking of the upper torso, jumping, gazing out of the corners of his eyes, repetitive tapping of objects, and repetitive vocalizing. He is also quite skillful at spinning and twirling objects such as coasters and saucepan lids. His parents report that while engaged in these behaviors Brady is "in another world," and that it is very difficult to "snap him out of it." His toy play is repetitive and unimaginative. He explores toys rather than plays with them and seldom uses them for their intended purposes. For example, if given a toy truck he will turn it over and spin the wheels in a self-stimulatory manner.

Several of Brady's behaviors seem inconsistent with the severe deficits so apparent in other areas of functioning. His mother describes his memory as "incredible." For example, she took him to a particular department store when he was approximately 18 months of age. He did not enter that store again until he was almost 4½, yet he remembered exactly where particular types of items were and correctly noted the absence of a counter that had been in the store three years earlier but was no longer there. He is fascinated by children's books and knows his own books so well that, even if the covers are separated from the contents, he can match them up immediately. The books are all very similar in content, style, and coloring, and his mother reports that it takes her over an hour to correctly sort all the covers and contents. He also learned the entire alphabet in a matter of minutes and can sing rather complex songs with perfect pitch.

On standardized intellectual assessments, Brady tests from the moderately to mildly retarded range. The variability is probably due to the different skills emphasized by particular tests. He scores highest on visual-spatial form recognition and memory tasks and scores less well on conceptual, abstract, and logic tasks. (Schreibman & Mills, 1983, pp. 141–143)

Infantile autism is one type of pervasive developmental disorder. Besides autism, DSM-III defines childhood-onset pervasive developmental disorder as "gross and sustained impairment of social relationships beginning between the ages of 30 months and 12 years," with the child exhibiting at least three of the following characteristics:

Sudden excessive anxiety, catastrophic reactions to everyday events, inability to be consoled when upset, or unexplained attacks of panic

Narrow or inappropriate affect and extreme lability of mood

Resistance to change in the environment or insistence on sameness

Odd movements, such as peculiar postures, hand movements, or walking movements

Abnormal speech characteristics

Oversensitivity or undersensitivity to stimuli

Self-mutilation

As in autism, there is the absence of delusions or hallucinations that characterize schizophrenia in adults.

Childhood schizophrenia is a severe disorder in which thinking is distorted. Children with schizophrenia frequently believe they are being controlled by alien forces. These children may have bizarre delusions and distorted perceptions, sometimes including hallucinations, and their affect is inappropriate for actual circumstances. Children with schizophrenia may also be enclosed in their own world, alone. Their withdrawal into their private world—their autism—sometimes makes it difficult or impossible to distinguish between schizophrenia and infantile autism. Systematized delusions and hallucinations are rare in preadolescents, but they are sometimes a part of severe disorders, as in the case of Thomas, an 11-year-old boy whose schizophrenia included a highly developed pattern of bizarre thinking.

Thomas

Thomas believes he is the son of a union between Christ and an unknown goddess. God stands at the top of a universe which is divided into two camps. Christ and those who strive for good in the world (including Thomas himself) are on one side, and the members of the Counter Gang, to whom Thomas eventually assigns a place in the "Community of Saints," are on the other.

The Gang, which incorporates the evil in the world and is in constant feud with the good, is an incessant threat to Thomas's body and life. As the son of Christ, he was a wild boar in a former existence. It is his task now to rid the world of the Gang which plans to prepare for him an agonizing death. Since nowadays no one is crucified, he will be crushed between two millstones until blood squirts from his fingers.

Among other things, the boy sees black men with horns. His explanations: "world regulators"; "dear, sweet little devils with radical power, recognized by the color of their tails"; "young female creatures" whose eyelid lines give them away as members of the Gang. (Stutte & Dauner, 1971, p. 416)

THE NECESSITY OF CLASSIFICATIONS

The search continues for reliable, valid classifications with relevance for intervention. Although classification of disordered behavior carries the risk that individuals will be needlessly stigmatized by labels for their differences, it would be foolish to abandon the task of classifying people's problems. Giving up all uses of classification is tantamount to abandoning the scientific study of social and behavioral difficulties. Indeed, we need labels for problems to communicate about them. Nevertheless, we must try to reduce the social stigma of the words that describe behavioral differences.

THE COMPLEXITY AND AMBIGUITY OF CLASSIFICATION

Classification is a complex undertaking, and scholars frequently disagree about how particular behavioral characteristics should be categorized. Furthermore, any set of categories yet devised leaves the categorical "home" of some behaviors in doubt. All comprehensive systems of classification produce a residual or miscellaneous category for behavioral odds and ends, or they result in arbitrary assignment of certain behaviors to a category of questionable homogeneity. As we shall see in Parts Three and Four, both the disorders of behavior and their causes are usually multidimensional; life seldom refines disorders or their causes into pure, unambiguous forms. Youngsters seldom show teachers or researchers a single disorder uncontaminated by elements of other problems, and the cause of a disorder is virtually never found to be a single factor. As a case in point, consider the interrelationships among hyperactivity, conduct disorder, and delinquency. Hyperactivity is a prominent feature of the behavior of many children who have a conduct disorder. Conduct disorder and delinquency are overlapping categories because conduct disorder is characterized by overt aggression or covert antisocial behavior, such as stealing, lying, and fire setting; delinquency is also often characterized by such behavior, but involves breaking the law. The same factors that cause conduct disorder and delinquency may also contribute to hyperactivity. Thus, grouping specific types of disorders is necessarily somewhat subjective, and classifications always contain a certain amount of ambiguity.

SUMMARY

Classification is basic to any science, including the science of human behavior. Classifications should help us understand the nature, origin, and course of whatever is being classified. Psychiatric classification systems have not been especially useful to educators because they are not highly reliable or valid for teaching purposes. Teachers will probably encounter the most widely accepted psychiatric classification system, that of the American Psychiatric Association (various editions and revisions of DSM, the official diagnostic and statistical manual).

Dimensional classifications more closely approximate the ideal system in terms of reliability, validity, and utility in education. An assumption underlying the dimensional approach is that all individuals exhibit behavior that is classifiable, but to varying degrees; thus we classify behavior, not individuals. The broadest categories in a quantitative, dimensional approach to disordered behavior are internalizing (withdrawal) and externalizing (acting out). Within these broad dimensions, more specific categories have been described. Some of these are called conduct disorder, socialized aggression, attention problem, immaturity, anxiety-withdrawal, and psychotic behavior. Students with behavior disorders typically obtain higher ratings on all or most problem dimensions than do students in other special education categories. Boys usually obtain higher problem scores than girls. Differences between behavior disordered and other students tend to be greatest for the conduct disorder dimension.

The severe disabilities called, in psychiatric terminology, *pervasive developmental disorders* (also sometimes called *childhood psychosis*) present particular difficulties for classification. The two most common categories are infantile autism and childhood schizophrenia. Autism is distinguished from schizophrenia primarily by age of onset, although other differences may be noted as well. Children whose characteristics are first noticed before the age of two-and-a-half or three years are usually considered autistic; if the onset is later, the child is usually said to have schizophrenia. Autistic children often lack functional language and do not usually show the disordered thought patterns of children with schizophrenia (which sometimes include hallucinations or delusions).

PART THREE

Causal Factors
in Behavior
Disorders

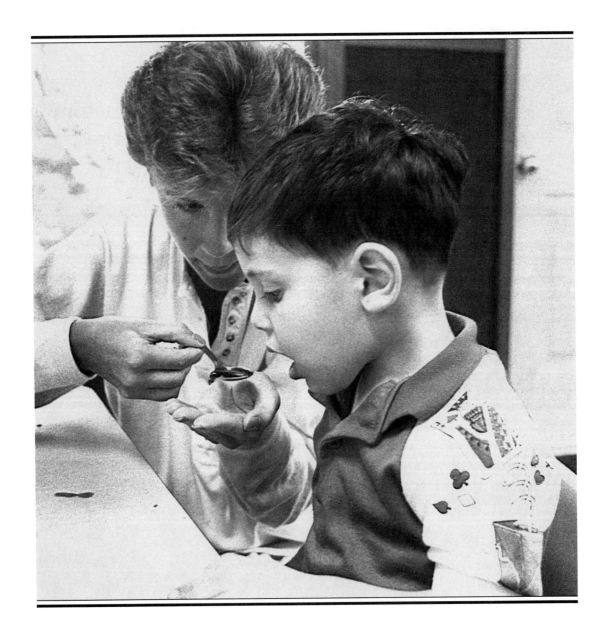

8

Biological Factors

As you read this chapter, keep these guiding questions in mind:

☐ What is the relationship between the cause of a behavior disorder and its cure?

☐ To what extent should youngsters with behavior disorders be held accountable for their conduct?

☐ Why do biological factors have such great appeal as explanations of deviant behavior?

☐ Under what conditions is it most likely that a person will develop schizophrenia?

☐ What can one conclude about the relationship between brain injury and disordered behavior?

☐ In what way might nutritional factors and youngsters' deviant behavior be interactional or exert reciprocal influence?

☐ What do we know about the relationship between disordered behavior and biochemical irregularities?

☐ How might disordered behavior be related to physical illness or disability?

☐ What is temperament, and how might it affect pupil-teacher interactions?

CAUSE, CURE, AND BLAME: AN INTRODUCTION TO CAUSAL FACTORS

When humans are confronted by another's deviant behavior, their first reaction is often to ask "Why?" A seemingly natural tendency is to seek a causal explanation that will allow us to assess blame and take corrective action—we want a conceptual model that will help us make sense of deviance and allow us to control it. As we discussed in Chapter 4, conceptual models differ greatly in their presumed causes, objects of blame, and curative courses of action. Although all conceptual models suggest causal factors that contribute to deviant behavior, none accounts for all deviance. In all but extremely rare cases, we are not able to answer the question "Why?" with much confidence.

Research does indicate, however, that behavior disorders are more or less likely to occur depending on certain biological, family, cultural, and school factors. We will discuss these factors in Part Three. Discussing the factors in separate chapters does not mean they are entirely separate issues. In fact, biological, family, cultural, and school factors are all interrelated; no one area acts entirely alone to cause a behavior disorder. Before we begin our discussion of biological factors, we will first consider the relationships between cause and cure and between presumed cause and blame.

The relationship between cause and cure requires careful interpretation. Knowing the cause does not always imply that we know a cure; we may know the cause of a disorder, but not how to intervene successfully. We may know that viewing televised violence increases the level of aggression in already hyperaggressive children, but we may not have effective means for preventing hyperaggressive children from watching violent programs. Moreover, an effective cure or intervention does not always imply that a cause has been identified. Drugs and/or behavior modification procedures can help reduce hyperactivity, but we cannot then conclude that the cause of hyperactivity is biochemical or social. Reasoning back from effective treatment to cause reveals an error of logic; *post hoc, ergo propter hoc* (after the fact, therefore because of it) is an argument that does not hold. To take an example from medicine, the observation that penicillin cures strep throat does not support the conclusion that a lack of penicillin causes strep throat. Similarly, in classroom practice, the observation that praise for on-task behavior increases attention to task does not support the conclusion that lack of reinforcement for on-task behavior causes inattention to task.

The relationship between presumed cause and blame has important implications for intervention and, indeed, for the survival of a humane society. An enduring moral precept of our society is that we do not hold people responsible for misfortunes that are beyond their control. Sick people are not usually blamed for their illness. To the extent that we assume behaviorally disordered students are suffering from mental illness or the work of social forces beyond their control, we do not blame them for their misconduct. In modern America, and in most Western cultures, we seldom blame children or youth for serious misconduct. In most cases, blame has shifted to biological disorder, parental mismanagement, dissolution of families, peer pressure, teachers' incompetence, school organization, societal pressures or disintegration, mismatch of the student and the social environment, or to some other target. Duke (1978) noted the depersonalization of blame for personal misconduct that characterizes the history of our society and the possible implications:

140

No longer do scholars seem to hold an individual responsible for his triumphs or his transgressions. Instead, what an individual does is regarded as the product of a variety of external factors. . . . Everyone becomes a victim of forces outside himself. The question arises, "Can a society in which everyone is a victim survive?" (p. 415)

In the final analysis, the resolution of the current "crisis" in school discipline will depend to a large extent on the ability of young people, and educators, to cease regarding themselves as victims of their environment and to start seeing themselves as responsible human beings able to determine a significant portion of their own behavior. (p. 434)

Duke's comments are consistent with the social cognitive conceptual model explained in Chapter 4—people make choices about some aspects of their behavior and some features of their environments; they are not merely passive recipients of external forces. It is important to recognize, however, that Duke's comments are about discipline problems, not about the serious and persistent social deviance that typically earns the label "behavioral disorder" or "emotional disturbance." That is, depersonalization of blame may carry somewhat different implications, depending on the nature, seriousness, or severity of the disorder. Blaming children and youth with autism or schizophrenia—holding them morally responsible for their deviant behavior—hardly seems justifiable on any grounds, partly because evidence so clearly connects these disorders with biological processes. Nevertheless, children and youth who exhibit disorders for which alternative causal explanations are less convincing—conduct disorders and juvenile delinquency, for example—might be expected to share a measure of moral responsibility for their behavior; to a significant degree, they can exercise personal choice in how they behave.

Attribution of cause and personal responsibility is a pervasive and critical issue in the field of behavior disorders. Duke (1978) pointed out that depersonalization of blame has undesirable outcomes, including the tendency to tolerate or even increase social benefits to youngsters who misbehave and the tendency to depreciate individual integrity. He calls for more research by social scientists to unravel the factors in assessing cause and responsibility, especially the causal factors related to person variables—those aspects of misbehavior that involve individual choice. In an era of greater concern for individual responsibility and self-actualization, special educators must carefully weigh the evidence that individual students are able to exercise self-control, as well as the evidence that they are victims of circumstances for which they have no personal moral responsibility.

THE APPEAL OF BIOLOGICAL FACTORS AS CAUSAL EXPLANATIONS

A biological view of behavior disorders has particular appeal. Psychological models of behavior cannot account for all behavioral variations in children. On the other hand, advances in medicine, genetics, and physiology make the suggestion of a biological basis for all behavior disorders plausible. The central nervous system is undeniably involved in all behavior, and all behavior involves neurochemical activity. Furthermore, scientists long ago established that genetic factors alone are *potentially* sufficient to explain all variation in human behavior (Eiduson, Eiduson, & Geller,

1962). It may seem reasonable to believe, therefore, that disordered behavior always implies a genetic accident, bacterial or viral disease, brain injury, brain dysfunction, or biochemical imbalance.

Attractive as biological explanations may appear on the surface, however, the assumption that disordered behavior is simply a result of biological misfortune is misleading. First, much of the so-called evidence linking biological factors to behavior disorders is presumptive. A case in point is the presumption of minimal brain dysfunction or damage (MBD) in children who are hyperactive and distractible. As we will see, many hyperactive children have been diagnosed as having MBD on the basis of their behavior alone—purely presumptive evidence that their brains are actually damaged or dysfunctioning. Second, biological factors, though pervasive, affect behavior only in interaction with environmental factors. In the case of genetics, "all human behavioral characteristics are products of an interaction between life experiences and a conglomerate of genetic factors" (Mednick, Moffitt, Gabrielli, & Hutchings, 1986). Indeed, the effects of all biological factors on behavior are influenced by their social context. Finally, as Lovaas (1979) points out, even with confirmation of a biological cause of troublesome behavior, knowledge of the cause is not likely to lead to a prescription for treatment. Although biological research may carry significant implications for prevention, it produces few direct implications for educators.

The effects of biological factors on behavioral development are considerable, but frequently neither demonstrable nor simple. While biological factors influence behavior, environmental conditions modify biological processes. At this juncture in the behavioral sciences, examining biological factors that increase the risk of behavioral maldevelopment and searching for factors that make individuals resistant to stress may be more useful than searching for direct and simple biological causes for behavior disorders (Garmezy, 1987). With these points in mind, we can discuss several representative biological factors that contribute to the development of disordered behavior. The biological processes involved in behavioral deviance are extremely complex, and new discoveries are being made rapidly. Moreover, nearly every type of biological factor has been suggested as a possible cause of nearly every type of psychopathology (see Werry, 1986a). Consequently, we will discuss only representative factors that are suspected of contributing to a few types of behavioral problems.

BIOLOGICAL MISFORTUNES WITH BEHAVIORAL IMPLICATIONS

Extreme deviation from the norm, whether in intelligence or social-emotional behavior, is more likely to have an identifiable biological cause than is less marked or normal deviation. More evidence can be found in support of a biological etiology of childhood psychosis than for milder forms of behavior disorder; severe mental retardation more often has an identifiable biological cause than does mild mental retardation. This fact should not, however, lead to the conclusion that we know the cause of all childhood psychosis; the causes remain a mystery in the vast majority of cases. Even though we cannot pinpoint causes for most severe disorders, it is helpful to examine what is known about the relationship of *suspected* causes to disordered behavior. Future research may show suspected causes to be actual causes or significant causal factors, leading eventually to effective prevention.

Genetic Accidents

Children inherit more than physical characteristics from their parents; they also inherit predispositions to certain behavioral characteristics. Not surprisingly, genes have been suggested as causal factors in every kind of behavioral difficulty, from criminality (Mednick et al., 1986) to hyperactivity (see Campbell & Werry, 1986). Nevertheless, these characteristics are not determined simply by genes. Environmental factors, particularly social learning, play an important role in modifying inherited behavioral predispositions. At the level of specific behaviors, social learning is nearly always far more important than genetics. Little or no evidence supports the suggestion that disturbed youngsters' specific behaviors are genetically transmitted; however, some type of genetic misfortune obviously contributes to the psychotic disorders of children and adolescents and to many other disorders as well (Nicol & Erlenmeyer-Kimling, 1986; Reed, 1975).

Schizophrenia and Autism

The exact genetic mechanisms responsible for a predisposition to schizophrenia are still unknown, but research clearly shows an increase in risk for schizophrenia and schizophreniclike behavior (often called **schizoid** or **schizophrenic spectrum** behavior) in the relatives of schizophrenics. The closer the genetic relationship between the child and a schizophrenic relative, the higher the risk that the child will develop the condition. Heightened risk cannot be attributed to the social environment or

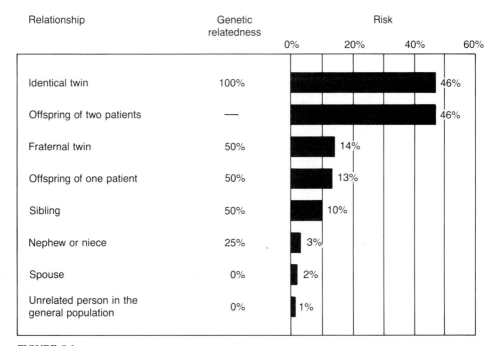

FIGURE 8.1

Lifetime Risk of Developing Schizophrenia

From "Clues to the Genetics and Neurobiology of Schizophrenia" by S.E. Nicol and I. Gottesman, 1983, *American Scientist, 71,* p. 399. Used with permission.

Schizophrenia: Genetic Factors and Their Implications

One of the most common severe mental disorders, schizophrenia strikes about one in every 100 people worldwide. Its victims are likely to suffer delusions, auditory hallucinations (hearing voices), outrageous fears of persecution and suspicions that others can "hear" their thoughts.

"Of all the babies born today, one percent of them will be diagnosed as schizophrenic by the time they reach the age of 55," said [Irving I.] Gottesman, who joined the U.VA. faculty as Commonwealth Professor of Psychology in 1985. "It's a major mental health problem, especially given the fact that it tends to have an early onset. Once it appears, it wipes you out with regard to future education or employability at the level you had before you became ill. It takes you out of the mainstream."

Over the course of a quarter century of research, Mr. Gottesman has found that schizophrenia is "importantly genetic in its origins." Schizophrenics inherit a predisposition—a genetic liability—for the illness, which in turn is set off by some environmental factor, perhaps severe trauma, brain damage, or even drug abuse. In the age-old "nature vs. nurture" debate, schizophrenia takes both sides.

Mr. Gottesman explained that nature's contribution to schizophrenia—the genetic link—was long obscured by the fact that most schizophrenics don't have a near relative who suffers from the condition. Paradoxically, only 10 percent of schizophrenics have a mother or father with the disorder, while in a more typical hereditary disease, such as Huntington's chorea, the victim always has at least one affected parent.

"How could it be that some 90 percent of individuals who are schizophrenic do *not* have a mother or father who is schizophrenic? What on earth kind of genetic disorder is that which does not appear to run vertically through families?" Mr. Gottesman asked rhetorically. "Well, it does run vertically through families, but in an irregular fashion. In Huntington's disease a single gene carries the disease. In schizophrenia we are dealing with a genetic system rather than a single gene that is doing all the work.

"Perhaps the best analogy is that of two short parents who produce tall children. If each parent has genes for height that are not expressed, then by chance one or more of their children could receive all the tall genes from one parent and all the tall genes from the other parent, so a child could have all the characteristics that neither parent has. . . ."

interpersonal factors alone. Figure 8.1 shows the increased level of risk that goes with increasingly close genetic relatedness to a person who has schizophrenia. Having an identical twin who has schizophrenia increases an individual's risk of developing schizophrenia by a factor of 46; having a sibling with schizophrenia carries 10 times the risk of the general population.

Many people misunderstand the implications of increased risk for schizophrenia or other disorders. Does a heightened genetic risk for schizophrenia mean a person will necessarily develop the disorder? Do the genetic factors in schizophrenia mean that prevention is impossible? The answer to both questions is no. "Not all people with the genetic potential to become schizophrenic will actually develop the clinical disorder" (Nicol & Erlenmeyer-Kimling, 1986, p. 33). Furthermore, risk factors can be lowered by altering the social environment and avoiding circumstances that might trigger the disorder. (The box summarizes some of the major findings of a leading researcher.)

But are genes really the culprit? Since relatives of schizophrenics share the same environment with victims of the disorder, could some kind of contagion be involved? Mr. Gottesman calls that notion naive, and he rules it out by pointing to studies of children who are adopted away from schizophrenic mothers. In one study, for instance, 16 percent of the children adopted away from schizophrenic mothers also became ill.

"Because those individuals are not exposed to their chronic schizophrenic parent, they should, on environmental grounds, be free of illness," said Mr. Gottesman. "Instead you find the same, relatively high risk that you see in the children of schizophrenics reared by their sick parents."

Mr. Gottesman . . . is quick to point out that genes rarely work alone to cause schizophrenia. While genetic makeup may weigh heavily against the high-risk individual, environmental factors must be added to tip the scale toward sickness. Those at risk are particularly sensitive to severe psychological trauma. The death of a parent, for example, might cause bereavement and short-term depression in most of us, but it could push someone with a high genetic risk into schizophrenia. Brain damage from an auto accident also could precipitate the illness.

But perhaps the most ominous environmental contributor to schizophrenia is drug abuse. Mr. Gottesman warns emphatically that anyone with a genetic predisposition for mental illness should stay away from cocaine, marijuana, LSD, PCP, amphetamines and other hallucinogenic drugs. "What may be simply a bad trip for the person on the street may be a disastrous *Lusitania*-like voyage for the relative of a psychotic," said Mr. Gottesman, adding that even some prescription drugs may have this effect. This warning is "one of the few practical pieces of advice we can give to a relative of a schizophrenic," said the psychologist, who also urges those with a high "genetic liability" to make sure they have adequate health insurance coverage.

Are there times when environmental contributors are the only cause of the illness? Very rarely, said Mr. Gottesman. For the vast majority of victims, the causes of schizophrenia are "multifactorial," a combination of heredity and environment.

From "Schizophrenia: Irving Gottesman Reveals the Genetic Factors." *University of Virginia Alumni News,* 1987, 75(5), pp. 12–14.

Schizophrenia occurs primarily in the 15- to 45-year age range. Most genetic studies of the disorder have involved only adults. Little evidence suggests, however, that bizarre behavior, distorted thinking and perception, and abnormal affect represent different genetic factors in childhood than in adulthood (Prior & Werry, 1986).

Nevertheless, early infantile autism apparently does not represent the same genetic accidents that are involved in childhood schizophrenia. One indication that autism is different from schizophrenia is that the incidence of psychosis in the relatives of autistic children is not as high as in the relatives of children with schizophrenia. It is comparatively unusual for an autistic child to have a close relative who is psychotic (except in the case of identical twins, who have the same genetic makeup). In studies of twins, Folstein and Rutter (1977) found an apparent genetic contribution to some cases of autism.

Implications of Genetic Factors

A common misperception is that disorders arising from genetic accidents are not treatable, that once the genetic code is set, the related deviant behavior is immutable. But this is not necessarily the case (Mednick et al, 1986). As with schizophrenia, environmental as well as biological factors are involved in the causation of deviant behavior. When the mechanisms underlying genetic transmission are discovered, there is hope that effective interventions will be found to prevent or alter the course of behavioral development.

The case of PKU (phenylketonuria, a genetically transmitted metabolic disorder) is perhaps the most dramatic instance in which identification of a genetic disorder has resulted in successful prevention of behavioral disorder (see Guthrie, 1984). The biochemical irregularity caused by the genes that produce PKU can be identified and treated to prevent mental retardation and accompanying behavior problems.

> PKU is a disorder of amino acid in which the enzyme phenylalanine hydroxylase is missing. This enzyme has a crucial role in the utilization of phenylalanine, a common component of the diet. In its absence, phenylalanine cannot be converted to tyrosine but instead accumulates in the tissues and is partly transformed into phenylpyruvic acid and other metabolites. In some way, as yet unknown but perhaps related to myelin formation, the accumulation of these abnormal metabolites prevents normal development of the brain, and mental retardation is the usual result. Other symptoms are irritability, athetoid movements, hyperactivity, and blond coloration. About one-third of the children have convulsive seizures. (Reed, 1975, p. 83)

If PKU is detected soon after birth and phenylalanine is eliminated from the diet until the child's brain is no longer damaged by abnormal metabolites (until middle childhood), mental retardation can be prevented. If the child is not treated, he or she may not only be retarded, but may also exhibit schizoid behavior, hyperactivity, uncontrollable temper tantrums, seizures, and athetoid movements (clumsy movements usually associated with cerebral palsy). Dietary restriction of phenylalanine after the child has become retarded will not reverse the mental retardation but may help to alleviate the behavior problems (Reed, 1975).

In summary, genetic factors are known to contribute to a variety of behavior disorders, perhaps even to most. In some cases of severe disorder, such as schizophrenia, the level of the genetic contribution is clear but how the gene system works remains obscure. For most types of behavior disorders, the genetic contributions remain unclear and environmental factors appear to be more important. In a few cases, such as PKU, the genetic mechanism is relatively well understood and effective prevention of behavior disorder is possible. Discovery of genetic mechanisms that contribute to disordered behavior may have important implications for prevention.

Brain Damage or Dysfunction

The brain can be traumatized in several different ways before, during, or after birth. Physical insult during an accident or during the birth process may destroy brain tissue. Prolonged high fever, infectious disease, toxic chemicals (such as drugs or poisons taken by the child or by a woman during pregnancy) may also damage the brain. The most frequently suspected or known cause of brain damage in children, however, is *hypoxia* (also known as *anoxia*), a seriously reduced supply of oxygen. Hypoxia often occurs during birth, but can also occur during accidents or as a result of disease or respiratory disorders later in life. The brain may function improperly due to accidental physical damage or such factors as congenital malformation or biochemical irregularity. Naturally, brain dysfunction *can* produce aberrant behavior, but the conclusion that disordered behavior necessarily results from brain dysfunction is not justified. Many children and adults exhibit disordered behaviors in the absence of any evidence of neurological malfunctioning.

Brain damage can run the gamut from massive destruction, resulting in a vegetative state or death, to imperceptible trauma that has no discernible effects on behavior or intellectual functioning. Along the continuum of insult from mild to severe are degrees of damage which, depending also on age and locus of the damage, may result in specific learning disabilities, epilepsy, cerebral palsy, mental retardation, or a variety of other disorders.

A child's brain can be, and often is, damaged. Moreover, all behavior is obviously related to brain function. Nevertheless, the behavioral manifestations of brain injury cannot be predicted, except within extremely broad limits (Werry, 1986a). Reviewing the literature, Sameroff and Chandler (1975) found little to support the contention that children who suffered perinatal trauma (including hypoxia) but show no obvious brain damage are greater risks for later deviance than children who have not suffered perinatal trauma (see also Koupernik, MacKeith, & Francis-Williams, 1975). In fact, the abnormal behavior of children with hypoxia or other birth complications appeared to decline with age unless the children were from homes in which child-rearing practices exacerbated behavioral difficulties. Thomas et al. (1968) found that one pattern of behavioral dysfunction could not be considered to fit all cases of brain damage. They further found that in cases in which a child's central nervous system was damaged, parental mismanagement and other features of the social environment determined whether or not behavior disorder was manifested (see also Thomas & Chess, 1975).

The diagnosis of brain damage is often difficult. The assumption that damage to the brain can be easily and reliably confirmed in cases that do not involve massive or obvious injury is not justified. Even with recent advances in neurology, the assessment of brain dysfunction leaves much room for error and speculation (Werry, 1986a). For example, the usefulness of an electroencephalogram (EEG), a method of recording the electrical activity of the brain, in diagnosing brain dysfunctions and behavior disorders is often grossly exaggerated (Feuerstein, Ward, & LeBaron, 1979; Freeman, 1967). Koupernik et al. (1975) comment, "It can sometimes tell us something about disorder of the brain; it cannot tell us about the person's abilities and disabilities. . . . It cannot, except in rare instances, tell us whether a person has a brain lesion or epilepsy but it may tell us what sort of epilepsy he has" (p. 118). Even with computerized study of EEG records, differences between the electroencephalographic features of autistic and nonautistic children appear to be small or nonspecific (Cantor, Thatcher, Hrybyk, & Kaye, 1986). Werry (1986a) summarizes as follows:

> Thus, the diagnosis of brain damage, unless gross, depends on a group of medical, historical, and psychological measures, most of which are of low or untested

reliability, discriminate poorly between normal and *mildly* brain-damaged populations, and apparently measure a variety of unrelated functions instead of some homogeneous variable "brain damage." Under the circumstances, the diagnosis of brain damage or dysfunction in the majority of children with nonorganic psychopathology is no more than an enlightened guess. Even where the diagnosis can be firmly established, there is as yet no way of proving that the damage is *causally* related to the behavior observed. What makes establishing this connection even more difficult is the repeated demonstration of the close relationship between the causes of brain damage and a host of sociofamilial variables that are disadvantageous to social adjustment *and* to physical health. (p. 303)

The assumption that behavior disorder implies brain dysfunction has led to much confusion and debate, especially in the case of what is referred to as **minimal brain dysfunction** (MBD). The term was coined to apply to children who have learning difficulties and exhibit other maladaptive behavior—usually hyperactivity, and sometimes distractibility, perceptual problems, motor awkwardness, or other "soft" neurological signs. Brain dysfunction in these cases is said to be "minimal" because, although it is assumed to exist, it cannot clearly be detected by reliable tests. "Soft" neurological signs are not diagnostic of MBD and not all MBD children show them. The signs include behaviors that are seen in a relatively high proportion of normal children—clumsiness in gross or fine motor movements, abnormal eye movements, frequent tics and grimaces, disturbed body position sense, left-right confusion, awkward gait, poor visual-motor performance, reading disabilities, and so on (Kornetsky, 1975). Thus, the term MBD is ill-defined and represents a presumed etiology (Kauffman & Hallahan, 1979).

In short, anything less than gross pathology or dysfunction of the central nervous system ordinarily leaves doubt as to the etiology of behavior disorder. The lack of knowledge regarding brain dysfunction as a factor in behavior disorders applies to cases of severe and profound disturbances, such as childhood psychosis, and to milder disorders as well. For most types of behavior disorders, brain dysfunction is only hypothetical. For a few severe disorders, brain dysfunction is known to be a causal factor, but the specifics of the dysfunction are a mystery. Autism, for example, is known to involve a dysfunction of the central nervous system, but the nature of the dysfunction, remains unknown (Prior & Werry, 1986; Rutter & Schopler, 1987). "So far . . . the meaning of the neurophysiological findings in autism remain obscure, and it is not at all clear how they might be linked to the findings on psychological deficits" (Rutter & Schopler, 1987, p. 171).

Nutritional Errors

Severe malnutrition has devastating effects on children's, especially young children's, development (Cravioto & DeLicardie, 1975). Malnutrition reduces the child's responsiveness to stimulation and produces apathy. The eventual result of serious malnutrition (especially severe protein deficiency) is retardation in brain growth, irreversible brain damage, mental retardation, or some combination of these effects. Apathy, social withdrawal, and school failure are expected long-term outcomes if children are improperly nourished (Ashem & Jones, 1978). Thus the concern for children's adequate nutrition in poor families is well justified. Some youngsters of affluent families may be malnourished because they or their parents choose nutritionally inadequate diets because of obsessive concern about avoiding obesity.

The belief that less severe nutritional inadequacies (such as not enough vitamins or minerals) or excesses (such as too much sugar or caffeine) cause children to misbehave has been popular for many years. Disorders ranging from hyperactivity to depression to autism to delinquency have been attributed to what youngsters eat or do not eat. Knapczyk (1979), for example, points out that hypoglycemia (low blood sugar), vitamin or mineral deficiencies, and allergies can influence behavior and that teachers should be aware of these potential problems. Subtle effects of sugar on the behavior and performance of preschoolers have been demonstrated (Goldman, Lerman, Contois, & Udall, 1986). Nevertheless, evidence that hypoglycemia and dietary deficiencies or excesses are causes of behavior disorders or learning problems, except in rare cases, is lacking (Silver, 1987; Werry, 1986a).

Several investigators have suggested that disordered behavior is, in some cases, a result of ingesting certain foods (for example, wheat flour or fresh fruits) or food additives (for example, colorings or preservatives) or of the absence of certain trace elements in the diet (Fishbein & Meduski, 1987). Feingold (1975) suggests that children's hyperactivity is often caused by food substances (specifically, salicylates). One theory is that some dietary substances are toxins (chemicals that cause direct damage to the body); another is that some foods produce an allergic reaction that causes behavior disorders (foods that trigger an immunological reaction). So far, evidence for dietary control of behavior problems is inconclusive. Although some studies show a relationship between problem behavior and food coloring (Rose, 1978; Swanson & Kinsbourne, 1980; Weiss et al., 1980) or certain classes of foods (O'Banion, Armstrong, Cummings, & Strange, 1978), others have failed to find any causal connection between food additives or nutritional adequacy and disordered behavior (Bird, Russo, & Cataldo, 1977; Harley, Matthews, & Eichman, 1978; Raiten & Massaro, 1986). Research strongly suggests that food chemicals do produce a highly reliable, negative behavioral response *in a very small percentage of children* (Rose, 1978; Swanson & Kinsbourne, 1980; Weiss et al., 1980). Research also suggests that food dyes can affect nerve functioning at a molecular level, that is, produce changes in the release of neurotransmitters (Augustine & Levitan, 1980; Fishbein & Meduski, 1987).

Controversy over the role of food additives and food substances continues (Blouin, 1983; Fishbein & Meduski, 1987; Silver, 1987; Trites & Tryphonas, 1983a, 1983b). Werry (1986a) notes that in many cases diet may be the result, not the cause, of disordered behavior; deviant youngsters may self-select diets that are high or low in food substances thought to be connected with psychopathology. Of course, nutritional factors could be both cause and effect, part of a vicious cycle of poor nutrition and deviant behavior. A youngster whose behavior is problematic might self-select a diet extremely high in sugar and low in other nutrients, and this diet might in turn contribute to higher levels of inappropriate behavior.

Biochemical Irregularities

Among the many supposed or suspected biological causes of disordered behavior are those in which toxins (poisons) or missing biochemicals alter an individual's cognitive abilities, affective responsiveness, or other behavioral characteristics. Besides genetically transmitted disorders such as PKU and dietary factors such as food additives, a variety of other biochemical processes may be involved. For example, the relationships of disordered behavior to metal poisoning (Marlowe et al., 1985), to abnormalities of the immune system (Warren, Margaretten, Pace, & Foster, 1986), and to fetal alcohol syndrome (Kavale & Karge, 1986) have been researched.

Evaluation of research on biochemical factors presents serious problems for educators. On the one hand, all behavior clearly represents biochemical processes, and the significance of biochemistry for behavior disorders is therefore undeniable. On the other hand, the evidence linking *most* disorders of behavior to specific biochemical irregularities is weak, and when a reliable link between troublesome behavior and a specific biochemical defect emerges, its implications for educators' day-to-day work are remote. Furthermore, biochemical origins have been suggested for almost every kind of behavioral deviance, making it hard to sift out the findings that are most reliable and relevant to education. Consequently, we will look at findings related to biochemical factors involved in only two disorders, childhood psychosis and hyperactivity.

Childhood Psychosis

It has long been suspected that psychotic individuals lack some biological substance essential for normal central nervous system functioning and/or produce a toxic biochemical that suppresses or destroys normal function. The body fluids and neural tissues of psychotic persons have thus been studied intensively, but efforts to find and treat biochemical irregularities related to psychosis have been generally disappointing. Missing or toxic biological substances have not been reliably linked to behavioral problems of psychotic children or children with other disorders, except in a few specific and relatively rare cases (Blouin, Blouin, & Kelly, 1983; Prior & Werry, 1986; Werry, 1986a,b).

Psychotic individuals have also been given a wide variety of chemicals in attempts to improve their behavior (Campbell, Cohen, & Perry, 1983; Campbell, Green, & Deutsch, 1985; Gittelman & Kanner, 1986). Although in some cases psychotic children's troublesome behavior improves with medication, a cure or even a uniform improvement has not been achieved.

Many types of deviant behavior are associated with childhood psychosis, and one can readily find competing psychological and biochemical explanations for most types of maladaptive behavior. For example, a perplexing and debilitating behavioral characteristic of many psychotic children, especially autistic children, is excessive *self-stimulation*. Self-stimulatory behavior is repetitive, stereotyped behavior that appears to produce sensory feedback but does not appear to have social consequences. "These behaviors take the form of prolonged body-rocking, head-nodding, flapping the hands at the wrists, tapping or shaking objects, gazing at lights, jumping up and down, etc." (Lovaas, Newsom, & Hickman, 1987, p. 45), and they are typically incompatible with learning other, more adaptive responses. Researchers usually attribute the causes of self-stimulatory behavior primarily to psychological or to biological factors, although all agree that both biochemistry and environmental conditions are involved to some extent.

Lovaas et al. (1987; Newsom & Lovaas, 1987) advance the idea that self-stimulatory behavior is acquired and maintained primarily by perceptual reinforcement—it is learned and continued because of the sensory consequences produced by the behavior itself. This view of self-stimulation has immediate implications for teachers because they can intervene by rearranging the consequences for behavior in the classroom, perhaps even by using self-stimulation as a reward for other, more appropriate behavior (Lovaas et al., 1987; Wolery, Kirk, & Gast, 1985). Lovaas's psychological explanation is challenged by Lewis, Baumeister, and Mailman (1987), who argue that biochemical flaws that interfere with proper functioning of the central nervous system are the primary cause of self-stimulation. Lewis et al. admit that the exact nature of the biochemical problem is unknown and suggest no interventions that carry direct implications for teachers.

Hyperactivity

Some proponents of a biological view argue that the apparent therapeutic response of many hyperactive and distractible children to stimulant drugs, massive doses of vitamins (**megavitamin** or **orthomolecular therapy**), or dietary elimination of food additives indicates a biological cause for such disorders. As we have seen, however, we must evaluate such evidence cautiously. The conclusion that hyperactivity and distractibility are usually caused by any known biological factor is not supported by reliable data (Campbell & Werry, 1986; Kauffman & Hallahan, 1979; Whalen, 1983).

Whalen (1983) points out the important influence of children's and adults' ideas about the causes of hyperactive behavior on successful strategies to control it. If youngsters believe that hyperactivity is caused by biological factors, then they may be less likely to blame themselves for misbehavior; if they attribute behavioral control to pills, then they may be less likely to believe self-control is possible. Lisa's case illustrates the power some youngsters ascribe to their medications.

Lisa, Age 11

CHILD: I wasn't at all—I didn't at all have hardly any friends. I only had two, and that was it. And last year I didn't take it [the medication] in the afternoon, but the last time I saw my doctor he said, "Why don't you have her start taking it in the afternoon?" And then since I've been doing that I've gotten about 20 more friends.

INTERVIEWER: How can you tell when you forget to take Ritalin?

CHILD: When I can tell that I'm not concentrating in school. Like she'll [the teacher] give us a half hour to do a math page, like there's about 20 problems, and I'll get about 6 done in 20 minutes, a half hour. But if I take it, I can get them all done in 10 minutes, 20 minutes, and have 10 minutes free.

INTERVIEWER: This is an "imagination" question. Let's say you stopped taking Ritalin altogether.

CHILD: Oh, wow, I'd stay home from school!

INTERVIEWER: How come?

CHILD: Because I know what would be happening if I didn't. I wouldn't get my work done at all.

INTERVIEWER: How about your friends?

CHILD: Nobody would like me then, if I didn't take it. They'd think in their minds, "Gosh, she doesn't even want to play. What a baby!"

INTERVIEWER: Pretend that a friend of yours was about to start taking Ritalin and she asked you what you thought. . . .

CHILD: They'd ask me, like "What does it do?" I'd just tell them, "Well, it helps you concentrate, get more friends, and you want to join in the games more. And you'd be invited more places." (From C.K. Whalen in *Handbook of Child Psychopathology* by T.H. Ollendick and M. Hersen [Eds.], 1983, New York: Plenum. Reprinted by permission.)

Physical Illness or Disability

A child who is physically ill is more prone to irritability, withdrawal, or other behavior problems. Some diseases (for example, **encephalitis**) can result in brain damage that can affect intelligence or social behavior or both. In most cases in which the youngster's behavior is disordered during a physical illness, however, the behavior problem is transitory; any residual effect is likely to be a function of solicitous attention by caretakers during the illness.

Changes in behavior may accompany certain physical disorders, such as rapid or protracted **salt depletion**, **hyperthyroidism**, or **hypoglycemia**. With appropriate medical treatment or dietary change, the behavior problems ordinarily resolve. Youngsters' physical status influences their perceptions and behavior. To the extent that a child is hungry, tired, or uncomfortable, he or she will be more prone to exhibit behavior that adults and peers find irritating and inappropriate.

Physical disability associated with chronic health impairment, crippling, or disfigurement can have a profound effect on psychological functioning, especially during adolescence and early adulthood (Johnson, 1986; Werry, 1986c). In some cases, physical disabilities appear to trigger depression or suicide (Bryan & Herjanic, 1980; Hawton, 1986).

Some researchers find a correlation between minor physical anomalies (minor "defects" such as facial asymmetry, malformed ears, curvature of the fifth finger, or two or more hair whorls) and hyperactivity or other disorders (Firestone & Prabhu, 1983). Krouse and Kauffman (1982) note problems in measuring such anomalies and question interpretations of the statistical relationship between anomalies and disordered behavior. There is no evidence that minor physical anomalies cause disordered behavior. Moreover, the hypothesis that behavior disorders are caused by a biological factor such as perinatal trauma, which is also associated with minor physical anomalies, is not supported by reliable research.

Physical illnesses or disorders believed to be caused by an individual's psychological state are called *psychosomatic* or **psychophysiological**. Disorders that are assumed to be psychophysiological involve disruption of normal biological processes: breathing, eating, eliminating, moving, sleeping, and the like. A few of the types of behavior problems traditionally considered psychophysiological are listed in Table 8.1, and some of these disorders are discussed in other chapters. Werry (1986b) notes that the terms *psychosomatic* and *psychophysiological* are now obsolete. In general, little sound evidence shows that psychological factors cause physiological disorders of any type, although both psychological and physiological factors are often involved in both physical and behavioral disorders (Hetherington & Martin, 1979; Werry, 1986c).

TABLE 8.1
Examples of Disorders Traditionally Believed to Have Psychophysiological Components

Breathing Disorders	Eating Disorders	Elimination Disorders	Movement Disorders	Sleep Disorders
Asthma (paroxysms of difficulty in breathing, particularly expiration)	Anorexia nervosa (severe self-starvation and marked weight loss, accompanied by intense fear of becoming obese) Bulimia (binge eating followed by purging [vomiting or enemas] or extreme dieting) Pica (eating nonnutritional substances [e.g., paint, paper, cloth])	Encopresis (incontinence of feces) Enuresis (incontinence of urine)	Tics (sudden, repetitive, involuntary movements)	Sleep walking Night terrors (motor activities [e.g., screaming, sitting up, walking] while asleep; child is impossible to wake or console)

Note: For more complete listing and discussion, see Werry (1986c).

Physiology does play a part in all behavior (more prominently in some than others), and children may be born with a predisposition for certain physiological disorders. Parental management and other environmental factors can, however, change the course of a disorder once it has been manifested. It could be, of course, that (a) physical symptoms and psychological disorders are merely coexistent and not causally related at all; that (b) physical illness causes psychological stress; or that (c) both physical illness and psychological stress are caused by a third factor or combination of factors. Consider the possible interactions between psychological and physiological factors in the case of Paul's fatal asthma. In this extreme case, both physical and emotional distress, along with parental mismanagement and problem behavior at home and school, were all mutual, reciprocal causative factors.

Paul

Paul was a 13-year-old white boy who was first diagnosed with asthma at the age of six. Mild and infrequent at first, his asthma became increasingly severe in the three years prior to admission. In the last year, his attacks required emergency room treatment with increasing frequency. . . . The importance of psychological factors was immediately recognized and psychiatric consultation was sought as part of a thorough evaluation.

His parents' history revealed that attacks were often precipitated by Paul's emotional reactions to stress, which had been increasing in recent months, both at home and at school. High parental expectations and Paul's failure to meet them led to periods of intense anxiety and sadness. A great deal of rivalry with two younger siblings was reported. Paul's father noted that on two occasions attacks had occurred shortly after he had pressured his son into Little League and into competitive swimming. His mother was especially negative in her assessment of Paul, describing him variously as cruel to animals, hyperactive, never affectionate, loud, and impulsive. His schoolwork had dropped off, and his C's and D's were a source of friction in the family.

Paul was a pudgy, early adolescent who repeatedly said he felt fine and had no tightness even when he was wheezing audibly. He was rather guarded in initial evaluation interviews but did acknowledge a number of sources of anxiety and unhappiness, including his father's intense involvement in his schoolwork and grades, a frightening nighttime police raid in his neighborhood, the death of an asthmatic schoolmate, his physical limitations, and a lack of friends. He said "a puff or two" on his inhaler was all it took to cure shortness of breath. This view was associated with use of it up to fifteen to twenty times per day.

His last hospitalization went smoothly. . . . An educational program addressed his lack of knowledge about asthma. Transfer to the psychosomatic unit was considered, but ongoing outpatient therapy was ultimately elected. Paul was discharged with minimal wheezing and widespread optimism about the overall therapeutic plan.

An enjoyable fishing trip with his father interrupted the psychiatric care. Two weeks after discharge and one day after a clinic visit that found him to be much improved, his parents discovered Paul at midnight huddled in the bathroom in marked respiratory distress and cyanotic. Resuscitation by parents and paramedics was unsuccessful; he was dead on arrival at a nearby hospital. (From "Psychological Factors in Fatal Childhood Asthma" by G.K. Fritz, S. Rubinstein, and N.J. Lewiston, 1987, *American Journal of Orthopsychiatry, 57,* 254–255. Reprinted, with permission, from The American Journal of Orthopsychiatry. Copyright [1987] by The American Orthopsychiatric Association, Inc.)

Difficult Temperament

During the past 25 years, researchers have begun to explore the centuries-old notion of temperament. The definition and measurement of temperament and the stability or continuity of temperament across time are matters of considerable controversy (Garrison & Earls, 1987; Worobey, 1986). Temperament has been variously defined as "behavioral style," or the *how* rather than the *what* and *how well* of behavior, as the "active and reactive qualities" of infant behavior, and as "measurable behavior" during infancy. It has been measured by questionnaires given to parents or teachers and by direct observation of children's behavior. Despite differences among researchers regarding definition and measurement, we can describe the concept of temperament in general terms: individuals tend to have consistent, predictable reactions to certain types of circumstances or events, and their typical way of responding—their temperament—is partly determined by basic biological processes as well as environmental factors.

Some of the earliest and most influential research on temperament was done by Thomas et al. (1968), who studied 141 mothers and their infants over a period of years. Thomas suggests that from birth all children exhibit a temperament—a behavioral style. Initial temperament seems to be determined by several factors that operate prenatally, including genetic makeup, the mother's physical status during pregnancy, and the occurrence of perinatal trauma. The point is that infants begin life with an inborn tendency to behave in certain ways. The newborn has a behavioral style that is determined predominantly by biological factors, and how a baby behaves at birth and in the first weeks and months thereafter will influence how others respond. But temperament can be changed by the environment in which the child develops; what the child experiences and how the child is managed may change temperament for better or worse. A difficult temperament may increase the child's risk for behavior disorder, but viewing temperament as anything other than an initial behavioral style that may interact with environmental influences to cause a behavior disorder would be inappropriate. As Thomas et al. (1968) state:

> Temperament is not immutable. Like any other characteristic of the organism, its features can undergo a developmental course that will be significantly affected by environmental circumstances. In this respect it is not different from height, weight, intellectual competence, or any other characteristics of the individual. The initially identified pattern of the young child may be relatively unchanged by environmental influences, or it may be reinforced and heightened, diminished, or otherwise modified during the developmental course. (pp. 4–5)
>
> Neither in theory nor in fact would we expect a one-to-one relation to exist between a specific pattern of temperament and the emergence of a behavior problem; temperament, in and of itself, does not produce a behavior disorder. (p. 9)

Based on their longitudinal study, Thomas et al. (1968) described nine categories of temperamental characteristics (see also Garrison & Earls, 1987):

1. Activity level—how much the child moves about during activities such as feeding, bathing, sleeping, and playing
2. Rhythmicity—the regularity or predictability with which the child eats, sleeps, eliminates, and so on
3. Approach or withdrawal—how the child responds initially to new events such as people, places, toys, and foods
4. Adaptability—how quickly the child becomes accustomed to or modifies an initial reaction to new situations or stimuli
5. Intensity of reaction—the amount of energy expended in reacting (positively or negatively) to situations or stimuli
6. Threshold of responsiveness—the amount or intensity of stimulation required to elicit a response from the child
7. Quality of mood—the amount of pleasant, joyful, and friendly behavior compared with unpleasant, crying, and unfriendly behavior exhibited by the child
8. Distractibility—the frequency with which extraneous or irrelevant stimuli interfere with the ongoing behavior of the child in a given situation
9. Attention span and persistence—the length of time a child will spend on a given activity and the tendency to maintain an activity in the face of obstacles to performance

Chess, Thomas, and their colleagues found that children with any kind of temperament might develop behavior disorders, depending on the child-rearing practices of their parents and other adults. Children with difficult temperaments, however, were

more likely to develop troublesome behavior. For their subjects, a difficult temperament was characterized by irregularity in biological functioning, mostly negative
(withdrawing) responses to new stimuli, slow adaptation to changes in the environment, frequent display of negative mood, and a predominance of intense reactions.
A difficult temperament may elicit negative responses from a child's caretakers—a
baby with a difficult temperament is not easy to care for and may increase parents'
irritability, negative mood, and tendency to ignore or punish the child. If infant and
parents adopt a pattern of mutual irritation, their negative interactions may increase
the probability that the youngster will exhibit inappropriate or undesirable behavior
in future years (see also Chess & Thomas, 1977).

The concept of difficult temperament has its critics (see Garrison & Earls, 1987).
Some suggest that what researchers believe are inborn biological characteristics of
infants are merely the subjective interpretations of mothers' reports. That is, "difficult
temperament" reflects social perceptions of an infant's behavior and may not be within-
the-individual characteristics. A baby is said to have a difficult temperament on the
basis of the mother's report rather than on the basis of more objective evaluations;
therefore, the mother's perceptions (and the researcher's) are being assessed, not a
biological characteristic. Thomas, Chess, and Korn (1982) and others, however, interpret their research as confirming the reality of inborn behavioral characteristics
or temperaments.

A central issue in research is whether difficult temperament actually contributes
to behavior disorders. Garrison and Earls (1987) offer this comment: "The dearth of
studies now available on a supposed relationship between early temperamental characteristics and subsequent child disorder precludes any definitive conclusions on this
matter. Data we do have, however, suggest a rather weak association that deterio-
rates as development proceeds" (p. 63). While research does not offer definitive conclusions, current interest in temperament seems likely to produce many studies that will
address the question of the relationship between temperament and psychopathology.

A few researchers have investigated teachers' ratings of children's temperaments
in the classroom (Martin et al., 1986; Paget, Nagle, & Martin, 1984; Pullis & Cadwell,
1982, 1985). Their general findings are that children do exhibit a consistent behavioral
style or temperament in the classroom and that teachers tend to take children's
temperaments into account in planning, instruction, and management. Pullis and
Cadwell (1985) found that teachers take temperament into consideration in making
decisions regarding instruction and behavior management, such as what group situation will best accommodate the student or choosing consequences for behavior.
They found no relationship between temperament ratings and decisions regarding
students' identification for special education or placement.

Three primary temperament characteristics have emerged from teachers' classroom ratings: (1) task orientation, related to the child's ability to stay in seat during
working activities, persist on tasks until they are completed, and resist distraction; (2)
adaptability, related to the child's positive reaction to new stimuli, appropriate modification of behavior when changes occur in routines, and positive response during
social interactions; and (3) reactivity, related to the child's tendency to overreact to
stressful circumstances and become very upset when frustrated (Pullis & Cadwell,
1982, 1985). Classroom research does not indicate that temperament is the direct

result of biological factors, but it does suggest that students exhibit a consistent behavioral style that teachers recognize and should consider in planning instruction.

IMPLICATIONS FOR EDUCATORS

It is erroneous to assume that all behavior disorders have a biological origin and that, therefore, all such disorders are best handled by medical intervention. Not only is the tie between behavior disorders and biological causative factors tenuous, but a biological cause may have no direct implications for change in educational methodology. To be sure, educators should work with other professionals to obtain the best possible medical care, nutrition, and physical environment for their students. Nevertheless, the implications of biological causal factors for the work of educators may be nil. Koupernik et al. (1975) commented on the nonimplications of brain injury for the work of teachers:

> Where the brain lesion or disorder is a nonprogressive one, there is often no advantage in treatment to identifying the cause or the anatomical or physiological disorder. All the child's various abilities and disabilities must be evaluated and then treatment given for his visual, auditory, language, motor, learning, emotional, and social deficits; his pre-, pari-, or postnatal insult is in the past and is untreatable. (p. 114)

Educators cannot provide medical intervention; they have only limited control over their students' physiologies. While teachers should be aware of possible biological factors in disordered behavior and refer students for evaluation by other professionals when appropriate, they must not allow speculation regarding biological etiologies to excuse them from teaching appropriate behavior to disturbed students.

SUMMARY

Humans seek explanations for deviant behavior; they want to know why people behave as they do. Assumptions about causal factors frequently determine what interventions will be selected and where blame will be placed. Assumptions that remove all personal responsibility or blame from youngsters for their misbehavior may be problematic, but personal accountability for some disorders is clearly inappropriate. The most common explanations of behavior disorders involve biological, family, cultural, and school factors.

Biological factors have special appeal because all behavior involves biochemical, neurological activity. Biological misfortunes that may contribute to the origins of behavior disorders include genetic accidents, brain damage or dysfunction, nutritional errors, biochemical irregularities, physical illnesses and disabilities, and difficult temperament.

Genetic accidents have been suggested as the causes of nearly every type of disorder, but the most reliable evidence of genetic factors are found for only the most extreme disorders. Genetic factors are known to be involved in the causation of schizophrenia, but little is known about how the gene system that causes the disorder works. Environmental factors appear to trigger schizophrenia in individuals who are genetically vulnerable.

Brain injury or dysfunction has been suggested as a cause of nearly every type of behavior disorder. The diagnosis of brain injury, however, is extremely imprecise. Furthermore, reliable evidence does not link brain damage or dysfunction to most behavior disorders. Likewise, evidence does not link nutritional substances, particular biochemical irregularities, or physical illnesses or disabilities to disordered behavior except in rare cases.

Temperament, or inborn behavioral style, is an old idea that has been researched for a relatively short time. The definition and measurement of temperament are matters of controversy. Some evidence suggests that temperament may be an important factor in parent-child interactions and in teachers' classroom planning for individual students.

Clearly, when biological factors contribute to behavioral disorders, they do not operate in isolation from or independently of environmental (psychological) forces. The most tenable view at this time is that biological and environmental factors interact with one another to cause behavior disorders. It seems reasonable to propose a continuum of biological causes ranging from minor, undetectable organic faults to profound accidents of nature and a related continuum of behavior disorders ranging from mild to profound to which these biological accidents contribute. Implications of biological factors for the day-to-day work of teachers are nil, but teachers should be aware of possible biological causes and refer students to other professionals when appropriate.

9

Family Factors

As you read this chapter, keep these guiding questions in mind:

☐ Why is the family considered an important source of disordered behavior?
☐ How do vulnerability and risk factors relate to development of behavior disorders?
☐ What are the implications of an interactional-transactional model of family influence for families with abused children?
☐ What is a negative reinforcement trap?
☐ How do coercive family interactions relate to development of antisocial behavior?
☐ Why might we need to revise assumptions about the strengths and weaknesses of the traditional family form?
☐ What are short-term and long-term effects of divorce on youngsters' behavior?
☐ How could one characterize the most and least desirable types of parental discipline?
☐ How can we explain family influences on the behavior of psychotic children?
☐ How do parenting practices contribute to juvenile delinquency?
☐ What do we know about family contributions to anxiety-withdrawal and depression?
☐ How can parents foster school success or school failure?

THE APPEAL OF FAMILY FACTORS

All societies consider the nuclear family (father, mother, and children) a central factor in early personality development (Martin, 1981). Parents have traditionally been held responsible for their children's conduct at least until they reach late adolescence. When youngsters misbehave, the natural tendency is to blame parental mismanagement or family disintegration.

While the nuclear family deserves close scrutiny as the primary setting for children's behavioral development, a substantial proportion of children are now reared in other social contexts, particularly single-parent families. Many children are being reared by parents who themselves are little more than children, often under adverse environmental conditions and in the context of family discord. Regardless of whether the family is intact or broken, however, a child's kin are usually the first people to whom he or she must become oriented, and kinship provides entry into the larger social context and culture.

Given the primacy of family relations in children's social development, it is understandable that we have sought the origins of behavior disorders in the structure, composition, and interactions of family units. Unfortunately, these elements do not provide a straightforward basis for predicting most behavioral disorders.

FAMILY CHARACTERISTICS AND PREDICTION OF BEHAVIOR DISORDER

Family characteristics appear to predict behavioral development only in complex interactions with other factors, such as socioeconomic status, sources of emotional support outside the family, and the child's age, sex, and temperamental characteristics. Nevertheless, broken homes, an absent father, parental separation, divorce, and chaotic or hostile family relationships are known to increase children's risk of developing behavior disorders (Hetherington & Martin, 1979; Martin, 1975; Rutter, 1979, 1985; Sameroff, Seifer, & Zax, 1982). When several risk factors occur together—for example, poverty, parental hostility, and illness requiring hospitalization—their effects are not merely additive, but multiplicative. That is, two such factors occurring together more than double the probability that a child will develop a behavior disorder; if a third factor is added, the chance of disorder is several times higher yet (Garmezy, 1987).

Rutter's (1979) review of research on maternal deprivation and related family factors in behavior disorders points out some of the complexities in family influences. A tempting conclusion, for example, is that separation of the child from one or both parents always works serious mischief with a youngster's psychological and behavioral development. But that conclusion is not valid, because a variety of other circumstances must be taken into account. In an intact family, parental discord may exert a more pernicious influence than parental separation. A good relationship with one parent may sustain a child even in the face of parental discord or separation. The interaction of the child's constitutional or temperamental characteristics with parental behavior may be more important than parental separation or disharmony. In addition, factors outside the home (school, for instance) may lessen or heighten the negative influence of family factors. For some reason, some children do not succumb to extreme dis-

162

ruption or disintegration of their families (Hetherington & Martin, 1986). Some children are amazingly invulnerable; factors that increase the risk for most youngsters simply do not phase them.

No one knows why some children are vulnerable and others invulnerable to negative family influences. Future research may reveal which family factors are causally related to disordered behavior and which ones protect children from stress. One strategy for unraveling the seemingly impossible tangle of family factors that can give rise to behavior disorders would be to experiment with families; that is, researchers could purposely manipulate family variables to induce behavior disorders in children, taking care to control extraneous variables that could cloud the outcome. If researchers could produce behavior disorders at will, then they could identify the etiological variables. For obvious ethical reasons, intervention research must be confined to therapeutic variables and amelioration of behavior disorders; experimentation in which we would cause behavioral disorders is out of the question.

An alternative is intensive longitudinal study of individuals for whom the *risk* of developing a behavior disorder is high (Sameroff & Seifer, 1983; Walker & Emory, 1983). "The definition of a high-risk child is one who is at a greater than average risk for later deviances in behavior because of membership in some identifiable population" (Sameroff & Seifer, 1983, p. 1254). Mosher and Gunderson (1974) suggest that risk research is a natural outgrowth of previous investigations that have shown the importance of both genetic and environmental factors. Attempts to identify factors associated with vulnerability and risk of schizophrenia are an example.

> Researchers seeking the origins of schizophrenia have traditionally concentrated their attention upon the systematic experimental analysis of schizophrenic patients' behavior. But although this approach has yielded any number of putative etiological clues, attempts to evaluate the significance of differences found between normal and schizophrenic subjects have been stymied by a major and seemingly insuperable methodological problem—the impossibility of determining whether abnormalities observed in already manifest, diagnosed schizophrenics reflect a cause or a consequence of illness. To circumvent this problem, a cadre of enterprising researchers have turned to a promising and relatively new research strategy: The study of individuals deemed particularly vulnerable to schizophrenia prior to the manifestation of illness. By following vulnerable individuals from their earliest years through the period of risk, these investigators hope to identify preexisting biochemical, physiological, psychological, or life-history characteristics which consistently differentiate those who ultimately develop schizophrenia from those who do not. (Mosher & Gunderson, 1974, p. 13)

The report of Sameroff et al. (1982) helps confirm the complex interaction of many variables in the causation of behavior disorders and indicates that parental pathology alone seldom, if ever, accounts for children's problems. Sameroff and his colleagues studied the infants and young children of several hundred mentally ill women and concluded that no simple biological or environmental model can account for the transmission of schizophrenia. In particular, their data appear to refute the notion that schizophrenic mothers cause their children to be mentally ill: "It is our impression from watching our sample of chronic schizophrenics rearing their children for the first few years of life that among their many incompetencies is the incompetence

163

to make their children crazy" (p. 65). Their data indicate that children of schizo-phrenics are indeed at risk for disordered behavior. Poor economic circumstance, low social status, unstable family organization, and a parent's prolonged, severe mental disturbance, regardless of the specific diagnosis of schizophrenia, however, were more notable risk factors than being reared by a schizophrenic parent.

The concept of heightened risk, as opposed to a simple cause-effect relationship, is important in all types of disordered behavior, not just schizophrenia. We can best understand risk in terms of a conceptual model of family influence. What happens in families in which risk of behavior disorder is high?

AN INTERACTIONAL-TRANSACTIONAL MODEL OF FAMILY INFLUENCE

Child development specialists are realizing that children's influence on their parents' behavior is as important as parents' influence on their children. Researchers are suggesting that negative family interactions and undesirable parenting behavior are as much a reaction of family members to a deviant youngster as they are a cause of disturbed behavior (Bell, 1968; Bell & Harper, 1977; Martin, 1981; Patterson, 1982, 1986a, 1986b; Sameroff & Chandler, 1975). As Martin (1975) stated:

> At the moment of birth, parent and child begin an interactive drama that will evolve
> its own unique character and destiny. Affection, joy, antagonism, openness, with-
> drawal, demands, and acquiescence will be interchanged according to each dyad's
> own pattern—a pattern that is likely to vary considerably according to circum-
> stances and over time. (p. 463)

In this view of family behavior, interactions and transactions among individuals are the central theme in interpreting developmental data. The data include reinforce-ment, punishment, imitation, and other teaching transactions consistent with social cognitive theory. Emphasis is on reciprocity of influence from the earliest parent-child interactions and on the pervasiveness of reciprocal influences of parents and children in all subsequent interactions.

Clarke-Stewart (1973) offers an example of the type of research on which an interactional-transactional model is based. She carefully recorded the interactions between 36 mothers and their firstborn children (9 to 18 months of age) over a nine-month period. Repeated observations were made in the homes, in both structured and spontaneous situations. Analysis of observational data indicated that mothers who were highly responsive to their infants and provided abundant stimulation in the form of talking and playing had more intelligent babies than less stimulating mothers. That is, maternal responsiveness and stimulation appeared to increase the child's cognitive growth. In the area of social development, however, the child's behavior appeared to have a controlling influence on the mother's behavior: the child's looking at, smiling at, and vocalizing to the mother seemed to increase the mother's responsiveness to demands and distress signals. Clarke-Stewart's findings, then, suggest a reciprocal pattern of influence in which the mother's responsiveness and stimulation facilitate the child's cognitive development and the child's positive social-emotional signals to the mother increase maternal responsiveness and sensitivity.

Martin (1981) studied interactions of mothers with their 10-month-old infants and followed up his initial observations when the children were 22 and 42 months old. His data (which were much clearer for boys than for girls) indicated that the beginnings of coercive, uncooperative mother-child relationships can be identified quite early in a child's life. Such relationships are particularly likely to arise in cases in which the mother is unresponsive to or uninvolved with her son and/or the son is highly demanding. The evidence suggests that in some cases "mothers and children force each other into a mode of interaction which is designed to accommodate different kinds of noncooperativeness in dyadic relations—autonomy (noninvolvement) on the part of the mother and noncompliance on the part of the child—but that these attempts at accommodation. . . have little influence on increased cooperation" (p. 42). As we shall see, interactions in which a parent and child try to force responses from each other appear to be characteristic of a coercive relationship that leads to disordered child behavior.

An interactional-transactional model is not confined to any one area of child behavior; it is being applied to nearly every conceivable topic in child development, including efforts to teach youngsters prosocial (helpful) behavior. Keller and Bell (1979), for example, investigated how children's behavior (looking at an adult and answering promptly when questioned) influenced adults' methods of trying to induce the children to perform acts of altruism. Two ideas associated with the interactional-transactional model represent a significant advance in theories of child development and psychopathology: (1) children have effects on adults that are equal to adults' effects on children; and (2) family interactions are understandable only when reciprocal influences of parent and children on each other are taken into account.

Sameroff and Chandler (1975) postulate that the outcome of child care is positive to the extent that the child elicits or is provided with nurturance, but that a child is at high risk for later difficulties to the extent that she or he elicits negative responses from the environment. They interpret even child abuse, which has traditionally been considered a result of negative psychological characteristics of the parents, in terms of interaction-transaction. The abused child's temperament may contribute to parents' tendencies to be abusive: "Children with difficult temperaments or physical disorders may increase their own chances of being abused, whereas siblings of a less bothersome nature are likely to receive only minimal abuse" (Sameroff & Chandler, 1975, p. 23).

Interactional-Transactional Effects in Child Abuse

Parke and Collmer (1975) found that certain parental sociocultural characteristics appear to increase the chance of child abuse: their own history of being abused as children, their social isolation from the community and from sources of emotional support, poverty and undereducation, having many children, and a cultural environment that condones violence and harsh physical discipline (see also Webster-Stratton, 1985). Evidence also indicates that abusive mothers are less able than nonabusive mothers to identify infants' emotions (Kropp & Haynes, 1987). Certain characteristics of children seem to invite abuse: they appear to become likely targets to the extent that they are unattractive, irritable, unresponsive to loving attention or to discipline, or difficult to care for because of illness or prematurity. Older children who are abused are characterized by physical unattractiveness and by behavior that commonly calls forth negative responses from adults: high activity level, irritability, and defiance of discipline, for example (see Zirpoli, 1986). Parents often see children with severe disabilities as unresponsive to attempts to involve them in social interactions (Zirpoli & Bell, 1987). Thus, although certain parental characteristics contribute to child abuse, so do certain characteristics of the child.

Research findings by George and Main (1979) and Mulhern and Passman (1979) are consistent with the interactional hypotheses of Parke and Collmer (1975) and Sameroff and Chandler (1975). George and Main found that abused toddlers in a day-care center exhibited a set of negative behaviors that distinguished them from non-abused youngsters. The abused children physically assaulted their peers, harassed and seldom made friendly advances toward their adult caregivers, and often avoided friendly overtures. These abused children's behaviors, according to George and Main, were similar to those of children who were rejected by their mothers.

One hypothesis about parent-child interaction in child abuse is that their children's responses to punishment *teach* parents to become increasingly punitive. For example, if the child exhibits behavior that is aversive to the parent (perhaps whining), the parent may punish the child (perhaps by slapping). If the punishment is successful and the child stops the aversive behavior, then the parent is negatively reinforced by the consequence; the parent is, in effect, rewarded by the child's stopping the aversive behavior. The next time the child whines, the parent is more likely to try slapping to get relief from the whining. If at first the child does not stop whining, the parent may slap harder or more often to try to make the child be quiet. Thus the punishment becomes increasingly harsh as a means of dealing with the child's increasingly aversive behavior. Supporting this hypothesis is the finding of Mulhern and Passman (1979) that mothers escalated punishment in attempts to teach their sons a new task, which is consistent with the hypothesis that abusive parents may rely on punishment in attempts to teach their children.

Although abusive parents are not usually successful in punishing their child, they continue to escalate punishment. They seem not to understand or be able to use alternative means of control. And although abused children suffer in the bargain, they usually hold their own in the battle with their parents; they stubbornly refuse to knuckle under to parental pressure. Parent and child are trapped in a mutually de-structive, coercive cycle in which they cause and are caused physical and/or psycho-logical pain (Webster-Stratton, 1985). Such a coercive struggle is characteristic of conduct disorder.

The conclusion that the child's behavior is *always* a reciprocal causal factor in an abusive relationship with a parent is not warranted, however. Abusive relationships are extremely varied, both in abusive behaviors and in abused-abuser relations. Sexual abuse in families, for example, takes many forms and may involve incestuous rela-tionships between siblings, parent and child, or other family members (for example, stepparent or grandparent) and child. Because it is a social problem surrounded by many taboos, sexual abuse is a difficult topic for research (Parker & Parker, 1986). Research does not justify the assumption that children contribute to their sexual abuse, particularly when the abused child is very young. The accompanying box describes a case that, though unusual and extreme, makes the point that an abusive relationship may begin with a completely innocent victim. Granted that an extended history of abuse can cause some children to learn sexually provocative behavior that contributes to their further abuse, it would be difficult to make the case that infants and young children initiate their own victimization by sexually abusing parents.

Maternal-Neonatal Incest: A Case Description

The mother had had no history of childhood incestuous exposure but at 19 years of age had been raped by an acquaintance. Although she had been exclusively hetero-sexual in her relationships, she did express some homosexual ideation. Mother and son had slept together since the child's birth. When the child was 18 months old, the mother revealed that within the first two weeks after birth she had begun to fondle and stimulate the child's genitals and had continued in her sexual interaction with him, performing fellatio on the child and using him for masturbation by rubbing him against her genitals, through 18 months of age. At the time these events came to light, the child had been having marked behavior problems and demonstrated significant delays in language and social development. The child, now three years of age, contin-ues to be physically aggressive and difficult to manage, with little speech development despite intensive intervention programs. Sexual acting out, whereby the child reached under other children's clothing and attempted to fondle their genitals, was reported in his interactions with peers at a preschool program.

From "Maternal-Neonatal Incest" by I. J. Chasnoff, W.J. Burns, S.H. Schnoll, K. Burns, G. Chisum, and L. Kyle-Spore, 1986, *American Journal of Orthopsychiatry, 50,* pp. 577–578. Reprinted, with permission, from American Journal of Ortho-psychiatry. Copyright 1986 by the American Orthopsychiatric Association, Inc.

Most people give little thought to children's and parents' interactive effects on each other in cases of abuse. Child abuse is often seen as a problem of parental behavior alone, and intervention has often been directed only at changing parents' responses to their children. The interactional-transactional model considers abused children's influence on their parents and suggests that intervention deal directly with the abused child's undesirable behavior as well as with the parents' abusive responses (see Patterson, 1980, 1982; Zirpoli, 1986). This perspective is valuable even when the child is not initially an instigator of abuse, but has been drawn into an abusive relationship and is exhibiting inappropriate behavior.

Interactional-Transactional Effects in Conduct Disorder

Conduct disorder is characterized by antisocial behavior of various kinds, including fighting and assault, temper tantrums, disobedience, quarreling, fire setting, stealing, truancy, and the like (see Chapter 7). Antisocial behavior generally falls into two categories: overt and covert (see Chapters 13 and 14). Both types of antisocial behavior are serious. When a conduct disorder involves both extreme noncompliance with adults' directions and serious deficits in social and work skills, the probability is high that the child will adopt a life-long, debilitating pattern of social deviance (see Dishion, Loeber, Stouthamer-Loeber, & Patterson, 1984; Kazdin, 1987; Patterson, 1986a).

The work of Patterson and his colleagues gives insights into the family charac-teristics of antisocial youngsters (Patterson, 1973, 1980, 1982, 1986a, 1986b; Patterson et al., 1975). Their methods involve direct observation and measuring parents' and children's behavior in the home, revealing an identifiable family pattern; that is, interaction in families with aggressive children is characterized by exchange of neg-ative, hostile behaviors, whereas the interaction in families with nonaggressive chil-dren tends to be mutually positive and gratifying for parents and children. In the families with aggressive children, not only do the children behave in ways that are highly irritating and aversive to their parents, but the parents rely primarily on aversive methods (hitting, shouting, threatening, and so forth) to control their children. Thus, children's aggression in the family seems both to produce counteraggression and to be produced by punitive parenting techniques.

Patterson (1980) studied mutually aversive interactions between mothers and children, particularly in families of aggressive children, and found that many of the behaviors are maintained by negative reinforcement. Negative reinforcement involves escape from or avoidance of an unpleasant condition, which is rewarding (negatively reinforcing) because it brings relief from psychological or physical pain or anxiety. An example of negative reinforcement in mother-child interactions is shown in Table 9.1. Patterson calls these interactions *negative reinforcement traps* because they set the stage for greater conflict and coercion; each person in the trap tends to reciprocate the other's aversive behavior and to escalate attempts to use coercion—controlling someone by negative reinforcement. Patterson and his colleagues have found that, unlike normal children, problem children tend to increase their disruptive behavior in response to parental punishment. Predictably, therefore, the families of aggressive children seem to foster undesirable child behavior.

In effect, the members of families with aggressive children *train* each other to be aggressive. While the major training occurs in transactions between an aggressive

TABLE 9.1
Some Reinforcement Traps

	Negative Reinforcement Arrangement		
Neutral Antecedent:	Time Frame 1	Time Frame 2	Time Frame 3
Behavior:	Mother ("clean your room")	Child (whine)	Mother (stops asking)
	Short Term Effect	Long Term Effect	
Mother	The pain (child's Whine) stops	Mother will be more likely to give in when child whines	
Child	The pain (mother's Nag) stops	Given a messy room, mother less likely to ask him to clean it up in the future	
Overall	The room was not cleaned	Child more likely to use whine to turn off future requests to clean room	

Explanation: Child's room is messy, an aversive condition for mother. When mother asks child to clean room, child whines. Child's whining is painfully aversive to mother, so mother stops asking or nagging. Mother's nagging is painfully aversive to child, who finds that his whining will stop mother's nagging. In short run, both mother and child escape pain—child stops whining and mother stops nagging—but child's room is not cleaned. In the long run, mother avoids asking child to clean room and child learns to use whining to stop mother's nagging. Both mother and child are negatively reinforced by avoidance of or escape from aversive consequences. However, problem condition (messy room) still exists as potential source of future negative interactions.

Note: From "Mothers: The Unacknowledged Victims" by G. R. Patterson, 1980, *Monographs of the Society for Research in Child Development, 45* (5, Serial no. 186) p. 5. Copyright 1980 by the University of Chicago Press. Reprinted by permission.

child and parent(s), it spills over to include siblings. Patterson (1986b) reports that siblings of an aggressive child are no more aggressive toward their parents than are children in families without an aggressive child. Interactions between siblings in families of antisocial youngsters, however, are more aggressive than those in families without an aggressive child. Coercive exchanges between aggressive children and their parents appear to teach siblings to be coercive with each other. Not surprisingly, these children then tend to be more aggressive in other social contexts, such as school. In fact, school conflict and school failure are frequently associated with antisocial behavior at home (cf. Patterson, 1986b; Stevenson-Hinde, Hinde, & Simpson, 1986).

What is the background of these coercive exchanges in families of aggressive children and the negative outcomes for their lives? How do these problems get started? The model emerging from Patterson's research group suggests that they arise from "failure by parents to effectively punish garden-variety, coercive behaviors" (Patterson, 1986b, p. 436). The child begins winning battles with the parents, and parents become increasingly punitive but ineffective in responding to coercion. Coercive exchanges escalate in number and intensity, increasing to hundreds per day and progressing from whining, yelling, and temper tantrums to hitting and other forms of physical assault. The child continues to win a high percentage of the battles with parents; parents continue to use ineffective punishment, setting the stage for another round of conflict. And this coercive family process often occurs in the context of other conditions associated with high risk for psychopathology of both parents and child: social and economic disadvantage, substance abuse, and a variety of other stressors such as parental discord and separation or divorce. During the process, the child receives little or no parental warmth and is often rejected by peers. School failure is another typical concomitant of the process. Understandably, the child usually develops a poor self-image.

Patterson's suggestion that parents of aggressive children do not punish their children effectively does not mean he believes punishment should be the focus of parental discipline. His work does suggest, however, that parents need to set clear limits for children's behavior, provide a warm and loving home environment, provide positive attention and approval for appropriate behavior, and follow through with nonhostile and nonphysical punishment for coercive conduct. Appropriate punishment might consist of withdrawing privileges or restricting the child's activities contingent upon specific types of misbehavior, particularly not minding.

The apparent homeliness of the coercive family process model—its emphasis on ordinary daily interactions rather than more interesting and mysterious unconscious processes—belies its importance. As Patterson (1986b) concluded,

> Perhaps it is curious that a process with such a myriad of effects and outcomes can be initiated by something as ordinary as the level of parents' family-management skills. That, however, is what the general model prompting these studies indicates. Findings from our clinical and the modeling studies also suggest that anger, rejection, poor self-esteem, and perhaps some forms of depression may have their beginnings in the prosaic daily round of parental mismanagement. What is being mismanaged is something as inherently banal as family coercive exchanges. What leads to things getting out of hand may be a relatively simple affair, whereas the process itself, once initiated, may be the stuff of which novels are made. (p. 442)

Patterson and other researchers have shown that the pattern of coercive exchanges characterizing families of antisocial children can be identified early (Patterson, 1986b; see also Stevenson-Hinde et al., 1986; Waters, Hay, & Richters, 1986). Martin (1981), for example, found indications that mutually uncooperative, coercive styles of mother-child interaction can be identified in some cases by the time the child is three-and-a-half years old. These and other findings suggest that conduct disordered children are at risk from an early age, partly because they are infants with difficult temperaments and have parents who lack skills in coping with the stress of having a difficult baby (cf. Kazdin, 1987; Patterson, 1986b). The pattern of coercive exchanges is established early and grows more intense and hurtful as the child becomes stronger and more skillful in counterattack as a response to parental irritability or lack of compliance with his wishes.

A wealth of research shows a pattern of punishment, negative reinforcement, and coercion in the families of aggressive children. Other research indicates that hostile, inconsistent discipline and family conflict are associated with disordered child behavior (Hetherington & Martin, 1986; Moore & Arthur, 1983; Willis, Swanson, & Walker, 1983). Nevertheless, these data do not demonstrate that punitive parents cause their children to become aggressive any more than difficult-to-manage, aggressive children cause their parents to become punitive. Fortunately, however, Patterson et al. (1975; Patterson, 1982) and other behavioral researchers have demonstrated that many parents can be trained to change their responses to their children to modify the children's aggression (see Patterson et al., 1975; Willis et al., 1983).

THE INFLUENCE OF FAMILY FORMS AND PARENTAL DISCIPLINE

Two factors assumed to have significant effects on youngsters' behavioral development are family intactness and how parents discipline their children. High rates of divorce and growing numbers of out-of-wedlock births, particularly to teenage mothers, have raised serious concerns about the effects on children of family forms that differ from the traditional or ideal. Parental discipline, forever a matter of social controversy, has become a topic for research.

Family Forms

Although the intact mother-father-children concept of family remains the ideal in American culture, discrepancies from this ideal are common. Society may need to revise its traditional assumptions about the strengths and weakness of diverse family forms to fit the realities of contemporary life (Hetherington & Camara, 1984). Effects of family size and birth order on behavioral development have been studied extensively, but such elements of family configuration are outweighed by factors of divorce and other circumstances resulting in single-parent homes (cf. Hetherington & Martin, 1986).

Of the voluminous research regarding effects of divorce and alternative family configurations, we will mention only a few generalizations. Family composition or configuration in itself is not known to be a significant causal factor in children's behavior disorders; other factors involving characteristics of family members and the social context in which they live are far more important. Level of conflict among family members, security of parent-child emotional attachment, temperamental characteristics of children and parents, and availability of extrafamilial resources appear to be important influences on behavioral development (Hetherington & Camara, 1984; Waters et al., 1986). These factors are overriding concerns, whether the family varies from the traditional ideal or is dissolved by death or divorce and reconstituted.

Nonetheless, divorce is traumatic—for parents and children and for extended family and friends. The lasting psychological pain and fear of many children whose parents divorce are well known (Wallerstein, 1987), along with the increased susceptibility of adolescents of divorced parents to negative peer pressure, even when the family is reconstituted with a stepparent (Steinberg, 1987). Yet the overwhelming finding is that most children adjust to divorce and go on with their lives without developing chronic behavior problems. "Most children manifest some disturbances— often a combination of anger, anxiety, depression, dependency, and noncompliance— in the immediate aftermath of divorce; however, most children and adults also recover and adjust to their new life situation by about three years after divorce" (Hetherington & Martin, 1986, p. 340).

How children adjust to divorce depends on a variety of circumstances besides family dissolution, including the child's age when the divorce occurs, the child's level of attachment to the custodial parent and to the noncustodial parent, level of parental conflict prior to and following the divorce, characteristics of the custodial parent, details of custody and visitation rights, behavior of the visiting parent, economic circumstances of the custodial parent, sources of extrafamilial support for members of the partial family, and the child's cognitive and affective characteristics related to coping with stress (see Johnson, 1986). There is no general formula for predicting child psychopathology following divorce.

Parental Discipline

Becker (1964) suggested two major dimensions along which parental discipline techniques can vary: *restrictiveness* versus *permissiveness,* and *warmth* versus *hostility.* His landmark review of research led him to conclude that warm, love-oriented methods of discipline and permissiveness (a high degree of tolerance in areas such as neatness, orderliness, toilet training, sex play, modesty, manners, noise, obedience, and so on) foster desirable social growth. Power-assertive, hostile methods of discipline and restrictiveness (strict rule enforcement) inhibit social development. At the same time, the two dimensions of warmth-hostility and restrictiveness-permissiveness interact to affect the child's social development.

Becker concluded that parents whose discipline is warm and restrictive are likely to have submissive, dependent, polite, neat children who are minimally aggressive, friendly, and creative. On the other hand, parents who use warm and permissive discipline are likely to have socially outgoing, active, creative, independent children who are able to assume adult roles and show minimal self-aggression. Hostile and restrictive parents will tend to have socially withdrawn, neurotic children who are shy and quarrelsome with their peers, show maximal self-aggression, and have difficulty assuming adult roles. Parents who are hostile and permissive in their discipline will tend to have highly aggressive, noncompliant, delinquent children. Furthermore, consistency in discipline—sameness over time, agreement between parents, predictability of consequences, and congruity between instructions, rewards, and models—is a crucial factor in the outcome. In general, consistency will smooth out difficulties and inconsistency will aggravate problems. Even though consistent, love-oriented, permissive discipline seems to facilitate socialization, and inconsistent, hostile, restrictive disciplinary measures are typically debilitating, Becker concluded that "There are probably many routes to becoming a 'good parent' which vary with the personality of both the parents and children and with pressures in the environment with which one must learn to cope" (p. 202).

Martin (1975) later reviewed research on discipline techniques and arrived at the same conclusions Becker reached regarding children's aggression: Parents who are generally lax, uncaring, and rejecting in their attitudes toward their children, but are also harsh, hostile, and inconsistent in discipline, tend to have hostile, aggressive children. Martin's review, however, did not support Becker's conclusion that parental restrictiveness produces withdrawn-neurotic behavior. Martin's analysis did reaffirm the pernicious effects of parental rejection and nonacceptance and the desirable outcome of sensitivity to children's needs, reinforcement for appropriate behavior, and love-oriented methods of dealing with misbehavior. Becker's and Martin's earlier conclusions regarding the negative influence of inconsistent discipline on child behavior and hostile, rejecting, disorganized family relationships are supported by more recent reviews by Doke and Flippo (1983), Moore and Arthur (1983), and Willis et al. (1983). Firm, consistent, but loving and responsive parental discipline is now known to be associated with the most positive outcomes for children (Hetherington & Martin, 1986).

The effects of discipline techniques are complex and not highly predictable without considering both the parents' and the child's behavioral characteristics. Parents who are most likely to avoid contributing to the development of behavioral problems, however, are sensitive to the child's individuality in exerting their control; they are firm, yet warm and accepting of the child's own temperament. These ideas are supported by the longitudinal study of Thomas et al. (1968; see also Chess & Thomas, 1977; Thomas & Chess, 1975, 1984). The thesis Thomas and Chess advance is that every child is born with a temperament or behavioral style (see Chapter 8). Temperament affects behavioral development only in interaction with environmental variables, including parental behavior and schooling. Some children have a difficult temperament, a behavioral style that includes negative mood, intense reactions, irregularity in biological functions, and slowness to adapt to new stimuli or environmental changes. Other children have an easy temperament, characterized by just the opposite behavioral style. Depending on how parents, teachers, and other adults manage them, both easy and difficult children may develop either behavior disorders or desirable behavior patterns. (The box describes different outcomes of parental management of difficult children.)

FAMILY FACTORS IN SPECIFIC BEHAVIOR DISORDERS

Childhood Psychosis

No sound evidence indicates that parents make their children psychotic—autistic or schizophrenic (Prior & Werry, 1986; Sameroff et al., 1982). The families of many

Managing Difficult Children

The differences in the developmental courses of difficult children which result from differences in parent-child interactions are illustrated by the contrasting behavioral courses of two of the study children. Both youngsters, one a girl and the other a boy, showed similar characteristics of behavioral functioning in the early years of life, with irregular sleep patterns, constipation and painful evacuations at times, slow acceptance of new foods, prolonged adjustment periods to new routines, and frequent and loud periods of crying. Adaptation to nursery school in the fourth year was also a problem for both children. Parental attitudes and practices, however, differed greatly. The girl's father was usually angry with her. In speaking of her, he gave the impression of disliking the youngster and was punitive and spent little or no recreational time with her. The mother was more concerned for the child, more understanding, and more permissive, but quite inconsistent. There was only one area in which there was firm but quiet parental consistency, namely, with regard to safety rules. The boy's parents, on the other hand, were unusually tolerant and consistent. The child's lengthy adjustment periods were accepted calmly; his strident altercations with his younger siblings were dealt with good-humoredly. The parents waited out his negative moods without getting angry. They tended to be very permissive, but set safety limits and consistently pointed out the needs and rights of his peers at play.

By age 5½ years, these two children, whose initial characteristics had been so similar, showed marked differences in behavior. The boy's initial difficulties in nursery school had disappeared, he was a constructive member of his class, had a group of friends with whom he exchanged visits, and functioned smoothly in most areas of daily living. The girl, on the other hand, had developed a number of symptoms of increasing severity. These included explosive anger, negativism, fear of the dark, encopresis, thumb sucking, insatiable demands for toys and sweets, poor peer relationships, and protective lying. It is of interest that there was no symptomatology or negativism in one area where parental practice had been firmly consistent, i.e., safety rules.

The boy, though his early handling had been difficult for his parents, was never considered by them to have a behavioral disturbance. They understood that the youngster's troublesome behavior was the expression of his own characteristics. With this constructive parental approach, these troublesome items of behavior did not become transformed into symptoms of a behavior disorder. The girl, in contrast, suffered the consequences of parental functioning which was excessively stressful for a child with her temperamental attributes and developed a neurotic behavior disorder. . . .

From *Temperament and Behavior Disorders in Children* (pp. 82–83) by A. Thomas, S. Chess, and H.G. Birch, 1968, New York: New York University Press.

severely and profoundly disturbed children are indistinguishable from the families of normal children. Suggestions that parental psychopathology is the cause of autistic children's disability have been thoroughly discredited (Bristol, 1985; Schreibman & Mills, 1983).

When family members other than the psychotic youngster also exhibit behavioral pathology, the problem may be as much a result of the disruptive influence of the psychotic child on the parents and siblings as a matter of pathogenic parental influence. The trauma parents and siblings experience when the family acquires a severely handicapped child is great, and all of the blame for the ensuing problems in the family cannot be ascribed to the parents (see Turnbull & Turnbull, 1986). Under the stress of coping with a severely handicapped youngster, parents and siblings may adopt undesirable patterns of interaction. As we have seen, when a child exhibits maladaptive behavior, parental or sibling responses to it may serve to maintain, attenuate, or otherwise modify it. In attempting to accomplish therapeutic goals for the psychotic child, therefore, intervention should be aimed at the entire family social system (Bristol, 1985).

Juvenile Delinquency

Delinquent or law-violating behavior is obviously learned from the child's social environment (see Chapter 15), although biological factors are suspected in aggression and criminality (Cairns & Cairns, 1986; McCord, 1986; Mednick et al., 1986; Olweus, 1986). The social environment includes the child's family, in which he or she learns attitudes and characteristic responses to social rules. Because delinquency may involve either overt aggression or covert antisocial behavior or both, it is reasonable to believe that the same coercive family process associated with conduct disorder is at work in family contributions to delinquency.

Until recently, there was little reason to question the assertion that "the family correlates of early antisocial aggression and most forms of delinquency appear to be similar" (Hetherington & Martin, 1979, p. 257). Becker (1964), Martin (1975), and Hetherington and Martin (1979) pointed to similar family factors related to law violations and the aggressive, acting out (but not necessarily delinquent) behavior known as conduct disorder. Moore, Chamberlain, and Mukai (1979), however, suggested that "aggressive behavior and adolescent criminal behavior represent different developmental tracks that are not necessarily related" (p. 346). They found that, while stealing was highly predictive of later contact with the juvenile court, aggression in the home was not. In this and other research, it has become apparent that there are differences in the families of children who steal and families of children who are aggressively antisocial but not stealers (see Patterson, 1982). Stealers are more coercive than nonproblem boys, but less coercive than boys who are highly aggressive but not stealers. Moreover, parents of boys who steal tend to be less involved with their children's supervision; they are more detached emotionally and attempt to blame someone else for the child's misbehavior.

Although Moore et al. (1979) studied a small sample, Loeber, Weissman, and Reid (1983) report similar findings. These findings, along with other evidence from Patterson's research group (1982, 1986b), suggest that the family factors in delinquency and those in conduct disorder are more quantitative than qualitative. Stealing is one behavior associated with conduct disorder, but research now suggests that stealers are a subgroup of youngsters with conduct disorders, most of whom are destined to become delinquent. Future research of family characteristics as they relate to specific types of antisocial behavior may reveal reliable differences in the family process that contributes to social maladjustment and the process that leads to criminal behavior.

Anxiety-Withdrawal

Anxiety-withdrawal (see Chapter 16) includes characteristics such as excessive shyness, lack of assertiveness, and excessive fears. We know much less about family contributions to anxiety-withdrawal than about conduct disorder, probably because anxiety and social withdrawal are perceived as less pressing social problems with less severe consequences for later adjustment. Hetherington and Martin (1986) reviewed research showing that anxious, withdrawn children tend to have at least one overprotective parent. It is certainly plausible that anxious, withdrawn parents teach their children to behave as they do. In many cases of withdrawal or fearfulness, one or both parents are overly restrictive, demanding, critical, or anxious and neurotic; however, we do not know precisely the extent to which family interaction, as opposed to biological factors or influences from outside the family, accounts for anxiety and withdrawal (Petti, 1983).

Depression

Although childhood and adolescent depression has become a topic of intense interest, there is considerable controversy regarding its assessment and causes (Forness, 1988; Quay & LaGreca, 1986). Some researchers prefer the term **dysphoria**, meaning a general feeling of unhappiness, because it is not yet clear that children experience depression in the same way as adults. We will use the terms interchangeably.

Parental conflict and divorce, the death of a family member (particularly a parent), or other traumatic life events may contribute to a child's depression, but relatively little research links specific family characteristics to children's depression. Hetherington and Martin (1986) conclude that "the theme that runs through all of the studies. . . is that childhood dysphoria is associated with unresponsive, uncaring parenting combined with some degree of parental overprotection" (p. 376). Research indicates that children of depressed parents tend to be depressed or exhibit other behavior problems (Billings & Moos, 1985; Forehand, McCombs, & Brody, 1987). In other studies, Cole and Rehm (1986) found that the standard-setting and rewarding behavior of mothers of depressed children differed from those of mothers of children who were not depressed. Mothers with depressed children tended both to set high standards for their children's performance and to seldom reward them for attempting to meet those standards. Thus their children constantly faced seemingly impossible expectations for performance and little recognition for accomplishment. If children internalize their mothers' standards and expectations, as seems likely, it is not surprising that those whose parents set high standards and provide few rewards experience dysphoric mood. (We will discuss depression in greater detail in Chapter 17.)

School Failure

The family's contribution to school failure in most cases plays a secondary role, for it is axiomatic that the school is responsible for the child's learning. Parents nevertheless contribute toward or detract from their child's success at school in several ways: their expressed attitudes toward school, academic learning, and teachers; their own competence or lack of success in school; and their disinterest in or reinforcement of appropriate school-related behaviors, such as attending regularly, completing homework, reading, and studying. Gesten, Scher, and Cowen (1978) found that "homes characterized by lack of educational stimulation appear to produce children who are prone to learning problems" (p. 254).

Studies of the effects of major psychiatric problems of parents on their children's competence in school show that the way peers and teachers perceive students cannot be predicted simply by the fact that their parents are considered to be mentally ill (Baldwin, Cole, & Baldwin, 1982). Rather, competence in school depends on the warmth and balance of parent-child interactions. A parent may have a major psychiatric problem, but if the parent and other family members are emotionally available and responsive and willing to interact sensitively, the youngster's school functioning is not necessarily affected by parental pathology.

Thomas et al. (1968) found that interaction between the child's temperament and the parents' behavior management techniques could add to or subtract from the child's adaptation to school (see also Thomas, 1971). When parental standards and family interactions differed markedly from the standards and characteristic situations the child faced at school, a problem sometimes resulted. This finding is consistent with what we know about cultural conflict and disordered behavior (see Chapter 11). If teachers, peers, or both rejected or ridiculed the child for behaving in ways that were acceptable at home, the child sometimes then developed a behavior disorder. "Easy" children for the parents then became "difficult" at school.

Hal

The parents of 4-year-old Hal... worried because he let the other children take his toys, did not defend himself but, instead, came home crying. This behavior represented qualities in their son of which his parents did not approve and never had approved. The basic issue, however, was that the other children as a group ganged up on Hal because of his inappropriately formal manners and his habit of asking with meticulous politeness to share their toys; they saw him as a strange creature. Hal's formalistic manners actually were the direct reflection of the standards and approaches imposed by his parents, who were not aware that his politeness would cause him to become the target of teasing. They considered the other children badly brought up but, even so, they wanted their son to be manly and capable of standing up for his rights.

Isobel

Another child, Isobel, ... who presented with a learning difficulty in second grade, was of concern to her parents because they honored education highly and knew the youngster to be above average in intelligence. On the surface it appeared that the child had not adapted, despite her intellectual ability, to their academic standards. However, Isobel's learning difficulty stemmed from her unwillingness to take instruction, and this, in turn, derived from the parental focus on uniqueness, the right of each person to be individual. They encouraged self-expression in the child, and simultaneously she developed a disregard for rules in play with peer groups and in learning situations in school. When engaged in dramatic play, Isobel was outstanding in her creative imagination and no problems arose. When in the classroom, however, she did not consider the group directions to be her concern and expected individual instruction. The net result was failure to build an educational base because the environment simply had no provision for the child who refused to avail herself of group instruction and required, no matter how pleasantly, the teacher's entire attention. (Thomas et al., 1968, p. 88)

Differences between cultural standards or expectations of home and school, however, are not the only factor to consider. Parent-child relationships, especially parental discipline style, can make a big difference in how the child performs at school. In contrast to the foregoing cases, parents of difficult youngsters contributed, through management attuned to their children's temperaments, to making them easy—or at least easier than otherwise—at school. Jimmy, a difficult child whose parents managed him well by good-natured but firm and consistent routine, is an example.

Jimmy

Homework had been done haphazardly in the earliest grades. The parents then established a firm and unvarying rule of no television during the week and gave him a specific time, place, and set of conditions for doing his homework. The initial tantrums when these rules were applied gradually gave way to compliance, and the youngster gave his full attention to mastering the work. There was still periodic distress when new subject material was introduced, and Jimmy would become absolutely certain that he would never learn it. During these periods the child would slam his way in and out of rooms and assure his family that he was the dumbest boy in the class. The parents laughed through such sessions, knowing that these would soon be displaced, as they were but a minor aspect in the child's eventual good adaptation. (Thomas et al., 1968, p. 84)

Other research indicates the important role of parental discipline, parent-school relations, and parent-child relationships in school success and school failure. Hess and Holloway (1984) identified five ways in which parents encourage school success:

Mothers engage in high levels of verbal interaction with their children

Parents express clear expectations for achievement

Parents maintain a warm and encouraging relationship with their children

Parents use an authoritative style of discipline (controlling, directive, warm, and supportive, not hostile, rigid, or permissive)

Parents believe their children can and will learn

Dornbusch, Ritter, Leiderman, Roberts, and Fraleigh (1987) provide further evidence that authoritative families—those characterized by neither authoritarian nor permissive discipline—are associated with higher school achievement in adolescents. They characterize authoritative parental discipline as follows:

In their family communication, parents tell the youth to look at both sides of issues, they admit that the youth sometimes knows more, they talk about politics within the family, and they emphasize that everyone should help with decisions in the family; as a response to good grades, parents praise the student, and give more freedom to make decisions; as a response to poor grades, they take away freedom, encourage the student to try harder, and offer to help. (Dornbusch et al., 1987, p. 1247)

Families in which a coercive process is at work are likely to send students to school unprepared to comply with teachers' instructions, to complete homework assignments, or to relate well to their peers. Unprepared for the demands of school, these students are virtually certain to fail to meet reasonable expectations for academic performance and social interaction (Patterson, 1986b). Parents who are caught up in coercive interactions with their children are not likely to be much involved with their children's schooling; parents who are more involved with education and invest energy in monitoring and facilitating their children's progress at school tend to have young-sters who perform at a higher academic level (Stevenson & Baker, 1987).

IMPLICATIONS FOR EDUCATORS

With what we know about the family's role in children's behavior disorders, educators would be foolish to ignore the influence of home conditions on school performance and conduct. Still, blaming parents of troubled students is unjustified. Particularly in the case of childhood psychosis, evidence does not show that parents cause their children's problems. The teacher must realize that the parents of a disturbed youngster have undergone a great deal of disappointment and frustration and that they too would like to see the child's behavior improve, both at home and at school.

We find the strongest indicators of family causal contributions for antisocial behavior, although even for conduct disorder and delinquency, the assumption that parents are the sole cause is not justified. Educators must be careful not to become entangled in the same coercive process that may characterize the antisocial student's family life. Harsh, hostile, verbal or physical punishment at school is likely to function as a new challenge for antisocial students, who have probably been trained, albeit inadvertently, by their parents to step up their own aversive behavior in response to punishment. To win the battle with such students, school personnel must employ the same strategies that are recommended for parents—clearly stated expectations for behavior, an emphasis on positive attention for appropriate conduct, and calm, firm, nonhostile and reasoned punishment for misbehavior.

In light of numerous studies showing that parents can be helped to intervene successfully in their children's behavior disorders, the educator should try to enlist the parents' cooperation. Although the teacher may be successful in working directly with parents, obtaining the help of a school psychologist, social worker, liaison teacher, or other professional whose role includes parent training may be necessary.

SUMMARY

The nuclear family provides the context for early nurturance, so it is not surprising that people tend to look to the family as a likely source of deviant behavior. Family factors do not account for children's disordered behavior, however, except in complex interaction with other factors. Some family factors, notably conflict and coercion, are known to increase a youngster's risk for developing a behavior disorder. No one knows why some children are more vulnerable to risk factors than others.

An interactional-transactional model of family influence suggests that children and parents exert reciprocal effects; children affect their parents' behavior as surely as parents affect their children's. We can view both child abuse and conduct disorder in terms of the interactions and transactions of parents and their children. In both cases, parent and child become involved in an aversive cycle of negative reinforcement; each escalates behavior that is aversive for the other until someone wins, obtaining reinforcement by getting the other person to withdraw from the battle. The youngster's difficult temperament and the parent's lack of coping skills may contribute to the initial difficulty; the coercive process then grows from nagging, whining, and yelling to more serious and assaultive behavior such as hitting.

Family form and parental discipline relate to children's behavior problems. Assumptions regarding the strengths and weakness of the traditional family unit may need to be reconsidered because of the prevailing high rates of divorce and single-parent families. Divorce does not usually produce chronic behavior disorders in children, although we can expect temporary negative effects.

The style of parental discipline is a significant factor in behavioral development. Although there may not be a single best style of discipline, one style is consistently associated with behavior disorders: discipline that is at once harsh and capricious, while the parent provides lax supervision.

The idea that parents cause their children to have schizophrenia or autism has been discredited, although families of psychotic children may experience stress because of the children's severe disabilities. Family contributions to juvenile delinquency are similar to family contributions to conduct disorder. Families of antisocial youngsters who steal, however, appear to be characterized by lower rates of coercive behavior than families of antisocial youngsters who do not steal. Moreover, parents of stealers appear to be more detached from their children and to provide less supervision. Family contributions to anxiety-withdrawal and depression are not well understood. Parental behavior, especially style of discipline, verbal interactions with their children, expressed attitudes toward school, expectations that their children will learn, and involvement with the school affect children's school performance and conduct.

Educators should be concerned about the family's influence on children's conduct at school, but they must not blame parents for children's misbehavior. School personnel must avoid becoming enmeshed in the same coercive process that antisocial students are probably experiencing at home and should use the same intervention strategies that are recommended for parents.

10

School Factors

As you read this chapter, keep these guiding questions in mind:

- ☐ Why should educators consider how the school might contribute to the development of disordered behavior?
- ☐ What do we know about the intelligence of students with behavior disorders?
- ☐ With what academic skill levels should teachers of disturbed students be prepared to deal?
- ☐ What characteristics of student behavior are associated with success in school?
- ☐ What behavioral characteristics are most likely to be associated with school failure?
- ☐ What is the relationship between school failure and later adjustment?
- ☐ How do educators demonstrate insensitivity to students' individual differences, and how might this insensitivity contribute to the development of undesirable conduct?
- ☐ What are appropriate expectations for students?
- ☐ How might inconsistent management in the classroom produce results similar to those produced by a coercive family process?
- ☐ How can one convince students that what they are asked to learn is functional and relevant to their lives?
- ☐ What reinforcement contingencies relate to student behavior and teacher attention in most classrooms?
- ☐ How can teachers use appropriate models to foster desirable classroom behavior?

THE APPEAL OF SCHOOL FACTORS

Educators need to scrutinize the role of the school in the development of behavior disorders, because the school environment is the causal factor over which teachers and principals have direct control. As we have seen in other chapters, conditions outside the school can influence students' in-school behavior. Some youngsters, of course, develop behavior problems before they begin school, but even if a child already has a behavior disorder, educators should consider how the school experience might ameliorate the problem or make it worse. And, since many youngsters do not exhibit behavior disorders until after they enter school, educators must recognize the possibility that the school experience could be a significant causal factor.

An ecological approach to understanding behavior includes the assumption that all aspects of a youngster's environment are interconnected; changes in one element of the ecology have implications for the other elements. Success or failure at school affects behavior at home and in the community; effects of school performance ripple outward. Consequently, success at school assumes even greater importance if a youngster's home and community environments are disastrous. Furthermore, prereferral strategies, required before a student is evaluated for special education, imply that the current classroom environment may be causally related to disordered behavior (see Chapter 6). Special educators recognize the importance of eliminating possible school contributions to misconduct before labeling the student as handicapped.

Besides the family, the school is probably the most important socializing influence on children and youth. In our culture, success or failure at school is tantamount to success or failure as a person; school is the occupation of all children and youth in our society—and sometimes it is their preoccupation. Academic success is fundamentally important for social development and postschool opportunity.

INTELLIGENCE

As mentioned in Chapter 6, intelligence tests are most reasonably viewed as tests of general learning in areas that are important to academic success. IQ refers only to performance on an intelligence test. IQs are moderately good predictors of how students will perform academically and how they will adapt to the demands of everyday life. Standardized tests are the best single means we have to measure IQ, even though performance on a test is not the only indicator of intelligence.

Intelligence of Mildly and Moderately Disturbed Students

Authorities on emotional disturbance have traditionally assumed that disturbed students fall within the normal range of intelligence. If the IQ falls below 70, the student is considered mentally retarded, even when behavior problems are a major concern. Occasionally, however, students with IQs in the retarded range are labeled *emotionally disturbed* or *learning disabled* rather than mentally retarded, on the presumption that emotional or perceptual disorders prevent them from performing up to their true capacity.

The average IQ for mildly and moderately disturbed students (those not considered psychotic) is in the low normal range, with a dispersion of scores from the severely mentally retarded to the highly gifted levels. Over the past 25 years, numerous studies have yielded the same general finding: average tested IQ for these students is in the low nineties (Bortner & Birch, 1969; Bower, 1981; Graubard, 1964; Kauffman et al., 1987; Lyons & Powers, 1963; Motto & Wilkins, 1968; Rubin & Balow, 1978). We have accumulated enough research on disturbed students' intelligence to draw this conclusion: although the majority of mildly and moderately disturbed students fall only slightly below average in IQ, a disproportionate number, compared to the normal distribution, score in the dull normal and mildly retarded range, and relatively few fall in the upper ranges. Research findings suggest a distribution like that in Figure 10.1. The hypothetical curve for mildly and moderately disturbed students shows a mean of about 90 to 95 IQ, with more students falling at the lower IQ levels and fewer at the higher levels than in the normal distribution. If this hypothetical distribution of intelligence is correct, then one can expect a greater-than-normal frequency of academic failure and socialization difficulties for mildly and moderately disturbed students.

Intelligence of Severely Disturbed (Psychotic) Students

Mental health professionals long suspected that psychotic students—those considered autistic or schizophrenic—are not really mentally retarded, even though they function at a retarded level in most areas of development. Kanner's (1943) description of early infantile autism strengthened the belief that such children are potentially normal in intelligence. DeMyer (1975) summarized Kanner's reasons for believing that autistic children have normal intelligence.

> The reasons for his belief were the presence of splinter skills, "intelligent" faces, few reports of motor dysfunction, and "refusal" to perform when age-appropriate items from intelligence tests were presented to them. One widely held theory

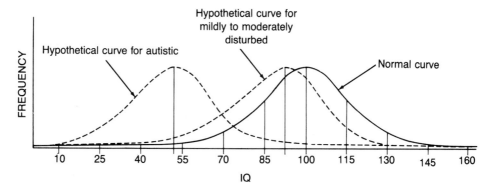

FIGURE 10.1
Hypothetical Frequency Distributions of IQ for Mildly to Moderately Disturbed and Autistic Students as Compared to a Normal Frequency Distribution

advanced to explain these "facts" was that most if not all autistic. . . children had anatomically normal brains and that relatively high splinter skills were a "true" reflection of their potential intelligence. If the right treatment key could be found, then the seriously delayed verbal intelligence would advance in an accelerated fashion to catch up with the splinter skills and with the norms of the child's chronological age. (pp. 109–110)

Within the past 25 years, data have been accumulated to indicate that most autistic children's IQs can be reliably determined and that the majority score in the moderately to severely mentally retarded range of intelligence (DeMyer, 1975; DeMyer et al., 1974; Lovaas et al., 1973; Prior & Werry, 1986; Rutter & Schopler, 1987). Only 20 to 25 percent of autistic children can be expected to score within the normal range of intelligence; few score far above average. On the basis of available data, the distribution of intelligence for autistic students is hypothesized as shown in Figure 10.1. The average IQ is probably around 50, with the vast majority of students falling between about 35 and about 70.

While the intelligence of schizophrenic students is generally higher than that of autistic students, the distribution for schizophrenic students is probably below that for the general population (Prior & Werry, 1986). If we were to plot a hypothetical distribution for schizophrenic students, it would be slightly lower than the distribution for mildly to moderately disturbed students.

Although severe behavior disorders occur across the entire spectrum of intelligence, they occur most frequently in individuals who have a lower than average IQ. Besides general intellectual deficiencies, psychotic children and youth tend to have particular problems dealing with tasks that require language or higher cognitive skills. These students' developmental retardation is associated with poorer prognosis; even with the best available behavioral interventions, it is often a life-long disability (Eggers, 1978; Prior & Werry, 1986). Advances in intensive early intervention, however, show promise for ameliorating or even eliminating the behavioral and cognitive deficits of a significant percentage of autistic students (Lovaas, 1987).

Implications of Low IQ

Research clearly suggests that students with behavior disorders tend to be lower than normal in IQ and that the most severely behaviorally disabled students also tend to be the lowest in IQ (DeMyer et al., 1974; Kauffman et al., 1987; Prior & Werry, 1986). The correlation between intelligence and level of behavior disorder does not imply a causal relationship. Even so, the IQs of disturbed students appear to be the best single predictor of educational achievement and later adjustment (see Prior & Werry, 1986). DeMyer (1975) and Rutter and Bartak (1973), for example, reported that their subjects' IQs at initial evaluation were good predictors of academic and social skill achievement in autistic children. The predictive power of IQ for less severely disturbed students' academic achievement and future social adjustment probably approximates the predictive power of IQ for students in the normal distribution.

Notwithstanding the bulk of available evidence, we may need to revise the conclusion that IQ is a good predictor of outcome for autistic students. Lovaas (1987) demonstrated that nearly half a group of autistic children who received intensive early intervention tested within normal limits on intelligence measures and were successful in school. These findings are a startling contrast to those of most researchers and must await replication by others. Nevertheless, Lovaas's results cannot be dismissed as an anomaly; the research meets rigorous scientific standards and suggests potential major revisions in assumptions about the nature of autism.

ACHIEVEMENT

Although academic achievement is usually assessed by standardized achievement tests, it is dangerous to place too much confidence in them, because they are not highly accurate measures of academic aptitude, nor highly precise measures of the academic attainment of the individual handicapped student. Scores on achievement tests do, however, allow comparisons between the performances of normative and disturbed groups, which are valuable in assessing and predicting disturbed students' school success.

Achievement of Mildly and Moderately Disturbed Students

The academic achievement of disturbed and delinquent students has been studied for many years (Bower, 1981; Graubard, 1964; Kauffman et al., 1987; Motto & Wilkins, 1968; Rubin & Balow, 1978; Silberberg & Silberberg, 1971; Stone & Rowley, 1964; Tamkin, 1960). Collectively, research leads to the conclusion that most mildly and moderately disturbed students are academically deficient even taking into account their mental ages, which are typically slightly below those of their chronological age mates. Although some disturbed students work at grade level and a very few are academically advanced, most function a year or more below grade level in most academic areas.

Achievement of Severely Disturbed (Psychotic) Students

Compared to their age mates, few autistic students are academically competent. Many require training in self-help skills (toileting, dressing, feeding, bathing, grooming), language, and play skills. The highly intelligent, academically competent autistic student is a rarity; most autistic children are severely deficient in academic attainment and require prolonged, directive instruction in a carefully controlled teaching environment to attain functional academic skills (Koegel et al., 1982; Lovaas, 1987; Schreibman, Charlop, & Britten, 1983).

The behavioral characteristics of children diagnosed as schizophrenic tend to persist into adulthood (Howells & Guirguis, 1984). Although there are no data specific to learning, schizophrenic students might be expected to have problems in academic achievement on the basis of their lower than average IQs, problems with language, attention, perception, and logic, and their deficits in social skills (Prior & Werry, 1986).

Implications of Academic Underachievement

Low achievement and behavior problems go hand in hand; they are highly related risk factors. Figure 10.2 shows data from a study in which children with a greater number of social problems were found to be more likely to have low achievement test scores. In a sample of 1,449 children in grades 2 through 5, Kupersmidt and Patterson (1987) found that about one-third of those who had three or more social problems scored below the 25th percentile on standardized achievement tests; fewer than 10 percent of the children who had no social problems obtained such low achievement scores. Social problems were defined by teacher and peer ratings of aggressive behavior, shy-withdrawn behavior, peer rejection, depression, low self-esteem, low parental involvement in education, and poor grooming and/or personal hygiene.

In most cases it is not clear whether disordered behavior causes underachievement or vice versa. Sometimes the weight of evidence may be more on one side of the issue than the other, but in the majority of instances the precise nature of the relationship is elusive. As we will see, there is reason to believe that underachievement and disordered behavior affect each other reciprocally. Disordered behavior apparently makes academic achievement less likely, and underachievement produces social consequences that are likely to foster inappropriate behavior. In any case, the effects of educational failure on future opportunity cause alarm for the plight of disturbed students.

> Educational attainment and opportunity are linked in many ways. Abundant evidence supports the view that education affects income, occupational choice, social and economic mobility, political participation, social deviance, etc. Indeed, educational attainment is related to opportunity in so many ways that the two terms seem inextricably intertwined in the mind of the layman and in the findings of the social scientist. (Levin, Guthrie, Kleindorfer, & Stout, 1971, p. 14)

FIGURE 10.2

Percent of Children with Academic Problems as a Function of Social Problems

From "Interim Report to the Charlottesville Public Schools on Children at Risk" by J. B. Kupersmidt and C. J. Patterson, 1987, unpublished manuscript, University of Virginia, Charlottesville, Virginia. Reprinted by permission.

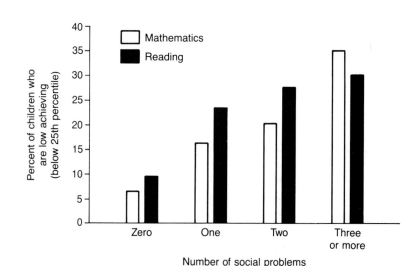

Autistic students and others with severe disabilities that require focus on self-care and daily living skills must achieve these nonacademic skills or be consigned to lives of stunted development and continuing dependence.

BEHAVIOR PREDICTIVE OF SCHOOL SUCCESS AND FAILURE

Intelligence tests were devised in the early twentieth century for predicting children's academic success or failure. Although IQ is not infallible, especially in the individual case, it is a fairly accurate predictor of academic success or failure on a statistical basis. Educational researchers have also become interested in identifying the overt classroom behavioral characteristics associated with academic accomplishment, in the hope that teachers can teach those behaviors. For instance, if attentiveness is found to correlate positively with achievement, then teaching students to pay better attention might improve academic performance. Similarly, if achievement correlates negatively with certain dependency behaviors, then reducing dependency behaviors might be successful. Implicit here is the assumption that the identified behavioral characteristics will have more than a correlational relationship to achievement; there will be a *causal* link between certain overt behaviors and achievement.

The causal relationship between overt classroom behavior and academic success or failure is not entirely clear. Although a frequent strategy of teachers and educational researchers has been to modify behavior (such as task attention) in the hope of improving performance on academic tasks, direct modification of academic skills has proved most effective in preventing failure or remediating deficits (Hallahan, Lloyd, Kauffman, & Loper, 1983; Lloyd & De Bettencourt, 1986). Direct reinforcement of academic performance has in some cases eliminated classroom behavior problems (Hallahan & Kauffman, 1975). Yet, classroom success or failure is determined by more than academic competence; doing the academic work is critical, but it is not the whole story.

Success and failure in school correlate with a variety of academic and social characteristics (McKinney, Mason, Perkerson, & Clifford, 1975; Shinn, Ramsey, Walker, Stieber, & O'Neill, 1987; Spivack & Swift, 1966, 1977; Swift & Spivack, 1968, 1969a, 1969b, 1973; Walker & McConnell, 1988; see also Hess & Holloway, 1984). Students who are low achieving and socially unsuccessful tend to exhibit the following characteristics:

Engaging in behavior that requires teacher intervention or control, such as teasing, annoying, or interfering with others

Overly dependent on the teacher for direction

Difficulty paying attention and concentrating

Offer fewer ideas and bring fewer materials to class than high achievers

Become upset under pressure

Work is sloppy and impulsively done

Low self-confidence; believe they cannot do what is expected

Highly opinionated and dogmatic, unreceptive to others' opinions

Exhibit nervousness and anxiety and/or social withdrawal

High achieving and popular students, on the other hand, exhibit the following characteristics:

Establish rapport with the teacher, engage in friendly conversation before and after class, and are responsive in class

Engage in appropriate verbal interaction, asking relevant questions, volunteering, and participating in class discussions

Do more than the minimum work required, taking care to understand directions and to master all details

Exhibit originality and reasoning ability, being quick to grasp new concepts and apply them and preparing homework in an interesting way

Walker and McConnell (1988) have devised a 43-item rating scale to identify the social skills deficits related to school failure of elementary age pupils, *The Walker-McConnell Scale of Social Competence and School Adjustment*. It identifies teacher-preferred behavior for success during classroom instruction, peer-preferred behavior, and interpersonal social skills. Teacher-preferred social behavior includes items such as "Shows sympathy for others," "Accepts constructive criticism from peers without becoming angry," "Is sensitive to the needs of others," "Cooperates with peers in group activities or situations," and "Controls temper." Representative items indicating peer-preferred behavior are "Plays or talks with peers for extended periods of time," "Interacts with a number of different peers," "Makes friends easily with other children," "Plays games and activities at recess skillfully," and "Voluntarily provides assistance to peers who require it." Interpersonal social skills related to school adjustment are represented by items such as "Displays independent study skills," "Uses free time appropriately," "Attends to assigned tasks," "Has good work habits," and "Listens carefully to teacher directions and instructions for assignments." The extent to which students do not exhibit these characteristics indicates social deficits that put them at risk for school failure. Friendly, supportive, popular with peers, involved with learning, task-oriented, intelligent, creative, anxious to please—these are characteristics that serve students well in school, but are not the typical characteristics of students with behavior disorders.

SCHOOL FAILURE AND LATER ADJUSTMENT

Low IQ and academic failure often foretell difficulty for students. A higher proportion of those with low IQ and achievement than of students high in IQ and achievement will experience adjustment difficulties as adults. A high proportion of schizophrenic and antisocial adults are known to have exhibited low academic achievement as children (Bower et. al., 1960; Kazdin, 1987; Robins, 1966, 1986; Watt, Stolorow, Lubensky, & McClelland, 1970).

Low IQ and achievement alone do not spell disaster for later adjustment, however. Most mildly retarded youngsters, whose achievement may lag behind even their mental ages, do not turn into social misfits, criminals, or institutional residents in adult life; they are considered problems only during their school years (Edgerton,

1984). The same can probably be said of most youngsters with learning disabilities, whose academic retardation usually marks them as school failures (see Hallahan, Kauffman, & Lloyd, 1985). Even among mildly and moderately disturbed children and youth, the prognosis is not necessarily poor just because the student has a low IQ or fails academically.

Follow-back studies, which research the childhoods of adults diagnosed as psychotic, antisocial, or sociopathic through interviews and examination of the records of schools, clinics, and courts, provide adulthood prognoses for youngsters who exhibited certain characteristics (Bower, Shellhammer, & Daily, 1960; Robins, 1966, 1986; Watt, Stolorow, Lubensky, & McClelland, 1970; see also Garmezy, 1974; Robins, 1974, 1979). In general, these studies reveal that school failure is a part of the pattern identified as **premorbid** (predictive of later mental illness), especially for boys. Premorbid girls are more prone to withdrawal, immaturity, and introversion, whereas premorbid boys are more likely to show underachievement, negativism, and antisocial behavior (Watt et al., 1970; Robins, 1986). Without maladaptive behavior of some sort, however, low intelligence and low achievement in childhood are not highly predictive of disordered behavior in adulthood. School failure, then, cannot be considered by itself to cause adult social failure.

When school failure is accompanied by serious and persistent antisocial behavior—conduct disorder—the risk for mental health problems in adulthood is most grave. And the earlier the onset and the greater the number of antisocial behaviors, the greater the risk (cf. Kazdin, 1985, 1987; Loeber, 1982; Robins, 1966, 1979, 1986; Shinn et al., 1987; Walker et al., 1987). Even when conduct disorder is accompanied by low intelligence and low achievement, we must be careful in drawing causal inferences; if a causal connection does exist between achievement and antisocial behavior, however, then it has implications for education.

> It is well known. . . that children with antisocial behavior are usually seriously retarded in academic performance. We do not know at this point whether academic failure usually preceded or followed the onset of antisocial behavior. If experiencing academic failure contributes to the occurrence of antisocial behavior disorders, then it is clear that preventive efforts should include efforts to forestall failure through programs such as those currently endeavoring to improve the IQs and academic success of disadvantaged children either by educating their parents to stimulate them as infants or through a variety of educationally oriented daycare and preschool programs. (Robins, 1974, p. 455)

To reiterate, low IQ and school failure alone are not as highly predictive of adult psychopathology as when they are combined with conduct disorder. The outlook for a youngster is particularly grim when he or she is at once relatively unintelligent, underachieving, and highly aggressive or extremely withdrawn. If conduct disorder is fostered by school failure, then programs to prevent school failure may also contribute to prevention of antisocial behavior.

Intelligence, Achievement, and Antisocial Behavior

Given that antisocial behavior (for example, hostile aggression, theft, incorrigibility, running away from home, truancy, vandalism, sexual misconduct), low intelligence, and low achievement are interrelated in a complex way, it may be important to clarify their apparent interrelationship. Figure 10.3 shows a hypothetical relationship among the three characteristics. The various shaded areas in the diagram represent the approximate (hypothesized) proportions in which various combinations of the three characteristics occur. The diagram illustrates the hypothesis that relatively few youngsters who exhibit antisocial behavior are above average in IQ and achievement (area A); most are below average in IQ and achievement (area D), and a few are below average in only IQ (area B) or only achievement (area C). Whereas the majority of underachieving youngsters are low in IQ (areas D and G), they are usually not antisocial (area G is much larger than area D). Some youngsters are low in IQ but not in achievement (areas B and E) or vice versa (areas C and F), but relatively few of these youngsters are antisocial (area E is much larger than area B, and area F is much larger than area C).

Keep in mind that additional factors enter the picture to determine the adult outcome for children and youth with a given combination of characteristics. The severity of the antisocial behavior, the parents' behavioral characteristics, and perhaps parental socioeconomic circumstances influence the probability that behavior difficulties will persist into adulthood. To the extent that youngsters exhibit many antisocial behaviors in a variety of settings and at high frequency, have parents who are themselves antisocial or abusive, and come from a lower social class, they have a greater

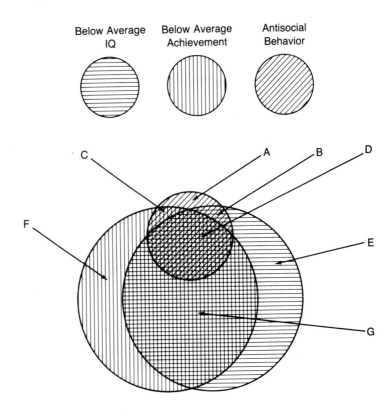

FIGURE 10.3
Hypothetical Relationships Among Below Average IQ, Below Average Achievement, and Antisocial Behavior

chance of being hospitalized as mentally ill or incarcerated as a criminal when they become adults (Loeber, 1982; Robins, 1979). Also, remember that many children and youth who are low in intelligence, low in achievement, antisocial, or some combination of these do not exhibit serious behavior disorders as adults. Any prediction of adult behavior based on childhood behavioral characteristics is subject to a great degree of error for the individual case.

THE SCHOOL'S CONTRIBUTIONS TO BEHAVIOR DISORDERS

Below average intellectual functioning and below expected academic achievement are characteristics of students with behavior disorders. Combined with conduct disorder, low intelligence and achievement provide a gloomy forecast for adulthood. Although school failure is not known to cause behavior disorders, it is a frequent concomitant of maladaptive behavior and a possible contributor to maladjustment. On the other hand, one could argue that maladaptive behavior makes academic success unlikely and contributes to school failure. Logically, one might take the position that school can contribute to both social difficulties and academic incompetence.

The demands of school and the student's social and academic repertoire probably affect each other reciprocally. A circular reaction occurs between the student and the social structure of the classroom (Glidewell, 1969; Glidewell, Kantor, Smith, & Stringer, 1966). Students who are healthy, intelligent, upper-middle class, high achieving, high in self-esteem, and adroit in interpersonal skills enter the classroom at a distinct advantage. They are likely to make approach responses to others, who in turn are likely to respond positively; and these advantaged students will be sensitive to others' responses toward them and able to use their intelligence to further enhance their personal power and social status. Intelligence and achievement beget social acceptability, self-esteem, accurate social perception, and status, all of which in turn induce positive social responses from others and facilitate achievement. This perspective on the student's reciprocal interaction with the social ecology of the classroom is entirely consistent with recent research (cf. Hess & Holloway, 1984). Moreover, the same coercive process found in families of antisocial boys (Patterson, 1986a, 1986b) can be found in schools. Among their peers and in interactions with teachers and administrators, students with conduct disorders may be caught in negative reinforcement traps. Educators (like parents) and classroom peers (like siblings) can become entangled in escalating contests of aversiveness, in which the individual who causes greater pain is the winner, obtaining negative reinforcement and digging in for the next round of conflict.

How the school affects a student's emotional or behavioral development depends, at least to some extent, on his or her characteristics upon entering the educational system. The same type of interaction between the student's temperament and the parents' child-rearing techniques appears to occur between the student's temperament and the school's social and academic demands. The student who is slow to approach others, has irregular work habits, is slow to adapt to new situations, and is predominantly negative in mood is most likely to have difficulty in school, though any temperamental characteristic is susceptible to modification with proper handling (Thomas et al., 1968).

The school, like the family and biological factors, does not operate unilaterally to determine students' behavioral development, but we can identify classroom conditions and teacher reactions to pupil behavior that make behavioral difficulties more likely to occur or that could be changed to reduce the likelihood of behavior disorders (Gelfand et al., 1986). There are six specific, but not mutually exclusive, ways the school might contribute to development of disordered behavior and academic failure:

1. Insensitivity to students' individuality
2. Inappropriate expectations for students
3. Inconsistent management of behavior
4. Instruction in nonfunctional and irrelevant skills
5. Destructive contingencies of reinforcement
6. Undesirable models of school conduct

Besides these, factors such as crowded and deteriorated schools and classrooms are associated with aggression and other problems (McAfee, 1987; Rutter, Maughan, Mortimer, Ouston, & Smith, 1979). The physical conditions under which students are taught will surely affect their behavior for better or worse.

Insensitivity to Students' Individuality

Special educators of all persuasions—psychoanalytic, psychoeducational, humanistic, ecological, and behavioral—recognize the necessity of meeting pupils' individual needs. Some speculate, in fact, that the large proportion of school children identified as having learning and behavior disorders reflects the refusal of the education system to accommodate individual differences (Reynolds, Wang, & Walberg, 1987; Rubin & Balow, 1971). While not making reasonable accommodations to individual needs undoubtedly contributes to some students' failure or maladjustment, reasonable requirements for conformity to rules and standards clearly do not account for the failure or deviance of many others.

Rigidity and failure to tolerate differences do demand consideration, however. By making the same academic and behavioral requirements of each student, schools can force many students who are only slightly different from most into roles of academic failures or social deviants. Through inflexibility and stultifying insistence on sameness, schools can create conditions that inhibit or punish healthy expression of individuality. In an atmosphere of regimentation and repression, many students will respond with resentment, hostility, vandalism, or passive resistance to the system (see Mayer, Nafpaktitis, Butterworth, & Hollingsworth, 1987).

Thus, by squelching individuality and demanding uniformity, schools may contribute to learning and behavior problems instead of facilitating optimum development. For students unfortunate enough to differ more than slightly from the norm in learning or behavior, the message in some classrooms is clear: "To be yourself is to be bad, inadequate, or unacceptable." These students' self-perceptions are likely to become negative, their perceptions of social situations distorted, and their intellectual efficiency and motivation weakened. They can become caught in a self-perpetuating cycle of conflict and negative influence as described by Long (1974) and Glidewell et al. (1966) for school environments and by Patterson and his colleagues for family environments (Patterson, 1982, 1986b).

Insensitivity to individuals does not, of course, emanate from the school as an abstraction. Administrators, teachers, and other pupils are the persons who are sensitive or insensitive to expressions of individuality. School administrators can create a tolerant or a repressive mood in the way they deal with students and in the way they deal with adults. Teachers are primarily responsible for the classroom emotional climate and for how restrictive or permissive, individualized or regimented the student's school day will be. Peers may demand strict conformity regarding dress, speech, or deportment for social acceptance, especially in the higher grades. On the other hand, peers may be an easygoing, open group in which a fellow student can find acceptance even though he or she is quite different from the group.

Although there is little experimental evidence to suggest that behavior disorders are caused by insensitivity, we can readily find anecdotal and descriptive evidence that insensitivity may be a feature of many students' school experience (Epstein, 1981; Rutter et al., 1979). Glidewell et al. (1966) found that the social structure of the classroom was profoundly affected by teacher behavior. When a teacher delegates power to students and shows acceptance of all pupils in the class, more pupil-to-pupil interaction, less interpersonal conflict and anxiety, and more autonomous work, independent thought, and moral responsibility tend to occur. Highly rigid, authoritarian teachers who show acceptance of only those pupils who please them most might be expected, then, to have students who exhibit many learning and behavior problems. Mayer et al. (1987) found correlations between vandalism and punitive school environments that did not recognize individual differences.

Thomas and Chess (1984) and Thomas et al. (1968) show that the growth of behavior disorders is accelerated by adults' failure to treat youngsters in accordance with their temperamental individuality. Richard's case illustrates how the rigidity of the school and the insensitivity of teachers and other students can play a part in creating behavior problems. In the first grade, Richard had temper tantrums (up to five per day), and the school threatened to force his parents to withdraw him unless both they and Richard undertook psychiatric treatment.

Richard

Initially, the tantrums were precipitated whenever Richard objected to stopping what he was doing and moving on to a new activity. As time passed, the number of incidents that would evoke a tantrum increased, especially since the other children had begun to laugh at his crying. Concurrently, he had begun, with much persistence, to ask his teacher that he be taught formal reading. This was not possible inasmuch as the school's educational philosophy emphasized reading readiness procedures in the first grade and the postponement of instruction in formal reading itself to the second or third grade. (Thomas et al., 1986, p. 154)

Richard's behavior greatly improved when his parents placed him in a different school where he was allowed to spend more time than other children on a given activity (such as reading or writing) before shifting to another task and received more instruction in reading, writing, and arithmetic. During the remainder of the first grade and throughout the second and third grades, his tantrums did not recur, because his teachers approved of his persistence in working on his assignments. In the fourth grade, however, his tantrums began again. One of the incidents in his fourth year at school is a particularly clear example of insensitivity on the part of teacher and peers.

Richard

Then a poster contest for public school children was announced. The teacher had obtained a specified number of poster papers, selected the children from the class who were to be permitted to enter the contest, and gave them paper. Richard did not get any and, quite innocently, assumed that it would be all right to get his own poster paper. He proceeded to do so and then brought in his finished poster. The teacher interpreted this as insubordination, scolded him for being disobedient, and tore up his poster. The other children laughed, and Richard erupted by flinging his notebook, which hit the teacher on the nose. The teacher reported this to the principal, which made the episode automatically an assault charge with mandatory dismissal of the child. (Thomas et al., 1968, p. 167)

The foregoing discussion is not intended as an indictment of all rules, regulations, or demands for conformity in the classroom or school. Certainly, reasonable rules must be maintained for the safety and well-being of all. No social institution can exist without some requirements of conformity, and one cannot interpret an appeal for tolerance of individual expression to mean that *anything* should be accepted. Nevertheless, insensitivity to students as individuals and needless repression of their uniqueness can contribute to behavior problems. Students like to have a piece of the action, and allowing them to participate in self-determination of their classroom lives often results in improved behavior and academic performance (Lovitt, 1977).

Inappropriate Expectations for Students

The expectations teachers hold for their students, and the expectations they should hold, are continuing sources of controversy in American education. Two facets of the problem of expectations are the effects of what teachers are led to believe about their students (especially the possible biasing effects of diagnostic or administrative labels) and teachers' classroom standards of behavior and academic performance.

The Biasing Effects of Labels

Ever since Rosenthal and Jacobson published *Pygmalion in the Classroom* (1968), many educators and critics of education have been concerned that teachers' expectations of students may become self-fulfilling prophecies (Weinstein, Marshall, Sharp, & Botkin, 1987). Dunn's now classic article, "Special Education for the Mildly Retarded—Is Much of It Justifiable" (1968), which was a rallying point for those opposed to the use of categorical labels in special education, added to the concern that students may fail because they are expected to fail. The assumption has been that a label, such as "emotionally disturbed," carries with it an expectation of misbehavior and lower academic performance. The teacher's lower expectation for students labeled "exceptional" will be communicated in subtle ways to them, and they will indeed fulfill this expectation. As it happens, students' expectations for themselves may also influence their performance (cf. Rappaport & Rappaport, 1975).

While we have no reliable experimental data to indicate that teachers' expectations in themselves influence students' behavior, it is plausible that teachers do behave differently toward pupils depending upon their expectations for them. If teachers have low expectations for a particular pupil, they may then treat that pupil differently than they treat another student for whom they have high expectations. The differences may involve types and difficulty of assignments and instructions, frequency of contact, amount of social praise and criticism, tone of responses to questions, objectivity of evaluation of performance, and other features of teacher behavior. Some differences in teacher behavior may be quite subtle and yet extremely powerful in their effects on students.

In early research on expectancy effects, Meichenbaum, Bowers, and Ross (1969) found that the teacher expectancy effect may be associated with changes in teacher behavior. Students for whom teachers were given the expectation that they would be potential intellectual bloomers improved significantly more in appropriate classroom behavior and objective measures of academic performance than control students for whom the expectation was not induced. Measurement of the teachers' behavior showed that they behaved differently toward students for whom the higher expectations were created, significantly increasing positive interactions or significantly decreasing negative interactions with the high expectancy pupils. Meichenbaum et al. (1969) concluded from their data: "It appears one means of modifying behavior of both teachers and pupils is to modify the teacher's perception or label of the students' academic potential" (p. 315).

If the hypothesis as to the relationship between teacher expectation and teacher behavior is correct, then it will be important to know whether labels that imply that a student's behavior is deviant carry with them a set of lowered expectations (see Herson, 1974). Studies by Foster, Ysseldyke, and Reese (1975) and Ysseldyke and Foster (1978) provide some evidence that the label "emotionally disturbed" may bias teachers toward an expectation of lower than normal academic performance and poorer than normal social adjustment. Foster et al. (1975) found that undergraduate and graduate special education students rated a normal child (shown on videotape in a variety of situations, including testing and free play) lower in behavior and performance if they were told the child was emotionally disturbed than if they were told the child was normal. Ysseldyke and Foster (1978) found the same biasing effect for the label "learning disabled" as for "emotionally disturbed." Admittedly, it is dangerous to generalize from these studies, but if "emotionally disturbed" and similar labels do negatively influence teachers' expectations, one might hypothesize this:

> A child is presented to the teacher bearing a deviancy label, and the teacher in turn approaches the child with a mental set based on preconceived expectancies. If the child shows signs of normalcy, these may, to some extent, alter the teacher's preconceived expectancies. This research suggests though that these normal behaviors can be misinterpreted as typical of negatively categorized children. Logic

dictates that an experimenter bias effect may then come into play, with the teacher behaving toward the child in ways consistent with the bias. If the child responds to the bias, he may in turn reinforce the teacher's expectancies. (Foster et al., 1975, p. 473)

Other research suggests that it is not necessarily the diagnostic or categorical label given to a student but the way behavior is characterized that sets teachers' expectations. DeStefano, Gesten, and Cowen (1977) compared the judgments of primary grade teachers and school mental health workers regarding hypothetical children with specific behavioral characteristics. The teachers viewed children with behavior problems as more difficult and less enjoyable to work with and as having a poorer prognosis than did the mental health workers. Coleman and Gilliam (1983) found that regular teachers in an elementary school had more negative attitudes toward students characterized as aggressive than toward those characterized as withdrawn from social contact. Lewin, Nelson, and Tollefson (1983) studied teachers' attitudes toward disruptive students and the changes that might be expected to occur in their attitudes toward disruptive children after they had successfully modified the children's disruptive behavior. They found that teachers carried negative, rejecting attitudes toward disruptive children, and, more importantly, the teachers' attitudes did not change after they reported success in decreasing the disruptive behavior. Clearly, teachers do tend to view disturbed students negatively, particularly if they are aggressive or disruptive (Johnson & Blankenship, 1984). These negative preconceptions likely carry expectations of negative teacher-pupil interactions and, perhaps, academic failure.

Which label—*emotionally disturbed* or *behaviorally disordered*—carries the more negative connotations for teachers? After studying teachers and teacher trainees' perceptions of students described by these two labels, Feldman et al. (1983) concluded that *behaviorally disordered* is significantly less negative in its meaning for teachers than is *emotionally disturbed*. Preservice and inservice teachers believed that children labeled *behaviorally disordered* were more teachable, more likely to be successful in a mainstream classroom, and more likely to have a good future than were children described as *emotionally disturbed*. Lloyd et al. (1987) reported similar findings.

The Effects of Classroom Standards

The research and speculation on effects of teacher bias does not lead logically to the conclusion that simply expecting normal behavior will help disturbed students improve. After all, it is quite clear that most disturbed students are lower in tested intelligence, academic achievement, and social adjustment than nondisturbed students; many are far below their age mates in numerous areas of development, and expecting normal performance is unrealistic. Perhaps a discrepancy between the child's ability and adults' expectations for performance contributes directly to the development of disordered behavior (Kirk, 1972). Kirk reasoned that teacher expectations that are too high or too low might contribute to the problem.

Kirk based his concept of discrepancy between potential and expectation on his own clinical observations and on extrapolations from experimental research with animals and children. He noted that experimental psychologists have found aggression, regression, and resignation to be frequent outcomes of frustration. Experimental situations in which animals or children were made to experience frustration caused the subjects to become aggressive in trying to reach their goal, to regress to an immature level of behavior, or to simply give up. Requiring students to perform in ways they cannot places them in a highly frustrating situation; a child may respond by becoming angry and upset, exhibiting silly, irrational, or immature behavior, or simply becoming truant. More direct evidence to support Kirk's hypothesis comes from Center, Deitz, and Kaufman (1982), who found that students' disruptive classroom behavior increased when they were given academic tasks that were too difficult for them. Kirk's discrepancy hypothesis is also consistent with research indicating that mothers of depressed children set high criteria for rewards, and then reward their children at a very low rate (Cole & Rehm, 1986). If the same high standard-low reward conditions prevail in the classroom, it is reasonable to assume the effect will be the same—the student's depression.

If expectations that are too low become self-fulfilling prophecies and if expectations that are too high are frustrating and depressing, then what level of expectation will avoid the risk of contributing to development of disordered behavior? Expectations for improvement are always in order, assuming, of course, that the teacher knows the student's current level of academic performance or adequate social behavior and can specify a reasonable level of improvement along a measurable dimension. If pupil and teacher define *reasonable* together, then the expectations should be neither too low nor too high.

Research does not suggest that teachers' expectations and demands are well attuned to disturbed students' abilities and characteristics. Investigating the standards and expectations of regular and special education teachers for students' academic performance and social-interpersonal behavior, Walker and Rankin (1983) found that teachers' expectations could be described as narrow, intense, and demanding. The typical teacher expressed little tolerance for pupils who could not keep up academically or who exhibited inappropriate social behavior. And teachers consistently saw youngsters' competence in peer relations as less important than academic competence; their expectations centered on behaviors related to academic adjustment. These findings suggest that teachers' expectations may be a significant problem for behavior disordered students regardless of whether they are in a special or regular class.

Elementary and secondary teachers' expectations and demands appear to be similar. Kerr and Zigmond (1986) studied the behavioral characteristics that high school teachers' considered critical for success and those they considered intolerable; their findings were similar to those of Walker and his associates, who studied elementary teachers' standards and expectations (Hersh & Walker, 1983; Walker & Rankin, 1983). Tables 10.1 and 10.2 list the skills elementary and high school teachers most often considered critical for success and those they considered intolerable. Note that students with externalizing problems, who act out aggressively or have conduct disorders, are extremely likely to fail to meet teachers' expectations and to violate teachers' standards of classroom decorum. Walker (1986) also reports that teachers resist placement in their classroom of a student who is at times uncontrollably aggressive, is **incontinent**, is **enuretic**, has deficient self-help skills, or is hyperactive. Given teachers' standards and expectations, it should not be surprising that disturbed

TABLE 10.1
Skills Considered Critical for Success in Regular Classrooms

1. Follows established classroom rules (85)
2. Listens to teacher instructions (84)
3. Can follow teacher-written instructions and directions (81)
4. Complies with teacher commands (78)
5. Does in-class assignments as directed (74)
6. Avoids breaking classroom rule(s) even when encouraged by a peer (67)
7. Produces work of acceptable quality given his/her skill level (67)
8. Has good work habits (e.g., makes efficient use of class time, is organized, stays on task, etc.) (67)
9. Makes her/his assistance needs known in an appropriate manner (64)
10. Copes with failure in an appropriate manner (64)
11. Uses academic tools correctly (63)
12. Uses classroom equipment and materials correctly (62)
13. Attends consistently to assigned tasks (60)
14. Can accept not getting his/her own way (59)
15. Expresses anger appropriately (58)
16. Listens while other students are speaking (56)
17. Observes rules governing movement around the room (53)
18. Behaves appropriately in nonclassroom settings, respects property and the rights of others (53)
19. Is honest with others (52)
20. Improves academic or social behavior in response to teacher feedback (51)
21. Questions rules, directions, or instructions that are not clear to her/him (51)
22. Has independent study skills (51)
23. Responds to requests and directions promptly (51)

Note: Items rated critical for success by 50 percent or more of secondary teachers in the study by Kerr and Zigmond (1986) (percentages indicated in parentheses following items). Items 1, 2, 4, 5, 6, 7, 9, 15, and 18 were nine of the ten items rated critical for success most often by elementary teachers in the study by Hersh and Walker (1983).

students and their teachers frequently disappoint each other, setting the stage for conflict and coercion.

We should not inappropriately generalize to all teachers, nor assume that high standards and low tolerance for misbehavior are undesirable. Walker (1986) reports great variability in teachers' responses to questions about their standards and tolerance; some teachers apparently make few demands and have great tolerance for deviance, and others are just the opposite. Compared to regular classroom teachers, special education teachers may be somewhat more tolerant of misbehavior and judge students' behavior as less deviant (Walker, 1986; Fabre & Walker, 1987; Safran & Safran, 1987. Teachers' expressed tolerance for troublesome behavior may be affected by several factors, including their self-perceived competence, the availability and quality of technical assistance, and the difficulty of the particular group of students they are teaching (Safran & Safran, 1987). Teachers who have higher standards and lower tolerance for disorderly behavior may also provide more effective instruction (Gersten, Walker, & Darch, 1988).

TABLE 10.2
Problems Considered Intolerable in Regular Classrooms

1. Engages in inappropriate sexual behavior (99)
2. Steals (98)
3. Is physically aggressive with others (98)
4. Behaves inappropriately in class when corrected (98)
5. Damages others' property (97)
6. Refuses to obey teacher-imposed classroom rules (97)
7. Disturbs or disrupts the activities of others (96)
8. Is self-abusive (96)
9. Makes lewd or obscene gestures (94)
10. Ignores teacher warnings or reprimands (94)
11. Creates a disturbance during class activities (93)
12. Cheats (93)
13. Is verbally aggressive with others (93)
14. Has tantrums (90)
15. Reacts with defiance to instructions or commands (90)
16. Uses obscene language (89)
17. Is inexcusably late for the beginning of class activities (86)
18. Does not ask permission to use others' property (85)
19. Forces the submission of peers by being dominant (82)
20. Engages in silly, attention-getting behavior (80)
21. Lies (77)
22. Argues and must have the last word in verbal exchanges (76)

Note: Items rated intolerable by 75 percent or more of secondary teachers in the study by Kerr and Zigmond (1986) (percentages indicated in parentheses following items). Items 1, 2, 3, 4, 5, 6, 8, 9, 10, and 14 were the ten items rated intolerable most often by elementary teachers in the study by Hersh and Walker (1983).

Inconsistent Management of Behavior

A major hypothesis underlying a structured approach to educating disturbed students is that a lack of structure or order in their daily lives contributes to their difficulties. When youngsters cannot predict adults' responses to their behavior, they become anxious, confused, and unable to choose appropriate behavioral alternatives. If at one time they are allowed to engage in a certain misbehavior without penalty and at another time are punished for the same misconduct, the unpredictability of the consequences of their behavior encourages them to act inappropriately. If they cannot depend on favorable consequences following good behavior, they have little incentive to perform well.

We find strong support for the contention that inconsistent behavior management fosters disordered behavior in the child development literature (Hetherington & Martin, 1986). If one can extrapolate from the findings that inconsistent parental discipline adversely affects children's behavioral development, then it seems highly likely that inconsistent behavior management techniques in the school will also have negative effects. Certainly one may surmise that capricious, inconsistent discipline in the classroom will contribute nothing toward helping students learn appropriate conduct. School-based studies of antisocial behavior, such as vandalism, also indicate a connection between punitive, inconsistent discipline and problem behavior (Mayer et al., 1987). Even though inconsistent management may not be the root of behavior disorders, it obviously contributes to perpetuation of behavioral difficulties.

Instruction in Nonfunctional and Irrelevant Skills

One way the school increases the probability that students will misbehave or be truant is in offering instruction for which pupils have no real or imagined use. Not only does this kind of education fail to engage pupils, it also hinders their social adaptation by wasting their time and substituting trivial information for knowledge that would allow them to pursue rewarding activities.

The problem of making education relevant to students' lives has plagued teachers for a long time. The question is more than whether the teacher or other adults know the instruction to be important for the student's future. To resolve the question, the youngster must be convinced that the learning he or she is asked to do is or will be important. The teacher must convince the student that the instruction is in some ways worthwhile, otherwise the classroom will be merely a place for the pupil to avoid or to disrupt. For some students with a history of school disorder, convincing them will require provision of artificial reasons to learn, such as extrinsic rewards for behavior and performance.

Destructive Contingencies of Reinforcement

From the viewpoint of behavioral psychology, the school can contribute to the development of behavior disorders in two obvious ways: by providing reinforcement for inappropriate behavior and by failing to provide reinforcement for desirable behavior. Ample evidence suggests that in many classrooms, destructive rather than constructive contingencies of reinforcement are in place—appropriate conduct typically goes unrewarded, while reinforcement for misconduct is frequent (Nelson, 1981; Strain, Lambert, Kerr, Stagg, & Lenkner, 1983). Yet a great deal of evidence suggests that constructive reinforcement contingencies can be arranged to teach appropriate behavior even to students whose behavior is seriously disordered (Kerr & Nelson, 1983; Kerr et al., 1987; Morris, 1985).

The classroom can offer many types of reinforcement, ranging from teacher praise to tangible reinforcers such as candy, trinkets, or money. Perhaps the most endemic reinforcer in the classroom is the teacher's attention. Time after time, experimental studies have shown that providing teacher attention during appropriate behavior but withholding it during undesirable behavior results in improvement (Kazdin, 1984; Morris, 1985; Nelson, 1981; Sherman & Bushell, 1975).

Consider that in many classrooms, contingencies of reinforcement are inadvertently arranged to promote the very behavior the teacher deems undesirable! Strain et al. (1983) corroborated the findings of several previous studies indicating that teachers tend to provide predominantly negative feedback to pupils and seldom reinforce appropriate behavior. The chance that any of the 130 children in their study would receive positive feedback (verbal compliment or gestural approval, such as a pat or hug) following compliance with a teacher's command, demand, or request was only one in 10. In addition, Strain et al. found that the 19 regular class teachers (kindergarten through third grade) they studied gave reinforcement (positive feedback) to poorly adjusted children following noncompliance behavior more often than they gave reinforcement for compliance. And the teachers tended to repeat the commands, demands, and requests more often for poorly adjusted than for well-adjusted pupils. Given these conditions, which apparently are common in classrooms, it is not surprising that many children's misbehavior becomes a greater problem as they advance through the grades. Fortunately, researchers have repeatedly demonstrated how changes in contingencies of reinforcement can improve children's behavior.

For decades, researchers have demonstrated how teacher attention and praise, as well as other reinforcers naturally available in the classroom, can be used to reduce misbehavior and increase teachers' positive control. In an early and now classic study, Hall, Panyon, Rabon, and Broden (1968) conducted an experiment in an inner-city sixth grade classroom (in which pupils exhibited high rates of disruption and other nonstudy behavior) that clearly illustrates the effects of teacher attention on appropriate behavior. They measured not only the time pupils spent in study behavior during a half-hour period each day, but also the teacher's attention to pupils who were engaged in study behavior during the period. As shown in Figure 10.4, the children spent only about 45 percent of their time studying, and the teacher seldom attended to children who were studying during the baseline phase (sessions 1 through 17). During the Reinforcement$_1$ phase, the teacher was told to attend more frequently to children who were studying, as shown in the graph of teacher attention to study. During this phase, studying students received more teacher attention for studying, and the pupils improved markedly in their study behavior. When, for the sake of experimentation, the teacher returned to his baseline mode of operation (paying little attention to pupils who were studying, as shown in the Reversal phase), study behavior dropped sharply. High rates of studying were then reinstated by returning to the procedure of having the teacher attend to studying children (as shown in the Reinforcement$_2$ phase). Postchecks up to five months later showed that the teacher was continuing to attend to studying children and the children were continuing to maintain a high percentage of study behavior. Similar effects have been demonstrated in numerous other studies.

Teachers are not the only school personnel who can effectively use positive attention to improve students' behavior. Copeland, Brown, and Hall (1974) found that having the school principal pay attention to appropriate pupil behavior was an effective means of improving problem behaviors shown by pupils in an inner-city elementary school. Chronically truant children began to attend school more often when the principal came into the classroom and gave them a few words of praise on the days they came to school. Low-achieving students improved their academic performance when they were sent to the principal's office for praise contingent on their achieving specified criteria. Having the principal recognize the improving students and the highest performing students in two classrooms resulted in an increase in pupils' achievement. By spending only a few minutes each day giving attention to desirable behavior, the principal was able to effectively improve academic and behavioral char-

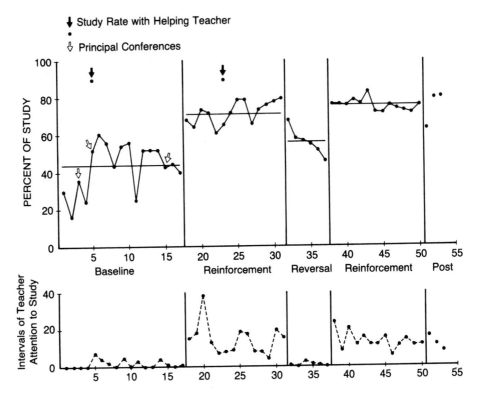

FIGURE 10.4
Record of Study Behavior and Teacher Attention for Study Behavior During Reading Period
in a Sixth Grade Classroom
(baseline = before experimental procedures; reinforcement₁ = increased teacher attention
for study; reversal = removal of teacher attention for study; reinforcement₂ = return to
increased teacher attention for study; post = follow-up checks up to 20 weeks after
termination of experimental procedures)

Note: From "Instructing Beginning Teachers in Reinforcement Procedures Which Improve Classroom Control" by R.V.
Hall, M. Panyan, D. Rabon, and M. Broden, 1968, *Journal of Applied Behavior Analysis, 1,* p. 317. Copyright 1968 by
Society for the Experimental Analysis of Behavior. Reprinted by permission.

acteristics. In all likelihood, any member of the school staff can be enlisted to use
contingent positive attention with similar results.

Compared to other types of intervention, rewarding consequences for desirable
behavior has often been found more effective and efficient. In a study with 12 seventh
grade boys who exhibited behavior problems, for example, Marlowe, Madsen, Bowen,
Reardon, and Logue (1978) found that teacher praise for following classroom rules,
especially when combined with token reinforcement (points exchangeable for snacks
on Friday), was effective in reducing rowdiness and off-task behaviors. Increasing
positive teacher attention to the boys' desirable behaviors was more effective by far
than a nondirective counseling approach.

The use of constructive consequences for adaptive behavior is consistent with a
conceptual model that assumes interactive effects of students' and teachers' responses.

An interactional or transactional model suggests that youngsters and adults exert reciprocal influence on each other. It is reasonable to believe that teachers' and problem students' mutual praise and criticism become important factors in the maintenance of behavior, and that mutual hostility could be defused beginning with either teacher or pupil. Polirstok and Greer (1977) trained an eighth grade girl who was frequently verbally abusive (and who received primarily disapproving, critical comments from her teachers) to increase her approving, complimentary comments to her teachers. In response to what they described as her remarkable socialization and new-found maturity, her teachers reversed their tendency to interact with her in a predominantly negative way. Morgan, Young, and Goldstein (1983) trained three behaviorally disordered boys in an elementary school to recruit social reinforcement and assistance from their teachers. The boys were trained to prompt their teachers to offer help on academic tasks, praise their teachers for helping them, and prompt their teachers to give them approval for good behavior and correct work. These studies demonstrated that destructive contingencies of reinforcement are not one-sided; classroom harmony and disharmony are a function of both teacher and student conduct. In the typical educational setting, however, the teacher is responsible for making the first move toward providing positive, constructive consequences for desirable behavior.

Students who have social adjustment problems are usually at odds with their peers as well as their teachers. The same type of mutual hostility and negative reciprocity that characterizes exchanges between some teachers and students also appears in social interactions of rejected students and their peers. Polirstok and her colleagues (Greer & Polirstok, 1982; Polirstok, 1986, 1987; Polirstok & Greer, 1986) report success in teaching adolescents with behavior problems to serve as tutors for their peers. Both tutors and tutees have benefited academically from the peer tutoring program. The problem students who served as tutors improved their on-task behavior and engaged in more positive reciprocal responses with their peers. A critical component of the tutoring program is the teacher's awarding points to tutors for giving verbal approval to tutees (Polirstok & Greer, 1986). By initiating reciprocal approval during tutoring, teachers apparently set in motion an interaction style that made the school a much more hospitable environment for everyone. Tutors and tutees exchanged approval; teachers rewarded tutors for their reinforcement of tutees; and tutors and tutees made more academic progress and behaved more appropriately in classes, rewarding teachers for their efforts and setting the stage for continued reciprocity of approval. Polirstok explains the benefits:

> If, as the evidence suggests, problematic adolescents can be taught to earn natural reinforcement in the environment, a unique shaping process between the school and the tutor will ensue. As a result of this shaping process, school life will become more reinforcing for tutors, who, in turn, will improve their academic and social behaviors and, as a consequence, will merit additional reinforcement from the school. (1986, p. 209)

Training students to tutor their peers is not a venture to undertake lightly (Gerber & Kauffman, 1981). Especially when the tutors are students with serious behavior problems, training and monitoring the tutors require considerable time and effort. Nevertheless, this strategy has demonstrated success in maintaining students with behavioral disorders in mainstream settings (Polirstok, 1987).

In summary, abundant empirical evidence shows that student's classroom behavior can be altered by manipulating the contingencies of reinforcement, even when the reinforcement is so natural a part of the classroom as teacher and peer attention. One needs neither a great backlog of classroom observation nor great acumen to see the potential implications of this evidence in the school's contributions to the development of behavior disorders. Students whose behavior is a problem often receive abundant attention for misbehavior but little or no attention for appropriate conduct. Even though the attention they receive for misbehavior is often in the form of criticism or punishment, it is still attention and is likely to reinforce whatever they are doing at the time it is dispensed. The effect of attention for misbehavior and nonattention for good deportment is likely to be perpetuation of the miscreant's deeds, regardless of the intentions of the teacher or other adult.

Undesirable Models of School Conduct

Children and youth are great imitators. Much of their learning is the result of watching others and mimicking their behavior. Youngsters are particularly likely to imitate the

Maltreatment in the Classroom

"Verbal abuse of kids in classrooms is rather common, especially in athletics," says Patrick Lynch, a professor of school law at Pennsylvania State University who has researched legal remedies for emotional abuse in school.

According to Lynch, educators who call children names like "stupid," "dummy" or "fat slob" and otherwise behave in ways meant to embarrass them typically defend their actions as a kind of stimulus or motivation. "Nothing in psychological research demonstrates [that] any positive value comes from verbal abuse," he says.

Research does show, however, that psychological injury can stem from verbal abuse. "There are unfortunate consequences," says Lynch. "Kids can be ruined. We don't know [to] what extent those who do suffer are affected. A lot of kids can shrug it off. But why take the risk?"

Cases of maltreatment in the classroom are easier to resolve than in the home, primarily because society more readily recognizes the boundaries in the teacher-child interaction than in the parent-child relationship. While cases against teachers have been brought to court under charges of violation of the civil rights law, of defamation, even of educational malpractice, the legal system consistently has seen it as a matter of administrative discipline. "The most common and only feasible remedy is teacher dismissal," says Lynch, adding that the dismissal usually results from incompetency charges rather than psychological abuse charges.

There have been exceptions. Lynch reports a Pennsylvania case in 1977 in which the teacher who called a 12-year-old girl a "slut" and a "dog" was fired solely on the basis of verbal abuse. "The psychological dimension of this being recognized in court is quite new and is happening more frequently," says Lynch. "We're not acting in a gray area that way. We know from studies that . . . you don't call kids names, you don't dump on them and you don't diminish them."

From "Child Abuse: The Emotional Side. Some Scars Aren't Found on the Body," by Don Oldenburg. *The Washington Post*, Tuesday, September 22, 1987.

behavior modeled by people who are socially or physically powerful, attractive, and in command of important reinforcers (Bandura, 1986). Understandably, the examples teachers set strongly influence the way students approach their academic work and the way they behave. Rutter et al. (1979) point out that "pupils are likely to be influenced—either for good or ill—by the models of behaviour provided by teachers both in the classroom and elsewhere" (p. 189). Exemplary behavior on the part of the teacher encourages like conduct in pupils.

Teachers whose attitude toward academic work is cavalier, who treat others cruelly or disrespectfully, or who are disorganized, for example, may foster similar undesirable attitudes and conduct in students. The box, "Maltreatment in the Classroom," suggests how teachers sometimes provide not merely destructive consequences, but occasionally outrageous models for their pupils.

Peers exert considerable social pressure on students' behavior in school, particularly at the high school level. Schools in which high status students refuse to perform academic tasks or exhibit serious misbehavior with impunity are likely to see the spread of academic failure and social misconduct (Arnold & Brungardt, 1983; Rutter et al., 1979).

IMPLICATIONS FOR EDUCATORS

The teacher of disturbed students must be prepared to work with pupils who are intellectually and academically deficient as well as deviant in their social behavior, although some disturbed students are superior intellectually and academically. Teaching disturbed students demands not only the ability to instruct pupils with an extremely wide range of intellectual and academic levels, but also the ability to teach social and other nonacademic behaviors that make scholastic success possible, such as good work habits, attention strategies, and independence. The most crucial tasks of the teacher as a preventive agent are to foster academic success and lessen the student's antisocial conduct. Academic failure and antisocial behavior predict limited future opportunities and probable future maladjustment.

The most valuable perspective for the teacher is to examine the student's present environment to detect factors that contribute to disordered behavior and those that encourage desirable behavior. The teacher's primary task is to modulate the school environment in ways that will contribute to adaptive, prosocial behavior and academic growth.

SUMMARY

The role of the school in causing behavior disorders is a particularly important consideration for educators. In our society, school failure is tantamount to personal failure. The school environment is not only critically important for social development, but is the factor over which educators have direct control.

As a group, students with behavior disorders score below average on intelligence tests and are academic underachievers. The behavior disturbed students exhibit is inimical to school success. Disordered behavior and underachievement appear to influence each other reciprocally; in an individual case, which causes the other is not as important as recognizing that they are interrelated. Academic failure and low intelligence, when combined with antisocial behavior or conduct disorder, portend social adjustment problems in adulthood.

The school may contribute to the development of behavior disorders in children in several ways:

- ☐ School administrators, teachers, and other pupils may be insensitive to the student's individuality.
- ☐ Teachers may hold inappropriate expectations for students.
- ☐ Teachers may be inconsistent in managing students' behavior.
- ☐ Instruction may be offered in nonfunctional (that is, seemingly irrelevant) skills.
- ☐ School personnel may arrange destructive contingencies of reinforcement.
- ☐ Peers and teachers may provide models of undesirable conduct.

Teachers of students with behavior disorders must be prepared to teach youngsters who are underachieving and difficult to instruct, and instruction must be provided in both academics and social skills.

11

Cultural Factors

As you read this chapter, keep these guiding questions in mind:

☐ How do conflicts between cultures create stress for children and youth?

☐ What steps can educators take to avoid the problems of bias and discrimination against students whose cultures differ from their own?

☐ Besides family and school, what major cultural factors may contribute to behavioral deviance? Why is it difficult to evaluate the effects of these factors?

☐ What relationships have been established between TV viewing and children's antisocial and prosocial behavior?

☐ By what processes do the mass media influence behavior?

☐ What types of behavior characterize high status peers and youngsters who are rejected by their peers?

☐ What social skills should we teach youngsters who are rejected by their peers, and how should we teach the skills?

☐ How would you characterize a neighborhood that provides support for development of children's appropriate social behavior?

☐ What conclusions can we draw about the effects on behavior of urbanization, ethnicity, and social class?

THE APPEAL OF CULTURAL FACTORS

Neither families nor schools include all the social influences that determine how youngsters behave. Children, families, and teachers are part of a larger culture that molds their behavior. Parents and teachers tend to hold values and set behavioral standards and expectations that are consistent with those of the cultures in which they live and work. Children's attitudes and behavior gravitate toward the cultural norms of their families, peers, and communities. Hetherington and Martin (1986) note that we must evaluate family factors in the context of cultural differences and changes.

> The patterns of parenting associated with adaptive or deviant behavior in children may differ in an inner-city environment, an affluent suburb, or an isolated Virginia mountain hollow, in times of war and peace, economic stability or depression. . . . It may be that results of the studies made in the 1960s have little relevance for today's changing families and that the findings of current studies will tell us little about American families in the 1990s. (p. 333)

When the child's, family's, or school's values or expectations conflict with other cultural norms, behavioral development may be adversely affected (Hinde, 1986; Willis et al., 1983). That is, to the extent that different cultural forces tug and pull a youngster's behavior in different directions, they create conflicting expectations and increase the probability that he or she will violate cultural norms and be labeled deviant. Comer (1988) notes that "Differences between home and school—whether of class, race, income, or culture—always create potential conflict" (p. 37). It is not surprising, therefore, that researchers have given a great deal of attention to cultural factors that contribute to disordered behavior.

CONFLICTING CULTURAL VALUES AND STANDARDS

It is easy to find examples of conflicting cultural values and standards and the stress they create for children and youth. Television shows, movies, and magazines glamorize the behavior and values of high status models that are incompatible with the standards of many children's families; youngsters' imitation of these models results in disapproval from parents. Religious groups may proscribe certain behaviors that are normative in the larger community (such as dancing, attending movies, dating, masturbating), and youngsters who conform to these religious teachings may be rejected by peers, stigmatized, or socially isolated, while those who violate the proscriptions may feel extreme guilt. The values children attach to certain possessions or behavior because they are highly regarded by their peers or teachers (such as wearing particular items of clothing or achieving at school) may be incomprehensible to their parents. Differences between parents' and children's values may become the focus of parental nattering. Children of interracial marriages may have difficulty developing a sense of identity, particularly during adolescence. They may have major problems reconciling their dual racial identifications into a single, personal identity that affirms the positive aspects of each heritage while acknowledging society's ambivalence toward biracial persons (Gibbs, 1987).

210

Teenage Pregnancy: What Are the Penalties?

Before the baby came, her bedroom was a dimly lighted chapel dedicated to the idols of rock 'n' roll. Now the posters of Duran Duran and Ozzy Osbourne have been swept away and the walls painted white. Angela Helton's room has become a nursery for six-week-old Corey Allen. Angie, who just turned 15, finds it hard to think of herself as a mother. "I'm still just as young as I was," she insists. "I haven't grown up any faster." Indeed, sitting in her parents' Louisville living room, she is the prototypical adolescent lobbying her mother for permission to attend a rock concert, asking if she can have a pet dog and complaining she is not allowed to do anything. The weight of her new responsibilities is just beginning to sink in. "Last night I couldn't get my homework done," she laments with a toss of her blond curls. "I kept feeding him and feeding him. Whenever you lay him down, he wants to get picked up." In retrospect she admits: "Babies are a big step. I should have thought more about it."

The rhythm of her typing is like a fox-trot, steady and deliberate. It is a hot summer day in San Francisco, and Michelle, a chubby black 14-year-old, is practicing her office skills with great fervor, beads of sweat trickling down her brow. She is worried about the future. "I have to get my money together," she frets. "I have to think ahead." Indeed she must. In three weeks this tenth-grader with her hair in braids is going to have a baby. "I have to stop doing all the childish things I've done before," she gravely resolves. "I used to think, ten years from now I'll be 24. Now I think, I'll be 24 and my child will be ten."

It is early afternoon, and the smells of dirty diapers and grease mingle in the bleak Minneapolis apartment. The TV is tuned to *All My Children*, and Stephanie Charette, 17, has collapsed on the sofa. Her rest is brief. Above the babble of the actors' voices comes a piercing wail. Larissa, her three-week-old daughter, is hungry. In an adjacent bedroom, Joey, 1½ years old and recovering from the flu, starts to stir. Stephanie, who is an American Indian and one of ten children herself, first became pregnant at 15. It was an "accident," she explains. So too was her second baby. "I'm always tired," she laments, "and I can't eat." Before Joey's birth, before she dropped out of school, Stephanie dreamed of being a stewardess. Now her aspirations are more down-to-earth. "I want to pay my bills, buy groceries and have a house and furniture. I want to feel good about myself so my kids can be proud of me." It has been a long, long while, she confides, "since I had a good time."

Conflicting cultural influences on behavior are sometimes perverse; the culture provides both inducements for a given type of behavior and severe penalties for engaging in it. This kind of temptation or pressure with one hand and punishment with the other is especially evident in the areas of violent behavior and sexuality. Our society fosters violence through its glorification of high status, violent models in the mass media, yet seeks severe punishment for youngsters' imitative social aggression. Consider teenage pregnancy—the cultural forces that foster it, and society's responses to it. Morse (1985) notes that sexual mores have changed during the past two decades, so that adolescents now have much greater freedom and added responsibilities for preventing pregnancy. Our society tempts adolescents, offering them freedoms and responsibilities they are not equipped to handle, yet does nothing to help them deal with the freedoms and responsibilities, and in fact punishes them for abusing freedom and behaving irresponsibly. Motion pictures, MTV, and commercials highlight sex appeal and sexual encounters, providing models of behavior that are incompatible with efforts to encourage sexual abstinence and avoid pregnancy. Teenagers often pressure their peers to become sexually active; at the same time, conservative politicians have attempted to restrict sex education and make contraceptives less available to teens. Education for family life and child rearing is not widely offered (see Hagenhoff, Lowe, Hovell, & Rugg, 1987). The box about teenage pregnancy illustrates some of the problems of teenage mothers. As you read, consider the many cultural pressures on teenage girls to become sexually active and to become pregnant, and also consider the penalties teenage mothers must pay. Hagenhoff et al. note the cultural and social inducements for teenagers to become sexually active and the penalties teenage parents pay in limited education, employment, and health risks for mothers and children.

A MULTICULTURAL PERSPECTIVE

Besides the conflicts that differing cultural standards create, children's and adults' own cultural values may bias their perceptions of others. A full discussion of cultural bias in education is far beyond the scope of this chapter, but it is important to note that problems of bias and discrimination carry serious implications for evaluating youngsters' behavior. Ultimately, nearly all behavioral standards and expectations—and therefore nearly all judgments regarding behavioral deviance—are culture-bound; value judgments cannot be entirely culture-free. In our pluralistic society, which values multicultural elements, the central question for educators is whether they have made sufficient allowance in their judgments for behavior that is a function of a child's particular cultural heritage (see Carlson & Stephens, 1986). Cultural differences that do not put the youngster at risk in the larger society should be accepted; only values and behaviors that are incompatible with achieving the larger goals of education (self-actualization, independence, and responsibility) should be modified.

It is not easy to establish rules for applying a multicultural perspective. Teachers and school administrators must make daily decisions as to which standards of conduct represent their personal value systems and which represent justifiable demands for adaptation to the larger society; for example, Is it really necessary for students to remove their hats in the classroom? What is "polite" English, and is it necessary that students use it to address adults in school? What values and behaviors are inconsistent with a youngster's success and happiness in society at large? When do the values of a particular culture place a student at risk for school failure? Under what conditions is risk of school failure a fault of the school itself—how it is organized and the demands it makes of students? These and similar questions have no ready answers. They will continue to be part of our struggle for fairness and justice in a multicultural society.

PROBLEMS IN EVALUATING THE EFFECTS OF CULTURAL FACTORS

Besides the family and the school, which are topics of separate chapters, the most frequently researched cultural factors include the mass media, the peer group, the neighborhood, ethnic origin, social class, religious institutions, urbanization, and health and welfare services. Evaluating the role of these factors in behavior disorders is extremely difficult, primarily for two reasons. First, the interrelationships among the many cultural influences are so strong that untangling the effects of most of the individual factors is impossible. Farrington (1986a) summarizes this problem well.

> The major problem in drawing conclusions about sociocultural factors in childhood psychopathology is that most possible predisposing factors tend to be interrelated. Children who live in deprived inner-city areas (at least in North America and Great Britain) tend to be from ethnic minorities, tend to have parents with low status, low-paid jobs, or no job at all, and tend to have friends who commit deviant acts. Furthermore, sociocultural factors tend to be related to individual characteristics and to family influences. . . . Children from low-income families tend to have many siblings, which may make peer influence more important relative to parental influence, tend to receive poor nutrition and medical care from conception on-wards, and tend to be exposed to lax and erratic child-management practices and to parental conflict, violence, and alcohol abuse. (Farrington, 1986a, p. 391)

Second, research related to several of the factors is limited or nearly nonexistent. Religious beliefs and institutions, for example, probably have a strong influence on family life and child behavior, particularly among ethnic families of color (Harrison, Serafica, & McAdoo, 1984); yet there is little research on the effects of religion on child behavior and family life. Bronfenbrenner, Moen, and Garbarino (1984) noted that "researchers concerned with the well-being of families and children would do well to attend to the part played by religious institutions within the community, but at present this area remains a scientific terra incognita" (p. 307). Maypole and Anderson (1987) highlight the importance of including the black church in culture-specific intervention programs for black youngsters. Despite these difficulties in understanding cultural factors, available research does suggest relationships between certain cultural features and the development of behavioral deviance.

THE MASS MEDIA

Mass media include printed materials, radio, television, and motion pictures. Societal concern for the effects of mass media on the behavior of children and youth began as long ago as when books and magazines became widely available (Donelson, 1987). A few generations ago, concerns about the effects of radio programs and comic books were frequently expressed. Present controversies rage over the effects of textbooks, pornographic magazines, novels, and motion pictures on the thinking and behavior of the young. That what people read, see, and hear influences their behavior is hardly questionable, yet relatively little sound research is available to explain how—with the exception of advertising material. Publishers and broadcasters do market research to show the effectiveness of sponsors' ads; they know a lot about what sells and what influences the buying habits of specific segments of their audiences, including children and adolescents. Nevertheless, the influence of the media on youngsters' *social* behavior is often dubious or hotly disputed. Ironically, the same individuals (television network executives) who express confidence in the behavioral effects of television commercials argue that the effects of TV violence on children's social behavior is negligible (Eron & Heusmann, 1986).

Today, the effects of television on behavioral development is by far the most serious media issue. Specifically, researchers and policy makers are interested in how watching TV may increase children's aggression and their **prosocial behavior** (for example, helping, sharing, cooperation). We can summarize some relevant findings from the now considerable body of research into the effects of TV viewing on children's antisocial and prosocial conduct (Eron & Huesmann, 1986; Gelfand et al., 1986; Sprafkin & Gadow, 1986; Sprafkin, Gadow, & Dussault, 1986; Sprafkin, Gadow, & Kant, 1988; Sprafkin, Kelly, & Gadow, 1987).

□ Viewing TV violence has been established as a causal factor in heightened aggression of children from preschool age through adolescence, although children seem to be especially susceptible to the effects of TV violence at the age of about third grade.

□ Watching prosocial programs, such as "Mr. Roger's Neighborhood," "Lassie," "Father Knows Best" (and probably programs like "Family Ties" and the "Cosby Show"), has been shown to increase prosocial behavior in children from preschool age up to 10 years; little research regarding prosocial effects has been conducted with older children.

□ Viewing TV violence, especially when the violence is committed by males, increases aggression in both boys and girls, but the effect appears to be stronger for girls than for boys.

□ Intense television viewing, particularly of violent programs, is associated with higher levels of aggressive behavior. "It is the incessant, inexorable, ubiquitous nature of day-to-day TV exposure that appears to have a profound effect on the socialization of children, at least in the United States" (Eron & Huesmann, 1986, p. 303).

□ Children who are lower achievers, less popular with their peers, strongly identify with TV characters, have difficulty discriminating fantasy from reality, and engage in high levels of aggressive fantasy appear to be more susceptible to the aggression-facilitating effects of TV violence.

□ The effect of TV violence is greater for children who more readily accept it as realistic, and disturbed children tend to watch more violent programs and to see TV violence as more "real" than do nondisturbed children.

□ The children who are most attracted to and affected by TV violence are those who are already hyperaggressive; that is, watching TV violence and behaving aggressively affect each other in a circular process. "The viewing of TV violence leads to heightened aggressiveness, which in turn leads to an increase in TV violence viewing" (Eron & Heusmann, 1986, p. 310).

Research clearly links watching TV violence to increases in aggression, but the link is a statistical probability, not a one-to-one correspondence. Some highly aggressive children do not watch much violent TV, while some children who watch TV violence almost incessantly are not aggressive. Yet violence-viewing is clearly a contributing factor in *some* children's antisocial conduct, and it is important to understand how TV violence can be involved in causation. One obvious way TV violence can facilitate aggressive conduct is observational learning; youngsters imitate what they see. This explanation is probably a gross oversimplification, however, as research now suggests that much more complicated processes are involved.

The most likely explanation of the effects of TV viewing fit Brandura's social cognitive model (see Chapter 4). The effects involve reciprocal influence among three components: person variables (thoughts and feelings), the social environment, and behavior. In the case of TV violence and aggression, Bandura's triadic reciprocality involves the child's thoughts and feelings about aggression and the TV characters who perform it, the child's environment (including school, home, and community), and the child's selection of violent TV programs and aggressive responses to problem situations. But general social circumstance—the social ecology in which aggression is exhibited, including friendship patterns and school performance—must also be considered. Eron and Heusmann (1986) summarize reciprocal influences among person variables, environment, and behavior in the social ecology of aggressive children.

> Children who behave aggressively are less popular and, perhaps because their relations with their peers tend to be unsatisfying, watch more TV and view more violence. The violence they see on TV may reassure them that their own behavior is appropriate or teach them new coercive techniques that they then attempt to use in their interactions with others. Thus, they behave more aggressively, which in turn makes them even less popular and drives them back to TV. The evidence supports a similar role for academic failure. Those children who fail in school watch more TV, perhaps because they find it more satisfying than schoolwork. Thus, they are exposed to more violence and have more opportunity to learn aggressive behavior. Because their intellectual capacities are more limited, the easy aggressive solutions they observe may be incorporated more readily into their behavioral repertoire. In any case, the high frequency of violence viewing isolates them from their peers and gives them less time to work toward academic success. And, of course, any resulting increase in aggression itself diminishes the child's popularity. Thus, the cycle continues with aggression, academic failure, social failure, and TV violence reinforcing each other. (pp. 310–311)

In summary, a large body of evidence indicates that viewing TV violence tends to increase antisocial behavior, particularly in children and youth who are already at risk for social and academic problems. Moreover, a convergence of research findings on peer relations and school failure as well as TV viewing now suggests plausible mechanisms underlying the effects of TV violence. Considerably less evidence is available, however, regarding prosocial TV programs' facilitation of prosocial behavior. Perhaps it is reasonable to suspect that TV viewing may be a contributing factor in a variety of social problems, such as delinquency and teenage pregnancy, but a relationship of other problems to TV has is not yet been demonstrated.

The role of the mass media (not just TV, but all print, film, and broadcast media) in the development of behavioral disorders is a concern to those who wish to construct a more prosocial and humane society. For example, teenage suicidal behavior appears to increase following media coverage of teen suicides (Eisenberg, 1984; Hawton, 1986). Motion pictures that glorify violent solutions to problems, such as the "Rambo" movies, may add to the effects of TV violence. It is difficult to conclude that print materials featuring violence and pornography play any positive role in behavioral development or conduct. Perhaps decreasing portrayal of undesirable behavior and increasing prosocial programming and reporting of prosocial acts would make our culture less self-destructive and more humane. Yet the solution to the media problem is not apparent; censorship is not compatible with the principles of a free society.

Personal choice and responsibility in patronage may be the only acceptable way to approach the problem.

THE PEER GROUP

Peer relationships are extremely important for behavioral development, especially during middle childhood and early adolescence, yet, until about a decade ago, research tended to focus more on family relationships than on socialization to the peer group (Hops, Finch, & McConnell, 1985). We can now identify problematic relations with peers in children as young as five years of age, and these problems tend to persist over time (Coie & Dodge, 1983). Behavioral characteristics associated with emergence and maintenance of social status in the peer group and relationships between peer status and later behavioral problems are becoming clearer (Coie, Dodge, & Kupersmidt, in press; Coie & Kupersmidt, 1983; Kupersmidt & Coie, 1987; Maccoby, 1986; Patterson, 1986b; Strain, 1981; Strain, Odom, & McConnell, 1984).

Research indicates that, in general, high status or social acceptance is associated with helpfulness, friendliness, and conformity to rules—to prosocial interaction with peers and positive attitudes toward others. Low status or social rejection is associated with hostility, disruptiveness, and aggression in the peer group. To complicate matters, aggressive youngsters, compared to nonaggressive, seem more likely to attribute hostile intentions to their peers' behavior; and they are more likely to respond aggressively even when they interpret their peers' intentions as nonhostile (Dodge & Somberg, 1987). Low social status among peers is also associated with academic failure and a variety of problems in later life, including suicide and delinquency (Farrington, 1986a; Gelfand et al., 1986). In fact, poor peer relations, academic incompetence, and low self-esteem are among the primary factors in an empirically derived model of the development of antisocial behavior (Patterson, 1986b).

The evidence that antisocial children and youth are typically in conflict with their peers as well as with adult authorities is overwhelming, as is the evidence that antisocial youngsters tend to gravitate toward deviant peers. Youngsters who do not learn about cooperation, empathy, and social reciprocity from their peers are at risk for inadequate relationships later in life. They are likely to have problems developing the intimate, enduring friendships that are necessary for adequate adjustment throughout life. Thus the peer group is a critical factor in creating social deviance.

These generalizations do not do justice to the complexity of the research on relationships between social status among peers and children's behavioral characteristics. Social status can be measured using peer nominations, teacher ratings, or direct behavioral observations. Depending on the source of data, different pictures of social acceptance or rejection emerge. Normal or expected behavior in the peer group differs with age and sex, so the same type of behavior can have different implications for peer relations depending on age and sex (Cairns & Cairns, 1986; Maccoby, 1986). The social processes that lead to social rejection may be quite different from those that lead to social isolation or neglect (Coie et al., in press). The same classroom conditions can produce different effects on social status and friendship patterns for students of different races (Hallinan & Teixeira, 1987). And bias in peers' social perceptions can produce different outcomes in terms of social acceptability for two individuals who exhibit similar behavior (Hollinger, 1987).

All sources of information regarding children's social acceptance indicate that better-liked youngsters are those who are considerate, helpful, and able to appeal to group norms or rules without alienating their peers. Social rejection is related to opposite characteristics—violating rules, hyperactivity, disruption, and aggression—although the antisocial behavior that characterizes rejected youngsters changes with age. As children grow older, they tend to exhibit less overt physical aggression. The ways they irritate others, and so become rejected, become more complex, subtle, and verbal. Physical aggression is more often a factor leading to rejection in boys' groups than in girls'.

Social withdrawal is often associated with peer rejection, but the causal relationship is not always clear. Apparently, social withdrawal is not as prominent as aggression in young children's thinking about relations with their peers (Younger & Boyko, 1987). As children grow older, however, withdrawal correlates more closely with rejection, perhaps because rejected children are acquiring a history of unsuccessful attempts to join social groups. This correlation suggests that withdrawal is the result of rejection, a way of dealing with repeated social rebuffs. Youngsters who withdraw following repeated rejection may become the targets of taunts and abuse, perpetuating a cycle of further withdrawal and further rejection.

We know less about the behavior of socially neglected children than about those who are actively rejected, partly because it is difficult to study the characteristics of children who are all but invisible to their peers. Nevertheless, it appears that their peers see them as shy and withdrawn, that they engage in solitary play more frequently than most children, and that they are less aggressive than even popular youngsters. Neglected children sometimes appear to exhibit relatively high levels of prosocial behavior, but their general lack of assertiveness apparently results in their peers' not perceiving them as socially competent.

Given that we have identified social skills in which rejected, withdrawn, and neglected youngsters are deficient, programs to teach those skills are logical interventions. Indeed, social skills training programs are now readily available (Goldstein, Sprafkin, Gershaw, & Klein, 1980; Jackson, Jackson, & Monroe, 1983; Stephens, 1978; Walker, McConnell, Holmes, Todis, Walker, & Golden, 1983). Teachers and psychologists are often pressured to provide social skills training that will address their students' or clients' apparent deficits (Hops et al., 1985). Nevertheless, social skills training often yields equivocal results, and exactly what skills to teach often remain in doubt. The notion that we can readily and reliably identify critical social skill deficits is a deceptive oversimplification. Research increasingly reveals that social competence is much more complex than previously thought. Social competence may relate to the ability to display specific skills in specific situations, but precise identification of skills and exact specification of performance in given situations are extremely difficult to determine (see Fox, 1987; Weissberg & Allen, 1986). Moreover, identifying social skill deficits that *cause* youngsters to have problems with their peers is not always possible; the causes of peer rejection or neglect are typically multiple and complex.

An important aspect of the analysis of peer relations and social skills training, and one that has not always been considered in research, is the development of expectations that bias youngsters' perceptions of their peers' behavior. If, for example, a youngster acquires a reputation among his or her peers, for aggression or for popularity, others respond to this reputation. They expect behavior that is consistent with their attributions of the motives of an individual whose reputation they accept as valid, and they interpret behavioral incidents accordingly. If one child throws a ball that hits another child on the head, peers are likely to interpret the incident in terms of their beliefs about the motives of the child who threw the ball. If the child is popular and does not have a reputation for aggression, they are likely to interpret the incident as an accident; if the child has a reputation for aggression, they are likely to interpret it as aggressive. The reciprocal interaction of biased perceptions and actual behavior must be taken into account in trying to understand why some youngsters are rejected while others who behave similarly are not. Hollinger (1987) summarized this phenomenon:

> Children learn to expect aggressive behavior from peers who have gained a reputation for being aggressive, although the peers may not actually engage in more aggressive behavior. A cyclical pattern develops in which children engage in more aggressive behavior toward peers who have a reputation of being aggressive. Thus aggressive children are both the recipients and instigators of more aggressive behavior than their peers. From the peers' perspective, [their] aggressive behavior is justified as a response to more aggression from the aggressive child. And the hostile attributions of aggressive boys justify their aggressive behavior. In the end, the more aggressive the child, the more likely it is that [he] will attribute hostile intentions in ambiguous situations and consequently get caught in the cycle that maintains aggressive interactions. (p. 23)

Effective social skills interventions must therefore include provisions for dealing with peer group response to the disturbed youngster as well as teaching skills that enhance social acceptance (Strain et al., 1984). Only when the social ecology of the peer group can be altered to support appropriate behavioral change are social skills likely to result in improved status of the target child. Knowing that a youngster lacks specific social skills necessary for social acceptance and being able to teach those skills is not enough; one must also change the youngster's reputation—the perceptions and attributions of peers.

THE NEIGHBORHOOD

Neighborhood refers not only to residents' social class and the quality of physical surroundings, but to the available psychological support systems as well. Separating the neighborhood from other causal factors in social deviance, particularly social class, has proved difficult, if not impossible (Farrington, 1986a). Only recently have serious attempts been made to examine neighborhood as a separate and distinctive effect on child development (Bryant, 1985). Bryant took seven- and ten-year-olds on a walk through their neighborhoods and then interviewed them to determine what they perceived as sources of support.

> Support was conceptualized to include both experiences of relatedness to others and experiences of autonomy from others. Three major categories of reported

support in this study using the Neighborhood Walk were considered: others as resources (e.g., persons in the peer, parent, grandparent generation; pets), intrapersonal sources of support (e.g., hobbies; fantasies—structured and unstructured; skill development), and environmental sources of support (e.g., places to get off to by oneself; formally sponsored organizations with both structured and unstructured activities; informal, unsponsored meeting places). (Bryant, 1985, p. 77)

Bryant found that ten-year-olds have more elaborate and coherent concepts of neighborhood than do seven-year-olds. Girls made greater use of intrapersonal support strategies (such as fantasy) and had a less extensive, casual network of relationships than boys. Compared to children from smaller families, children from larger families turned to peers, grandparents, and pets more often for sources of support. These results only hint at the effects of neighborhood on social deviance; they are limited because the children represented a narrow age range and came from nonurban, white, two-parent families in which there was little apparent stress. Nevertheless, Bryant's study is significant as an initial attempt to study a neglected aspect of the ecology of childhood. Professionals who work with troubled children, should consider the sources of social support defined in her study since research suggests that social support can help offset stressful events (cf. Hetherington & Martin, 1986; Johnson, 1986). In all likelihood, future research will show that neighborhood sources of support contribute significantly to children's behavioral development.

The neighborhood and community may play important roles in the prevention of certain types of highly visible behavioral deviance, such as juvenile crime. For example, a community sense of moral order, social control, safety, and solidarity may be extremely difficult to achieve in a neighborhood in which crime rates are high. Interventions aimed at individuals will probably not succeed because of the lack of neighborhood monitoring and mutual support. Group-oriented, community interventions that promote a shared sense of being able to cope with deviance may be more likely to help prevent juvenile delinquency and crime in high-crime neighborhoods (Nietzel & Himelein, 1986).

URBANIZATION

Despite lack of evidence, the belief that city life is not conducive to mental health has persisted for well over a century (cf. Jarvis, 1852). Today, researchers are attempting to determine whether reliable differences in behavioral deviance are associated with rural or urban settings, such as urban-rural differences in rates of delinquency. When they find differences, they must look for explanations as to why some environments are associated with higher levels of problem behavior. Higher rates of delinquency frequently occur in urban than in rural areas, but a major difficulty in establishing urban environments as a causal factor in social deviance is that urbanization cannot be easily separated from other factors, such as crowding, quality of housing, community or neighborhood supports, social class, and so on (Farrington, 1986a).

Evidence from case studies suggests that, when children and families experience a sudden shift from rural to urban life, urbanization may play a role in the development of behavioral disorders. School age boys in Khartoum, Sudan, for example, showed three times the number of behavioral problems in 1980 as had boys of the same age in that culture in 1965. Rapid urbanization, including exposure to cultural values that conflicted with home values, may have been a significant factor in this increase or urbanization may have been merely the vehicle for the clash of values (Rahim & Cederblad, 1984). The opposite shift from urban to rural environment might be expected to unsettle children's and families' behavior as well. In rural environments with relatively sparse population, however, there may be less opportunity to engage in conflict with others outside the family. In addition, individuals' behavior is usually less closely monitored by police and social services in rural settings, which alone could account for some of the usual downward shift in reported deviance in rural areas.

Despite enthusiasm for the virtues and healing powers of rural retreats and agrarian cultures, there is not much evidence that they are superior to urban environments in producing mentally healthy children. The overriding factors associated with deviance appear to be low socioeconomic status and the breakdown of family and community ties.

ETHNICITY

In one of the largest and most carefully controlled studies of prevalence of behavioral problems in children and adolescents, Achenbach and Edelbrock (1981) found very few racial differences. They did, however, find substantial differences in behavioral ratings from different social classes, with children of lower class exhibiting higher problem scores and lower social competence scores than those from higher class. When the effects of social class are controlled, ethnicity apparently has little or no relationship to behavior disorders. The risk factors that may appear to accompany ethnicity are probably a function of the poverty of many ethnic minority families (Garmezy, 1987).

Ethnicity is often suggested as a factor in juvenile delinquency because studies show higher delinquency rates among black than among white youngsters, but we must question the meaning of differences in rate for at least two reasons. First, discrimination in processing may account for higher official delinquency rates among blacks. Second, ethnic origin is difficult or impossible to separate from other causal factors, including family, neighborhood, and social class. Thus, it is not clear that ethnicity is related to delinquency independently of other factors (Farrington, 1986a).

SOCIAL CLASS

One ordinarily measures children's social class in terms of parental occupation, with children of laborers and domestic workers representing one of the lower classes and children of professional or managerial workers representing one of the higher classes. Studies (Achenbach & Edelbrock, 1981) and reviews of studies (Farrington, 1986a) frequently link behavioral problems, lack of social competence, and delinquency to lower social class. Although lower social class is often associated with psychopathology, the meaning of this finding is controversial. The relationship between social class and specific types of disordered behavior does not hold up as well as the relationship to behavior problems in general. Furthermore, family discord and disintegration, low parental intelligence, parental criminality, and deteriorated living conditions seem to be much more influential than parents' occupational prestige in accounting for children's behavior. While it is true that many parents in low prestige occupations may be described by the characteristics just cited, it is not clear that low social class in itself is a contributing factor in children's social deviance; that is, social class may be a factor only in the context of these other parental and family characteristics. Economic disadvantage, with all its deprivations and stress, is apparently a factor in development of disordered behavior; social class, at least as measured by occupational prestige of parents, is probably not.

IMPLICATIONS FOR EDUCATORS

Educators should be aware of how cultural factors may be contributing to their students' behavior problems, and of the possibility of cultural bias in evaluating behavioral problems. Recall Farrington's (1986a) comments regarding the interrelationships among predisposing sociocultural factors in behavioral deviance. We can seldom untangle the effects of isolated factors from the mix of circumstances and conditions associated with disordered behavior. Nevertheless, research on specific factors that may give rise to disorders has important implications for prevention, especially if intervention can be aimed at improving children's individual circumstances. Strong evidence now suggests a basis for corrective action in many cases; reducing TV violence and providing more prosocial TV programming, for example, would probably help reduce the level of aggression in our society. Much could be done to address the needs of children reared under adverse conditions in which their health and safety, not to mention intellectual stimulation and emotional development, are at stake. These kinds of social changes demand large-scale efforts that educators cannot achieve alone; indeed, the politicization of issues regarding the physical and mental health risks of children and youth calls for all Americans to speak out. As Garmezy (1987) points out, decisions about child welfare programs have consequences for the nation's future.

Of the causal factors discussed in this chapter, the peer relations of rejected and neglected students are perhaps the most important consideration for the daily work of educators. Developing school-based interventions for target children and their peers should be a priority for researchers and teachers; these interventions may play an important role in prevention of social adjustment problems (Weissberg & Allen, 1986). Although we now recognize the great significance of disturbed students' poor peer relations, we know relatively little about the most effective means of intervening to improve their status. As Simpson (1987) says, educators agree that behaviorally disordered students should have more opportunities to interact productively with others, but fundamental questions remain as to appropriate goals: "For instance, should the goal be 'full-fledged membership' in an informal group of nonhandicapped peers or simple coexistence in school and community (e.g., increased tolerance, understanding, and acceptance of behaviorally disordered youth by others) without

The Health and Welfare of Children: How
Important Are They in American Culture?

The Children's Defense Fund has gathered some disquieting, even grim, statistics that attest to the crisis of risk for subsets of America's children. Compared to five years ago, the Fund reports, America's black children are now *twice* as likely as white children to die in the first year, be born prematurely, suffer low birth weight, have mothers who received late or no prenatal care, and have no employed parent. They are *three* times as likely to have their mothers die in childbirth, be in foster care, or die of known child abuse. They are *four* times as likely to live with neither parent and be supervised by a child welfare agency and to be murdered before one year of age or as a teenager. They are *five* times as likely to be dependent on welfare or become pregnant as teenagers. They are *twelve* times as likely to live with a parent who never married. Nor is this an issue limited to black children; it touches white children, Chicano children and other American racial and ethnic groups as well. After all, two of every three poor children in this country are white; almost one-half of all black children in America live in poverty; almost two of every five Hispanic children in America occupy a similar status; and more than half the children in female-headed households are poor. It is evident that poverty in America's families traverses a broad range of our varied population.

From "Stress, Competence, and Development: Continuities in the Study of Schizophrenic Adults, Children Vulnerable to Psychopathology, and the Search for Stress-resistant Children" by N. Garmezy, 1987, *American Journal of Orthopsychiatry*, 57, pp. 171–172. Reprinted, with permission, from American Journal of Orthopsychiatry. Copyright 1987 by the American Orthopsychiatric Association, Inc.

striving for total acceptance or membership?" (p. 293). The issues of choosing social skills for instruction, teaching these skills most effectively, and getting students to apply the skills in a variety of circumstances have not been resolved. Thus, teachers cannot yet look to the literature for prescriptions; they must in many cases develop their own procedures based on broad suggestions from research.

SUMMARY

Children, families, and teachers are influenced by the standards and values of the larger cultures in which they live and work. Conflicts between cultures can contribute to youngsters' stress and to their problem behavior. Not only conflicts between different cultures, but mixed messages from the same culture can be a negative influence on behavior. Cultures sometimes both encourage and punish certain types of behavior; for example, youngsters may be tempted or encouraged by the media to engage in sexual behavior, yet our society creates penalties for teenage pregnancy.

We must guard against bias and discrimination in our pluralistic, multicultural society. Cultural differences in behavior that do not put the child or youth at risk in the larger society must be accepted. Educators should seek to change only behavior that is incompatible with achievement of the larger goals of education. Clear rules for applying a multicultural perspective are not established, however. Teachers and school administrators must continue to struggle with decisions about what behavior puts a child at risk in society at large.

Besides family and school, cultural factors that influence behavior include mass media, peer group, neighborhood, urbanization, ethnicity, and social class. A major difficulty in assessing most of these and other cultural factors is that they are so intimately intertwined. It is difficult, for example, to untangle the factors of social class, ethnicity, neighborhood, urbanization, and peer group. Social class, ethnicity, the neighborhood, and urbanization have not been shown to be, in themselves, significant causal factors in behavior disorders. They are apparently significant only in the context of economic deprivation and family conflict.

Other cultural factors are more clearly involved in causing disordered behavior. Watching TV violence causes rising levels of aggression among children who are already aggressive. Rejection by peers also increases the upward spiral of aggression among youngsters who are uncooperative, unhelpful, disruptive, and aggressive. In both cases—TV violence and peer rejection—youngsters' behavior, their environments (including others' reactions to their behavior), and their perceptions are factors in the development of increasing social deviance.

The literatures on peer relations and social skills training have the clearest and most direct implications for educators. Teachers must be concerned with both the social skills deviant students need and the responses and perceptions of the peer group. Unfortunately, research does not yet allow confident recommendations about which social skills are essential or how best to teach them.

A FINAL NOTE ON CAUSAL FACTORS

We know much more today about the origins of behavior disorders than we knew 25 or even 10 years ago, but researchers now realize that causal mechanisms are far more complex than previously assumed. At the same time that research is revealing the incredible complexity and interconnectedness of causal factors, it is opening up new possibilities for intervention. Old ideas that the course of psychopathology was set by early life experiences and impervious to intervention have given way to more hopeful attitudes. Reflecting on the causal factors we have reviewed in Part 3 and anticipating discussion in the next part, the conclusions of a noted authority in child psychopathology are an appropriate epilogue. Rutter (1985) ended a review of family and school influences on behavioral development with these comments, which could be also apply also to biological and cultural influences.

> It is apparent that there are important family and school influences on behavioural development. The effects are sizable but they vary markedly across individuals and according to the ecological context; moreover, they are transactional, rather than unidirectional, in nature. The evidence runs counter to the view that early experiences irrevocably change personality development... and also runs counter to the suggestion that any single process is involved...; nevertheless, in some circumstances the indirect effects may be quite long-lasting. Even so, such long-term effects are far from independent from intervening circumstances. Rather, the continuities stem from a multitude of links over time.... Because each link is incomplete, subject to marked individual variation and open to modification, recurrent opportunities to break the chain continue right into adult life. (Rutter, 1985, pp. 364–365)

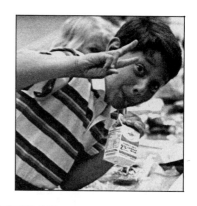

PART FOUR

Facets of
Disordered
Behavior

12

Hyperactivity and Related Problems

As you read this chapter, keep these guiding questions in mind:

☐ Why do we not define *hyperactivity* simply as being highly active?

☐ What types of behavior are most closely related to hyperactivity?

☐ What diagnostic or technical terms are used to describe hyperactivity?

☐ What are some popular myths about hyperactivity?

☐ What is the relationship between brain damage and hyperactivity?

☐ What biological and psychological causal factors probably contribute to hyperactivity?

☐ Why is prevention of hyperactivity now necessarily a matter of secondary prevention?

☐ In assessing hyperactivity, what kind of information is most useful for teachers?

☐ Which is the preferred treatment for hyperactivity—stimulant drugs or behavior modification? Why?

☐ What behavioral interventions are frequently used to manage hyperactivity and related problems?

☐ What general conclusions have been reached regarding the use of self-monitoring to manage off-task behavior and improve academic performance?

☐ What steps are generally followed in teaching students to use self-instruction?

☐ What types of intervention have not been used with hyperactivity?

DEFINITION AND PREVALENCE OF HYPERACTIVITY

Hyperactivity is not defined by high activity alone. Some children have extremely high activity levels but are socially well adapted and high achieving. These highly active children are apt to be labeled energetic, enthusiastic, hard working, or brilliant rather than hyperactive. The socially unacceptable character of the hyperactive child's behavior and the presence of other undesirable behavioral characteristics, in addition to inappropriate overactivity, are implicit in the definition of hyperactivity.

We said in Chapter 1 that disturbed youngsters induce negative feelings and behaviors in others. Among the many characteristics that are bothersome or irritating to others and that induce others to respond negatively is *hyperactivity*. Distractibility and impulsivity are closely related to hyperactivity, and together they reduce to shambles whatever social skills a youngster may have.

Hyperactive, distractible, impulsive children upset their parents and siblings because they are difficult to live with at home; at school they drive their teachers to distraction (Campbell & Werry, 1986; Conners & Wells, 1986; Mash & Johnston, 1983). These children are usually unpopular with their peers; they do not make charming playmates or helpful workmates (Grenell, Glass, & Katz, 1987; Whalen, Henker, Dotemoto, & Hinshaw, 1983). Incessant movement, impulsiveness, noisiness, irritability, destructiveness, unpredictability, flightiness, and other similar characteristics of hyperactive children are not endearing to anyone—parents, siblings, teachers, and schoolmates included. Hyperactivity makes children unpleasant companions and entails serious problems in behavior management for reasons illustrated in this description:

> A hyperactive child's mother might report that he has difficulty remembering not to trail his dirty hand along the clean wall as he runs from the front door to the kitchen. His peers may find that he spontaneously changes the rules while playing Monopoly or soccer. His teacher notes that he asks what he is supposed to do immediately after detailed instructions were presented to the entire class. He may make warbling noises or other strange sounds that inadvertently disturb anyone nearby. He may seem to have more than his share of accidents—knocking over the "tower" his classmates are erecting, spilling his cranberry juice on the linen tablecloth, or tripping over the television cord while retrieving the family cat, thereby disconnecting the set in the middle of the Superbowl game.
>
> A hyperactive child is all too frequently "in trouble"—with his peers, his teachers, his family, his community. His social faux pas do not seem to stem from negativism and maliciousness. In fact, he is often quite surprised when his behaviors elicit anger and rejection from others. (Whalen, 1983, pp. 151–152)

The types of behavior problems that bring hyperactive youngsters to the attention of therapists and special educators are further illustrated in Figure 12.1. Note that problems in school are the symptom most clearly associated with differences between hyperactive and nonreferred children.

Ross and Ross (1982) offer the definition of hyperactivity that perhaps best suits educational concerns. They conceptualize hyperactivity as "a class of heterogeneous behavior disorders in which a high level of activity is exhibited at inappropriate times and cannot be inhibited upon command" (p. 14). The teacher who deals with hyperactive children must understand that such students exhibit extremely varied types of inappropriate behavior. The problem of hyperactivity is not merely high activity

228

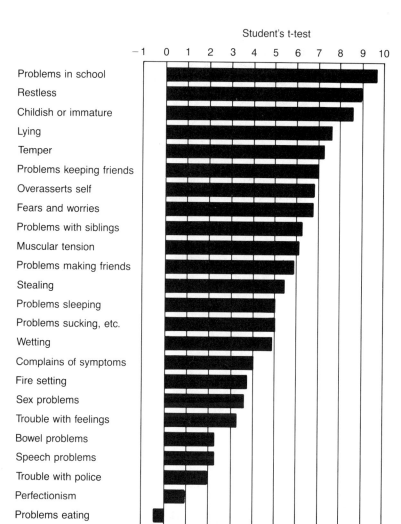

FIGURE 12.1

Symptoms in Clinic vs. Control Patients

From C.K. Conners & K.C. Wells, *Hyperkinetic children: A neuropsychosocial approach*. Copyright© 1986 by Sage Publications, Inc. Reprinted by permission of Sage Publications, Inc.

Note: Student's *t* test refers to a test of statistical significance. Significant at the 5% level means that differences as large or larger than approximately 2.0 could be expected to occur less than 5% of the time purely by chance. Thus, in common parlance, differences represented by a *t* score greater than 2.0 are probably reliable (i.e., true) differences.

levels, but high levels of *inappropriate* activity—behavior inappropriate for its context. Moreover, the student has not learned to control this kind of misbehavior; the misbehavior is not deliberate. The student has not learned the skills of maintaining attention and inhibiting impulses.

Teachers need to know about the developmental aspects of hyperactivity, distractibility, and impulsivity. We frequently see a high level of seemingly undirected activity, short attention span, and impulsive behavior in normally developing young

229

children. As children grow older, however, they gradually become better able to direct their activity into socially constructive channels, to pay attention for longer periods and more efficiently, and to consider alternatives before responding. Thus, only when motoric activity level, attentional skills, and impulse control are markedly discrepant from those expected at a particular age is the child's behavior considered to require intervention. Besides age, the child's sex may be an important developmental factor in these characteristics. Boys are far more frequently referred for problems of hyperactivity, distractibility, and impulsivity than are girls. Sociocultural differences also appear to be related to these problems, since hyperactive, distractible and impulsive children are seen more often in lower-income or culturally disadvantaged groups (Campbell, Breaux, Ewing, & Szumowski, 1986; Campbell & Werry, 1986; Werry, Elkind, & Reeves, 1987).

Controversy Regarding Definition and Terminology

For decades we have known that hyperactive children exhibit a typical cluster of interrelated behaviors:

Excessive motor activity of an inappropriate nature, often referred to as **hyperactivity** or **hyperkinesis**

Inability to sustain attention to the appropriate or relevant stimuli in a given situation, often referred to as **distractibility**

Disinhibition, or a tendency to respond to stimuli quickly and without considering alternatives, often referred to as **impulsivity**

Nevertheless, confusion and controversy persist over the definition of hyperactivity, its causes, and its treatment. One of the ironies about hyperactivity is that although it is frequently talked and written about, it is still imprecisely defined (Ross & Ross, 1982). Researchers and therapists continue to disagree as to the behaviors that signify it (that are necessary and sufficient for its diagnosis), its relationship to conduct disorder, the characteristics that accompany it, its causes, and the most effective approach to management (Campbell & Werry, 1986; Conners & Wells, 1986).

The overlap between hyperactivity and conduct disorder is a particularly relevant controversy for special educators. Comparison of the types of symptoms listed in Figure 12.1 to those that characterize conduct disorder suggests that it will be difficult to separate hyperactive and conduct disordered groups on the basis of behavior alone. The literature supports the assumption that hyperactive and conduct disordered youngsters often behave similarly, that the causes of their problems are often similar, and that intervention and education will be much the same (see Campbell & Werry, 1986). Nevertheless, this assumption does not hold for all cases; some hyperactive youngsters are not antisocial in the same ways as conduct disordered youngsters.

Regardless of how clinicians define it, hyperactivity is now one of the most frequent reasons for referral to child guidance clinics and one of the most written about disorders of childhood (see Ross & Ross, 1982; Whalen & Henker, 1980a). Yet the terminology of hyperactivity is not consistent. Over the years, a variety of terms have been used to refer to this type of problem: hyperactivity, hyperkinesis, hyperkinetic impulse disorder, minimal brain dysfunction, dyslexia, and Strauss Syndrome (after A.A. Strauss), for example. The American Psychiatric Association (in DSM-III-R, 1987) uses the term *attention-deficit hyperactivity disorder*. Very seldom do youngsters with attention deficits *not* exhibit hyperactivity as well (Barkley, 1982). The characteristics associated with hyperactivity are particularly important for special educators because they consist of behaviors that appear to preclude good social adaptation and school achievement (Barkley, 1985; Safer, 1982b; Whalen, 1983).

Prevalence

The prevalence of hyperactivity is difficult to determine precisely because of the lack of agreement over the criteria for defining the disorder. Generally, studies indicate that about two percent of elementary school children are diagnosed as hyperactive, but when cases of hyperactivity and conduct disorder combined are counted, the prevalence is closer to four percent (Campbell & Werry, 1986). Most authorities estimate that three to five percent of the child population is hyperactive (Barkley, 1983). Boys outnumber girls by a ratio of three or more to one.

Myths

Like other controversial and complex phenomena, hyperactivity has generated myths that die slowly. Henker and Whalen (1980) listed seven myths about hyperactivity that are slowly disappearing as more research is done. Each myth contains a kernel of truth, yet the statement is misleading—it is not supported by reliable empirical evidence. Keep in mind these myths, summarized in the box, and the more accurate statements that follow while reading this chapter.

In contrast to the myths that Henker and Whalen list, the following statements more accurately represent current understanding of hyperactivity:

> Hyperactivity is a problem of child behavior and environmental responses to it (e.g., parental attitudes and child management skills, cultural standards for behavior).

Disappearing Myths about Hyperactivity
MYTH 1: Hyperactivity resides in the child: The child deficit view
MYTH 2: Hyperactivity is in the eyes of the beholder
MYTH 3: Hyperactivity vanishes with adolescence
MYTH 4: Psychostimulant treatment is increasing to epidemic proportions
MYTH 5: There is an optimal response to psychostimulant medication
MYTH 6: Hyperactive children respond paradoxically to stimulant medication
MYTH 7: Psychostimulants are necessary and sufficient for the treatment of hyperactivity

From "The Changing Faces of Hyperactivity: Retrospect and Prospect" by B. Henker and C.K. Whalen. In *Hyperactive Children* (pp. 321–325) by B. Henker and C.K. Whalen (Eds.), 1980, New York: Academic Press. Reprinted by permission.

Hyperactivity is a problem of inappropriate and inadequate child behavior, plus others' perceptions of that behavior.

The attentional and social problems of hyperactive children tend to continue into adulthood.

Stimulant drug treatment of hyperactivity may be decreasing.

Response to stimulant drugs is idiosyncratic and complex.

Hyperactive and normal children tend to show similar reactions to stimulant drugs.

Stimulant drugs are helpful in the treatment of some hyperactive children, but in many cases they are not a necessary component of treatment, and they are never sufficient by themselves to solve the problems of a hyperactive child.

CAUSAL FACTORS AND PREVENTION

A link between hyperactivity and brain damage or brain dysfunction has been presumed for many years. Careful examination of the literature, however, only confirms the long-standing conclusion that "hyperactivity and cerebral dysfunction are neither synonymous nor mutually exclusive" (Keogh, 1971, p. 102). Some hyperactive youngsters show definite clinical signs of brain damage, but most do not; and some who show signs of neurological damage are not hyperactive (see Barkley, 1985; Campbell & Werry, 1986; Werry, 1986a). Not only is the definition of hyperactivity vague, but the pathogenic mechanism responsible for its appearance is also obscure. The link between hyperactivity and brain damage—indeed the link between brain damage and any specific behavior disorder—is so weak that the educational usefulness of the concept of brain damage is questionable (cf. Campbell & Werry, 1986; Werry, 1986a). The term *minimal brain dysfunction,* though it appears frequently in the literature on hyperactivity and learning disabilities, has no clear meaning and is of no value to educators or psychologists (Hallahan, Kauffman, & Lloyd, 1985; Kauffman & Hallahan, 1979).

Koupernik et al. (1975) pointed out that high activity levels are common among many different kinds of children, including:

Normal 2- and 3-year-old children

Older children with mental ages of 2 or 3 years

Very intelligent children who are highly exploratory

Children being nagged by parents or teachers

Anxious or depressed children

Environmentally deprived children

Some autistic children

Some epileptic children

The observations of Koupernik and his colleagues highlight the diversity of contexts in which high activity levels occur and indicate that the characteristics known collectively as hyperactivity probably have multiple origins. Brain damage (or brain dysfunction), the most common hypothesized cause of hyperactivity, can result from any of a number of circumstances, such as oxygen deprivation, physical insult, and lead poisoning. Furthermore, many factors that have been found detrimental to a child's development, such as poor prenatal nutrition and care, the mother's drinking or taking drugs during pregnancy, malnutrition, and abusive home environments, are also potential sources of brain trauma. Thus, while we cannot rule out the suggestion that brain damage is often a factor in hyperactivity, neither can we demonstrate that it is in fact often a cause. Knowing that a child's brain has been damaged is of little or no value in devising an effective educational program for the youngster.

Several other causes of hyperactivity have been suggested. Some hypotheses point to biological factors other than brain damage; others point to psychological causes—nonbiological, environmental factors. One of the alternative biological explanations is that hyperactivity is inherited. Research to date offers some evidence that hyperactivity or a predisposition to develop problems of inattention and impulsivity is genetically organized, but this genetic connection is not fully understood (Alberts-Corush, Firestone, & Goodman, 1986). It is plausible that genetic factors may give some individuals a predisposition to learn disturbed behavior or may be one of several biological factors that, in combination with other physiological characteristics or environmental stress, lead to hyperactivity (Barkley, 1982, 1983; Campbell & Werry, 1986).

Another hypothesis involves food additives or food allergies (see Chapter 8). Nonexperimental case studies and testimonies might support the belief that food additives are often at fault in hyperactivity. On the other hand, replicable data from carefully controlled experiments that made it possible to eliminate alternative explanations offer but scant supportive evidence; food additives or food substances can in a *very few* cases be considered causal factors in hyperactivity (Henker & Whalen, 1980; Swanson & Kinsbourne, 1980; Trites & Tryphonas, 1983a, 1983b; Weiss et al., 1980). Environmental lead or other environmental toxins, allergies, and deficiencies in neurochemicals are other suggested but unproven etiological factors (Barkley, 1985; Whalen, 1983); another unproven factor is fluorescent lighting (Fletcher, 1983).

A difficult temperament—an inborn behavioral style characterized by irritability, high activity level, short attention span, distractibility, and so on—has been suggested as the starting point for hyperactivity (see Chapter 8). Hyperactive children are often identifiable when they are toddlers or preschoolers. Temperamentally, they fit the description of the difficult child. They are children who "in the early preschool years show a mixture of problems in attention, impulse control, noncompliance, and aggression" (Campbell et al., 1986, p. 232). Yet temperament alone does not explain the problems of hyperactive youngsters. A difficult temperament may increase a child's risk for hyperactivity, but it is not a direct cause. If difficult temperament contributes to hyperactivity, it does so in interaction with parenting behavior. The parents and families of hyperactive children are often highly stressed. The stress may be partly a reaction to having a hyperactive child, and the stress may partly contribute to the child's hyperactivity. Not surprisingly, hyperactive children come, more frequently than expected by chance, from families characterized by conflict and deprivation (see Barkley, 1985).

In short, evidence does not clearly link any particular biological factor to hyperactivity. It is plausible that biological factors are involved in most cases, but precisely what they are and how they operate remain unknown.

Hypothesized psychological causes of hyperactivity range from psychoanalytic explanations to those involving social learning theory. One idea is that hyperactive children are understimulated or overstimulated in particular circumstances—their hyperactive behavior is an attempt to optimize their sensory stimulation for the demands of a particular task or social situation (Zentall, 1975, 1979; Zentall & Zentall, 1983). This hypothesis may be correct for some youngsters (Hastings & Barkley, 1978).

For the majority of children, other psychological causes are more plausible and supported by more data. For instance, numerous studies of modeling and imitation illustrate how children could acquire disturbed behavior through observation of frenetically active parents or siblings. The literature is replete with examples of how children's inappropriate behavior can be manipulated by social attention, suggesting that parents and teachers may inadvertently teach hyperactivity (see Ayllon & Rosenbaum, 1977; Kazdin, 1984; Ross & Ross, 1982). Nevertheless, research has not demonstrated that hyperactivity is exclusively a matter of undesirable social learning (Barkley, 1983, 1985; Campbell & Werry, 1986).

To summarize, no one really knows at this time why children become hyperactive. We know more about how to control hyperactivity once it has appeared than about its origins, but we can assume it is probably a result of multiple biological and psychological causes.

Prevention

Prevention of hyperactivity is largely a matter of intervening in the families and classrooms of youngsters who are difficult to manage. Effective primary prevention—keeping hyperactivity from emerging during development—would require parent training in child care and management and eliminating possible environmental factors. Secondary prevention—reduction and management of problems that have emerged—is the most feasible approach (cf. Gelfand et al., 1986). Much of the responsibility for secondary prevention falls upon educators, who must manage the child's behavior in school and provide instructional programs that will foster academic success.

Below-average performance on intelligence tests and learning difficulties are among the characteristics associated with hyperactivity (Barkley, 1985; Hechtman & Weiss, 1983). Hyperactivity interferes with academic achievement and peer relations; lack of achievement, feelings of failure, social isolation or rejection, and low motivation make for high rates of socially inappropriate behavior. The hyperactive student becomes trapped in a self-perpetuating negative interaction between hyperactive behavior and school failure. Prevention of later and more serious difficulties depends on breaking this cycle.

Hyperactivity does not seem to disappear automatically as the child matures. Without effective intervention, the young child who is hyperactive today stands a good chance of being hyperactive and/or having serious social and academic problems several years hence. Furthermore, hyperactivity and its negative concomitant characteristics (poor cognitive, academic, and social skills) appear to persist into adolescence and adulthood (Campbell & Werry, 1986; Hechtman & Weiss, 1983).

ASSESSMENT

Part of the problem in defining hyperactivity is the difficulty in measuring it. We can measure it, although imprecisely, through direct observation, mechanical devices attached to the child's body (actometers), or rating scales completed by parents or teachers (see Barkley, 1985; Conners & Wells, 1986; Eaton, 1983; Luk, Thorley, & Taylor, 1987). Direct observation is susceptible to error and unreliability. Mechanical devices are expensive and susceptible to failure. Both direct observation and mechanical devices carry the danger of reaction to measurement (the possibility that the youngsters will behave differently while their behavior is being recorded than while they are not being observed or recorded). The problem of reaction might eventually be overcome after the youngster adapts to the observer's presence or becomes accustomed to having the mechanical gadget attached to his or her body. Even so, one cannot assume that the measures obtained by observers or actometers are truly representative of children's behavior when they are not being observed. Even more problematic, however, is determining how much activity represents *hyper*activity.

Because hyperactivity is defined partly by observers' judgments about the appropriateness, meaning, or intention of behavior, it is typically assessed with behavior rating scales. Among the best known of the scales designed to measure hyperactivity are the *Teacher Questionnaire* (TQ) and the *Parent Questionnaire* (PQ) developed by Conners (1969, 1973). The TQ and PQ were devised for measuring children's responses to drugs, but have also been used to choose samples of hyperactive children for research studies and to measure responses to other than medical interventions. Other behavior rating scales, including most of those discussed in Chapter 6, include items related to hyperactivity. Teachers' ratings are useful as screening instruments, although they may not correspond well to actual counts of inappropriate behavior (Kazdin, Esveldt-Dawson, & Loar, 1983; Schachar, Sandberg, & Rutter, 1986). As Conners and Werry (1979) point out, even though they are not direct counts of the child's responses, rating scales "are, in essence, algebraic summations, over variable periods of time and numbers of social situations, of many discrete observations by parents, teachers, or other caretakers in which an unconscious data reduction process operates to produce a global score or frequency estimate" (p. 341).

An adequate clinical assessment of hyperactivity will include information from a variety of sources, including parents, teachers, and the youngster, that provides an account of the duration, severity, and nature of the problem. A critical aspect of assessment is obtaining significant others' perceptions of the youngster and their responses to his or her behavior, because hyperactivity is partly defined by others' perceptions and because other people's responses to appropriate and inappropriate behavior may serve to maintain it. The most useful assessment information for teachers, however, is probably what they obtain by direct observation and record as anecdotes in diaries or as frequencies of specific behaviors (Kazdin et al., 1983). Direct observations provide the best foundation for devising teaching and management strategies and for evaluating progress.

Assessment of Attention Problems

Krupski (1981) believes we must study attentional problems as an interaction of three factors: the student's characteristics, the nature of the task, and the demands of the setting. The student will demonstrate different attentional patterns depending on what he or she is asked to do and the structure of the environment in which attention is requested; for example, a hyperactive student may show very different attentional characteristics when given an arithmetic task in the regular class and when given an art project in a special self-contained class. A student may also have more than one type of attentional problem: difficulty coming to attention ("getting into" a task or focusing on it initially), making decisions (choosing a response after considering alternatives), or giving sustained attention (sticking with a task until it is completed) (Hallahan et al., 1985). The obvious implication is that one must assess attention problems in specific contexts (see Krupski, 1987).

Assessment of Impulsivity

Laboratory measures of behavior ordinarily offer relatively little information that teachers can use directly in instruction. In fact, laboratory tasks may require skills only remotely like those used to perform academic tasks or to get along with others in the classroom. To obtain information that is relevant to educational programming, teachers must adapt laboratory measures to more closely approximate classroom tasks or rely totally on direct observation.

A laboratory tool to measure impulsivity and reflectivity (the tendency to take one's time and consider alternatives before responding) is the *Matching Familiar Figures Test* (MFFT) (Kagan, 1965; Kagan, Rosman, Day, Albert, & Phillips, 1964). The MFFT requires children to chose from among several alternatives a line drawing of a familiar figure (for example, an airplane) that matches a standard. Each of the alternatives is slightly different from the standard, except the one that matches the standard exactly (see Figure 12.2). The child must match a series of figures, and the latency of response (that is, the length of time to make the first choice) and errors are recorded for each trial. The impulsive child tends to respond quickly and make many errors; the reflective child tends to have long response latencies and make few errors.

Impulsivity as measured by the MFFT correlates only moderately with other measures of impulsivity and with other characteristics of exceptional children, such as hyperactivity and distractibility (McClure & Gordon, 1984). Brown and Quay (1977) found that behaviorally disordered children show a developmental lag in impulse control, as indicated by their performance on the MFFT. Children with an impulsive cognitive tempo, as indicated by the MFFT, also do poorer academic work than reflective children (see Epstein, Hallahan, & Kauffman, 1975; Finch & Spirito, 1980). Nevertheless, the MFFT appears to tap features of cognitive style that are strongly

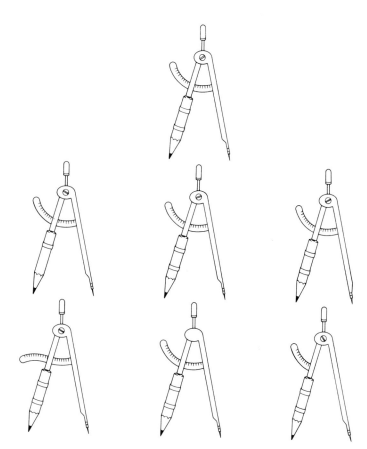

FIGURE 12.2
MFFT-type Item

Note: Adapted from "Impulsivity and
Academic Performance in Learning
and Behavior Disordered Children"
by K.B. Bower (Doctoral dissertation,
University of Virginia, 1975). *Disser-
tation Abstracts International,* 367A
(University Microfilms No. 76–1071).
Adapted by permission.

correlated with intelligence; therefore, MFFT scores may merely reflect level of overall cognitive development, and findings linking impulsivity as measured by the MFFT to disordered behavior may be a function of the fact that behaviorally disordered students tend to have lower than average IQs (see Chapter 10). If the MFFT correlates highly with IQ, then a student's score may give a teacher little in the way of new information. By constructing and using an analog of the MFFT, however, a teacher may learn something about how a student approaches academic tasks.

Children's performance on the Matching Familiar Figures Test (MFFT) may be compared to their performance on analogous academic tasks. Bower (1975) tested behaviorally disordered and learning disabled children using MFFT-type items (Figure 12.2) and analogously constructed match-to-sample arithmetic and reading items. These are examples of the analogous arithmetic and reading items[1]:

---

[1]Adapted from "Impulsivity and Academic Performance in Learning and Behavior Disordered Children" by K.B. Bower (Doctoral dissertation, University of Virginia, 1975), *Dissertation Abstracts International,* 367A (University Microfilms No. 76–1071). Adapted by permission.

```
  221
 −12
  209
```

```
  221    211
 −21    −12
  209    209
```

If you find the ring don't keep it.

If you fix the ring don't keep it.   *If you find her ring don't keep it.*

```
  221    221
 −12    +12
  901    209
```

When you find the ring don't keep it.   *If you find the ring just keep it.*

If you find the ring don't drop it.   *If you find the ring don't keep it.*

```
  221    221
 −12    −12
  209    219
```

Bower found that children took much longer to respond and made far fewer errors on the academic tasks than on tasks involving line drawings of objects; that is, children appeared to be much more reflective in cognitive tempo on the academic tasks than they were on the MFFT-type tasks. Further analysis of Bower's data, however, showed that children's performance on the MFFT significantly correlated with performance on the arithmetic and reading tasks; that is, latencies and errors tended to be high or low on all three measures. Thus, children tended to be slower and more accurate in an absolute sense when confronted with academic tasks than when asked to perform on the MFFT, but their relative impulsivity or reflectivity did not typically change—children who were quick and inaccurate tended to be so on each measure, and quickness of response was associated with errors. The academic analogs of the MFFT provide more useful information for teachers than the task of matching familiar objects because they indicate how children approach tasks more directly related to classroom performance.

Notwithstanding possible use of the MFFT and analogous tasks in assessing impulsivity, the teacher will need to observe and record impulsive behavior anecdotally or as frequency counts. Descriptions of slapdash performance on actual academic tasks and counts of impulsive acts in everyday school situations are likely to be far more useful in communicating with others and monitoring students' performance than are scores from laboratory measures or even classroom-relevant analogs.

INTERVENTION AND EDUCATION

Because hyperactivity tends to involve a cluster of related characteristics, including distractibility and impulsivity, many control techniques are designed to manage more than a high level of inappropriate motor activity. We will focus primarily on the usefulness of various intervention techniques in controlling excessive inappropriate motoric activity, some of which may represent impulsive responding to irrelevant or distracting stimuli. Techniques include medication, behavior modification, cognitive strategy training, and a variety of other interventions. We will discuss how to use these techniques in educational settings to help the hyperactive student achieve academic progress and social success.

Medication

Perhaps the most widespread notion about controlling hyperactivity is that drugs can be used to "slow children down." Lay persons, as well as professionals in education, psychology, and medicine, often suggest medicating a youngster if he or she is seriously and chronically disturbing to others. Many physicians believe it is appropriate to prescribe drugs in such cases, usually stimulant drugs such as methylphenidate (Ritalin) or dextroamphetamine (Dexedrine) (Campbell et al., 1985).

Perhaps no method of control has been so controversial as medication. Advocates of medication make totally unsupported claims for the effectiveness of drugs. Opponents raise questions about the drugs' undesirable side effects, long-term detrimental effects on growth and health, adverse effects on learning, negative effects on habits and perceptions of self-control, and the possibility of encouraging drug abuse. Some objections of opponents of drugs are unfounded and hysterical; others are thoughtful, cautious, and based on reliable data. Research does clearly indicate that the right dosage of the right drug can result in marked improvement of hyperactive students' behavior (Abikoff & Gittelman, 1985; Henker, Astor-Dubin, & Varni, 1986).

The effects of stimulant drugs, though frequently helpful, are neither simple to understand nor highly predictable for the individual child. The effects of medications are idiosyncratic and depend to some extent on social and psychological factors, such as the child's attitude toward his or her behavior and parental skill in managing the behavior (Whalen & Henker, 1980a). Given their potentially powerful effects on hyperactive behavior and their possible negative side effects, stimulant drugs are not an issue to take lightly (Campbell et al., 1985).

Whalen and Henker (1980b) note that children often attribute more power to the medicines they take than to their own efforts or skills. These attributions of control can enhance the drugs' effects, but can also present difficulties in teaching children self-control strategies. The accompanying box, with excerpts from interviews of hyperactive children, illustrates the extent to which children may believe their behavior is controlled by pills.

Prescribing medications for hyperactive children seems to have become a fad that waxes and wanes (Hollander, 1983). Responsible clinicians use drugs carefully as one approach to treatment when other solutions to the problem of hyperactivity are not feasible or when there is reason to suspect that drugs in addition to other interventions will produce a better result (cf. Barkley, 1985; Campbell & Werry, 1986). When a drug is prescribed, an important aspect of evaluating its effectiveness is the observation and judgment of the classroom teacher (Forness & Kavale, 1988; Gadow, 1986; Rapport, Stoner, DuPaul, Birmingham, & Tucker, 1985). It is never safe to presume that a drug will have desirable effects.

What Do Children Make of the Pills They Take?

The following excerpt is from an interview with a 9-year-old boy who described himself as being "on the borderline between hyperkinetic and a regular person."

INTERVIEWER: You were giving me a good example of times when you take an extra pill. Can you think back to another time?

CHILD: Yes, at Catalina. Another fishing story.

INTERVIEWER: Great, another fishing story.

CHILD: In the fishing I got bored, 'cause we couldn't catch the goldfish. There's goldfish in the ocean. . . . So we wouldn't catch them and I got bored waiting for another Catalina perch. We were bored. And I needed a pill—so I had to have another pill. And I didn't have one that morning. Then I had two. My Dad brought a case of them.

INTERVIEWER: He carries them with him?

CHILD: Yeah.

INTERVIEWER: So, how did you know you were bored and that you needed a pill?

CHILD: 'Cause my legs started kicking and my hands got all loose. . . then my feet start kicking all around and stuff. . . . My body gets all out of control and I need another pill.

The following excerpt is from an interview with a 10-year-old boy.

INTERVIEWER: How can other people tell when you forget to take Ritalin?

CHILD: Yeah, people can tell when I'm not taking it, because I'm running around.

INTERVIEWER: Tell me about the last time you remember that happening. When was that?

CHILD: Sunday, yesterday.

INTERVIEWER: And what happened?

CHILD: I was trying to run in the water, swimming pretty fast, bumping into the girls, my sisters, and diving in, and diving in and bouncing in and diving in and turn around and spring off your feet like a bowling pin in the water.

INTERVIEWER: And they didn't like it very much?

Behavior Modification

Behavior modification is not a foolproof method of controlling hyperactivity or any other behavior problem, but research has demonstrated that hyperactive youngsters' noisy, destructive, disruptive, and inattentive behavior can usually be changed for the better by controlling contingencies of reinforcement (see Ayllon & Rosenbaum, 1977; Barkley, 1985; Hallahan et al., 1985; Kerr & Nelson, 1983; Kerr et al., 1987). Behavior modification will not automatically bring improvement. To use it successfully one must apply the principles of learning to rearranging environmental events (such as changing when the student receives attention from teacher or parents). Unless the person who is trying to use behavior modification techniques understands behavior principles and is attuned to the student's individual characteristics and preferences, the behavior is not likely to change—at least not in the desired direction. Like medication, behavior modification can be abused and misused. Even with skillful use, it is a powerful method that can have unanticipated or undesirable outcomes, and it will not necessarily make the hyperactive student appear normal (Abikoff & Gittelman, 1984).

CHILD: Uh, uh, and so they told my Mom and my Mom called me in and I had to take my Ritalin.

The next excerpt is from an interview with an 11-year-old boy.

INTERVIEWER: How can people tell when you forget to take Ritalin?
CHILD: I'm acting horrible.
INTERVIEWER: What kinds of things do they see?
CHILD: I'll be bouncing the ball all around the room, that kind of stuff. Like say it's past 11:30 and I'm doing "wah-wah-wah" [pretends to bounce ball], he [the teacher] can see when you forget.
INTERVIEWER: OK, so one thing [the teacher] can see when you forget to take Ritalin is bouncing the ball around, doing that kind of thing. What else, what else does he see?
CHILD: Running around the room. Like, like there's a girl named Vicki and sometimes I go, "Sticky-Vicky is very picky about her diet. All she has on her diet is fat." And that really, and then she sometimes goes and tells the teacher.
INTERVIEWER: What else, any more samples? Those are good examples for me.
CHILD: Running out of the room, kicking people, beating people up, cussing them out, things like that.
INTERVIEWER: How come?
CHILD: [laughs] I don't know. I just wanna. I just feel like it.
INTERVIEWER: What does that feel like?
CHILD: Like, I don't know what it feels like, really.
INTERVIEWER: Think about it for a minute.
CHILD: I can't. Let's see, how it feels. It feels just like you can't hold it in. It has to come out.
INTERVIEWER: How do you know?
CHILD: Because I can tell by the way I'm acting. You know, like if I'm acting really goofy, I know I haven't taken my pill.

From Whalen and Henker, 1980b, pp. 28–29.

Modifying the hyperactive youngster's behavior ordinarily means making certain that rewarding consequences follow desirable behavior and that either no consequences or punishing consequences follow undesirable behavior. Rearranging environmental events this way may involve so simple a change as shifting the teacher's attention from inappropriate to appropriate behavior, or more complicated techniques such as token reinforcement. The emphasis must be on positive consequences for appropriate behavior, but prudent negative consequences for misbehavior are often necessary (Rosen, O'Leary, Joyce, Conway, & Pfiffner, 1984; see also Chapter 13). Etscheidt and Ayllon (1987) used contingent exercise, along with positive reinforcement for academic performance, to decrease the distractible, off-task behavior and improve the academic performance of a 13-year-old hyperactive boy. In their program, failure to meet criteria for academic performance resulted in the student's having to engage in exercise (sit-ups, push-ups, running in place, and so forth) for five minutes.

Both individual and group contingencies of reinforcement have been successful with hyperactive, disruptive students (Shapiro, Albright, & Ager, 1986). In one of the earliest studies to apply behavior modification techniques to hyperactivity, Patterson (1965a) employed a combination of group and individual contingencies. He arranged reinforcement for the nonhyperactive behavior of Earl, a nine-year-old second grader, and his classmates. Earl's inappropriate behavior included very frequent talking, pushing, hitting, pinching, looking about the room or out of the window, walking around the room, moving his desk, and tapping or handling objects. Patterson used a special device, a small box containing a digital counter and a light that could be remotely controlled, to deliver points for reinforcement. Patterson explained to Earl and his classmates that whenever Earl was sitting still and paying attention for a few minutes, the counter would turn to indicate points and the light would flash. Each point accumulated on the counter earned one penny or one small piece of candy, and the earned rewards were divided evenly among Earl and his classmates. With immediate and frequent reward for his appropriate behavior and motivation for his classmates to help him behave well, Earl's behavior quickly improved.

The now classic case of Henry is another example of combining individual and group contingencies of reinforcement to alter hyperactive behavior.

Henry

Henry was a bright (IQ 120) 6-year-old described not only as hyperactive, but also loud, demanding, oppositional, and disruptive. He piled his desk with debris and refused to sit with the other children. His teacher found that scolding and reprimanding him only made his behavior worse. As shown in Figure 12.3, his behavior was a se-

FIGURE 12.3

Henry's Disruptive Behavior During Baseline and Reinforcement Phases

From "The Good Behavior Clock: A Reinforcement Time Out Procedure for Reducing Disruptive Classroom Behavior" by E.S Kubany, L.E. Weiss, and B.B. Slogget, 1971, *Journal of Behavior Therapy and Experimental Psychiatry, 2*, p. 175. Copyright 1971 by Pergamon. Reprinted by permission.

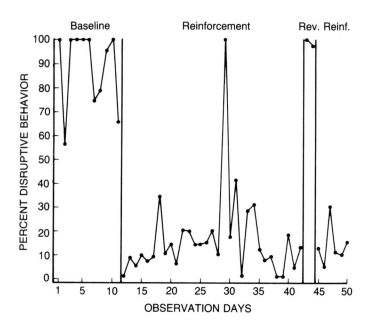

vere problem during baseline sessions (when the teacher ignored most of his misbe-havior but provided no explicit reinforcement for appropriate conduct). The behavior modification procedure devised for Henry was as follows: For each two minutes (15 minutes after the first day) that Henry was in his seat and quiet, a candy or trinket was dropped into a "sharing jar," and Henry was allowed to distribute the "earned" good-ies to his classmates at the end of the day. The accumulation of "good behavior time" was shown on a large 15-minute timer hung at the front of the room and labeled "Henry's Clock." The teacher controlled the clock by turning it off whenever Henry misbehaved and turning it on again after he had been well behaved for 15 seconds. Figure 12.3 shows that this procedure was effective in improving Henry's behavior. A reversal (return to baseline procedures) and reinstatement of the reinforcement con-tingency demonstrated clearly the causal link between reinforcement and Henry's be-havior. (Kubaney, Weiss, & Sloggett, 1971)

An important question regarding modification of task attention is whether, once the child is ostensibly paying attention (looking at the teacher or work), academic performance improves. That is, does reinforcing attention improve both task attention and academic performance? Alternatively, does reinforcing academic performance increase both performance and attention? The answer to both questions depends on the student's level of attention, ability to use attentional strategies, and ability to perform the academic tasks (Hallahan & Kauffman, 1975; Hallahan et al., 1983, 1985). Reinforcement for merely paying attention will probably help the student whose attention is initially at a very low level, since increased attending makes correct responding more likely. On the other hand, a student who already pays attention most of the time will not greatly benefit from reinforcement for attending. The student who does not know how to pay attention, what to look for, or how to search for information, needs direct instruction in attentional strategies. Otherwise, reinforce-ment for looking at the teacher or task will reinforce only looking, not performing. Reinforcing correct responses to academic tasks will probably increase attention only when the tasks are within the student's capacity and the percentage of time attending to tasks is below average (below about 75 percent) to begin with; offering reinforce-ment for a performance the student cannot give is futile, and expecting any student to pay attention to work all of the time is unreasonable.

When positive reinforcement of appropriate behavior is insufficient to correct the hyperactive student's conduct, carefully administered punishment may be in order. By themselves, punishment contingencies are never sufficient, nor are they, when used alone, an acceptable means of controlling behavior. When punishment is nec-essary, response cost (withdrawal of privileges or rewards) is the preferable type of contingency (see Walker, 1983). Other negative consequences are time out and ov-ercorrection (see Chapter 13 for more extensive discussion of punishment).

Briefly, behavior modification techniques have been used frequently and effec-tively to control hyperactive behaviors in the classroom as well as at home. Hyperactive behavior, like other behaviors of unknown origin, is usually susceptible to environ-mental influence and can be brought under control by systematically rewarding ap-propriate responses and withholding rewards for or punishing undesirable activity. But controlling hyperactive behavior will not make hyperactive students indistinguishable from their nonhyperactive peers. Social learning interventions (discussed in Chapter 13) are also appropriate with hyperactive behavior.

Drugs Versus Behavior Modification

One controversy in the literature has been whether medication or behavior modification is preferable for hyperactivity. Proponents of behavior modification have argued that such techniques are an effective alternative to medication, but they have not always backed up their claim with research data. Some researchers, however, have made direct experimental comparisons of the two interventions. Ayllon, Layman, and Kandel (1975) reported one such study that clearly showed that behavior modification controlled hyperactivity as well as drugs and produced better academic performance. Subsequent studies indicated that both drugs and cognitive or behavioral therapies produced improvement in hyperactive boys. The combination of pharmacological and behavioral interventions did not produce better results than either treatment alone (Brown, Wynne, & Medenis, 1985; Pollard, Ward & Barkley, 1984).

Kauffman and Hallahan (1979) reviewed studies that compared drug treatment and behavior modification, and concluded that drugs are sometimes helpful in controlling behavior. Still, drug effects are always interactive with environmental effects; how a child responds to medication depends not only on the dosage but also on the classroom or home environment (cf. Barkley, 1985; Whalen & Henker, 1980b). With or without drugs, behavior modification is usually effective, with some distinct advantages over medication:

It tends to have more specific effects than drugs.

It encourages a focus on teaching appropriate behavior in addition to concern for eliminating maladaptive responses.

It demands improvement of the child's environment rather than allowing exclusive attention to the misbehavior.

It may be used to increase the child's tendency to attribute behavior change to his/her own action rather than to the chemical effects of pills (that is, it may tend to foster personal responsibility rather than explanations having to do with external agents).

Cognitive Strategy Training

Since the mid-1970s, there has been a surge of interest in teaching children with learning and behavioral disorders to use a variety of strategies to control their own behavior (see Hallahan et al., 1983; Harris et al., 1985; Larson & Gerber, 1987; Meichenbaum, 1977, 1979, 1980; Wallace & Kauffman, 1986). Much of the research with cognitive strategies has dealt with impulsive behavior of youngsters labeled hyperactive. Cognitive strategies have sometimes been highly successful (Bornstein & Quevillon, 1976; Hallahan, Marshall, & Lloyd, 1981; Varni & Henker 1979).

The techniques referred to as cognitive strategy training may include self-observation, self-recording, self-monitoring, self-reinforcement, and self-punishment. Individually and as a group, the techniques are described by a variety of labels, including *cognitive-behavior modification, strategy training, cognitive training, cognitive strat-*

egy training, and so on. All have the goal of helping children become more aware of their own behavior and actively engage in control of their own responses to academic tasks and social situations. They are based on social cognitive theory (see Bandura, 1986), which highlights the importance of people's cognitive and affective as well as behavioral responses to their social environments. Notwithstanding the many reports of success with a wide variety of self-management procedures, unresolved theoretical issues remain (Mace & West, 1986).

We will discuss only two strategies, self-monitoring and self-instruction, because they are the most widely used in educational settings. Other strategies that involve students cognitively in self-management, such as goal-setting, are also valuable in dealing with hyperactive youngsters (Lyman, 1984; Maher, 1987).

Self-Monitoring

Self-monitoring, which requires self-assessment and self-recording, has been successful with hyperactive students who have difficulty staying on task. The procedure is usually used during seatwork, when on-task behavior can be unambiguously defined. A tape recorder is used to produce tones (prerecorded to sound at random intervals ranging from 10 to 90 seconds, with an average interval of 45 seconds) that cue the student to self-assess and self-record. The student is trained to ask himself, when he hears the tone, "Was I paying attention?" and to check a yes or no column on a simple recording form. The same procedure, with slight modifications, has been used during small group instruction. The teacher writes "Was I paying attention?" on the chalkboard, and students use mechanical counters to tally their answers.

Research on self-monitoring has led to the following general conclusions (Hallahan, Hall et al., 1983; Kneedler & Hallahan, 1981):

Self-monitoring of on-task behavior has resulted in increased on-task behavior in most cases.

Self-monitoring of on-task behavior has also tended to result in increases in academic productivity.

Improvement in behavior and performance has been found to last for at least two-and-a-half months after the procedure was discontinued.

The beneficial effects of self-monitoring have been achieved without the use of back-up reinforcers; extrinsic rewards, such as tokens or treats for improved behavior, have not been necessary.

Cues (tones) are a necessary element of the initial training procedure, although students can be weaned from them after initial training.

Students' self-recording responses—marking the answers to their self-questions—are a necessary element of the initial training, but can be discontinued after students learn the full procedure.

Self-recording appears to be more effective when the student assesses his or her own attentional behavior than when the teacher assesses it.

Accuracy in self-monitoring is not critically important; some students are in close agreement with the teacher's assessment of their on-task behavior, but others are not.

The cuing tones and other aspects of the procedure are minimally disruptive to other students in the class.

Self-monitoring procedures of various kinds have been used with students of all ages and with disruptive students labeled emotionally disturbed or behaviorally disordered as well as with students labeled learning disabled (Hughes & Hendrickson, 1987; Kiburz, Miller, & Morrow, 1984). Figure 12.4 shows a recording form used by a teacher of adolescent behaviorally disordered students who self-monitored several of their inappropriate off-task behaviors during seatwork (talking out without permission, telling off-task stories, humming or singing, and playing with objects). When these students heard the tape-recorded tone, they made a slash through the appropriate symbol of any target behavior they had exhibited during the previous interval (McManus, 1985). Partial results of their self-monitoring are shown in Figure 12.5.

The self-monitoring procedures described here are simple and straightforward, but they cannot be implemented without preparing the students. A brief training session in which the teacher talks with the student about the nature of off-task and appropriate behavior, explains the procedure, role plays the procedure, and has the student practice is necessary (see Hallahan, Lloyd et al., 1983).

Self-Instruction

Teaching students to use verbal labels for stimuli and to rehearse the instructions they have been given or the stimuli they have been shown appears to have merit as

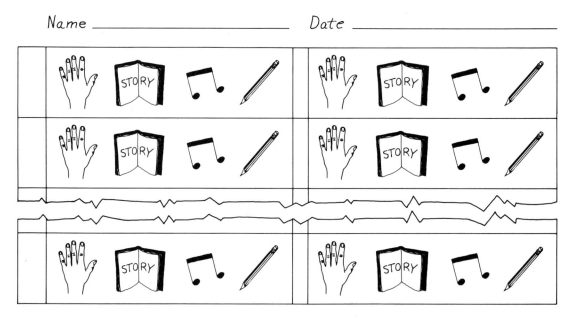

FIGURE 12.4
Sample Recording Form for Off-Task Behaviors

From "Modification of Adolescent Students' Off-Task Behaviors Using Self-Monitoring Procedures" by M. McManus, 1985, unpublished manuscript. Reprinted by permission.

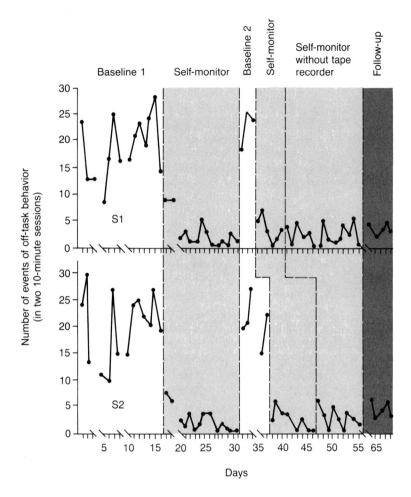

FIGURE 12.5

A Record of Off-Task Behavior of Two Behavior Disordered Students

From "Modification of Adolescent Students' Off-Task Behaviors Using Self-Monitoring Procedures" by M. McManus, 1985, unpublished manuscript. Reprinted by permission.

an instructional strategy (Hallahan & Kauffman, 1975). For example, a student may be told to verbalize each arithmetic problem or its operation sign while working the problem, to say each letter of a word aloud while writing it, or to rehearse a reading passage (Lovitt, 1977); however, this method of managing hyperactivity and related problems has limits (O'Leary, 1980). Verbal self-instruction can be a cumbersome procedure and is, at least for some students, no better than direct instruction by the teacher (Hallahan, Lloyd et al., 1983). Verbal labeling and rehearsal may benefit younger or developmentally delayed children who have no strategy for deploying their attention, but may actually hinder nondelayed children (Hagen, Meacham, & Mesibov, 1970). Thus, one must take into account the student's developmental level and specific attentional abilities and disabilities in selecting instructional strategies.

Teaching students to use their own language to regulate behavior has been a successful approach with some impulsive children and youth (Goodwin & Mahoney, 1975; Larson & Gerber, 1987; Mahoney, 1974). Meichenbaum and Goodman (1969, 1971), Palkes, Stewart, and Freedman (1971) and Palkes, Stewart, and Kahana (1968), for example, found that having youngsters instruct themselves to be more reflective reduced impulsive errors on experimental tasks. To instruct impulsive students to slow down and be careful in responding may not be enough to help them, but it may be helpful if the same students can be induced to tell *themselves* to stop and think before they give a response. Practical applications of a form of self-instruction to academic tasks appear in literature by Lovitt and Curtiss (1968) and Parsons (1972), who found that requiring children who made many careless or impulsive errors in arithmetic computation to verbalize each problem or operation sign before writing their answers improved accuracy. Larson and Gerber (1987) taught delinquent youths verbal self-instruction skills in which the youngsters cued themselves to stop and think before responding to social situations in which there was risk of danger, harm, or rule violation. The self-instruction training reduced negative reports and increased staff ratings on rehabilitation achievement.

Typically, self-instructional training of impulsive students involves a series of steps in which verbal control of behavior is first modeled by an adult, then imitated by the student, and finally used independently by the student. On a given task, the adult first performs the task while verbalizing thoughts about the task requirements, relevant stimuli, strategies, task performance, and coping and self-reinforcement statements. For example, suppose the training task were to find matching arithmetic problems (like the task shown on page 238). The teacher might model self-instruction by saying aloud something like this: "OK, now, what do I have to do? I have to find a problem down here that is just exactly the same as this one up here. This is going to be tough, but I just need to relax and get through it. Let's see, now. This problem is 221 minus 12 equals 209. I need to remember to make sure every part of the one I find down here is just the same. I'd better take it one part at a time just to make sure I get it right, because every part has to be the same. I know what I'll do, I'll just take it slow, one step at a time, and I'll cross off each one down here if I find something that's different. Because once I find something wrong, I don't have to check that one again because I know it can't be the one. Now, it's got to have 221 at the top. Let's see. This one has 221. But this one has 211 at the top, not 221, so it can't be right. So I'll mark it off. This one has 221, and this one, and this one, and this one, so they're OK. Now, it's got to be minus 12. This is minus 21, so it gets marked off. Minus 12 here is OK. Plus 12 can't be it. Minus 12 here is OK and here is OK. Boy, I'm really being careful, and I'm going to get it right. OK. Now I've got to find 209 for the answer. Let's see, 901 is wrong, 209 is right. Looks like I've got it now. But I'd better check this other one too. No, 219 is wrong, so it must be this one here. I'm going to double check just to make sure. Up here 221, down here, 221. Up here minus 12, down here minus 12. Up here 209, down here 209. Got it. Wow, did I do a great job on that!"

Next, the student might run through similar problems, imitating the teacher's verbalizations. The teacher might coach the student about appropriate verbalizations. Then trials might consist of first the teacher, then the student, whispering the self-instructions. Finally, the teacher might model the appropriate task behavior with covert verbalization (but pointing and comparing), after which the student does the same. In most training programs, the teacher also models making occasional errors and dealing with them constructively, like this: "Now I've got to find minus 12. Let's see, minus 12—cross it off. Oops! I almost made a mistake. But I caught it, and I can just erase that line, I'm still OK, because I'm thinking and being careful. Let's see, plus 12 is not minus 12, so I'll cross it off. Now I'm getting it." This type of self-instruction training, adapted to the particulars of the task and the student's characteristics, has great intuitive appeal, and research indicates that the techniques hold promise when skillfully applied (Meichenbaum, 1980; O'Leary, 1980).

Cognitive training and other self-control procedures are clearly not a panacea for the problems presented by impulsive children. Moreover, cognitive training is not as simple as it might at first appear. The teacher who wishes to implement the techniques effectively must understand their theoretical basis and carefully construct procedures to fit the individual case (see Gelfand & Hartmann, 1984; Meichenbaum, 1983; Rooney & Hallahan, 1985; Wallace & Kauffman, 1986 for further discussion). Future research will undoubtedly lead to refinements in teaching self-control and reveal the circumstances under which self-instruction and other cognitive training methods are and are not the treatment of choice (cf. Hallahan, Lloyd et al., 1983; Harris et al., 1985; Polsgrove, 1979).

Self-Control Training: A Psychoeducational Curriculum

Fagen et al. (1975) present a sequence of instructional units for teaching students to be, among other things, less impulsive and more reflective. Units of instruction include activities calculated to help the student learn to focus attention, avoid distractions, develop memory skills, plan sequences of behavior, anticipate consequences, appreciate feelings, tolerate frustration, inhibit or delay responding, and relax.

> Taken together, the... skills represent an integration of cognitive and affective factors which mediate possibilities for regulating action. The presence of these skills enables a learner to make personally and socially acceptable choices regarding task requirements—choices which preclude the feelings of inadequacy which so often accompany task performance or nonperformance. Through mastery of these self-control skills, the learner incorporates the necessary self-pride and respect for open-minded reflection on available alternatives. (p. 44)

This approach emphasizes the importance of feelings, self-understanding, introspection, and insight in changing behavior, although Fagan's curriculum goes well beyond the methods described in early writings about the psychoeducational approach and includes some techniques associated with cognitive strategy training. Fagen and Long (1979) present data to support their self-control curriculum; but unlike the cognitive-behavior modification research, which emphasizes careful analyses involving single subjects, their research involves comparison of averages for groups of children. (The self-control curriculum is discussed further in Chapter 13.)

Other Methods

Besides the methods of control we have discussed so far, many others have been tried, such as various forms of psychotherapy. In fact, almost every type of intervention that has been used with any kind of troublesome behavior has been tried with hyperactivity (Ross & Ross, 1982). Perhaps that in itself is a commentary on the seriousness with which adults approach hyperactivity, the prevalence of hyperactivity in exceptional children, and our lack of knowledge about the origins of such behavior.

Life Space Interview

The life space interview (LSI) was devised by Redl (1959b) and his colleagues (see also Redl & Wineman, 1951, 1952) as a means of building ego strength in impulsive, aggressive children and youth. The LSI is a way of talking therapeutically with young-sters about their behavior. A life space interview is usually held immediately after a behavioral "crisis," since crises provide opportunities to explore with the youngster what happened, why it happened, and what can be done to prevent future difficulties. The assumption underlying the LSI technique is that discussing children's behavior with them in the proper way will help them gain insight into their problems and work out solutions to their dilemmas. Insight, LSI proponents believe, will provide the basis for volitional or ego control.

The LSI has great appeal to many people who oppose, on philosophical grounds, explicit behavior modification techniques. It also appeals to those whose perspective is predominantly psychiatric. Although there is a great deal of descriptive literature regarding the rationale and use of the LSI with disturbed children and youth, exper-imental research of its effects on behavior has not been forthcoming. Proponents of the LSI must, unfortunately, base their conviction of its value on testimonial or an-ecdotal evidence from case reports.

Structured Environment: Consistency and Teacher Direction

The structured approach emphasizes clear expectations about children's movement about the classroom, and the classroom routine is highly predictable (cf. Cruickshank et al., 1961; Haring & Phillips, 1962). Consistent consequences (actually an elementary form of behavior modification) are thus applied to hyperactive and nonhyperactive behavior. The teacher is highly directive, making nearly all decisions for children until they can wisely manage themselves. The structured classroom of Cruickshank, Haring, and their co-workers is designed to control the distractible, impulsive behavior as-sociated with hyperactivity. Research (Haring and Phillips, 1962; Haring and Whelan, 1965) indicated that a highly structured classroom has a salutary effect on disturbed children's behavior. The structured approach, pioneered decades ago, is consistent with contemporary research indicating the effectiveness of maintaining a highly con-sistent classroom environment that offers reward for appropriate behavior and mild punishment for misconduct (cf. Rosenberg, 1986).

Optimal Sensory Stimulation

The concept of optimal stimulation suggests that youngsters will not respond favorably to excessive stimulation or to extreme sensory deprivation (see Ross & Ross, 1982); that is, an optimal level of sensory stimulation produces normal behavior. Cruickshank (1975) hypothesizes that the ordinary classroom environment contains too much stimulation for the distractible child. An alternative hypothesis is that distractible children often need more stimulation than is found in the normal classroom if they are to perform normally (Zentall, 1975, 1979). A thorough review of research by Zentall (1983b) indicates that children's behavior, especially hyperactive behavior, is adversely affected by too much or too little stimulation. The relationship of various types of environmental stimuli (visual, auditory, social) to behavior and achievement is too complex to cover here, but an important general conclusion of Zentall is that hyperactive children may be helped by a highly stimulating environment (bright colors and decorations, for example) when working on familiar, repetitive tasks and by an environment with low stimulation when working on complex or unusual tasks.

Biofeedback and Relaxation Training

Biofeedback is a way of teaching individuals to control their overt behavior or internal biological processes by feeding back to them information about their physiological status. A person may be taught to control blood pressure or brain waves by training him or her to monitor these internal activities continuously with the help of an oscilloscope or similar device. Braud, Lupin, and Braud (1975) reported a case in which a six-year-old hyperactive boy was taught to reduce his muscular activity and tension by training him to monitor his own muscle tension. His training was carried out in a laboratory situation, but some generalized improvement of his behavior was observed at home and at school. Schulman, Stevens, Suran, Kupst, and Naughton (1978) decreased the activity level of a highly active 11-year-old boy using a combination of biofeedback (from a portable activity-measuring device worn at the child's waist) and behavior modification techniques. They also increased the activity level of a lethargic (hypoactive) ten-year-old boy using the same methods in an experimental classroom.

Raymer and Poppen (1985) used relaxation training and feedback in the clinic, plus training in the home provided by the mother, to reduce muscle tension and hyperactivity in three boys. The intent of the training was to help tense individuals adopt more relaxed postures and behaviors. The results suggest methods that could be adapted for classroom use; "for example, in classroom study period, or at home watching TV, children could be taught to slow their breathing, drop their jaw, remain quiet, and so forth" (p. 315). Combined biofeedback and relaxation training has improved the performance of hyperactive boys on laboratory measures of memory (Omizo, Cubberly, Semands, & Omizo, 1986). Future research and development of biofeedback and relaxation training techniques could provide practical methods for controlling hyperactive behavior in everyday classroom settings (see also Christie, Dewitt, Kaltenback & Reed, 1984; Ross & Ross, 1982; Tansey & Bruner, 1983).

Dietary Control

Well-controlled studies indicate that a few youngsters' hyperactivity is at least partly a function of the food substances they ingest, and that younger children may more often be affected by food chemicals than are older children. Feingold's (1975, 1976) claims that most hyperactive children will be significantly helped by following his diet, however, are apparently extravagant. Research supports a considerably more cautious view of how many children are adversely affected by foods, how many children's behavior would be improved by following the diet, and how much improvement could be obtained by dietary control alone (Blouin, 1983; Swanson & Kinsbourne, 1980; Trites & Tryphonas, 1983a, 1983b; Varley, 1984; Whalen, 1983). Not many children can be expected to respond significantly to dietary control (Campbell et al., 1985), and it is an intervention that is primarily the responsibility of parents; teachers are in no position to recommend it, nor are they able to implement it.

SUMMARY

Hyperactivity is not defined simply by a high rate of activity; it is a high rate of inappropriate behavior of various kinds that the youngster cannot control at will. Closely related to hyperactivity are distractibility (attention problems) and impulsivity (acting without thinking). We see many of the hyperactive child's characteristics in normally developing young children, whereas the hyperactive child exhibits developmentally deviant behavior.

There is persistent controversy as to the definition of hyperactivity and the appropriate terminology for it. Conduct disorder and hyperactivity are often difficult to distinguish. Besides hyperactive, hyperkinetic, minimal brain dysfunction, and a variety of other labels have been used. The American Psychiatric Association now uses the term *attention-deficit hyperactivity disorder* to refer to hyperactivity and related problems. Most authorities estimate that three to five percent of the child population is hyperactive, and boys outnumber girls by a ratio of three or more to one.

Brain damage is the favorite causal explanation for hyperactivity, but there is little evidence to confirm brain injury as the cause in most cases. Hyperactivity may be genetically organized in many cases, but no one knows how this genetic factor works. There is little evidence for any other possible biological cause, such as allergies, toxins, or deficits in neurochemicals. Social learning is a plausible causal factor, but does not explain most cases fully. Because we understand so little about the causes of hyperactivity, secondary prevention is the only feasible approach.

Assessment of hyperactivity requires obtaining multiple perspectives on the youngster's behavior and its contexts. Rating scales are useful for screening and initial evaluation, but assessment for educational programming and evaluation of progress demands direct observation. Adequate assessment of attention calls for measuring the student's attention in relation to specific tasks in specific contexts. One might assess impulsivity by adapting laboratory instruments and by direct observation.

Nearly every type of intervention that has been tried with any kind of behavior problem has been tried with hyperactivity. The most useful approaches to date are medication (stimulant drugs), behavior modification, and cognitive strategy training. The right dosage of the right drug tends to reduce hyperactive behavior, but the effects on academic performance may not be significant. Drug effects are idiosyncratic and require careful monitoring. Behavior modification typically leads to improvement in both hyperactivity and academic performance, but it is not a panacea. Positive reinforcement of on-task behavior is the typical behavior modification approach. Behavior modification has certain advantages over drugs: it tends to have more specific effects, keeps the focus on learning, demands improvement of the youngster's environment, and fosters personal responsibility for behavioral change.

Cognitive strategy training includes a wide variety of techniques for helping individuals become more aware of their behavior and active in changing it. Self-monitoring and self-instruction have been successful with hyperactive youngsters. Self-monitoring involves training the student to record his or her own behavior on cue; self-instruction requires teaching the student to talk himself or herself through a systematic approach to a problem. A psychoeducational self-control curriculum incorporates many of the principles of cognitive strategy training.

A variety of other techniques have been used with hyperactive students, including Life Space Interviewing, a structured classroom approach, optimal sensory stimulation, biofeedback and relaxation training, and dietary control.

Conduct Disorder: Overt Aggression

As you read this chapter, keep these guiding questions in mind:

- ☐ What distinguishes the aggressive antisocial youngster from one who is developing normally?
- ☐ What behavior characterizes the three subtypes of conduct disorder?
- ☐ From a psychodynamic viewpoint, what causes aggression?
- ☐ What is the frustration-aggression hypothesis, and to what extent is it supported by research?
- ☐ According to social learning theory, how is aggression learned?
- ☐ What factors put youngsters at high risk for conduct disorder?
- ☐ How does one assess conduct disorder?
- ☐ Which clinical interventions have been most successful with conduct disorder?
- ☐ Why have educators largely abandoned the psychodynamic approach to managing aggression?
- ☐ How are psychoeducational and social learning approaches to managing aggression becoming similar, and how are they different?
- ☐ What common intervention techniques does a social learning approach to aggression use?
- ☐ How is punishment defined, and why is it a dangerous and controversial but common approach to dealing with aggression?
- ☐ When punishment is necessary, what guidelines should one follow?
- ☐ What is countercontrol, and how might one manage it?

DEFINITION AND PREVALENCE

Normally developing children and adolescents occasionally exhibit antisocial behavior of various descriptions. They may throw temper tantrums, fight with their siblings or peers, cheat, lie, be physically cruel to animals or to other people, refuse to obey their parents, or destroy their own or others' possessions. Normally developing youngsters do not, however, perform antisocial acts in most social contexts, nor with such frequency as to become pariahs among their peers or excessively burdensome to their parents and teachers. A child who has a conduct disorder exhibits a persistent pattern of antisocial behavior that significantly impairs everyday functioning at home or school or that leads others to conclude that the youngster is unmanageable (Kazdin, 1987).

Some youngsters exhibit conduct disorder that is characterized primarily by acts of overt aggression, and their behavior is classified as *undersocialized aggressive conduct disorder* (Quay, 1986a, 1986b). Their behavior includes characteristics such as hyperactivity, impulsiveness, irritability, stubbornness, demandingness, arguing, teasing, poor peer relations, loudness, threatening and attacking others, cruelty, fighting, showing off, bragging, swearing, blaming others, sassiness, and disobedience. Other youngsters exhibit *socialized aggressive conduct disorder,* characterized by more covert antisocial acts such as negativism, lying, destructiveness, stealing, setting fires, associating with bad companions, belonging to a gang, running away, truancy, and alcohol and/or drug abuse. Still other youngsters are described as *versatile* if they show both overt and covert forms of antisocial conduct (Loeber & Schmaling, 1985a, 1985b). (The socialized, undersocialized, and versatile forms of conduct disorder correspond roughly to the three types of conduct disorder called group, solitary, and undifferentiated in DSM-III-R.) In this chapter, we will discuss overtly aggressive and versatile forms of conduct disorder; covert antisocial behavior is covered in Chapter 14.

Most youngsters normally exhibit aggressive, antisocial behavior to some degree and in some contexts. Ordinarily, for example, children are more aggressive on the playground than in the classroom, and they tend to exhibit less overt aggression as they grow older. Compared to nonaggressive youngsters, children and youth with aggressive conduct disorder typically show age-inappropriate aggression from an earlier age, develop a larger repertoire of aggressive acts, exhibit aggression across a wider range of social situations, and persist in aggressive behavior for a longer time (see Harris, 1979; Loeber, 1982).

The prevalence of conduct disorder has been estimated at four to ten percent of the child population, although reliable statistics are not available (Quay, 1986b). Nevertheless, the consensus among researchers is that the problem affects a sizable percentage of children and youth. "Even though it is difficult to pinpoint how many children might be defined as conduct disordered at a particular age, data consistently reveal that the problem is great by most definitions" (Kazdin, 1987, p. 16). Boys with aggressive conduct disorder outnumber girls by a wide margin, probably three or more to one. Given that conduct disorder is among the most prevalent types of behavior disorders, the seriousness of the problem for our society and the implications of overt aggression for children's futures must be addressed.

Perspective on Aggression

"Aggression and America have long been intimate companions" (Goldstein, Carr, Davidson, & Wehr, 1981). Aggression is not new to American children, their homes and families, or their schools. Even cursory examination of *Children and Youth in America* (Bremner, 1970, 1971) and other similar sources quickly reveals that coercion, violence, and brutality have been practiced by and toward children and youth since the founding of this nation. Recognizing the historical presence of violence does not in any way, however, reduce the crisis proportions of aggression in the present-day lives of American children. Both violent adult crime and violent juvenile delinquency have increased dramatically during the past few decades (Doke & Flippo, 1983). Through the media, children are exposed to brutal acts of aggression at a rate unprecedented in the history of civilization (Comstock, 1983; Eron & Heusmann, 1986). Assaultive behavior, disruptiveness, and property destruction in schools have grown commonplace (Harootunian & Apter, 1983; Mayer et al., 1987; Morse, 1985; Ruhl & Hughes, 1985).

Regular classroom teachers must be prepared to deal with aggression, since it is likely that at least one of their students will be highly disruptive, destructive, or assaultive toward other students or the teacher. Teachers of disturbed students must be ready to handle an especially large dose of aggression (Ruhl & Hughes, 1985). As you recall from previous chapters, conduct disorder is the variety of exasperating deportment that most frequently obtains a deviance label and results in the student's referral for special education services. The prospective special education teacher who expects most disturbed students to be withdrawn or who believes that students with conduct disorder will quickly learn to reciprocate a kindly social demeanor will be shocked. Without effective means for controlling aggression, the teacher of behavior disordered students must develop a superhuman tolerance for interpersonal nastiness.

Aggressive youngsters about whom we are concerned here perform noxious behaviors at a much higher rate and at a much later age than normally developing children. A youngster with aggressive conduct disorder may match the noxious behaviors of the normally developing child two-to-one or more; and whereas the normally developing child exhibits social aggression at a decreasing rate as he or she grows older, the conduct disordered youngster usually does not (Patterson et al., 1975). Table 13.1 lists fourteen noxious behaviors that aggressive and normally developing youngsters exhibit. Patterson and his colleagues identified the behaviors and typical rates of occurrence through many hours of naturalistic observation in the homes of families with socially aggressive and nonaggressive children. Note the marked differences between rates of aggressive behaviors in aggressive and nonaggressive children. According to the data in Table 13.1, an aggressive child can be expected to be noncompliant about every ten minutes, as well as to hit and to tease about every half hour; a nonaggressive child, on the other hand, might be expected to be noncompliant once in twenty minutes, to tease once in about fifty minutes, and to hit once in a couple of hours. While this list is certainly not exhaustive, it does represent the most common means by which children inflict suffering on others.

TABLE 13.1

Noxious Behaviors and Average Time between Occurrences in Aggressive and Nonaggressive Children

Noxious Behavior	Description	Average Number of Minutes between Occurrences[a]	
		Aggressive Children	Nonaggressive Children
Disapproval	Disapproving of another's behavior by words or gestures	7	12
Negativism	Stating something neutral in content but in negative tone of voice	9	41
Noncompliance	Not doing what is requested	11	20
Yell	Shouting, yelling, or talking loudly; if carried on for sufficient time it becomes extremely unpleasant	18	54
Tease	Teasing that produces displeasure, disapproval, or disruption of current activity of person being teased	20	51
High rate activity	Activity that is aversive to others if carried on for a long period (e.g., running in the house or jumping up and down)	23	71
Negative physical act	Attacking or attempting to attack another with enough intensity to potentially inflict pain (e.g., biting, kicking, slapping, hitting, spanking, throwing, grabbing)	24	108
Whine	Saying something in a slurring, nasal, high-pitched, or falsetto voice	28	26
Destructive	Destroying, damaging, or trying to damage or destroy any object	33	156
Humiliation	Making fun of, shaming, or embarrassing another intentionally	50	100
Cry	Any type of crying	52	455
Negative command	Commanding another to do something and demanding immediate compliance, plus threatening aversive consequences (explicitly or implicitly) if compliance not immediate; also directing sarcasm or humiliation at another	120	500
Dependent	Requesting help with task the child is capable of doing himself (e.g., a 16-year-old boy asking his mother to comb his hair)	149	370
Ignore	Appearing to recognize that someone has directed behavior toward oneself but not responding in an active fashion	185	244

[a]Minutes between occurrences expressed as approximations of reported average rates per minute (e.g., for aggressive children's "whine," reported rate per minute equals 0.0360, or approximately once every 28 minutes.)

Note: Adapted from "A Social Learning Approach to Family Intervention," by G. R. Patterson, J. B. Reid, R. R. Jones, and R. E. Conger. In *Families with Aggressive Children,* Vol. 1 (p.5), 1975, Eugene, OR: Castilia. Reprinted by permission.

Observations in schools and studies of school records suggest that we may expect classroom behaviors similar to those in Table 13.1 from aggressive youngsters (Patterson, Cobb, & Ray, 1972; Ruhl & Hughes, 1985). These behaviors are frequently accompanied by academic failure. Not surprisingly, students who exhibit aggressive conduct disorder are often rejected by their peers and perceive their peers as hostile toward them (Dodge & Somberg, 1987; Konstantareas & Homatidis, 1985; Panella & Henggeler, 1986). When children exhibit aggressive antisocial behavior and academic failure beginning in the early elementary grades, the prognosis is particularly grim, unless effective early intervention is provided (Kelso & Stewart, 1986; Ledingham & Schwartzman, 1984; Safer, 1984; Walker et al., 1987).

The high rates of antisocial behavior and the significant impairment of everyday functioning of youngsters with undersocialized aggressive conduct disorder do not bode well for their futures. Such youngsters tend to exhibit a relatively stable pattern of aggressive behavior over time; their problems do not tend to dissipate, but to continue into adulthood (Olweus, 1979; Quay, 1986b; Robins, 1986). Consequently, the prognosis for later adjustment is poor, and the pattern of antisocial conduct is often transmitted over generations. Because aggressive antisocial behavior tends to keep people in contact with mental health and criminal justice systems, and because the behavior inflicts considerable suffering on victims of physical assault and property loss, the cost to society is enormous (Kazdin, 1985, 1987). While for boys, a history of serious antisocial conduct before age fifteen increases the chances of externalizing psychopathology (aggression, criminal behavior, alcohol and drug abuse) in adulthood, for girls this kind of childhood history increases the probability of adulthood externalizing disorders and internalizing disorders (depression, phobias) as well (Robins, 1986). "Clearly, no other disorder of childhood and adolescence is so widespread and disruptive of the lives of those who suffer it and of the lives of others" (Quay, 1986b, p. 64). Thus, finding effective interventions for conduct disorder is a priority among social scientists (Doke & Flippo, 1983; Goldstein, 1983a, 1983b, 1987; Goldstein & Keller, 1983; Kazdin & Frame, 1983).

The case of Don illustrates the type of behavior extremely socially aggressive children exhibit at home and at school. Notice that Don's interactions with his family are characterized by coercive exchanges. Without effective intervention to break the coercive cycle at home and at school, Don seems virtually certain to experience a high rate of failure in school and continuing conflict in the community.

Don

When I met him, he was 6½ years of age. . . . A trim four-footer, he had a sleazy look about him, like a postcard carried too long in a hip pocket. He sat in the reception room, slouched down in the chair and coolly looked me over as I approached. . . . The violence of his temper outbursts was frightening and seemed to be triggered by relatively minor provocations. At school, a simple request to turn in his homework, a mild rebuke, or a suggestion that he had erred in his work could lead to shouted obscenities, overturned desks, or attacks on other children with a pencil held as a dagger. The observers commented that in the home he ruled whatever territory he occupied. . . .

During the intervals when he was absent from home, telephone calls would often mark his progress through the neighborhood, e.g., he left school two hours early, stole candy from a store, and appropriated a toy from a neighborhood child.

No baby-sitter would brave this storm center, so the parents had long ago given up the idea of a private life, movies, or weekends together. Both parents worked. The mother (not yet 30 and physically attractive) looked as if she was in the throes of a severe illness. The family physician provided medication for her chronic depression and accompanying fatigue. Work was a reprieve from her morning and afternoon bouts with her son, Don. . . . Typically, her day began at 7:00 a.m., rousing him from his wet sheets (which she changed), then scolding until he went sullenly to his tub. Once there, she washed and dried him as if he were an infant or visiting royalty.

He often dawdled while dressing, which produced a stream of prompts and commands from his mother. Suggested items of clothing were refused; this led to bitter exchanges with the now thoroughly exasperated mother. He emphasized their disagreements by kicking the door and throwing things around the room. Through all of this the mother hovered about, helping to get him dressed. She alternately cajoled and scolded, wheedled and glared.

She stood in attendance while he dined. Not only did she serve, but she finally fed him whenever he deigned to open his mouth. Through it all ran a steady cacophony of yells, cries, and arguments about whether his mother had any right to force these unreasonable requests upon him. The mother alternated between patient and antagonistic answers to his arguments and threats. At one point, she brought a stick from behind the refrigerator door. Her menacing demeanor left little doubt that she regularly employed this weapon. In the face of this ultimate threat, Don showed temporary compliance and moved forward in his glacial progress toward leaving for school.

In the afternoon Don returned from school to pick up the morning refrain. His 4-year-old brother was also available as a partner. The latter (a Machiavellian of considerable stature) knew when to probe, when to attack, and when to withdraw with tearful protestations to the protection afforded by his parents. For example, as Don sat eating his ice cream (with his fingers), the younger brother surreptitiously slipped a more efficient spoon into the mess and ran triumphantly down the hall to hide behind the door in his bedroom. Don ran shrieking after him, grabbed the door, and repeatedly slammed it into his younger brother. The screams brought both parents to the scene. The father listened for a moment to their shouted claims and counterclaims. After a brief pause, he simply began to slap both children. With that, the mother turned, walked quietly back into the kitchen and sat staring out the window.

Later the family was to go for a ride in the car. Both parents began shouting commands. In the rush of the moment, they often overlapped in their targets; e.g., the mother said, "Don, wash your face right now," while the father ordered, "Put on your jacket, Don. Hurry up now." A steady stream of commands was given as they moved toward the car. The children moved at their own pace, largely ignoring both parents.

During the day, the observers noted periods where the interactions seemed warm and positive. For example, on numerous occasions one parent would read to the children, who would often sit for long periods of time entranced with the story. At these times they seemed to be the prototypical loving family unit. (Patterson, 1982, pp. 294–295)

CAUSAL FACTORS AND PREVENTION

Why do children begin to hurt and threaten others, and why do they persist in aggression? These questions have no ready answers, although we have learned a great deal about the causes of aggression. How to prevent social aggression and how to control it once it emerges must become topics of major concern to educators and parents if schools and families are to be humane social institutions.

Aggression has historically been a concern of social scientists, and many alternative explanations have been offered for it. In psychodynamic analyses, aggression is assumed to be instinctual; aggressive instinct is assumed to cause people to behave aggressively. Aggression is viewed as an entity in itself, a force behind behavior rather than the behavior itself. Redl and Wineman (1951), for example, suggested that "We have ample materials on the various disguises which particles of aggression and hate have to assume in order to sneak close to the scene of action or find open expression in fantasy or thought" (p. 25). Of aggressive children they stated, "Then, under the impact of trauma or fright, the full blast of their aggression rides herd over them" (p. 29), and of a passive child who became aggressive they said, "Behind the seemingly empty and childlike stare of his detached eyes lay an ocean of unbridled aggression, destruction, and counter hatred, which was the response to years of earlier cruelty and neglect, but which had been frozen into apathetic immobility at the time" (p. 28). Berkowitz and Rothman (1960) offered this summary of aggression from a psychoanalytic perspective:

> Aggression is an innate instinctual impulse which may give rise to a need for aggressive behavior. Aggression which can be successfully sublimated may become socially useful, while overt aggression which is destructive in nature is an acting out of the child's need to inflict pain and punishment upon himself or upon others. Aggressive behavior which is uncontrolled is an easily observed, obvious indicator of maladjustment. (p. 89)

Psychodynamic theories of aggression appear to have lost adherents in recent years, primarily because the hypotheses such theories generate are not empirically testable. Moreover, psychodynamic theory is of limited value in designing effective intervention techniques, and other conceptual models are now supported by abundant empirical data and have direct implications for intervention.

Another alternative explanation of aggression that enjoyed acclaim is the hypothesis that frustration (defined as the blocking or thwarting of any ongoing goal-directed activity) always results in aggression and that aggression always arises from frustration (Dollard, Doob, Miller, Mowrer, & Sears, 1939). Rather than ascribing aggression to innate instincts, Dollard et al. argued that frustration induces an aggressive drive that motivates aggressive behavior. Encountering frustration automatically induces the aggressive drive, which must be given expression before the drive can be reduced. The popularity of the frustration-aggression hypothesis among proponents of psychodynamic theory in the 1950s is exemplified by comments of Redl and Wineman (1951).

> The various studies in "Frustration and Aggression" have documented Freud's old suspicions along that line and have shown statistically that the mere frustration of

basic needs or important goals in a child's life may be enough to produce unmanageable quantities of aggression and destructiveness or other disturbance even
in children who otherwise wouldn't have had to hate so much. (pp. 25–26)

While frustration-aggression theory was indeed constructed on the basis of
empirical data showing that frustration *can* produce aggression, the theory has been
laid to rest by additional research (see Achenbach, 1982b; Bandura, 1973; Goldstein,
1983a, 1983b, 1987). In brief, this research has shown that aggression is not an
inevitable outcome of frustration and that several other factors besides frustration can
contribute to the development and maintenance of aggression. Furthermore, the
concept of an aggressive *drive* is superfluous; it is not needed to explain the instigation
and perpetuation of aggressive behavior. Biological and social learning analyses now
offer appealing alternatives to earlier explanations of aggression.

Biological Factors

Hypotheses regarding the biological bases of aggressive conduct disorder usually
follow one of three lines of argument:

Aggression is genetically organized and shaped through evolutionary processes

Aggression is primarily a response to hormonal or other biochemical action

Aggression reflects aberrant central nervous system function

In actuality, biological causal factors are not so neatly separable; genetic, biochemical,
and neurological factors are interlocking biological processes, all of which are affected
by environmental factors.

Evolutionary processes have probably shaped human aggression, although aggressive behavior may no longer serve its original purposes. Sociobiology presently
has little to offer developmental psychologists who are seeking more immediate causes
of aggression (Hinde, 1986). Nevertheless, studies of twins and adopted children
clearly indicate a genetic factor in extremely hyperaggressive and criminal behavior
(Kazdin, 1987; Mednick et al., 1986), although how this genetic factor operates, its
relationship to hormonal levels and central nervous system function, and its implications are not understood. Hormonal changes and drugs apparently can induce
aggressive tendencies, but the available evidence is far from sufficient to justify the
conclusion that biochemical processes are the cause of most human aggression (Achenbach, 1982b; Bandura, 1973; Olweus, 1986). Genetic factors involved in criminality
may produce an autonomic nervous system that is slow to respond (Mednick et al.,
1986), yet neurological processes alone do not explain why people behave aggressively
(Delgado, 1969; Kety, 1979; Simmel, Hahn, & Walters, 1983). All behavior, including
aggression, involves neurobiological processes, but these biological forces alone do
not determine how a person will behave. In fact, present knowledge strongly suggests
that an individual's social environment is a powerful regulator of neurobiological
processes and behavior; social learning may be the most important determinant of
aggression and prosocial behavior (Bandura, 1973). While biological factors apparently
contribute to the most severe cases of conduct disorder, their role in milder cases of

aggression is not clear; in both severe and mild forms of conduct disorder, the social environment obviously contributes to the problem (Wells & Forehand, 1985).

Social Learning Factors

A social learning (or social cognitive) analysis of aggression includes three major controlling influences: the environmental conditions that set the occasion for behavior or that reinforce or punish it, the behavior itself, and cognitive/affective (person) variables (Bandura, 1973, 1986; see Chapter 4). Whether or not a person exhibits aggressive behavior depends on the reciprocal effects of these three factors and the individual's social history. Social learning theory suggests that aggression is learned through the direct consequences of aggressive and nonaggressive acts and through observation of aggression and its consequences. Research in social learning supports several generalizations (see Bandura, 1973; Goldstein, 1983a, 1983b; Patterson, 1986a, 1986b).

☐ Children learn many aggressive responses by observing models or examples. The models may be family members, members of the child's subculture (friends, acquaintances, peers and adults in the community), or individuals portrayed in the mass media (including real and fictional, human and nonhuman).

☐ Children are more likely to imitate aggressive models when the models are of high social status and when they see that the models receive reinforcement (positive consequences or rewards) or do not receive punishment for their aggression.

☐ Children learn aggressive behavior when, given opportunities to practice aggressive responses, they experience either no aversive consequences or succeed in obtaining rewards by harming or overcoming their victims.

☐ Aggression is more likely to occur when children are aversively stimulated, perhaps by physical assault, verbal threats, taunts, or insults; by thwarting of goal-directed behavior; or by decreases in or termination of positive reinforcement. Children may learn through observation and/or practice that they can obtain rewarding consequences by engaging in aggressive behavior. The probability of aggression under such circumstances is especially high when alternative (appropriate) means of obtaining reinforcement are not readily available or have not been learned, and when aggression is sanctioned by social authorities.

☐ Factors that maintain aggression include three types of reinforcement: *external reinforcement* (tangible rewards, social status rewards, removal of aversive conditions, expressions of injury or suffering by the victim); *vicarious reinforcement* (gratification obtained by observing others gain rewards through aggression), and *self-reinforcement* (self-congratulation or increased self-esteem following successful aggression).

☐ Aggression may be perpetuated by cognitive processes that justify hostile action: comparing one's deeds advantageously to more horrific deeds of others, appealing to higher principles (such as protection of self or others), placing responsibility on others (the familiar "I didn't start it" and "He made me do it" ploys), and dehumanizing the victims (perhaps with demeaning labels such as nerd, trash, pig, drooler).

☐ Punishment may serve to heighten or maintain aggression when it causes pain, when there are no positive alternatives to the punished response, when punishment is delayed or inconsistent, or when punishment provides a model of aggressive behavior. When counterattack against the punisher seems likely to succeed, punishment maintains aggression. The adult who punishes a child by striking not only causes pain, which increases the probability of aggression, but provides a model of aggression as well.

A social learning analysis of aggression generates testable predictions about environmental conditions that foster aggressive behavior. Research over several decades has led to empirically confirmed predictions about the genesis of aggression (cf. Goldstein, 1983a; Goldstein & Segall, 1983; Olweus, Block, & Radke-Yarrow, 1986).

Viewing televised aggression will increase aggressive behavior, especially in males and in children who have a history of aggressiveness (Eron & Huesmann, 1986).

Delinquent subcultures, such as street gangs, will maintain aggressive behavior in their members by modeling and reinforcing aggression (Buehler, Patterson, & Furniss, 1966; Farrington, 1986a).

Families of aggressive children are characterized by high rates of aggression on the part of all members, by coercive exchanges between the aggressive child and other family members, and by parents' inconsistent punitive control techniques (Patterson, 1986a, 1986b).

Aggression begets aggression. When one person presents an aversive condition for another (hitting, yelling, whining) the affronted individual is likely to reply by presenting a negative condition of his or her own, resulting in a coercive process (Patterson, 1982). The coercive interaction will continue until one individual withdraws his or her aversive condition, providing negative reinforcement (escape from aversive stimulation) for the victor (see also Tedeschi, Smith, & Brown, 1974).

Family, school, and cultural factors involving social learning were discussed in Chapters 9, 10, and 11, respectively. These factors undoubtedly play a major role in the development of aggressive conduct disorders. By providing models of aggression and supplying reinforcement for aggressive behavior, families, schools, and the larger society teach youngsters (albeit inadvertently) to behave aggressively. This insidious teaching process is most effective for youngsters who are already predisposed to aggressive behavior by their biological endowment and/or their previous social learning. And the process is maintained by reciprocity of effects among the behavior, the social environment, and the child's cognitive and affective characteristics. The teaching/learning process involved in aggression includes reciprocal effects such as these:

The social environment provides aversive conditions (noxious stimuli)

The youngster perceives the social environment as both threatening and likely to reward aggression

The youngster's behavior is noxious to others, who attempt to control it by threats and punitive responses

In coercive bouts, the youngster is frequently successful in overcoming others by being more aversive or persistent, thereby obtaining reinforcement for aggression and confirming his or her perceptions of the social environment as threatening and controlled by aggressive behavior

Risk Factors

A wide range of experiences and conditions are known to put youngsters at risk for conduct disorders. These are among the known risk factors, which involve social learning in addition to biological predispositions:

Difficult temperament (see Chapter 8)

Early development of antisocial behavior

Academic failure and school discipline problems

Parental psychopathology or criminality

Lax supervision and erratic discipline at home

Abuse

Broken home and marital discord

Environmental conditions associated with low social class

Punitive, deteriorated, poorly managed, crowded, and inadequate school environments (Kazdin, 1987)

This list could be greatly extended; it could include an enormous variety of circumstances and conditions inimical to normal child development. Most of the risk factors are highly interrelated; for example, any combination—teenage parents, poor economic conditions, child abuse, parental deviance, parental discord, poor parental discipline, and inadequate schooling—place a child at high risk for conduct disorder.

Prevention

Prevention of aggressive conduct disorder presents enormous problems. Given the nature of aggressive youngsters' problems, efforts to help them develop empathy for and relationships with others, develop social problem-solving skills, acquire academic and work skills, and participate in community-based recreation programs have intuitive appeal. Yet, "in general, the data available at this time do not seem to support implementation of any large-scale prevention program to alter antisocial behavior" (Kazdin, 1987, p. 107). In fact, some prevention efforts have had the opposite results— participation in the program has *increased* the antisocial behavior of youths at risk.

Preventing conduct disorder from becoming worse—secondary prevention—may be accomplished by early treatment with promising intervention programs; deterring development of antisocial behavior of youngsters who do not exhibit conduct disorder—primary prevention—is much more problematic. Despite the many risk factors associated with conduct disorder, it is not possible to accurately predict which children will develop a conduct disorder and which will not. Thus, efforts to select high-risk youngsters for preventive efforts yield many false positives (those who are at high risk based on current research, but who will not become conduct disordered). As Kazdin (1987) points out, inclusion of these false positives in prevention programs may *increase* the likelihood of negative outcomes, perhaps because the children are labeled as problems when they are not, or because the prevention program is not actually effective. Still, we must continue to try to devise effective prevention programs.

Intervention programs for conduct disordered youngsters (secondary prevention) appear to offer greater promise than primary prevention. Secondary prevention poses a dilemma because, on the one hand, youngsters who exhibit earlier and more diverse forms of antisocial behavior carry a worse prognosis (Robins, 1986), but are less responsive to intervention (Kazdin, 1987). It is thus not clear whether concentrating efforts on mild or severe conduct disorders would be the more efficient and effective approach to secondary prevention.

ASSESSMENT

Since conduct disorder is a dimension that consistently appears in analyses of behavior problem checklists, assessment by parents' and teachers' behavior ratings seems straightforward (see Chapter 7; Quay, 1986a, 1986b); however, "exactly how to measure conduct disorder is not well worked out" (Kazdin, 1987). Besides behavior checklists or rating scales, measures of social skills, peer relations, self-reports, cognitive processes, and academic achievement may also be employed. Direct observation of aggressive acts is also a useful tool in assessing antisocial conduct. But assessments that use various sources of data (such as parent, teacher, and self-ratings) often yield very different results—the different measures do not converge to provide a consistent picture of the problem. Nor do we have clear-cut criteria for diagnosis or classification on any given type of measure. Thus, to conclude that a youngster exhibits conduct disorder is largely a matter of clinical judgment. Ideally, judgment is based on information from a variety of behavior measures and others' perceptions of the behavior. In school, measuring aggressive behavior through direct observation, evaluating academic skills, and assessing social skills provide the most useful information for educational programming (Polsgrove, 1987).

INTERVENTION AND EDUCATION

Strategies for controlling aggressive antisocial behavior depend on the presumed causes of aggression. Those who view humans as inherently aggressive, driven by merciless and unalterable instincts, offer little advice except to accept aggressive behavior or, perhaps, try to channel aggression into constructive pursuits or resolve underlying conflicts through long-term psychotherapy. Alternatively, those who believe that social forces are primarily responsible for aggression will recommend modulating the social environment to support more acceptable behavior. One who assumes aggression can be altered through biological processes may recommend drugs or surgery as the treatment of choice. Many mental health workers suggest combinations or variations of psychodynamic, behavioral, or biological interventions.

Prediction and social control of violent behavior are among the most contro-versial and critical issues involving American youth today (Eisenberg, 1984; Monahan, 1984; Nietzel & Himelein, 1986). A variety of conceptual approaches, ranging from psychodynamic to behavioral, have been suggested. An even wider variety of treat-ments has been offered, none of which has been clearly and reliably effective. Table 13.2 summarizes major types of treatment for antisocial aggression. Kazdin (1987) notes that parent management training, problem-solving training, family therapy based on systems theory and behaviorism, and community-based treatments are the most promising approaches. Interventions based on social learning principles (Patterson, 1982, 1986a, 1986b) have generally been more successful than those based on psy-chodynamic theory.

Approaches to Education

The interventions summarized in Table 13.2 are typically implemented by psychol-ogists, psychiatrists, and social workers; they do not have an educational focus, al-though educators may be involved to some extent. We will focus on intervention strategies as they are conceptualized and implemented in psychodynamic, psycho-educational, and social learning theory.

Psychodynamic Theory

From a psychodynamic perspective, aggression is a pervasive and unalterable aspect of every child's personality, and the objective must be to help the child express aggression constructively. Two ways a teacher can help the aggressive youngster are, first, by accepting the child's behavior and feelings, and, second, by providing op-portunities for **catharsis** (literally, cleansing). Accepting the child's feelings and be-havior helps in developing a therapeutic relationship, which is supremely important in psychodynamic theory (see Ack, 1970; Bettelheim, 1950). Providing opportunities for catharsis is important because to reduce aggression, the child must express ag-gressive impulses.

Proponents of a psychodynamic approach to education for disturbed children recommend a permissive environment, compared to the traditional school. They believe a permissive environment allows students to feel accepted and free to express themselves, which promotes a secure and reassuring relationship with the teacher. This relationship is the key to academic progress and emotional growth. Relaxation of formal restrictions encourages a feeling of acceptance. The classroom atmosphere should be noncompetitive and friendly, permitting individuality and self-expression. To build the student's trust, the teacher must make it clear that no matter how the student behaves, he or she will be accepted as an individual. Teachers must sometimes allow themselves to be manipulated, playing a subservient role to serve the students'

TABLE 13.2
Therapeutic Focus and Processes of Major Classes of Treatment for Antisocial Behavior

Types of Treatment	Focus	Key Processes
Child-Focused Treatments		
Individual Psychotherapy	Focus on intrapsychic bases of antisocial behavior especially conflicts and psychological processes that were adversely affected over the course of development.	Relationship with the therapist is the primary medium through which change is achieved. Treatment provides a corrective emotional experience by providing insight and exploring new ways of behaving.
Group Psychotherapy	Processes of individual therapy, as noted above. Additional processes are reassurance, feedback, and vicarious gains by peers. Group processes such as cohesion, leadership also serve as the focus.	Relationship with the therapist and peers as part of the group. Group processes emerge to provide children with experiences and feelings of others and opportunities to test their own views and behaviors.
Behavior Therapy	Problematic behaviors presented as target symptoms or behaviors designed to controvert these symptoms (e.g., prosocial behaviors).	Learning of new behaviors through direct training, via modeling, reinforcement, practice, and role playing. Training in the situations (e.g., at home, in the community) where the problematic behaviors occur.
Problem-Solving Skills Training	Cognitive processes and interpersonal cognitive problem-solving skills that underlie social behavior.	Teach problem-solving skills to children by engaging in a step-by-step approach to interpersonal situations. Use of modeling, practice, rehearsal and role play to develop problem-solving skills. Development of an internal dialogue or private speech that utilizes the processes of identifying prosocial solutions to problems.

emotional needs (see Ack, 1970; Berkowitz & Rothman, 1960; Bettelheim, 1950; Grossman, 1965). Popularity of the psychodynamic approach has declined probably for three reasons: (1) there is hardly any evidence to support its efficacy in reducing aggression; (2) other evidence suggests that it is destructive and actually has a pernicious effect; and (3) alternative methods are supported by reliable empirical data.

The notion of catharsis has been part of the popular imagination for so long that it has practically become a cultural truism (Berkowitz, 1973). Theories that postulate an aggressive drive or instinct imply that aggression is cumulative. The only way to get rid of aggression, therefore, is to drain off this reservoir, cleansing or purging the self

TABLE 13.2
continued

Types of Treatment	Focus	Key Processes
Child-Focused Treatments—Continued		
Pharmacotherapy	Designed to affect the biological substrates of behavior, especially in light of laboratory-based findings on neurohumors, biological cycles, and other physiological correlates of aggressive and emotional behavior.	Administration of psychotropic agents to control antisocial behavior. Lithium carbonate and haloperidol have been used because of their anti-aggressive effects.
Residential Treatments	Means of administrating other techniques in day treatment or residential setting. Foci of other techniques apply.	Processes of other techniques apply. Also, separation of the child from parents or removal from the home situation may help reduce untoward processes or crises that contribute to the clinical problem.
Family-Focused Treatments		
Family Therapy	Family as a functioning system serves as focus rather than the identified patient. Interpersonal relationships, organization, roles, and dynamics of the family.	Communication, relationships, and structure within the family and processes as autonomy, problem solving, and negotiation.
Parent Management Training	Interactions in the home, especially those involving coercive exchanges.	Direct training of parents to develop prosocial behavior in their children. Explicit use of social learning techniques to influence the child.
Community-Based Treatments		
Community-wide Interventions	Focus on activities and community programs to foster competence and peer relations.	Develop prosocial behavior and connections with peers. Activities are seen to promote prosocial behavior and to be incompatible with antisocial behavior.

Source: From *Conduct Disorders in Childhood and Adolescence* (pp. 75–76) by A. E. Kazdin, 1987. Beverly Hills, CA: Sage. Reprinted by permission.

by expressing aggression in one way or another. Catharsis can be achieved through *sublimation* (expressing aggression directly but in a socially sanctioned way, such as participation in contact sports), *displacement* (aggressing against a substitute and socially acceptable target, such as a punching bag or doll), or *fantasy,* in which aggressive acts are imagined or observed. Proponents of catharsis suggest that children's aggression might be lessened by allowing them to observe others' aggressive behavior in motion pictures or on television or by allowing them to repeatedly paint scenes of violence to express their hostility (cf. Berkowitz & Rothman, 1960).

Contrary to the catharsis hypothesis, research indicates that viewing, imagining, and practicing aggression tend to increase aggressive behavior, particularly in those who are already more aggressive than most (Bandura, 1973; Comstock, 1983; Eron & Heusmann, 1986). Exposure to TV violence decreases children's and adults' emotional sensitivity to acts of aggression, blunting their sensitivity to watching other people being hurt (Thomas, Horton, Lippincott, & Drabman, 1977). Arguments for cathartic activities are thus without support, and research indicates that youngsters are likely to become more aggressive as a result of cathartic activities.

Psychoeducational Approach

Proponents of a psychoeducational approach suggest that, although one should consider psychoanalytic concepts of unconscious instincts and drives, intervention should focus on conscious cognitive and affective problems—children's **ego** needs. An assumption underlying this approach is that if cognitive and affective problems can be resolved by helping children gain insight into their needs and motivations, they will change their behavior (cf. Morse, 1974, 1985; Morse & Wineman, 1965; Redl & Wineman, 1951, 1952; Rezmierski et al., 1982).

At this point, experimental evidence supporting the psychoeducational approach to managing aggression is weak; for example, the link between insight and behavioral change is tenuous (Bandura, 1986; Hobbs, 1974). The literature strongly suggests that insight into personal motivations is, by itself, not likely to produce a change in behavior (Bandura, 1973), although there is reason to suspect that cognitive and affective factors can be effective *components* of strategies for reducing aggressive behavior. A part of behavioral or social learning strategies, for example, may be calling the youngster's attention to the hurtful consequences of aggression, labeling aggression as bad or unacceptable, or making the child aware through discussion that victims of aggression have some desirable characteristics or share some of the child's own characteristics. Cognitive awareness of one's affective responses to aggression-inducing situations and cognitive analysis of the sequence of events may help in controlling aggressive behavior, although the mechanisms of control are probably built through explicit training rather than insight into motivations (cf. Bandura, 1973, 1986; Goldstein, 1983a, 1983b, 1987).

A significant extension of the psychoeducational approach is a self-control curriculum developed by Fagen et al. (1975; see also Fagen, 1979; Fagen & Long, 1979). Their curriculum includes eight skill clusters:

Selection—ability to perceive incoming information accurately

Storage—ability to retain the information received

Sequencing and ordering—ability to organize actions on the basis of a planned order

Anticipating consequences—ability to relate actions to expected outcomes

Managing frustration—ability to cope with external obstacles that produce stress

Inhibition and delay—ability to postpone or restrain action tendencies

Relaxation—ability to reduce internal tension (Fagen & Long, 1979)

The methods Fagen and Long suggest for teaching these skills include many of those used in a cognitive behavioral approach: self-instruction, problem solving, modeling and rehearsal, self-determination of goals and reinforcement standards, self-observation, self-evaluation, and self-reward. Their curriculum seems designed primarily as a skill-building, primary prevention approach that includes group instruction and role playing. Cognitive-behavioral strategies, on the other hand, are characterized by *in situ* analyses of specific behaviors of individual students. The Fagen-Long curriculum, however, clearly could be applied to work on specific behavior problems of individual students in everyday classroom situations.

Goldstein and his colleagues also describe "a psychoeducational intervention, designed specifically to enhance the prosocial, interpersonal, stress management, and planning skills of aggressive, withdrawn, immature, and 'normal' but developmentally lagging adolescents—all of whom are, by our definition, skill deficient" (Goldstein, Sprafkin, Gershaw, & Klein, 1986, p. 312; see also Goldstein, 1987; Goldstein et al., 1980). Their "structured learning" approach includes modeling, role playing, feedback, and transfer of training activities designed to teach specific social skills and alternative responses to aggression. Lessons in alternatives to aggression include instruction in asking permission, sharing something, helping others, negotiating, using self-control, standing up for one's rights, responding to teasing, avoiding trouble with others, and keeping out of fights (Goldstein et al., 1986, p. 319).

The Fagen and Long and Goldstein et al. instructional programs share some of the characteristics of behavioral and social learning strategies. They are representative of two trends in approaches to managing disruptive, hyperaggressive behavior: (1) movement of proponents of the psychoeducational approach away from the subjective psychodynamic interpretation of behavior and toward a firmer empirical foundation for theory and methodology; and (2) movement of proponents of the behavioral approach away from total reliance on direct observation and toward recognition of the importance of internal dialogue and affective states in behavioral control. The result of these trends has been a rapprochement between psychoeducational and cognitive behavioral interventions. The reconciliation of these two points of view has its critics, who prefer the theoretical and methodological purity of mid-century behaviorism or humanism. Nevertheless, many special educators view the rapprochement as a welcome step.

The movement by psychoeducational proponents toward empirical data and experimental methods, coupled with behaviorists' willingness to experiment with cognitive-affective interventions, could have a desirable result; perhaps it will produce reliable experimental evidence to support some psychoeducational methods that heretofore have been accepted on the basis of subjective clinical experience and dogma. This remains speculation, however; as Gresham (1985) notes, the empirical literature does not yet support the notion that changing youngsters' thought and problem-solving processes will change their behavior in naturalistic settings such as the classroom or that such changes will result in improved peer acceptance or social adjustment.

Social Learning

Among the approaches to control of aggression, those based on behavior principles or social learning have the most reliable experimental support. As we use it, the term *social learning* includes behavioral and cognitive-behavioral interventions. A social learning approach to the control of aggression includes three primary components: specific behavioral objectives, techniques for changing behavior, and precise measurement of behavioral change (Carr, 1981). Consequently, one can judge the outcome of intervention quantitatively as well as qualitatively against an objective goal. Behavior change techniques are employed by those who have the most continuous contact with the aggressive child and the greatest amount of control over his or her immediate environment—usually parents, siblings, teachers, or peers, as opposed to therapists who see the youngster infrequently and work in highly artificial or contrived settings. The focus is on modifying the youngster's current social environment (rather than unconscious, internal processes) to foster and reward adaptive, nonaggressive behavior, although there may be some attention to cognitive and affective responses to aggressive acts (Goldstein, 1983a).

School-based social learning interventions designed to reduce aggression may include one or more of these procedures:

☐ *Modeling* nonaggressive responses to aggression-provoking situations (for example, demonstrating repeatedly how to behave unaggressively under aversive conditions by using models, who may be adults or peers, live or filmed, human or nonhuman)

☐ Giving *feedback* on behavior or performance (for example, making videotapes of the youngster becoming angry or having a temper tantrum, then showing them to the youngster to illustrate what the behavior looks like to others and help identify early stages of maladaptive behavior)

☐ Giving *guided practice* or *coaching* in nonaggressive behavior in real life and in activities such as role playing and rehearsal in hypothetical situations (the teacher breaks the task down into steps and helps the youngster master the component skills through rehearsal and coaching)

☐ Providing *reinforcement* for nonaggressive behaviors by giving rewards for specific alternatives to aggressive responses (following the rules in a game or playing without hitting) or for adaptive behaviors that increase the youngster's social competence (accepting criticism or giving compliments)

☐ Using *extinction* by withholding rewards for aggressive responses (for example, refusing to give into, and thus reinforce, temper tantrums or whining)

☐ Providing *nonhostile, humane punishment* of aggressive behaviors; punishment may involve presenting a mild aversive stimulus, such as a reprimand, or withdrawing positive reinforcers such as subtracting points already earned or withholding a favorite activity, or time out, a brief period during which the youngster is not able to engage in pleasurable activities or earn rewards

In brief, the theory behind social learning interventions is that since most aggressive behavior is learned, nonaggressive behavior can be taught directly. To teach it, nonaggressive modes of behavior must be made salient and rewarding, and the rewarding consequences for aggression must be removed or prevented. Furthermore, social incompetence, including academic failure and lack of skills in social interaction, must be remediated. Finally, aversive, inhumane social conditions, including poverty, oppression, and lack of opportunity, contribute to aggression and must be rectified if other attempts to reduce aggression are to be highly successful.

Do not misinterpret the social learning approach as an attempt to decrease socially appropriate assertiveness. Socially appropriate assertiveness includes the expression of feelings, needs, preferences, or opinions verbally or nonverbally in a way that is self-enhancing and self-protective. Assertiveness may be encouraged or even specifically taught as part of social learning interventions when youngsters lack these skills. Inappropriate assertiveness and coercive aggression are extremely similar. Both carry a demand for immediate reaction and an implied threat if the demand is not met (see Patterson, 1982). Social learning interventions target aggressive behavior that is inappropriate for its context and socially destructive.

There are many types of techniques and specific procedures for managing aggression from a social learning perspective. Although punishment may be part of the approach, the focus is on positive consequences for nonaggressive behavior and helping the youngster learn self-management. We are considering only three types of techniques: positive reinforcement of nonaggressive behavior, contingency contracting, and self-instruction. These and other techniques are described in much more detail in texts on behavior management (Alberto & Troutman, 1986; Gelfand & Hartmann, 1984; Kazdin, 1984; Kerr & Nelson, 1983; Kerr et al., 1987; Morris, 1985).

The stock technique of social learning interventions is positive reinforcement of nonaggressive behavior. Combined with ignoring aggression or carefully crafted punishment of aggressive acts, it is a powerful means of changing behavior. The following description of an intervention for a six-year-old hyperaggressive preschooler illustrates the use of positive consequences.

Tom

He had a long history of brutal treatment and neglect by his natural parents and was living in a foster home. Because Tom was so cruel toward other children, his peers were afraid of him and tried their best to avoid playing with him. He would often hit or kick other children. Sometimes he would climb several feet high on a play apparatus and jump off onto other children or deliberately stomp their toys. His play was extremely rough, and he often broke toys by throwing, banging, stomping on them, or using them in ways other than the manufacturer intended.

The teacher was at her wit's end, having tried with no discernible success to ignore Tom's misbehavior (often impossible and inadvisable because he could so easily damage other people and things) or place him in time out (the only place available that even resembled seclusion was an area under a movable water-play table, so of course, time out didn't work). She was quite hesitant to intervene sternly in Tom's aggressive acts, for the little Hun had vented his fury against her, at one time ripping her hose with his teeth. She also tended to ignore him (probably because of exhaustion) during the brief but identifiable periods when he was reasonably well behaved. Figure 13.1 shows the frequency of Tom's rough physical behaviors (defined as hitting, kicking, biting, pushing, or otherwise hurting another person, or throwing, kicking, breaking, or otherwise abusing equipment or materials) during half an hour of free play each day.

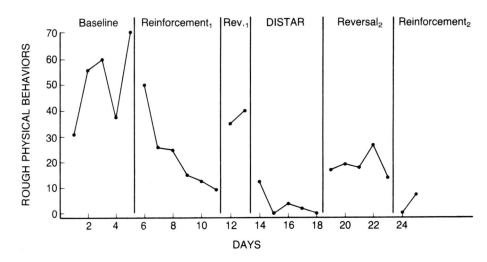

FIGURE 13.1

Frequency of Rough Physical Behaviors per 30-minute Observation Session

Reprinted with permission of publisher from: Kauffman, J. M. & Hallahan, D. P. Control of rough physical behavior using novel contingencies and directive teaching. PERCEPTUAL AND MOTOR SKILLS, 1973, 36, 1225–1226, Figure 1.

Before any intervention began, Tom was performing one of his rough physical behaviors at an average rate of nearly two per minute. Because he was getting essentially no reinforcement for appropriate behavior, the first intervention strategy was to reinforce behavior incompatible with aggression. Beginning on Day 6, the teacher provided positive reinforcement for appropriate behavior after variable intervals of time averaging three minutes. Whenever Tom had been behaving appropriately for a short time (as little as 20 seconds in the beginning) the teacher went to him, patted him, and praised his behavior ("I like the way you're playing gently with Sam"). She also let him turn over a playing card in a previously shuffled deck (a device described by Kauffman, Cullinan, Scranton, & Wallace, 1972) and earn a prize: the same number of Froot Loops as the number on the card, a penny candy for an ace, and a chance to shoot a toy revolver eight times (no caps, and aimed at no one) for a face card. The result was a noticeable drop in roughhousing, as shown for Days 6 through 11. To test whether the reinforcement contingency was responsible for the behavioral change, reinforcement was discontinued for two days. Figure 13.1 shows that Tom started to return to his violent ways (Days 12 and 13).

From Day 14 through Day 18, Tom's behavior was recorded during a DISTAR session that temporarily replaced the free play activities in which his behavior had previously been observed. DISTAR is a highly structured, sequential teaching system in which each child in a small group is expected to respond according to rules the teacher establishes and models. Children are reinforced individually with praise, pats, and/or food (for example, juice or raisins) for appropriate behavior and/or correct responses. Misbehaving children are ignored while well-behaved children are reinforced, thus providing a model for the miscreant and vicarious reinforcement for good behavior. As Figure 13.1 shows, Tom's aggressive behavior fell to near zero during DISTAR. A return to baseline during free play (Days 19 through 23) and reinstatement of the reinforcement condition (Days 24 and 25) were undertaken to show the relationship between aggressive behavior and classroom conditions. It is apparent from Figure 13.1 that both novel reinforcement for nonaggression and the combined elements (modeling, ignoring, reinforcement) of the DISTAR program were effective in reducing Tom's aggression. (Kauffman & Hallahan, 1973)

A contingency contract is a written agreement regarding certain of the student's aggressive and nonaggressive behaviors and their consequences. Figure 13.2 is an example of a contract for George, a student in middle school. Contracts must be written with the student's age and intelligence in mind. They may be simple statements or quite elaborate and technical, like George's, depending on the characteristics of the student. Note that George's contract involves both his parents and his teacher and specifies consequences of both desirable and aggressive behavior. Successful contingency contracts must be clearly written, emphasize the positive consequences for appropriate conduct, specify fair consequences to which all parties agree, and be strictly adhered to by the adults who sign the document.

Self-instruction is one type of cognitive strategy that has been used to manage aggression. Kazdin and Frame (1983) describe the use of self-instruction with Dave, an eleven-year-old who had severe, versatile conduct disorders. He was extremely abusive toward other children and adults; in addition, he stole and was truant. Three times per week, Dave received cognitive problem-solving training that could be applied in everyday situations. Training steps included teaching Dave to ask himself the following questions or make the following statements to himself:

What am I supposed to do?

I need to look at all of my possibilities.

I have to focus in (concentrate).

I have to make a choice.

How well did I do?

At first, Dave was taught to use these steps while working on preacademic or academic tasks. Later, after he had become proficient at using the steps in nonthreatening situations, he was taught to use them in provocative interactions with others in a variety of social encounters, such as being blamed by a teacher, arguing with a peer, or being confronted by the police. In role playing, the therapist first modeled the approach and Dave served as the other person in the interaction; then the therapist and Dave switched roles so that Dave could practice using the steps and receive feedback from the therapist on his performance. The training was quite successful in helping Dave control his aggression, at least immediately and during an eight-month follow-up. He used the steps in a variety of provocative situations where he previously would have responded by fighting. Although Kazdin and Frame provided Dave's cognitive training in a clinical (hospital) setting, similar procedures can be implemented in public schools (see Kerr et al., 1987; Spivack & Shure, 1982).

Other techniques involving cognitive strategies used in educational settings include rational-emotive therapy, in which internal dialogue and irrational beliefs are examined (Zionts, 1985); problem-solving training (Goldstein et al., 1986; Spivack & Shure, 1982); goal setting, in which students participate in choosing what they intend

Preamble

This contract is an agreement among George Reiner, his parents, his teacher, and his principal. All parties agree by signing this contract that they will do their best to live up to the terms of the agreement.

Article 1: Purpose

The purpose of this contract is to help George behave better and get better grades in school, and to make sure that George gets the privileges and rewards he earns.

Article 2: General Provisions

The general provisions of the contract are (1) that George will be able to earn points at school by behaving appropriately and doing his work, (2) that George will be able to exchange his earned points for things he likes to do at home, and (3) that George will be restricted each time he gets involved in a fight.

Article 3: Points Awarded and Point Fines

George will be given 60 points by his teacher (Ms. Laver) each morning when he arrives at school. Ms. Laver will keep track of George's points on a card placed on her desk. At the end of each school day, Ms. Laver will phone George's mother and report the number of points George earned. George will be fined 5 points each time he breaks one of the following rules:

1. Do what Ms. Laver or any other teacher tells you to do.
2. Complete all in-class assignments and homework on time.
3. Keep your hands to yourself during class.
4. Stay in your seat unless you have permission to get out.
5. Talk in a normal voice (don't yell) in class and only when you have permission.
6. Take turns in conversations (don't interrupt).

Whenever George breaks one of these rules, Ms. Laver will tell him in a quiet way which rule he broke and subtract 5 points from his total points.

Article 4: Exchanging Points

George's mother and father agree that George will be allowed to watch TV each evening for exactly the number of minutes as he has earned points for that day (1 minute per point). George can choose the programs he wants to watch. His mother and father will tell George when his time has expired, and George will turn off the TV then.

On weekends, George will be allowed to watch TV for 2 hours per day (2 hours on Saturday and 2 hours on Sunday), except that he can watch an extra ½ hour each day on weekends if he has earned a total of 250 points or more during the preceding week. George's mother will keep track of the points he earns each day and post them on the door of the refrigerator.

Article 5: Restrictions for Fighting

If George gets involved in a fight anytime during the school day, Ms. Laver will report the incident to the school principal (Mr. Christian), who will call George's father or mother at work. Either George's father or his mother will take George home as soon as possible (within 30 minutes). At home, George will do chores around the house as directed by his mother or father until the time school is normally out. He must stay in the house for the rest of the day and will not be allowed to watch any TV until the next day that he has remained in school all day.

Also, if George is sent home for fighting, Ms. Laver will send all his assignments for the day home with him, and he must complete all the assignments before he will be allowed to return to school the next day. If George misses more than two days of school in a week because of fighting or failure to complete his assigned work, then he will be required to stay in the house and will not be allowed to watch any TV the following weekend (Saturday and Sunday).

Article 6: Renegotiation

The terms of this contract will become effective on Monday, October 1, 1984. After it is in effect for two weeks, everyone involved will evaluate how the contract is working and renegotiate the terms of the contract if it is not satisfactory.

Signatures

FIGURE 13.2
A Contingency
Contract

George	_____	Teacher	_____
Mother	_____	Principal	_____
Father	_____	Date	_____

to accomplish (Lyman, 1984; Maher, 1987); and social **metacognitive** training, in which students are taught to observe and modify their own thought processes about problem situations (Larson & Gerber, 1987).

The Uses and Misuses of Punishment

Although teaching appropriate behavior is important in social learning interventions, some behaviors may require punishment because they are intolerable or dangerous and unresponsive to alternative positive interventions (Axelrod & Apsche, 1983; Braaten, Simpson, Rosell, & Reilly, 1988; Polsgrove, 1983). It may be difficult or impossible to establish adequate classroom control, particularly with students who have learning and behavior problems, without using negative consequences for misbehavior in addition to positive reinforcement for appropriate conduct. Judicious use of negative consequences for misconduct can even enhance the effectiveness of positive consequences (Pfiffner & O'Leary, 1987; Pfiffner, Rosen, & O'Leary, 1985).

One must be extremely careful in the use of punishment, however, because ill-timed, vengeful, and capricious punishment without incentives for appropriate behavior will only provide a vicious model and encourage further misbehavior. Extremely aversive punishment provokes counteraggression and coercion. Punishment is a seductive, easily abused approach to controlling behavior. Harsh punishment has an immediate effect; because it frequently results in immediate cessation of the individual's irritating or inappropriate behavior, it provides powerful negative reinforcement for the punisher. Thus it is often the beginning point of a coercive style of interaction in which the punished and the punisher vie for the dubious honor of winning an aversive contest. And because people mistakenly believe that punishment makes the individual suffer, physical punishment is frequently thought to be more effective than milder forms. These dangers, misconceptions, and abuses of punishment appear to underlie the coercive relationships that characterize families of aggressive antisocial children (cf. Patterson, 1982, 1986b). Consequently, it is critical to carefully consider punishment in educational settings to avoid having the school become another battleground for aversive control.

A pervasive misconception about punishment is that it requires inflicting physical pain, psychological trauma, or social embarrassment. None of these is required; punishment can be defined as any consequence that results in a decline in the rate or strength of the punished behavior. Thus a mild, quiet reprimand, temporary withdrawal of attention, or loss of a small privilege may often be effective punishment. For persistent and serious misbehavior, stronger punishment may be necessary, but mild forms of social punishment such as restrictions or loss of rewards are most effective if the youngster's environment also provides many opportunities for positive reinforcement of appropriate behavior.

The social learning literature clearly supports the assertion that punishment, carefully and appropriately administered, is a humane and effective tool for controlling misbehavior (cf. Axelrod & Apsche, 1983; Braaten et al., 1988; Bandura, 1973; Kauffman, Boland, Hopkins, & Birnbrauer, 1980; Polsgrove, 1983). Effective punishment may actually be necessary to rear a nonaggressive, socialized child (Patterson, 1982), but clumsy, vindictive, or malicious punishment is the teacher's downfall.

Punishment: What Are the Priority Behaviors?

Braaten (1982) proposed a model for dividing disturbing behaviors into five priority levels. This priority scale views a problem behavior as the primary variable in deciding whether or not punishers are appropriate and how intense an intervention should be.

☐ *Low priority* behaviors include those that are annoying, but not harmful to others, and those that may impede goal achievement. Examples include teasing, disrupting, and various other off-task behaviors that do not substantially interfere with class routine.

☐ *Mild priority* behaviors frequently interfere with or prohibit achievement of adaptive goals, involve minor property damage, and result in minor injury to self or others. Examples include defiance or off-task behaviors, defacing desktops, pushing, poking, or other provocative behaviors. These behaviors require teacher intervention.

☐ *Moderate priority* behaviors interfere repeatedly and significantly with achievement of adaptive goals or with other members of the class and may require the involvement of support staff, administrators, and parents. Examples include fighting, avoidance of schoolwork, throwing objects or engaging in other behaviors likely to result in injury, exaggerated temper outbursts, and abuse of staff.

☐ *High priority* behaviors are characterized by a generalized alienation or agitation that is excessively disruptive to self and others. These are behaviors that have persisted despite interventions by teachers, support staff, administrators, and parents, and they may require use of nontraditional interventions. Examples vary from physical assault to the ritualistic behaviors of autism.

The final level is reserved for *urgent priority* behaviors, which involve extreme risk and may require immediate expert intervention. Examples include life-threatening and potentially injurious behaviors.

Source: "Using Punishment with Exceptional Children: A Dilemma for Educators" by S. R. Braaten, R. Simpson, J. Rosell, and T. Reilly, 1988, *Teaching Exceptional Children, 20*(2), p. 80. Copyright 1988 by The Council for Exceptional Children. Reprinted by permission.

Before using punishment procedures, educators must be sure a strong program of teaching and positive consequences for appropriate behavior is in place, and they must carefully consider the types of behavior that are priorities for punishment (see box). Teachers should study the use of punishment procedures in depth before implementing them in the classroom. After deciding to use punishment, the teacher may want to consider one of three common techniques: **response cost, time out,** or **overcorrection**.

Response cost implies that an inappropriate response costs something of value, such as earned rewards or privileges; it means a fine in terms of whatever the punished individual is required to forfeit (Walker, 1983). This type of punishment is usually preferred, because it is less likely to result in abusive treatment or to produce counteraggression, but it is not effective without careful planning (see Walker, 1983, for recommendations).

279 CHAPTER 13: CONDUCT DISORDER: OVERT AGGRESSION

Time out means that for a specified, brief period, the child loses the opportunity to earn positive reinforcement. The procedure may involve withdrawing attention, requiring the student to sit out of an activity, or isolating the student from social contact. Time out has been effective in helping to bring severe behavior problems under control. It can be easily abused, however, and one must take care to avoid unethical practices and violations of students' rights, such as secluding the student in a frightening or dangerous place or placing the student in time out for extended periods (see Brantner & Doherty, 1983; Nelson & Rutherford, 1983; Zabel, 1986, for discussion and guidelines). Time out is not effective unless the situation from which the student is removed is one that offers the possibility of ample rewards for desirable behavior.

Overcorrection implies either requiring the student to make restitution or to engage in a more appropriate form of behavior (Foxx & Azrin, 1972, 1973; Foxx & Bechtel, 1983; Foxx & Livesay, 1984). Restitution may mean repairing damaged property and working to improve the damaged environment, or returning stolen property plus giving something in addition. To use positive practice overcorrection, one has the individual repeatedly practice a more desirable or correct form of behavior, such as raising a hand and requesting permission to get out of seat. It requires expenditure of effort, contingent upon misbehavior, to perform an appropriate behavior. Although overcorrection can be a useful tool, it cannot be implemented without considerable effort on the teacher's part, and it should be used only with carefully written guidelines (Braaten et al., 1988).

These are general guidelines for humane and effective use of punishment:

- ☐ Punishment should be used only after positive correction methods have failed and allowing the behavior to continue will result in more serious negative consequences than the proposed level of punishment. Punishment should be instituted only in the context of ongoing classroom management and instructional programs that emphasize positive consequences for appropriate conduct and achievement.
- ☐ Punishment should be used only by people who are warm and loving toward the individual when his or her behavior is acceptable and who offer ample positive reinforcement for nonaggressive behavior.
- ☐ Punishment should be administered matter-of-factly, without anger, threats, or moralizing.
- ☐ Punishment should be fair, consistent, and immediate. If the youngster is able to understand descriptions of the contingency, punishment should be applied only to behavior that he or she has been warned is punishable. In short, punishment should be predictable and swift, not capricious or delayed.
- ☐ Punishment should be of reasonable intensity. Relatively minor misbehavior should evoke only mild punishment, and more serious offenses or problems should generally result in stronger punishment.
- ☐ Whenever possible, punishment should involve response cost (loss of privileges or rewards or withdrawal of attention) rather than aversives.
- ☐ Whenever possible, punishment should be related to the misbehavior, enabling the youngster to make restitution and/or practice a more adaptive alternate behavior.

□ Positive reinforcement should not be delivered immediately following punishment; if it is, the child may learn to misbehave and endure the punishment so as to obtain reinforcement. Positive reinforcement should, however, be provided for any appropriate behavior that follows punishment.

□ Punishment should be discontinued if it is not quickly apparent that it is effective. Unlike positive reinforcement, which may not have an immediate effect on behavior, effective punishment usually results in an almost immediate decline in the misbehavior. It is better not to punish than to punish ineffectively, as ineffective punishment may merely increase the individual's tolerance for aversive consequences. Punishment will not necessarily be more effective if it becomes harsher or more intense; a different type of punishment may be more effective.

□ There should be written guidelines for using specific punishment procedures. All concerned parties—students, parents, teachers, and school administrators—should know what punishment procedures will be used. Before implementing specific punishment procedures, especially those involving time out or aversive consequences, they should be approved by school authorities (see Braaten et al., 1988; Wood & Braaten, 1983).

Countercontrol

Aggressive youngsters sometimes engage in countercontrol of those who try to modify their behavior (Seay, Suppa, Schoen, & Roberts, 1984). A component of some aggressive antisocial youngsters' behavior is what Mahoney (1974) calls the "screw you" phenomenon—behaving exactly opposite to the way the behavior manager urges and entices them to act. Some youngsters delight in frustrating adults by being oppositional and derive much more pleasure from opposition than from the rewards and reinforcers offered by well-meaning teachers or parents. Youngsters frequently endure punishment they could easily avoid, behaving in an obstinate and self-defeating way (but perhaps in a way *they* perceive as self-enhancing in the face of a pig-headed adult). Mahoney (1974) makes some astute observations about countercontrolling children and youth and the role of personal choice in overcoming opposition, as in the case of Aaron.

Aaron

My experiences in the group home environment and a handful of pilot investigations over the past two years have suggested a number of possibly relevant variables in countercontrol phenomena. First, it appears that the presence or absence of choice may moderate oppositional patterns. This possibility was first impressed upon me by 6-year-old Aaron, our rebellious enuretic. Aaron was also a terror at bedtime—he refused to take his shower, threw temper tantrums, etc. We had painstakingly programmed reinforcement for more appropriate responses (e.g., with after-shower snacks) and consistently used the removal of privileges as negative consequences for transgressions (response cost and time-out). Nevertheless, Aaron's rebellious patterns persisted. One night, I serendipitously said, "Aaron, do you want to take your shower in the upstairs or downstairs bathroom?" He stopped, smiled broadly, and said,

"Downstairs!" His compliance surprised me (partly because he usually showered downstairs). An equally amazed staff member asked me what I had done to win Aaron's cooperation. We set about a naturalistic experiment. Was it the choice? We arranged a series of ministudies which varied the presence or absence of choice and the type of choice involved (which bathroom, color of towel, and so forth). Aaron's data were impressively consistent—when we gave him a choice, he complied enthusiastically. When we did not, he countercontrolled. Several subsequent experiences added to my hunch that choice may be an important variable in the moderation of oppositional patterns. It is interesting to note that some of the most effective treatment programs for delinquency have incorporated substantial choice options—the delinquents have some say-so in their own contingency management. . . . (Mahoney, 1974, p. 245)

Other writers also note that oppositional behavior often improves when youngsters are given a say in their affairs (Lovitt, 1977). Mahoney (1974) suggests that the conspicuousness of reinforcement contingencies, modeling, and other variables probably contribute to the phenomenon of countercontrol, but he notes, along with others, that there has been little research on how best to handle this form of aggression (see also Bateson, Day, McClosky, Meehl, & Michael, 1975; Seay et al., 1984).

Summary of Social Learning Interventions

Although social learning interventions have been the most effective attempts to alter aggressive behavior, current methods have limitations (lack of generalization and lack of maintenance of improvement) that researchers are seeking to overcome. Aggression can be changed quickly and dramatically in many cases by using behavior modification or cognitive-behavioral techniques, but there is little evidence that the changes extend to all facets of the youngster's environment or are long-lasting (Kazdin, 1987; Kazdin & Frame, 1983). Efforts to overcome these limitations have recently centered on three strategies:

1. Teaching aggressive youngsters social skills that will allow them to obtain gratification in more socially acceptable ways
2. Teaching aggressive youngsters cognitive strategies or self-instruction skills that will help them exercise firmer self-control in aggression-provoking situations
3. Retraining the families of aggressive youngsters (see Doke & Flippo, 1983; Goldstein, 1983a; Griest & Wells, 1983; Kazdin & Frame, 1983; Patterson, 1982).

Each approach shows promise, but none has resolved the problems of generalization and maintenance. Social skills research does not yet yield convincing evidence that an aggressive youngster's adjustment is generally enhanced through training (Schloss, Schloss, Wood, & Kiehl, 1986). Cognitive-behavioral strategies have not yet produced generalized and permanent change (Gresham, 1985), and family retraining has not yet provided the unfailing and permanent solution to childhood aggression (Patterson, 1986b). Aggression in its many forms remains the most serious and intractable form of disordered behavior (Kazdin, 1987).

Social learning interventions sometimes appear quite simple, but the apparent simplicity is deceptive, because it is often necessary to make subtle and intricate adjustments in technique to make them work. An exquisite sensitivity to human communication is necessary to master humane and effective application of behavior principles. The range of possible techniques for an individual case is extensive, calling for a high degree of creativity to formulate an effective and ethical plan of action.

COMPARISONS AMONG INTERVENTION APPROACHES

There are several critical distinctions among psychodynamic, psychoeducational, and social learning strategies for changing aggressive behavior. The following descriptions are oversimplifications of the three approaches to classroom interventions, but our purpose is to show as clearly as possible their contrasting emphases.

Psychodynamic Approach

As depicted in Figure 13.3, psychodynamic intervention aims to uncover unconscious instincts, drives, or needs that find expression in cognitive and affective problems. The hypothesis is that creating an atmosphere of permissiveness and trust in which unconscious forces can be freely expressed will help the youngster develop insight resulting in resolution of behavior problems. For example, if a boy who has uncon-

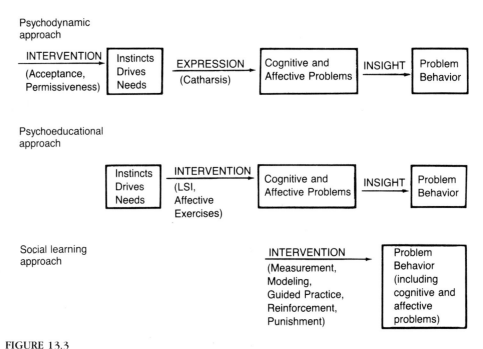

FIGURE 13.3

Diagrammatic Representation of Psychodynamic, Psychoeducational, and Social Learning Approaches to Intervention

scious aggressive wishes about his father is allowed to express the need to aggress without censure by verbally assaulting his teacher (who, by **transference** has unconsciously become his symbolic father), then he may be able to gain insight into the fact that hostile wishes toward his father are acceptable and manageable and thus learn to control his aggression. Or if a student is allowed to act out aggressive impulses by destroying a picture she has just drawn, then helped to talk about what she just did, she may gain insight into her unconscious motivations, understand why she attacked her own work, and so be able to control such urges in the future.

Psychoeducational Approach

In contrast, psychoeducational intervention focuses on faulty cognitive and affective states rather than on their unconscious antecedents, at the same time recognizing the existence of needs, drives, and so forth. The assumption is that making youngsters aware of their feelings and discussing the nature of their aggression will help them gain insight into their maladaptive behavior and thus gain ego control (volitional control) over their aggressive behavior. For example, if the student can become aware that he or she has angry feelings when another student teases or hassles, and can learn to think through alternatives to counteraggression (ignoring rather than hitting the tormentor), then the student may start using self-control skills and become less aggressive. Recent developments in the psychoeducational approach involve teaching specific skills for managing aggressive, impulsive behavior that are similar in many respects to cognitive-behavioral or social learning interventions.

Social Learning Approach

Social learning intervention focuses on the problem behavior itself, which may include cognitive and affective responses to aggressive behavior and aggression-provoking situations. For example, if the youngster frequently hits others, then intervention is directed toward reducing the hitting behavior. To the extent that the student can identify and record cognitive or affective responses (hateful thoughts, inability to predict the consequences of teasing others, high level of tension, and so on), they can be dealt with directly, perhaps at first with the help of the teacher. Social learning interventions may involve training in specific social skills that reduce the likelihood of aggressive behavior.

SUMMARY

Conduct disorder is characterized by persistent antisocial behavior that seriously impairs the youngster's functioning in everyday life or results in adults' concluding that the youngster is unmanageable. Subtypes of conduct disorder include overt aggressive (undersocialized); covert antisocial (socialized), such as theft, lying, and arson; and versatile (socialized and undersocialized). We distinguish youngsters with conduct disorder from those who are developing normally by their higher rates of noxious behaviors and by the persistence of such conduct beyond the age at which most children have adopted less aggressive behavior.

We do not know the prevalence of conduct disorder, but it is among the most common disorders; it is a frequent reason for referral to clinics and to special education. Boys with undersocialized conduct disorder outnumber girls by three to one or more.

Undersocialized conduct disorder carries a particularly poor prognosis for adult adjustment; it is a serious disorder that is extremely costly to society and to individuals. Development of effective prevention programs presents numerous problems, and at this time, we know little about how to prevent the disorder effectively.

Psychodynamic theories and the hypothesis that aggression is always produced by frustration have been largely discounted. We know that genetic factors contribute to extreme aggression and criminality, but not how the factors work. We know that social learning factors help cause conduct disorder; the social environment, through processes of modeling, reinforcement of aggression, and ineffective punishment, contributes to the development of aggressive youngsters' problems. Risk increases through a wide variety of biological and social factors, and the social conditions that increase risk tend to be highly interrelated.

Assessment of undersocialized conduct disorder requires evaluation of aggression and related behavior from a variety of perspectives, including that of the parents, teachers, and the youngster. Of the many different clinical interventions that have been tried, none has produced generalized and long-lasting changes in aggressive behavior. Interventions that emphasize family retraining, problem-solving training, and community-based intervention have been the most successful, especially when social learning principles are the basis for behavior change.

Educational interventions include psychodynamic, psychoeducational, and social learning approaches. Psychodynamic strategies, especially catharsis, are not well supported by research. Psychoeducational strategies, especially recently developed social-skills and self-control training programs, are promising. Social learning strategies are supported by a large body of empirical data showing that aggressive behavior can be reduced, although generalization and maintenance of behavioral gains are elusive. Common techniques associated with social learning interventions are contingency contracting, reinforcement of nonaggressive behavior, and self-control training. Punishment is sometimes necessary in managing aggression in school, but is frequently misunderstood, dangerous, and controversial. It should be implemented carefully according to written guidelines. Countercontrol often emerges in working with aggressive youngsters and can often be managed effectively by offering reasonable choices based on personal preferences.

14

Conduct Disorder: Covert Antisocial Behavior

As you read this chapter, keep these guiding questions in mind:

☐ If we conceptualize overt and covert antisocial behavior as different ends of a single dimension or continuum, what type of behavior is shared by both?

☐ What specific covert antisocial behaviors are typically thought to be "masculine," and what types are considered "feminine"?

☐ What family process characteristics may distinguish youngsters with covert antisocial behavior?

☐ What type of prevention programs are particularly relevant for covert antisocial behavior?

☐ What special problems does one encounter in assessing covert antisocial behavior?

☐ Why is intervention in the families of stealers particularly difficult?

☐ What guidelines for management of theft should school personnel follow?

☐ Why is children's lying a major concern of parents and teachers?

☐ What are the probable risk factors in fire setting by children and youth?

☐ How do successful programs to decrease school vandalism differ from the usual response to increased violence and destructiveness in schools?

☐ What general suggestions can one offer for decreasing truancy?

DEFINITION AND PREVALENCE OF COVERT ANTISOCIAL BEHAVIOR

As we saw in Chapter 13, antisocial behavior may involve overt acts, such as physical and verbal aggression, covert acts, such as stealing, lying, and fire setting, or both overt and covert forms of disordered conduct. Loeber and Schmaling (1985a) suggest that overt and covert antisocial behavior may represent different ends of a single behavioral dimension, with noncompliance—sassy, negative, persistent disobedience—as the most common or keystone characteristic of both extremes (see also Patterson, 1982, 1986b). Figure 14.1 depicts this conceptualization of overt and covert forms of conduct disorder.

Awareness of different forms of conduct disorder has existed for decades, but reliable empirical evidence of the different forms has emerged from large-scale studies only relatively recently (Loeber & Schmaling, 1985a, 1985b; Quay, 1986b). These studies are based on statistical probabilities; thus, a particular child is not necessarily characterized by behavior at one end of the continuum shown in Figure 14.1. As noted in Chapter 13, some children are versatile in their antisocial conduct, showing both overt and covert forms. Youngsters who show versatile antisocial behavior generally have more severe problems, and their prognosis is usually poorer compared to those who exhibit only one type of antisocial behavior (Kazdin, 1987; Loeber & Schmaling, 1985a). Versatility is a matter of degree; some individuals are much more versatile or exclusive in their antisocial conduct than others. Conduct disorder of both types is often difficult to distinguish from other disorders, especially juvenile delinquency. In fact, the socialized (covert) form typically involves delinquent activities (Quay, 1986b). Delinquency is a legal term, however, and connotes behavior that is the topic of Chapter 15. (Although socialized or covert antisocial behavior may include substance abuse, drug abuse will be discussed with delinquency in Chapter 15, because it ordinarily involves law violation.) The focus of this chapter is the covert antisocial behavior problems of the type listed on the lower, arithmetically negative area of the scale shown in Figure 14.1.

As you know, conduct disorder is one of the most common and serious behavior problems of children and youth, with prevalence estimates ranging from four to ten percent of the child population. The prevalence of each subtype of conduct disorder has not been estimated precisely. Robins (1986) indicates that conduct disorders are on the increase for both boys and girls, but boys and girls have tended to exhibit somewhat different patterns of antisocial misconduct. In Robins's research, relatively more "masculine" antisocial behaviors included vandalism, fighting, and stealing, whereas lying, running away, and substance abuse were typed as more "feminine." Four school-related problems (truancy, expulsion, underachievement, and discipline) clustered together for both males and females. Vandalism, lying, and stealing clustered together for girls, but not for boys (Robins, 1986); that is, girls who vandalized, lied, or stole tended to do all three, whereas boys tended to perform antisocial acts in different patterns (vandalism with fighting and substance abuse, lying with truancy and underachievement, and stealing with running away).

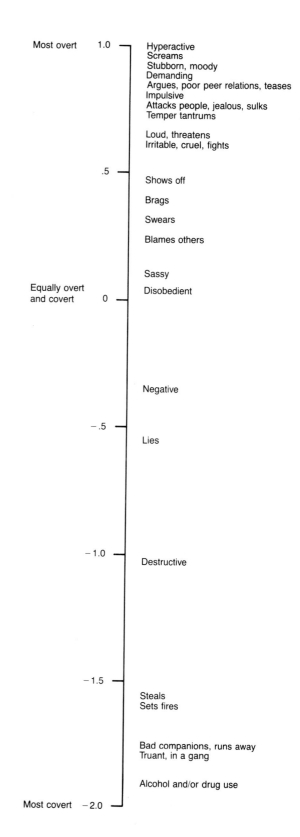

Most overt   1.0 ─┐ Hyperactive
                   │ Screams
                   │ Stubborn, moody
                   │ Demanding
                   │ Argues, poor peer relations, teases
                   │ Impulsive
                   │ Attacks people, jealous, sulks
                   │ Temper tantrums
                   │
                   │ Loud, threatens
                   │ Irritable, cruel, fights
                   │
           .5 ─┤
                   │ Shows off
                   │
                   │ Brags
                   │
                   │ Swears
                   │
                   │ Blames others
                   │
                   │
                   │ Sassy
Equally overt   │
and covert   0 ─┤ Disobedient
                   │
                   │
                   │
                   │
                   │
                   │ Negative
                   │
         − .5 ─┤
                   │ Lies
                   │
                   │
                   │
                   │
        − 1.0 ─┤
                   │ Destructive
                   │
                   │
                   │
                   │
        − 1.5 ─┤
                   │ Steals
                   │ Sets fires
                   │
                   │ Bad companions, runs away
                   │ Truant, in a gang
                   │
                   │ Alcohol and/or drug use
Most covert − 2.0 ─┘

FIGURE 14.1

Overt and Covert Behaviors in One Dimension

From "Empirical Evidence for Overt and Covert Patterns of
Antisocial Conduct Problems: A Metaanalysis" by R. Loeber
and K. B. Schmaling, 1985, *Journal of Abnormal Child Psychology*, 13, p. 347. Copyright © by Plenum Publishing Corp.
Reprinted by permission.

CAUSAL FACTORS AND PREVENTION

In general, the same causal factors seem to underlie overt aggression and covert antisocial conduct. In some studies comparing overt to covert antisocial children, families of those who exhibit covert antisocial behavior are characterized by lower rates of aversive, coercive behavior on the part of parents and children and less supervision or monitoring on the part of parents. Other studies, however, found no differences between overtly and covertly antisocial youngsters on family process variables such as parental rejection. A fairly consistent finding is that youngsters with versatile antisocial behavior come from the most disturbed families in which child rearing practices are the most inadequate (Loeber & Schmaling, 1985a).

Prevention of covert antisocial behavior in many ways parallels prevention of overt aggression. Character training or moral education seems particularly relevant to prevention of stealing, lying, vandalism, and so on. A few studies indicate that deficits in moral reasoning are associated with conduct problems and peer conformity among delinquents (Bear & Richards, 1981; Gibbs, Arnold, Ahlborn, & Chessman, 1984; Krouse, 1982; Sigman, Ungerer, & Russell, 1983). The effects of typical moral and character education, however, have been nil or very slight (Zimmerman, 1983). Moral behavior often does not match moral judgment—children and youth, as well as adults, often do wrong even though they know what is right. Moral behavior tends to be controlled at least as much by situational factors as by moral or character traits; youngsters are honest or altruistic at some times and in some situations but not in others (Walker, de Vries, & Trevethan, 1987). Teachers' talk about classroom conventions, procedures, and moral issues has little effect on children's reasoning about morals (Blumenfeld, Pintrich, & Hamilton, 1987). For schools to have much influence in teaching prosocial values, they must develop coherent and pervasive programs of character education that include discussion, role playing, and social-skills training to help students recognize moral dilemmas, adopt moral values, and select moral behavioral alternatives (Edelman & Goldstein, 1981). This training may be particularly important for disturbed students (Zionts, 1985).

ASSESSMENT

As with prevention, assessment of covert antisocial conduct disorder seems to parallel assessment of overt aggression. A particularly difficult problem, however, is direct observation of behavior; the behavior is, by definition, not usually observed by others. Often, the antisocial deed is not discovered until long after it is committed, and even then there may be doubt as to who was responsible. Although extremely serious, the behavior may occur at a relatively low rate compared to overt acts of aggression; thus, comparison of baseline rates to treatment may require lengthy evaluation. Assessment can therefore involve long periods of observation, and research may employ self-reports of acts such as stealing, lying, truancy, and vandalism.

INTERVENTION AND EDUCATION

Because of similarities in the nature and causes of the problems, intervention and education in overt and covert forms of conduct disorder share many features, along with important differences. "The treatment of covert antisocial acts such as theft is necessarily more complicated than that of overt antisocial acts because the covert acts are less easily detected and defined, and consequences therefore cannot as quickly and consistently be applied" (Loeber & Schmaling, 1985b, p. 333). Consequently, the particular problems as well as the approaches to intervention may differ somewhat for specific types of covert antisocial acts. Families of children who steal, more often than families of aggressive children who do not steal, are extremely difficult treatment targets (Patterson, 1982). Sometimes family therapy or parent discipline training is simply infeasible or ineffective. Vandalism is often a particular problem in schools, and some intervention programs may therefore be primarily school-based. Fire setting may be only tangentially related to school programs; truancy, on the other hand, is by definition an educational problem, although programs to encourage school attendance may involve both the school and other community agencies.

Stealing

A common behavior problem that parents of young children report is that they do not recognize and respect the property rights of others. Many young children simply take what they want when they see it without regard for ownership; in short, they steal. If this behavior persists beyond the age of five or six, the child may become known as a stealer and get into trouble with peers and adults. The most useful analyses of the origins and management of stealing come from a behavioral or social learning perspective.

In an early case study, Wetzel (1966) found that he could modify a disturbed boy's compulsive stealing by means of behavior modification principles. Reid and Patterson and their associates (Loeber et al., 1983; Moore et al., 1979; Patterson, 1982; Patterson et al., 1975; Reid & Hendricks, 1973; Reid & Patterson, 1976) have systematically researched the characteristics and behavior modification of aggressive children who steal. Their subjects were primarily predelinquent children referred for treatment of social aggression; about half were also in trouble because of stealing. Reid and Hendricks (1973) found that children who stole exhibited a lower rate of positive-friendly behaviors at home than did nonstealers or nonreferred children. In turn, stealers also exhibited a higher rate of negative-coercive acts than nonreferred children. Compared to aggressive children who did not steal, however, stealers showed a *lower* rate of negative-coercive acts. In all three groups (nonreferred, stealers, and nonstealers) the fathers interacted less than mothers with their families, but there were no significant differences in the interaction of fathers in the three groups. Mothers of stealers exhibited a lower rate of positive-friendly interaction than mothers of nonstealers or nonreferred children. The rate of negative-coercive acts of mothers of stealers fell between the rates for mothers of nonreferred children and mothers of nonstealers. These generalizations emerged.

> Stealers exhibited lower rates of observable out-of-control (negative-coercive and antisocial) behavior than aggressive children who did not steal.
>
> Families of stealers demonstrated lower rates of both positive-friendly and negative-coercive behaviors than families of aggressive children who did not steal.
>
> The differences in positive-friendly and negative-coercive behavior rates were due almost completely to the mothers' behavior.

Reid and Hendricks also found that stealers did not respond as well as non-stealers to treatment based on social learning theory. They base their speculation on the nature of the child's behavior and the nature of the family's social interaction. Many stealers appear to exhibit high rates of antisocial behavior only away from home or at home when no observers are present. Many stealers are likely to confine their antisocial behavior to settings outside the home, disturbing the community rather than their parents by their theft and leaving their parents with little motivation to work on the problem. Parents of stealers tend to blame the stealing on someone else, thus refusing to recognize the problem and failing to follow through on intervention plans (see Patterson, 1982; Patterson et al., 1975; Reid & Patterson, 1976). Families of stealers appear to be loosely structured and characterized by lack of parental supervision or emotional attachment to the children (Patterson, 1982; Reid & Patterson, 1976). The stealer may, therefore, learn that taking others' possessions is acceptable behavior, that no one will care what he or she takes, and that no adverse consequences will follow theft. The child who learns to steal may be motivated to seek stimulation and reinforcement outside the family.

Despite the difficult and destructive family interaction patterns of stealers, relatively successful behavioral interventions have been devised. Patterson et al. (1975) believe a behavioral antistealing program has several essential components. Before instituting the actual antistealing program, however, one must resolve a fundamental problem—parental definition of stealing. Parents of stealers are usually hesitant to accuse the child of theft and loath to take disciplinary action. Since they are unlikely to observe the child in the act of taking something, the parents feel obliged to accept their child's explanation for how something came into his or her possession. Many parents blindly accept the child's claims of finding, borrowing, trading, winning, or receiving as payment whatever item was stolen. When their child is accused by teachers, peers, or police, parents of stealers argue that the child is being unjustly attacked. By blaming others—making it somebody else's problem—the parents avoid having to deal with the problem themselves. Even when the behavior occurs at home, parents often do not adequately define stealing. Some parents consider it theft to take food from the refrigerator without specific permission, while others view all family possessions as common property. The value of an item is also an issue, as many parents of stealers cannot bring themselves to apply consequences for stealing something they consider to be worth very little.

As Patterson et al. (1975) point out, the first step in dealing with theft is to recognize that the child is in difficulty because he or she steals more than other children of the same age, may steal valuable objects, and has been labeled by others as a thief. The antitheft strategy must include steps to help the child stop being accused of theft and being viewed with suspicion. The child will not lose the stigma associated with the label until he or she learns to avoid even the appearance of wrongdoing.

Patterson et al. (see also Patterson, 1982; Reid & Patterson, 1976) promote the following strategy to help the family deal with theft:

1. Agree to define stealing as the child's possession of anything that does not belong to him or her or taking anything he or she does not own.

2. Only the parents decide whether a theft has occurred. They may base their judgment on either their own observation or on the report of a reliable informant.

3. When it is determined that the child has stolen, the parents merely state that, according to the rules, the child has taken the item, and then apply the consequences. The parents must not shame or counsel the child at the time they discover the theft and apply the consequences, but they are encouraged to discuss the theft with him or her at another time.

4. Every instance of stealing must receive consequences.

5. Parents are advised to keep their eyes open and ask about "new" property rather than use detective tactics such as searching the child's room or clothing.

6. Consequences for stealing are either a specified interval of useful work or a period of "grounding" or restriction. Stealing more expensive items receives more severe consequences. Harsh consequences, such as humiliation or beating, are prohibited.

7. No positive reinforcement is given for periods of nonstealing, since it is impossible to know that successful covert stealing has not occurred.

8. The program should stay in effect at least six months following the last episode of stealing.

Teachers could implement similar strategies for managing stealing in school (Switzer, Deal, & Bailey, 1977). Rosen and Rosen (1983) worked with a first grader who frequently took other students' and classroom property without permission. They marked all his personal and school items with a green circle and defined stealing as having items not marked with a green circle on his person or in his desk or supply box. During intervention, the teacher awarded points (which he later could exchange for work breaks, extra reading time, trinkets, and candy) and praised him contingent on his having possession of only green-marked items; the teacher also reprimanded and "fined" him by taking away points for having unmarked items. This intervention quickly reduced stealing to a very low rate. A form of overcorrection—restitution, requiring that the stealer give back what was taken plus another identical or similar item—is sometimes effective in reducing stealing (Azrin & Wesolowski, 1974).

If the child steals both at home and at school, parents and teachers must implement consistent antitheft programs in both environments. Effective and early management of stealing is particularly important; the younger the age at which children begin stealing and the longer they persist, the more likely they are to become chronic stealers and adjudicated delinquents (Henderson, 1983; Loeber & Schmaling, 1985b; Moore et al., 1979). In general, the more severe the conduct disorder, the less likely it is that intervention will be successful (Kazdin, 1987). Management of stealing at school can present legal problems, particularly with older students, and the school must avoid illegal searches and seizures. The box provides general guidelines for managing stealing in school.

Lying

Parents and teachers consistently rate lying as a serious problem behavior of childhood, yet there has been little research on the subject (Stouthamer-Loeber & Loeber,

Dealing with Stealing: General Guidelines for School Personnel

Stevens (1980) reports that the child does have some rights to privacy in the dignity of his body and his place of residence. Similarly, Trosch, Williams, and Devore (1982) maintain that the fourth amendment of the United States Constitution protects children in school from unreasonable searches conducted by teachers or administrators without first establishing probable cause. Defining probable cause is not easy; however, known facts and tips from reliable sources are admissible in the courts. Teachers and school officials are often in a better position than parents to identify, interpret, and record the totality of circumstances necessary to establish probable cause (Trosch et al., 1982). Teachers can observe children from hour to hour on a daily basis and in relationship to other children. A student's individual actions, such as unusual secretiveness, departures from normal schedules or travel patterns, possession of questionable items, and instances of lying or other "rule-breaking" behaviors, may provide the documentation necessary for establishing probable cause for searches in schools not in violation of the child's Fourth Amendment rights.

In addition to those guidelines offered for dealing with instances of theft, common sense suggests the following approach may be considered with regard to theft detection:

1. Clearly state rules and authority to search a child's possessions based upon establishment of probable cause, particularly for older children and youth;
2. Carefully observe and monitor the behavior of all children and record instances of unusual behavior;
3. Refrain from being a "detective" and indiscriminately searching a child's possessions;
4. Ask children about unusual behavior or possession of questionable objects. . . .

Only by clearly establishing rules, and firmly and fairly enforcing those rules within an atmosphere of loving concern and respect for the child, can parents and teachers hope to eliminate stealing behavior in children.

From "Children's Stealing: A Review of Theft-control Procedures for Parents and Teachers" by R. L. M. Williams, 1985, *Remedial and Special Education, 6*(2), pp. 21–22.

1986). Developmental changes clearly occur in the understanding of lies and liars (Peterson, Peterson, & Seeto, 1983), but the relationship of these changes to the development of pathological lying is not understood. Apparently, children often lie in attempts to escape punishment. Adults consider lying a serious problem not only because it is an attempt at concealment, but also because it is associated with other antisocial behavior such as stealing and truancy. In the classroom, lying and cheating are functionally similar behaviors.

As one might expect, lying is related to the same sort of family process variables, especially lack of parental monitoring or supervision, that characterize stealing (Stouthamer-Loeber & Loeber, 1986). Although lying is a serious problem and may be a stepping-stone to the development of other conduct problems (Patterson, 1982), no body of research is available to guide intervention.

Fire Setting

The fires that children set frequently cause injury, loss of life, and property damage. In fact, youthful arsonists account for more than half of all set fires. The United States has the highest arson rate in the world, and arson has been the fastest growing crime (Wooden & Berkey, 1984). "Few problem behaviors provoke as much anxiety in the community because of the possible harm to life, safety, and property" (Koles & Jenson, 1985).

Although fire setting has been a behavior of scientific interest for over 150 years (Wooden & Berkey, 1984), we still do not understand the causes and management of this behavior in children. Fanciful psychodynamic explanations that connect fire setting to sexual excitement have only recently begun to give way to conceptualizations grounded in reliable empirical evidence. Kolko and Kazdin (1986) propose a social learning model for conceptualizing risk factors of fire play and fire setting that consists of three primary factors: learning experiences and cues, personal repertoires (cognitive, behavioral, and motivational), and parent and family influences and stressors. Kolko and Kazdin note that children learn attitudes and behaviors from early experiences, such as watching parents or older siblings working or playing with fire. Children of fire fighters, furnace stokers, smokers, and adults who otherwise model behavior dealing with fire may be more likely to set fires. We see interest in fire and playing with fire in a high percentage of young children. The ready availability of incendiary materials to children who are interested in fire and observe models who set or manage fires may set the stage for fire setting. Another major factor, however, is the personal repertoires that may heighten the risk of fire setting. Children may be more likely to set fires if they do not understand the danger of fire or the importance of fire safety; if they do not have the necessary social skills to obtain gratification in appropriate ways; if they engage in other antisocial behaviors; or if they are motivated by anger and revenge. Finally, stressful life events, parental psychopathology, and lack of parental supervision, monitoring, and involvement can increase the chances that a child will set fires.

Although research does not clearly distinguish different types of fire setters, all fires obviously are not set under the same conditions or for the same reasons. Some fires are set accidentally by children playing with matches or lighters, some by angry children who are seeking revenge but do not understand the awful consequences, others by delinquents who know full well the consequences of arson, and still others by youngsters whose behavior is related to anxiety and obsessions or compulsions. Future research should attempt to delineate the various forms of fire setting to help identify the particular risk factors associated with each (Kolko & Kazdin, 1986).

Most school age youngsters who set fires have a history of school failure and multiple behavior problems (Wooden & Berkey, 1984), and schools are sometimes their targets, so educators are among the many who have an interest in identifying and treating fire setters. At this point, however, we can make few research-based recommendations for intervention or prevention. Both will probably require efforts similar to those suggested for managing other covert antisocial behaviors such as stealing, vandalism, and truancy (cf. Koles & Jenson, 1985; Kolko & Kazdin, 1986).

Vandalism

Deliberate destruction of school property costs hundreds of millions of dollars each year, and vandalism in other community settings results in much higher costs. Destructiveness and violence against people are often linked, and both are on the increase. The typical response of school administrators and justice officials to violence and vandalism is to tighten security measures and provide harsher punishment. Unfortunately, punitive measures may only aggravate the problems (Mayer, Nafpaktitis, Butterworth, & Hollingsworth, 1987).

Vandalism in schools appears to be, at least in part, a response to aversive environments (Mayer & Butterworth, 1981; Mayer, Butterworth, Nafpaktitis, & Sulzer-Azaroff, 1983; Mayer et al., 1987). More specifically, students tend to be disruptive and destructive when school rules are vague, discipline is punitive, punishment is rigidly applied regardless of students' individual differences, relationships between students and school personnel are impersonal, the school curriculum is mismatched with students' interests and abilities, and when students receive little recognition for appropriate conduct or achievement (see also Chapter 10). Decreasing the aversiveness of the school environment by adjusting school rules, teachers' expectations, and consequences for desirable and undesirable behavior might be more effective in preventing vandalism than increasing security and making punishment more severe.

Mayer et al. (1983) provide evidence of the effectiveness of a positive approach to dealing with disruption and destruction in schools. They worked with students and school personnel in 18 junior high schools over a three-year period to try to prevent school vandalism and improve discipline by emphasizing positive management rather than sterner punishment. The intervention consisted of workshops to train school personnel in behavioral strategies. The effort was to establish a positive rather than a punitive atmosphere in the schools. The cooperation of community citizens and students was enlisted by focusing on campus improvement projects and activities such as neighborhood walks to inform people of the school's efforts to stop vandalism. The program achieved significant increases in teachers' positive behavior (such as praise for appropriate student conduct) and significant reductions in students' vandalism and off-task behavior. In fact, Mayer and his colleagues have found that this type of program helped decrease the average cost of vandalism in 23 elementary and junior high schools by 73.5 percent (Mayer et al., 1987).

Truancy

Berg (1985) notes that truancy is easier to describe than to define or measure because the reasons for students' school absences vary so much and because parents' and teachers' awareness and records of absences are often inaccurate. Truancy generally means unjustified absence from school, although, as used in this chapter, the term does not include cases in which anxiety about school attendance is the major reason for absence. Anxiety regarding school attendance (often referred to as **school phobia**) is discussed in Chapter 16. The issue here is a student's choice not to attend school because of dissatisfaction with the school program and the lure of alternative activities.

Although attendance at school certainly does not guarantee academic success, chronic unexcused absence virtually assures failure. Frequent truancy is serious not only because of probable school failure but because chronic truants are at risk for later unemployment or employment failure, criminal convictions, substance abuse, and a variety of other difficulties. Dissatisfaction with school programs and failure to attend school regularly are important signals that the student may drop out (Edgar, 1987).

The traditional approach of attendance officers' counseling truants has not been remarkably successful. Researchers have already shown that alternative behavioral strategies can be highly effective. Copeland et al. (1974) found that truants from an elementary school improved their attendance when the school principal stopped by their classrooms to compliment them on their presence (see Chapter 10). Working with older children and adolescents, Tharp and Wetzel (1969) improved school attendance by making participation in certain events or interaction with certain individuals in the community contingent on attendance. The contingencies of reinforcement were often administered with the aid of "natural mediators," persons living in the community who could control the youngster's access to rewards and could themselves be rewarding to the child or youth, as in the case of Cowboy Gaines.

Case #98

Cowboy Gaines operated a riding stable on the outskirts of the city. Cowboy and his plumpish, fortyish wife were warm, homespun people, and they enjoyed the role of counselors to mixed-up youths. Cowboy himself was full of rustic figures of speech, and he dispensed his rough and ready ranch philosophy generously. Cowboy and his wife, Irma, proved to be highly effective mediators.

Case #98 was an extraordinarily truant seventh grader who was powerfully attracted to animals, especially horses. There was no adult person with whom he had a positive relationship.

The Behavior Analyst asked Cowboy and Irma if they would help with Billy, and they at once agreed. The arrangement was simple: Billy could earn time at Cowboy's stables by staying in school. Billy was allowed to ride the horses in return for attending to minor chores when he was not riding.

Billy responded perfectly and thereafter never missed an hour of school. Cowboy and Irma had a little trouble with him at first because the undersized boy complained in smart-alec terms when he felt he wasn't getting enough riding. Cowboy gave him a few bits of rough advice and Irma was obliged to become a disciplinarian. Billy sulked and made plain his displeasure, but the horses and riding were too important to give up. (Tharp & Wetzel, 1969, pp. 95–96)

MacDonald, Gallimore, and MacDonald (1970) compared similar contingencies to more traditional attendance counseling and found the contingency arrangements superior in increasing the attendance of ninth, and tenth, and twelfth grade pupils.

Interventions based on social learning principles continue to produce better results than other approaches (see Kerr, Nelson, & Lambert, 1987). Lawrence, Litynsky, and D'Lugoff (1982) reduced truancy dramatically using behavioral interventions and counseling in a special day school. Students earned points for school attendance and appropriate behavior, which they could exchange for a variety of activities and treats during special recreation periods. Schloss, Kane, and Miller (1981) suggest that a

Suggestions for Dealing with Behaviorally Disordered Adolescents' Truancy

Increase satisfaction obtained by school attendance:

☐ Reduce academic demands on the student to increase the likelihood of success

☐ Monitor and intervene in peer relations to reduce peer tensions

☐ Provide more frequent social reinforcement for completed work

☐ Frequently communicate successful school experiences to parents

☐ Encourage parents to equate favorable reports with special after-school and weekend activities

☐ Encourage parents to send the student to bed at a reasonable time

☐ Engage the student in frequent conferences with the teacher, in which concerns about the school program can be openly expressed

Decrease satisfaction obtained by being absent from school:

☐ Have someone make a home visit immediately if the student does not come to school

☐ If the student is ill, send home the day's schoolwork

☐ If the student is not ill but is at home, escort the student to school (accompanied by parents if possible)

☐ If the student is not willing to be escorted to school, impose prearranged sanctions such as removing television privileges for the day or decreasing allowance

Actively teach skills that enhance ability to benefit from school attendance:

☐ Provide small group activities designed to develop social skills

☐ Include special interest areas in which the student is highly motivated in the academic program (shop, art, athletics)

(Schloss et al., 1981, p. 178)

truancy intervention program for disturbed adolescents might include features like those described in the accompanying box.

SUMMARY

Covert antisocial behavior consists of acts such as stealing, lying, fire setting, vandalism, and truancy. Overt and covert antisocial behavior may represent different ends of a continuum, with noncompliance as the keystone behavior or common origin of both extremes.

Researchers note sex differences in antisocial behavior. Vandalism, fighting, and stealing are typed as "masculine," while lying, substance abuse, and running away are considered "feminine." Four school-related problems (truancy, expulsion, under-achievement, and discipline) characterize both boys and girls with conduct disorders.

In general, the same types of causal factors seem to underlie overt and covert forms of conduct disorder. Some studies indicate, however, that families of youngsters who steal and exhibit other covert forms of antisocial behavior are characterized by lower rates of aversive, coercive behavior and lower rates of parental supervision and monitoring. A particularly relevant preventive strategy for covert antisocial behavior is moral education or character training, although typical moral education seems ineffective, suggesting the need for comprehensive, pervasive programs.

Because the acts are usually unobserved and are performed at relatively low rates, assessment of covert antisocial conduct disorder presents special problems and often involves self-reports in addition to other measures. Intervention and education for youngsters with covert antisocial problems are similar to those for overt aggression but are more complicated because covert acts are harder to detect and the consequences often cannot be applied immediately and consistently. Specific covert behaviors may thus require special treatment.

Families of stealers differ from families of aggressive youngsters who do not steal, showing less parental supervision and involvement with their children. Intervention in families of stealers is often particularly difficult because the parents do not recognize or do not want to be bothered with the problem. Effective management of stealing includes careful supervision of the child and consistent, appropriate punishment of all instances of stealing. When theft-management procedures are implemented in schools, care must be taken not to violate students' constitutional rights.

Lying is considered a major child behavior problem because it is often part of other covert antisocial behavior. There is little research on lying and no guidelines for handling it.

Fire setting is a growing and dangerous problem among children and youth. There is little understanding of the causes of fire setting behavior and little research for managing it. A social learning model suggests that early learning experiences, personal repertoires (cognitive, behavioral, and motivational), and parent and family influences and stressors may put children at risk for fire setting. Research to distinguish different types of fire setters is needed.

Rising rates of violence and destructiveness in schools are typically met by tightening security measures and applying more punitive discipline, but these measures may be counterproductive. Vandalism may represent a response to an aversive school environment. Programs to make the school environment less aversive for students by increasing positive attention to appropriate conduct, making the school curriculum more relevant, and improving school discipline practices have dramatically reduced school vandalism.

Chronic truancy virtually ensures school failure and is associated with a variety of negative outcomes in adulthood. Traditional counseling approaches have not been very effective. Behavioral interventions that make school attendance more rewarding and nonattendance less attractive have been successful with many truants.

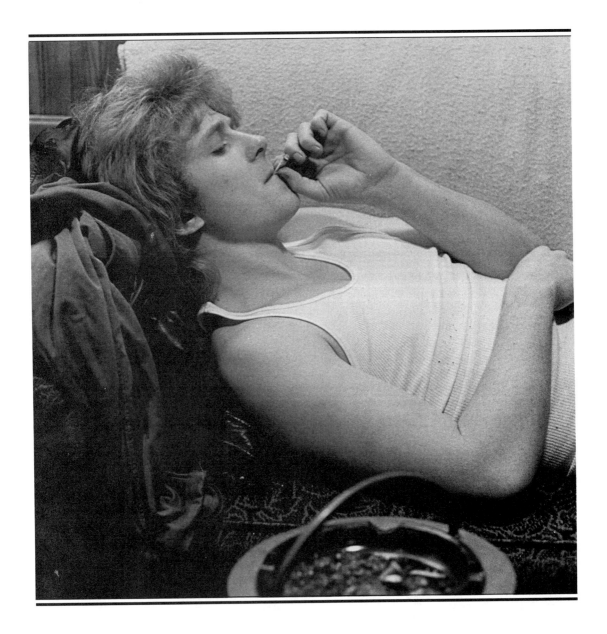

15

Delinquency and Substance Abuse

As you read this chapter, keep these guiding questions in mind:

- ☐ What makes juvenile delinquency difficult to define precisely?
- ☐ What is the difference between a status offense and an index crime?
- ☐ What arguments support the assertion that youngsters who become "official" delinquents are those most likely to have psychopathological disorders?
- ☐ What sex differences do we find in delinquent behavior and punishment for delinquent acts?
- ☐ What arguments support the assumption that all (or nearly all) incarcerated youngsters are behaviorally handicapped?
- ☐ How does control theory explain the causes of delinquent behavior?
- ☐ Why is it often extremely difficult to assess delinquents' educational needs?
- ☐ What are the ostensible advantages of the juvenile justice system over the adult justice system, and why are these not often realities?
- ☐ What training characterizes effective intervention in families of delinquents?
- ☐ What characterizes schools that most successfully manage disruptive and delinquent behavior?
- ☐ What are the features of a good special education program in a corrections facility, and why is it so difficult to achieve these features?
- ☐ What is necessary for an effective delinquency prevention program?
- ☐ Which substances do children and youth most commonly abuse?
- ☐ What are the progressive stages in substance abuse?
- ☐ What can educators do to help prevent and manage substance abuse?

DEFINITION AND PREVALENCE OF JUVENILE DELINQUENCY

Juvenile delinquency is not easy to define precisely because it has various legal meanings, as well as meanings that connote individual perceptions or personal evaluations of behavior. That is, behavior that some adults perceive to be intolerable or highly inappropriate is sometimes mistakenly called delinquent, although it is not prohibited by law. Strictly speaking, delinquency is a legal term that denotes violation of the law. We will discuss substance abuse in this chapter because for juveniles it almost always involves law-violating behavior and is often part of a pattern of other delinquent conduct.

When someone who is not legally an adult (a juvenile) commits an act that could result in apprehension by police, he or she is said to have committed a *delinquent* act. Because many delinquent acts do not result in arrests, the extent of juvenile delinquency is difficult to determine. Some laws are vague or loosely worded, so that delinquency is not clearly defined. Some acts are illegal if committed by a juvenile but not if they are committed by an adult (such as buying or drinking alcoholic beverages). Other delinquent acts are clearly criminal; they are considered morally wrong and punishable by law regardless of the age of the person who commits them. The following cases illustrate instances in which juveniles were accused of offenses that are criminal, whether committed by juveniles or adults.

V. K.

V. K., a teenager serving a 15-year sentence for the second degree murder of a 16-year-old classmate, will not have her sentence reduced. She was a 15-year-old senior when she became involved in a knife fight with another student at a school bus stop. Testimony in her trial indicated that dozens of students and adults stood by without intervening as the two fought. The girl who was stabbed bled to death from a wound in her neck, one of several she received in the fight.

Seven-year-old Murderer

An eight-year-old boy is charged with murder in a housefire that killed a 66-year-old woman. The boy, who was seven at the time of the fire, is the youngest person ever charged with murder in this state. He is also charged with arson in two other fires in which there were no injuries.

"Scarface"

The child, nicknamed "Scarface" because of the cuts and scars on his face, was ten years old, only five feet tall, and weighed just 90 pounds. His spindly legs barely touched the floor as he sat in detention, waiting for his court-appointed lawyer. He was accused of molesting a ten-year-old girl on the schoolgrounds while one of his friends held her down. The judge released him into the custody of his parents. Over the next ten weeks, he was arrested five more times—more times than any other juvenile in Washington, D.C. in that year, 1985. His other arrests were for holding up and robbing two men, threatening a woman with an iron pipe, participating in a brawl, illegally entering a car, and roughing up a woman and snatching her purse.

Not all delinquent behavior is so clearly illegal or criminal as that in these cases. Many aggressive children's behavior just skirts legal delinquency. Much of the behavior of incarcerated youths is irritating, threatening, or disruptive, but not clearly delinquent in a legal sense. Consider, for example, the case of "The Whiz," described by Wolford (1983). Some of the Whiz's behavior might or might not be defined as delinquent; some is clearly criminal; some is merely socially inappropriate.

The Whiz

The Whiz, as the young man in this story came to be known in the correctional institution where I was working as an educational counselor, gained his prison nickname as a result of his near wizardry in the assembly, disassembly, and repair of electronic equipment. None of the school's audiovisual equipment was left unexamined. Although this self-trained technician could quickly repair nearly any malfunctioning gadget, one was never sure what added component the machine might have gained while upon the Whiz's workbench. During his 18-month stay in a medium security prison he managed to adapt every piece of the school's audio equipment so it could be quickly converted into a speaker for his beloved electric guitar.

The Whiz was clearly an individual with talents and capability for contributing to our society. So why did I meet him in a prison where he was serving a 3-to-10-year sentence for a variety of theft and drug-related convictions? The Whiz could not make it in a public school; despite his measurable potential he continued to fail. His home and family, though neither affluent nor overly supportive, was not characterized by abuse as is the case for so many institutionalized offenders.

I believe the Whiz could have been classified as behaviorally disordered and/or emotionally disturbed although no formal assessment of such a condition was ever made. He failed in public school, not from a lack of capacity to learn, but rather because of behaviors that were disruptive to the process of learning and the educational system. The Whiz was a youth of excess. His behavior, like his zeal for electronics, was intense, and he exhibited wide swings in mood and behavior.

I recall a story told to me by a co-worker in charge of the prison's recreational services. The Whiz was the leader of an inmate rock group patterned after "The Who"—a band known as much for its flamboyant stage antics as for its hard-driving music. The Whiz, demonstrating his excessive behaviors, during long rehearsal sessions tutored his band not in playing the songs but in practicing the intricacies of jumping off the stage at the close of their concert.

To match his excesses were deficits in behavior and personal social development. The Whiz had little sense of appropriate social distance and would routinely invade the space of others around him. He had not acquired the skills of social interaction that one would expect of one his age. He had not been able to learn from appropriate models, or had not been exposed to them. He also exhibited many self-abusive behaviors, and his body was marred by cigarette burns, needle tracks, and crudely applied tattoos.

The Whiz did not finish his freshman year in high school. He turned to the streets. He began to experiment with drugs. The idle time, his developing drug addiction, and circle of acquaintances helped to lead him to crime. (From "Correctional Education and Special Education—An Emerging Partnership, or 'Born to Lose,' " by B. I. Wolford. In *Monograph in Behavioral Disorders* [pp. 13–14]. Copyright 1983 by The Council for Exceptional Children. Reprinted with permission.)

Delinquent Behavior and Official Delinquency

Any act that has legal constraints on its occurrence may be considered delinquent behavior. Juveniles may commit *index crimes,* crimes that are illegal regardless of a person's age and that include the full range of criminal offenses from misdemeanors to first-degree murder. Common index crimes committed by juveniles are vandalism, shoplifting and various other forms of theft such as auto theft and armed robbery, and assault. Other illegal behavior may be against the law only because of the offender's age. Acts that are illegal only when committed by a minor are called **status offenses**. Status offenses include truancy, running away from home, buying or possessing alcoholic beverages, and sexual promiscuity. They also include a variety of ill-defined behaviors described by labels such as "incorrigible," "unmanageable," or "beyond parental control." Status offenses are a grab-bag category that can be abused in determining whether a child is a juvenile delinquent; it is a category that encompasses serious misdeeds but which adult authorities can expand to include mere suspicion or the appearance of misconduct.

The differences between official delinquency and delinquent behavior are significant. Surveys in which children and adolescents report whether they engage in specific delinquent acts indicate that the vast majority (80 to 90 percent) have done so. Self-reports appear to be by far the best way to estimate the true extent of delinquent behavior (Arnold & Brungardt, 1983). Self-reported delinquent behavior does not correlate with social class or race. In contrast, about 20 percent of all minors are at some time officially delinquent; in a given year, approximately three percent of all American children are adjudicated. We find a disproportionate number of official delinquents among lower classes and racial minorities (Arnold & Brungardt, 1983).

Moore and Arthur (1983) suggest an explanation for the discrepancy between delinquent behavior and official delinquency. "Official" delinquents are children and youth who commit more serious delinquent acts at a higher rate. The delinquents who are arrested are usually the ones who *should* be arrested, as indicated by their self-reports and what they were caught doing. If we can assume that some types of delinquency represent psychopathology, then the rate and severity of delinquent acts should be the criteria for judging pathological delinquent behavior. In other words, the "sickness" of delinquent behavior should be judged by how frequently and how seriously the child or youth offends the law. For this reason, official delinquency is better than self-reported delinquency as a gauge of behavior disorder or psychopathology. Moore and Arthur (1983) summarize the difference between official and self-reported delinquency:

> Delinquent behavior is widespread and common, but the majority is not of concern to juvenile justice authorities. Populations that engage in higher rates of more severe delinquent behaviors are overly represented by children from lower social classes and minority groups. These types of offenses are of concern to community agents and would lead to adjudication if the offender were caught. Because number and severity of delinquent acts are implicit in the definition of delinquency-as-psychopathology, official records of delinquency constitute the best current source of data with which to investigate this area. (p. 360)

Nature and Extent of Delinquency

Statistics regarding juvenile delinquency clearly show that most children and youth commit at least one delinquent act. But because authorities do not detect most illegal acts, "hidden" delinquency remains a major problem. About half the juveniles who become official delinquents are adjudicated for only one offense before they become adults. Juveniles who commit repeated offenses (*recidivists*) account for the majority of official delinquency. Recidivists commit more serious offenses and begin performing delinquent acts at an earlier age, usually before they are 12, and tend to continue their antisocial behavior as adults (Tolan, 1987).

Males commit most juvenile offenses, particularly serious crimes against persons and property. Females may be increasingly involved in major offenses, but males still far outnumber females in official delinquency statistics (Moore & Arthur, 1983). Interestingly, the juvenile justice system tends to deal much more harshly with females than males (Arnold & Brungardt, 1983). Nearly all sources of information indicate that official delinquency and delinquent behavior have become more prevalent, violent, and destructive during the past 20 years (Arnold & Brungardt, 1983; Wolford, 1983). Orientation to drugs and delinquency related to drugs, especially alcohol abuse, are pervasive concerns of parents and adult authorities (Achenbach, 1982b; Milgram & Nathan, 1986; Safer, 1982b).

The nature of delinquency is not just law-violating behavior, but also the responses of adult authority to it. Incarceration and other forms of punishment have been miserable failures in controlling delinquency. The problem seems to be not only a surge in young people's criminal behavior, but adult responses that tend to exacerbate rather than reduce delinquency (Arnold & Brungardt, 1983). The scope of the problem is so great and the issues in delinquency have such complex legal, moral, psychological, and sociological implications that the reader is referred to volumes specifically on juvenile delinquency (Arnold & Brungardt, 1983; Griffin & Griffin, 1978; Kittrie, 1971; Nelson et al., 1987).

Types of Delinquents

Researchers have attempted to delineate homogeneous groups of delinquents based on behavioral characteristics, types of offenses, and membership in subcultural groups. As Arnold and Brungardt (1983) point out, none of these attempts have produced a classification system that is of much value in explaining the origins of delinquency or planning intervention programs. Achenbach (1982a) and Quay (1975, 1986a), however, suggest subtypes of the delinquent population similar to those they have found for nondelinquent disturbed children. Achenbach (1982b) discusses three major subtypes: socialized-subcultural, unsocialized-psychopathic, and neurotic-disturbed. Socialized-subcultural delinquents, who tend to be lower in IQ and socioeconomic status, experience less parental rejection than the other types. They relate socially to bad companions, engage in gang activities, and maintain their social status among their delinquent peers by their illegal behavior. Unsocialized-psychopathic delinquents are aggressive, assaultive individuals who tend to feel persecuted and respond poorly to praise or punishment. They tend to be irritable, defiant, explosive, and extremely insensitive to other people's feelings. Disturbed-neurotic delinquents are overly sensitive, shy, and worried, and unhappy with themselves and their lives.

If we can identify distinctly different subgroups of delinquents, then we should be able to distinguish different causes and particular treatments for each subgroup. Unfortunately, there is considerable overlap among the different subgroups in terms of overt behavior, causal factors, and treatment effectiveness. Future research may result in more meaningful subclassifications, but for now, it is not easy to explain most aspects of delinquency by reference to subtypes.

Delinquency, Handicapping Conditions, and Need for Special Education

Educating juvenile delinquents presents difficult problems for public schools and correctional institutions because of unclear definitions of handicapping conditions (Nelson et al., 1987; Safer, 1982b, Wolford, 1983). Are juvenile delinquents handicapped and, therefore, included under PL 94-142? Some psychologists and educators contend that most or all *adjudicated* delinquents logically fall into the PL 94-142 category of "seriously emotionally disturbed." But the current federal definition specifically excludes youngsters who are "socially maladjusted but not seriously emotionally disturbed." Since delinquent behavior is considered to reflect social maladjustment rather than emotional disturbance, juvenile delinquents are often excluded under PL 94-142 unless they are mentally retarded, learning disabled, physically or sensorially impaired, or mentally ill as determined by a psychiatrist (see Murphy, 1986b; Nelson, 1987; Wolford, 1987; Wood, 1987b).

Most authorities admit that a percentage of incarcerated delinquents are handicapped in some way, with learning disability the most prevalent handicapping condition (Murphy, 1986b; Nelson et al., 1987). Nevertheless, the fact that a child or youth has been adjudicated and assigned to a correctional institution is apparently not in itself considered an indication that he or she is handicapped or in need of special education (Gilliam & Scott, 1987). It requires curious turns of logic, however, to conclude that many incarcerated youth are *not* behaviorally disordered and *not* entitled to special education under the law. If behavioral disorders include both overt and covert antisocial behavior (socialized and undersocialized conduct disorder as described by Kazdin, 1987, Quay, 1986a, 1986b, and others), then finding incarcerated youths who are *not* behaviorally disordered is a logical impossibility (except, of course, children or youth who are held unjustly). If Arnold and Brungardt's (1983) contention regarding the relationship between delinquency and psychopathology is correct (higher levels of delinquent conduct indicate higher levels of psychopathology) and if youths who commit more frequent and more serious delinquent acts are more likely to be incarcerated, then the argument that all or nearly all incarcerated youths are handicapped is supported. Finally, if behavioral disorders are *not* defined as handicapping conditions under the law, then logically indefensible distinctions are drawn between emotional disturbance and social maladjustment, as discussed in Chapter 1. Wolf, Braukman, and Ramp (1987) concluded that "evidence and consensus are growing that delinquent behavior, especially when persistent and serious, may often be part of a durable, significantly handicapping condition that is composed of multiple antisocial and dysfunctional behaviors, and that sometimes appears to be familially transmitted" (p. 350).

CAUSAL FACTORS AND PREVENTION OF DELINQUENCY

Among the most popular early theories of delinquency were those of Miller (1958), who hypothesized that the lower-class culture is a generating milieu for gang delinquency, and of Cohen (1955) and Cloward and Ohlin (1960), who believed that gang delinquency may result from social structure and anomie (normlessness).

Miller's idea is that the lower class culture has a long tradition of behavior and values of its own and that life in lower-class society focuses on concerns that foster delinquent patterns of behavior. Miller noted six focal concerns of lower-class culture:

1. Trouble (emphasis on law-violating versus law-abiding behavior)
2. Toughness (physical prowess combined with masculinity, lack of sentimentality, an exploitive attitude toward women, and avoidance of any behavior that might be interpreted as weakness)
3. Smartness (the ability to "con," "take," outwit, or dupe others and to avoid being "taken" by others)
4. Excitement (periods of intense excitement breaking an overall rhythm of boredom and routine)
5. Fate (the belief that luck rather than personal control or decision determines what happens in one's life)
6. Autonomy (the desire to be free from constraint and control by authority, mixed with the wish to be cared for)

Miller suggested that lower-class adolescents can achieve status and a sense of belonging by exhibiting behavior that is in line with the focal concerns of their culture, which often meant behaving as a delinquent.

The concept of *anomie,* or normlessness, has to do with the absence of norms for moral conduct among lower-class individuals who aspire to transcend class lines (to achieve success according to American middle-class values) but are blocked in achieving material goals by legitimate means (Cohen, 1955). The lower-class person who cannot achieve middle-class status in an acceptable way may turn to delinquent (lawless or normless) means of acquiring material goods and "the good life." Cloward and Ohlin (1960) hypothesize that out of the several types of delinquent subcultures—*criminal* (stealing for profit), *conflict* (seeking status through violence), or *retreatist* (taking drugs)—one subculture may develop into a substitute for the dominant culture, which lower-class youths cannot achieve or have rejected.

Long-standing theories of juvenile delinquency as a lower-class problem have been largely discredited by studies showing that growing up in a high delinquency area does not necessarily mean a child will become delinquent (Dinitz, Scarpitti, & Reckless, 1962; Scarpitti, Murray, Dinitz, & Reckless, 1960). According to these studies, boys who were not likely to become delinquent saw themselves clearly as nondelinquents by the age of twelve, were "good citizens" and favorably inclined toward school (though not necessarily outstanding students), admitted to little delinquent behavior, had favorable attitudes toward police, felt their parents accepted them and used the right amount of discipline, avoided association with delinquent peers, and expected to finish high school. These findings, combined with data showing that most recidivist delinquents have committed their first delinquent acts before the age of twelve, suggest that (1) the subculture of lower class and minority groups is not in itself sufficient to produce delinquency; and (2) the clear self-perception that one is not a delinquent, at least if it is developed by the age of twelve, may prevent a child from becoming delinquent even if he lives in a high delinquency area.

More recently, Arnold and Brungardt (1983) proposed a control theory of delinquency that is generally consistent with principles of social learning. They suggest that delinquency is the end result of a causal chain; a chain reaction in the variables that can lead to delinquency, as shown in Figure 15.1. An increase in any link in the chain will produce increases in all the succeeding links that lead, ultimately, to misconduct. The links in the chain are defined as follows:

> Biological capacity—the ability (as socially defined) of individuals to carry out actions (including perceiving and thinking) with their bodies.
>
> Ecological access—subject to contact in space and time, the objects of contact including physical objects and ideas and values contacted personally, through other persons, or through the media.

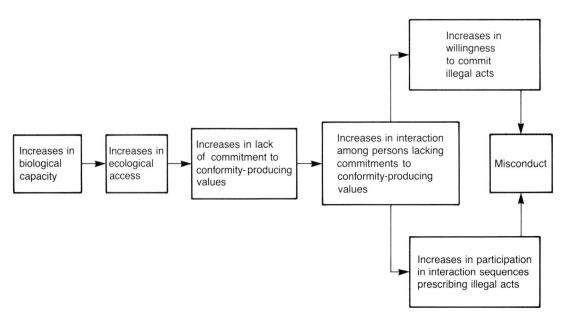

FIGURE 15.1
A Causal Chain Control Theory

From *Juvenile Misconduct and Delinquency* (p. 66) by W. R. Arnold and T. M. Brungardt, 1983, Boston: Houghton Mifflin. Reprinted by permission.

Lack of commitment to conformity-producing status—relative weakness or absence of whole-hearted acceptance and application of values that insulate or defend against illegal acts.

Interaction with others lacking conformity-producing values—actions carried out (usually, but not necessarily, face to face) because of awareness of others who are similarly uncommitted to conformity-producing values.

Willingness to carry out illegal acts—feelings condoning illegal behavior, varying from neutrality to whole-hearted approval, depending essentially upon the dynamic interpretation of any given situation.

Interaction sequence prescribing an illegal act—interaction (usually, but not necessarily, verbal) in a more or less sequential series that indicated an illegal act is acceptable and/or expected and/or rewarding.

Misconduct—an act that, at least in the perception of social scientists, is contrary to the juvenile code of the pertinent area. (Arnold & Brungardt, 1983, p. 64)

In more common terminology, one can interpret Figure 15.1 and the Arnold-Brungardt theory to mean that:

Increases in physical and cognitive capacities to perform delinquent acts will increase opportunities to perform them.

Increases in opportunities to perform delinquent acts will increase lack of personal commitment to law-abiding behavior.

Increases in lack of personal commitment to law- abiding behavior will increase association with others who lack commitment to law-abiding behavior.

Increases in association with others who lack commitment to law-abiding behavior will simultaneously increase willingness to commit illegal acts and expectations or demands to participate in such acts.

Willingness to commit illegal acts and the expectation or demand to commit them are necessary and sufficient conditions for delinquent behavior.

No conclusive evidence supports any single theory of delinquency (Achenbach, 1982b; Arnold & Brungardt, 1983; O'Leary & Wilson, 1975), but we have a considerable body of research regarding the kinds of experiences and social environments that are predictive of delinquency and persistent antisocial behavior (see Chapters 13 and 14). Factors that increase the probability that a youngster will exhibit delinquent behavior include, but are not necessarily limited to:

☐ Problems at school
☐ Low verbal intelligence
☐ Alcoholism and arrest record of parents
☐ Reliance on welfare or poor management of family income
☐ Crowded, disorderly, or broken home
☐ Erratic supervision and lax or inconsistent parental discipline
☐ Indifference or hostility of parents and siblings toward the child
☐ Substance abuse

As discussed in previous chapters, antisocial behavior in combination with low academic achievement and low intelligence offer a very pessimistic outlook for the child. Perhaps the most important group of causal factors in delinquency, however, are those related to the home (see Moore & Arthur, 1983; Patterson, 1982, 1986b; Tolan, 1987; Wolf et al., 1987). Parents who provide little emotional warmth, little supervision or control of the child's activities, erratic and punitive discipline, and a model of lawless behavior are most likely to have delinquent children.

An important concept related to the Arnold-Brungardt control theory is that delinquency is not so much caused as it is not prevented. Their theory emphasizes lack of controls that prevent someone from conforming to the law and moral precepts. One of their basic assumptions is that human nature is somewhat on the bad side of neutral; that without socially imposed controls, people's behavior will tend to be self-centered and antisocial. Not surprisingly, the permissiveness of contemporary American society—with the lack of clear and immediate sanctions for delinquent behavior, aggressive models in the media, the breakdown of families, and the declining influence of religion—tends to weaken control factors that suppress delinquent behavior. Research with families of aggressive children tends to support this notion. Patterson's (1982, 1986a, 1986b) research suggests that parents of aggressive children fail to confront and punish their coercive behavior effectively, whereas parents of nonaggressive children provide a generally attentive, loving environment and know how to use nonviolent punishment effectively. This research could have important implications for designing intervention programs (cf. Wolf et al., 1987).

Genetic factors also appear significant in seriously delinquent behavior (Mednick et al., 1986; Wolf et al., 1987). As we saw in Chapter 8, evidence does not suggest that genes directly cause delinquency; rather, children may inherit a vulnerability to environmental conditions that are conducive to delinquent conduct. Genetics may be one reason that delinquency and criminality sometimes run in families, with family interaction patterns and social and economic circumstances as additional reasons.

Prevention of delinquency presents a difficult challenge. Because of the overwhelming evidence of family influence in delinquent conduct, it is logical to aim preventive programs at families. As Wolf et al. (1987) observe, however, many seriously delinquent youths either have no parents or have parents who are themselves models of antisocial conduct and unwilling to learn more effective child rearing skills. The parents are thus part of the problem in many cases of serious delinquency, so trying to channel any kind of prevention or intervention through them is difficult or impossible. Furthermore, ethical considerations and legal constraints do not allow the degree of intrusion into family life that appears necessary to prevent delinquency until youngsters have established a pattern of seriously antisocial behavior. Thus, primary prevention is seldom possible, given present understanding of delinquency and its treatment.

ASSESSMENT OF DELINQUENTS' EDUCATIONAL NEEDS

Assessment of delinquent students' educational needs does not essentially differ from assessment of other needs, and evaluation should relate directly to the skills in which instruction is to be offered (cf. Howell, 1985, 1987; Howell & Morehead, 1987). It is often difficult to assess delinquents' educational needs, because their disruptive behavior and bravado can make them inaccessible or uncooperative, or successful in covering up their academic deficits. Because many delinquents have cognitive and academic deficits in addition to social and vocational skill deficits, their assessment must often be multifaceted. Because they are often in detention centers or special facilities where student populations are transient, educational records are unavailable, and communication with other agencies is difficult, assessment must often be done hurriedly and without relevant background information. Finally, because there is little agreement as to what are the most important skills for delinquents—social, academic, or vocational—the focus of assessment is often questionable.

INTERVENTION AND EDUCATION: COURTS, FAMILIES, SCHOOLS, AND CORRECTIONS

Intervention by the Courts

Juvenile courts were instituted in the United States at the turn of the century to offer more humane treatment of juvenile offenders than the nineteenth-century reform schools had provided. Judges were empowered to use their discretion in determining the consequences of a child's misconduct, with the idea that the judge would consider the case carefully and then act as a wise father in its disposition. Although the intent was good, the institution has become mired in an overload of cases. Judges are often not "wise fathers," and the rights of children—if children are considered to have constitutional rights equal to those of all other citizens—have been blatantly abridged (Arnold & Brungardt, 1983; Kittrie, 1971; Silberman, 1978). Consequently, the juvenile court system and the question of children's legal rights are now under close scrutiny (see Snarr, 1987; Warboys & Shauffer, 1986; Wood, 1987b). A central issue is the role of the family versus the role of the court. As Judge Noah Weinstein says,

> Implementing the concept that children are people with rights faces the dilemma that our social structure is based on the family; and the courts, and the community as well, are at the very least reluctant to take any action which they erroneously believe will undermine the family unit. It is this mistaken apprehension which causes the courts to disregard children's rights and to seek out a security blanket of vague parental fitness to avoid equal consideration of the protection of children. (Kirk, 1976, p. 396)

Although we frequently hear proposals for drastic reform, the juvenile court system is likely to remain as it is for a considerable time. Since a sizable proportion of children and youth will make appearances before a juvenile court during their school years, teachers could profit from familiarity with the court's workings (see Arnold & Brungardt, 1983; Silberman, 1978; Snarr, 1987; Wolford, 1987).

Achenbach (1975) notes that society's attempts to deal with juvenile delinquency are characterized by a recurrent pattern of enthusiasm for proposed solutions that have no social foundation in research, followed by failure to win enough support for the new ideas to make them fulfill the hopes they arouse. Other writers also comment on the history of our legal structures' failure to deal with the problems of crime and violence, including delinquency of minors (Silberman, 1978). Whatever the failures in the social systems of families and schools, one can find equal disasters in the procedures and institutions devised by lawyers and judges. The court system and the instruments of probation, parole, and correctional institutions offer no promise of solving the problems of juvenile misconduct and delinquency (cf. Wolf et al., 1987; Wolford, 1987).

Arnold and Brungardt (1983) list many types of juvenile correctional facilities: "reception and diagnostic centers, halfway houses, group homes, ranches, forestry camps, farms, training schools, and community-based nonresidential treatment centers" (p. 393). Juvenile court judges may assign delinquent children and youth to any of these types of facilities or place them on probation. Regardless of the facility, the prospect for permanently reforming the delinquent's behavior is not good. Even the best innovative programs for chronically delinquent youth have not yielded dramatic changes in long-term behavior patterns, although some have produced significant short-term changes (Wolf et al., 1987).

When should the court treat a child or youth charged with a serious crime as an adult? The rights of children and their treatment under the adult system of justice are crucial matters of moral judgment. Given the present court systems and their options for dealing with adult criminals and juvenile delinquents, it perhaps makes little difference whether a young person encounters the adult world of justice or is "sheltered" by juvenile justice. This seems to have been the sad conclusion of the judge in the case of V. K. Here we pick up the story again, as it illustrates some of the dilemmas of juvenile versus adult justice.

V. K.

The judge of the circuit court said he was pleased to hear testimony from the prisoner, her relatives, a prison counselor, and several guards that the girl, now 18, has adjusted well to prison life. Guards described her as a model prisoner who has taken advantage of rehabilitation and training programs during her incarceration. She told the judge that she had "learned my lesson" and had "changed my life around" while in jail.

The public defender, who made an impassioned plea for her release or reduction of her 15-year sentence, said that she is one of the youngest prisoners in the facility and is often "hassled" by older women. The judge answered that the guards' testimony clearly showed their awareness of her special needs because of her age, and he expressed the hope that she will eventually obtain the cosmetology training she has applied for at the prison so that she will be a productive citizen when she is eventually released.

At the beginning of today's proceedings, the judge clarified a statement he made three years ago during a hearing at which he decided to try the girl as an adult. The State Court of Special Appeals had remanded the case to the judge out of concern over a remark he had made which seemed to imply that the same rehabilitation is available in juvenile and adult correctional facilities. The judge said that he had meant to add the word "none." He stated further that he is not convinced there is any real rehabilitation available anywhere in the state's prison system, thereby denying any grounds for a new trial.

> The girl left the courtroom sobbing uncontrollably, supported on either side by the prison guards who had testified in her behalf. Her parole will be considered again in about 18 months.

Probation, parole, incarceration, and traditional counseling or psychotherapy have been obvious failures in reducing recidivism among delinquents. Relatively successful programs have focused on specific interventions for specific behavior problems, developed the cognitive and communication skills of youths and their families, and initiated intervention shortly after the youths' first delinquent acts (Romig, 1978).

Intervention in Families

As noted, many families of aggressive, antisocial, persistently delinquent children and youth provide inadequate environments for teaching appropriate behavior. Whether these families initially cause youngsters to become aggressive and later delinquent, or are disrupted by children's aggression and delinquency, is moot; evidence suggests a mutually pernicious influence of aggressive, delinquent children and their families on each other.

The typical parents of chronic delinquents do not punish aggressive, delinquent behavior effectively. (Not every parent of a delinquent can be faulted.) When their children misbehave, they either do not punish, or they punish violently, rather than providing consistent, aversive but nonviolent consequences, such as time out or restriction. They do not provide appropriate supervision and seem to have little interest in teaching their children how to behave. They show little concern when their children offend the community by stealing or fighting outside the home. As long as they do not have to deal with the misbehavior, they tend not to see their children as a serious problem. Within the home, they show little motivation to change their own behavior to decrease the coercion and violence that characterize their interactions with their children (cf. Patterson, 1982, 1986b).

Intervention in the families of chronic offenders is extremely difficult. Changing long-standing patterns of coercion may be impossible in families where parents are unmotivated and have few cognitive and social skills. Patterson and his colleagues report success in significantly reducing aggressive behavior and stealing in many families of aggressive children; however, the long-term outcome for stealers and chronic adolescent delinquents is guarded. Although delinquent behavior may be significantly reduced during behavioral intervention, research does not show that the improvement will persist after treatment is terminated (Patterson, 1982). Follow-up of juvenile offenders who were placed in group homes that used a teaching-family method (a behaviorally-oriented program designed to provide an appropriate family atmosphere) also shows that behavioral improvement during treatment is not maintained (Kirigin, Braukman, Atwater, & Wolf, 1982; Wolf et al., 1987).

At this time there appears to be no effective intervention in or substitute for a family social system that has failed—at least when the criterion for effectiveness is "cure" or permanent behavioral change that requires no further treatment. Wolf and his colleagues have suggested that serious delinquency should be considered a social disability requiring long-term supportive environments. Effective long-term intervention in this disability may require placing the delinquent with a foster or surrogate family in which trained parents provide appropriate behavioral controls, models, and supports throughout adolescence and into adulthood (Wolf et al., 1987).

Intervention in Schools

Students and teachers frequently observe delinquent behavior in the classroom, in other areas of the school, and on the way to and from school, as in the descriptions of "Scarface" and V. K. Many of the delinquent behaviors result in psychological trauma for victims and observers, costly damage to school property, total disruption of instruction, serious injury, or death. Each month during the academic year, thousands of teachers and millions of children in America's schools are assaulted or otherwise victimized. Theft, assault, drug and alcohol abuse, extortion, sexual promiscuity, and vandalism occur all too frequently, not just in deteriorated inner-city schools but in affluent suburban and rural communities as well (Bybee & Gee, 1982).

Punishment is the school's usual response to highly disruptive or delinquent behavior. Typical punishments (detention or corporal punishment) or exclusion (office referral, suspension, disciplinary transfer, or expulsion) are usually ineffective in reducing the problem behavior and improving the student's academic progress. In short, the school's typical response to disruptive behavior is woefully inadequate, and does little more than maintain a semblance of order and prevent total abandonment of its traditional programs (Mayer et al., 1987; Safer, 1982c).

Public schools fail many of their students. Many students experience constant academic failure, are functionally illiterate when they end their schooling, do not acquire the skills that will allow for gainful employment, are social misfits, and drop out of school before the age of 16 (see Edgar, 1987; Edgar, Webb, & Maddox, 1987). One point of view is that the schools have been "set up" for failure by public expectations that they will deal effectively with all problems of all children. Yet, the schools receive little financial or moral support. In any case, many disruptive and delinquent students pass through the public schools without anyone's ever addressing their individual needs for learning academic and social skills (Cullinan & Epstein, 1979; Nelson & Kauffman, 1977; Nelson et al., 1987; Safer, 1982b).

Safer (1982c) discusses the many interventions that schools have tried to decrease disruption:

Referrals to the school office (on the assumption that the principal or assistant principal will "straighten the child out")

After-school detention, extra assignments, grade reductions, exclusion from extracurricular activities

Suspension (both in- school and out-of-school)

Expulsion or encouragement to drop out

Retention in grade

Corporal punishment (see also Rose, 1983)

Remedial instruction

Codes of conduct

Security guards

Alternative schools (see also Fizzell, 1987; Knoblock, 1979; Nelson, 1977)

Inservice training for teachers

School-based counseling

Medication

Parent support for good school behavior

As Safer notes, school programs that are highly structured, focused on academic remediation and improved social skills, and based on principles of reinforcement for desirable behavior can produce improvements in several areas: school attendance, academic achievement, passing grades, progress toward graduation, and decreased delinquent behavior and suspensions. But research does not show that school intervention programs for disruptive youth produce long-term improvements in academic skills or in social behavior in or out of school. Moreover, nearly all school intervention programs for disruptive, delinquent youth are supported by federal or state grants, and once funding ends, the programs are usually discontinued even if they have produced positive results.

We have found no satisfactory answers to the problems of disruptive, delinquent behavior in schools. The most promising possibilities are often not implemented on a sustained basis, even when supported by rational arguments and research evidence. As Safer (1982a) suggests, widespread public tolerance of disruptive adolescents, most of whom seldom profit from sporadic school attendance, may be the crux of the problem:

> If one takes the position that it is the responsibility of the public schools to meet the educational needs of all students, including the disruptive and the disenchanted, then the large number of students who are not attending school can not be reasonably ignored. However, America tolerates a high degree of handgun abuse, petty delinquency, crowded jails, alcoholism, unwed motherhood, inefficiency and waste in the military, and white collar crime, and it also seems to tolerate having many adolescents engaged in no productive activity from ages 14 to 18. (p. 78)

Education in the Corrections System

Providing appropriate education for children and youth who are in jails or other detention facilities presents enormous problems. Implementing the essential components of an effective correctional education program and applying them to individual students, especially to those who have handicapping conditions in addition to behavioral disabilities, is extremely difficult. These are important components that Nelson, Rutherford, and Wolford mention:

Functional assessments of the deficits and learning needs of handicapped offenders

A functional curriculum (that is, one that meets a student's individual needs)

Vocational training opportunities specifically tailored to the needs of handicapped persons

Transition services that effectively link the correctional education program to a student's previous educational program, as well as to the educational and human services needed to support the handicapped offender following incarceration

A comprehensive system for providing a full range of educational and related services to handicapped offenders

Effective training in correctional special education to improve skills of educators currently serving handicapped offenders and develop skills in preservice special educators (1987, pp. 14–15)

Education of handicapped children and youth in detention is governed by the same federal laws and regulations as education of youngsters in public schools. Handicapped youngsters in detention facilities are guaranteed all the procedural protections and requirements for nonbiased individualized assessment, individualized education programs, and so on afforded under PL 94-142 and related laws and regulations (Leone, Price, & Vitolo, 1986; Wood, 1987b). Ideally, therefore, assessment of students in detention is functionally related to an appropriate curriculum (Howell, 1987), and the instruction of students is data-based and prepares them with critical life skills (Fredericks & Evans, 1987; Leone, 1985). Nevertheless, incarcerated children and youth often do not receive assessment and education. Leone et al. (1986) and Nelson (1987) summarize the problems and impediments:

☐ Criminal justice officials and the public often take the attitude that delinquent and criminal young people are not entitled to the same educational opportunities as law-abiding citizens.
☐ Some psychologists, psychiatrists, and educators take the position that many incarcerated youths are not handicapped.
☐ There is a shortage of qualified personnel to staff good special education programs in correction facilities.
☐ Some of the provisions of PL 94-142, such as regulations requiring education in the least restrictive environment and parental involvement in educational planning, are particularly difficult to implement in correction facilities.
☐ The student population of correctional facilities is transient, making educational assessment and planning especially difficult.
☐ Interagency cooperation and understanding is often limited, which hampers obtaining student records, designating responsibility for specific services, and working out transition from detention to community.
☐ Administrators of correction facilities often consider security and institutional rules more important than education.
☐ Funds for educational programs in correction facilities are limited.

Given these difficulties, it is not surprising that many delinquent youngsters' needs are not met. Recall the story of the Whiz, as Wolford (1983) goes on to describe how social systems, including correctional education, failed this lad.

The Whiz

I have stated that the Whiz was poorly served by three very important groups—public schools, the criminal justice system, and correctional education.

The public schools labeled him as a failure and helped to develop in him an image of himself as a reject, as someone without the skills needed to succeed in life and, more importantly, without a sense of direction or purpose.

The juvenile and adult criminal justice systems through courts, probation programs, and prisons continued the lead of the public schools. The Whiz was never diagnosed as having a problem other than his criminal behavior and drug addiction. He was not recognized as having failed in life for a particular reason or set of reasons, but rather as a criminal who was in need of punishment and correction.

Then came the correctional educational system which did not consider what led to the Whiz's failures. The correctional education program felt this youth needed an education and enrolled him in Adult Basic Education and General Equivalency Diploma prep. He also needed a trade, so the system helped to get him into a correspondence electronics program and a vocational training course in office machine repair.

The Whiz established what has been identified by Hans Touche as a niche. . . . He found a safe harbor at the school from the stormy climate of the prison. In this small and highly structured environment he was accepted and able to function as part of a unit. Although this niche assisted him in mental and physical survival in the prison, it is questionable whether the long-term effects of such an experience were in his best interests.

Never in his progression through public schools, the criminal justice system, or correctional education had the real needs of the youth been identified. No one had really considered what had made it difficult for him to succeed.

Whiz got his GED, dropped out of vocational school, and finished his correspondence program. Soon thereafter he was released on parole. Because of his obvious talents correctional educators helped him line up a job interview with an electronics shop upon his release. By some measures Whiz was a parolee with a bright future: he had an education, a trade, and the possibility of a job.

Some who knew him were surprised when he never showed up for the job interview, and when he called the prison 8 months after his release and 6 months after he had been declared a parole violator to ask for a letter of reference and tell us how well he was doing. Some were even surprised when we heard he had been arrested and charged with another series of drug offenses coupled with violent crimes.

No one should have been surprised. The Whiz left with the same problems he had when he dropped out of public school and when he entered the criminal justice system. He lacked the life skills needed to make it on the streets. He neither understood nor did he have the skills necessary to control his own behavior. (From "Correctional Education and Special Education—An Emerging Partnership, or 'Born to Lose'," by B. I. Wolford, 1983, *Monograph in Behavioral Disorders,* pp. 14–15. Copyright 1983 by The Council for Exceptional Children.)

What were the real needs of the Whiz? What skills did he need to control his own behavior? Research does not answer these questions, nor similar questions that could be posed for the majority of disruptive, delinquent students in schools, jails, or detention centers.

Final Notes on Intervention and Prevention

After assessing the outcomes of intervention in delinquency, regardless of the social agency or system involved, the future looks bleak. Improving the outlook for delinquents and their victims could require significant social change, in which the juvenile justice system, families, schools, and detention facilities apply nonviolent and consistent constraints on aggressive, coercive behavior. Love is not enough. In the absence of appropriate punishment for transgression, affection does not teach social skills. Punishment is not enough. In the absence of love, punishment produces only countercontrol and aggression. Perhaps the government, whether through the courts or the public schools or detention facilities, is incapable of providing an effective substitute for loving, controlling parental care.

Is truly effective intervention possible at any age? Certainly there is little to suggest that short-term intervention produces permanent behavioral change after a child or youth has been repeatedly apprehended (cf. Kirigin et al., 1982; Wolf et al., 1987). To help incarcerated delinquents or chronically disruptive, aggressive youth, we must at least give them an effective education that will meet their needs for employment and independent living (Edgar et al., 1987; Goldstein, 1987; Leone et al., 1986). Unfortunately, we don't really know what kind of education will best help delinquents lead a law-abiding life. Obviously, they will need basic academic and social skills so they can get jobs and cope with frustration. Many will need to be taught specific vocational skills as well. But at what age and for what types of delinquents can we set specific educational goals? No one knows.

We do know that to have a chance of preventing delinquent behavior, intervention must begin early in the child's life and, if that is not possible, immediately after the child's first delinquent act. Early intervention in the families of aggressive, coercive children can be effective, both in the short term for many and in the long run for at least some (cf. Patterson, 1982; Strain, Steele, Ellis, & Timm, 1982). A program to teach parenting skills to all young parents would very likely help prevent delinquency. Combined with other measures, such as reducing victims' vulnerability and developing young people's cognitive, behavioral, academic, and vocational skills, family retraining might significantly reduce delinquency and crime (Feldman, 1983; Nietzel & Himelein, 1986). Yet for youths whose serious delinquency and criminal conduct represents the second generation or more of antisocial behavior, nothing short of long-term care by a socialized surrogate family seems likely to be effective (Wolf et al., 1987).

SUBSTANCE ABUSE: NATURE AND SCOPE OF THE PROBLEM

We use the term *substance abuse* rather than *drug abuse* because not all abused chemicals are drugs. Abused substances other than drugs include gasoline, cleaning fluids, glue, and other chemicals that can cause psychological effects. A substance is considered abused if it is deliberately used to induce physiological or psychological effects (or both) for other than therapeutic purposes and when its use contributes to health risks, disruption of psychological functioning, adverse social consequences, or some combination of these.

A common misperception is that substance abuse has to do primarily with illegal drugs such as cocaine, marijuana, and heroin, or with illicit use of prescription medications such as barbiturates, but as Werry (1986b) notes, "*alcohol and tobacco are, as ever, the real drug problem*" (p. 228). Alcohol and tobacco are the largest problems because they are readily available to adults, they are advertised for sale, most people view their use by adults as socially acceptable, and children usually receive their first exposure to and first experiment with these substances in the home. The earlier the child's first experience with alcohol and tobacco, the more likely he or she will become a regular user. Early use of alcohol and tobacco, as well as other substances, correlates with family problems, low socioeconomic status, and school failure. Because the negative health consequences of alcohol and tobacco are staggering, Werry suggests that "it seems wisest to concentrate on preventing children and young people from starting smoking and drinking, not overtargeting the high-risk but numerically small group of illicit drug users" (1986b, p. 228).

Some youngsters, primarily adolescents fifteen years or older, do abuse substances other than alcohol and tobacco. Table 15.1 lists major drugs of abuse (some of which are prescribed for therapeutic purposes) along with the most typical effects of drug intoxication and withdrawal. Table 15.2 lists several classes of drugs frequently prescribed for specific therapeutic purposes; these drugs may also be abused—obtained and taken without prescription for the purpose of experiencing side effects. In addition to those listed in Tables 15.1 and 15.2, people may abuse many other preparations, including *designer drugs,* new concoctions made up in illegal laboratories and represented as well-known drugs or touted to produce euphoria.

These are necessary terms in a discussion of substance use:

Intoxication—indicates symptoms of a toxic amount of a substance in the bloodstream (enough to have physiological and/or psychological effects)

Tolerance—refers to physiological adaptation to a substance such that an increasing amount is required to produce the same effects; tolerance typically increases with repeated usage and decreases after a period of abstinence

Addiction—indicates compulsive use of a substance and that obtaining and using the substance has become a central concern and pattern of behavior

Dependence—refers to need to continue using a substance to avoid physical or emotional discomfort or both

Withdrawal—designates physical and/or emotional discomfort associated with a period of abstinence

An important feature of advanced substance abuse is its insidious onset, progressing through various stages. A substance abuser rarely becomes a habitual user immediately; rather, experimentation, perhaps under peer pressure, is followed by occasional social or recreational use, then use in certain circumstances or situations (perhaps to relax after a stressful event, to stay awake to perform a demanding task, or to sleep). Situational use may intensify and become part of daily routine; eventually, the substance can become the individual's central focus. Miksic (1987) summarizes patterns of progressive drug use (delineated by the National Institute on Drug Abuse, 1982),

TABLE 15.1
Major Drugs of Abuse and Their Prominent Effects

Drug Class	Representative Drugs	Prominent Effects	
		Intoxication	Withdrawal
Depressants	alcohol phenobarbital Valium Quaalude	relaxation sedation drowsiness irritability	tremulousness fever hallucinations psychological dependence
Marijuana	cigarettes (joints) hashish (resin)	relaxation sleepiness poor concentration confusion anxiety distortion of perception	psychological distress
Stimulants	amphetamines cocaine nicotine caffeine phencyclidine (PCP)	pupil dilation restlessness loss of appetite paranoia hallucinations	mental and physical depression fatigue

Hallucinogens	lysergic-acid-diethylamide
	   (LSD)
	mescaline
	psilocybin
	cannabis (marijuana)
	scopolamine
		pupil dilation
		disturbed attention
		hallucinations
		altered body concept
		distortions of time
		   perception
		emotional fluctuations
			inconsistent
			   evidence—little or
			   none noted

Inhalants	aerosols glue paint thinner cleaning fluid	exhilaration confusion loss of balance drowsiness depression hallucinations frequent coughing	inconsistent
Narcotics	morphine Darvon methadone codeine Dilaudid	analgesia slurred speech drowsiness constricted pupils poor coordination	fever vomiting cramps sweating "goose flesh" chills irritability running nose tearing

Source: From *Strategies for Managing Problems in the Classroom* (p. 255) by M. M. Kerr and C. M. Nelson, 1983, Columbus, OH: Merrill Publishing Company. Copyright 1983 by Merrill Publishing Company. Reprinted with permission.

TABLE 15.2
Therapeutic Drugs and Their Side Effects

Drug Class	Representative Drugs	Therapeutic Application	Side Effects
Psychotropics (psychiatric)	Tranquilizers Librium Valium	anxiety reduction muscle relaxation	intoxication physical dependency drowsiness
	Antipsychotics chlorpromazine (Thorazine) Mellaril haloperidol	reduced irritability control of hallucinations control of delusions control of thought process	lethargy social withdrawal sedation restlessness muscular spasm altered muscle control
	Stimulants amphetamine methylphenidate (Ritalin) pemoline	improved concentration reduced acting out increased behavior control	anorexia toxic psychosis
	Antidepressants imipramine	reduced depression decreased anxiety bed wetting (enuresis)	loss of balance visual disturbance restlessness dry mouth
Antiseizure	Barbiturates phenobarbital Phenytoin (Dilantin) Tegretol	seizure control seizure prevention	intoxication physical dependence
Tubercular	isoniazid Seromycin	tuberculosis	anxiety paranoia confusion
Hormonal Agents	Corticosteroids	hormone imbalance	hallucinations confusion delirium
Anticholinergics	scopolamine	Parkinson's disease asthma sleep disturbance	dry mouth blurred vision fever increased heart rate
Antihypertensives	methyldopa (Aldomet) guanethidine	high blood pressure	depression fatigue
Levo-dopa	L-Dopa	Parkinson's disease	paranoia restlessness delusions
Cardiovascular agents	digitalis propranolol (Inderal)	heart failure chest pain arrythmia	depression confusion fatigue hallucinations
Contraceptives	estrogen preparations	pregnancy prevention other gynecologic reasons	depression

Source: From *Strategies for Managing Behavior Problems in the Classroom* (p. 265) by M. M. Kerr and C. M. Nelson, 1983, Columbus, OH: Merrill Publishing Company. Copyright 1983 by Merrill Publishing Company. Reprinted with permission.

Coke Is It? Changing Social Attitudes Toward Substances

The Coke you sit down with today is still basically Priestly's carbon dioxide-in-water mix. There have been only one or two small changes. When in 1888 a pharmacist in Atlanta, Georgia, bottled a variant of Priestly's water as something he called "Coca-Cola," he was so proud of the medicinal pedigree that he marketed it as a mouthwash and gargle, guaranteed, in company advertising of the time, to "whiten the teeth, cleanse the mouth, and cure tender and bleeding gums." That was useful, but apparently of limited attraction. In time the gargle angle was dropped, and drinking the water, carbon dioxide, and sugar concoction was encouraged instead. There were still judicious amounts of cocaine poured in. To us that might seem excessive, especially as it was designed as a beverage for all the family, but this was before the first food and drug acts of the U.S. Brandy was common in children's tonic, morphine was available in many places without prescription, and by the end of the century a brand-new powder pick-me-up was being sold over the counter by an aspirin company: this was heroin. In that pharmacological flurry a little crushed coca leaf was not to be remarked upon. In 1903 it was dropped, though, with labels of that date noting "Cocaine Removed."

David Bodanis, *The Secret House.* New York: Simon & Schuster, 1986, pp. 72–73. Copyright © 1986 by David Bodanis. Reprinted by permission of Simon & Schuster, Inc.

shown in Table 15.3. Clearly, substance use and abuse does not always progress to the obsessive/dependent stage, but as Miksic points out, teachers and other adults should be aware of the danger signals of the transitions from experimentation to social/recreational and to situational/circumstantial use. Teachers may first observe changes in social behavior and academic performance at the point of transition to situational use.

It is difficult to estimate the extent of substance abuse among children and adolescents. The level of abuse of specific substances reflects both fads and social attitudes and prohibitions (Wong, 1979). Use of hallucinogenic drugs has been lower in the 1980s than in the previous two decades, but designer drugs (such as "crack," a form of cocaine) have become major concerns, and marijuana use, which in previous decades caused much alarm and sometimes resulted in legal penalties of absurd proportions, is now considered comparatively safe (cf. Miksic, 1987).

SUBSTANCE ABUSE: INTERVENTION AND EDUCATION

Children's substance abuse is a social problem of extraordinary proportions. A successful attack on the problem involves families, schools, communities, and child and adolescent peer groups. We need programs for prevention, control, crisis intervention, and long-term rehabilitation. The chaotic and frantic efforts of the sixties and seventies have become more focused and coherent. Substance abuse educators now recognize

TABLE 15.3
Patterns of Progressive Drug Abuse

Stage of Use	Behavior	Frequency of Use	Emotional State
Experimentation	Little effect Denial of negative consequences	1 to 5 times (total)	Excitement/daring Mild euphoria Possible discomfort Mild guilt
Social/ situational	Decreased academic performance Loss of interest in hobbies Loss of interest in special activities Begins to seek out drug- using friends Changes in clothing habits Some uncharacteristic behavior	2 to 4 times per week	Excitement Being "in" with the crowd Feels better with drug than without it Less guilt—"Drugs are OK, I can handle them"
Habitual	Most friends use drugs Beginning of family problems due to drug use Major loss of interest in school and other activities Impulsiveness Erratic mood swings Uses drug alone	Daily use	"Need" for euphoric state Highs are very high, and lows are very uncomfortable More guilt and depression
Obsessive/ dependent	Skips school regularly Weight loss or gain Messy, unclean appearance Loss of ability to concentrate Severe paranoid or depressed thoughts Dangerous aggression Suicidal thoughts Pathologic lying Stealing to obtain drugs Family chaos	Multiple times per day depending on drug	Needs drug to feel "normal" Severe discomfort if drug not available Disorganized thoughts Erratic behavior May become psychotic or suicidal

Source: From *Helping Adolescents with Learning and Behavior Problems* (p. 288) by M. M. Kerr, C. M. Nelson, and D. M. Lambert, 1987, Columbus, OH: Merrill Publishing Company.

Getting Help for Substance Abuse Education

Information about drug abuse education is available from the National Institute on Drug Abuse, 5600 Fishers Lane, Rockville, MD 29857. NIDA will provide a list of regional drug abuse education coordinators. Various government publications are also available, including *Treatment Services for Adolescent Substance Abusers* by A. Friedman and G. Beschner (1985, NIDA Monograph No. ADM 85-1342).

Drug education curriculum materials for specific grade levels are available from The Addiction Research Foundation, 83 Russell Street, Toronto, Canada M5S 2S1.

TABLE 15.4
Drug Information Guide

Drug Used	Alcohol (beer, wine, liquor)	Cocaine (coke, rock, crack, base)	Depressants Barbiturates, Sedatives, Tranquilizers, (downers, tranks, ludes, reds, Valium, yellow jackets, alcohol)
Physical Symptoms	Intoxication, slurred speech, unsteady walk, relaxation, relaxed inhibitions, impaired coordination, slowed reflexes.	Brief intense euphoria, elevated blood pressure & heart rate, restlessness, excitement, feeling of well-being followed by depression.	Depressed breathing and heartbeat, intoxication, drowsiness, uncoordinated movements.
Look for	Smell of alcohol on clothes or breath, intoxicated behavior, hangover, glazed eyes.	Glass vials, glass pipe, white crystalline powder, razor blades, syringes, needle marks.	Capsules and pills, confused behavior, longer periods of sleep, slurred speech.
Dangers	Addiction, accidents as result of impaired ability and judgment, overdose when mixed with other depressants, heart and liver damage.	Addiction, heart attack, seizures, lung damage, severe depression, paranoia (see Stimulants).	Possible overdose, especially in combination w/alcohol, muscle rigidity, addiction, withdrawal & overdose require medical treatment.

Seven POSSIBLE symptoms of Drug Involvement
1. Change in school or work attendance or performance.
2. Alteration of personal appearance.
3. Mood swings or attitude changes.

An important feature of successful substance abuse education programs is getting accurate and useful information into the hands of teachers, parents, and students in an accessible, abbreviated form. Table 15.4 is an example of the type and amount of information that can be put on a three-by-five-inch "slideguide," a card that pulls through an outer sleeve. Headings and other information (such as hot line numbers) are printed on both sides of the sleeve. As one pulls the card through the sleeve (which has windows in it), information on both sides of the card appears under the headings.

Hallucinogens (acid, LSD, PCP, MDMA, Ecstasy, psilocybin mushrooms, peyote)	Inhalants (gas, aerosols, glue, nitrites, Rush, White out)	Marijuana (pot, dope, grass, weed, herb, hash, joint)	Narcotics Heroin (junk, dope, Black tar, China white), Demerol, Dilaudid (D's), Morphine, Codeine	Stimulants (speed, uppers, crank, Bam, black beauties, crystal, dexies, caffeine, nicotine, cocaine, amphetamines)
Altered mood and perceptions, focus on detail, anxiety, panic, nausea, synaesthesia (ex: smell colors, see sounds).	Nausea, dizziness, headaches, lack of coordination and control.	Altered perceptions, red eyes, dry mouth, reduced concentration and coordination, euphoria, laughing, hunger.	Euphoria, drowsiness, insensitivity to pain, nausea, vomiting, watery eyes, runny nose (see Depressants).	Alertness, talkativeness, wakefulness, increased blood pressure, loss of appetite, mood elevation.
Capsules, tablets, "microdots", blotter squares.	Odor of substance on clothing and breath, intoxication, drowsiness, poor muscular control.	Rolling papers, pipes, dried plant material, odor of burnt hemp rope, roach clips.	Needle marks on arms, needles, syringes, spoons, pinpoint pupils, cold moist skin.	Pills and capsules, loss of sleep and appetite, irritability or anxiety, weight loss, hyperactivity.
Unpredictable behavior, emotional instability, violent behavior (with PCP).	Unconsciousness, suffocation, nausea and vomiting, damage to brain and central nervous system, sudden death.	Panic reaction, impaired short term memory, addiction.	Addiction, lethargy, weight loss, contamination from unsterile needles (hepatitis, AIDS), accidental overdose.	Fatigue leading to exhaustion, addiction, paranoia, depression, confusion, possibly hallucinations.

4. Withdrawal from responsibilities/family contacts.
5. Association with drug-using peers.
6. Unusual patterns of behavior.
7. Defensive attitude concerning drugs.

Source: Drug Information Guide. Promotional Slideguide Corp., 33 Rockwell Place, Brooklyn, NY 11217. Used with permission.

that "America is a drug-using society" (Wong, 1979, p. 186), that there are no sure-fire solutions, and that, in today's social context, the problem will never be entirely resolved (Miksic, 1987; Wong, 1979). Because the problem is so complex, educators who wish to know more about how to approach substance abuse issues should seek information from government and private agencies.

Not all substance abuse is preventable; as Werry (1986b) and others argue, the focus should probably be on the substances that cause the most damaging consequences for the greatest number—alcohol and tobacco (see also Elder, Stern, Anderson, Hovell, Molgaard, & Seidman, 1987; Milgram & Nathan, 1986). Still, educational programs can keep many youngsters from wasting years of their lives and damaging their health. Miksic (1987) outlines the major actions in a successful substance abuse education program.

1. Establish a clear, well-defined policy for teachers and students spelling out how teachers and administrators will deal with apparent or substantiated drug use or possession.
2. Encourage teachers to establish a basic drug education curriculum for their grade levels—keeping it simple, brief, and nonjudgmental and emphasizing the teachers' concern for the students' physical and psychological welfare.
3. Help teachers increase their awareness of local drug problems and community service agencies.
4. Provide an atmosphere in which the teacher can develop the skills and sensitivity for resolving classroom and individual problems and for leading group discussions about topics such as adolescent development and drug use.
5. Develop an intervention program that involves families as well as students by offering both one-to-one and group counseling and by utilizing community resources such as community counseling centers and drop-in centers within the school. (A drop-in center could be staffed by an education counselor with some training in drug abuse counseling.)
6. Try to get all teachers to review their role perceptions. If they feel their jobs are basically unfulfilling and that they are unable to empathize with students and deal with affective as well as cognitive training, this may lead to constructive career reorientation.
7. Develop peer-group approaches with positive role models for group or individual support. Different types of peer programs are discussed in the National Institute on Drug Abuse publication, "Adolescent Peer Pressure" (NIDA Publication No. ADM 83-1152).
8. Promote understanding of the emotional structure and perceptions that often accompany drug use. Many drug-using students feel they are incompetent and unreasonably rejected by adults and peers. They need a sympathetic approach rather than a disciplinary and judgmental attitude that confirms their belief that teachers and administrators are only concerned about keeping order, not about helping students. (See Kerr et al., 1987, p. 245.)

Family involvement and programs that are consistent with cultural traditions are critical features of prevention and intervention efforts (Bry, Conboy, & Bisgay, 1986;

Maypole & Anderson, 1987). Although successful programs use a variety of cognitive and affective approaches to prevention, control, and rehabilitation, we cannot overlook the consequences of abstinence and use. Positive consequences for remaining drug free and aversive consequences for substance use have been highly effective components of some interventions (Bry et al., 1986; Elder et al., 1987).

Teachers need to know how to manage suspected substance abuse episodes and suspected intoxication or withdrawal crises in school. Their role is to manage and refer students appropriately, not to become investigators or counselors. While educators must be aware of indications of substance abuse, they should not automatically assume that certain physical or psychological symptoms are the result of intoxication or withdrawal. Referral to counselors or medical personnel is appropriate to determine the cause. A clear school policy regarding detection and management helps teachers and administrators to respond correctly to suspected abuse and crisis situations. In the event of an emotional-behavioral crisis, the teacher should remain calm and nonconfrontational; safety is more important than demonstrating disciplinary control (Miksic, 1987).

SUMMARY

Juvenile delinquency is a legal term that indicates violation of the law by an individual who is not yet an adult. Acts that are illegal only if committed by a minor are status offenses; index crimes are illegal regardless of the individual's age. The vast majority of youngsters commit delinquent acts; a small percentage are apprehended. About 20 percent of all children and youth are at some time officially delinquent, and about three percent are adjudicated each year.

Self-reported delinquent behavior is not related to social class, but official delinquency appears more often among lower social classes and minorities. Juveniles who are apprehended and adjudicated tend to be those who commit the greatest number of serious delinquent acts and are most logically considered behaviorally disordered. Recidivists tend to have committed their first delinquent act before the age of twelve. Males commit more serious crimes against persons and property than females, but the juvenile justice system tends to deal more harshly with females than with males.

Subtypes of delinquents (socialized-subcultural, unsocialized psychopathic, and neurotic-disturbed) have been identified, but there is a great deal of overlap among the groups. A high percentage of incarcerated delinquents have handicapping conditions, primarily learning disabilities, but the Department of Education does not interpret incarceration in itself to indicate that a youngster is entitled to special education. Arguments can be made that all or nearly all incarcerated children and youths are behaviorally handicapped and in need of special education. Seriously delinquent and criminal behavior may be considered a handicapping condition, a social disability that requires long-term supportive intervention.

Early theories of delinquency attributed delinquent behavior to the characteristics and focal concerns of lower-class culture. More recent and empirically defensible control theories based on social learning principles attribute delinquent behavior to a causal chain with these links: physical and cognitive capacities to commit delinquent acts, opportunities for delinquent acts, lack of personal commitment to law-abiding behavior, association with others who lack commitment to law-abiding behavior, and willingness to commit delinquent acts. Other factors that also increase the risk for delinquency are problems in school, low verbal intelligence, parents' alcoholism and arrest records, low socioeconomic status, disrupted families, lax parental supervision, indifference or hostility of parents and siblings, and substance abuse. Control theory suggests that delinquency is not so much caused as it is not prevented; breakdowns in societal controls set the stage for delinquency. Both family interaction patterns and genetic factors are contributing causes of delinquency.

Assessment of delinquents' educational needs is extremely difficult because of the delinquents' characteristics and those of the social agencies that serve them. Intervention in delinquency comes from juvenile courts, family retraining, school programs, and correctional education. In general, interventions of the juvenile justice system have been a failure. More successful programs focus on specific responses to specific types of behavior, improve the cognitive and communication skills of young-sters and their families, and begin shortly after the youngster's first delinquent act. Family retraining with delinquents is extremely difficult; long-term outcomes for chronic offenders are guarded. Effective intervention may require long-term care by socialized surrogate families. Schools typically respond to disruptive and delinquent behavior with heightened punishment, and this approach has failed. The most suc-cessful school programs are highly structured, focus on academic remediation and improvement of social skills, and reinforce desirable behavior. Education in the cor-rections system should include functional assessment of students' needs, a curriculum that teaches important life skills, vocational training, supportive transition back to the community, and a full range of educational and related services from collaborating agencies.

A substance is abused when it is deliberately used to induce physiological or psychological effects (or both) for other than therapeutic purposes and when its use contributes to greater health risks, disruption of psychological functioning, adverse social consequences, or some combination of these. The most serious substance abuse problems involve alcohol and tobacco. Prevention efforts should focus on keeping youngsters from beginning to use these substances. Substance abuse typically pro-gresses through several stages, from experimentation, to social-recreational use, to circumstantial-situational use, which may become intensified and lead to obsessional dependency. Teachers are most likely to observe the first indications of substance use during the transition from experimentation to social-recreational or to circumstantial-situational use.

Substance abuse is deeply ingrained in cultural patterns of behavior. Americans are a drug-using society; the problem has no immediate solutions, and not all substance abuse can be prevented. Well-implemented drug education programs can, however, prevent some youngsters from wasting their lives or endangering their health. An effective educational program begins with rational and clearly communicated school policies that make teachers' and administrators' responsibilities and legitimate actions known to all. Family and community involvement are critical aspects of effective education programs. Providing appropriate consequences for both abstinence and substance use is an important feature of management.

16

Anxiety-Withdrawal and Other Disorders

As you read this chapter, keep these guiding questions in mind:

- [ ] What types of behavior are associated with anxiety-withdrawal?
- [ ] Under what conditions should educators and others be concerned when a youngster exhibits behavior characteristics of anxiety-withdrawal?
- [ ] What are the most likely causes of social isolation?
- [ ] What is the role of the peer group in intervening effectively in social isolation?
- [ ] What strategies are most effective in helping adolescents overcome social withdrawal and social ineptitude?
- [ ] How do children acquire fears and phobias, and how can maladaptive fears and phobias be prevented?
- [ ] What are guidelines for dealing with school phobia?
- [ ] Under what conditions should intervention be implemented for a youngster's rituals or compulsive behavior?
- [ ] What strategies might one try with a youngster who is extremely reluctant to speak to others in school?
- [ ] What behavioral, cognitive, and affective characteristics do anorexics and bulimics share?
- [ ] What are the best ways to treat enuresis and encopresis?
- [ ] What is the relationship between extremely feminine behavior in young boys and later homosexuality?
- [ ] What criteria should lead adults to be concerned about a youngster's tics?

Chapters 12 through 15 centered on problems that fall under the general dimension of *externalizing disorders*. This chapter turns to problems designated generally as *internalizing*. Although the broad band classification *internalizing* is well established in empirical studies of behavioral dimensions (Quay, 1986a), most of the specific categories and disorders that fall under it are not. In short, there is more confusion and controversy over terminology and classification for internalizing problems than for externalizing problems. Grouping internalizing problems for discussion therefore presents unavoidable difficulties. Social withdrawal and other internalizing behavior problems often occur together (Strauss, Forehand, Smith, & Frame, 1986). Other writers comment on the difficulties as follows: "We will, owing to the nature of the literature, sometimes be discussing findings based on the study of symptoms, sometimes on the study of broadly defined 'disorder,' and sometimes also on the study of a more circumscribed disorder" (Quay & La Greca, 1986, p. 75).

The relationships among the various problems are for the most part tenuous, and since they are so varied and loosely related, we will not attempt to summarize definition, prevalence, causal factors, prevention, assessment, intervention, or education for the general case; these subheadings are included for specific disorders where we have sufficient information for discussion. In discussing anxiety-withdrawal, social isolation and ineptitude, fears and phobias, obsessions and compulsions, reluctant speech, eating disorders, elimination disorders, sexual disorders, and stereotyped movement disorders, you will find they are not mutually exclusive categories; eating disorders and reluctant speech may both involve fears or phobias, sexual disorders may involve obsessions or compulsions or both, and so on. The problems we will discuss are representative of those most frequently described in the literature. We will concentrate on the disorders that are most relevant to educational practice: anxiety-withdrawal, social isolation and ineptitude, and fears and phobias.

ANXIETY-WITHDRAWAL

In analyses of behavior problem checklists, Quay and Peterson (1987) describe anxiety-withdrawal as a behavioral dimension with characteristics such as feelings of inferiority and inability to succeed, self-consciousness and easy embarrassment, shyness, bashfulness, anxiousness and fearfulness, feelings of being unloved and depressed, reluctance to try new things for fear of failure, and hypersensitivity (easily hurt feelings). The shy, anxious, socially withdrawn youngster described by this dimension (often labeled **neurotic** in psychodynamic literature) has traditionally been assumed to be more disturbed and to have a worse prognosis for adult adjustment than the hostile, acting out child or youth. Research does not bear out this assumption. Characteristics associated with anxiety-withdrawal are more transitory than those associated with conduct disorder, and anxiety-withdrawal does not put a child at risk for later development of schizophrenia or other major psychiatric disorder in adulthood (Quay & La Greca, 1986; Robins, 1966, 1986).

Quay and La Greca (1986) estimate that *persistent* anxiety-withdrawal may characterize two percent of the child population, and that about five percent may be affected by such behavior problems at one time or another. Anxiety-withdrawal may be part of the problems of 20 to 30 percent of youngsters referred to clinics for treatment of behavioral disorders. Boys and girls are referred for these problems in about equal percentages, but these are only rough estimates, because there have been no extensive studies of prevalence.

Anxiety-withdrawal in its typical form is not, then, a great concern to knowledgeable professionals who work with children and youth. It is not the most prevalent type of disorder, nor does it usually carry serious implications for future development. But in their extreme form, some of the characteristics of anxiety-withdrawal and some associated disorders *do* carry serious implications. Extreme social isolation, extreme and persistent anxiety, and persistent extreme fears, for example, can seriously endanger social and personal development and demand effective intervention.

SOCIAL ISOLATION AND INEPTITUDE

Social isolation may result from excessive behavior, such as hyperactivity or aggression, that drives others away, or it may result from deficiencies in behavior, such as lack of social initiative. Some isolated youngsters exhibit both excessive and deficient behavior. As we have seen, hyperactive and hyperaggressive children and youth are often rejected by their peers; they are most obviously isolated because of behavior that is highly aversive to others. This chapter focuses on children and youth who are socially isolated primarily for other reasons—deficits in social approach and responsiveness.

Definition and Prevalence

Some socially isolated youngsters lack social approach skills, such as looking at, initiating conversation with, asking to play with, and appropriately touching their peers or adults. Usually, they also lack responsiveness to others' initiations of social contact. Indeed, research on social interaction in field settings and in the laboratory strongly suggests that the severely withdrawn or socially isolated child does not engage in the social reciprocity (exchange of mutual and equitable reinforcement between pairs of individuals) that is characteristic of normal social development (McConnell, 1987; Strain et al., 1984). The withdrawn or isolated child or youth lacks specific social skills for making and keeping friends.

Social isolation is not an all-or-nothing problem. All children and youth sometimes exhibit withdrawn behavior and are socially inept. This behavior may occur with any degree of severity, ranging along a continuum from a normal social reticence in new situations to the profound isolation of psychosis. In nearly any classroom, from preschool through adulthood, however, some individuals are distinguished by their lack of social interaction. Their social isolation is often accompanied by immature or inadequate behavior that makes them targets of ridicule or taunts. They are friendless loners who are apparently unable to avail themselves of the joy and satisfaction of social reciprocity. Unless their behavior and that of their peers can be changed, they are likely to remain isolated from close and frequent human contact and the attendant developmental advantages afforded by social interaction. Their prognosis, then, is not good (McEvoy & Odom, 1987). Lack of research makes it impossible to estimate the prevalence of social skills deficits among children and youth (Hops, Finch, & McConnell, 1985).

Causal Factors and Prevention

Social learning theory predicts that some children, particularly those who have not been taught appropriate social interaction skills and those who have been punished for attempts at social interaction, will be withdrawn. A mildly or moderately withdrawn youngster is likely to be anxious and have a low self-concept, but the conclusion that anxiety and low self-concept cause withdrawal and social isolation is not justifiable. It is more plausible that anxiety and low self-concept result from the child's lack of social competence.

Parental overrestrictiveness or social incompetence, lack of opportunity for social learning, and early rebuffs in social interaction with peers may contribute to a child's learning to play in isolation from others and to avoid social contact. Parents who are socially obtuse are likely to have children whose social skills are not well developed (Sherman & Farina, 1974), probably because socially awkward parents provide models of undesirable behavior and are unable to teach their children the skills that will help them become socially attractive. Aversive social experiences may indeed produce anxious children who have little self-confidence and evaluate themselves negatively. Anxiety and self-derogation may thereafter contribute to reticence in social situations and help to perpetuate social incompetence. Nevertheless, the child's temperamental characteristics, in combination with early socialization experiences and the nature of the current social environment, probably account for the development of social isolation. The social learning view of isolate behavior, which focuses on the factors of reinforcement, punishment, and imitation, carries direct implications for intervention and suggests ways to remediate isolation by teaching social skills (see Field, 1981; Fundis, 1981; Hops et al., 1985; McConnell, 1987). Effective prevention of social isolation, however, involves more than teaching youngsters how to approach and respond to others; it requires arranging a social environment that is conducive to positive interactions.

Assessment

The definition of social isolation includes rejection or nonacceptance by peers. Measurement of rejection and acceptance frequently includes use of a questionnaire or sociometric game that asks youngsters to choose or nominate classmates for various roles. Students may be asked to indicate which of their peers they would most like to play, sit, work, or party with, and with whom they would least like to interact. The results of this procedure are then analyzed to see which individuals have high social status in the group (to whom many peers are attracted), those who are isolates (not chosen as playfellows or workmates by anyone), and those who are rejected (with whom peers want to avoid social contact) (Hops & Lewin, 1984; Sabornie, 1987). More precise measurement of social interaction may be obtained by direct daily observation and recording of behavior. We can thus define social isolates as children who have a markedly lower number of social interactions than do their peers. Sociometric status and direct measurement of social interactions, though both valuable in assessment, do not necessarily reveal what causes a youngster to experience social isolation. A student could, for example, have a relatively high rate of positive social interaction and still be a relative social isolate: his or her interactions might involve relatively few peers and be characterized by a superficial or artificial quality (Walker, Greenwood, Hops, & Todd, 1979). Consequently, assessment should also include teacher ratings and self-reports. Thus, adequate measurement of social skills or social isolation requires attention to the *rate* of interactive behaviors, *qualitative* aspects of social interaction, and children's *perceptions* of social status (Asher & Taylor, 1981; Hops et al., 1985; McEvoy & Odom, 1987).

Although interest in assessing and improving exceptional children's social skill deficits has risen dramatically, problems of definition and measurement remain critical issues (Bellack, 1983; Hops et al., 1985; Schloss, Schloss, Wood, & Kiehl, 1986; Shores, 1987; Simpson, 1987; Strain et al., 1984). People accept the notion that withdrawn and socially isolated children lack social skills, but do not know precisely what those skills are and how to measure them reliably. One might assume that eye contact during conversation is an important social skill, for example, and observe that a disturbed youngster avoids eye contact when engaged in conversation. The confusion arises in defining appropriate eye contact and measuring it precisely. Should one record the cumulative amount of time the youngster gazes at a conversational partner, the duration of gazes, or the number of gazes? "These measures are not equivalent. . .; they reflect different affective states and parameters of social skill. The distinction is well illustrated by contrasting a [youngster] who makes frequent 'furtive' glances, with one who stares fixedly for part of the time, with one who gazes for several short periods" (Bellack, 1983, p. 31). Who, other than the youngster's conversational partner, can record eye contact accurately? In what social contexts and with what conversational partners should one measure eye contact? Different patterns of eye contact are socially appropriate under different circumstances and with different people, which complicates the matter further.

As social skills research becomes more sophisticated, the nuances of appropriate social interaction become more difficult to capture. Much of our knowledge about the nature of children's social skills is superficial. Children's social *intentions* (*why* as well as *what* they do) may be an important area to research; we may need to assess their pragmatic reasons for interacting with peers in specified ways to fully understand social isolation and social acceptance (McEvoy & Odom, 1987).

Intervention and Education

One approach to the problem of withdrawal is to try to improve the youngster's self-concept, on the assumption that this will result in a tendency to engage more often in social interactions. We can encourage children to express their feelings about their behavior and social relationships in play therapy or in therapeutic conversations with a warm, accepting adult. As they come to feel accepted and able to express their feelings openly, their self-concepts will presumably become more positive. The incidence of positive social interactions should then increase as well. Attempts to remediate social isolation without teaching specific social skills or manipulating the social environment are usually ineffectual, however. Few data show that self-concept can be improved without first improving behavior. If youngsters' appraisals of their own behavior are unrealistic, then bringing self-perceptions into line with reality is, to be sure, a worthy goal. If youngsters are indeed socially isolated, then attempting to convince them of their social adequacy without first helping them learn the skills for social reciprocity may be misleading. Once their behavior has been improved, however, there is a foundation for improving self-image (cf. Morena & Litrownik, 1974).

Arranging appropriate environmental conditions helps teach socially isolated youngsters to reciprocate positive behavior with their peers. Situations that are conducive to social interaction, that contain toys or equipment that promote social play, bring the isolated youngster into proximity with others who have social interaction skills or who require social interaction from the target child. Specific intervention strategies based on social learning principles include (1) reinforcing social interaction (perhaps with praise, points, or tokens); (2) providing peer models of social interaction; (3) providing training (models, instruction, rehearsal, and feedback) in specific social skills; and (4) enlisting peer confederates to initiate social interactions and reinforce appropriate social responses. Of course, all four strategies may be used together, and experimental research shows the effectiveness of these procedures in modifying certain behaviors (Hops et al., 1985; McConnell, 1987; Strain, 1981). An intervention program for increasing withdrawn children's social interactions in kindergarten through third grade—PEERS (Procedures for Establishing Effective Relationship Skills)—includes this combination of strategies (Hops et al., 1978).

Social learning strategies for defining, measuring, and changing handicapped youngsters' deficient social behavior show great promise. Nevertheless, current social skills training methods do not adequately address the problems of producing behavioral changes that actually make handicapped children and youth more socially acceptable, that generalize across a variety of social situations, and that are maintained after intervention is terminated (Bellack, 1983; McConnell, 1987). As Strain et al. (1984) note, social skills involve reciprocity—an exchange of behavior between two people. Interventions that focus exclusively on changing the isolated individual's behavior miss that vital aspect of social adaptation—social interaction. The goal of intervention must be to help the socially isolated individual become enmeshed or entrapped in positive, reciprocal, self-perpetuating social exchanges, which can be done only by carefully choosing the target skills. One must select target skills with these questions in mind: Are the particular social behaviors likely to be maintained after intervention is terminated? Are the skills likely to generalize across different settings (such as in different areas of the school and during different types of activities)? Do the target skills relate to peers' social behavior, so that peer behavior prompts and reinforces performance of the skill (that is, are the skills part of naturally occurring, positive social interactions)? If these questions generate affirmative answers, then social skills training is more likely to last (McConnell, 1987).

Perhaps the most promising approach is peer-mediated intervention that includes both the isolated youngster's behavior and that of peers. Sainato, Maheady, and Shook (1986) and Twardosz, Nordquist, Simon, and Botkin (1983) have experimented with this approach. Twardosz et al. encouraged preschoolers and their teachers to engage in games and group activities in which affectionate behavior is demonstrated naturally. Socially isolated children are not singled out for treatment, but their social interaction has increased following participation in the group affection activities. Matthew's social interactions increased using group affection activities.

Matthew

Matthew was a five-year-old enrolled in a nursery school that served about 15 children three to six years of age. He had been variously diagnosed as autisticlike, learning disabled, and minimally brain damaged. He exhibited a variety of peculiar and inappropriate behaviors that caused other children to avoid him. He did not like anyone to touch him and resisted other children's approaches with statements such as "I hate you," "Get away from me," and "Don't look." He was videotaped for 15 minutes during 30-minute free-play periods several times per week; the videotapes were later reviewed and scored to measure the percentage of time he spent in interaction with his peers. During baseline observations, Matthew interacted with his peers only about 15 percent of the time (as shown in Figure 16.1). Twardosz et al. (1983) designed an intervention with group affection activities, conducted for 10 minutes each day, to increase his social interaction. The activities consisted of gradually more intimate and extended physical contact between Matthew and his peers and included nine other children and two teachers. Children were encouraged but not required to participate. The activities began with shaking hands and saying hello and progressed to clasping arms, hugging, and tickling. As we see in Figure 16.1, the affection training had a marked effect on Matthew's interaction with his peers. The affection activities were discontinued during the reversal phase, and peer interaction declined; later they were reintroduced and again produced increased interaction.

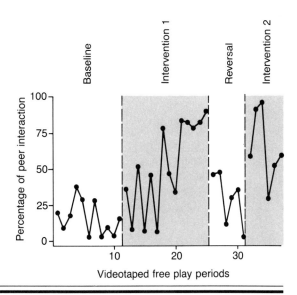

FIGURE 16.1

Matthew's Percentage of Peer Interaction for Baseline and Intervention Conditions

Source: From "The Effect of Group Affection Activities on the Interaction of Socially Isolate Children" by S. Twardosz, V. M. Nordquist, R. Simon, and D. Botkin, 1983. *Analysis and Intervention in Developmental Disabilities, 3,* 318. Copyright 1983 by *Analysis and Intervention in Developmental Disabilities.* Reprinted by permission.

Sainato et al. (1986) explored the effects of serving as a classroom manager on the social interaction of three withdrawn kindergartners (as described in the box). As class managers, the withdrawn children made more positive social initiations to

The Labor of Management: Increasing Social Status by Role Assignment

A [procedure] was implemented to determine if the assignment of a "manager" role would influence the interpersonal attraction and interaction patterns of three socially isolated children. During baseline, all subjects were observed interacting in the free-play setting without any experimenter-manipulated changes in the routine. The teacher monitored the play activities and offered ideas, but generally did not prompt the children to engage in social interactions. Following a 5-day baseline, the teacher announced to the class that she had selected a new helper (Brendan) in the class-room. She then called Brendan to the front of the class and awarded him a large "manager" button to wear for the next 2 weeks. His "job" consisted of leading and/or directing the class in previously rated, highly preferred activities, which included di-recting the feeding of the class guinea pig, collecting milk money and taking lunch count, ringing the bell for clean-up time, and handing out the "keys" to the barber shop and shoe store areas. Prior to beginning school each day, the teacher reviewed the manager's duties with the target child and the rest of the class. In addition, a pic-ture board depicting the manager's major tasks was displayed in front of the class-room to prompt the target child not to forget an assignment. This was the first time the teacher had used a student in the "manager" role.

Brendan remained the classroom "manager" over the next 10-day period. On Day 16, the teacher complimented Brendan publicly on the "great job" he had done as manager and suggested that the entire class applaud him for this efforts. The teacher then announced that Ilene would be the new manager for the next 2-week period. Procedures used with [Ilene] were identical to those described previously. Fol-lowing 2 weeks under Ilene's management, the same procedures were implemented with [Linda].

From "The Effects of a Classroom Manager Role on the Social Interaction Patterns and Social Status of Withdrawn Kinder-garten Students" by D. M. Sainato, L. Maheady, and G. L. Shook, 1986, *Journal of Applied Behavior Analysis, 19,* p. 190.

their peers during free-play time, received more positive and fewer negative social bids from their peers, and were chosen more often as best friends by their peers.

Social Ineptitude

Some children and youth are not social isolates but still do not fit in well with their peers and are hampered by inadequate social sensitivity or ineptness in delicate social situations. Children whose previous social experience is at odds with the majority of their peers, adolescents making their first approaches to members of the opposite sex, and adolescents interviewing for their first jobs are often quite tactless or unskilled in the social graces demanded for acceptance. Some individuals have irritating per-sonal habits that detract from social adequacy. The results of social ineptitude may be negative self-image, anxiety, and withdrawal.

One can often eliminate or avoid bungling social behaviors by teaching im-portant social cues and appropriate responses. Offering group and individual coun-seling, showing the youngster videotaped replays of his or her own behavior, modeling appropriate behavior, and providing guided practice (or some combination of these strategies) have been used to teach social skills (see Cartledge & Milburn, 1986; Hops et al., 1985, for reviews). A social learning view of the origin and remediation of interpersonal ineptness is clearly a functional view for the special educator, for it implies that direct instruction is most effective. The following descriptions, based on research by Franco, Christoff, Crimmins, and Kelly (1983), show how an adolescent's extreme shyness and social ineptitude were altered through social skills training. The youngster is described as somewhat depressed; social isolation and depression are similar but not synonymous.

Norbert

Norbert was a 14-year-old referred to a clinic by his parents because they were concerned about his shyness and lack of peer relationships. He associated primarily with children 5 to 8 years younger than he, spent a great deal of time alone in his bed-

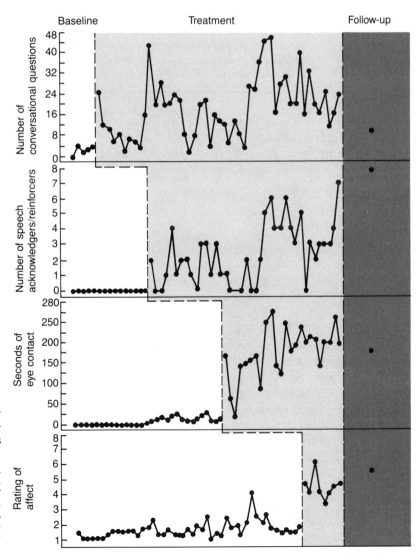

FIGURE 16.2

Frequency of Skill Behaviors During 10-Minute Unstructured Conversations with Novel Partners

Source: From "Social Skills Training for an Extremely Shy Young Adolescent: An Empirical Case Study" by D. P. Franco, K. A. Christoff, D. B. Crimmins, and J. A. Kelly, 1983, *Behavior Therapy, 14,* p. 573. Copyright 1983 by *Behavior Therapy.* Reprinted by permission.

room, and seldom talked to anyone at all. At school he had few friends and was often teased by peers, who referred to him as a "dope," "nerd," and so on. He did not seem to be particularly anxious but "appeared to be a somewhat depressed young person with minimal conversational skills, no friends, and a longstanding socially isolated life-style" (p. 570). Franco and colleagues set up a series of videotaped 10-minute sessions involving conversations between Norbert and conversational partners who were teenagers or young adults. They scored the videotapes to assess Norbert's interactional skills along four dimensions that are important in social relationships: asking conversational questions, verbally acknowledging and verbally reinforcing what one's conversational partner says, making eye contact during conversation, and showing affective warmth. After five baseline sessions, Norbert was trained in each of the four conversational skills in succession. Training consisted of 20 to 30 minutes discussing the importance of the particular skill, the trainer's modeling the skill, and guiding Norbert in rehearsing the skill. Improvement resulted from each component of the training (see Figure 16.2, preceding page). Other information Franco et al. obtained indicated that Norbert's skills generalized to situations outside the training sessions. In fact, follow-up data 16 months after intervention ended indicated that Norbert's social relationships remained improved; he "now had classmates visit the house, had begun to date, and was trying out for a school athletic team" (Franco et al., 1983, p. 574).

It is often more effective to teach social skills in group situations, where role playing affords a more realistic context for practice. Research shows the feasibility of group training in social skills for shy young adolescents (Christoff, Scott, Kelley, Schlundt, Baer, & Kelly, 1985).

FEARS AND PHOBIAS

At birth, infants have a fear of falling and of loud noise; fear of other stimuli (strange persons, objects, situations) ordinarily develops during the first few months. These fears probably have survival value, and they are considered normal and adaptive, not deviant. As children grow into the middle childhood years, they develop additional fears, especially about imaginary creatures or events (Morris & Kratochwill, 1983a, 1983b; Siegel & Ridley-Johnson, 1985). Unless the fears become excessive or debilitative and prevent the child from engaging in normal social interaction, sleep, school attendance, or exploring the environment, they are not maladaptive. Indeed, a child who has no fears at all is not only highly unusual, but also likely to be hurt or killed because of inappropriate brashness.

Humans learn fears in several different ways (see Morris & Kratochwill, 1983b; Siegel & Ridley-Johnson, 1985, for detailed analyses of fear acquisition). Infants and young children especially may learn fear through classical or respondent conditioning. If an already fright-producing stimulus is paired with another object or event, the child may come to fear that object or event. Comments, remonstrations, and other verbal communications of parents (especially the mother) and other adults about objects, activities, places, persons, or situations induce fearfulness in children who have acquired language skills. Adults' and other children's nonverbal behavior can also have a powerful influence on a child's learning fear. A child who is overly fearful of dogs may have acquired the fear in one or a combination of ways: a dog may have frightened the child by barking or growling, jumping, knocking the child down, biting, and so on; the parents or someone else may have warned the child in an emotional way about the dangers of dogs, or the child may have heard people talk about a dog's meanness and dangerousness; the child may have seen a parent, sibling, or other child (or someone in a movie or on TV) attacked by or frightened by dogs.

Children's fears may be mild and short-lived enough that they do not seriously interfere with social growth. When fear unnecessarily restricts the child's activity, however, intervention is called for. Extreme, irrational fear that is out of proportion to reality and leads to automatic avoidance of the feared situation is often called a **phobia**. Morris and Kratochwill (1983a) describe acquisition of an excessive fear or phobia.

Mary

When Mary was 6 years old, her parents decided to have an alarm system installed throughout their house. It seemed that in the past year a number of burglaries had been committed in their neighborhood and Mr. and Mrs. Frank wanted to have an alarm system in their house so that they could feel more "safe and secure" at night. Mary "always" had difficulty falling asleep at night, and needed to have a nightlight on each night near her bed to provide some light in her room and help her feel more comfortable in her darkened room.

Mary asked her parents many questions concerning the new alarm system—especially concerning why it had to be turned on at night. Her parents explained to her about the recent robberies in the neighborhood and how they felt more comfortable knowing that they had an alarm system that would go off if someone tried to break into their house.

The first night after the alarm was installed, there was a false alarm at about 2:00 A.M. The alarm woke up Mary and her parents. Mary began yelling and crying, and Mr. and Mrs. Frank started walking nervously throughout the house. After deciding that it was a false alarm, they returned to Mary to comfort her. To help Mary fall back to sleep, Mrs. Frank allowed Mary to keep the light on next to her bed for the whole night. This continued for the next several days, with Mary going to bed at night with her lamp on next to her bed.

Whenever Mrs. Frank tried to have Mary go to sleep without her lamp on, she would cry and become upset. As a result, for the next three months she was allowed to sleep at night with her lamp on in her room—afraid of being in her room alone when it was dark. Her fear of the dark was found to transfer to movie theaters and to going out on Halloween night (activities that she had always previously enjoyed doing). She also became fearful of sleeping at a friend's house, because she was concerned that she could not have a light on at night. (Morris & Kratochwill, 1983a, pp. 54–55.)

Social learning principles can help resolve both children's and adults' excessive or irrational fears. Three approaches, which can be used in combination, have been particularly successful: modeling, **desensitization**, and self-control training. With these techniques, clinicians have helped children and youth overcome a wide array of fears and phobias (Morris & Kratochwill, 1983a, 1983b; Siegel & Ridley-Johnson, 1985).

Having fearful children watch movies in which other youngsters are having fun (at a party or playing games) while approaching the feared object without hesitation (for example, the youngsters in the movie may be handling dogs or snakes while playing) reduces fear in the observers and makes them more willing to approach the thing they fear. Having individuals with phobias watch several different peer models unanxiously approach several different feared objects and showing films that display the actual feared object (rather than a replica) have increased the effectiveness of this method of fear reduction. Positive reinforcement of the fearful person's approach to the feared object adds to the fear-reducing effects of watching models. Filmed modeling procedures have been highly effective in preventing children from acquiring maladaptive fears of medical and dental procedures as well as in dealing with children who have already become fearful (King, Hamilton, & Murphy, 1983).

Procedures variously referred to as **systematic desensitization, reciprocal inhibition,** and **counterconditioning** have also been effective in lowering fears of children and adults. The central feature of these procedures involves the individual's gradual and repeated approach to the fear-provoking stimuli (either in real life—*in vivo*—or in purposeful fantasy of them) while the person remains unanxious and perhaps engaged in an activity that is incompatible with or inhibits anxiety (such as eating a favorite treat or relaxing comfortably in a chair). The gradual approach to the feared object, repeated exposure to it, and maintenance of an unanxious state during exposure are thought to weaken the conditioned or learned bond between the object and the fear response it elicits (cf. Wolpe, 1975).

In self-control training, fearful individuals learn to talk through a variety of techniques for managing anxiety. They may learn relaxation, self-reinforcement, self-punishment, self-instruction, visual imagery, or problem-solving strategies. Mary, for example, might say to herself, "I'm a brave girl. I can take care of myself. Kids who can take care of themselves go to sleep in the dark," and so on. The trainer might help the individual develop mental images that represent calm or pleasant feelings that are incompatible with anxiety and that the subject can recall when he or she encounters anxiety-provoking circumstances.

School Phobia

Some children who show a specific fear of going to school are said to have school phobia. (School phobia should not be confused with truancy—failure to attend school—discussed in Chapter 14.) School phobic children usually exhibit symptoms of anxiety about attendance and may develop abdominal pain, nausea, or other physical complaints before the time to go to school in the morning. The nature and causes of school phobia are so far unresolved (Atkinson, Quarrington, & Cyr, 1985). The psychodynamic notion that school phobia represents anxiety about separation from the mother (cf. Eisenberg, 1958) does not hold, because school phobia often does not develop until after the child has attended school (and been separated from the mother) without problems for several years (cf. Levental & Sills, 1964). It is more likely that traumatic incidents in school or threatening and stressful demands for academic or social performance induce the fear. When school becomes threatening or aversive, the child may seek refuge and protection at home (Yates, 1970).

Behavior principles have been quite successful in remediating the problem of school phobia (Blagg & Yule, 1984; Gelfand, 1978; Patterson, 1965b). Specific techniques vary from case to case, but general procedures include one or more of the following:

1. Desensitization of the child's fear through role playing or in vivo approximations of attending school for an entire day
2. Reinforcement for attending school even for a brief period, gradually lengthening the time the child is required to stay in school
3. Matter-of-fact parental statements that the child will go back to school, avoiding lengthy or emotional discussion
4. Removal of reinforcers for staying home (such as being allowed to watch television, play a favorite game, stay close to mother, or engage in other pleasurable activities)

King et al. (1983) suggest that many maladaptive fears in the school setting are preventable. Prevention would involve desensitizing young children to school by introducing future teachers, school routines, play activities, and so on. Transitions to middle school and senior high school likewise can be made less anxiety-provoking by preparing students for their new environments and new expectations. While many schools attempt to provide orientation experiences, they are often not carefully planned. Individual students may need to learn coping skills to deal with irrational thoughts and to learn adaptive behavior (such as asking a teacher or peer for assistance) through modeling, rehearsal, feedback, and reinforcement.

OBSESSIONS AND COMPULSIONS

Obsessions are repetitive, persistent, intrusive impulses, images, or thoughts about something. *Compulsions* are repetitive, stereotyped acts the individual feels he or she must perform. Both obsessions and compulsions may be part of some ritualistic behavior an individual performs in attempts to reduce anxiety. Lyon (1983) describes a 12-year-old sixth grader of superior intelligence who was a compulsive lip-biter. He bit his lip, then wiped off excess saliva with his sleeve. He repeated this behavior so frequently that he had created a three-inch red line with open sores from the edge of his mouth diagonally across his left cheek, resulting in taunts and negative comments from his classmates. Teachers reported that he had engaged in this behavior since kindergarten. In spite of his annoyance with his own behavior and teasing from his classmates, the boy was not able to stop the habit.

Descriptions and treatment of children's obsessive and compulsive behavior are primarily psychodynamic in orientation (cf. Easson, 1969; Rapoport, 1986; Rubin, 1962). Obsessions and compulsions have seldom been topics of behavioral research. The social learning view of obsessive and compulsive behavior is that obsessions and compulsions, like phobias, represent failure to learn socially acceptable or correct responses to specific circumstances (Ullmann & Krasner, 1969). The study of obsessive and compulsive behavior in children is complicated by its close relationship not only to phobic behavior but also to excessive self-stimulation and fantasy. Obsession, fear, related fantasy or delusions, and compulsive rituals are often interconnected (Kennedy, 1983; Milby, Wendorf, and Meredith, 1983).

Although obsessive-compulsive disorders of children are rare (Rapoport, 1986), Milby et al. (1983) list these types:

Compulsive rituals that often assume the form of washing, checking, or other kinds of repetitive motoric behavior.

Cognitive compulsions consisting of words, phrases, prayers, sequence of numbers, or other forms of counting, and so forth.

Primary obsessional slowness in which simple tasks of living require excessive time to complete.

Doubting and other anxiety-elevating obsessions in which specific cognitive patterns (e.g., questioning adequacy of specific behaviors) increase distress or discomfort. (p. 17)

Milby provides an example of the first type of obsessive-compulsive behavior.

Ritualistic Behavior

The youngster was a 15-year-old male of above average intelligence enrolled in a suburban Catholic high school and working part-time as a busboy. He presented with excessive hand washing and showering rituals related to a fear of contamination from feces, body fluids, and related materials. Rituals averaged 30 minutes for hand-washing and 65 minutes for showering per day. He was also obsessed about punishment from God and prayed ritualistically to allay these fears. The ritualistic praying ceased spontaneously during the pretreatment assessment.

Washing rituals began 2 years prior to treatment. No precipitating events were recalled, although his uncle was described as having washed excessively due to a preoccupation with germs, especially related to venereal disease. The uncle had warned the patient to avoid various situations for fear of contamination.

At the time of treatment, the patient's fears and rituals began to interfere with scholastic performance, but not work functioning. Sexual development, family relationships, and peer relationships appeared relatively normal. No previous psychiatric treatment had been attempted. (Milby et al., 1983, p. 19.)

Kennedy (1983) offers a reasonable criterion for deciding whether a youngster's obsessive, compulsive, or ritualistic behavior requires intervention. "The major issue to remember is that we do not want to tidy up children as far as their small rituals are concerned. Most parents do well to leave these alone, with the advice that he will outgrow them. Only when the ritual is highly elaborate and expensive, as well as precarious, can it justify treatment as a clinical problem" (p. 289). The most effective interventions appear to be based on social learning principles, particularly strategies employed for fear reduction (Kennedy, 1983; Milby et al., 1983).

RELUCTANT SPEECH

Children who are extremely reluctant to speak, although they know how to converse normally, are said to be *electively mute*—they choose to speak only to a certain individual or small groups of persons and refuse to talk to all others. These children present a puzzling behavior problem to teachers. Kratochwill, Brody, and Piersel (1979) point out the many different perspectives on this problem and the many terms used to describe it. Sanok and Ascione (1979) suggest the term *selective mutism* to indicate that the child is mute only under specific environmental circumstances. Ollendick and Matson (1983) describe a representative case of selective mutism.

Selective Mutism

The boy treated was 9 years of age and had had normal speech until the age of 6. He was from a poor family in the Appalachian area of West Virginia. His school performance was average with respect to grades and standard academic achievement tests. For the previous 3 years he had not spoken to anyone, and the problem had progressed to the point that he would not initiate sounds. An example of the latter problem can be exemplified by an instance in which he was punched in the nose (making it bleed) soon after being admitted to the hospital where the study was conducted. He neither said anything to the child who had hit him nor, for that matter, did he make a sound. (p. 245)

Because the electively mute youngster does not need to acquire normal speech but merely to learn to use speech under ordinary circumstances, remediation is often considerably easier than that of the mute or echolalic child. The electively mute child is, at least to some degree, socially withdrawn, although he or she may be withdrawn only from adults or only from peers (Griffith, Schnelle, McNees, Bissinger, & Huff, 1975). Elective mutism appears to be social withdrawal based, in most cases, on a rather specific fear of talking to certain adolescents or groups of people. The causes of elective mutism are apparently diverse, however, and many children who exhibit this behavior have multiple behavior problems and disturbed families (Cunningham, Cataldo, Mallion, & Keyes, 1984).

As with other fears, social learning principles have been the basis for the most successful approaches to elective mutism (Sanok & Ascione, 1979). Strategies involve altering the demands or conditions under which the child is expected to speak, desensitization to the fear of speaking, and reinforcement for gradual approximations of speaking freely to the person(s) in whose presence the child has been mute (Cunningham et al., 1984; Mace & West, 1986; Ollendick & Matson, 1983).

EATING DISORDERS

Eating disorders receive much attention in the press, because the nation's affluence makes food a wastable commodity and because of the near obsession many people—

particularly of high social status—have with slenderness. Among eating disorders, **anorexia nervosa** (or simply anorexia) and **bulimia** (sometimes called bulimarexia or bulimia nervosa) garner the most attention.

Anorexia (literally, loss of appetite) is a misnomer, for anorexics do not report absence of hunger, and the problem is clearly a refusal to eat a proper diet. Individuals with anorexia are obsessively concerned with losing weight and extremely anxious about getting fat. Anorexics starve themselves down to an abnormally low weight, often exercising compulsively as well as severely restricting caloric intake. They endanger their health and sometimes even die from their self-starvation. Anorexia occurs most often in females (by a ratio of about ten to one), usually in the early adolescent to young adult age range. Leon and Dinklage's (1983) description exemplifies the problem.

Wendy

Wendy was 16 years old when her parents insisted that she be seen by the family pediatrician because of severe weight loss. Wendy was 5 feet, 3 inches tall and weighed 78 pounds. She had been dieting for the past 2 years, since she decided, at a weight of 110 pounds, that she was too fat. Wendy had begun menstruating at age 13, but she had not had a menstrual period for the previous 1½ years. She indicated that she was not concerned that her periods had stopped, but she was extremely concerned that she was still too fat. At the time she was seen, Wendy was consuming an average of about 500 calories of food per day.

Over the course of her past 2 years' dieting efforts, Wendy had become increasingly stricter about how much she would eat, and each mealtime ended in a battle with her parents over her food intake. If possible, she tried to avoid eating meals with her parents and two older brothers, saying that she was not hungry at that time and that she would eat more if she ate alone at a later time. If her parents insisted that she eat with them, she toyed with her food, cut it up into small portions, and piled the left-over food on one part of her plate in order to make it look as if she had eaten more than she actually had. Typically, her daily food consumption consisted of an egg, a small portion of bread, a carrot stick, and some water or diet soda.

Wendy had always been a good student in school. However, both of her brothers had consistently been on the honor roll and had excelled in academic and extracurricular activities. Wendy worked hard to get good grades, but her academic performance was taken for granted by her parents in the context of the superior achievements of her older brothers.

Wendy was described by her parents as having been an obedient child who always complied with her parents' wishes. They indicated that they were fairly structured in raising Wendy, setting limits on her outside activities, the time she went to bed each night, and who the youngsters were that she played with. Wendy was described as agreeable to this structure. Her parents were therefore amazed and helpless in dealing with her intractable stubbornness in relation to eating, given her compliant behavior in all other areas since childhood.

As Wendy grew thinner, she became increasingly more preoccupied with planning how much she was going to eat each day, and how to avoid situations in which she would be pressured to eat more than she had planned to. Wendy began an exercise program at the time she started dieting, and her daily exercises, carried out in a strictly ordered routine, became lengthier and more strenuous each day. Wendy always swam a given number of laps four times a day. During the summer, she would swim these laps outdoors even if there were lightning or thunder outside. Over time, even though feeling exhausted, she added an extra swimming session at night without her parents' knowledge, jumping out of her second-story bedroom window to go outside to swim. Wendy felt extremely hungry, tired, and irritable almost all of the time. She was also preoccupied with thoughts of food and how she looked. Her weight continued to drop and her school work suffered. She stopped interacting with the few girls she talked to at school and became quite isolated from others.

Despite the efforts of her parents and her pediatrician, Wendy refused to stop dieting. She indicated that she felt extremely good about herself, knowing that she could control her bodily urges to the extent that she would not eat when hungry, and could exercise strenuously even though she felt exhausted. Eventually, Wendy was hospitalized for treatment, despite her strong objections that there was nothing wrong with her. Her weight at the time of hospitalization was 68 pounds. (Leon & Dinklage, 1983, pp. 270–271)

Bulimia involves binge eating followed by self-induced vomiting. Bulimics typically try to keep their eating binges and vomiting a secret. They often feel depressed and unable to control their eating habits. In some cases they attempt to lose weight through extremely restrictive diets (except during binges), enemas, or laxatives, in addition to vomiting.

Despite public fascination with anorexia and bulimia and the relatively high estimates of prevalence of these disorders among high school and college females, not much is understood about causes or effective treatment (Andersen, 1987; Mizes, 1985). Researchers now recognize that the problems are multidimensional and require multimodal treatment approaches (Bemis, 1987; Foreyt & Kondo, 1985; Fundudis, 1986; Garner, Fairburn, & Davis, 1987; Rosen, 1987). Behavioral analyses of causes (cf. Chiodo, 1987) and behavioral or cognitive-behavioral interventions have been encouraging in the short run, but long-term follow-up evaluations indicate the need for more comprehensive assessment and treatment approaches (cf. Andersen, 1987; Bemis, 1987). Effective intervention requires consideration of the eating behaviors themselves and the thoughts and feelings associated with anorexia and bulimia, plus the social environment in which the patterns have developed and are maintained.

Other eating disorders include **pica** (eating inedible substances such as paint, hair, cloth, or dirt), **rumination** (self-induced vomiting, which usually begins in infancy), highly exclusive food preferences, and obesity (Foreyt & Kondo, 1985; Leon & Dinklage, 1983; Siegel, 1983; Werry, 1986c). These problems severely limit a child's social acceptability and endanger health. Childhood and adolescent obesity is a growing problem in most Western cultures and carries significant health risks, usually results in poor self-image, often contributes to poor social relations, and tends to persist into adulthood (McKenzie, 1986; Spence, 1986). Although causes of obesity include genetic, physiological, and environmental factors, "the basic problem is a negative imbalance between calorific intake and energy expenditure, resulting in the storage of fat in adipose cells" (Spence, 1986, p. 447). Successful management of obesity therefore requires not only changing eating habits but increasing physical activity (McKenzie, 1986).

Specific fear of obesity, but without all the characteristics of anorexia or bulimia, has been described by Pugliese, Lifshitz, Grad, Fort, and Marks-Katz (1983). They found that some children and youth restrict their caloric intake because of a specific fear of obesity and its alleged consequences, such as physical unattractiveness, poor health, and shortened life span. These children showed retardation in growth and delayed puberty as a result of their extremely limited diets, but resumed normal eating patterns and recovered normal growth and sexual development following nutritional and psychiatric counseling. Schleimer (1983) and Davies and Furnham (1986) found that most adolescent girls diet frequently without adverse long-term effects, although health complications occur in some cases.

Leon and Dinklage (1983) and Csapo (1987) note that severe eating disorders, especially anorexia and bulimia, are related to societal influence. "In countries in which food is scarce, most persons do not have the luxury of overeating to the point of obesity, or gaining attention through refusing to eat. In countries such as India and Sri Lanka, where food is scarce and obesity has traditionally been highly valued as a sign of wealth, extremely low rates of anorexia nervosa are manifested. Both obesity and anorexia nervosa are most common in more affluent countries of the Western hemisphere" (Leon & Dinklage, 1983, p. 271).

ELIMINATION DISORDERS

Attitudes toward toileting vary widely among cultures and within social groups. In Western culture, toilet training is considered very important and is generally begun at a young age. Although the extreme practice of beginning toilet training in the first few weeks of life is ill-advised, behavioral research shows that most children can be taught by 16 or 18 months (see O'Leary & Wilson, 1975). When children continue to wet or soil themselves after the age of five or six years, they are considered to have a problem that demands intervention. *Enuresis* may be either diurnal (wetting during waking hours) or nocturnal (bedwetting). About twice as many boys as girls are enuretic, and two or three percent of children are enuretic at age 14. At the time they begin first grade, approximately 13 to 20 percent of children are enuretic. **Encopresis,** or soiling, usually occurs during the day and is a rarer problem than enuresis.

Toilet training is usually a gradual process, and stress and illness have an effect on bowel and bladder control. Thus, the younger the child and the more stressful the circumstances, the more one can expect accidents to occur. Enuresis and encopresis are not matters of infrequent accidents; the enuretic or encopretic child has a chronic problem in retaining urine or feces and releasing it only in the toilet (Doleys, 1983, 1985; Siegel, 1983).

Psychodynamic theory assumes that enuresis and encopresis are symptoms of underlying emotional conflicts usually involving the family. Whether or not one accepts psychodynamic ideas, family factors obviously play an important role if the family is inconsistent or unreasonable in toilet training. At the least, wetting and soiling can sour parent-child relationships regardless of the cause of the problem. Not many parents can face these problems with complete equanimity, and rare is the child who is completely unaffected by adults' reactions to misplaced excrement. Thus one must recognize that negative feelings about the problem often run high in families of encopretic or enuretic children. Treatment must be planned to avoid further parental anger and abuse of the child. Enuresis is seldom the child's only problem; the enuretic child often has other difficulties—perhaps stealing, overeating, or underachievement (cf. Doleys, 1983; Siegel, 1983; Vivian, Fischel, & Liebert, 1986). Diurnal enuresis and encopresis at school are intolerable problems for teachers and result in peer rejection. Understandably, most enuretic and encopretic youngsters have low self-esteem.

A few cases of enuresis have physical causes that can be corrected by surgery or medication, but the vast majority of cases have no known anatomical defect, and medication is not particularly helpful. The most effective methods of treating enuresis derive from the assumption that the problem is a deficiency in habit training or practice. Intervention may thus involve training the child in urine retention, rapid awakening, and practice in toileting as well as reward for appropriate toileting or mild punishment for wetting (cf. Azrin, Sneed & Fox, 1974; Breit, Kaplan, Gauthier, & Weinhold, 1984). For many children, a urine alarm system in the bed or pants has successfully eliminated enuresis (cf. Mountjoy, Ruben, & Bradford, 1984; Taylor & Turner, 1975). While many approaches to enuresis have been tried and many behavioral techniques have been highly successful, no single approach has been successful for every child, and combinations of techniques are often used. Selecting a successful technique depends on careful assessment of the individual case (Leon & Dinklage, 1983; Siegel, 1983).

Encopresis may involve either of two conditions: (1) prolonged retention of feces which causes constipation, compaction of feces, and eventual passage of small, hard feces or leakage of mucous around the compacted mass which is pressing against the anal sphincter; or (2) a chronically dilated anal sphincter that allows for constant fecal discharge. Medical causes or complications of encopresis include congenital defects of the anus or colon, spinal defects that prevent anal sphincter control, and acquired dysfunction of the colon or anal sphincter from extreme chronic constipation. A social learning view of encopresis suggests that inadequate habit training or conditioning or fear of the toilet is the problem when there are no known medical causes (cf. O'Brien, Ross, & Christophersen, 1986).

Regardless of the causes, passage of feces or feces-laden mucous anywhere but in the toilet is extremely unacceptable and stigmatizing. Once past infancy, the child who soils or plays with feces is revolting to peers and adults alike, and unless effective intervention stops the encopretic behavior, the child will suffer social stigma in addition to any medical problems he or she may have. Fortunately encopresis is relatively rare, for the encopretic child is seriously handicapped in social relationships and may be rejected for placement in regular classes (O'Leary & Wilson, 1975). Strategies based on behavior principles have been successful in cases in which the child had not learned to regulate sphincter pressure or the release of feces in the toilet (O'Leary & Wilson, 1975; Werry, 1986c). Even in seemingly intransigent cases where psychodynamic therapy and medical treatment have failed, behavior modification (providing rewards for sphincter control or for producing feces in the pot, and, in some instances, mild punishment for incontinence) has frequently been successful. Ferinden and Handel (1970) found that a seven-year-old boy, with a long history of soiling himself several times a day in the classroom, began soiling much less and interacted more positively with his peers when the following procedure was used: the boy brought a change of clothing to school; he was made responsible for washing out his soiled clothing; he was asked to clean himself with strong soap and cool water; and he was required to stay after school to make up for time lost in cleaning his clothes and himself. In brief, encopretic behavior has repeatedly responded to systematic application of consequences in the context of appropriate diet and training (Blechman, 1979; Bornstein et al., 1983; Doleys, 1985; O'Brien et al., 1986; Rolider & Van Houten, 1985).

SEXUAL PROBLEMS

A wide variety of sexual behavior is of concern to parents, teachers, and other adults who manage children and youth (Rekers, 1985; Werry, 1986c). Promiscuous sexual conduct is often thought to connote moral misjudgment, and promiscuity is often involved in delinquency. Teenage pregnancy is a problem of enormous proportions (Hagenhoff et al., 1987). Dating and related heterosexual relationships are of great concern to teens and their adult caretakers. Scarcely anyone condones exhibitionism, sadomasochism, incest, prostitution, fetishism, transvestism, and sexual relations involving children, and these behaviors usually carry serious social penalties. Contemporary sexual freedom notwithstanding, American social mores do not condone all sex practices—some sexual behavior is clearly taboo. We will discuss only two specific types of sexual conduct: public masturbation and childhood gender problems.

Public Masturbation

Most mental health authorities do not consider autoerotic activity by itself maladaptive, although it is viewed as undesirable by some religious groups. When carried to excess or done publicly, however, sexual self-stimulation is considered disordered behavior by nearly everyone. Although many or most teachers have observed children masturbating publicly, relatively little research has been done on the problem, perhaps because masturbation has for so long been looked upon as evil (Hare, 1962; Stribling, 1842). Rekers (1978) mentions one report (a nonexperimental study) in which public masturbation was modified by means of behavioral reinforcement and punishment techniques. An 11-year-old girl's masturbation in the classroom was eliminated by using verbal reprimands for autoerotic behavior and social reinforcement for attention to academic tasks and participation in classroom activities (Wagner, 1968). Cook, Altman, Shaw, and Blaylock (1978) successfully reduced a seven-year-old severely retarded boy's public masturbation by squirting lemon juice in his mouth contingent on masturbation.

Childhood Gender Problems

Probably the most widely known work on childhood gender problems is that of Rekers and his research group (see Rekers, 1977a, 1977b, 1978, 1981, 1985). According to Rekers (1977b), gender problems can involve excessive masculinity or excessive femininity in either boys or girls, but research has dealt almost exclusively with one type: extreme femininity in boys. What Rekers refers to as *gender behavior disturbance* involves, for boys, a preference for girls' clothing, actual or imagined use of cosmetics, and feminine gestures, mannerisms, vocal inflections, and speech content. It also involves preference for girls' play and girl playmates. Boys with cross-gender identification not only exhibit these characteristics but truly wish to be or fantasize that they are girls (Zucker, Finegan, Doering, & Bradley, 1984). DSM-III-R defines gender identity disorder of childhood as persistent and intense distress about being an individual of one's sex and an intense desire to be a member of the opposite sex. In some instances, the child insists that he or she *is* a member of the opposite sex. This disorder is accompanied by persistent aversion to normative clothing for one's sex and preoccupation with clothing of the opposite sex, intense desire to participate in stereotypical behavior of the opposite sex, or persistent repudiation of one's sexual anatomy. Transsexualism is the term applied to "persistent discomfort and sense of inappropriateness about one's assigned sex in a person who has reached puberty" (APA, 1987, p. 74).

Rekers and his colleagues have identified specific sex-typed mannerisms and ways of scaling gender problems from profound to mild. Identification and assessment of gender disturbance require careful psychological and physical examination, interviews with the child and parents, and direct observation in different settings, sometimes including the classroom (Rekers, 1985). The gender-disturbed child does not just occasionally exhibit the characteristics of the opposite sex, but persistently shows cross-gender behavior that his peers reject. Rekers (1981) notes that young children typically "try out" behaviors and clothing of the opposite sex. This kind of cross-sex behavior is of no clinical significance.

> In rare cases, however, the child deviates from the normal pattern of trying out the opposite sex-role behaviors and develops a persistent, compulsive, and rigidly stereotyped pattern. At one extreme is the excessive hypermasculinity of boys who are interpersonally violent, destructive, uncontrolled, and belligerent and who lack gentle and socially sensitive behaviors (Harrington, 1970). Behavioral intervention is required for those exaggeratedly "super masculine" boys who have adopted a caricature of the masculine social role. The opposite extreme is observed in boys who reject their male role to the extent of insisting that they are girls or that they want to grow up to be mothers and to bear children. Such a boy frequently dresses in girls' clothes; avoids boys' clothing; plays predominantly with girls; tries on cosmetics, wigs, and other feminine attire; and displays stereotypically feminine arm movements, gait, and body gestures. Such hyperfemininity in boys goes beyond normal curiosity-induced exploration of feminine stereotypic behavior to constitute a serious clinical problem. Although there has been a dearth of research on female childhood gender disorders, it is theoretically possible to identify the parallel conditions of hyperfemininity and hypermasculinity in girls. (Rekers, 1981, pp. 483-484)

Behavioral intervention in childhood gender problems shows considerable promise, but more longitudinal research is necessary to draw firm conclusions. Current treatment procedures include a wide array of behavior modification techniques, including reinforcement (often at home and at school) for sex-appropriate mannerisms, dress, and play; self-observation, self-recording of behavior and self-reinforcement; and instruction in athletic activities (Rekers, 1977a, 1978, 1985).

Zuger (1984) evaluated the long-term behavior of 55 boys who showed markedly effeminate behavior before they were of school age. Green (1987), in a 15-year study of highly effeminate boys, found that 75 percent became homosexual. "Taken together, prospective and retrospective studies point unmistakably to the high incidence of adult homosexuality as the final outcome in male children manifesting early effeminate behavior" (Zuger, 1984, p. 96). The effeminate behavior of these young boys could not, in Zuger's opinion, be accounted for by family or other environmental factors but seemed to be determined by genetic or other biological factors.

Classifying gender-related behavior of any kind as a *disorder* raises serious questions of cultural bias and discrimination. The consensus is that *some* forms of sexual expression are deviant and should be prevented—incest and public masturbation, for example. Today, however, many people feel there is nothing deviant about other sex-related behaviors, such as preference for clothing styles, stereotypical masculine or feminine mannerisms, and homosexuality. Clothing styles and accepted sex roles have changed dramatically during the past two decades. *Androgyny* (having the characteristics of both sexes) is apparent in many fashions and in role models. Problems related to sexual preference may be seen as primarily a matter of cultural or personal intolerance, so we must be sensitive to the possibility of cultural and personal bias in judging sex-related behavior, just as we must be aware of personal biases toward racial and ethnic identity.

STEREOTYPED MOVEMENT PROBLEMS

Stereotyped movements are involuntary, repetitive, persistent, and nonfunctional acts over which the individual can exert at least some voluntary control. Stereotyped movements include self-stimulation and self-injury, discussed in Chapter 18. They may also include repetitive movements related to obsessions or compulsions (Werry, 1986c).

Most stereotyped movements that are not labeled self-stimulation or self-injury are referred to as **tics**. Tics that involve only the facial muscles and last only a short time are common; nearly one-fourth of all children will at some time during their development display this kind of tic, and it is best to ignore them. If the tic involves the entire head, neck, and shoulders, however, then biofeedback and overcorrection training, in which the youngster practices a more correct form of movement, are recommended (Wesolowski & Jawlocki, 1985).

Chronic motor tics that last more than a year and involve at least three muscle groups simultaneously are more serious. **Tourette's disorder** is a little understood disorder involving a variety of tics and ticlike behavior, including impulsive swearing and obscene gestures, or both (Bauer & Shea, 1984). The problem usually appears before the youngster is 15 and follows an unpredictable course. Management of severe tics may require behavior modification or drugs or both (Werry, 1986c; Wesolowski & Jawlocki, 1985).

SUMMARY

Subcategories of internalizing problems are not well defined. Characteristics associated with anxiety-withdrawal (feelings of inferiority, self-consciousness, shyness, fearfulness, and hypersensitivity, for example) are generally more transient and are associated with lower risk for adulthood psychiatric disorder than are behaviors related to externalizing disorders. Anxiety-withdrawal may characterize two to five percent of the child population and 20 to 30 percent of youngsters referred to clinics for behavior problems. Behaviors associated with anxiety-withdrawal call for intervention only when they are extreme and persistent.

Socially isolated children and youth do not have the social approach and response skills necessary to develop reciprocally reinforcing relationships. They may lack these skills because of inappropriate models of social behavior at home, inadequate instruction or opportunity to practice social skills, or other circumstances that inhibit social development. Intervention and prevention call for teaching social skills that are assumed important for social development, but there is a great deal of controversy concerning which are the most appropriate skills and the most effective instructional methods. In general, social skills training involves modeling, rehearsal, guided practice, and feedback, either for individual students or for groups. Peer-mediated interventions that alter both the socially isolated youngster's behaviors and those of peers in naturally occurring interactions may be the most effective strategies.

Most children develop specific fears, but their fears are not persistent and do not interfere with their activities. Maladaptive fears and phobias severely restrict a person's activities and call for intervention. Modeling, desensitization, and self-control training have effectively reduced fears. School phobia is usually best managed by making school attendance more reinforcing and staying at home less attractive. Obsessions (repetitive thoughts) and compulsions (repetitive acts) are rare in children and may be related to fears. Intervention is called for if the obsessive or compulsive behavior begins to interfere seriously with everyday activities. Extreme reluctance to talk, known as elective or selective mutism, may be related to feared situations that involve conversation. Youngsters who are electively mute often come from disturbed families, but we know relatively little about the causes of elective mutism. As with other fears, elective mutism is usually most effectively managed with procedures based on social learning—models, desensitization, and reinforcement for talking.

Eating disorders that receive the most attention in the media are anorexia (self-starvation) and bulimia (binge eating followed by self-induced vomiting). These disorders appear almost exclusively in affluent cultures. The causes are not well understood, and management demands a multimodal approach. Both anorexia and bulimia involve excessive anxiety about getting fat. Not all teenage dieting and fear of obesity lead to anorexia or bulimia. Obesity in children is a serious health and social problem. Intervention requires procedures to correct eating habits and encourage exercise. Other eating disorders include pica (eating inedible substances), rumination (self-induced vomiting usually beginning in infancy), and highly exclusive food preferences.

Enuresis (wetting) and encopresis (soiling) can seriously limit a child's social acceptance and damage self-image. Behavior modification procedures with these problems have been quite successful.

Sexual disorders include a wide variety of socially sanctioned behaviors. Two problems are public masturbation and childhood gender problems. Public masturbation can usually be managed with behavior modification techniques. The childhood gender identity problem that has been studied most intensively is extremely feminine behavior in young boys. This problem has been approached by training boys in sex-appropriate behavior and dress, reinforcement for engaging in masculine activities, and other behavior modification techniques. Extremely feminine young boys appear more likely to become homosexual than those who adopt masculine patterns of behavior.

Stereotyped movement disorders involve persistent, involuntary, repetitive, and nonfunctional acts (tics). These often involve only facial muscles and are transitory, requiring no intervention. Intervention is called for when tics involve multiple muscle groups and are persistent. Relatively little is known about the causes of tics. Treatment may involve medication, behavior modification procedures, or both.

17

Depression and Suicidal Behavior

As you read this chapter, keep these guiding questions in mind:

☐ How does the federal definition of "seriously emotionally disturbed" include *depression*?

☐ To what extent is childhood depression like depression in adults?

☐ What is the concept of *masked depression,* and of what value is it?

☐ What are the primary indications that a child or youth is depressed?

☐ How might parents contribute to their children's depression, and how might children contribute to the parents' depressed feelings?

☐ What are the theoretical bases for cognitive strategies and self-control training as interventions in depression?

☐ Why is it difficult to define suicide and to estimate its prevalence?

☐ What is *parasuicide,* and what do we know about its prevalence?

☐ What evidence suggests a genetic factor in suicide?

☐ What psychological factors are probably related to increased suicidal behavior among children and youth during the past several decades?

☐ Why are problems of false positives and false negatives so difficult to resolve in identifying students who are at risk for suicide?

☐ How do hopelessness and feelings of invisibility relate to suicidal behavior?

☐ What risk factors indicate that an adolescent may be planning to attempt suicide?

☐ How can teachers help reduce suicide risk, and how should they manage students following following a suicide threat or attempt?

One of the five distinguishing characteristics of children defined in federal regulations as seriously emotionally disturbed is "a general, pervasive mood of unhappiness or depression" (see Chapter 1). What youngsters federal officials meant to identify by this characteristic is not clear (Forness, 1988). A general, pervasive mood of unhappiness or depression is more narrow and restrictive than the broad-band behavioral dimension *internalizing,* yet it does not correspond exactly with other narrower dimensions, such as social withdrawal (see Chapters 7 and 16). Neither is it consistent with the DSM-III-R's (APA, 1987) clinical criteria for major depressive episode which include disturbance of vegetative functions (such as eating and sleeping) in additon to depressed affect. A reasonable conclusion is that the federal definition of seriously emotionally disturbed includes a wide range of internalizing disorders such as anxiety-withdrawal and clinical depression.

Depression has been relatively neglected in special education research, yet its close relationship to a variety of other disorders and to academic and social difficulties is now clear, especially for older girls (Epstein, Kauffman, & Cullinan, 1985; Forness, 1988). The relationship between depression and suicidal behavior—a problem for all educators, but especially those who work with psychologically disturbed students—makes these important topics (Harris & Ammerman, 1987).

DEPRESSION

Definition and Prevalence

Depression has only recently become a topic of serious study in child psychopathology (Earls, 1984; Forness, 1988; Kaslow & Rehm, 1985; Petti, 1983), and there is so far no general agreement as to a definition of childhood depression. In fact, some even question its existence in children who have not yet reached puberty (Quay & La Greca, 1986). Kaslow and Rehm (1983) note the controversy that has characterized the concept of childhood depression. Traditional psychoanalytic theory has held that depression cannot occur in childhood because psychological self-representation is not sufficiently developed. Some scholars suggest that children's depression is "masked" by other symptoms—expressed indirectly through symptoms such as enuresis, temper tantrums, hyperactivity, learning disabilities, truancy, and so on. Other writers suggest that childhood depression is a common, transitory phenomenon that typically works itself out without clinical intervention—a pervasive problem usually resolved by spontaneous remission. Researchers now are arriving at a consensus that depression in childhood parallels adult depression in many ways, but the specific types of behavior the depressed person exhibits will be developmentally age appropriate (Costello, 1981; Harris & Ammerman, 1987; Kovacs, Feinberg, Crouse-Novak, Paulauskas, & Finkelstein, 1984). Both children and adults can thus be characterized by depressed mood and loss of interest in productive activity, but adults may develop problems around work and marriage, while children may have academic problems and exhibit a variety of inappropriate conduct such as aggression, stealing, social withdrawal, and so forth.

The assumption that depression in childhood is similar to depression in adulthood is evident in DSM-III-R (APA, 1987). Depression is not listed among the disorders that are usually evident in infancy, childhood, or adolescence, and depressed children are classified under the section on adults' affective disorders. To some extent, however, the assumption that depression is the same phenomenon in children and adults may be premature. As Cantwell (1982) notes, "We know very little from an empirical standpoint about how mood is experienced and manifested at different ages" (p. 87), although there are striking similarities between depressed children and depressed adults. One must remember, however, that children are not merely scaled-down versions of adults, that childhood depression may be accompanied by other disorders (enuresis, encopresis, school phobia, school failure, suicidal behavior, and so on), and that children's limited experience and cognitive capacity may make them perceive depression differently from an adult.

At the same time, we cannot simply infer depression from nearly any kind of problem behavior. When aggression, hyperactivity, noncompliance, learning disabilities, school failure, or problems of nearly any sort are attributed to underlying depression in the absence of core features of depressed behavior, depression becomes meaningless as both a concept and diagnostic category. Consequently, we should discard the idea of masked depression. Assessment should focus on identifying key indications of depression, which may or may not be accompanied by other maladaptive behavior.

With the definition in doubt, the prevalence of childhood depression cannot be estimated with much accuracy. Depending on diagnostic criteria, perhaps four percent of the child population and 10 to 15 percent of the adolescent population could be considered depressed. Among children and youth who receive special education services, 20 to 25 percent may have depression or something approximating depression as the primary complaint. Students who have symptoms of depression in addition to other difficulties (learning disability or other behavior disorders) may comprise 50 to 60 percent of the special education population (Forness, 1988). The prevalence of depression is higher among older adolescents, especially girls, and sex differences are typical—older girls tend toward depression, and older boys tend toward aggression (Epstein et al., 1985; Harris & Howard, 1987).

Assessment

According to DSM-III-R, a major depression typically involves several of the following problems over a period of at least two weeks.

- ☐ Anhedonia (inability to experience pleasure) or depressed mood
- ☐ Disturbance of appetite or significant weight gain or loss
- ☐ Disturbance of sleep (insomnia or hypersomnia)
- ☐ Psychomotor agitation or retardation
- ☐ Loss of energy, feelings of fatigue
- ☐ Feelings of worthlessness, self-reproach, or excessive or inappropriate guilt
- ☐ Diminished ability to think or concentrate, or indecisiveness
- ☐ Ideas of suicide or suicide threats or attempts

Other suggested diagnostic criteria usually include four categories of problems: affective, cognitive, motivational, and physiological. We may expect the depressed child to be sad, lonely, and apathetic; to show low self-esteem, excessive guilt, and pessimism; to avoid tasks and social experiences; and/or to have physical complaints or problems in sleeping and eating. Kaslow and Rehm (1983) recommend basing assessment on several sources of information: self-reports, parental reports, peer nominations, and clinical ratings. Costello (1981) discusses the psychiatric interview, questionnaires and behavioral checklists, reinforcement and pleasant event surveys, and evaluations of social skills and mood. One should never assume that data from a single source or representing a single perspective are valid. One should assume a child is depressed only when a constellation of behaviors assessed from a variety of perspectives consistently indicate depression. Costello notes, "It would be unethical to assume that a child manifesting no clear signs of depression is nevertheless depressed" (p. 340).

As yet, no consistent diagnostic criteria or methods of assessment have emerged (Kerr, Hoier, & Versi, 1987). Most studies of children's depression rely primarily on self-ratings, with little direct observation of classroom behavior—perhaps because researchers assume that internalized disorders such as depression are not open to assessment by such methods.

A persistent problem with rating scales is that parents tend to rate their children's depression more severely than do the children themselves (Kazdin, Colbus, & Rodgers, 1986; Kazdin, French, & Unis, 1983; Kazdin, French, Unis, & Esveldt-Dawson, 1983). Self-rating scales are valuable sources of information nevertheless, because affective states are probably best judged by the individual's own experience rather than someone else's interpretations (Kazdin, 1981). Still, teachers' judgments of children's depression should not be overlooked, as some studies show that teachers' and children's ratings correlate more highly than do parents' and children's ratings (Fauber, Forehand, Long, Burke, & Faust, 1987).

Causal Factors and Prevention

In most cases, we do not know the causes of depression. Some cases are evidently *endogenous* (a response to unknown genetic, biochemical, or other biological factors); other cases are apparently *reactive* (a response to environmental events, such as death of a loved one or academic failure) (Seligmann, 1975). Predictably, child abuse, parental psychopathology, and family conflict and disorganization are frequently linked to children's depression (Harris & Ammerman, 1987).

Evidence is accumulating that there is a significant correlation between parents' depression and a variety of problems in their children, including depression (Billings & Moos, 1985; Cole & Rehm, 1986; Forehand et al., 1987; Kaslow & Rehm, 1983). This relationship could, of course, reflect genetic influences on behavior, but it can reflect family process as well. Depressed parents may provide models of depressed behavior (which their children imitate), reinforce depressive behaviors in their children, or create a home environment that is conducive to depression (by setting unreasonable expectations, providing few rewards for achievement or initiative, emphasizing punishment, or providing noncontingent rewards and punishments). Depressed mothers are known to lack parenting skills, which could account for at least some of their children's behavioral and affective problems (Kaslow & Rehm, 1985).

Forehand et al. (1987) analyze the complexity of the relationships between parental depression and child functioning. They note that in families with clinically depressed parents, the direction of causal effects probably runs from parents to children because the parents are unable to implement parenting practices that induce children's social competence.

> Such parents have been found to be less involved with and affectionate toward their children, to feel more guilt and resentment, and to experience more general difficulty in managing and communicating with their children than do nondepressed parents. . . .
>
> For families in which the parents are not clinically depressed, we speculate that the obtained relations between parental depressive mood and child functioning may best be described by a transactional model. (Forehand et al., 1987, p. 9)

In the transactional model, parents and children mutually alter each other's perceptions through their tolerance for and attention to each other's behavior. They may "get on each other's nerves," disappoint and anger each other, and pull each other into a coercive cycle that results in both parties feeling depressed. In this case, children are as much a cause of their parents' depressive state as parents are a cause of their children's depression. The interactional model is consistent with Patterson's (1982; 1986b) research with aggressive families. In all likelihood, parental influence on a child's depression depends on a variety of factors, including idiosyncratic characteristics of parents and child, the child's age and sex, and the characteristics of siblings and members of an extended family (Harris & Howard, 1987). From an interactional perspective, one can assume that a certain parental behavior will not influence all children in the same family in the same way.

Educators should give special attention to the ways a student's depression may affect and be affected by school performance. Depression appears to be associated with lowered performance on some cognitive tasks, lowered self-esteem, lowered social competence, deficits in self-control, and a depressive attributional style in which children tend to believe bad outcomes are a result of their own unmodifiable and global inadequacies (Fauber et al., 1987; Kaslow, Rehm, & Siegel, 1984). These findings suggest that school failure and depression may be reciprocal causal factors: depression makes the student less competent and less confident, both academically and socially; failing academically and socially makes the student feel and act more depressed, and reinforces the attribution of failure to unalterable personal characteristics. Depression and failure may thus become a vicious cycle that is hard to break.

Preventing depression is important because childhood depression, at least in its severe and chronic form, is linked to adult maladjustment and to suicidal behavior (Harris & Ammerman, 1987). An accumulation of stressful life events is an important factor in some youngsters' depression and suicide (Johnson, 1986). Primary prevention may therefore involve efforts to reduce all manner of stressful life events for all children, but such broad-based, unfocused efforts are unlikely to receive much political or fiscal support. There is a better chance for support and success if efforts focus on relieving stress for abused and neglected youngsters and others whose lives are obviously extremely stressful. Another approach to primary prevention, somewhat more focused and feasible, is parenting training for depressed parents (Harris & Ammerman, 1987). Secondary and third-level prevention are still more focused and feasible, giving depressed youngsters behavioral or cognitive-behavioral training in overcoming their specific difficulties. This training is preventive in that it keeps the child's current situation from worsening and forestalls the development of long-term negative outcomes.

Johnson (1986) describes the case of Jason, a 10-year-old referred for psychological evaluation, in part because his father felt that Jason was quite depressed and might have ideas of suicide. The father was also concerned because Jason's school work was deteriorating and his behavior was becoming difficult to manage because of extreme fits of seemingly unprovoked anger, destruction of his sister's toys, and attempts to run away.

Jason

When Jason was about 2 years old, a younger sibling was born. Shortly after this, Jason's parents were separated and divorced, with the father getting custody of both children. When he was about 3 years old, his sister was diagnosed as having a chronic life-threatening illness that subsequently resulted in her having to be hospitalized on numerous occasions. At age 4 or 5 he and his sister were kidnapped by their natural mother. At around the age of 6 his father remarried and was divorced again within a period of eight months. Within the six months prior to Jason's referral to a mental health facility, he watched as a horse his uncle was trying to train fell on his uncle's head, which resulted in the uncle's eye being dislodged from its socket and subsequent blindness in both eyes. Finally, within three months of the referral, his uncle's wife (of whom Jason was very fond) unexpectedly committed suicide. (Johnson, 1986, p. 87)

Intervention and Education

Antidepressant drugs may be quite helpful, particularly in cases of endogenous depression. The side effects can be problematic, however (Campbell et al., 1985), and when drugs are prescribed, teachers need to carefully monitor the effects on behavior and learning. Teachers are most likely to be directly involved in interventions that are behavioral or cognitive-behavioral. These interventions are based on theories of depression that highlight the roles of social skills, productive and pleasurable activity, causal attributions, cognitive assertions, and self-control.

Depressed individuals often appear to lack the social skills necessary to obtain reinforcement from their social environments. People may also become depressed because many of their primary activities, such as work, play, school, or homemaking, result in very little reinforcement. Consequently, they engage in fewer activities and obtain even less pleasure from them. Programs based on this theory teach social skills to help increase the depressed person's participation in a variety of pleasurable and rewarding activities.

Another theory is that depression is a form of learned helplessness. Depressed people have learned to attribute failure to highly predictable, global, internal factors. They do not seem to recognize that they are not responsible for all negative events or that they can change what will happen to them. Intervention therefore consists of strategies for changing the depressed person's causal attributions of success and failure.

A cognitive theory of depression suggests that depressed people have adopted a negative bias in their thinking and view themselves, the rest of the world, and the future in predominantly negative terms. They distort reality to make it conform to negative patterns of thinking that developed early in life. Intervention based on a cognitive theory consists of behavioral activities and cognitive exercises for changing the person's characteristically negative behavior and belief system.

Finally, intervention may be based on a theory of self-control deficits. According to this theory, a depressed person has deficits in self-monitoring, self-evaluation, and self-reinforcement. He or she selectively attends to negative events and their imme-diate consequences, sets criteria for self-evaluation that are too stringent, makes in-accurate attributions of responsibility for his or her behavior, does not engage in enough self-reinforcement, and engages in too much self-criticism and self-punish-ment. Intervention consists of training in self-monitoring, self-evaluation, and self-reinforcement to make the person's interpretation of and responses to events more realistic and gratifying (Cantwell, 1982; Kaslow & Rehm, 1983, 1985).

Kaslow and Rehm (1983) proposed a schema for making decisions about in-tervention in children's depression, as shown in Figure 17.1. Note that if a child is diagnosed as depressed, then other behavior disorders are addressed first, since other disorders may contribute to the depression. Social skills are addressed next, since they may be prerequisite for appropriate activities. The flow chart is based on the assumption that overt behavior change should precede attempts to change distorted thinking.

Kaslow and Rehm (1985) provide case studies of children for whom various intervention strategies were chosen. Their descriptions of Jack, Yvette, Sandra, and Don provide a glimpse of the kinds of difficulties for which four types of intervention are appropriate. Jack's major problems appear to center around low levels of activity, partly because of social skills deficits. Consequently, his treatment consisted of pro-grams to get him engaged in pleasurable, age-appropriate activities and teach him social skills that would help him relate to his peers. Yvette appears to have adopted an attributional style in which she blames herself for all kinds of misfortune, so her therapy focused on attribution retraining. Sandra was given cognitive therapy to help correct her distorted thinking about herself, and Don received self-control training to help him adopt more realistic goals and reinforce himself for reasonable accomplishments.

Behavioral Strategies: Jack

Jack, a nine-year-old male, was brought to the clinic by his parents. Data obtained at the initial evaluation revealed that Jack was feeling sad and lonely, he felt isolated from his peers, he did not enjoy any in-school activities, and he was not involved in

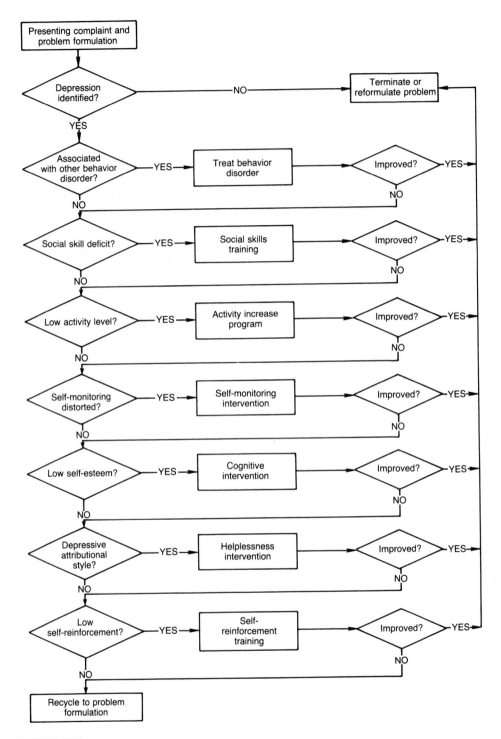

FIGURE 17.1

Flow Chart for Ordering Decisions About Intervention Targets in Treating Depression in Children

From "Childhood Depression" by N. J. Kaslow and L. P. Rehm. In *The Practice of Childhood Therapy* (pp. 27–51) by R. J. Morris and T. R. Kratochwill (Eds.), 1983, New York: Pergamon. Reprinted by permission.

much activity after school. Further, Jack stated that he was hesitant to approach other children and was reluctant to assert himself. Jack was a good student in school, although he was not feeling interested in his school work. No suicidal ideation was present. (p. 622)

Helplessness Strategies: Yvette

Yvette, a 12-year-old female, was referred for a psychological evaluation by her pediatrician. She had recently been diagnosed as having juvenile onset diabetes and was feeling sad, helpless, and hopeless, was blaming herself for her physical problems, and was feeling like everything that went bad was her fault. She did not want to try to do anything at school or with her peers because she felt that nothing would turn out well for her. (pp. 626–627)

Cognitive Strategies: Sandra

Sandra, a 13-year-old female, was referred for treatment by her school counselor. Her teachers were concerned that, despite the fact that she was performing adequately at school, she frequently made self-deprecatory comments. At the initial interview, Sandra acknowledged feeling sad. She stated that she did not like anything about herself—not her brains, her looks, or her personality. She felt as if things would never get better for her and that she was in a dark tunnel and there was no light at the end. When queried, she admitted to having thoughts about killing herself; however, she claimed that she would not do that because she did not have enough courage. (p. 629)

Self-Control Strategies: Don

Don, an 11-year-old, was brought to the clinic by his mother who was concerned about his continued sad mood, which appeared to be in response to marital tension. Although Don was typically an above-average student, he was not doing well in school. He did not like doing anything anymore, and he spent his free time at home watching TV or napping. He frequently complained of stomachaches, which had no known organic etiology. At the interview, Don said very little, he appeared hypoactive, and he complained of feeling tired all of the time. He denied feeling sad. He did say that nothing good ever happened in his life, and he felt that he never got praised for anything he did. He stated the reason for staying at home was that he used to want to be a football player, but since he did not make his junior high school team, he had given up. (p. 633)

Source: These four cases are from "Conceptualization, Assessment, and Treatment of Depression in Children" by Nadine J. Kaslow and Lynn P. Rehm, in P. H. Bornstein and Alan E. Kazdin (Eds.), *Handbook of Clinical Behavior Therapy with Children.* © 1985 by The Dorsey Press, Chicago, IL. Reprinted by permission.

SUICIDAL BEHAVIOR

Definition and Prevalence

The definition of suicide is sometimes clouded because the circumstances of untimely death, particularly the intentions of the deceased, are often in question. Suicide is socially stigmatizing, so the label "suicide" is often avoided if death can be attributed to accident. Since accidents are the leading cause of death among adolescents in the 15 to 24 age bracket, it is suspected that, in this age group, many deaths attributed to accident are disguised or misreported suicides (Guetzloe, 1987; Hawton, 1986; Langone, 1981; Underwood, 1987). It is sometimes impossible to determine the precise circumstances of death that would clarify the issue of suicide. Consequently, suicide is undoubtedly underreported, especially for children and adolescents.

The term **parasuicide** sometimes refers to unsuccessful suicidal behavior. Attempted suicide is difficult to define because studies often differ in distinctions between *suicidal gestures* (interpreted as suicidal behavior that is not "serious" in intent), thoughts of suicide, threats of suicide, and self-inflicted injury that requires medical treatment. There is no commonly accepted definition of *suicide attempt* (Hawton, 1986).

However we define them, it is clear that suicide and suicide attempts of adolescents, and to a lesser extent younger children, have increased dramatically during the past several decades (Harris & Ammerman, 1986; Hawton, 1986). Only accidents and homicides are more often the cause of death among youths between the ages of 15 and 24 (Eisenberg, 1984). In this age group, males commit suicide at a higher rate than females, and this sex difference becomes more marked with age. Among older adolescents and young adults, parasuicides are more common for females than for males. Among children the sex difference is reversed, with suicide attempts more common for boys than for girls. In the U.S., blacks have significantly lower suicide rates than whites. Rates are higher for married than for unmarried teenagers. Suicide methods appear to relate to the availability of means; firearms are more commonly used in the U.S. than in most other countries (Hawton, 1986).

Although suicide is rarely reported in children under ten years and is relatively infrequent even in prepubertal children, we do occasionally encounter reports of suicide attempts and successful suicides of very young children. Rosenthal and Rosenthal (1984) presented case descriptions of 16 preschoolers who they believed were suicidal. The Rosenthals' work raises the possibility that depression and suicide are much more common among very young children than many mental health workers believe.

Rising suicidal behavior among young persons and the high rate at which children and youth kill or attempt to kill themselves are alarming. Greater understanding of the causes and more effective prevention programs must be priorities. We also need better means of dealing with suicidal individuals after an attempted suicide, and with survivors after a completed suicide.

Causal Factors and Prevention

The many complex factors that contribute to children's and adolescents' suicidal behavior include psychosis, feelings of hopelessness, impulsivity, naive concepts of death, drug abuse, social isolation, abuse and neglect by parents, family conflict and disorganization, a family history of suicide and parasuicide, and cultural factors, including stress caused by the educational system and attention to suicide in the mass media (Hawton, 1986; Rotheram, 1987; Sheras, 1983). The common thread among all factors, Sheras feels, is that suicidal individuals believe they have little impact on the world around them. "They have no means of gaining acknowledgment of their very existence. In short, they feel invisible" (p. 774). They then become convinced that the only way they can achieve recognition is to die. Suicide is a highly visible act, a way to leave one's mark.

Most authorities agree that biological and nonbiological factors interact in complex ways in the causation of suicide and depression, but this complexity does not make it impossible to assess the strength of biological contributions. Studies of adoptive and biological relatives of individuals with certain disorders, for example, help reveal the degree of heritability. As we saw in Chapter 8, studies have revealed a genetic factor in schizophrenia. The work of Kety (1979) and his associates suggests a genetic factor in suicide as well. Figure 17.2 shows data for adopted individuals only, meaning that the observed differences between groups cannot be attributed to the variable of adoption and that the effects of biological relationship and psychological environment can therefore be untangled. If living with depressed people in the family were the dominant factor in suicide, then the adoptive relatives of adoptees who are depressed (C) ought to have a higher rate of suicide than the biological relatives of those who are adopted and depressed (A). Furthermore, if suicide has primarily psychogenic causes, then the adoptive relatives of depressed adoptees (C) ought to have a higher suicide rate than the adoptive relatives of nondepressed adoptees (D). But Figure 17.2 shows a suicide rate 13 times higher for group A than for group B; 6.5 times higher for group A than for group C; and equal rates for groups C and D, thus indicating a genetic link to suicidal behavior. At the same time, the data in Figure 17.2 do not rule out psychological factors in suicide.

Hawton (1986) summarizes three probable psychological factors in suicidal behavior, which may be interrelated. First, changes in the social environment during the past several decades have created additional psychological stress for young people. Rising divorce rates, pressure for sexual experiences and adopting other adult responsibilities at a younger age, loss of a sense of community, and decreases in extended families and other supportive relationships, for example, may have produced higher rates of depression. Second, the greater acceptability of suicide as an option for handling stress (especially as highlighted in sensational news coverage) may have led many youngsters to imitate other suicides or attempts. Related factors may be the growing tendency to question the reasons for personal existence, the constant threat of nuclear annihilation, and declining religious faith. Third, the increasing tendency to rely on mood-altering drugs to resolve personal problems and higher rates of substance abuse among young people may have diminished their skills in coping with stress, their willingness to consider other ways of dealing with problems, and their capacity to consider alternatives while under the influence of drugs. The ready availability and greater acceptability of dangerous drugs may also have led to more accidental overdoses.

Many children and adolescents who commit suicide or parasuicide have a history of behavior disorders and school failure (Hawton, 1986; Rotheram, 1987). In fact, school performance of adolescents who show suicidal behavior is almost uniformly poor, and a large proportion of teenagers' suicides and parasuicides occurs in the spring months, when school problems (grades, graduation, college admission) are highlighted. Outbreaks of suicide attempts are particularly likely to occur in institutional settings and psychiatric hospitals, probably partly as a result of imitation or competitive bids for attention and status.

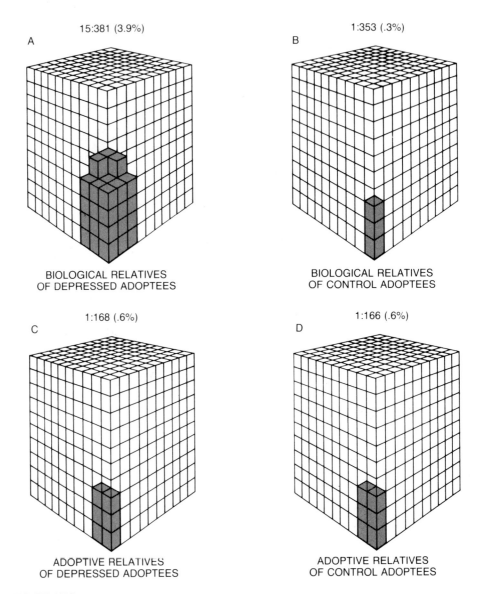

15:381 (3.9%)

1:353 (.3%)

1:168 (.6%)

1:166 (.6%)

BIOLOGICAL RELATIVES
OF DEPRESSED ADOPTEES

BIOLOGICAL RELATIVES
OF CONTROL ADOPTEES

ADOPTIVE RELATIVES
OF DEPRESSED ADOPTEES

ADOPTIVE RELATIVES
OF CONTROL ADOPTEES

FIGURE 17.2

Incidence of Suicide in Biological and Adoptive Relatives of Depressed and Control
Adoptees

From "Disorders of the Human Brain" by Seymour A. Kety, 1979, *Scientific American, 241*(3), p. 206.

Primary suicide prevention presents enormous problems of identifying individuals who are at risk, because in any attempt to make predictions, the number of false
positives is extremely high and the consequences of false negatives are extremely
severe. That is, because only a relatively small percentage of the population commits
or attempts suicide, and because suicidal and nonsuicidal individuals have many

common characteristics, any general screening procedure turns up many false positives—individuals who are not actually at high risk. But the consequences of identifying as "not at risk" those who are in fact likely to attempt or commit suicide (the false negatives) are obviously grim. Consequently, most primary prevention programs are aimed at entire school populations.

Eisenberg (1984) believes there are three major preventive measures: (1) limiting access to devices often used in impulsive self-destruction (as through enacting effective gun control); (2) limiting the publicity given to suicides, because extensive publicity is almost always followed by a sharp increase in suicidal acts; and (3) improving early detection of depression in children and youth.

Assessment

Suicidal behavior is not always preceded by recognizable signals, although some characteristics and circumstances are danger signals for which educators and other adults should be on the lookout. Adults' and peers' awareness of indications that a child or youth might be at risk for suicidal behavior is an important aspect of assessing the general school population (Guetzloe, 1987; Underwood, 1987). These are some indications of risk in the general school population:

☐ Sudden changes in usual behavior or affect
☐ Serious academic, social, or disciplinary problems at school
☐ Family or home problems, including parental separation or divorce or child abuse
☐ Disturbed or disrupted peer relations, including peer rejection and breakup of boy/girl relationships
☐ Health problems, such as insomnia, loss of appetite, sudden weight change, and so on
☐ Substance abuse
☐ Giving away possessions or talk of not being present in the future
☐ Talk of suicide or presence of a suicide plan
☐ Situational crisis such as death of a family member or close friend, pregnancy or abortion, legal arrest, loss of employment of self or family member, etc.

Part of any assessment of risk involves systematic evaluation of the characteristics of individuals who are thought to be at higher than usual risk. A personal characteristic associated with most suicides, parasuicides, and thoughts of suicide is depression, so it is important to assess depression (Bettes & Walker, 1986; Harris & Ammerman, 1987). Pfeffer (1984) notes specific factors that distinguish suicidal from nonsuicidal children: they express extreme depression, hopelessness, feelings of worthlessness, wishes to die, and intense preoccupation with death. Their parents often have been seriously depressed or have shown suicidal tendencies.

A sense of hopelessness is apparently more closely linked to suicidal intent than is depression (Dwyer & Kreitman, 1984; Kazdin, French, Unis, Esveldt-Dawson, & Sherick, 1983; Pfeffer, 1984). Table 17.1 lists items from a scale for measuring a child's sense of hopelessness. Youngsters who score high on this measure of hopelessness tend to score high on a measure of depression; however, hopelessness and intent to

TABLE 17.1
The Hopelessness Scale for Children

Key	Item
True	2. I might as well give up, because I can't make things better for myself.
	8. I don't have good luck, and there's no reason to think I will when I grow up.
	9. All I can see ahead of me are bad things, not good things.
	10. I don't think I will get what I really want.
	12. Things just don't work out the way I want them to.
	13. I never get what I want, so it's dumb to want anything.
	14. I don't think I will have any real fun when I grow up.
	15. Tomorrow seems unclear and confusing to me.
	17. There's no use in really trying to get something I want, because I probably won't get it.
False	1. I want to grow up because I think things will be better.
	3. When things are going badly, I know that they won't be bad all of the time.
	4. I can imagine what my life will be like when I'm ____ (10 years older).
	5. I have enough time to finish the things I really want to do.
	6. Someday I will be good at doing the things I really care about.
	7. I will get more good things in life than most other kids.
	11. When I grow up, I think I will be happier than I am now.
	16. I will have more good times than bad times.

Note: From "Hopelessness, Depression, and Suicidal Intent Among Psychiatrically Disturbed Inpatient Children," by A. E. Kazdin, N. H. French, A. S. Unis, K. Esveldt-Dawson, and R. B. Sherick, 1983, *Journal of Consulting and Clinical Psychology, 51,* p. 506. Reprinted by permission.

commit suicide correlate more highly than depression and suicidal intent. Apparently, all individuals who feel hopeless are depressed, but not all who are depressed feel hopeless. Hopelessness may represent the final stage of depression that tends to precede suicidal intent, the stage at which an individual concludes that suicide is justified (Dwyer & Kreitman, 1984; Sheras, 1983). Hopelessness and alienation justify the act of ultimate withdrawal from the world.

Rotheram (1987) suggests procedures for evaluating imminent danger of suicide. These consist of an initial ten-minute interview in which statistically-based risk factors are considered: male sex, past attempt with method other than ingestion, more than one previous attempt, history of antisocial behavior, close friend or family member committed suicide, frequent drug and alcohol use, depression, incompatible social environment. If five or more of these indicators are present, then the youngster is judged to be potentially in imminent danger of suicide; if two or more are present, or if it is found that the youth has current ideas or plans for suicide, the next step in evaluation is recommended. The second phase requires about 20 to 30 minutes and evaluates the youngster's ability to behave in a nonsuicidal manner as demonstrated in four ways: (1) ability to make a written promise not to engage in suicidal behavior for a specified period of time, such as two weeks; (2) ability to deliver compliments to self and others, which is inconsistent with a pessimistic and hopeless outlook; (3) capacity to assess feelings by rating own feelings, including those associated with emotional discomfort and suicidal ideation; and (4) capacity to plan ahead for suicidal situations, including specific steps for coping with threatening circumstances. Roth-eram (1987) notes that "In practice, most youths are able to accomplish all of the tasks outlined or none of them. Failure to perform these tasks is a behavioral indication of imminent danger: coping skills to ward off suicidal tendencies are not available" (p. 108).

Intervention and Education

Sheras (1983) suggests three general considerations for responding to the suicidal child or adolescent. Adults should

1. Take all suicide threats and attempts seriously
2. Seek to reestablish communication
3. Provide emotional support or sustenance that relieves alienation

While dealing adequately with the problem of suicidal behavior requires a complex, multifaceted effort, the general notion is that the suicidal individual must be helped to establish and maintain as many points of contact as possible with significant others, including adults and peers. The child or adolescent must be shown unself-destructive ways to leave a mark or to become visible. Teachers can aid in suicide prevention, Sheras believes, by realizing that they can identify students who are at risk; school systems can play a part in prevention by providing curricula that acquaint students with others' experience of normal physical and social development (Guetzloe, 1987; Underwood, 1987).

The educator's role in intervention is primarily to provide information about suicide and refer students who appear at risk to other professionals. A comprehensive program of suicide awareness and prevention has several parts: administrative guidelines specifying school policy, faculty inservice to obtain support of teachers and provide them with basic information and skills in dealing with students, and curricular programs for students (Underwood, 1987). In addition, hotlines, peer counseling, and programs designed to reduce and manage stress may be implemented (Guetzloe, 1987). Figure 17.3 shows a wallet-sized card that is printed on both sides and folds in the middle. Prepared by a guidance counselor, it addresses adolescents in plain language, without technical jargon, but is also appropriate for adults. Its convenient size makes it more likely to be kept and used than would a sheet of paper. This is how Underwood describes programs for students:

> Two basic premises, which should underlie any programming in this area, are the recognition that adolescence is a difficult time and that suicide is the inappropriate choice some teens make to use death as a way to deal with life. Keeping adolescent development issues in mind, both the positive and negative impacts of peer pressure must also be recognized. The positive aspect, of course, is that peers are usually the first to know about a friend's troubles; but in a negative sense, peer culture may often apply pressure to keep this information a secret. For students,

MYTHS AND FACTS ABOUT SUICIDE

- It is a **myth** that talking to someone about suicidal feelings will cause them to commit suicide.
  Fact: Asking someone about their suicidal feelings may make the person feel relieved that someone finally recognized their emotional pain.
- It is a **myth** that all suicidal people want to die and there is nothing that can be done about it.
  Fact: Most suicidal people are ambivalent, that is, part of them is saying: **"I want to live."**
- It is a **myth** that people who talk about committing suicide never actually do it.
  Fact: When someone talks about committing suicide, he/she may be giving a warning that should not be ignored by others who hear such comments.
- It is a **myth** that there is a "typical" type of person who commits suicide.
  Fact: The potential for suicide exists in all of us. There is no "typical" type of suicidal person.
- It is a **myth** that suicide occurs without warning.
  Fact: Many people, including adolescents, give warnings of their suicidal intent.

SOME SIGNS OF SUICIDE

Often people who are contemplating ending their lives will give signs or signals of their intent. One sign alone does not mean that a person is suicidal. Several signs at one time, however, may mean that the person is seeking help. A few of these signs are:

- Verbal suicide threats.
- Previous suicide attempts.
- Personality changes (unusual withdrawal, aggression or moodiness).
- Depression (changes in normal appetite, sleep disturbances, sudden drop in school performance, etc.)
- Final arrangements (making a will, giving away prized possessions.)

When you suspect that a friend or a family member may be suicidal, you may become nervous and anxious. This is a normal feeling. It may help if you remember the following:

WHAT NOT TO DO

Do not allow yourself to be sworn to secrecy by the suicidal person. You may lose a friendship but you may save a life.
Do not leave the person alone if you believe the risk for suicide is immediate.
Do not act shocked at what the person tells you.
Do not counsel the person yourself.
Do not debate whether suicide is right or wrong. This may make the person feel more guilty.

L·I·F·E·L·I·N·E·S

**St. Clare's Hospital
Department of Consultation & Education**

ADOLESCENT SUICIDE
WHY?

The suicidal person feels a tremendous sense of loneliness, isolation, helplessness and hopelessness. For the young person these feelings may be caused by family conflicts, a divorce or separation, the death of a parent, the break-up of a romance, the move to a new school or pressure to succeed at school.

Suicidal people feel that they can no longer cope with their problems and that suicide may be the only way out. Most people think about suicide at some point in their life. Most people find that these thoughts are temporary and that things do get better. Suicide is a needless and permanent solution to short-term problems.

WHAT TO DO

Believe or trust your suspicions that the person may be self-destructive.
Communicate your concern for the well-being of the person. Be an active listener and show your support.
Be direct. Talk openly and freely and ask direct questions about the person's intentions. Try to determine if the person has a plan for suicide (how, where, when). The more detailed the plan, the greater the risk.
Get professional help. Encourage the person to seek help from a school counselor, minister, or someone who would know what else to do. If the person resists, you should get help for them anyway.

MORRIS COUNTY
24 HOUR CRISIS PHONE LINES

Contact Morris/Passaic	831-1870
St. Clare's Hospital	625-0280
Morristown Memorial Hospital	540-5045
Pequannock Valley Mental Health Center	839-0770

HOSPITAL EMERGENCY SERVICES

St. Clare's Hospital	625-6063
Morristown Memorial Hospital	540-5004
Dover General Hospital	989-3200
Chilton Memorial Hospital	831-5000

POISON CONTROL CENTER
800-962-1253

LOCAL POLICE
Inside cover of phone directory or 911.

FIGURE 17.3
St. Clare's "Lifelines" Card

The author gratefully acknowledges John Kalafat, Ph.D., Department of Education, St. Clare's Riverside Medical Center, Denville, NJ 07834, for giving permission to reproduce the card.

a shift must be made so that secret-keeping is viewed as a burden and telling someone as a responsible act that requires courage. As with the faculty, this "responsible act" does not include solving a friend's problem, but simply telling someone else who is in a better position to help.... While teachers often feel identifying an at-risk student is burdensome, the initial response of students often is to not want to tell anyone but to keep the responsibility to themselves. The task is to persuade both groups that referral is in their best interests. This may be easier to do with teachers who appropriately welcome the opportunity to pass the buck than with teens who are sometimes caught up in omnipotent fantasies of rescue.

Another critical element in the construction of a student program is to confront the developmental movement of adolescents from dependence to independence and convince them that the paradox of independence means knowing when to ask for help. From our perspective as adults, we appreciate that shuttling back and forth between dependence and independence in order to gain strength is the optimal way to negotiate this developmental challenge, but a lot of stereotypes must be broken to convince urban males in particular that help-seeking behavior is an indication of strength.

Unfortunately, the typical school community also does not reinforce the concept that asking for help is acceptable. Schools encourage competition. Sharing, collaboration, collective problem solving are often just synonyms for "cheating" in academic vocabulary. Students are frequently led to believe early on that there are only so many As to go around, that helping a peer to do well may be at their own expense. Certainly knowing how to compete appropriately is a necessary life-skill, but knowing when and how to be independent is equally important. Making students aware of resources both within the school and local community is pointless if their resistance to using them is not addressed.

Most programs for students incorporate these principles by using creative, interactive methods that capture a student's attention and capitalize on the adolescent's current life experiences. Their counterpart is a program for parents that acknowledges the challenges that parents of teenagers face today. The program also provides information about how to recognize when teens are in trouble, and outlines local resources. (Underwood, 1987, pp. 35–36)

Managing children and adolescents following their suicide attempts or threats is the joint responsibility of counselors or other mental health personnel and teachers. While teachers should not attempt to offer counseling or therapy themselves, they can provide critical support by encouraging students and families to obtain help from qualified counselors or therapists. Teachers can also help by reducing unnecessary stress on students and being willing and empathic listeners.

Schools need to work out plans for dealing with the aftermath of a student's suicide. The plan should be suited to the needs of students and faculty of the particular school, but the procedures must be designed to avoid contagion. Peers of the student who died may be at risk for emulating the suicide, especially if they were close friends or were depressed at the time of the suicide.

School-based intervention and prevention programs can inadvertently increase suicide risk. By focusing too much attention on suicide, particularly if suicidal behavior is glamorized or glorified, students may be more rather than less inclined to engage in this behavior. If the program dispenses information that is not simple, factual, and practical, it is not likely to decrease suicide risk. And if school personnel and professionals in community agencies are not able and willing to follow through with appropriate support and services to students who seek help for themselves and their friends, the information provided in an educational program will be useless or worse (Guetzloe, 1987).

SUMMARY

The federal definition of seriously emotionally disturbed suggests that youngsters with internalizing problems, including depression, should be eligible for special education, although the definition describes depression ambiguously. Childhood depression has only recently become a topic of serious research, and there is still controversy over the definition. Consensus is emerging that childhood depression parallels adult depression in many respects, but particular behaviors exhibited in response to depressed affect will be developmentally age appropriate. Both adults and children who are depressed experience depressed mood and lose interest in productive activity. Depressed children may exhibit a variety of inappropriate conduct, including problems such as aggression, stealing, and social withdrawal. The concept of masked depression, which allows attribution of any kind of misbehavior to depression with or without evidence of key features of depression, is useless. No reliable prevalence estimates for childhood depression are available. A large percentage of children served by special education, however, are known to suffer from depression. Prevalence of depression is higher among older adolescents, especially girls.

Diagnostic criteria for depression under DSM-III and most other classification systems include affective, cognitive, motivational, and physiological indications. Assessment of depression must be multifaceted and should include self-reports, parental reports, peer nominations, and clinical ratings. The judgments of teachers should not be overlooked. Most researchers have relied primarily on children's self-reports to assess depression, but as yet no consistent criteria for diagnosis have emerged.

Some cases of depression clearly result from unknown biological factors, but the causal factors in most cases are indeterminable. In some cases depression represents a reaction to stressful or traumatic environmental events. We find significant correlations between parents' depression and problems of their children, including depression. Clinically depressed parents are probably a major cause of their children's depression, but in other cases it appears that depressed children and adults affect each other reciprocally. Educators should give special attention to how depression and school failure can be reciprocal causal factors. Prevention of depression is important because severe, chronic depression is associated with adult maladjustment and suicidal behavior. Prevention may involve reducing stress, parenting training, or teaching specific cognitive or behavioral skills.

Antidepressant drugs may be useful in some cases of depression, but their effects and side effects should be monitored carefully. Interventions in which educators may play a role include cognitive and cognitive-behavioral retraining. These interventions are based on theories that attribute depression to inadequate social skills, maladaptive thought patterns, and lack of self-control. Selecting intervention strategies depends on analyzing the depressed individual's specific cognitive and social characteristics.

Suicide and attempted suicide present serious problems of definition because the stigma attached to suicidal behavior results in deliberate misreporting. In addition, the prevalence of suicide and suicide attempts is difficult to establish because the precise circumstances of death are often impossible to determine. Nevertheless, we know that both suicides and suicide attempts of children and youth, especially of adolescents and young adults, have increased dramatically in the past several decades. The causes of suicide are mostly unknown, but include a genetic factor and many complex psychological factors. Probable causal factors related to increased suicide rates of children and adolescents include changes in the social environment, greater acceptability of suicidal behavior, and rising substance abuse and reliance on mood altering drugs as ways to cope with stress. Many students who engage in suicidal behavior have a history of difficulty or failure in school.

Prevention of suicide is extremely difficult because of the problems associated with false positives and false negatives. Most students who share the characteristics of suicide attempters are not at risk for suicide, so that any screening procedure will turn up many false positives. Yet the consequences of failing to identify those who are in fact at risk—the false negatives—are unacceptable. Prevention programs are typically aimed at entire school populations and consist of guidelines for teaching, inservice for teachers, and instructional programs for students and parents.

Assessment of suicide risk involves recognizing danger signals and evaluating the individual's sense of hopelessness. Evaluation of statistically-based risk factors and the student's ability to perform specific coping tasks are required to determine whether a suicide attempt is imminent.

Adults should take all suicide threats and attempts seriously, seek to reestablish communication with students who feel alienated and help them establish as many points of contact as possible with significant others, and provide emotional sustenance and support. In addition, intervention programs call for instruction for adolescents regarding human development, coping mechanisms, and the meaning and management of suicidal behavior. Management of the student and significant others following a suicide threat or attempt is critically important. Schools should have a plan for follow-up intervention when a suicide occurs, but must be careful in implementing prevention and intervention programs so that suicide risk is not inadvertently increased.

18

Psychotic
Behavior

As you read this chapter, keep these guiding questions in mind:

☐ What is the relationship between psychotic behavior and classifying an individual as having a disorder?

☐ Regarding the causes and assessment of psychotic behavior, what are the most important types of information for teachers?

☐ What kinds of research regarding psychotic behavior would be the greatest help to educators?

☐ What behavioral characteristics are associated with autistic withdrawal?

☐ What hypothesis about the cause of self-stimulation has the greatest implications for educators?

☐ What are the indications that self-stimulation requires intervention?

☐ How is the self-injurious behavior of individuals with severe behavioral disorders different from that of individuals who are considered normal?

☐ Why is it important to assess the environments in which self-stimulation and self-injury occur?

M ajor features of childhood psychosis—infantile autism, childhood schizophrenia, and related disorders—were sketched in Chapters 1 and 7. This chapter presents more detailed information regarding several aspects of psychotic behavior. We will give closer consideration to three types of psychotic behavior that are often seen in youngsters with severe disabilities, regardless of their diagnostic labels: autistic withdrawal, self-stimulation, and self-injury.

PSYCHOTIC BEHAVIOR

Definition and Prevalence

Prior and Werry (1986) offer one definition of psychotic behavior: "The interpretation of oneself, of the world, and of one's place in it, is so seriously at variance with the actual facts of the matter as to interfere with everyday adaptation and to strike the impartial observer as incomprehensible" (p. 156). Since this definition implies that the individual has the cognitive skills required for social interpretation of behavior, it applies primarily to the distorted thought processes and bizarre behavior of older

---

Notes on the Personal Experience of Autism

I was living in a world of daydreaming and Fear revolving aboud my self I had no care about Human feelings or other people. I was afraid of everything! I was terrified to go in the water swimming, (and of) loud noises; in the dark I had severe, repetitive Nightmares and occasionally hearing electronic noises with nightmares. I would wake up so terrified and disoriented I wasnt able to Find my way out of the room for a few miniuts. I felt like I was being draged to Hell. I was afraid of simple things such as going into the shower, getting my nails cliped, soap in my eyes, rides in the carnival— except the Spook house I love it, I allso like Hellish envirments such as spookhouses at the Carnival, Halloween, and movies—horror. I daydreamed a lot and tryed to actvly communicate and get into that world. I rember Yale Child Study Ctr. I ignored the doctors and did my own thing such as make something and played or idolize it not caring that anybody was in the room. I was also very hat(e)full and sneakey. I struggled and breathed hard because I wanted to kill the gunia pig; as soon as the examiner turned her back I killed it. I hated my mother becaus she try to stop me from being in my world and doing what I liked; so I stoped and as soon as she turn her back I went at it agen. I was very Rebellious and sneaky and distructive. I would plot to kill my mother and destroy the world. Evil thing astonished me such as an H.Bomb. I loved cartoons and their envirments. I also (had) a very warp sence of humor and learn(ed) perveted thing(s) verry quickly. I used to lash out of controll and repeat sick, perverted Phrases as well as telling people violent, wild, untrue things to impress them.

In school I learned somethings verry quickly but other were beyond learning comprehenshion. I used to disrupt the whole class and love to drive the teachers nuts. . . .

After I left (this school) The physical problems continued and The list gets longer. I lived with my father and the(n) saw the so call(ed) normal, sick teenage world. I was 14. I set my will (to) be normal like everybody else. (I) look(ed) up to

---

children and youth with intelligence above the severe-profound range of mental retardation. As we use the term *psychotic behavior,* however, it also applies to the seriously deviant behavior of very young children, including those who are severely mentally retarded. These children, and older youngsters and adults with severe cognitive limitations, may exhibit behavior that is incompatible with normal development, although it may not represent cognitive interpretation of self, the world, and one's place in it. The behavior may be stereotypic, repetitive, self-injurious, or incompatible with learning and social acceptance to such a degree that it must be altered, however.

Tony W. was initially referred for evaluation at the age of 26 months. At the age of 22 years, he wrote of his experiences as a child and youth. He was then working, living alone, and had a few superficial friendships. His IQ was 93. The accompanying feature presents excerpts from his description of his experiences as a child and youth and shows that his cognitive, affective, and social problems have persisted into adulthood.

The prevalence of psychotic behavior is impossible to estimate precisely because psychotic behavior and the clinical diagnosis "psychotic" are not synonymous. The

---

people in school and did what they did to be accepted and put (up) more of a show to hide the problems and be Normal. I force(d) my self to Know all the top rock groups, smoke pot, and drink and (tried to) have a girl friend. This was the 9th grade and 10th. I constantly got in trouble in school and did som(e) real crazy things to be cool. Like everybody else I thought I was normal. Most of it was a failure. More people hated me then ever. My interests were destroyed becouse I thought they wernt normal. Things were going bad at home. My Father and I were not getting along becouse of trouble in school. I wasn't getting along with No one. I got my (drivers) license and tried to impress people at school and girls by driving like a nut. IN tenth grade I quit school and worked washing cars and work(ed) many other Jobs too. I was verry derpressed and Hyper at work. I got along with my boss at all my Jobs. I tend to get lazy and had trouble getting along with other people. So in (an) effort to keep my Jobs I avoided many people. I found It a lot easeyer to get along with older people and FEARED People my age because of school. I went to the army and got in lots of Fights with people. So I got discarged (discharged). I allso have great Troub(l)e getting thing(s) organized and missunderstand allmost everything. I worked a few more Jobs and hung around w/some Crazy people I knew from school and got drunk a lot and did distructive things,Magnified Fears and Peronia on pot. I never got Fired from a job. My problems havn't changed at ALL from early childhood. I was Just able to Function. And it still (is) the same today—1983. Plus more physical problems in 1982 knowing that NONE of these problems are gone but only sepressed (suppressed) by Physcatric (Psychiatric) treatment. Then (I) insisted on their was a medical problem but IT programed that Medical Help was a cop out and after (I) Find out more truth about lie and rebelling and hating its and doubting it. And then all the childhood problems and physical problems starting eating me like a cancer. I then felt The medical help in one of the only hopes for my well being and (that of) Approx. 500,000+ Autistic kids (pp. 49–52).

From "The Experience of Infantile Autism: A First-person Account by Tony W." by F. R. Volkmar and D. J. Cohen, 1985, *Journal of Autism and Developmental Disorders, 15,* pp. 47–54. Copyright © 1985 by Plenum Publishing Corp. Reprinted by permission.

definition of the behavior is not quite the same as the criteria for classifying individuals. Psychotic individuals may exhibit behavior that is not typically labeled psychotic (such as hyperactivity or anxiety-withdrawal). And not everyone who exhibits behavior that is seemingly psychotic is labeled a psychotic person. Thus we may see psychotic behavior in people who are diagnosed as mentally retarded, or who carry other diagnostic labels, or who even have no clinical diagnosis (those considered normal). Notwithstanding this range of persons who may exhibit psychotic behavior, we see the behavior problems most often in individuals who are considered autistic, schizophrenic, or mentally retarded. It is reasonable to guess that approximately two percent of children and youth exhibit psychotic behavior so persistently as to require intervention.

Causal Factors and Prevention

The causes and prevention of psychotic behavior were discussed in Part Three. Briefly summarized, the notion that parents make their children psychotic has been effectively refuted, although family interactions can certainly contribute to shaping and maintaining deviant behavior. Understanding of this parental role has resulted in recruiting parents as therapeutic agents in many treatment programs (see Bristol, 1985; Lovaas, 1987). A biological basis for most psychotic behavior is suspected, although the nature of the genetic or biochemical defect has been identified only in rare cases. Schizophrenic behavior is known to be organized in part by genetics, but the genetic mechanism is not understood. Recent research regarding the etiology of autism has explored factors such as abnormalities of the immune system (Warren et al., 1986) and brain opioids (which control sensitivity to pain) (Sahley & Panksepp, 1987), but this research has not led to pinpointing causes or effective therapies. Regarding autism, Rutter and Schopler (1987) summarized, "So far..., the meaning of the neurophysiological findings in autism remain obscure, and it is not at all clear how they might be linked to the findings on psychological deficits" (p. 171).

Prevention consists primarily of efforts to manage psychotic behavior after it appears, through medication and various forms of psychotherapy or behavior modification (see Lovaas, 1987; Ornitz, 1986; Prior & Werry, 1986; Rutter & Schopler, 1987). Searches for nonmedical factors have the greatest relevance for the everyday practice of educators.

Assessment

Behavioral disorders that feature psychotic behavior tend to be among the most complex problems of children and youth. Consequently, adequate assessment demands thorough evaluation of the whole child (medical, social, cognitive, and educational aspects). Assessment should include behavior ratings, interviews, and psychological and educational tests, as well as informal and formal observations in a variety of settings. (Discussion of comprehensive evaluation procedures for autism and other severe disorders is available from Dunlap, Koegel, & O'Neill, 1985; Koegel et al., 1982; Newsom & Rincover, 1981; and Strain, 1987, among others.)

From the educator's perspective, direct observation under a variety of environmental conditions yields the most important information for programming. The most critical data are those that indicate the student's responsiveness to various conditions. Changes in the student's environment, including physical surroundings, learning tasks, expectations for performance, and consequences for behavior are the focus of teaching.

Intervention and Education

Treatment of psychotic children has long been a matter of heated controversy (Kauffman, 1974a, 1974b, 1986a; Lovaas, 1979, 1982). Behavioral interventions have emerged as the most effective and relevant approaches for teachers, if not clinicians (Koegel et al., 1982). Early, intensive intervention is critical, particularly with autism (Fenske, Zalenski, Krantz, & McClannahan, 1985; Lovaas, 1987). Advances in behavioral interventions suggest that some children with autism (perhaps about 50 percent) may recover from the disorder if they receive early and intensive treatment (Lovaas, 1987), in stark contrast to previous research that showed recovery for only a very small percentage (10 percent or less). Other researchers have found that appropriate behavioral intervention allows some psychotic children (some with autism or other severe developmental disabilities) to be taught in classes with nonhandicapped peers (Strain, 1983, 1984). Intensive early intervention for psychotic children typically involves training parents and teachers (and all those who participate in the child's daily management) in behavior management procedures.

Behavioral interventions have been highly successful with psychotic children in many research situations, which indicates what teaching strategies and instructional techniques are most likely to succeed, but has not always yielded direct, practical implications for teachers. It is essential to find procedures that teachers can apply in everyday environments without the extensive support found in research settings (see Donnellan, Mesaros, & Anderson, 1985; Valcante, 1986). A significant trend in behavioral intervention research is toward more natural, less intrusive, and less aversive instructional methods (cf. Koegel, O'Dell, & Koegel, 1987; Winterling, Dunlap, & O'Neill, 1987).

Although recent research creates the hope that many psychotic children will eventually function normally (Lovaas, 1987), educators must not lose sight of the fact that for the foreseeable future many psychotic children, adolescents, and adults will require teaching in basic life skills such as personal hygiene, cooking, and community travel (Smith & Belcher, 1985).

Psychopharmacological interventions in psychotic behavior consist primarily of *neuroleptics* (antipsychotic drugs) such as Thorazine, Mellaril, and Haldol (Campbell et al., 1985; Gittelman & Kanner, 1986). Although the medications sometimes give symptomatic relief, responses to the drugs are idiosyncratic—they depend on the individual child. Even when drugs are helpful, behavior management and instruction by parents and teachers is still critical.

AUTISTIC WITHDRAWAL

A primary feature of infantile autism is the child's unrelatedness to people, although extreme withdrawal does not appear exclusively in children categorized as autistic. Many psychotic children and some who are severely mentally retarded effectively shut out the world to such a degree that their withdrawal may be considered autistic, due to their profound isolation. We will focuses on five characteristics of extreme withdrawal that children with severe disorders may exhibit, regardless of whether they have been labeled autistic. The term *autistic withdrawal,* then, means extreme social isolation, irrespective of the child's diagnostic label. Five important behavioral characteristics associated with autistic withdrawal are

1. Unresponsiveness to social stimuli
2. Gaze aversion
3. Overselective responding
4. Language disorders (including muteness and echolalia)
5. Excessive and inappropriate fantasy and delusions

Unresponsiveness to Social Stimuli

During the first year of life, children normally show growing awareness of and responsiveness to their social environment. They recognize their mothers and other familiar faces, develop a social smile in response to hearing or seeing familiar persons, lift their arms in anticipation of being picked up, engage in social games with glee (such as babbling, patty-cake, peek-a-boo, and so on), delight in close physical contact with their parents, and interact positively and reciprocally with people in many other ways. Children who do not display social responsiveness early in life are often thought to be autistic, retarded, brain injured, or even deaf or blind. They seem completely oblivious to what is going on around them, and it is no surprise that their parents and other adults begin to wonder if they can see or hear. Lack of social contact and failure to cuddle or to adapt their posture to that of the adult who is holding them give the impression that they lack interest in or even reject human relationships. If children do not respond to language as they get older (do not come when called or follow verbal directions), they become a management problem for their parents and other adults.

Autistic withdrawal often goes beyond simple unresponsiveness to stimuli. It may become obvious, because of adept locomotion and manipulation of objects and avoidance of certain visual stimuli, that a child can see. It may also become obvious, because of sensitive response to some auditory stimuli, that a child can hear. In these cases it is not clear whether withdrawal involves perceptual or information processing problems. Can these children make sense of what they see and hear? Or are they deliberately "screening out" certain social stimuli to maintain their isolation in a private world? Because some profoundly withdrawn children often respond with the opposite of what is requested, we know that they can "make sense" of auditory and visual social stimuli (Steucher, 1972).

Negativism is a frequent feature of some autistic children's behavior, and it requires attention to and understanding of social stimuli (Wallace, 1975). Negativism is a highly effective way of keeping people at bay and maintaining social isolation. In fact, combined with the bizarre mannerisms and self-injurious behavior that many psychotic children exhibit, negativism quickly produces perplexity or even revulsion in most adult caretakers. But negativism may also result from repeated experiences of failure and lack of reinforcement for performance; it may be part of a pattern of learned helplessness (Koegel & Mentis, 1985).

Unresponsiveness and negativism have most often been approached with highly directive, consistent, intrusive teaching procedures. More recently, researchers have sought to avoid negativism and noncompliance with methods that attenuate task demands, such as varying task presentation and allowing the child more choices during instruction (Koegel et al., 1987; Winterling et al., 1987). Very basic social skills are taught with behavior modification techniques. Skills and reinforcers must be chosen to fit the child's developmental level and to provide powerful motivation.

Gaze Aversion

During social interactions, people normally look at each other's faces and gaze into each other's eyes at least occasionally. How often and for how long one fixes a gaze on the other, as well as where she or he directs the gaze, depend on a variety of factors, including social status, physical proximity, and the emotional valence of the interaction (Grumet, 1983). Lack of eye contact is often interpreted as inattention or unwillingness to enter into an interpersonal relationship. Continuous eye contact extending over an unusually long time, especially in close physical proximity, is usually perceived as either threatening assertiveness or amorousness. Thus, the significance of gaze fixation in social interaction is readily apparent—it is a basic social skill.

Gaze aversion is a frequent component of autistic withdrawal. Failure to establish eye contact with others makes autistic children seem to look "through" or "beyond" other people or to appear "out of it." Rather than focus on others' faces, autistic children often rely on peripheral vision and quick, furtive glances to interpret social cues. This gaze aversion makes adults feel ill-at-ease and shut out; it also has the function of appeasing or inhibiting attacks from other children. Failing to look at people's faces could also be one reason autistic children have difficulty interpreting others' emotions and learning communication skills (Hobson, 1986; Tiegerman & Primavera, 1984). Because gaze aversion is obviously a disturbing and debilitating social behavior, one of the first steps in teaching children who avert their gaze must be to establish appropriate eye contact. Methods for overcoming averted gaze include games that require looking at another person, prompts, imitating the child's behavior, and reinforcement for eye contact (Koegel et al., 1982; Tiegerman & Primavera, 1984).

Overselective Responding

Most children observe and respond to a variety of features of complex stimuli. They learn to recognize their parents' faces, for example, from a variety of the stimuli that characterize them—eyes, hair, noses, and so on. They learn language by attending to the many components of speech, such as its sounds, pitch, rhythm, and intonation patterns. Unlike most normally developing youngsters, many psychotic and mentally retarded children are overselective in responding to complex stimuli. They respond to only a narrow range or a single dimension of complex social stimuli. When presented with a written word, for example, they may pay attention to only one letter or even to an irrelevant mark on the paper. An autistic child may learn to recognize his father only when the father is wearing his glasses, because the glasses are all the child has really paid attention to.

Since the early 1970s, researchers have suspected that overselectivity accounts for many psychotic and retarded youngsters' learning problems. As a consequence of overselectivity they learn relatively little from ordinary instruction, and they are usually handicapped in social situations because they do not recognize people or pick up the nuances of social intercourse. They may fail to make the critical associations required for learning appropriate affect and for learning to respond to social rewards (Dunlap, Koegel, & Burke, 1981; Gersten, 1983; Koegel et al., 1982; Lovaas, Koegel, & Schreibman, 1979). Overselective attention to a single dimension of spoken language, such as the content or intonation of speech, may be the basis for nonverbal and echolalic children's difficulties in language learning (Schreibman, Kohlenberg, & Britten, 1986).

To learn from instruction, an overselective child needs special teaching procedures. Procedures may include repeated exposure to multiple cues, overtraining, interspersing reinforced and unreinforced training trials, carefully constructed prompts that are intrinsic to the stimuli to be discriminated, equivalence training that shifts discriminations from objects to photographs to line drawings, or some combination of these procedures. (For further explanation, see Dunlap et al., 1981; Hedbring & Newsom, 1985; Koegel et al., 1982; and Rincover, 1978b).

Language Disorders: Muteness and Echolalia

Most autistically withdrawn children exhibit severe language disorders (Rutter & Schopler, 1987). A high proportion of children diagnosed as autistic are mute; approximately 50 percent have no functional oral language. Many are echolalic, parroting back whatever they hear. Their echolalia may be immediate or delayed. Psychotic children's speech often seems mechanical and monotonous, without appropriate patterns of stress or intonation. Some psychotic youngsters refer to themselves in the third person, using *he* for *I*, for example, or *her* for *me*. Some profoundly withdrawn children are neither mute nor echolalic, but have no functional language, as their speech consists of random jargon or **neologisms** that cannot be used for meaningful communication. A few very withdrawn children (seldom considered autistic) are electively mute (see Chapter 16).

Psychotic children seem to exhibit more echolalia in unfamiliar settings and with unfamiliar persons (Charlop, 1986). Unquestionably, autistically withdrawn children's language problems represent an extreme detriment to social development. Because language is a primary vehicle for social interaction, some researchers have gone so far as to suggest that severe language deficiency is the necessary and sufficient cause underlying the behavior that characterizes autistic and schizophrenic children (see Churchill, 1978).

Many mute and echolalic children can learn functional language skills through operant conditioning. Operant procedures first teach the child a repertoire of motor and verbal imitations (this is not necessary with echolalic children, who already imitate excessively) and then transfer control of those responses to appropriate social stimuli, such as the questions "What is this?" or "What is Bobby doing?" The language instruction is specific, highly structured, carefully sequenced, and constitutes many thousands of learning trials. The teacher reinforces each successive approximation of functional speech. The child is gradually taught longer sentences under more varied conditions. The ultimate goal is to generalize language skills to everyday circumstances (Devany et al., 1981; Dunlap et al., 1985; Lovaas, 1977, 1987; Schreibman et al., 1983).

Some autistic children do not acquire truly functional language under an operant training regimen, and training is extremely time-consuming in the face of slow progress. Manual signing (like that used by deaf persons) and simultaneous signing and spoken language have been tried. Carr, Binkoff, Kiloginsky, and Edd (1978) taught four autistic children to use manual signs for common objects, but found that even though the children said the names of the words during the manual communication training, three of the four children apparently learned nothing about oral language from their training; they responded only to the visual stimuli. Carr (1979) concludes that simultaneous communication training (signing and talking) does not seem likely to be successful in getting mute children to talk. Children who have good skills in verbal imitation, however, show gains in speech following simultaneous communication training. Other researchers (Konstantareas, Webster, & Oxman, 1979) have found that training in simultaneous communication has improved not only communication skills but behavior in other areas as well, but further research is needed about the value and limitations of manual signing and simultaneous communication with psychotic children.

A promising alternative to typical operant training is what Koegel calls a "Natural Language Teaching Paradigm" (Koegel et al., 1987), using social learning principles to make teaching more closely approximate the interactions that take place in normal language learning. Koegel compared the natural language paradigm to the more typical operant (analogue) approach in an experimental study. Table 18.1 shows how the two instructional programs differ. The natural language paradigm resulted in more imitative responses and greater generalization of language learning. More natural language interactions in instructional programs appear promising and are consistent with recent research in language development (cf. Butler, 1986).

Excessive Fantasy and Delusions

Fantasy is a private activity that must be inferred from what people do—how they behave, pictures they draw, or what they say. Undeniably, fantasy is characteristic of emotional health and behavioral normality. When fantasy dominates thought and interferes with ongoing behavior and reality-oriented demands, however, it represents pathological withdrawal. Excessive, debilitating fantasy (which could be considered covert or cognitive self-stimulation) is sometimes evident in the extremely withdrawn individual. Thomas's case in Chapter 7 illustrates delusional behavior. Delusional thinking is rare in children, but they are sometimes convinced of the reality of their fantasies or the delusions of other people (Milby et al., 1983; Simonds & Glenn, 1976).

Some psychotic children cannot tell the difference between fantasy and reality. They may engage in wild fantasies during play, and therapists often attempt to use the fantasies to help children "work through emotional conflicts" (see Wundheiler, 1976). The case of Wanda illustrates the extent to which psychotic children can become

TABLE 18.1

Differences Between the Analogue and the Natural Language Paradigm Conditions

	Analogue Condition	NLP Condition
Stimulus items	a. Chosen by clinician b. Repeated until criterion is met c. Phonologically easy to produce, irrespective of whether they were functional in the natural environment	a. Chosen by child b. Varied every few trials c. Age-appropriate items that can be found in child's natural environment
Prompts	a. Manual (e.g., touch tip of tongue, or hold lips together)	a. Clinician repeats item
Interaction	a. Clinician holds up stimulus item; stimulus item not functional within interaction	a. Clinician and child play with stimulus item (i.e., stimulus item is functional within interaction)
Response	a. Correct responses or successive approximations reinforced	a. Looser shaping contingency so that attempts to respond verbally (except self-stimulation) are also reinforced
Consequences	a. Edible reinforcers paired with social reinforcers	a. Natural reinforcer (e.g., opportunity to play with the item) paired with social reinforcers

From "A Natural Language Teaching Paradigm for Nonverbal Autistic Children" by R. L. Koegel, M. C. O'Dell, and L. C. Koegel, 1987, *Journal of Autism and Developmental Disorders, 17,* p. 191. Copyright © 1987 by Plenum. Reprinted by permission.

caught up in their fantasies, which makes them relatively inaccessible to teaching. Note the frustration of Wanda's teacher.

Wanda

I was aware, of course, that emotionally disturbed children sometimes have wild fantasies, but I was not prepared for Wanda. Wanda was 11 years old when I met her. She had a tested IQ of about 160, but it didn't do her much good except, perhaps, to enrich her fantasy life. I was never able to find a topic of conversation, an area of the curriculum, a place, or a time that was free of her bizarre imaginings. She had fantasies about jeans—she "wore" special 40-pocket and 100-pocket jeans with zippers in the front and drew stylized pictures of them. She had fantasies about the president and the governor and crucifixes and *The Pit and the Pendulum,* doctors, nurses, swimming pools, toilets, injections, physical examinations..., moles (she had one on her arm that was a microphone into which she talked and one on her leg that was a thermostat controlling her body temperature)... there was no end.

When she engaged in her fantasies, Wanda got a peculiar, fixed grin on her face, her eyes became glazed, she giggled, and she talked (often apparently to herself) in a high-pitched, squeaky voice. Frequently, she drew pictures with captions representing fantasied objects and activities. Sometimes she engaged in other bizarre behaviors, such as flattening herself on the floor or wall, kissing it, caressing it, and talking to it. It was impossible to teach Wanda or to have a rational conversation with her while she was fantasizing, and she was "in" fantasy most of the time. It was impossible to predict when, during times of lucidity and reality-oriented behavior, she would suddenly enter her fantasy world again. (Patton et al., 1987, pp. 27–28)

Severely and profoundly disturbed children with high intelligence and verbal skills are relatively rare, but their cases provide grist for psychoanalytic interpreters. We know little about controlling children's maladaptive fantasies or delusions. Conjecture about treatment is usually based on research of children's other verbal behavior and adults' psychotic speech, obsessions, and delusions. Responding to a psychotic child's inappropriate fantasies probably merely reinforces and perpetuates the problem (see Kazdin, 1984; O'Leary & Wilson, 1975).

SELF-STIMULATION

Definition and Prevalence

We have already described the repetitive, stereotyped nature of self-stimulation. It can take an almost infinite variety of forms, such as staring blankly into space, body rocking, hand flapping, eye rubbing, lip licking, or repeating the same vocalization over and over. Depending on the *topography* (particular movements) of self-stimulation and the rate or intensity, it can result in physical injury; for example, eye rubbing at a high rate and pressure. It is sometimes difficult to know whether to consider a psychotic individual's behavior self-stimulation or self-injury. Koegel, Firestone, Kramme, and Dunlap's (1974) study illustrates the great variety this behavior may take. Table 18.2 also illustrates the diversity of self-stimulation that a given individual may exhibit. Control procedures with over 50 different forms or topographies of self-stimulation have been studied (LaGrow & Repp, 1984).

Self-stimulation is apparently a way to obtain self-reinforcing or self-perpetuating sensory feedback. It is not likely to stop for long unless demands for other incompatible responses are made or it is actively suppressed. This appears to be true of psychotic or retarded individuals' self-stimulation, as well as for some self-stimulatory behavior (such as nail biting) of ordinary people. As Sroufe, Steucher, and Stutzer (1975) suggest, we could probably find some form of self-stimulation in everyone's behavior, varying only in subtlety, social appropriateness, and rate. It is a pervasive characteristic of normally developing infants, and nearly everyone engages in higher rates of self-stimulatory behavior when bored or tired. Thus, like most behaviors, self-stimulation is considered normal or pathological depending on its social context and rate.

Epstein et al. (1985) find different levels of self-stimulation, ranging from low-level motor behaviors (rocking, spinning, hand flapping) to higher level behaviors that apparently have more cognitive content (echolalia, preoccupation with spelling

TABLE 18.2

Complete List of Self-stimulatory Responses for Subject 1 and Subject 2

Subject 1
1. Eye crossing
2. Finger manipulations (moving the hands with continuous flexion and extension)
3. Repetitive vocalizations (excluding recognizable words)
4. Feet contortions (tight sustained flexions)
5. Leg contortions (tight sustained flexions)
6. Rhythmic manipulation of objects (repeatedly rubbing, rotating, or tapping objects with fingers)
7. Grimacing (corners of mouth drawn out and down, revealing the upper set of teeth)
8. Staring or gazing (a fixed glassy-eyed look lasting more than 3 seconds)
9. Hands repetitively rubbing mouth
10. Hands repetitively rubbing face
11. Mouthing of objects (holding nonedible objects in contact with the mouth)
12. Locking hands behind head
13. Hands pressing on or twisting ears

Subject 2
1. Staring or gazing (a fixed glassy-eyed look lasting more than 3 seconds)
2. Grimacing (corners of mouth drawn out and down, revealing the upper set of teeth)
3. Hand waving vertically or horizontally with fingers outstretched in front of eyes
4. Hands vigorously and repetitively rubbing eyes
5. Hands vigorously and repetitively rubbing nose
6. Hands vigorously and repetitively rubbing mouth
7. Hands vigorously and repetitively rubbing ears
8. Hands vigorously and repetitively rubbing hair
9. Hands vigorously and repetitively rubbing clothes
10. Hands vigorously and repetitively rubbing objects
11. Hand flapping in air
12. Hand wringing (hands alternately rubbing and clutching each other)
13. Finger contortions (tight sustained flexions)
14. Tapping fingers against part of body or an object
15. Tapping whole hand against part of body or object
16. Mouthing of objects (holding nonedible objects in contact with the mouth)
17. Rocking (moving the trunk at the hips rhythmically back and forth or from side to side)
18. Head weaving (moving head from side to side in a figure-eight pattern)
19. Body contortions (sustained flexions or extensions of the torso)
20. Repetitive vocalizations (excluding recognizable words)
21. Teeth clicking (audibly and rapidly closing teeth together)
22. Tongue rolling and clicking
23. Audible saliva swishing in mouth
24. Repetitive tapping feet on floor
25. Repetitive tapping toes inside shoes (visible through canvas tennis shoes)
26. Leg contortions (tight sustained flexions)
27. Repetitive knocking knees against each other
28. Repetitive knocking ankles against each other
29. Tensing legs and suspending feet off the ground
30. Head shaking (rapid small movements from side to side)
31. Tensing whole body and shaking

From "Increasing Spontaneous Play by Suppressing Self-stimulation in Autistic Children" by R. L. Koegel, P. B. Firestone, K. W. Kramme, and G. Dunlap, 1974, *Journal of Applied Behavior Analysis, 7*, p. 523. Copyright 1974 by Society for the Experimental Analysis of Behavior, Inc. Reprinted by permission.

or numbers). In autistically withdrawn children, self-stimulation is often low level, socially inappropriate, and exhibited at such high rates that the children engage in few other pursuits.

It is hard to estimate the prevalence of self-stimulation, because it is difficult to define it precisely and because it takes so many different forms. The rate and type of self-stimulation are also likely to change as a function of treatment and environmental conditions (Epstein et al., 1985; Runco, Charlop, & Schreibman, 1986). Among psychotic youngsters, self-stimulation is common; it is one of the defining characteristics of infantile autism, but it is frequently seen in other psychotic and retarded individuals.

Causal Factors and Prevention

What factors cause children to become pathological self-stimulators are a topic of conjecture with no conclusive evidence to support any of the speculation. Among the various schools of thought, two now receive the majority of attention—neurobiological and perceptual reinforcement. The neurobiological school suggests that stereotyped behavior such as self-stimulation is primarily a result of anatomical or neurochemical abnormalities (or both) (Lewis et al., 1987). The perceptual reinforcement school argues that self-stimulation is acquired and maintained because of the sensory consequences it produces; it results in powerful perceptual reinforcement (Lovaas et al., 1987; Newsom & Lovaas, 1987). The perceptual reinforcement hypothesis has clearer implications for teachers, because it is based on research that links causal factors and intervention procedures.

Prevention of pathological self-stimulation presents many difficult problems. Self-stimulation is typical behavior for normally developing infants and older individuals under various conditions. Pathological self-stimulation is such a common feature of individuals with severe developmental disabilities that to pinpoint biological causes and prevent them appear impossible. Thus realistic prevention efforts are directed at providing environments in which developmentally disabled individuals have ample alternatives for obtaining perceptual reinforcement and using teaching procedures that encourage higher level, more appropriate forms of self-stimulation or perceptual reinforcement.

Assessment

Assessment of self-stimulation requires direct observation and behavior recording in various contexts. Ratings and subjective judgments of the level or appropriateness of self-stimulation may be helpful but are not an adequate substitute for direct observation, which indicates more precisely if and how self-stimulation is changing (see Dunlap et al., 1985; Koegel et al., 1982). It is particularly important to evaluate the environment to see whether inappropriate self-stimulation is encouraged by the absence of alternatives; the environment should offer adequate sensory stimulation for appropriate conduct (Runco et al., 1986).

Intervention and Education

Self-stimulation is inversely related to autistic children's learning and appropriate play—when self-stimulation increases, learning and appropriate play decrease (Epstein et al., 1985; Koegel & Covert, 1972; Koegel et al., 1974). If children engage in high rates of self-stimulation, their self-stimulation must be brought under control so they can learn new skills and adopt more acceptable behaviors.

Treatment of self-stimulation often requires highly intrusive, directive teaching procedures. Many procedures have been researched, among them using self-stimulation or alternative sensory stimulation as a reinforcer for appropriate behavior, sensory extinction, overcorrection, and a variety of other aversive consequences.

Self-stimulation apparently serves a variety of functions, including reinforcement. Thus, creative researchers have sometimes used opportunity to engage in self-stimulation as a reinforcing consequence for correct responses to training tasks or other appropriate behavior (Wolery et al., 1985). Rincover, Newsom, Lovaas, and Koegel (1977) used various types of sensory stimulation (music, flickering light, a windshield wiper) as reinforcement for a simple motor response. What type of sensory stimulation served as an effective reinforcer was idiosyncratic for a particular child, and making small changes in the stimuli (to avoid satiation) helped maintain a child's responding for long periods. The sensory stimuli appeared to function similarly to self-stimulation and might be effective reinforcers in therapeutic work or teaching.

Sensory extinction is based on the hypothesis that removing the sensory consequences will extinguish self-stimulation. For example, if a child spins a plate on hard surfaces and the self-stimulation is maintained by its auditory consequences (the noise made by the spinning plate), then carpeting the surfaces where the child spins the plate should prevent the auditory consequences and extinguish the behavior. If spinning the plate is reinforced by its visual consequences, however, then blindfolding the child should prevent the consequences and extinguish the behavior. Self-stimulation has been successfully reduced through sensory extinction procedures tailored for the individual child (e.g., Maag, Wolchik, Rutherford, & Parks, 1986; Rincover, 1978a; Rincover, Cook, Peoples, & Packard, 1979).

Azrin and his colleagues (Azrin, Kaplan, & Foxx, 1973; Foxx & Azrin, 1973; Foxx & Bechtel, 1983; Foxx & Livesay, 1984) devised overcorrection or autism reversal. They noted that self-stimulation has been suppressed through punishment (for example, slaps, shock), medication (for example, Thorazine), and reinforcement for non-self-stimulatory behavior, but that in each case the methods were ineffective with some children, had only temporary effects, or required very painful stimuli. Hence, they sought a method that has general application, is quick and powerful, and inflicts a minimum of pain.

Overcorrection is the technique of requiring the child who self-stimulates to practice a more correct mode of behavior under the direction of the teacher or therapist for a specific period of time. In a sense, it requires the child to "overcorrect" a behavioral error. The child who self-stimulates by flapping hands or flicking fingers may be required, when observed performing these responses, to perform "functional" hand exercises. The exercises, performed for a period of time under the teacher's direction, are different hand movements from those used in self-stimulation. The original overcorrection procedures were enforced for five to ten minutes; more recent research suggests that in some cases, overcorrection that lasts only 20 or 30 seconds is as effective as longer periods (Maag, Rutherford, Wolchik, & Parks, 1986).

Overcorrection involves several components, one of which is a verbal warning to stop the self-stimulatory behavior before requiring the corrective movement (see

Foxx & Bechtel, 1983). Wells, Forehand, and Hickey (1977) found that stern verbal warnings alone were effective in suppressing two children's self-stimulation. The warnings did not result in either child's increasing appropriate play, but positive practice overcorrection not only suppressed both children's self-stimulation, but increased one child's appropriate play.

Researchers have experimented with a variety of other aversive consequences for self-stimulation, including sharp verbal reprimands, unpleasant odors (ammonia fumes held under the nose), tastes (lemon juice or vinegar in the mouth), tactile sensations (water mist on the face), facial screening (putting a towel over the face), and unpleasant sounds (distortion in recorded music) (see Bailey, 1983; LaGrow & Repp, 1984). Procedures that were considered only mildly aversive (water mist or a towel on the face) were sometimes effective in reducing self-stimulation (Friman, Cook, & Finney, 1984; Horton, 1987). Kern, Koegel, and Dunlap (1984) obtained reductions in self-stimulation following 15-minute periods of vigorous exercise (jogging).

The best method of self-stimulation control varies according to the individual. Intervention in self-stimulation is not always justified; for some, reducing self-stimulation may serve no therapeutic purpose. When self-stimulation does not result in physical injury or deformity, interfere significantly with learning, or prevent participation in normal activities, then intervention may not be justified (O'Brien, 1981). Whether to intervene depends on the topography, rate, duration, and typical social consequences of the behavior.

SELF-INJURIOUS BEHAVIOR (SIB)

Definition and Prevalence

There are no more pitiable creatures than those who voraciously attack themselves. Until one has seen severe self-injurious behavior, it is difficult to grasp the human capacity for self-torture. Seeing a child battered by adults is somehow easier to believe than seeing a child who is self-brutalized. Ordinary human decency demands that we seek the causes and cures of self-injurious behavior. Unfortunately, current knowledge is limited, and some effective control techniques are abhorrent to those who find punishment of any kind for any reason morally unpalatable.

Types of Self-Injury

Some psychotic youngsters injure themselves repeatedly and deliberately in the most brutal fashion. We find this kind of SIB in individuals who are severely mentally retarded but not labeled psychotic, but it is a characteristic often associated with multiple disabilities—mental retardation *and* psychosis (see Zirpoli & Lloyd, 1987). These *atavistic* (primitive) behaviors take a variety of forms, but left unchecked, they share the consequence of bodily injury. Without physical restraint, or effective intervention, there is risk that the youngster will permanently disfigure, incapacitate, or kill himself or herself. This behavior may seem aggressive and suicidal, but it is unlike aggressive conduct disorder in that it arises from different causal factors, and unlike suicide or parasuicide in that it does not appear to be contemplated in the same way.

Self-Injury

The subject was a moderately retarded, 9-year-old autistic girl resident of. . ., a community-based, short-term residential treatment facility for seriously disturbed, developmentally disabled children. She had been referred for residential treatment because of severe self-injurious behavior and other autisticlike behaviors such as self-stimulation, poor social interaction, lack of speech and repetitive, nonmeaningful vocalizations. Her self-injurious behavior consisted of biting either hand or forearm. Previous care providers reported that self-biting resulted in skin lesions which became infected frequently and required medical attention. Additionally, it was reported that her arm had once been broken when a caretaker in another setting had attempted to restrain her intense self-biting behavior. Prior to her placement. . ., various nonrestrictive treatment strategies had been employed (e.g., edible positive reinforcement and response cost). These had not been effective in eliminating the self-injurious behavior. Outbursts of self-biting appeared to occur in response to verbal directives. In addition to arm biting, these intense temper outbursts included extremely loud, repetitive sequences of nonmeaningful vocalizations.

Journal of Behavior Therapy and Experimental Psychiatry, 15, A. Neufeld & J. W. Fantuzzo, "Contingent Application of a Protective Device to Treat the Severe Self-Biting Behavior of a Disturbed Autistic Child." Copyright 1984 by Pergamon Journals, Ltd.

These are only a few examples of specific self-injurious responses: youngsters may slap themselves or hit themselves with their fists; bang their heads against the wall, floor, or pieces of furniture; bite or chew themselves, perhaps biting their fingers, the backs of their hands, their arms, or their shoulders; pull out their hair, including eyebrows, eyelashes, and pubic hair; scratch themselves with their fingernails or sharp objects; stick sharp objects, such as pins and needles, into their skin, joints, eyes, or ears; slash themselves with sharp objects such as knives or razors; burn themselves with cigarettes; or ingest poisonous substances. Bachman (1972) noted the range in severity of various self-injurious behaviors.

The physical damage sustained by such behavior varies. Some individuals are "careful" and produce only minor lesions with few permanent consequences. Others, however, produce serious, permanent damage to themselves, such as blindness, loss of limb, severe bleeding, concussion, etc. These people are often physically restrained (for example, tied down to their beds) lest they produce further injury or kill themselves. As soon as their restraints are removed, the [self-injurious behavior] begins. . . . Very little other behavior is observed in these chronic self-injurers. (p. 212)

The amazing and deviant aspects of SIB are its rate, intensity, and persistence. Normally developing children and ordinary adults sometimes perform some of the behaviors listed above; perhaps 10 percent of young, nonhandicapped children under the age of five engage occasionally in self-injurious behavior (cf. Zirpoli & Lloyd, 1987). It is considered normal, for example, for young children in fits of temper to bang their heads or hit themselves, for older children to play by pushing pins under the callouses on their hands, for women to pluck out some of the hairs of their eyebrows, and for adults to drink alcohol. Nondeviants' self-directed acts are performed seldom enough and gently enough so that incapacitation, early death, or permanent disfigurement are highly improbable. Deviant self-injury, however, occurs so frequently and is of such intensity and duration that the youngster cannot develop normal social relationships or learn self-care skills and is in danger of becoming even more severely disabled.

We do not know the prevalence of self-injury among psychotic youngsters. Part of the problem in establishing prevalence estimates is the overlap in mental retardation and childhood psychosis; another problem is that self-stimulation, self-injury, and other stereotypic movement disorders may be confused. The only statement about prevalence that we can make with much confidence is that SIB is quite common among youngsters diagnosed as autistic.

Causal Factors and Prevention

Psychodynamic, biological, and social learning etiologies of self-injury have been suggested. Psychoanalytic formulations of the causes of SIB cannot be scientifically confirmed and offer no effective treatment (see Lovaas, 1982; Schroeder, Schroeder, Rojahn, & Mulick, 1981).

Evidence indicates that SIB could in some cases be a result of deficiencies in biochemicals required for normal brain functioning, inadequate development of the central nervous system, early experiences of pain and isolation, sensory problems, insensitivity to pain, or the body's ability to produce opiatelike substances in response to pain or injury. But no single biological explanation is now supported by research (Cataldo & Harris, 1982; Zirpoli & Lloyd, 1987).

Biological factors need not, and probably do not, operate independently of social factors in causing SIB. Perhaps in many cases biological factors cause initial self-injury, but social learning factors exacerbate and maintain the problem (see deCatanzaro, 1978; Demchak & Halle, 1985; Edelson, Taubman, & Lovaas, 1983; Kety, 1979). Self-injury, like other types of behavior, may be reinforced by social attention. This notion has important implications for intervention. Nonbehavioral approaches offer few specific and effective suggestions for managing truly atavistic children; for this reason, the literature consists primarily of behavior modification and social learning studies (see Schroeder, et al., 1981; Zirpoli & Lloyd, 1987).

Social learning analyses of the causes of SIB remain speculative. Social learning interventions appear to be more effective than drugs (e.g., Luiselli, 1985; Singh & Millichamp, 1985), and other treatment alternatives (such as psychotherapy or psychosurgery) are typically ineffective or infeasible. Yet there is no direct evidence that social learning causes SIB, and for obvious ethical reasons, SIB cannot be experimentally induced merely to demonstrate its origins. Social learning analyses do suggest that reinforcement may exacerbate and maintain self-injury, even when the reinforcement is positive, as when a self-injurious child obtains solicitous attention. Experimental studies show that for some children, adult attention reinforces SIB; when attention has been withdrawn contingent upon SIB, self-injury has been extinguished (see Lovaas, 1982).

Carr, Newsom, and Binkoff (1976) suggested that SIB may sometimes be induced or maintained by negative reinforcement—escape from an aversive circumstance. They observed that some children appear to use SIB as a means of getting adults to withdraw demands for performance, which the children experience as aversive. That is, when presented with a task that demands their attention and performance, these children begin to injure themselves; the demands are then withdrawn. The social interaction and attention involved in teaching and learning is reinforcing for some children, and withdrawal of attention contingent upon SIB is an effective extinction or punishment procedure. The same type of interaction and attention is apparently aversive for other children, and withdrawal of attention contingent upon SIB is negatively reinforcing for them; it makes the problem worse instead of better.

For each case, the factors that cause and maintain SIB must be analyzed as carefully as possible; otherwise, effective interventions cannot be devised. At this point, interventions based on behavior principles or social learning theory are the only feasible alternatives for educators.

Assessment

Assessment of self-injury is at once straightforward and complex. It is straightforward in that assessment involves direct observation and measurement; that is, self-injurious behaviors should be defined, observed, and recorded daily in the different environments in which they occur. It is complex in that the causes are not well understood, and care must be taken to eliminate possible biological and subtle environmental causes. In some cases, SIB is a direct result of metabolic disorder, as in **Lesch-Nyhan syndrome** (see Ball, Datta, Rios, & Constantine, 1985; Zirpoli & Lloyd, 1987). Possible biological causes, including genetic anomalies and factors such as ear infections and sensory deficits, must be assessed. SIB may occur more often in some environments than in others, and a change in environmental conditions (such as demands for performance) may dramatically alter the problem (Edelson et al., 1983). It is thus important to assess the quality of the youngster's surroundings and social environment as well as the behavior itself, and it is particularly important to assess the social consequences.

Intervention and Education

Intervention in SIB has included physical restraint, drugs, extraction of teeth, psychosurgery, psychotherapy, and a variety of behavior modification techniques. Because other techniques for controlling severe atavistic behavior have failed so miserably, we will discuss only those based on behavioral or social learning principles. The most common and most effective methods involve reinforcement of noninjurious behavior and punishment of SIB.

For practical purposes, clinical and educational interventions in SIB tend to be the same. SIB is typically incompatible with learning other, more adaptive behavior. It must be controlled in the classroom and other settings if the youngster is to be helped to learn new skills. To obtain generalized improvement, control procedures must be implemented not only in the classroom but in other settings such as the home.

Reinforcement of noninjurious behavior is an important component of nearly all procedures for reducing SIB. In some cases, it is sufficient merely to use extinction of SIB in combination with reinforcement of noninjurious behavior—to remove the social attention that typically follows SIB. In other cases, however, punishment produces better results. Punishment may take the form of time out, response cost, overcorrection, or presentation of aversive consequences. Aversive consequences can take many forms, including slaps, shouts, or water mist in the face (see Lovaas, 1982; Zirpoli & Lloyd, 1987). When using punishment procedures, one must carefully adhere to guidelines that protect the youngster from abuse (see Chapter 13).

Researchers are constantly seeking more effective and humane treatments for SIB. Some have found that simply preventing SIB from occurring, encouraging alternate forms of sensory feedback, altering the sensory feedback it produces, or self-control procedures are effective. Azrin, Besalel, and Wisotzek (1982) reduced SIB by reinforcing appropriate behavior combined with brief interruptions of self-injury (holding the child's hands or arms for a couple of minutes when SIB was attempted, for example). Favell, McGimsey, and Schell (1982) successfully reduced SIB by providing toys, objects, or food that children could use for noninjurious self-stimulation and play. Rincover and Devany (1982) used a sensory extinction procedure with several young children. A child who banged his head, for example, was fitted with a padded helmet, and a girl who scratched her face was required to wear thin rubber gloves. These procedures prevented the children from obtaining the usual sensory feedback from their SIB and were, combined with reinforcement for appropriate behavior, successful in reducing self-injury to a low level. As a follow-up to Rincover and Devany's sensory extinction procedures, Neufeld and Fantuzzo (1984, 1987) fitted severely self-injurious individuals with clear plastic bubble helmets designed to minimally restrict vision, hearing, and vocalizations and that therapists or teachers could quickly fit and remove. The helmets prevented self-injury of various kinds, such as biting and head hitting. Using the helmet in conjunction with positive reinforcement of appropriate behavior effectively reduced SIB and allowed placement in less restrictive settings. Osborne, Kiburz, and Miller (1986), working with a severely behaviorally disordered 15-year-old boy in a resource room and math and English classes, used self-control techniques to decrease self-injury. The boy frequently hit himself in the face with a closed fist and engaged in other aberrant behaviors. Showing him videotapes of his behavior and giving him graphic feedback on the number of times he hit himself reduced his SIB.

SUMMARY

We define psychotic behavior to include distorted interpretations of the self or the environment and seriously deviant behavior that is incompatible with normal development. Three types of psychotic behavior are autistic withdrawal, self-stimulation, and self-injury. The prevalence of psychotic behavior is difficult to determine because exhibiting psychotic behavior is not the same as receiving a clinical diagnosis of "psychotic." The causes of psychotic behavior are not known except in rare cases, although biological factors are suspected. Prevention consists mainly of efforts to manage psychotic behavior once it emerges. Assessment demands comprehensive evaluation with data from many sources. The most useful assessment information for teachers derives from direct observation of psychotic behavior under a variety of environmental conditions, as the behavior is typically sensitive to environmental changes that teachers can effect.

The most effective current interventions are behavioral. Intensive early intervention using behavioral methods may help children to learn successfully in mainstream environments; an increasing percentage (perhaps 50 percent as opposed to 10 percent or less without intensive early behavioral intervention) may even recover from autism and other severe disorders. We need behavioral research with more practical implications for teachers, along with research into methods for teaching basic life skills to adolescents and adults.

Unresponsiveness to social stimuli usually requires instruction in basic social skills. Highly directive, consistent, intrusive teaching procedures have been used, but recent research focuses on finding more natural, less intrusive, and less aversive methods. Overcoming gaze aversion through prompts, imitation, and reinforcement may be required before other behaviors can be taught successfully. Overselective responding refers to the tendency to learn from only a very narrow range of stimuli or a single element of a complex stimulus. Overselectivity may be an underlying problem in learning language and other social skills. Systematic operant conditioning procedures may be successful in teaching basic language skills to children who are mute or echolalic. Alternatives to the usual operant training are being sought. A natural language teaching approach, in which teaching procedures more closely approximate natural interactions, appears promising. Treatment of excessive fantasy and delusions of psychotic children is based on intervention with adults' psychotic speech, obsessions, and delusions.

Self-stimulation consists of repetitive, stereotyped acts that seem to provide reinforcing sensory feedback. High rates of self-stimulation are incompatible with learning and may result in self-injury. Two leading hypotheses attribute the cause to neurobiological factors and perceptual reinforcement. Adequate assessment of self-stimulation requires evaluating the behavior under various environmental conditions, because the behavior is typically sensitive to environmental changes. Intervention in self-stimulation consists of behavior modification methods such as sensory extinction and overcorrection.

Self-injurious behavior is seen in many psychotic and retarded individuals; its causes may be biochemical or environmental or both. As with self-stimulation, assessing self-injury demands evaluation of the environment as well as the behavior itself; and, as with self-stimulation, effective interventions are behavioral. Common interventions include reinforcement of noninjurious behavior, mild punishment, and sensory extinction.

PART FIVE

Implications:
A Beginning
Point

19

A Personal Statement

M y purpose in this chapter is to discuss what I consider the primary considerations in educating children and youth with behavior disorders. These include definition and measurement of behavior; causal factors and the teacher's role; essential experiences of work, play, love, and fun; communication, directness, and honesty; modeling and self-control; and finally, a look at the past to predict the future.

In previous chapters I have concentrated on the characteristics of disordered behavior; I now focus on the amelioration or resolution of behavior problems. These comments are only a preface or brief orientation to educational methodology, and they are based primarily on the research findings summarized in other sections of the text. Kerr and Nelson (1983) and Kerr et al. (1987) give details of educational methods and behavior management that are consistent with my orientation.

DEFINITION AND MEASUREMENT OF BEHAVIOR

Defining and classifying behavior disorders are persistent problems—problems that appear to defy a truly satisfactory resolution. The intractability of defining and classifying youngsters' behavior *disorders* does not, fortunately, preclude useful definition and measurement of behavior. The teacher of disturbed youngsters can define and measure precisely the behaviors that bring children and youth into conflict with others. Indeed, the teacher who cannot or will not pinpoint and measure the relevant behaviors of the students he or she is teaching is probably not going to be very effective. As we have seen in previous chapters, disturbed students are considered to need help primarily because they exhibit behavioral excesses or deficiencies. Not to define precisely and to measure these behavioral excesses and deficiencies, then, is a fundamental error; it is akin to the malpractice of a nurse who decides not to measure vital signs (heart rate, respiration rate, temperature, and blood pressure), perhaps arguing that he or she is too busy, that subjective estimates of vital signs are quite adequate, that vital signs are only superficial estimates of the patient's health, or that vital signs do not signify the nature of the underlying pathology. The teaching profession is dedicated to the task of changing behavior demonstrably for the better. What can one say, then, of educational practice that does not include precise definition and reliable measurement of the behavior change induced by the teacher's methodology? *It is indefensible*. Measurement need not be sophisticated to be extremely valuable. Vance's story illustrates this type of definition and measurement.

The technology of behavioral definition and measurement is readily available to teachers (Alberto & Troutman, 1986; Cooper et al., 1987; Haring, Lovitt, Eaton, & Hansen, 1978; Smith, 1984; Kerr & Nelson, 1983; Kerr et al., 1987; Lovitt, 1977). With relatively little investment of effort, the teacher can learn behavior measurement techniques and teach them to students (see Hallahan et al., 1983; Wallace & Kauffman, 1986). When students know how to define and measure their own behavior and the responses of those with whom they live, two additional benefits accrue: (1) the teacher is relieved of some of the mechanical aspects of teaching, and (2) the students have an opportunity to gain an extra degree of control over their own environments.

My suggestion is not that every behavior of every student should be measured, or that the teacher should become preoccupied with measurement to the exclusion

Vance

Vance was placed in Ms. Sullivan's class in mid-February. His progress in a self-contained classroom for the behavior disordered called for placement in the least restrictive environment, specifically the regular classroom. Ms. Sullivan is the type of teacher who provides a lot of structure for her students. She gives very clear directions, has rules for her classroom that she reviews with all the children and, most important, she provides consequences when students either follow or disobey those rules. She has a schedule that sets a brisk pace for instruction and activities throughout the school day. She is the type of teacher that multidisciplinary teams love to have as a resource for [behaviorally disordered] student placement. Vance was placed in her class for this reason. Vance is a very impulsive student who acts without thinking. He blurts out answers in class, speaks out of turn, and frequently jumps at answers before considering what might be the best response. Of course, he has many other problems, but Ms. Sullivan can tolerate his impulsiveness the least, and thus it is the first target for intervention. Ms. Sullivan has also determined when this problem is worst—during reading group instruction, when she simply can't tolerate interruptions. During this 20-minute period, she has counted Vance's interruptions and found that they occur about every two minutes (median number of interruptions: 12).

From "Methods of Instruction" by G. J. Williams, 1987, in *Assessing and Managing Behavior Disabilities*, N. G. Haring, Ed., pp. 287–288. Seattle: University of Washington Press.

of other crucial concerns. Teaching is much more than measurement. A mechanical approach to teaching that excludes affective concerns is no more justifiable than an approach that neglects cognitive and behavioral goals. If the student's most important behavioral characteristics are not monitored, however, then it will be almost impossible for the teacher to communicate anything of substance about the student's progress to the youngster or to anyone else.

The importance of behavioral measurement is demonstrated so clearly and frequently that one is prompted to ask why many teachers of disturbed students still do not measure their pupils' behavior. Measurement has probably been neglected for at least these reasons:

> There is a strong bias among special educators in support of theoretical models (such as psychodynamic or humanistic) that do not include direct measurement of behavior and, in fact, include the presumption that measurable responses are unimportant or a superficial aspect of psychopathology.
>
> Parents of disturbed students have placidly accepted less than adequate evidence of teachers' effectiveness as the best that the education profession can offer.
>
> Many teachers are still uninformed about the value of direct measurement of behavior or are untutored in the appropriate methodology.
>
> Some teachers are incompetent and negligent.
>
> Although measurement of behavior is invaluable for precise assessment of therapeutic effects, measurement is often not a prerequisite for behavioral change.
>
> Informal and subjective estimates of students' behavioral status, which include anecdotal records and statements such as "She is much improved this week"

without any objective data to back up the claim, give the impression that more precise measurement is unnecessary.

Admittedly, some qualitative or affective aspects of pupils' behavior and teachers' methodology cannot be measured directly, and these affective variables may be extremely important. I do not mean to imply that one should ignore everything that cannot be measured. But for a teacher of disturbed students not to ask "Exactly what is it this student does or does not do that is causing a problem?" and then not set about measuring the behavior in question as objectively and precisely as possible is unconscionable. Without direct measurement of behavior, the teacher risks being misled by subjective impressions of the student's responses and the effects of instructional and behavior management techniques. It is reasonable to expect that the teacher show objective and precise evidence of pupils' behavioral change as well as describe the quality of his or her relationship to students in more subjective and affective terms.

CAUSAL FACTORS AND THE ROLE OF THE TEACHER

The first or ultimate causes of behavior disorders almost always remain unknown. A realistic and productive approach is to consider contributing factors that may interact to cause disordered behavior. Contributing factors may be predisposing or precipitating; both increase the probability that a behavior disorder will occur under given circumstances. Precipitating factors may trigger a maladaptive response, given a set of predisposing variables. An important task of the teacher is to identify the contributing factors that account for the student's current behavioral status.

The focus of the special educator's concern should be on the contributing factors that the teacher can alter. Factors over which the teacher has no control may determine how the child or youth is approached initially, but the teacher of disturbed students is called upon to begin working with specific pupils after behavior disorders have appeared. The special educator has two primary responsibilities: first, to make sure that he or she does no further disservice to the student; and second, to manipulate the student's present environment to foster development of more appropriate behavior in spite of unalterable past and present circumstances. Emphasis must be on the present and future, not the past. And although other environments may be important, the teacher's focus must be on the classroom environment. Certainly teachers may profitably extend their influence beyond the classroom, perhaps working with parents to improve the home environment or using community resources for the child's benefit. But talk of influence beyond the classroom, including such high-sounding phrases as ecological management, is patent nonsense until the teacher has demonstrated that he or she can make the classroom environment conducive to improved behavior.

This is not to say that collaboration of school personnel with families and communities is unimportant. Comer's (1988) observations on working with troubled schools are timely: "We realized that no single group—parents, teachers, administrators, students—was at fault. We recognized that no single intervention—curriculum change, behavior modification method, physical environment improvement—would make a significant and sustained difference" (p. 38). Yet we must recognize that many teachers work under conditions in which administrators and consultants do not facilitate home-school or community-school ties. Teachers are often on their own, and the individual contribution they can make outside the classroom is limited.

The stance of the special educator, therefore, must be that behavior is predictable and controllable; in the case of disordered behavior, enough controlling factors can be found and changed in the classroom to produce a therapeutic result in that context. We cannot change the past, and the teacher cannot alter many of the contributing factors operating in the present. Educators must have faith that the proper classroom environment alone *can* make a difference in the student's life, even if nothing else can be altered. They must also hope that more than classroom environment can be changed and work toward that end.

I agree with the suggestion of Forness, Sinclair, and Russell (1984) that teachers must have the primary role in determining students' eligibility for special education and deciding how disturbed children and youth will be served. Teachers' tolerance for and knowledge of individual students' behavior in the context of their classrooms must become the ultimate criteria for deciding where a student can be educated appropriately (Gerber, 1988).

WORK, PLAY, LOVE, AND FUN

It does not take great wisdom to see that disturbed children and youth do not usually do productive work or know how to play, give and receive love, and have fun. Yet these four experiences—work, play, love, and fun—are nearly the essence of satisfying and meaningful existence. Education of disturbed students requires a curriculum that brings these essential experiences into sharp focus. This is not to imply that a curriculum must try to teach these experiences directly; in fact, someone who wishes to teach a youngster how to work, play, love, or have fun must have a curriculum with a content of useful specific skills, but the skills in themselves do not constitute essential life experiences. The vapid antics of "fun-seekers" and the desperate "play" of professional athletes illustrate the difficulty in apprehending fun and play through concentrated effort alone. Relations among events—the structure of experience as well as events themselves—teach a person to work, play, love, and enjoy.

The teacher's primary task is to structure or order the environment for the pupil in such a way that work is accomplished, play is learned, love is felt, and fun is enjoyed—by the student and the teacher. The teacher does not provide structure and order by allowing the student complete freedom to choose what to do. Disturbed youngsters are in difficulty because they make unguided and unfortunate choices about how to conduct themselves. One must make value judgments as to what a student should learn. Hobbs (1974, p. 156) writes, "A child simply must know how to read, write, spell, and do arithmetic, and it is good for him to know how to hit a ball, to play a guitar, to scull a canoe, to lash a table, and to travel by bus across town." The teacher must have confidence in his or her own judgment about what is good for the youngster to learn and how the student should behave, or effective structuring of the student's environment is impossible. This does not mean the teacher should determine every skill the pupil learns or every way of behaving. The point is not to make students mindlessly conform to ridiculous behavioral standards, but to require a reasonable standard of conduct and learning that will allow them greater personal choice and fulfillment in a free society.

Besides the value judgments and difficult decisions one must make about what to teach disturbed children and youth, questions remain as to how to best arrange the teaching environment. Two fundamental principles guide the organization of an effective teaching environment: choosing tasks that are appropriate for the pupil (tasks that are at the right level and at which the student can usually succeed), and arranging appropriate consequences for performance. One does not learn work, play, love, and fun through failure, but through success and mastery. We do not learn pride, dignity, self-worth, and other attributes of good mental health by having our wishes immediately gratified, but by struggling to overcome difficulties, meeting requirements, and finding that our own efforts will achieve desired goals.

We cannot depend on disturbed youngsters to learn by some magical, mysterious, internally guided process; their learning will be assured only by a skillful and sensitive adult who makes the expectations for their behavior appropriately difficult. Hobbs (1974) describes the appropriate level of expectation as the "Principle of Just Manageable Difficulties." The "J.M.D. Principle" is that people are most well adjusted or in the best mental health when they choose for themselves problems or tasks that are just about, but not quite, insurmountable.

> Part of the art of choosing difficulties is to select those that are indeed just manageable. If the difficulties chosen are too easy, life is boring; if they are too hard, life is defeating. The trick is to choose trouble for oneself in the direction of what he would like to become at a level of difficulty close to the edge of his competence. When one achieves this fine tuning of his life, he will know zest and joy and deep fulfillment. (Hobbs, 1974, p. 165)

The teacher's task is to choose at first just manageable tasks for disturbed students, then gradually allow them to set their own goals as they become attuned to their true capabilities and desires.

Ample evidence indicates that the order in which events are structured has a profound influence on students' learning—specifically, that making highly preferred events (play) contingent or dependent upon less preferred events (such as work) improves the individual's work performance (cf. Bandura, 1986; Haring & Phillips, 1962; Hewett, 1968; Lovitt, 1977). The expectation "work before play (or pay)" is a fundamental principle of behavior modification. An environment in which rewards and privileges (beyond those that are everyone's right) are gratis is stultifying. "Earning your way," on the other hand, builds self-esteem. Rothman (1970), who worked with disturbed and delinquent girls in New York City, comments on the value of work and pay:

> If I had my way, all children in school would work and be paid for the work they do. If the work of children is to learn, then children should be paid for learning. Money is a powerful motivator. I daresay that truancy might decrease and that more children would learn, even those children who have been relegated to the substratum of the nonachiever, if they were paid for services rendered. Someday,

> I would like a fund to pay girls for increasing their reading and arithmetic skills. Supposing I could say to a girl, "You increased your reading from fourth grade to fifth. You have earned five dollars." How great! If only we could do it. (p. 211)

It *can* be done, if not with money, then with special privileges, goods, or services that are meaningful to the child. The fundamental principle underlying a token economy is payment of a fair wage for work. Rothman (1970) also notes one of the usual outcomes of work: "Pride—an essential personal ingredient. All the girls who work find it" (p. 232).

I will not be so presumptuous as to try to define play, love, or fun; a definition of work—purposeful and necessary expenditure of effort to achieve a desired goal—is daring enough. Suffice to say that for the emotionally healthy individual, work, play, love, and fun are inextricably intertwined, and for the emotionally disturbed person, they are unrelated or unattainable. When a youngster's behavior has become disordered, the most effective strategy for restoring a "vital balance" or "zest, joy, and deep fulfillment" is to provide appropriate work and consistent consequences for performance. Play, love, and fun are likely to follow the experience of accomplishing a valued task and earning a reward by one's own labor. To work is to build a sound basis for self-esteem.

COMMUNICATION, DIRECTNESS, AND HONESTY

Some advocates of a structured approach and some behavior modification enthusiasts imply that consistent consequences for behavior alone will be enough to bring about therapeutic change in disturbed children and youth. Teaching is more than just providing a structured relationship among events, however. How the environment is arranged may be as important as the structure itself in determining the outcome for the student.

How one listens and talks to students will have an effect on their perceptions and their responses to other environmental events. In describing the consequences of behavior, for example, the teacher can emphasize either the positive or the negative aspects of an arrangement. A teacher may say, "You may not go to recess until your math is finished." Another teacher might phrase it, "You may go to recess as soon as you finish your math." Whereas both teachers have described the response-consequence relationship, and both statements are equally correct, the second draws attention to the positive consequences of appropriate performance, and the first to the negative results of nonperformance. Each statement will obviously affect the student differently. Nonverbal communication, too, is important and should be consistent with what is said. To be therapeutic, teachers must listen, talk, and act in ways that communicate respect, caring, and confidence, both in themselves and in their students.

It does not follow that the teacher must always communicate approval or positive regard for the student's behavior. In fact, the teacher of disturbed pupils must communicate disapproval with great clarity. We cannot expect a disturbed youngster to learn to behave appropriately if we respond to all behavior with approval or equanimity. Candor, including honest appraisal of inappropriate behavior, will serve the teacher of disturbed students well. Consistent follow-through with positive and negative consequences for desirable and undesirable behavior, combined with extremely clear communication of expectations, will be successful in managing most behavior problems. Recall Vance and his teacher, Ms. Sullivan. Ms. Sullivan was assisted by a consulting teacher, Mr. Nottingham. Together, they decided to implement a nonseclusionary time out procedure for Vance's interruptions. Vance would be sent to a chair outside the reading group for three minutes when he interrupted; there he would be ignored. When he was behaving appropriately, he would be praised, especially for waiting to be called on before talking. Continuing Vance's story, we can see the kind of directness, honesty, and consistency in applying consequences that serves all teachers well.

Communication is a two-way affair, and teachers of disturbed students will not be successful unless they learn to listen skillfully, to watch students' behavior with understanding, and to accurately interpret the relation between childrens' verbal and nonverbal behavior. Youngsters who do not believe they are being listened to will go to extreme lengths to make themselves understood, often getting into additional trouble by their efforts to establish communication. Rothman (1970) offers excep-

Follow-Through With Vance

Having decided upon this plan of action, on Tuesday morning Ms. Sullivan called Vance aside. She carefully told him what the target behavior was. "Vance, every time you interrupt our reading group by talking out when you haven't been called on, you are going to have to sit in this chair [she points to a chair next to the reading group area] for three minutes. At the end of the three-minute period, I will tell you to come back and join the group. In order to come back, though, you must be sitting quietly. If you are talking, or bugging other students, you will have to stay in time out until you are quiet. Every time you talk out, you will have to sit there for three minutes."

And so reading group instruction began. Ms. Sullivan was pleased when after about seven or eight minutes, she noted that Vance was obviously attempting to control his talk-outs. After about 12 minutes, however, Vance did blurt out, "Johnny, quit looking at me that way!" Ms. Sullivan immediately told Vance, "Vance, you can't talk out like that in class, go to that chair until I tell you to return to the group." Well, Vance didn't want to go—that was obvious from the look on his face—but slowly, he got up and went to sit in the chair. Ms. Sullivan went on with the group activity, not even looking in Vance's direction. She remembered what Mr. Nottingham had said about not paying any attention to the student in time out. To Ms. Sullivan's surprise, Vance sat quietly the entire three minutes. She made sure to actively engage all the other students' attention during that time so they wouldn't be tempted to look in Vance's direction. At the end of the three minutes, she said, "Vance, you're sitting quietly, you may return to the group." Vance walked to his seat, sat down, and participated in the group activity. Ms. Sullivan, remembering what Mr. Nottingham had said, praised him soon thereafter for sitting quietly and (most important) for waiting to be called on before talking. That day, Vance spoke out inappropriately only twice. The number of his inappropriate interruptions remained between one and three for the rest of the week.

From "Methods of Instruction" by G. J. Williams, 1987, in *Assessing and Managing Behavior Disabilities*, N. G. Haring, Ed., pp. 287–288. Seattle: University of Washington Press.

tionally clear and refreshing examples of how a teacher can communicate with disturbed students.

Directness in talking to disturbed children and youth facilitates communication. Many teachers and parents tend to be tentative, noncommittal, and obfuscatory in their conversations with disturbed youngsters, perhaps out of fear of rejecting or being rejected, or perhaps from the misguided notion that to help disturbed youngsters, one must never direct them. Disturbed youngsters do not profit from having to guess about adults' wishes or intentions. A few, in fact, will improve their behavior almost immediately if the teacher merely states clearly, forthrightly, and unequivocally how they are to behave.

Disturbed children are sure to test the teacher's honesty. Honesty is more than candor in expressing opinions and reporting facts accurately. The disturbed youngster wants to know whether teachers are as good as their word. A teacher who makes idle threats or fails to deliver positive consequences as promised will surely run afoul of disturbed students.

MODELING AND SELF-CONTROL

There is overwhelming evidence that children learn much through observing others' behavior (Bandura, 1986). Teachers whose own behavior is not exemplary may corrupt rather than help students, regardless of their finesse with other teaching strategies. To be blunt, teaching disturbed students is not an appropriate job for social misfits or the psychologically unstable. Imitating the teacher should lead to behavioral improvement, not to maladaptive conduct. Hobbs (1966) sums up the kind of model a teacher (in this example a teacher-counselor in Project Re-ED) should provide:

> But most of all a teacher-counselor is a decent adult; educated, well trained; able to give and receive affection, to live relaxed, and to be firm; a person with private resources for the nourishment and refreshment of his own life; not an itinerant worker but a professional through and through; a person with a sense of the significance of time, of the usefulness of today and the promise of tomorrow; a person of hope, quiet confidence, and joy; one who has committed himself to children and to the proposition that children who are emotionally disturbed can be helped by the process of re-education. (pp. 106–107)

A teacher of disturbed students should be a model of self-control. Not only should one model self-control; one should also teach through direct instruction. Every pupil, disturbed pupils included, should be allowed free choice and self-determination, for appropriate self-guidance is both inherent in the concept of individual rights and inimical to the loss of control that characterizes disordered behavior. This statement does not mean that disturbed students should always be allowed to behave as they will without interference, or that the teacher is always wrong to require a pupil to behave willy-nilly. Students should be allowed to choose for themselves how they will behave except when they choose to behave in ways that are self-defeating, ways that clearly are not in their best interests, or in ways that violate the rights of others. The teacher's role should be to structure the classroom environment so that the student is aware of options, can exercise choice in as many areas of behavior as possible, and is tutored in and rewarded for appropriate decisions. Students should be taught cognitive behavior modification techniques, such as self-instruction, rehearsal, and guided practice, to make them as self-sufficient as possible in controlling their own behavior. External control may be required at first to humanize the pupil, but the task of truly humanistic education is not completed until control is internalized to the greatest extent possible.

THE PAST

Textbooks often end with speculation about the future. I have chosen instead to comment on the past because I believe the best prediction of future developments derives from analysis of past events. In the past, we have seen an ebb and flow of concern for the plight of disturbed students and periods of progress and regression in effective intervention. Professionals have expressed enthusiasm for new methods and disillusionment when the solution turned out to be less than final. A solely legal-bureaucratic approach to fulfilling society's obligation to handicapped students has failed in the past, and shows no particular promise for the future. Public Law 94-142 and its successors may set forth legal standards and promises, but these can easily be circumvented. Effective and humane education of disturbed students has always depended on the individual actions of competent, caring teachers, and this will be the case in the future regardless of legal mandates or prohibitions.

The issues today parallel those of the last century, though the potential for helping disturbed students is greater today than it was then because of our broader base of knowledge and experience. We have reason, then, for guarded optimism. Quick and easy cures are unlikely, but as long as people care and go beyond caring to search diligently for answers to the questions of how youngsters come to be disturbed and how they can be helped to develop appropriate behavior, we can have confidence that periods of progress will outweigh periods of regression.

Glossary

Adjustment disorders Maladaptive reactions to an identifiable and stressful life event or circumstance. Includes impairment of social/occupational functioning. Maladaptive behavior is expected to change when stress is removed.

Affective disorders *See* Mood disorders.

Amnesia Chronic or severe inability to remember; loss of memory that is general or more than temporary.

Anomie Normlessness; especially, absence of norms for moral conduct among lower-class persons who aspire to achieve a higher class status.

Anorexia nervosa Severe self-starvation and marked weight loss that may be life threatening; occurs most often in adolescent girls.

Anoxia; Hypoxia Deprivation of oxygen for a long enough time to result in brain trauma.

Anxiety disorders Disorders in which anxiety is the primary feature. Anxiety may focus on specific situations, such as separation or social contact with strangers, or it may be generalized and pervasive.

Anxiety-withdrawal Behavior characterized by anxiety, feelings of inadequacy, embarrassment, shyness, and withdrawal from social contact.

Athetoid movement Involuntary, jerky, writhing movements (especially of the fingers and wrists) associated with athetoid cerebral palsy.

Attention-deficit hyperactivity disorder A disorder, described in DSM-III-R, that includes inattention, impulsivity, and hyperactivity; begins before the age of seven years.

Attentional strategies Use of verbal labeling, rehearsal, self-instruction, or other techniques to improve a child's ability to attend efficiently to appropriate stimuli.

Atypical childhood psychosis Profound disturbance in relations with other people, accompanied by many bizarre behaviors; characteristics appear after 30 months but before 12 years of age.

Autism, autistic Severe disturbance or psychosis of childhood characterized by extreme social isolation, bizarre behavior, and delayed development, beginning in the first 2½ years. *See also* Child psychosis, Psychosis.

Behavior modification Systematic control of environmental events, especially of consequences, to produce specific changes in observable responses. May include reinforcement, punishment, modeling,

409

self-instruction, desensitization, guided practice, or any other technique for strengthening or eliminating a particular response.

Behavioral model Assumptions that behavior disorders result primarily from inappropriate learning and that the most effective preventive actions and therapeutic interventions involve controlling the child's environment so as to teach appropriate behaviors.

Biological model Assumptions that behavior disorders result primarily from dysfunction of the central nervous system (because of brain lesions, neurochemical irregularities, or genetic defects) and that the most effective preventive actions and therapeutic interventions involve prevention or correction of such biological defects.

Brain syndrome *See* Organic brain syndrome.

Bulimia Binge eating followed by purging (by vomiting or enemas); binges often alternate with extreme dieting.

Catharsis Cleansing; in psychoanalytic theory, the notion that it is therapeutic to express one's feelings freely under certain conditions (e.g., that aggressive drive can be reduced by free expression of aggression in a safe way, such as hitting a punching bag or doll).

Cerebral palsy A developmental disability resulting from brain damage before, during, or soon after birth and having as a primary feature weakness or paralysis of the extremities. Often accompanied by mental retardation, sensory deficiencies, and/or behavior disorders.

Character disorder Acting-out, aggressive behavior with little or no indication of associated anxiety or guilt.

Childhood psychosis Used to denote a wide range of severe and profound disorders of children, including autism, schizophrenia, and symbiotic psychosis.

Choreoathetoid Involuntary, purposeless, uncontrolled movement characteristic of some types of neurological disorders.

Conceptual model A theory; in behavior disorders, a set of assumptions regarding the origins and nature of the problem and the nature of therapeutic mechanisms; a set of assumptions guiding research and practice.

Conduct disorder; Conduct problem Disorder characterized by overt, aggressive, disruptive behavior or covert antisocial acts such as stealing, lying, and fire setting, or both overt and covert antisocial behavior.

Contingency contract In behavior modification, a written agreement between a child and adult(s) specifying the consequences for specific behavior.

Counterconditioning Behavior therapy that teaches, by means of classical and operant conditioning, adaptive responses that are incompatible with maladaptive responses.

Countertheorists *See* Humanistic education.

Desensitization; Systematic desensitization Elimination of fears or phobias by gradually subjecting the fearful individual to successively more anxiety-provoking stimuli (real or imagined), while the individual remains relaxed and free of fear.

Developmental deviations; Developmental disorders Behavior disorders apparently caused by the child's failure to develop at a normal rate or according to the usual sequence.

Distractibility Inability to direct and sustain attention to the appropriate or relevant stimuli in a given situation. *See also* Selective attention.

Down syndrome A genetic defect in which the child is born with an extra chromosome (number 21 in the 22 pairs; hence, trisomy 21) in each cell; a syndrome associated with characteristic mongoloid facial features, mental retardation, and other congenital defects. (Previously called *mongolism*.)

DSM *Diagnostic and Statistical Manual of the American Psychiatric Association;* editions designated by roman numerals, as DSM-III for third edition. Revised third edition is referred to as DSM-III-R.

Dynamic psychiatry The study of emotional processes, mental mechanisms, and their origins; study of evolution, progression, or regression in human behavior and its motivation. Distinguished from *descriptive psychiatry,* in which focus is on static clinical patterns, symptoms, and classification.

Dysphoria General feeling of unhappiness or unwellness, especially when disproportionate to its cause or inappropriate to one's life circumstances. Opposite of *euphoria.*

Echolalia; echolalic The parroting repetition of words or phrases either immediately after they are heard or later; usually observed only in psychotic, schizophrenic, or autistic children.

Ecological model Assumptions that behavior disorders result primarily from flaws in a complex social system in which various elements of the system (e.g., child, school, family, church, community) are highly interdependent, and that the most effective preventive actions and therapeutic interventions involve changes in the entire social system.

Educateur An individual broadly trained to enhance social development of children and youth in various community contexts; someone trained in education and related disciplines to intervene in the social ecology of troubled children and youth.

Ego The conscious mind; in Freudian psychology, the volitional aspect of behavior.

Ego psychology Psychological theories or models emphasizing the ego.

Elective mutism, Selective mutism Muteness of a child who is able to talk. The child chooses to be mute, usually except in the presence of the mother or a few other select people.

Electroencephalogram (EEG) A graphic record of changes in the electrical potential of the brain; used in neurological and psychiatric research.

Emotional lability Unstable or rapidly shifting emotional states.

Encephalitis Inflammation of the brain, usually as a result of infection and often accompanied by behavioral manifestations such as lethargy.

Encopresis Incontinence of feces, which may consist of passing feces into the clothing or bed at regular intervals or leaking mucus and feces into the clothing or bed almost continuously.

Endogenous depression Depression apparently precipitated by biological factors rather than adverse environmental circumstances.

Enuresis Incontinence of urine, which may be diurnal (wetting oneself during the day) or nocturnal (bedwetting).

Epilepsy Abnormal electrical discharge in the brain that causes a seizure. A person is not considered epileptic unless repeated seizures occur.

Ethology Scientific comparative study of animal and human behavior, especially study of the development of human character.

Eugenics Belief that human qualities can be improved through selective mating; a science dealing with improving inherited characteristics of a race or breed.

Follow-back studies Studies in which adults with a given disorder are "followed back" in an attempt to find the antecedents of their condition in their medical, educational, or social histories.

Frustration-aggression hypothesis Hypothesis that frustration always produces aggression and that aggression is always the result of frustration.

Humanistic education Education suggested by "countertheorists" who call for radical school reform and/or greater self-determination by the child; education in which freedom, openness, innovation, self-direction, and self-evaluation by students and mutual sharing between students and teachers are practiced.

Hyperactivity High level of motor activity accompanied by socially inappropriate behavior, often including conduct problems, distractibility, and impulsivity.

Hyperkinesis Excessive motor activity.

Hyperkinetic; hyperkinetic impulse disorder; Hyperkinetic reaction; Hyperkinetic syndrome Characterized by excessive motor activity or hyperactivity.

Hyperthyroidism Enlargement of and excessive secretion of hormones from the thyroid gland that may result in nervousness, weakness, and restless overactivity.

Hypoglycemia Abnormally low level of blood sugar that may produce behavioral symptoms such as irritability, fretfulness, confusion, negativism, or aggression; may be associated with diabetes.

Hypoxia Severely reduced supply of oxygen. *See* Anoxia.

Immaturity-inadequacy Disorder characterized by social incompetence, passivity, daydreaming, and behavior typical of younger children.

Impulsivity Tendency to react quickly and inappropriately to a situation rather than take time to consider alternatives and choose carefully.

Incontinent Releasing urine or feces at inappropriate times or places; lack of control of bladder or bowel function.

Induction approach Use of reasoning, explanation, modeling, and expressions of love and concern in discipline, especially in teaching or enforcing moral standards.

Infantile autism *See* Autism.

Interactional-transactional model Assumptions that behavior disorders result primarily from the mutual influence of the child and other persons on each other and that the most effective preventive actions and therapeutic interventions involve changing the nature of interactions and transactions between the child and others.

Intervention Method or strategy used in treatment of a behavior disorder.

Intrapsychic; Intrapsychic causal factors Having to do with the mind; in the mind itself; conflict or disequilibrium between parts of the mind (in psychoanalytic theory, the id, ego, and superego); especially conflict in the unconscious.

Kanner's syndrome Early infantile autism (originally described by Leo Kanner in 1943), the primary symptoms of which are extreme isolation or aloneness from the first years of life and obsessive insistence on preservation of sameness. Generally replaced by the terms *autism* and *childhood psychosis. See also* Autism.

Lesch-Nyhan syndrome Severe neurologic disorder resulting from a genetically transmitted metabolic defect. Symptoms first appear at about six months of age, and children with the defect rarely live beyond their teens.

Life space interview Therapeutic way of talking with disturbed children about their behavior; a set of techniques for managing behavior by means of therapeutic communication.

Locus of control Belief that one's behavior is under internal or external control. Individuals have an *internal* locus to the extent that they believe they are responsible for their actions; an *external* locus to the extent that they believe chance or others' actions determine their behavior.

Megavitamin therapy Administration of extremely large doses of vitamins in the hope of improving or curing behavior disorders.

Metacognition; metacognitive Thinking about thinking; awareness and analysis of one's thought processes; controlling one's cognitive processes.

Minimal brain dysfunction; Minimal brain damage Term applied to children who exhibit behavioral characteristics (e.g., hyperactivity, distractibility) thought to be associated with brain damage, in the absence of other evidence that their brains have been damaged.

Minimal cerebral dysfunction *See* Minimal brain dysfunction.

Modeling Providing an example which, it is hoped, the child will imitate; behavior modification technique in which a clear model of the desired behavior is provided (typically, reinforcement is given for imitation of the model).

Mood disorders Disorders of emotion that color outlook on life. Usually characterized by either elation or depression. May be episodic or chronic, manic or depressive.

Moral therapy; Moral treatment Treatment provided in the late 18th and early 19th centuries characterized by humane and kindly care, therapeutic activity, and consistent consequences for behavior.

Neologism A coined word that is meaningless to others; meaningless word in the speech of a psychotic person.

Neuroleptics Antipsychotic drugs; drugs that suppress or prevent symptoms of psychosis; major tranquilizers.

Neurosis; Neurotic behavior Behavior disorder characterized by emotional conflict but not loss of contact with reality.

Operant conditioning Changing behavior by altering its consequences; altering the future probability of a response by providing reinforcement or punishment as a consequence.

Organic brain syndrome; Organic psychosis Behavior disorder caused by brain damage.

Organic mental disorders Disorders of behavior caused by transient or permanent brain dysfunction, often resulting from anoxia, ingestion of drugs or other toxic substances, or injury to brain tissue.

Organicity Behavioral indications of brain damage or organic defects.

Orthomolecular therapy Administration of chemical substances, vitamins, or drugs on the assumption that they will correct a basic chemical or molecular error that causes behavior disorders.

Overcorrection Set of procedures designed to "overcorrect" behavioral errors; may be *positive practice* overcorrection (requiring the individual to practice a more adaptive or appropriate form of behavior) or *restitution* overcorrection (requiring the individual to restore the environment to a condition better than its status before the misbehavior occurred).

Overselective attention *See* Selective attention.

Parasuicide Attempted suicide.

Permissive approach to education Allowing children to behave as they wish within broad or loosely defined limits, on the assumptions that it is therapeutic to allow them to "act out" their feelings (unless they endanger someone) and that the teacher must be permissive to build a sound relationship with children; derived mostly from psychoanalytic theory.

Personality disorders Deeply ingrained, inflexible, maladaptive patterns of relating to, perceiving, and thinking about the environment and oneself that impair adaptive functioning or cause subject distress.

Personality problem Disorder characterized by neurotic behavior, depression, and withdrawal.

Person variables Thoughts, feelings, and perceptions; private events or states.

Pervasive developmental disorder Distortion of or lag in all or most areas of development, as in autism or other childhood psychosis.

Phenomenological model Assumptions that behavior disorders result primarily from inadequate or distorted conscious experience with life events and that the most effective preventive actions and therapeutic interventions involve helping individuals examine their conscious experience of the world.

Phobia Irrational and debilitating fear.

Pica Persistent eating of nonnutritional substances (e.g., paint, plaster, cloth).

Play therapy Therapeutic treatment in which the child's play is used as the theme for communication between therapist and child.

Positive practice *See* Overcorrection.

Postencephalitic behavior syndrome Abnormal behavior following encephalitis (inflammation of the brain).

Premorbid; premorbid personality Condition or personality characteristics predictive of later onset of illness or disorder.

Primary process thinking Psychoanalytic concept that disorganized or primitive thought or activity represents direct expression of unconscious mental processes; distinguished from *secondary* process (rational, logical) thinking.

Prosocial behavior Behavior that facilitates or maintains positive social contacts; desirable or appropriate social behavior.

Pseudoretardation Level of functioning associated with mental retardation that increases to normal level of functioning when environmental factors are changed; falsely diagnosed mental retardation.

Psychoactive substance use disorders Disorders involving abuse of mood-altering substances (e.g., alcohol or other drugs).

Psychoanalytic model Assumptions that behavior disorders result primarily from unconscious conflicts and that the most effective preventive actions and therapeutic interventions involve uncovering and understanding unconscious motivations.

Psychodynamic model *See* Psychoanalytic model.

Psychoeducational Approach to education of disturbed children that takes into account psychodynamic concepts such as unconscious motivation but focuses intervention on the "ego processes" by which the child gains insight into his or her behavior.

Psychoneurosis; Psychoneurotic *See* Neurosis.

Psychopath; Psychopathic An individual who exhibits mostly amoral or antisocial behavior and is usually impulsive, irresponsible, and self-gratifying without consideration for others. Also called *sociopath* or *sociopathic.*

Psychopathology Mental illness; in psychiatry, the study of significant causes and development of mental illness; more generally, behavior disorder.

Psychophysiological Physical disorders thought to be caused by psychological (emotional) conflict.

Psychosexual disorder Disorders involving sexual functioning or sex-typed behavior.

Psychosis; Psychotic behavior; Psychotic reaction Behavior disorder characterized by major departure from normal patterns of acting, thinking, and feeling.

Psychosomatic; Psychosomaticization *See* Psychophysiological.

Psychotherapy Any type of treatment relying primarily on verbal and nonverbal communication between patient and therapist rather than on medical procedures; not typically defined to include behavior modification; typically administered by a psychiatrist or clinical psychologist.

Punishment Consequences that reduce future probability of a behavior; may be *response cost* (removal of a valued object or commodity) or *aversive conditioning* (presentation of an aversive stimulus such as a slap or electric shock).

Reactive depression Depression apparently precipitated by a specific event; depression that is a reaction to adverse circumstances.

Reactive disorders Behavior disorders apparently caused by reaction to stressful circumstances.

Reciprocal inhibition *See* Desensitization.

Reinforcement Presenting or removing stimuli following a behavior to increase its future probability. *Positive reinforcement* refers to presenting positive stimuli (rewards); *negative reinforcement* refers to removing negative stimuli (punishers) contingent on a response. Both positive and negative reinforcement increase rate or strength of the response.

Respondent behavior An elicited response; reflexive behavior elicited automatically by presenting a stimulus (e.g., pupillary contraction elicited by shining a light in the eye).

Respondent conditioning Process by which a previously neutral stimulus comes to elicit a respondent behavior after the neutral stimulus has been paired with presentation of another stimulus (an unconditioned stimulus that already elicits a response) on one or more trials.

Response cost Punishment technique consisting of taking away a valued object or commodity contingent on a behavior; a fine; making an inappropriate response "cost" something to the misbehaving child.

Response topography The particular movements that comprise a response; how the response looks to an observer, as opposed to the effect of the response on the environment.

Restitution *See* Overcorrection.

Rumination (Mercyism) Regurgitation with loss of weight or failure to thrive.

Salt depletion Abnormally low level of chloride (salt) in the blood that may result in behavioral symptoms. In rapid depletion, weakness, dizziness, stupor, and profuse perspiration may be manifestations; in protracted (long) depletion, headaches, tremors, nervousness, apprehension, depression, and restlessness may be manifestations.

Schizoaffective disorders Depression or manic behavior lasting at least one week and concurrent with psychotic behavior not consistent with a purely affective disorder.

Schizoid; Schizophrenic spectrum behavior Behavior like that of schizophrenics but occurring in individuals not diagnosed as schizophrenic; schizophreniclike behavior not as deviant as that typically seen in schizophrenia. *See* Schizophrenia.

Schizophrenia; Schizophrenic Psychotic disorder characterized by distortion of thinking, abnormal perception, and bizarre behavior and emotions.

Schizophrenic disorders *See* Schizophrenia.

Schizophreniform disorders *See* Schizoid.

School phobia Fear of going to school, usually accompanied by indications of anxiety about attendance, such as abdominal pain, nausea, or other physical complaints just before leaving for school in the morning.

Selective attention Ability to direct and sustain one's attention to the appropriate and relevant stimuli in a given situation. Disorders of selective attention include *underselective* attention (inability to focus attention only on relevant stimuli or to disregard irrelevant stimuli) and *overselective* attention (inability to attend to all the relevant stimuli or tendency to focus on an irrelevant stimulus).

Self-instruction Telling oneself what to do or how to perform; technique for teaching children self-control or how to improve their performance by talking to themselves about what they are doing.

Self-stimulation Any repetitive, stereotyped activity that seems only to provide sensory feedback.

Sensitization approach Use of harsh punishment, threats, and overpowering force in discipline, especially in teaching or enforcing moral standards.

Social learning theory Assumptions that antecedent or setting events (e.g., models, instructions), consequences (rewards and punishments), and cognitive processes (perceiving, thinking, feeling) influence behavior; includes features of behavioral model or behavior modification with additional consideration of cognitive factors.

Socialized delinquency; Subcultural delinquency Delinquent behavior in the context of an antisocial peer group.

Sociological model Approximate equivalent of *Ecological Model.*

Sociopath; Sociopathic *See* Psychopath.

Soft neurological signs Behavioral indications, such as incoordination, distractibility, impulsivity, perceptual problems, and certain patterns of nerve reflexes, that may occur in individuals who are not brain damaged as well as in those who are; signs that an individual may be brain damaged, but that cannot be said to indicate the certainty of brain damage.

Somatoform disorders   Physical symptoms suggesting a physical disorder, in the absence of demonstrable organic findings to explain the symptoms.

Status offense   Act that is illegal only if committed by a minor.

Stereotype   Persistent repetition of speech or motor activity characteristic of psychosis.

Strauss syndrome   Group of behavioral characteristics, including hyperactivity, distractibility, impulsivity, perceptual disturbances, no family history of mental retardation, and medical history suggestive of brain damage; named after Alfred A. Strauss.

Structured approach to education   Making the classroom environment highly predictable by providing clear directions for behavior, firm expectations that students will behave as directed, and consistent consequences for behavior. Assumes that children lack order and predictability in everyday life and will learn self-control in a highly structured (predictable) environment; derives primarily from learning theory.

Systematic desensitization   *See* Desensitization.

Target assessment   Definition and direct measurement (counting) of behaviors that are considered to be a problem (as opposed to administering psychological tests designed to measure behavioral traits or mental characteristics).

Temperament   Inborn behavioral style, including general level of activity, regularity or predictability, approach or withdrawal, adaptability, intensity of reaction, responsiveness, mood, distractibility, and persistence.

Therapeutic milieu   Total treatment setting that is therapeutic; environment that includes attention to therapeutic value of both physical and social surroundings.

Tic   Stereotyped movement disorder in which there is disregulation of gross motor movement; recurrent, involuntary, repetitive, rapid, purposeless movement; may be transient or chronic.

Time out   Technically, time out from positive reinforcement; interval during which reinforcement (rewards) cannot be earned. In classroom practice, usually a brief period of social isolation during which the child cannot receive attention or earn rewards.

Token economy; Token reinforcement; Token system   System of behavior modification in which tangible or "token" reinforcers, such as points, plastic chips, metal washers, poker chips, or play money are given as rewards and later exchanged for "backup" reinforcers that have value in themselves (e.g., food, trinkets, play time, books); a miniature economic system used to foster desirable behavior.

Tourette's disorder   Motor tics accompanied by multiple vocal tics, which are frequently obscene (coprolalic).

Transference   Unconscious redirection of feelings toward a different person (e.g., responding to teacher as if to parent); in psychoanalytic theory, responding to the therapist as if to another person, usually a parent.

Underselective attention   *See* Selective attention.

Unsocialized aggression   Unbridled aggressive behavior characterized by hostility, impulsivity, and alienation.

Vicarious extinction   Extinction of a fear response by watching someone else engage in an anxiety-provoking activity without apparent fear; loss of fear (or other response) by observing others' behavior.

Vicarious reinforcement   Reinforcement obtained by watching someone else obtain reinforcers (rewards) for a particular response.

References

Abikoff, H., & Gittelman, R. (1984). Does behavior therapy normalize the classroom behavior of hyperactive children? *Archives of General Psychiatry, 41,* 449–454.

Abikoff, H., & Gittelman, R. (1985). The normalizing effects of methylphenidate on the classroom behavior of ADDH children. *Journal of Abnormal Child Psychology, 13,* 33–44.

Achenbach, T. M. (1975). The historical context of treatment for delinquent and maladjusted children: Past, present, and future. *Behavioral Disorders, 1*(1), 3–14.

Achenbach, T. M. (1982a). Assessment and taxonomy of children's behavior disorders. In B. B. Lahey & A. E. Kazdin (Eds.), *Advances in clinical child psychology* (Vol. 5). New York: Plenum.

Achenbach, T. M. (1982b). *Developmental psychopathology* (2nd ed.). New York: Ronald Press.

Achenbach, T. M. (1985). *Assessment and taxonomy of child and adolescent psychopathology.* Beverly Hills, CA: Sage.

Achenbach, T. M., & Edelbrock, C. S. (1981). Behavior problems and competencies reported by parents of normal and disturbed children aged four through sixteen. *Monographs of the Society for Research in Child Development, 46* (1, Serial No. 188).

Achenbach, T. M., & Edelbrock, C. S. (1983). Taxonomic issues in child psychopathology. In T. H. Ollendick & M. Hersen (Eds.), *Handbook of child psychopathology.* New York: Plenum.

Achenbach, T. M., & Edelbrock, C. S. (1984). *Child Behavior Checklist—Teacher's Report.* Burlington, VT: University Associates in Psychiatry.

Achenbach, T. M., & Edelbrock, C. S. (1989). Diagnostic, taxonomic, and assessment issues. In T. H. Ollendick & M. Hersen (Eds.), *Handbook of child psychopathology* (2nd ed.). New York: Plenum.

Ack, M. (1970). Some principles of education for the emotionally disturbed. In P. A. Gallagher & L. L. Edwards (Eds.), *Educating the emotionally disturbed: Theory to practice.* Lawrence, KS: University of Kansas.

Ackerson, L. (1942). *Children's behavior problems.* Chicago: University of Chicago Press.

Aichorn, A. (1935). *Wayward youth.* New York: Viking Press.

Alberto, P., & Troutman, A. (1986). *Applied behavior analysis for teachers.* Columbus, OH: Merrill.

Alberts-Corush, J., Firestone, P., & Goodman, J. T. (1986). Attention and impulsivity characteristics of the biological and adoptive parents of hyperactive and normal control children. *American Journal of Orthopsychiatry, 56,* 413–423.

Alexander, F. G., & Selsnick, S. T. (1966). *The history of psychiatry: An evaluation of psychiatric thought from prehistoric times to the present.* New York: Harper & Row.

American Psychiatric Association. (1980). *Diagnostic and statistical manual of mental disorders* (3rd ed.). Washington, DC: Author.

American Psychiatric Association. (1987). *Diagnostic and statistical manual of mental disorders* (3rd ed., revised). Washington, DC: Author.

Andersen, A. E. (1987). Contrast and comparison of behavioral, cognitive-behavioral, and comprehensive treatment methods for anorexia nervosa and bulimia nervosa. *Behavior Therapy, 11,* 522–543.

Apter, S. J., & Conoley, J. C. (1984). *Childhood behavior disorders and emotional disturbance.* Englewood Cliffs, NJ: Prentice-Hall.

Arnold, W. R., & Brungardt, T. M. (1983). *Juvenile misconduct and delinquency.* Boston: Houghton Mifflin.

Ashem, B., & Jones, M. D. (1978). Deleterious effects of chronic undernutrition on cognitive abilities. *Journal of Child Psychology and Psychiatry, 19,* 23–31.

Asher, S. R., & Taylor, A. R. (1981). Social outcomes of mainstreaming: Sociometric assessment and beyond. *Exceptional Education Quarterly, 1*(4), 13–20.

Atkinson, L., Quarrington, B., & Cyr, J. J. (1985). School refusal: The heterogeneity of a concept. *American Journal of Orthopsychiatry, 55,* 83–101.

Augustine, G. J., & Levitan, H. (1980). Neurotransmitter release from a vertebrate neuromuscular synapse affected by a food dye. *Science, 207,* 1489–1490.

Axelrod, S., & Apsche, J. (Eds.). (1983). *The effects of punishment on human behavior.* New York: Academic Press.

Axline, V. (1947). *Play therapy.* Boston: Houghton Mifflin.

Ayllon, T., Layman, D., & Kandel, H. J. (1975). A behavioral-educational alternative to drug control of hyperactive children. *Journal of Applied Behavior Analysis, 8,* 137–146.

Ayllon, T., & Rosenbaum, M. S. (1977). The behavioral treatment of disruption and hyperactivity in school settings. In B. B. Lahey & A. E. Kazdin (Eds.), *Ad-*

vances in clinical child psychology (Vol. 1). New York: Plenum.

Azrin, N. H., Besalel, V. A., & Wisotzek, I. E. (1982). Treatment of self-injury by a reinforcement plus interruption procedure. *Analysis and Intervention in Developmental Disabilities, 2,* 105–114.

Azrin, N. H., Kaplan, S. J., & Foxx, R. M. (1973). Autism reversal: Eliminating stereotyped self-stimulation of retarded individuals. *American Journal of Mental Deficiency, 78,* 241–248.

Azrin, N. H., Sneed, T. J., & Foxx, R. M. (1974). Dry-bed training: Rapid elimination of childhood enuresis. *Behaviour Research and Therapy, 12,* 147–156.

Azrin, N. H., & Wesolowski, M. D. (1974). Theft reversal: An overcorrection procedure for eliminating stealing by retarded persons. *Journal of Applied Behavior Analysis, 7,* 577–581.

Bachman, J. A. (1972). Self-injurious behavior. A behavioral analysis. *Journal of Abnormal Psychology, 80,* 211–224.

Bailey, S. L. (1983). Extraneous aversives. In S. Axelrod & J. Apsche (Eds.), *The effects of punishment on human behavior.* New York: Academic Press.

Baker, E. M., & Stullken, E. H. (1938). American research studies concerning the "behavior" type of exceptional child. *Journal of Exceptional Children, 4,* 36–45.

Baldwin, A. L., Cole, R. E., & Baldwin, C. P. (Eds.). (1982). Parental pathology, family interaction, and the competence of the child in school. *Monographs of the Society for Research in Child Development, 47* (5, Serial No. 197).

Ball, T. S., Datta, P. C., Rios, M., & Constantine, C. (1985). Flexible arm splints in the control of a Lesch-Nyhan victim's finger biting and a profoundly retarded client's finger sucking. *Journal of Autism and Developmental Disorders, 15,* 177–184.

Balthazar, E., & Stevens, H. (1975). *The emotionally disturbed mentally retarded.* Englewood Cliffs, NJ: Prentice-Hall.

Bandura, A. (1973). *Aggression: A social learning analysis.* Englewood Cliffs, NJ: Prentice-Hall.

Bandura, A. (1977). *Social learning theory.* Englewood Cliffs, NJ: Prentice-Hall.

Bandura, A. (1978). The self-system in reciprocal determinism. *American Psychologist, 33,* 344–358.

Bandura, A. (1986). *Social foundations of thought and action: A social cognitive theory.* Englewood Cliffs, NJ: Prentice-Hall.

Barker, R. G. (1968). *Ecological psychology: Concepts and methods for studying the environment of human behavior.* Palo Alto, CA: Stanford University Press.

Barker, R. G., & Wright, H. F. (1949). Psychological ecology and the problem of psychosocial development. *Child Development, 20,* 131–143.

Barker, R. G., & Wright, H. F. (1954). *Midwest and its children.* Evanston, IL: Row, Peterson.

Barkley, R. A. (1982). Guidelines for defining hyperactivity in children: Attention deficit disorder with hyperactivity. In B. B. Lahey & A. E. Kazdin (Eds.), *Advances in clinical child psychology* (Vol. 5). New York: Plenum.

Barkley, R. A. (1983). Hyperactivity. In R. J. Morris & T. R. Krotchwill (Eds.), *The practice of child therapy.* New York: Pergamon.

Barkley, R. A. (1985). Attention deficit disorder. In P. H. Bornstein & A. E. Kazdin (Eds.), *Handbook of clinical behavior therapy with children.* Homewood, IL: Dorsey Press.

Barrett, R. P. (Ed.) (1986). *Severe behavior disorders in the mentally retarded.* New York: Plenum.

Bateman, B. D., & Herr, C. L. (1981). Law and special education. In J. M. Kauffman & D. P. Hallahan (Eds.), *Handbook of special education.* Englewood Cliffs, NJ: Prentice-Hall.

Bateson, P., Day, W. F., McClosky, H., Meehl, P. E., & Michael, J. (1975). Control and countercontrol: A panel discussion. In T. Thompson & W. S. Dockens (Eds.), *Applications of behavior modification.* New York: Academic Press.

Bauer, A. M., & Shea, T. M. (1984). Tourette Syndrome: A review and educational implications. *Journal of Autism and Developmental Disorders, 14,* 69–80.

Bear, G. G., & Richards, H. C. (1981). Moral reasoning and conduct problems in the classroom. *Journal of Educational Psychology, 73,* 664–670.

Becker, W. C. (1964). Consequences of different kinds of parental discipline. In M. L. Hoffman & L. W. Hoffman (Eds.), *Review of child development research* (Vol. 1). New York: Russell Sage Foundation.

Beers, C. W. (1908). *A mind that found itself: An autobiography.* New York: Longmans, Green.

Bell, R. Q. (1968). A reinterpretation of the direction of effects in studies of socialization. *Psychological Review, 75,* 81–95.

Bell, R. Q., & Harper, L. V. (1977). *Child effects on adults.* Hillsdale, NJ: Erlbaum.

Bellack, A. S. (1983). Recurrent problems in the behavioral assessment of social skills. *Behaviour Research and Therapy, 21,* 29–41.

Bemis, K. M. (1987). The present status of operant conditioning for the treatment of anorexia nervosa. *Behavior Modification, 11,* 432–463.

Bender, L. (1948). Genesis of hostility in children. *American Journal of Psychiatry, 105,* 241–245.

Bender, L. (1956). Childhood schizophrenia—Its recognition, description, and treatment. *American Journal of Orthopsychiatry, 26,* 499–506.

Bender, L. (1969). The nature of childhood psychosis. In J. G. Howells (Ed.), *Modern perspectives in international child psychiatry.* New York: Brunner/Mazel.

Berg, I. (1985). The management of truancy. *Journal of Child Psychology and Psychiatry, 26,* 325–331.

Bergman, P., & Escalona, S. (1949). Unusual sensitivities in very young children. *Psychoanalytic Study of the Child, 3-4,* 333–352.

Berkowitz, L. (1973). Control of aggression. In B. M. Caldwell & H. N. Ricciuti (Eds.), *Review of child development research* (Vol. 3). Chicago: University of Chicago Press.

Berkowitz, P. H. (1967). Public schools in treatment centers: An evaluation. In P. H. Berkowitz & E. P. Rothman (Eds.), *Public education for disturbed children in New York City.* Springfield, IL: Charles C. Thomas.

Berkowitz, P. H. (1974). Pearl H. Berkowitz. In J. M. Kauffman & C. D. Lewis (Eds.), *Teaching children with behavior disorders: Personal perspectives.* Columbus, OH: Merrill.

Berkowitz, P. H., & Rothman, E. P. (1960). *The disturbed child: Recognition and psychoeducational therapy in the classroom.* New York: New York University Press.

Berkowitz, P. H., & Rothman, E. P. (1967a). Educating disturbed children in New York City: An historical overview. In P. H. Berkowitz & E. P. Rothman (Eds.), *Public education for disturbed children in New York City.* Springfield, IL: Charles C. Thomas.

Berkowitz, P. H., & Rothman, E. P. (Eds.). (1967b). *Public education for disturbed children in New York City*. Springfield, IL: Charles C. Thomas.

Bettelheim, B. (1950). *Love is not enough*. New York: Macmillan.

Bettelheim, B. (1961). The decision to fail. *The School Review, 69,* 389–412.

Bettelheim, B. (1967). *The empty fortress*. New York: Free Press.

Bettelheim, B. (1970). Listening to children. In P. A. Gallagher & L. L. Edwards (Eds.), *Educating the emotionally disturbed: Theory to practice*. Lawrence: University of Kansas.

Bettelheim, B., & Sylvester, E. (1948). A therapeutic milieu. *American Journal of Orthopsychiatry, 18,* 191–206.

Bettes, B. A., & Walker, E. (1986). Symptoms associated with suicidal behavior in childhood and adolescence. *Journal of Abnormal Child Psychology, 14,* 591–604.

Billings, A. G., & Moos, R. H. (1985). Children of parents with unipolar depression: A controlled 1-year follow-up. *Journal of Abnormal Child Psychology, 14,* 149–166.

Bird, B. L., Russo, D. C., & Cataldo, M. F. (1977). Considerations in the analysis and treatment of dietary effects on behavior: A case study. *Journal of Autism and Childhood Schizophrenia, 7,* 373–382.

Blanton, S. (1925). The function of the mental hygiene clinic in schools and colleges. *New Republic, 122,* 93–101.

Blagg, N. R., & Yule, W. (1984). The behavioural treatment of school refusal—A comparative study. *Behaviour Research and Therapy, 22,* 119–127.

Blatt, B. (1975). Toward an understanding of people with special needs. In J. M. Kauffman & J. S. Payne (Eds.), *Mental retardation: Introduction and personal perspectives*. Columbus, OH: Merrill.

Blatt, B., & Kaplan, F. (1966). *Christmas in purgatory: A photographic essay on mental retardation*. Boston: Allyn & Bacon.

Blechman, E. A. (1979). Short- and long-term results of positive homebased treatment of childhood chronic constipation and encopresis. *Child Behavior Therapy, 1,* 237–247.

Blouin, A. G. (1983). Diet and behavior in children: Methodological considerations. *Topics in Early Childhood Special Education, 3*(2), 1–8.

Blouin, A. G., Blouin, J. H., & Kelly, T. C. (1983). Lead, trace mineral intake, and behavior of children. *Topics in Early Childhood Special Education, 3*(2), 63–71.

Blumenfeld, P. C., Pintrich, P. R., & Hamilton, V. L. (1987). Teacher talk and students' reasoning about morals, conventions, and achievement. *Child Development, 58,* 1389–1401.

Bockoven, J. S. (1956). Moral treatment in American psychiatry. *Journal of Nervous and Mental Disease, 124,* 167–194, 292–321.

Bockoven, J. S. (1972). *Moral treatment in community mental health*. New York: Springer.

Bodanis, D. (1986). *The secret house*. New York: Simon & Shuster.

Bornstein, P. H., Balleweg, B. J., McLellarn, R. W., Wilson, G. L., Sturm, C. A., Andre, J. C., & Van Den Pol, R. A. (1983). The "bathroom game": A systematic program for the elimination of encopretic behavior. *Journal of Behavior Therapy and Experimental Psychiatry, 14,* 67–71.

Bornstein, P. H., & Kazdin, A. E. (Eds.). (1985). *Handbook of clinical behavior therapy with children*. Homewood, IL: Dorsey Press.

Bornstein, P. H., & Quevillon, R. P. (1976). The effects of a self-instructional package on overactive preschool boys. *Journal of Applied Behavior Analysis, 9,* 179–188.

Bortner, M., & Birch, H. G. (1969). Patterns of intellectual ability in emotionally disturbed and brain-damaged children. *Journal of Special Education, 3,* 351–369.

Bower, E. M. (Ed.). (1980). *The handicapped in literature: A psychosocial perspective*. Denver: Love.

Bower, E. M. (1981). *Early identification of emotionally handicapped children in school* (3rd ed.). Springfield, IL: Charles C. Thomas.

Bower, E. M. (1982). Defining emotional disturbance: Public policy and research. *Psychology in the Schools, 19,* 55–60.

Bower, E. M., & Lambert, N. M. (1962). *A process for in-school screening of children with emotional handicaps*. Princeton, NJ: Educational Testing Service.

Bower, E. M., Shellhammer, T. A., & Daily, J. M. (1960). School characteristics of male adolescents who later became schizophrenic. *American Journal of Orthopsychiatry, 30,* 712–729.

Bower, K. B. (1975). Impulsivity and academic performance in learning and behavior disordered children. (Doctoral dissertation, University of Virginia, 1975). *Dissertation Abstracts International,* 367A. (University Microfilms No. 76-1071)

Braaten, S. R. (1982). A model for the differential assessment and placement of emotionally disturbed students in special education programs. In M. M. Noel & N. G. Haring (Eds.), *Progress or change: Issues in educating the emotionally disturbed: Vol. 1. Identification and program planning.* Seattle: University of Washington.

Braaten, S. R. (1985). Adolescent needs and behavior in the schools: Current and historical perspectives. In S. R. Braaten, R. B. Rutherford, & W. Evans (Eds.), *Programming for adolescents with behavioral disorders* (Vol. 2, pp. 1–10). Reston, VA: Council for Children with Behavioral Disorders.

Braaten, S. R., Kauffman, J. M., Braaten, B., Polsgrove, L., & Nelson, C. M. (in press). The regular education initiative: Patent medicine for behavioral disorders. *Exceptional Children.*

Braaten, S. R., Simpson, R., Rosell, J., & Reilly, T. (1988). Using punishment with exceptional children: A dilemma for educators. *Teaching Exceptional Children, 20*(2), 79–81.

Brantner, J. P., & Doherty, M. A. (1983). A review of timeout: A conceptual and methodological analysis. In S. Axelrod & J. Apsche (Eds.), *The effects of punishment on human behavior.* New York: Academic Press.

Braud, L., Lupin, M. N., & Braud, W. G. (1975). The use of electromyographic biofeedback in the control of hyperactivity. *Journal of Learning Disabilities, 8,* 420–425.

Breit, M., Kaplan, S. L., Gauthier, B., & Weinhold, C. (1984). The dry-bed method for the treatment of enuresis: A failure to duplicate previous reports. *Child and Family Behavior Therapy, 6*(3), 17–23.

Bremner, R. H. (Ed.). (1970). *Children and youth in America: A documentary history: Vol. 1. 1600–1865.* Cambridge, MA: Harvard University Press.

Bremner, R. H. (Ed.). (1971). *Children and youth in America: A documentary history: Vol. 2. 1866–1932.* Cambridge, MA: Harvard University Press.

Brigham, A. (1845). Schools in lunatic asylums. *American Journal of Insanity, 1,* 326–340.

Brigham, A. (1847). The moral treatment of insanity. *American Journal of Insanity, 4,* 1–15.

Brigham, A. (1848). Schools and asylums for the idiotic and imbecile. *American Journal of Insanity, 5,* 19–33.

Bristol, M. M. (1985). Designing programs for young developmentally disabled children: A family systems approach to autism. *Remedial and Special Education, 6*(4), 46–53.

Bronfenbrenner, U., Moen, P., & Garbarino, J. (1984). Child, family, and community. In R. D. Parke (Ed.), *Review of child development research* (Vol. 7). Chicago: University of Chicago Press.

Brown, L. L. (1987). Assessing socioemotional development. In D. D. Hammill (Ed.), *Assessing the abilities and instructional needs of students.* Austin, TX: Pro-Ed.

Brown, L. L., & Hammill, D. D. (1983). *Behavior Rating Profile: An Ecological Approach to Behavioral Assessment.* Austin, TX: Pro-Ed.

Brown, R. T., & Quay, L. C. (1977). Reflection-impulsivity in normal and behavior-disordered children. *Journal of Abnormal Child Psychology, 5,* 457–462.

Brown, R. T., Wynne, M. E., & Medenis, R. (1985). Methylphenidate and cognitive therapy: A comparison of treatment approaches with hyperactive boys. *Journal of Abnormal Child Psychology, 13,* 69–87.

Bry, B. H., Conboy, C., & Bisgay, K. (1986). Decreasing adolescent drug use and school failure: Long-term effects of targeted family problem-solving training. *Child and Family Behavior Therapy, 8*(1), 43–59.

Bryan, D. P., & Herjanic, B. (1980). Depression and suicide in handicapped adolescents and young adults. *Exceptional Education Quarterly, 1*(2), 57–65.

Bryant, B. K. (1985). The neighborhood walk: Sources of support in middle childhood. *Monographs of the Society for Research in Child Development, 50*(3, Serial No. 210).

Buehler, R. E., Patterson, G. R., & Furniss, J. M. (1966). The reinforcement of behavior in institutional settings. *Behaviour Research and Therapy, 4,* 157–167.

Burbach, H. J. (1981). The labeling process: A sociological analysis. In J. M. Kauffman & D. P. Hallahan (Eds.), *Handbook of special education* (pp. 361–377). Englewood Cliffs, NJ: Prentice-Hall.

Burke, D. (1972). Countertheoretical interventions in emotional disturbance. In W. C. Rhodes & M. L. Tracy (Eds.), *A study of child variance: Vol. 2. Interventions.* Ann Arbor: University of Michigan.

Burlton-Bennet, J. A., & Robinson, V. M. J. (1987). A single subject evaluation of the K-P diet for hyperkinesis. *Journal of Learning Disabilities, 20,* 331–335.

Butler, K. G. (1986). Language research and practice: A major contribution to special education. In R. J. Morris & B. Blatt (Eds.), *Special education: Research and trends.* New York: Pergamon.

Bybee, R. W., & Gee, E. G. (1982). *Violence, values, and justice in the schools.* Boston: Allyn & Bacon.

Cairns, R. B., & Cairns, B. D. (1986). The developmental-interactional view of social behavior: Four issues of adolescent aggression. In D. Olweus, J. Block, & M. Radke-Yarrow (Eds.), *Development of antisocial and prosocial behavior: Research, theories, and issues.* New York: Academic Press.

Campbell, M., Cohen, I. L., & Perry, R. (1983). Psychopharmacological treatment. In T. H. Ollendick & M. Hersen (Eds.), *Handbook of child psychopathology.* New York: Plenum.

Campbell, M., Green, W. H., & Deutsch, S. I. (1985). *Child and adolescent psychopharmacology.* Beverly Hills, CA: Sage.

Campbell, S. B. (1983). Developmental perspectives in child psychopathology. In T. H. Ollendick & M. Hersen (Eds.), *Handbook of child psychopathology* (pp. 13–40). New York: Plenum.

Campbell, S. B., Breaux, A. M., Ewing, L. J., & Szumowski, E. K. (1986). Correlates and predictors of hyperactivity and aggression: A longitudinal study of parent-referred problem preschoolers. *Journal of Abnormal Child Psychology, 14,* 217–234.

Campbell, S. B., & Werry, J. S. (1986). Attention deficit disorder (hyperactivity). In H. C. Quay & J. S. Werry (Eds.), *Psychopathological disorders of childhood* (3rd ed.). New York: Wiley.

Cantor, D. S., Thatcher, R. W., Hrybyk, M., & Kaye, H. (1986). Computerized EEG analyses of autistic children. *Journal of Autism and Developmental Disorders, 16,* 169–187.

Cantwell, D. P. (1982). Childhood depression: A review of current research. In B. B. Lahey & A. E. Kazdin (Eds.), *Advances in clinical child psychology* (Vol. 5). New York: Plenum.

Caplan, R. B. (1969). *Psychiatry and the community in nineteenth century America.* New York: Basic Books.

Carlson, E. T., & Dain, N. (1960). The psychotherapy that was moral treatment. *American Journal of Psychiatry, 117,* 519–524.

Carlson, P. E., & Stephens, T. M. (1986). Cultural bias and identification of behaviorally disordered children. *Behavioral Disorders, 11,* 191–199.

Carr, E. G. (1979). Teaching autistic children to use sign language: Some clinical research issues. *Journal of Autism and Developmental Disorders, 9,* 345–359.

Carr, E. G. (1981). Contingency management. In A. P. Goldstein, E. G. Carr, & W. S. Davidson (Eds.), *In response to aggression.* New York: Pergamon.

Carr, E. G., Binkoff, J. A., Kologinsky, E., & Eddy, M. (1978). Acquisition of sign language by autistic children. I: Expressive labeling. *Journal of Applied Behavior Analysis, 11,* 489–501.

Carr, E. G., Newsom, C. D., & Binkoff, J. A. (1976). Stimulus control of self-destructive behavior in a psychotic child. *Journal of Abnormal Child Psychology, 4,* 139–153.

Cartledge, G., & Milburn, J. F. (Eds.). (1986) *Teaching social skills to children.* New York: Pergamon.

Cataldo, M. R., & Harris, J. (1982). The biological basis for self-injury in the mentally retarded. *Analysis and Intervention in Developmental Disabilities, 2,* 21–40.

Center, D. B., Deitz, S. M., & Kaufman, M. E. (1982). Student ability, task difficulty, and inappropriate classroom behavior: A study of children with behavior disorders. *Behavior Modification, 6,* 355–374.

Center, D. B., & Obringer, J. (1987). A search for variables affecting underidentification of behaviorally disordered students. *Behavioral Disorders, 12,* 147–169.

Charlop, M. H. (1986). Setting effects on the occurrence of autistic children's immediate echolalia. *Journal of Autism and Developmental Disorders, 16,* 473–482.

Chasnoff, I. J., Burns, W. J., Schnoll, S. H., Burns, K., Chisum, G., & Kyle-Spore, L. (1986). Maternal-neonatal incest. *American Journal of Orthopsychiatry, 56,* 577–580.

Chess, S., & Thomas, A. (1977). Temperamental individuality from childhood to adolescence. *Journal of the American Academy of Child Psychiatry, 16,* 218–226.

Chiodo, J. (1987). Bulimia: An individual behavioral analysis. *Journal of Behavior Therapy and Experimental Psychiatry, 18,* 41–49.

Christie, D. J., Dewitt, R. A., Kaltenbach, P., & Reed, D. (1984). Using EMG biofeedback to signal hyperactive children when to relax. *Exceptional Children, 50,* 547–548.

Christoff, K. A., Scott, W. O. N., Kelley, M. L., Schlundt, D., Baer, G., & Kelly, J. A. (1985). Social skills and social problem-solving training for shy young adolescents. *Behavior Therapy, 16,* 468–477.

Churchill, D. W. (1978). *Language of autistic children.* New York: Wiley.

Clarke-Stewart, A. K. (1973). Interactions between mothers and their young children: Characteristics and consequences. *Monographs of the Society for Research in Child Development, 38* (6–7, Serial No. 153).

Cloward, R., & Ohlin, L. (1960). *Delinquency and opportunity: A theory of delinquent gangs.* Glencoe, IL: Free Press.

Coffey, O. D. (1987). Foreword. In C. M. Nelson, R. B. Rutherford, & B. I. Wolford (Eds.), *Special education in the criminal justice system.* Columbus, OH: Merrill.

Cohen, A. K. (1955). *Delinquent boys.* Glencoe, IL: Free Press.

Coie, J. D., & Dodge, K. A. (1983). Continuities and changes in children's social status: A five-year longitudinal study. *Merrill-Palmer Quarterly, 29,* 261–282.

Coie, J. D., Dodge, K. A., & Kupersmidt, J. (in press). Peer group behavior and social status. In S. R. Asher & J. D. Coie (Eds.), *Peer rejection in childhood: Origins, consequences, and intervention.* New York: Cambridge University Press.

Coie, J. D., & Kupersmidt, J. B. (1983). A behavioral analysis of emerging social status in boys' groups. *Child Development, 54,* 1400–1416.

Cole, D. A., & Rehm, L. P. (1986). Family interaction patterns and childhood depression. *Journal of Abnormal Child Psychology, 14,* 297–314.

Coleman, M. C., & Gilliam, J. E. (1983). Disturbing behaviors in the classroom: A survey of teacher attitudes. *Journal of Special Education, 17,* 121–129.

Comer, J. P. (1988). Is "parenting" essential to good teaching? *NEA Today, 6*(6), 34–40.

Comstock, G. (1983). Media influences on aggression. In A. P. Goldstein (Ed.), *Prevention and control of aggression.* New York: Pergamon.

Conners, C. K. (1969). A teacher rating scale for use in drug studies with children. *American Journal of Psychiatry, 126,* 884–888.

Conners, C. K. (1973). Rating scales for use in drug studies in children. Pharmoacotherapy of children [Special issue]. *Psychopharmacology Bulletin,* 24–84.

Conners, C. K., & Wells, K. C. (1986). *Hyperkinetic children: A neuropsychological approach.* Beverly Hills, CA: Sage.

Conners, C. K., & Werry, J. S. (1979). Pharmacotherapy. In H. C. Quay & J. S. Werry (Eds.), *Psychopathological disorders of childhood* (2nd ed.). New York: Wiley.

Cook, J. W., Altman, K., Shaw, J., & Blaylock, M. (1978). Use of contingent lemon juice to eliminate public masturbation by a severely retarded boy. *Behaviour Research and Therapy, 16,* 131–134.

Cooper, J. O., Heron, T. E., & Heward, W. L. (1987). *Applied behavior analysis.* Columbus, OH: Merrill.

Copeland, R. E., Brown, R. E., & Hall, R. V. (1974). The effects of principal-implemented techniques on the behavior of pupils. *Journal of Applied Behavior Analysis, 7,* 77–86.

Cossairt, A., Marlowe, M., Stellern, J., & Jacobs, J. (1985). Biofeedback assessment of behaviorally disordered students' stress levels and performance with a parent present during academic tasks. *Journal of Child and Adolescent Psychotherapy, 2,* 197–200.

Costello, C. G. (1981). Childhood depression. In E. J. Mash & L. G. Terdal (Eds.), *Behavioral assessment of childhood disorders.* New York: Guilford.

Council for Children with Behavioral Disorders, Executive Committee. (1987). Position paper on definition and identification of students with behavioral disorders. *Behavioral Disorders, 13,* 9–19.

Cravioto, J., & DeLicardie, E. R. (1975). Environmental and nutritional deprivation in children with learning disabilities. In W. M. Cruickshank & D. P. Hallahan (Eds.), *Perceptual and learning disabilities in children: Vol. 2. Research and theory.* Syracuse, NY: Syracuse University Press.

Crissy, M. S. (1975). Mental retardation: Past, present, and future. *American Psychologist, 30,* 800–808.

Cruickshank, W. M. (1975). The learning environment. In W. M. Cruickshank & D. P. Hallahan (Eds.), *Perceptual and learning disabilities in children: Vol. 1. Psychoeducational practices.* Syracuse, NY: Syracuse University Press.

Cruickshank, W. M., Bentzen, F., Ratzeburg, F., & Tannhauser, M. A. (1961). *A teaching method for brain-injured and hyperactive children.* Syracuse, NY: Syracuse University Press.

Cruickshank, W. M., Paul, J. L., & Junkala, J. B. (1969). *Misfits in the public schools.* Syracuse, NY: Syracuse University Press.

Csapo, M. (1987). Anorexia nervosa and bulimia. *British Columbia Journal of Special Education, 11,* 251–288.

Cullinan, D., & Epstein, M. H. (1979). Administrative definitions of behavior disorders: Status and directions. In F. H. Wood & K. C. Lakin (Eds.), *Disturbing, disordered, or disturbed? Perspectives on the definition of problem behavior in educational settings* (pp. 17–28). Minneapolis: Advanced Training Institute, Department of Psychoeducational Studies, University of Minnesota.

Cullinan, D., Epstein, M. H., & Kauffman, J. M. (1982). The behavioral model and children's behavior disorders: Foundations and evaluation. In R. L. McDowell, G. W. Adamson, & F. H. Wood (Eds.), *Teaching emotionally disturbed children.* Boston: Little, Brown.

Cullinan, D., Epstein, M. H., & Kauffman, J. M. (1984). Teachers' ratings of students' behaviors: What constitutes behavior disorder in schools? *Behavioral Disorders, 10,* 9–19.

Cunningham, C. E., Cataldo, M. F., Mallion, C., & Keyes, J. B. (1984). A review and controlled single case evaluation of behavioral approaches to the management of elective mutism. *Child and Family Behavior Therapy, 5*(4), 25–49.

Daly, P. M. (1985). The educateur: An atypical child-care worker. *Behavioral Disorders, 11,* 35–41.

Dain, N., & Carlson, E. T. (1960). Milieu therapy in the nineteenth century: Patient care at the Friend's Asylum, Frankford, Pennsylvania, 1817–1861. *Journal of Nervous and Mental Disease, 131,* 277–290.

Davids, L. (1975). Therapeutic approaches to children in residential treatment: Changes from the mid-1950s to the mid-1970s. *American Psychologist, 84,* 161–164.

Davies, E., & Furnham, A. (1986). The dieting and body shape concerns of adolescent females. *Journal of Child Psychology and Psychiatry, 27,* 417–428.

deCatanzaro, D. A. (1978). Self-injurious behavior: A biological analysis. *Motivation and Emotion, 2,* 45–65.

Delgado, J. M. R. (1969). *Physical control of the mind: Toward a psychocivilized society.* New York: Harper.

Dembinski, R. J., Schultz, E. W., & Walton, W. T. (1982). Curriculum intervention with the emotionally disturbed student: A psychoeducational perspective. In R. L. McDowell, G. W. Adamson, & F. H. Wood (Eds.), *Teaching emotionally disturbed children.* Boston: Little, Brown.

Demchak, M. A., & Halle, J. W. (1985). Motivational assessment: A potential means of enhancing treatment success of self-injurious individuals. *Education and Training of the Mentally Retarded, 20,* 25–38.

DeMyer, M. K. (1975). The nature of neuropsychological disability in autistic children. *Journal of Autism and Childhood Schizophrenia, 5,* 109–128.

DeMyer, M. K., Barton, S., Alpern, G. D., Kimberlin, C., Allen, J., & Steele, R. (1974). The measured intelligence of autistic children. *Journal of Autism and Childhood Schizophrenia, 4,* 42–60.

Dennison, G. (1969). *The lives of children.* New York: Random House.

Deno, S. L. (1985). Curriculum-based measurement: The emerging alternative. *Exceptional Children, 52,* 219–232.

Deno, S. L. (1987). Curriculum-based measurement. *Teaching Exceptional Children, 20,* 41–42.

DesLauriers, A. M., & Carlson, C. F. (1969). *Your child is asleep: Early infantile autism.* Homewood, IL: Dorsey Press.

Despert, J. L. (1965). *The emotionally disturbed child—Then and now.* New York: Brunner.

Despert, J. L. (1968). *Schizophrenia in children.* New York: Brunner.

DeStefano, M. A., Gesten, E. L., & Cowen, E. L. (1977). Teachers' views of the treatability of children's school adjustment problems. *Journal of Special Education, 11,* 275–280.

Deutsch, A. (1948). *The shame of the states.* New York: Harcourt, Brace, & World.

Devany, J., Rincover, A., & Lovaas, O. I. (1981). Teaching speech to nonverbal children. In J. M. Kauffman & D. P. Hallahan (Eds.), *Handbook of special education.* Englewood Cliffs, NJ: Prentice-Hall.

Dinitz, S., Scarpitti, F. R., & Reckless, W. C. (1962). Delinquency vulnerability: A cross group and longitudinal analysis. *American Sociological Review, 27,* 515–517.

Dishion, T. J., Loeber, R., Stouthamer-Loeber, M., & Patterson, G. R. (1984). Skill deficits and male adolescent delinquency. *Journal of Abnormal Child Psychology, 12,* 37–54.

Dodge, K. A., & Somberg, D. R. (1987). Hostile attributional biases among aggressive boys are exacerbated under conditions of threats to self. *Child Development, 58,* 213–224.

Doke, L. A., & Flippo, J. R. (1983). Aggressive and oppositional behavior. In T. H. Ollendick & M. Hersen (Eds.), *Handbook of child psychopathology.* New York: Plenum.

Dokecki, P. R., Strain, B. A., Bernal, J. J., Brown, C. S., & Robinson, M. E. (1975). Low-income and minority groups. In N. Hobbs (Ed.), *Issues in the classification of children* (Vol. 1). San Francisco: Jossey-Bass.

Doleys, D. M. (1983). Enuresis and encopresis. In T. H. Ollendick & M. Hersen (Eds.), *Handbook of child psychopathology.* New York: Plenum.

Doleys, D. M. (1985). Enuresis and encopresis. In P. H. Bornstein & A. E. Kazdin (Eds.), *Handbook of clinical behavior therapy with children.* Homewood, IL: Dorsey Press.

Doll, E. A. (1967). Trends and problems in the education of the mentally retarded: 1900–1940.

American Journal of Mental Deficiency, 72, 175–183.

Dollard, J., Doob, L. W., Miller, N. E., Mowrer, O. H., & Sears, R. R. (1939). *Frustration and aggression.* New Haven, CT: Yale University Press.

Donelson, K. (1987). Six statements/questions from the censors. *Phi Delta Kappan, 69,* 208–214.

Donnellan, A. M., Mesaros, R. A., & Anderson, J. L. (1985). Teaching students with autism in natural environments: What educators need from researchers. *Journal of Special Education, 18,* 505–522.

Dornbusch, S. M., Ritter, P. L., Leiderman, P. H., Roberts, D. F., & Fraleigh, M. J. (1987). The relation of parent style to adolescent school performance. *Child Development, 58,* 1244–1257.

Duke, D. L. (1978). The etiology of student misbehavior and the depersonalization of blame. *Review of Educational Research, 48,* 415–437.

Dumont, M. P. (1987). A diagnostic parable (first edition-unrevised). *Readings: A Journal of Reviews and Commentary in Mental Health, 2*(4), 9–12.

Dunlap, G., Koegel, R. L., & Burke, J. C. (1981). Educational implications of stimulus overselectivity in autistic children. *Exceptional Education Quarterly, 2*(3), 37–50.

Dunlap, G., Koegel, R. L., & O'Neill, R. (1985). Pervasive developmental disorders. In P. H. Bornstein & A. E. Kazdin (Eds.), *Handbook of clinical behavior therapy with children.* Homewood, IL: Dorsey Press.

Dunn, L. M. (1968). Special education for the mildly retarded—Is much of it justifiable? *Exceptional Children, 35,* 5–22.

Dwyer, J. A. T., & Kreitman, N. (1984). Hopelessness, depression, and suicidal intent. *British Journal of Psychiatry, 144,* 127–133.

Earls, F. (1984). The epidemiology of depression in children and adolescents. *Pediatric Annals, 13,* 23–31.

Easson, W. M. (1969). *The severely disturbed adolescent.* New York: International Universities Press.

Eaton, W. O. (1983). Measuring activity level with actometers: Reliability, validity, and arm length. *Child Development, 54,* 720–726.

Edelman, E. M., & Goldstein, A. P. (1981). Moral education. In A. P. Goldstein, E. G. Carr, W. S. Davidson, & P. Wehr (Eds.), *In response to aggression.* New York: Pergamon.

Edelson, S. M., Taubman, M. T., & Lovaas, O. I. (1983). Some social contexts of self-destructive behavior. *Journal of Abnormal Child Psychology, 11,* 299–312.

Edgar, E. B. (1987). Secondary programs in special education: Are many of them justifiable? *Exceptional Children, 53,* 555–561.

Edgar, E. B., Webb, S. L., & Maddox, M. (1987). Issues in transition: Transfer of youth from correctional facilities to public schools. In C. M. Nelson, R. B. Rutherford, & B. I. Wolford (Eds.), *Special education in the criminal justice system.* Columbus, OH: Merrill.

Edgerton, R. B. (1984). Mental retardation: An anthropologist's changing view. In B. Blatt & R. J. Morris (Eds.), *Perspectives in special education: Personal orientations.* Glenview, IL: Scott, Foresman.

Eggers, C. (1978). Course and prognosis of childhood schizophrenia. *Journal of Autism and Childhood Schizophrenia, 8,* 21–36.

Eggleston, C. (1987). Correctional special education: Our rich history. In C. M. Nelson, R. B. Rutherford, & B. I. Wolford (Eds.), *Special education in the criminal justice system.* Columbus, OH: Merrill.

Eiduson, B. T., Eiduson, S., & Geller, E. (1962). Biochemistry, genetics, and the nature-nurture problem. *American Psychologist, 119,* 342–350.

Eisenberg, L. (1958). School phobia: A study in the communication of anxieties. *American Journal of Psychiatry, 114,* 712–718.

Eisenberg, L. (1969). Child psychiatry: The past quarter century. *American Journal of Orthopsychiatry, 39,* 389–401.

Eisenberg, L. (1984). The epidemiology of suicide in adolescents. *Pediatric Annals, 13,* 47–54.

Eisenberg, L., & Kanner, L. (1956). Early infantile autism, 1943–55. *American Journal of Orthopsychiatry, 26,* 556–566.

Eissler, K. R. (1949). *Searchlights on delinquency.* New York: International Universities Press.

Elder, J. P., Stern, R. A., Anderson, M., Hovell, M. F., Molgaard, C. A., & Seidman, R. L. (1987). Contingency-based strategies for preventing alcohol, drug, and tobacco use: Missing or unwanted components of adolescent health promotion? *Education and Treatment of Children, 10,* 33–47.

Emery, R. E., Binkoff, J. A., Houts, A. C., & Carr, E. G. (1983). Children as independent variables: Some clinical implications of child effects. *Behavior Therapy, 14,* 398–412.

Epstein, J. L. (1981). *The quality of school life.* Lexington, MA: D. C. Heath.

Epstein, L. J., Taubman, M. T., & Lovaas, O. I. (1985). Changes in self-stimulatory behaviors with treatment. *Journal of Abnormal Child Psychology, 13,* 281–294.

Epstein, M. H., Cullinan, D., & Polloway, E. A. (1986). Patterns of maladjustment among the mentally retarded. *American Journal of Mental Deficiency, 91,* 127–134.

Epstein, M. H., Cullinan, D., & Sabatino, D. A. (1977). State definitions of behavior disorders. *Journal of Special Education, 11,* 417–425.

Epstein, M. H., Hallahan, D. P., & Kauffman, J. M. (1975). Implications of the reflectivity-impulsivity dimension for special education. *Journal of Special Education, 9,* 11–25.

Epstein, M. H., Kauffman, J. M., & Cullinan, D. (1985). Patterns of maladjustment among the behaviorally disordered: II. Boys aged 6–11, boys aged 12–18, girls aged 6–11, and girls aged 12–18. *Behavioral Disorders, 10,* 125–135.

Epstein, M. H., & Repp, A. (1987, November). *Project SAVE.* Paper presented at Eleventh Annual Conference on Severe Behavior Disorders of Children and Youth, Tempe, AZ.

Eron, L. D., & Huesmann, L. R. (1986). The role of television in the development of prosocial and antisocial behavior. In D. Olweus, J. Block, & M. Radke-Yarrow (Eds.), *Development of antisocial and prosocial behavior: Research, theories, and issues.* New York: Academic Press.

Esquirol, E. (1845). *Mental maladies: A treatise on insanity* (E. K. Hunt, Trans.). Philadelphia: Lea & Blanchard.

Etscheidt, M. A., & Ayllon, T. (1987). Contingent exercise to decrease hyperactivity. *Journal of Child and Adolescent Psychotherapy, 4,* 192–198.

Fabre, T. R., & Walker, H. M. (1987). Teacher perceptions of the behavioral adjustment of primary grade level handicapped pupils within regular and special education settings. *Remedial and Special Education, 8*(5), 34–39.

Fagen, S. A. (1979). Psychoeducational management and self-control. In D. Cullinan & M. H. Epstein

(Eds.), *Special education for adolescents: Issues and perspectives*. Columbus, OH: Merrill.

Fagen, S. A., & Long, N. J. (1979). A psychoeducational curriculum approach to teaching self-control. *Behavioral Disorders, 4,* 68–82.

Fagen, S. A., Long, N. J., & Stevens, D. J. (1975). *Teaching children self-control*. Columbus, OH: Merrill.

Farrington, D. P. (1986a). The sociocultural context of childhood disorders. In H. C. Quay & J. S. Werry (Eds.), *Psychopathological disorders of childhood* (3rd ed.). New York: Wiley.

Farrington, D. P. (1986b). Stepping stones to adult criminal careers. In D. Olweus, J. Block, & M. Radke-Yarrow (Eds.), *Development of antisocial and prosocial behavior: Research, theories, and issues*. New York: Academic Press.

Fauber, R., Forehand, R., Long, N., Burke, M., & Faust, J. (1987). The relationship of young adolescent Children's Depression Inventory (CDI) scores to their social and cognitive functioning. *Journal of Psychopathology and Behavioral Assessment, 9,* 161–172.

Favell, J. E., McGimsey, J. F., & Schell, R. M. (1982). Treatment of self-injury by providing alternate sensory activities. *Analysis and Intervention in Developmental Disabilities, 2,* 83–104.

Feingold, B. F. (1975). *Why your child is hyperactive*. New York: Random House.

Feingold, B. F. (1976). Hyperkinesis and learning disabilities linked to the ingestion of artificial food colors and flavors. *Journal of Learning Disabilities, 9,* 551–559.

Feldman, D., Kinnison, L., Jay, R., & Harth, R. (1983). The effects of differential labeling on professional concepts and attitudes toward the emotionally disturbed/behaviorally disordered. *Behavioral Disorders, 8,* 191–198.

Feldman, P. (1983). Juvenile offending: Behavioral approaches to prevention and intervention. *Child and Family Behavior Therapy, 5*(1), 37–50.

Fenichel, C. (1966). Psychoeducational approaches for seriously disturbed children in the classroom. In P. Knoblock (Ed.), *Intervention approaches in educating emotionally disturbed children*. Syracuse, NY: Syracuse University Press.

Fenichel, C. (1974). Carl Fenichel. In J. M. Kauffman & C. D. Lewis (Eds.), *Teaching children with behavior disorders: Personal perspectives*. Columbus, OH: Merrill.

Fenichel, C., Freedman, A. M., & Klapper, Z. (1960). A day school for schizophrenic children. *American Journal of Orthopsychiatry, 30,* 130–143.

Fenske, E. C., Zalenski, S., Krantz, P. J., & McClannahan, L. E. (1985). Age at intervention and treatment outcome for autistic children in a comprehensive intervention program. *Analysis and Intervention in Developmental Disabilities, 5,* 49–58.

Ferinden, W., & Handel, D. V. (1970). Elimination of soiling behavior in an elementary school child. *Journal of School Psychology, 8,* 207–209.

Feuerstein, M., Ward, M. M., & LeBaron, S. W. M. (1979). Neuropsychological and neurophysiological assessment of children with learning and behavior problems: A critical appraisal. In B. B. Lahey & A. E. Kazdin (Eds.), *Advances in clinical child psychology* (Vol. 2). New York: Plenum.

Field, T. (1981). Early peer relations. In P. S. Strain (Ed.), *The utilization of classroom peers as behavior change agents*. New York: Plenum.

Finch, A. J., & Spirito, A. (1980). Use of cognitive training to train cognitive processes. *Exceptional Education Quarterly, 1*(1), 31–39.

Firestone, P., & Prabhu, A. N. (1983). Minor physical anomalies and obstetrical complications: Their relationship to hyperactive, psychoneurotic, and normal children and their families. *Journal of Abnormal Child Psychology, 11,* 207–216.

Fishbein, D., & Meduski, J. (1987). Nutritional biochemistry and behavioral disabilities. *Journal of Learning Disabilities, 20,* 505–512.

Fizzell, R. L. (1987). Inside a school of choice. *Phi Delta Kappan, 68,* 758–760.

Fletcher, D. (1983). Effects of classroom lighting on the behavior of exceptional children. *Exceptional Education Quarterly, 4*(2), 75–89.

Folstein, S., & Rutter, M. (1977). Infantile autism: A genetic study of 21 twin pairs. *Journal of Child Psychology and Psychiatry, 18,* 297–321.

Forehand, R., McCombs, A., & Brody, G. H. (1987). The relationship between parental depressive mood states and child functioning. *Advances in Behavior Research and Therapy, 9,* 1–20.

Foreyt, J. P., & Kondo, A. T. (1985). Eating disorders. In P. H. Bornstein & A. E. Kazdin (Eds.), *Handbook of clinical behavior therapy with children*. Homewood, IL: Dorsey Press.

Forness, S. R. (1988). School characteristics of children and adolescents with depression. In R. B. Rutherford, C. M. Nelson, & S. R. Forness (Eds.), *Bases of severe behavioral disorders of children and youth*. Boston: Little, Brown.

Forness, S. R., & Kavale, K. A. (1988). Psychopharmacologic treatment: A note on classroom effects. *Journal of Learning Disabilities, 21* 144–147.

Forness, S. R., & MacMillan, D. L. (1970). The origins of behavior modification with exceptional children. *Exceptional Children, 37,* 93–99.

Forness, S. R., Sinclair, E., & Russell, A. T. (1984). Serving children with emotional or behavioral disorders: Implications for educational policy. *American Journal of Orthopsychiatry, 54,* 22–32.

Foster, G. G., Ysseldyke, J. E., & Reese, J. H. (1975). "I wouldn't have seen it if I hadn't believed it." *Exceptional Children, 41,* 469–473.

Foster, H. L. (1986). *Ribbin', jivin', & playin' the dozens: The persistent dilemma in our schools* (2nd ed.). Cambridge, MA: Ballinger.

Fox, J. J. (Ed.). (1987). Social interactions of behaviorally disordered children and youth [Special issue]. *Behavioral Disorders, 12*(4).

Foxx, R. M., & Azrin, N. H. (1972). Restitution: A method of eliminating aggressive-disruptive behavior of retarded and brain damaged patients. *Behaviour Research and Therapy, 10,* 15–27.

Foxx, R. M., & Azrin, N. H. (1973). The elimination of autistic self-stimulatory behavior by overcorrection. *Journal of Applied Behavior Analysis, 6,* 1–14.

Foxx, R. M., & Bechtel, D. R. (1983). Overcorrection: A review and analysis. In S. Axelrod & J. Apsche (Eds.), *The effects of punishment on human behavior*. New York: Academic Press.

Foxx, R. M., & Livesay, J. (1984). Maintenance of response suppression following overcorrection: A 10-year retrospective examination of eight cases. *Analysis and Intervention in Developmental Disabilities, 4,* 65–79.

Franco, D. P., Christoff, K. A., Crimmins, D. B., & Kelly, J. A. (1983). Social skills training for an extremely shy young adolescent: An empirical case study. *Behavior Therapy, 14,* 568–575.

Fredericks, B., & Evans, V. (1987). Functional curriculum. In C. M. Nelson, R. B. Rutherford, & B. I. Wolford (Eds.), *Special education in the criminal justice system*. Columbus, OH: Merrill.

Freeman, R. D. (1967). Special education and the electroencephalogram: Marriage of convenience. *Journal of Special Education, 2,* 67–74.

Freud, A. (1946). *The ego and the mechanisms of defense*. New York: International Universities Press.

Freud, A. (1965). The relation between psychoanalysis and pedagogy. In N. J. Long, W. C. Morse, & R. G. Newman (Eds.), *Conflict in the classroom*. Belmont, CA: Wadsworth.

Friedman, A., & Beschner, G. (1985). *Treatment services for adolescent substance abusers*. NIDA Monograph No. ADM 85-1342. Rockville, MD: National Institute on Drug Abuse.

Friman, P. C., Cook, J. W., & Finney, J. W. (1984). Effects of punishment procedures on the self-stimulatory behavior of an autistic child. *Analysis and Intervention in Developmental Disabilities, 4,* 39–46.

Fritz, G. K., Rubinstein, S., & Lewiston, N. J. (1987). Psychological factors in fatal childhood asthma. *American Journal of Orthopsychiatry, 57,* 253–257.

Frostig, M. (1976). Marianne Frostig. In J. M. Kauffman & D. P. Hallahan (Eds.), *Teaching children with learning disabilities: Personal perspectives*. Columbus, OH: Merrill.

Fundis, A. T. (1981). Social interaction with peers: A developmental perspective on social isolation. *Exceptional Education Quarterly, 1*(4), 1–12.

Fundudis, T. (1986). Anorexia nervosa in a pre-adolescent girl: A multimodal behaviour therapy approach. *Journal of Child Psychology and Psychiatry, 27,* 261–273.

Gadow, K. D. (1986). *Children on medication: Vol. II. Epilepsy, emotional disturbance, and adolescent disorders*. San Diego, CA: College Hill Press.

Garmezy, N. (1974). Children at risk: The search for the antecedents of schizophrenia. Part I. Conceptual models and research methods. *Schizophrenia Bulletin, 8,* 14–89.

Garmezy, N. (1987). Stress, competence, and development: Continuities in the study of schizophrenic adults, children vulnerable to psychopathology, and the search for stress-resistant children. *American Journal of Orthopsychiatry, 57,* 159–174.

Garner, D. M., Fairburn, C. G., & Davis, R. (1987). Cognitive-behavioral treatment of bulimia nervosa: A critical appraisal. *Behavior Modification, 11,* 398–431.

Garrison, W. T., & Earls, F. J. (1987). *Temperament and child psychopathology*. Newbury Park, CA: Sage.

Gartner, A. F. (1985). Countertransference issues in the psychotherapy of adolescents. *Child and Adolescent Psychotherapy, 2,* 187–196.

Gelfand, D. M. (1978). Social withdrawal and negative emotional states. In B. B. Wolman (Ed.), *Handbook of treatment of mental disorders in childhood and adolescence*. Englewood Cliffs, NJ: Prentice-Hall.

Gelfand, D. M., Ficula, T., & Zarbatany, L. (1986). Prevention of childhood behavior disorders. In B. A. Edelstein & L. Michelson (Eds.), *Handbook of prevention*. New York: Plenum.

Gelfand, D. M., & Hartmann, D. P. (1984). *Child behavior analysis and therapy* (2nd ed.). New York: Pergamon.

Gelfand, D. M., & Peterson, L. (1985). *Child development and psychopathology*. Beverly Hills, CA: Sage.

George, C., & Main, M. (1979). Social interactions of young abused children: Approach, avoidance, and aggression. *Child Development, 50,* 306–318.

Gerber, M. M. (1988). Tolerance and technology of instruction: Implications for special education reform. *Exceptional Children, 54,* 309–314.

Gerber, M. M., & Kauffman, J. M. (1981). Peer tutoring in academic settings. In P. S. Strain (Ed.), *The utilization of classroom peers as behavior change agents*. New York: Plenum.

Gerber, M. M., & Semmel, M. I. (1984). Teacher as imperfect test: Reconceptualizing the referral process. *Educational Psychologist, 19,* 137–148.

Germann, G., & Tindal, G. (1985). An application of curriculum-based assessment: The use of direct and repeated measurement. *Exceptional Children, 52,* 244–265.

Gersten, R. (1983). Stimulus overselectivity in autistic, trainable mentally retarded, and nonhandicapped children: Comparative research controlling chronological (rather than mental) age. *Journal of Abnormal Child Psychology, 11,* 61–76.

Gersten, R., Walker, H. M., & Darch, C. (1988). Relationships between teachers' effectiveness and their tolerance for handicapped students: An exploratory study. *Exceptional Children, 54,* 433–438.

Gesten, E. L., Scher, K., & Cowen, E. L. (1978). Judged school problems and competencies of referred children from varying family background characteristics. *Journal of Abnormal Child Psychology, 6,* 247–255.

Gibbs, J. C., Arnold, K. D., Ahlborn, H. H., & Chessman, F. L. (1984). Facilitation of sociomoral reasoning in delinquents. *Journal of Consulting and Clinical Psychology, 52,* 37–45.

Gibbs, J. T. (1987). Identity and marginality: Issues in the treatment of biracial adolescents. *American Journal of Orthopsychiatry, 57,* 265–278.

Gilliam, J. E., & Scott, B. K. (1987). The behaviorally disordered offender. In C. M. Nelson, R. B. Rutherford, & B. I. Wolford (Eds.), *Special education in the criminal justice system*. Columbus, OH: Merrill.

Gittelman, R., & Kanner, A. (1986). Psychopharmacotherapy. In H. C. Quay & J. S. Werry (Eds.), *Psychopathological disorders of childhood* (3rd ed.). New York: Wiley.

Glidewell, J. C. (1969). The child at school. In J. G. Howells (Ed.), *Modern perspectives in international child psychiatry*. New York: Brunner/Mazel.

Glidewell, J. C., Kantor, M. B., Smith, L. M., & Stringer, L. A. (1966). Socialization and social structure in the classroom. In L. W. Hoffman & M. L. Hoffman (Eds.), *Review of child development research* (Vol. 2). New York: Russel Sage Foundation.

Glidewell, J. C., & Swallow, C. S. (1968, July). *The prevalence of maladjustment in elementary schools*. Report prepared for the Joint Commission on the Mental Health of Children, University of Chicago.

Glosser, G., & Koppell, S. (1987). Emotional-behavioral patterns in children with learning disabilities: Lateralized hemispheric differences. *Journal of Learning Disabilities, 20,* 365–368.

Glueck, S., & Glueck, E. (1950). *Unraveling juvenile delinquency*. Cambridge, MA: Harvard University Press.

Glueck, S., & Glueck, E. (1962). *Family environment and delinquency*. Boston: Houghton Mifflin.

Glueck, S., & Glueck, E. (1970). *Toward a typology of juvenile offenders: Implications for therapy and prevention*. New York: Grune & Stratton.

Goldfarb, W. (1961). *Childhood schizophrenia*. Cambridge, MA: Harvard University Press.

Goldman, J. A., Lerman, R. H., Contois, J. H., & Udall, J. N. (1986). Behavioral effects of sucrose on preschool children. *Journal of Abnormal Child Psychology, 14,* 565–577.

Goldstein, A. P. (1983a). Behavior modification approaches to aggression prevention and control. In A. P. Goldstein (Ed.), *Prevention and control of aggression.* New York: Pergamon.

Goldstein, A. P. (1983b). United States: Causes, controls, and alternatives to aggression. In A. P. Goldstein & M. H. Segall (Eds.), *Aggression in global perspective.* New York: Pergamon.

Goldstein, A. P. (1987). Teaching prosocial skills to antisocial adolescents. In C. M. Nelson, R. B. Rutherford, & B. I. Wolford (Eds.), *Special education in the criminal justice system.* Columbus, OH: Merrill.

Goldstein, A. P., Carr, E. G., Davidson, W. S., & Wehr, P. (Eds.). (1981). *In response to aggression.* New York: Pergamon.

Goldstein, A. P., & Keller, H. R. (1983). Aggression prevention and control: multi-targeted, multi-channel, multi-process, multi-disciplinary. In A. P. Goldstein (Ed.), *Prevention and control of aggression.* New York: Pergamon.

Goldstein, A. P., & Segall, M. H. (Eds.). (1983). *Aggression in global perspective.* New York: Pergamon.

Goldstein, A. P., Sprafkin, R. P., Gershaw, N. J., & Klein, P. (1980). *Skillstreaming the adolescent: A structured learning approach to teaching prosocial skills.* Champaign, IL: Research Press.

Goldstein, A. P., Sprafkin, R. P., Gershaw, N. J., & Klein, P. (1986). The adolescent: Social skills training through structured learning. In G. Cartledge & J. F. Milburn (Eds.), *Teaching social skills to children* (2nd ed.). New York: Pergamon.

Goodall, K. (1972). Shapers at work. *Psychology Today, 6*(6), 53–63, 132–138.

Goodwin, S. E., & Mahoney, M. J. (1975). Modification of aggression through modeling: An experimental probe. *Journal of Behavior Therapy and Experimental Psychiatry, 6,* 200–202.

Gottesman, I. (1987). Schizophrenia: Irving Gottesman reveals the genetic factors. *University of Virginia Alumni News, 75*(5), 12–14.

Graham, P. J. (1979). Epidemiological studies. In H. C. Quay & J. S. Werry (Eds.), *Psychopathological disorders of childhood* (2nd ed.). New York: Wiley.

Graubard, P. S. (1964). The extent of academic retardation in a residential treatment center. *Journal of Educational Research, 58,* 78–80.

Graubard, P. S. (1971). The relationship between academic achievement and behavior dimensions. *Exceptional Children, 37,* 755–757.

Graubard, P. S. (1976). The use of indigenous grouping as the reinforcing agent in teaching disturbed delinquents to learn. In N. J. Long, W. C. Morse, & R. G. Newman (Eds.), *Conflict in the classroom* (3rd ed.). Belmont, CA: Wadsworth.

Graubard, P. S., Rosenberg, H., & Miller, M. (1971). Ecological approaches to social deviancy. In B. L. Hopkins & E. Ramp (Eds.), *A new direction for education: Behavior analysis 1971.* Lawrence: Kansas University Department of Human Development.

Green, R. (1987). *The "sissy boy syndrome" and the development of homosexuality.* New Haven, CT: Yale University Press.

Greer, R. D., & Polirstok, S. R. (1982). Collateral gains and short-term maintenance in reading and on-task responses by inner-city adolescents as a function of their use of social reinforcement while tutoring. *Journal of Applied Behavior Analysis, 15,* 123–139.

Grenell, M. M., Glass, C. R., & Katz, K. S. (1987). Hyperactive children and peer interaction: Knowledge and performance of social skills. *Journal of Abnormal Child Psychology, 15,* 1–13.

Gresham, F. M. (1985). Utility of cognitive-behavioral procedures for social skills training with children: A critical review. *Journal of Abnormal Child Psychology, 13,* 411–423.

Griest, D. L., & Wells, K. C. (1983). Behavioral family therapy with conduct disorders in children. *Behavior Therapy, 14,* 37–53.

Griffin, B. S., & Griffin, C. T. (1978). *Juvenile delinquency in perspective.* New York: Harper & Row.

Griffith, E. E., Schnelle, J. F., McNees, M. P., Bissinger, C., & Huff, T. M. (1975). Elective mutism in a first grader: The remediation of a complex behavioral problem. *Journal of Abnormal Child Psychology, 3,* 127–134.

Griffiths, W. (1952). *Behavior difficulties of children as perceived and judged by parents, teachers, and children themselves.* Minneapolis: University of Minnesota Press.

Grob, G. N. (1973). *Mental institutions in America: Social policy to 1875.* New York: Free Press.

Grosenick, J. K., & Huntze, S. L. (1979). *National needs analysis in behavior disorders: A model for a comprehensive needs analysis in behavior disorders*. Columbia: University of Missouri, Department of Special Education.

Grosenick, J. K., & Huntze, S. L. (1983). *More questions than answers: Review and analysis of programs for behaviorally disordered children and youth*. Columbia: University of Missouri, Department of Special Education.

Grossman, H. (1965). *Teaching the emotionally disturbed: A casebook*. New York: Holt, Rinehart, & Winston.

Grossman, H. (1972). *Nine rotten lousy kids*. New York: Holt, Rinehart, & Winston.

Grumet, G. W. (1983). Eye contact: The core of interpersonal relatedness. *Psychiatry, 46,* 172–180.

Guetzloe, E. (1987). *Suicide and depression, the adolescent epidemic: Education's responsibility* (rev. ed.). Orlando, FL: Advantage Consultants.

Gump, P. V. (1975). Ecological psychology and children. In E. M. Hetherington (Ed.), *Review of child development research* (Vol. 5). Chicago: University of Chicago Press.

Guthrie, R. (1984). Explorations in prevention. In B. Blatt & R. J. Morris (Eds.), *Perspectives in special education: Personal orientations*. Glenview, IL: Scott, Foresman.

Hagen, J. W., Meacham, J. A., & Mesibov, G. (1970). Verbal learning, rehearsal, and short-term memory. *Cognitive Psychology, 1,* 47–58.

Hagenhoff, C., Lowe, A., Hovell, M. F., & Rugg, D. (1987). Prevention of the teenage pregnancy epidemic: A social learning theory approach. *Education and Treatment of Children, 10,* 67–83.

Haines, T. H. (1925). State laws relating to special classes and schools for mentally handicapped children in the public schools. *Mental Hygiene, 9,* 545–551.

Hall, R. V., Panyon, M., Rabon, D., & Broden, M. (1968). Instructing beginning teachers in reinforcement procedures which improve classroom control. *Journal of Applied Behavior Analysis, 1,* 315–322.

Hallahan, D. P., Hall, R. J., Ianna, S. O., Kneedler, R. D., Lloyd, J. W., Loper, A. B., & Reeve, R. E. (1983). Summary of research findings at the University of Virginia Learning Disabilities Research Institute. *Exceptional Education Quarterly, 4*(1), 95–114.

Hallahan, D. P., & Kauffman, J. M. (1975). Research on the education of distractible and hyperactive children. In W. M. Cruickshank & D. P. Hallahan (Eds.), *Perceptual and learning disabilities in children: Vol. 2. Research and theory*. Syracuse, NY: Syracuse University Press.

Hallahan, D. P., & Kauffman, J. M. (1977). Categories, labels, behavioral characteristics: ED, LD, and EMR reconsidered. *Journal of Special Education, 11,* 139–149.

Hallahan, D. P., & Kauffman, J. M. (1988). *Exceptional children: Introduction to special education* (4th ed). Englewood Cliffs, NJ: Prentice-Hall.

Hallahan, D. P., Kauffman, J. M., & Lloyd, J. W. (1985). *Introduction to learning disabilities* (2nd ed.). Englewood Cliffs, NJ: Prentice-Hall.

Hallahan, D. P., Kauffman, J. M., Lloyd, J. W., & McKinney, J. D. (Eds.). (1988). The regular education initiative [Special issue]. *Journal of Learning Disabilities, 21*(1).

Hallahan, D. P., Keller, C. E., & Ball, D. W. (1986). A comparison of prevalence rate variability from state to state for each of the categories of special education. *Remedial and Special Education, 7*(2), 8–14.

Hallahan, D. P., Lloyd, J. W., Kauffman, J. M., & Loper, A. B. (1983). Academic problems. In R. J. Morris & T. R. Krotchwill (Eds.), *The practice of child therapy*. New York: Pergamon.

Hallahan, D. P., Marshall, K. J., & Lloyd, J. W. (1981). Self-recording during group instruction: Effects on attention-to-task. *Learning Disability Quarterly, 4,* 407–413.

Hallinan, M. T., & Teixeira, R. A. (1987). Opportunities and constraints: Black-white differences in the formation of interracial friendships. *Child Development, 58,* 1358–1371.

Hammill, D. D. (Ed.). (1987). *Assessing the abilities and instructional needs of students*. Austin, TX: Pro-Ed.

Hammond, W. A. (1891). *A treatise on insanity and its medical relations*. New York: Appleton.

Hare, E. H. (1962). Masturbatory insanity: The history of an idea. *Journal of Mental Science, 108,* 1–25.

Hargrove, L. J., & Poteet, J. A. (1984). *Assessment in special education: The educational evaluation*. Englewood Cliffs, NJ: Prentice-Hall.

Haring, N. G. (1968). *Attending and responding*. San Rafael, CA: Dimensions.

Haring, N. G. (1974a). Norris G. Haring. In J. M. Kauffman & C. D. Lewis (Eds.), *Teaching children with behavior disorders: Personal perspectives*. Columbus, OH: Merrill.

Haring, N. G. (1974b). Social and emotional behavior disorders. In N. G. Haring (Ed.), *Behavior of exceptional children*. Columbus, OH: Merrill.

Haring, N. G., Lovitt, T. C., Eaton, M. D., & Hansen, C. L. (1978). *The fourth R: Research in the classroom*. Columbus, OH: Merrill.

Haring, N. G., & Phillips, E. L. (1962). *Educating emotionally disturbed children*. New York: McGraw-Hill.

Haring, N. G., & Phillips, E. L. (1972). *Analysis and modification of classroom behavior*. Englewood Cliffs, NJ: Prentice-Hall.

Haring, N. G., & Schiefelbusch, R. L. (Eds.). (1976). *Teaching special children*. New York: McGraw-Hill.

Haring, N. G., & Whelan, R. J. (1965). Experimental methods in education and management. In N. J. Long, W. C. Morse, & R. G. Newman (Eds.), *Conflict in the classroom*. Belmont, CA: Wadsworth.

Harley, J. P., Matthews, C. G., & Eichman, P. (1978). Synthetic food colors and hyperactivity in children: A double-blind challenge experiment. *Pediatrics, 62*, 975–983.

Harms, E. (1967). *Origins of modern psychiatry*. Springfield, IL: Charles C. Thomas.

Harootunian, B., & Apter, S. J. (1983). Violence in school. In A. P. Goldstein (Ed.), *Prevention and control of aggression*. New York: Pergamon.

Harrington, C. C. (1970). *Errors in sex-role behavior in teenage boys*. New York: Teachers College Press.

Harrington, M. (1962). *The other America: Poverty in the United States*. New York: Macmillan.

Harris, A. (1979). An empirical test of the situation specificity/consistency of aggressive behavior. *Child Behavior Therapy, 1*, 257–270.

Harris, F. C., & Ammerman, R. T. (1986). Depression and suicide in children and adolescents. *Education and Treatment of Children, 9*, 334–343.

Harris, I. D., & Howard, K. I. (1987). Correlates of depression and anger in adolescence. *Journal of Child and Adolescent Psychotherapy, 4*, 199–203.

Harris, K. R., Wong, B. Y. L., & Keogh, B. K. (Eds.). (1985). Cognitive-behavior modification with children: A critical review of the state-of-the-art [Special issue]. *Journal of Abnormal Child Psychology, 13*(3).

Harrison, A., Serafica, F., & McAdoo, H. (1984). Ethnic families of color. In R. D. Parke (Ed.), *Review of child development research* (Vol. 7). Chicago: University of Chicago Press.

Hartshorne, H., & May, M. A. (1928–1930). *Studies in the nature of character: Vol. 1. Studies in deceit; Vol. 2. Studies in self-control; Vol. 3. Studies in the organization of character*. New York: Macmillan.

Hastings, J. E., & Barkley, R. A. (1978). A review of psychophysiological research with hyperkinetic children. *Journal of Abnormal Child Psychology, 6*, 413–447.

Hawton, K. (1986). *Suicide and attempted suicide among children and adolescents*. Beverly Hills, CA: Sage.

Hay, L. (1953). A new school channel for helping the troubled child. *American Journal of Orthopsychiatry, 23*, 678–683.

Hayman, M. (1939). The interrelations between mental defect and mental disorder. *Journal of Mental Science, 85*, 1183–1193.

Healy, W. (1915a). *The individual delinquent*. Boston: Little, Brown.

Healy, W. (1915b). *Mental conflicts and misconduct*. Boston: Little, Brown.

Healy, W. (1931). *Reconstructing behavior in youth: A study of problem children in foster homes*. New York: Alfred A. Knopf.

Healy, W., & Bronner, A. F. (1969). *Delinquents and criminals: Their making and unmaking*. New York: Batterson-Smith. (Original work published 1926) Hechtman, L., & Weiss, G. (1983). Long-term outcome of hyperactive children. *American Journal of Orthopsychiatry, 53*, 532–541.

Hechtman, L., & Weiss, G. (1983). Long-term outcome of hyperactive children. *American Journal of Orthopsychiatry, 53* 532–541.

Hedbring, C., & Newsom, C. (1985). Visual overselectivity: A comparison of two instructional remediation procedures with autistic children. *Journal of Autism and Developmental Disorders, 15*, 9–22.

Henderson, J. Q. (1983). Follow-up of stealing behavior in 27 youths after a variety of treatment programs. *Journal of Behavior Therapy and Experimental Psychiatry, 14*, 331–337.

Henker, B., Astor-Dubin, L., & Varni, J. W. (1986). Psychostimulant medication and perceived intensity in hyperactive children. *Journal of Abnormal Child Psychology, 14,* 105–114.

Henker, B., & Whalen, C. K. (1980). The changing faces of hyperactivity: Retrospect and prospect. In C. K. Whalen & B. Henker (Eds.), *Hyperactive children: The social ecology of identification and treatment.* New York: Academic Press.

Henry, N. B. (Ed.). (1950). The education of exceptional children. *Forty-ninth yearbook of the National Society for the Study of Education, Part II.* Chicago: University of Chicago Press.

Hersh, R. H., & Walker, H. M. (1983). Great expectations: Making schools effective for all students. *Policy Studies Review, 2*(1), 147–188.

Herson, P. F. (1974). Biasing effects of diagnostic labels and sex of pupil on teachers' views of pupils' mental health. *Journal of Educational Psychology, 66,* 117–122.

Hess, R. D., & Holloway, S. D. (1984). Family and school as educational institutions. In R. D. Parke (Ed.), *Review of child development research* (Vol. 7). Chicago: University of Chicago Press.

Hetherington, E. M., & Camara, K. A. (1984). Families in transition: The process of dissolution and reconstruction. In R. D. Parke (Ed.), *Review of child development research* (Vol. 7). Chicago: University of Chicago Press.

Hetherington, E. M., & Martin, B. (1979). Family interaction. In H. C. Quay & J. S. Werry (Eds.), *Psychopathological disorders of childhood* (2nd ed.). New York: Wiley.

Hetherington, E. M., & Martin, B. (1986). Family factors and psychopathology in children. In H. C. Quay & J. S. Werry (Eds.), *Psychopathological disorders of childhood* (3rd ed.). New York: Wiley.

Heuchert, C. M., & Long, N. J. (1980). A brief history of life-space interviewing. *The Pointer, 25*(2), 5–8.

Hewett, F. M. (1964a). A hierarchy of educational tasks for children with learning disorders. *Exceptional Children, 31,* 207–214.

Hewett, F. M. (1964b). Teaching reading to an autistic boy through operant conditioning. *The Reading Teacher, 18,* 613–618.

Hewett, F. M. (1965). Teaching speech to an autistic boy through operant conditioning. *American Journal of Orthopsychiatry, 35,* 927–936.

Hewett, F. M. (1966). A hierarchy of competencies for teachers of emotionally handicapped children. *Exceptional Children, 33,* 7–11.

Hewett, F. M. (1967). Educational engineering with emotionally disturbed children. *Exceptional Children, 33,* 459–471.

Hewett, F. M. (1968). *The emotionally disturbed child in the classroom.* Boston: Allyn & Bacon.

Hewett, F. M. (1970, November). The Madison Plan really swings. *Today's Education, 59,* 15–17.

Hewett, F. M. (1971). Introduction to the behavior modification approach to special education: A shaping procedure. In N. J. Long, W. C. Morse, & R. G. Newman (Eds.), *Conflict in the classroom* (2nd ed.). Belmont, CA: Wadsworth.

Hewett, F. M. (1974). Frank M. Hewett. In J. M. Kauffman & C. D. Lewis (Eds.), *Teaching children with behavior disorders: Personal perspectives.* Columbus, OH: Merrill.

Hewett, F. M., & Forness, S. R. (1974). *Education of exceptional learners.* Boston: Allyn & Bacon.

Hewitt, L. E., & Jenkins, R. L. (1946). *Fundamental patterns of maladjustment: The dynamics of their origin.* Springfield, IL: State of Illinois.

Hinde, R. A. (1986). Some implications of evolutionary theory and comparative data for the study of human prosocial and aggressive behaviour. In D. Olweus, J. Block, & M. Radke-Yarrow (Eds.), *Development of antisocial and prosocial behavior: Research, theories, and issues.* New York: Academic Press.

Hirschberg, J. C. (1953). The role of education in the treatment of emotionally disturbed children through planned ego development. *American Journal of Orthopsychiatry, 23,* 684–690.

Hobbs, N. (1965). How the Re-ED plan developed. In N. J. Long, W. C. Morse, & R. G. Newman (Eds.), *Conflict in the classroom.* Belmont, CA: Wadsworth.

Hobbs, N. (1966). Helping the disturbed child: Psychological and ecological strategies. *American Psychologist, 21,* 1105–1115.

Hobbs, N. (1974). Nicholas Hobbs. In J. M. Kauffman & C. D. Lewis (Eds.), *Teaching children with behavior disorders: Personal perspectives.* Columbus, OH: Merrill.

Hobbs, N. (1975a). *The futures of children.* San Francisco: Jossey-Bass.

Hobbs, N. (1975b). *Issues in the classification of children* (Vols. I and II). San Francisco: Jossey-Bass.

Hobson, R. P. (1986). The autistic child's appraisal of expressions of emotion. *Journal of Child Psychology and Psychiatry, 27,* 321–342.

Hoffman, E. (1974). The treatment of deviance by the educational system: History. In W. C. Rhodes & S. Head (Eds.), *A study of child variance: Vol. 3. Service delivery systems.* Ann Arbor: University of Michigan.

Hoffman, E. (1975). The American public school and the deviant child: The origins of their involvement. *Journal of Special Education, 9,* 415–423.

Hollander, S. K. (1983). Patterns of interest in the pharmacological management of hyperactivity. *American Journal of Orthopsychiatry, 53,* 353–356.

Hollinger, J. D. (1987). Social skills for behaviorally disordered children as preparation for mainstreaming: Theory, practice, and new directions. *Remedial and Special Education, 8*(4), 17–27.

Hollister, W. G., & Goldston, S. E. (1962). *Considerations for planning classes for the emotionally disturbed.* Washington, DC: Council for Exceptional Children.

Hops, H., Finch, M., & McConnell, S. (1985). Social skills deficits. In P. H. Bornstein & A. E. Kazdin (Eds.), *Handbook of clinical behavior therapy with children.* Homewood, IL: Dorsey Press.

Hops, H., Guild, J. J., Fleischman, D. H., Paine, S. C., Street, A., Walker, H. M., & Greenwood, C. R. (1978). *PEERS (Procedures for Establishing Effective Relationship Skills).* Eugene: University of Oregon, Center at Oregon for Behavioral Education of the Handicapped.

Hops, H., & Lewin, L. (1984). Peer sociometric forms. In T. H. Ollendick & M. Hersen (Eds.), *Child behavioral assessment: Principles and procedures.* New York: Pergamon.

Horton, S. V. (1987). Reduction of maladaptive mouthing behavior by facial screening. *Journal of Behavior Therapy and Experimental Psychiatry, 18,* 185–190.

Howe, S. G. (1851). On training and educating idiots: The second annual report to the legislature of Massachusetts. *American Journal of Insanity, 8,* 97–118.

Howe, S. G. (1852). Third and final report of the Experimental School for Teaching and Training Idiotic Children; also, the first report of the trustees of the Massachusetts School for Idiotic and Feebleminded Youth. *American Journal of Insanity, 9,* 20–36.

Howell, K. W. (1985). A task-analytical approach to social behavior. *Remedial and Special Education, 6*(2), 24–30.

Howell, K. W. (1987). Functional assessment in correctional settings. In C. M. Nelson, R. B. Rutherford, & B. I. Wolford (Eds.), *Special education in the criminal justice system.* Columbus, OH: Merrill.

Howell, K. W., & Morehead, M. K. (1987). *Curriculum-based evaluation for special and remedial education.* Columbus, OH: Merrill.

Howells, J. G. (Ed.). (1971). *Modern perspectives in international child psychiatry.* New York: Brunner/Mazel.

Howells, J. G., & Guirguis, W. R. (1984). Childhood schizophrenia 20 years later. *Archives of General Psychiatry, 41,* 123–128.

Hresko, W. P., & Brown, L. L. (1984). *Test of Early Socioemotional Development.* Austin, TX: Pro-Ed.

Hughes, C. A., & Hendrickson, J. M. (1987). Self-monitoring with at-risk students in the regular class setting. *Education and Treatment of Children, 10,* 225–236.

Hunter, R., & Macalpine, I. (Eds.). (1963). *Three hundred years of psychiatry, 1535–1860: A history in selected English tests.* London: Oxford University Press.

Hunter, R., & Macalpine, I. (1974). *Psychiatry for the poor. 1851 Colney Hatch Asylum-Friern Hospital. 1973: A medical and social history.* Kent, England: Dawsons of Pall Mall.

Huntze, S. (1985). A position paper of the Council for Children with Behavioral Disorders. *Behavioral Disorders, 10,* 167–174.

Hutton, J. B., & Roberts, T. G. (1986). *Social-emotional Dimension Scale: A Measure of School Behavior.* Austin, TX: Pro-Ed.

Hymes, J. L. (1949). *Teacher listen: The children speak.* New York: State Charities Aid Association.

Itard, J. M. G. (1962). *The wild boy of Aveyron.* New York: Appleton-Century-Crofts (Prentice-Hall).

Jackson, N. F., Jackson, D. A., & Monroe, C. (1983). *Getting along with others: Teaching social effectiveness to children.* Champaign, IL: Research Press.

Jarvis, E. (1852). On the supposed increase of insanity. *American Journal of Insanity, 8,* 333–364.

Jersild, A. T., & Holmes, F. B. (1935). Methods of overcoming children's fears. *Journal of Psychology, 1,* 75–104.

Johnson, J. H. (1986). *Life events as stressors in childhood and adolescence.* Beverly Hills, CA: Sage.

Johnson, J. L. (1969). Special education and the inner city: A challenge for the future or another means of cooling the mark out? *Journal of Special Education, 3,* 241–251.

Johnson, J. L. (1971). Croton-on-campus: Experiment in the use of the behavioral sciences to educate black ghetto children. In N. J. Long, W. C. Morse, & R. G. Newman (Eds.), *Conflict in the classroom* (2nd ed.). Belmont, CA: Wadsworth.

Johnson, L. J., & Blankenship, C. S. (1984). A comparison of label-induced expectancy bias in two preservice teacher education programs. *Behavioral Disorders, 9,* 167–174.

Juul, K. D. (1986). Epidemiological studies of behavior disorders in children: An international survey. *International Journal of Special Education, 1,* 1–20.

Kalfus, G. R. (1984). Peer mediated intervention: A critical review. *Child and Family Behavior Therapy, 6,* 17–43.

Kagan, J. (1965). Impulsive and reflective children. In J. Krumboltz (Ed.), *Learning and the educational process.* Chicago: Rand McNally.

Kagan, J., Rosman, B., Day, D., Albert, J., & Phillips, W. (1964). Information processing in the child: Significance of analytic and reflective attitudes. *Psychological Monographs, 78* (Whole No. 578).

Kanfer, F. H., & Grimm, L. G. (1977). Behavioral analysis: Selecting target behaviors in the interview. *Behavior Modification, 1,* 7–28.

Kanner, L. (1943). Autistic disturbances of affective contact. *Nervous Child, 2,* 217–250.

Kanner, L. (1957). *Child psychiatry.* Springfield, IL: Charles C. Thomas.

Kanner, L. (1960). Child psychiatry: Retrospect and prospect. *American Journal of Psychiatry, 117,* 15–22.

Kanner, L. (1962). Emotionally disturbed children: A historical review. *Child Development, 33,* 97–102.

Kanner, L. (1964). *History of the care and treatment of the mentally retarded.* Springfield, IL: Charles C. Thomas.

Kanner, L. (1973a). The birth of early infantile autism. *Journal of Autism and Childhood Schizophrenia, 3,* 93–95.

Kanner, L. (1973b). *Childhood psychosis: Initial studies and new insights.* Washington, DC: V. H. Winston.

Kanner, L. (1973c). Historical perspective on developmental deviations. *Journal of Autism and Childhood Schizophrenia, 3,* 187–198.

Kanner, L., Rodriguez, A., & Ashenden, B. (1972). How far can autistic children go in matters of social adaptation? *Journal of Autism and Childhood Schizophrenia, 2,* 9–33.

Kaplan, B. (Ed.). (1964). *The inner world of mental illness.* New York: Harper & Row.

Kaslow, N. J., & Rehm, L. P. (1983). Childhood depression. In R. J. Morris & T. R. Kratochwill (Eds.), *The practice of child therapy.* New York: Pergamon.

Kaslow, N. J., & Rehm, L. P. (1985). Conceptualization, assessment, and treatment of depression in children. In P. H. Bornstein & A. E. Kazdin (Eds.), *Handbook of behavior therapy with children.* Homewood, IL: Dorsey Press.

Kaslow, N. J., Rehm, L. P., & Siegel, A. W. (1984). Social-cognitive and cognitive correlates of depression in children. *Journal of Abnormal Child Psychology, 12,* 605–620.

Kauffman, J. M. (1974a). Conclusion: Issues. In J. M. Kauffman & C. D. Lewis (Eds.), *Teaching children with behavior disorders: Personal perspectives.* Columbus, OH: Merrill.

Kauffman, J. M. (1974b). Severely emotionally disturbed. In N. G. Haring (Ed.), *Behavior of exceptional children.* Columbus, OH: Merrill.

Kauffman, J. M. (1976). Nineteenth century views of children's behavior disorders: Historical contributions and continuing issues. *Journal of Special Education, 10,* 335–349.

Kauffman, J. M. (1979). An historical perspective on disordered behavior and an alternative conceptualization of exceptionality. In F. H. Wood & K. C. Lakin (Eds.), *Disturbing, disordered, or disturbed? Perspectives on the definition of problem behavior in educational settings* (pp. 49–70). Minneapolis: Advanced Training Institute, Department of Psychoeducational Studies, University of Minnesota.

Kauffman, J. M. (1980). Where special education for emotionally disturbed children is going: A personal view. *Exceptional Children, 48,* 522–527.

Kauffman, J. M. (1981). Historical trends and contemporary issues in special education in the United

States. In J. M. Kauffman & D. P. Hallahan (Eds.), *Handbook of special education*. Englewood Cliffs, NJ: Prentice-Hall.

Kauffman, J. M. (1984). Saving children in the age of Big Brother: Moral and ethical issues in the identification of deviance. *Behavioral Disorders, 10,* 60–70.

Kauffman, J. M. (1986a). Educating children with behavior disorders. In R. J. Morris & B. Blatt (Eds.), *Special education: Research and trends* (pp. 249–271). New York: Pergamon.

Kauffman, J. M. (1986b). Growing out of adolescence: Reflections on change in special education for the behaviorally disordered. *Behavioral Disorders, 11,* 290–296.

Kauffman, J. M. (1987). Research in special education: A commentary. *Remedial and Special Education, 8*(6), 57–62.

Kauffman, J. M. (1988). Lessons in the nonrecognition of deviance. In R. B. Rutherford, C. M. Nelson, & S. R. Forness (Eds.), *Bases of severe behavioral disorders of children and youth*. Boston: Little, Brown.

Kauffman, J. M., Boland, J., Hopkins, N., & Birnbrauer, J. S. (1980). *Managing and teaching the severely disturbed and retarded: A guide for teachers*. Columbus, OH: Special Press.

Kauffman, J. M., Cullinan, D., & Epstein, M. H. (1987). Characteristics of students placed in special programs for the seriously emotionally disturbed. *Behavioral Disorders, 12,* 175–184.

Kauffman, J. M., Cullinan, D., Scranton, T. R., & Wallace, G. (1972). An inexpensive device for programming ratio reinforcement. *The Psychological Record, 22,* 543–544.

Kauffman, J. M., Gerber, M. M., & Semmel, M. I. (1988). Questionable assumptions underlying the regular education initiative. *Journal of Learning Disabilities, 21*(1), 6–11.

Kauffman, J. M., & Hallahan, D. P. (1973). Control of rough physical behavior using novel contingencies and directive teaching. *Psychological Reports, 36,* 1225–1226.

Kauffman, J. M., & Hallahan, D. P. (1979). Learning disability and hyperactivity (with comments on minimal brain dysfunction). In B. B. Lahey & A. E. Kazdin (Eds.), *Advances in clinical child psychology* (Vol. 2). New York: Plenum.

Kauffman, J. M., & Kneedler, R. D. (1981). Behavior disorders. In J. M. Kauffman & D. P. Hallahan (Eds.), *Handbook of special education*. Englewood Cliffs, NJ: Prentice-Hall.

Kauffman, J. M., & Lewis, C. D. (Eds.). (1974). *Teaching children with behavior disorders: Personal perspectives*. Columbus, OH: Merrill.

Kavale, K. A., & Karge, B. D. (1986). Fetal alcohol syndrome: A behavioral teratology. *The Exceptional Child, 33,* 4–16.

Kazdin, A. E. (1977). Assessing the clinical or applied importance of behavior change through social validation. *Behavior Modification, 1,* 427–452.

Kazdin, A. E. (1978). *History of behavior modification: Experimental foundations of contemporary research*. Baltimore, MD: University Park Press.

Kazdin, A. E. (1981). Assessment techniques for childhood depression: A critical appraisal. *Journal of the American Academy of Child Psychiatry, 20,* 358–375.

Kazdin, A. E. (1984). *Behavior modification in applied settings* (3rd ed.). Homewood, IL: Dorsey Press.

Kazdin, A. E. (1985). *Treatment of antisocial behavior in children and adolescents*. Homewood, IL: Dorsey Press.

Kazdin, A. E. (1987). *Conduct disorders in childhood and adolescence*. Beverly Hills, CA: Sage.

Kazdin, A. E., Colbus, D., & Rodgers, A. (1986). Assessment of depression and diagnosis of depressive disorder among psychiatrically disturbed children. *Journal of Abnormal Child Psychology, 14,* 499–515.

Kazdin, A. E., Esveldt-Dawson, K., & Loar, L. L. (1983). Correspondence of teacher ratings and direct observations of classroom behavior of psychiatric inpatient children. *Journal of Abnormal Child Psychology, 11,* 549–564.

Kazdin, A. E., & Frame, C. (1983). Aggressive behavior and conduct disorders. In R. J. Morris & T. R. Krotchwill (Eds.), *The practice of child therapy*. New York: Pergamon.

Kazdin, A. E., French, N. H., & Unis, A. S. (1983). Child, mother, and father evaluations of depression in psychiatric inpatient children. *Journal of Abnormal Child Psychology, 11,* 167–180.

Kazdin, A. E., French, N. H., Unis, A. S., & Esveldt-Dawson, K. (1983). Assessment of childhood depression: Correspondence of child and parent ratings. *Journal of the American Academy of Child Psychiatry, 22,* 157–164.

Kazdin, A. E., French, N. H., Unis, A. S., Esveldt-Dawson, K., & Sherick, R. B. (1983). Hopelessness, depression, and suicidal intent among psychiatrically disturbed inpatient children. *Journal of Consulting and Clinical Psychology, 51,* 504–511.

Keller, B. B., & Bell, R. Q. (1979). Child effects on adults' method of eliciting altruistic behavior. *Child Development, 50,* 1004–1009.

Kelso, J., & Stewart, M. A. (1986). Factors which predict the persistence of aggressive conduct disorder. *Journal of Child Psychology and Psychiatry, 27,* 77–86.

Kennedy, W. A. (1983). Obsessive-compulsive and phobic reactions. In T. H. Ollendick & M. Hersen (Eds.), *Handbook of child psychopathology.* New York: Plenum.

Keogh, B. K. (1971). Hyperactivity and learning disorders: Review and speculation. *Exceptional Children, 40,* 5–11.

Kern, L., Koegel, R. L., & Dunlap, G. (1984). The influence of vigorous versus mild exercise on autistic stereotyped behaviors. *Journal of Autism and Developmental Disorders, 14,* 57–67.

Kerr, M. M., Hoier, T. S., & Versi, M. (1987). Methodological issues in childhood depression: A review of literature. *American Journal of Orthopsychiatry, 57,* 193–198.

Kerr, M. M., & Nelson, C. M. (1983). *Strategies for managing behavior problems in the classroom.* Columbus, OH: Merrill.

Kerr, M. M., Nelson, C. M., & Lambert, D. L. (1987). *Helping adolescents with learning and behavior problems.* Columbus, OH: Merrill.

Kerr, M. M., & Zigmond, N. (1986). What do high school teachers want? A study of expectations and standards. *Education and Treatment of Children, 9,* 239–249.

Kety, S. S. (1979). Disorders of the human brain. *Scientific American, 241*(3), 202–214.

Key, E. (1909). *The century of the child.* New York: Putnam.

Kiburz, C. S., Miller, S. R., & Morrow, L. W. (1984). Structured learning using self-monitoring to promote maintenance and generalization of social skills across settings for a behaviorally disordered student. *Behavioral Disorders, 10,* 47–55.

King, N. J., Hamilton, D. I., & Murphy, G. C. (1983). The prevention of children's maladaptive fears. *Child and Family Behavior Therapy, 5*(2), 43–57.

Kirigin, K. A., Braukman, C. J., Atwater, J. D., & Wolf, M. M. (1982). An evaluation of Teaching-Family (Achievement Place) group homes for juvenile offenders. *Journal of Applied Behavior Analysis, 15,* 1–16.

Kirk, S. A. (1972). *Educating exceptional children* (2nd ed.). Boston: Houghton Mifflin.

Kirk, W. J. (1976). Juvenile justice and delinquency. *Phi Delta Kappan, 57,* 395–398.

Kittrie, N. N. (1971). *The right to be different: Deviance and enforced therapy.* Baltimore: Johns Hopkins Press.

Klerman, G. L., Vaillant, G. E., Spitzer, R. L., & Michels, R. (1984). A debate on DSM-III. *American Journal of Psychiatry, 141,* 539–553.

Knapczyk, D. R. (1979). Diet control in the management of behavior disorders. *Behavioral Disorders, 5,* 2–9.

Kneedler, R. D., & Hallahan, D. P. (1981). Self-monitoring of on-task behavior with learning disabled children: Current studies and directions. *Exceptional Education Quarterly, 2*(3), 73–82.

Knitzer, J. (1982). *Unclaimed children: The failure of public responsibility to children and adolescents in need of mental health services.* Washington, DC: Children's Defense Fund.

Knoblock, P. (Ed.). (1965). *Educational programming for emotionally disturbed children: The decade ahead.* Syracuse, NY: Syracuse University Press.

Knoblock, P. (Ed.). (1966). *Intervention approaches in educating emotionally disturbed children.* Syracuse, NY: Syracuse University Press.

Knoblock, P. (1970). A new humanism for special education. The concept of the open classroom for emotionally disturbed children. In P. A. Gallagher & L. L. Edwards (Eds.), *Educating the emotionally disturbed: Theory to practice.* Lawrence: University of Kansas.

Knoblock, P. (1973). Open education for emotionally disturbed children. *Exceptional Children, 39,* 358–365.

Knoblock, P. (1979). Educational alternatives for adolescents labeled emotionally disturbed. In D. Cullinan & M. H. Epstein (Eds.), *Special education for adolescents: Issues and perspectives.* Columbus, OH: Merrill.

Knoblock, P., & Goldstein, A. (1971). *The lonely teacher*. Boston: Allyn & Bacon.

Knoblock, P., & Johnson, J. L. (Eds.). (1966). *The teaching-learning process in educating emotionally disturbed children*. Syracuse, NY: Syracuse University Press.

Koegel, R. L., & Covert, A. (1972). The relationship of self-stimulation to learning in autistic children. *Journal of Applied Behavior Analysis, 5,* 381–387.

Koegel, R. L., Firestone, P. B., Kramme, K. W., & Dunlap, G. (1974). Increasing spontaneous play by suppressing self-stimulation in autistic children. *Journal of Applied Behavior Analysis, 7,* 521–528.

Koegel, R. L., & Mentis, M. (1985). Motivation in childhood autism: Can they or won't they? *Journal of Child Psychology and Psychiatry, 26,* 185–191.

Koegel, R. L., O'Dell, M. C., & Koegel, L. Y. (1987). A natural language teaching paradigm for nonverbal autistic children. *Journal of Autism and Developmental Disorders, 17,* 187–200.

Koegel, R. L., Rincover, A., & Egel, A. L. (1982). *Educating and understanding autistic children*. San Diego, CA: College-Hill.

Kohl, H. (1970). *The open classroom*. New York: Vintage.

Koles, M. R., & Jenson, W. R. (1985). Comprehensive treatment of chronic fire setting in a severely disordered boy. *Journal of Behavior Therapy and Experimental Psychiatry, 16,* 81–85.

Kolko, D. J., & Kazdin, A. E. (1986). A conceptualization of fire setting in children and adolescents. *Journal of Abnormal Child Psychology, 14,* 49–61.

Konstantareas, M. M., & Homatidis, S. (1985). Dominance hierarchies in normal and conduct-disordered children. *Journal of Abnormal Child Psychology, 13,* 259–268.

Konstantareas, M. M., Webster, C. D., & Oxman, J. (1979). Manual language acquisition and its influence on other areas of functioning in four autistic and autistic-like children. *Journal of Child Psychology and Psychiatry, 20,* 337–350.

Kornberg, L. (1955). *A class for disturbed children: A case study and its meaning for education*. New York: Teachers College Press.

Kornetsky, C. (1975). Minimal brain dysfunction and drugs. In W. M. Cruickshank & D. P. Hallahan (Eds.), *Perceptual and learning disabilities in children:*

Vol. 2. Research and theory. Syracuse, NY: Syracuse University Press.

Koupernik, C., MacKeith, R., & Francis-Williams, J. (1975). Neurological correlates of motor and perceptual development. In W. M. Cruickshank & D. P. Hallahan (Eds.), *Perceptual and learning disabilities in children: Vol. 2. Research and theory*. Syracuse, NY: Syracuse University Press.

Kovacs, M., Feinberg, T. L., Crouse-Novak, M. A., Paulauskas, S. L., & Finkelstein, R. (1984). Depressive disorders in childhood. *Archives of General Psychiatry, 41,* 229–237.

Kozol, J. (1967). *Death at an early age*. New York: Bantam.

Kozol, J. (1972). *Free schools*. Boston: Houghton Mifflin.

Kratochwill, T. R., Brody, G. H., & Piersel, W. C. (1979). Elective mutism in children. In B. B. Lahey & A. E. Kazdin (Eds.), *Advances in clinical child psychology* (Vol. 2). New York: Plenum.

Kropp, J. P., & Haynes, O. M. (1987). Abusive and nonabusive mothers' ability to identify general and specific emotion signals of infants. *Child Development, 58,* 187–190.

Krouse, J. P. (1982). *Peer conformity among delinquent subtypes*. Unpublished doctoral dissertation, University of Virginia.

Krouse, J. P., & Kauffman, J. M. (1982). Minor physical anomalies in exceptional children: A review and critique of research. *Journal of Abnormal Child Psychology, 10,* 247–264.

Krugman, M. (Chairman). (1953). Symposium: The education of emotionally disturbed children. *American Journal of Orthopsychiatry, 23,* 667–731.

Krupski, A. (1981). An interactional approach to the study of attention problems in children with learning handicaps. *Exceptional Education Quarterly, 2*(3), 1–12.

Krupski, A. (1987). Attention: The verbal phantom strikes again—A response to Samuels. *Exceptional Children, 54,* 62–65.

Kubaney, E. S., Weiss, L. E., & Sloggett, B. B. (1971). The good behavior clock: A reinforcement/time-out procedure for reducing disruptive classroom behavior. *Journal of Behavior Therapy and Experimental Psychiatry, 2,* 173–179.

Kupersmidt, J. B., & Coie, J. D. (1987). *Preadolescent*

peer status and aggression as predictors of externalizing problems in adolescence. Manuscript submitted for publication, University of Virginia, Charlottesville, VA.

Kupersmidt, J. B., & Patterson, C. J. (1987). *Interim report to the Charlottesville Public Schools on children at risk.* Unpublished manuscript, University of Virginia, Charlottesville, VA.

LaGrow, S. J., & Repp, A. C. (1984). Stereotypic responding: A review of intervention research. *American Journal of Mental Deficiency, 88,* 595–609.

Lane, H. (1976). *The wild boy of Aveyron.* Cambridge, MA: Harvard University Press.

Langone, H. (1981). "Too weary to go on." *Discover, 1*(11), 72–76.

Larsen, S. C., & Poplin, M. S. (1980). *Methods for educating the handicapped: An individualized education program approach.* Boston: Allyn & Bacon.

Larson, K. A., & Gerber, M. M. (1987). Effects of social metacognitive training for enhancing overt behavior in learning disabled and low achieving delinquents. *Exceptional Children, 54,* 201–211.

Lawrence, C., Litynsky, M., & D'Lugoff, B. (1982). A day school intervention for truant and delinquent youth. In D. J. Safer (Ed.), *School programs for disruptive adolescents.* Baltimore, MD: University Park Press.

Ledingham, J. E., & Schwartzman, A. E. (1984). A 3-year follow-up of aggressive and withdrawn behavior in childhood: Preliminary findings. *Journal of Abnormal Child Psychology, 12,* 157–168.

Lee, B. (1971). Curriculum design: The re-education approach. In N. J. Long, W. C. Morse, & R. G. Newman (Eds.), *Conflict in the classroom* (2nd ed.). Belmont, CA: Wadsworth.

Leon, G. R., & Dinklage, D. (1983). Childhood obesity and anorexia nervosa. In T. H. Ollendick & M. Hersen (Eds.), *Handbook of child psychopathology.* New York: Plenum.

Leonard, G. (1968). *Education and ecstasy.* New York: Delacorte.

Leone, P. E. (1985). Data-based instruction in correctional education. *Journal of Correctional Education, 36,* 77–85.

Leone, P. E. (1987). Teaching handicapped learners in correctional education programs. In C. M. Nelson, R. B. Rutherford, & B. I. Wolford (Eds.), *Special*

education in the criminal justice system. Columbus, OH: Merrill.

Leone, P. E., Price, T., & Vitolo, R. K. (1986). Appropriate education for all incarcerated youth: Meeting the spirit of P. L. 94–142 in youth detention facilities. *Remedial and Special Education, 7*(4), 9–14.

Levental, T., & Sills, M. (1964). Self-image in school phobia. *American Journal of Orthopsychiatry, 34,* 685–695.

Levin, H. M., Guthrie, J. W., Kleindorfer, G. B., & Stout, R. T. (1971). School achievement and post-school success: A review. *Review of Educational Research, 41,* 1–16.

Lewin, P., Nelson, R. E., & Tollefson, N. (1983). Teacher attitudes toward disruptive children. *Elementary School Guidance and Counseling, 17,* 188–193.

Lewis, C. D. (1974). Introduction: Landmarks. In J. M. Kauffman & C. D. Lewis (Eds.), *Teaching children with behavior disorders: Personal perspectives.* Columbus, OH: Merrill.

Lewis, M. H., Baumeister, A. A., & Mailman, R. B. (1987). A neurobiological alternative to the perceptual reinforcement hypothesis of stereotyped behavior: A commentary on "self-stimulatory behavior and perceptual reinforcement." *Journal of Applied Behavior Analysis, 20,* 253–258.

Lewis, W. W. (1982). Ecological factors in successful residential treatment. *Behavioral Disorders, 7,* 149–156.

Linton, T. E. (1969). The European educateur program for disturbed children. *American Journal of Orthopsychiatry, 39,* 125–133.

Linton, T. E. (1970). The European educateur model: An alternative and effective approach to the mental health of children. *Journal of Special Education, 3,* 319–327.

Lloyd, J. W., Crowley, E. P., Kohler, F. W., & Strain, P. S. (1988). Redefining the applied research agenda: Cooperative learning, prereferral, teacher consultation, and peer-mediated interventions. *Journal of Learning Disabilities, 21,* 43–52.

Lloyd, J. W., & De Bettencourt, L. U. (1986). Prevention of achievement deficits. In B. A. Edelstein & L. Michelson (Eds.), *Handbook of prevention.* New York: Plenum.

Lloyd, J. W., Kauffman, J. M., & Gansneder, B. (1987). Differential teacher response to descriptions of aberrant behavior. In R. B. Rutherford, C. M. Nelson, & S. R. Forness (Eds.), *Severe behavior disorders of children and youth* (pp. 41–52). Boston: College Hill.

Lloyd, J. W., Kauffman, J. M., & Kupersmidt, J. B. (1987, November). *The Virginia Behavior Disorders Project*. Paper presented at Eleventh Annual Conference on Severe Behavior Disorders of Children and Youth, Tempe, AZ.

Loeber, R. (1982). The stability of antisocial and delinquent child behavior: A review. *Child Development, 53,* 1431–1446.

Loeber, R., & Schmaling, K. B. (1985a). Empirical evidence for overt and covert patterns of antisocial conduct problems: A metaanalysis. *Journal of Abnormal Child Psychology, 13,* 337–352.

Loeber, R., & Schmaling, K. B. (1985b). The utility of differentiating between mixed and pure forms of antisocial child behavior. *Journal of Abnormal Child Psychology, 13,* 315–336.

Loeber, R., Weissman, W., & Reid, J. B. (1983). Family interactions of assaultive adolescents, stealers, and nondelinquents. *Journal of Abnormal Child Psychology, 11,* 1–14.

Long, N. J. (1974). Nicholas J. Long. In J. M. Kauffman & C. D. Lewis (Eds.), *Teaching children with behavior disorders: Personal perspectives.* Columbus, OH: Merrill.

Long, N. J., Morse, W. C., & Newman, R. G. (Eds.). (1965). *Conflict in the classroom.* Belmont, CA: Wadsworth.

Long, N. J., & Newman, R. G. (1965). Managing surface behavior of children in school. In N. J. Long, W. C. Morse, & R. G. Newman (Eds.), *Conflict in the classroom.* Belmont, CA: Wadsworth.

Lovaas, O. I. (1966). A program for the establishment of speech in psychotic children. In J. K. Wing (Ed.), *Early childhood autism: Clinical, educational and social aspects.* New York: Pergamon.

Lovaas, O. I. (1967). A behavior therapy approach to the treatment of childhood schizophrenia. In J. P. Hill (Ed.), *Minnesota symposia on child psychology.* Minneapolis: University of Minnesota Press.

Lovaas, O. I. (1969). *Behavior modification: Teaching language to psychotic children* (16mm film). New York: Appleton-Century-Crofts.

Lovaas, O. I. (1977). *The autistic child: Language development through behavior modification.* New York: Irvington.

Lovaas, O. I. (1979). Contrasting illness and behavioral models for the treatment of autistic children: A historical perspective. *Journal of Autism and Developmental Disorders, 9,* 315–323.

Lovaas, O. I. (1982). Comments on self-destructive behaviors. *Analysis and Intervention in Developmental Disabilities, 2,* 115–124.

Lovaas, O. I. (1987). Behavioral treatment and normal educational and intellectual functioning in young autistic children. *Journal of Consulting and Clinical Psychology, 55,* 3–9.

Lovaas, O. I., Freitag, G., Gold, V. J., & Kassorla, I.C. (1965). Experimental studies in childhood schizophrenia: Analysis of self-destructive behavior. *Journal of Experimental Child Psychology, 2,* 67–81.

Lovaas, O. I., & Koegel, R. L. (1973). Behavior therapy with autistic children. In C. Thoresen (Ed.), *Behavior modification in education.* Chicago: University of Chicago Press.

Lovaas, O. I., Koegel, R. L., & Schriebman, L. (1979). Stimulus overselectivity in autism: A review of research. *Psychological Bulletin, 86,* 1236–1254.

Lovaas, O. I., Koegel, R. L., Simmons, J. Q., & Long, J. S. (1973). Some generalization and follow-up measures on autistic children in behavior therapy. *Journal of Applied Behavior Analysis, 6,* 131–166.

Lovaas, O. I., Newsom, C., & Hickman, C. (1987). Self-stimulatory behavior and perceptual reinforcement. *Journal of Applied Behavior Analysis, 20,* 45–68.

Lovaas, O. I., Schaeffer, B., & Simmons, J. Q. (1965). Building social behavior in autistic children by use of electric shock. *Journal of Experimental Research in Personality, 1,* 99–109.

Lovaas, O. I., & Simmons, J. Q. (1969). Manipulation of self-destruction in three retarded children. *Journal of Applied Behavior Analysis, 2,* 143–157.

Lovaas, O. I., Young, D. B., & Newsom, C. D. (1978). Childhood psychosis: Behavioral treatment. In B. B. Wolman (Ed.), *Handbook of treatment of mental disorders in childhood and adolescence.* Englewood Cliffs, NJ: Prentice-Hall.

Lovitt, T. C. (1977). *In spite of my resistance—I've learned from children.* Columbus, OH: Merrill.

Lovitt, T. C. (1980). *Writing and implementing an IEP: A step-by-step plan.* Belmont, CA: Pitman.

Lovitt, T. C., & Curtiss, K. A. (1968). Effects of manipulating an antecedent event on mathematics response rate. *Journal of Applied Behavior Analysis, 1,* 329–333.

Luiselli, J. K. (1985). Behavior analysis of pharmacological and contingency management interventions for self-injury. *Journal of Behaviour Therapy and Experimental Psychiatry, 17,* 275–284.

Luk, S., Thorley, G., & Taylor, E. (1987). Gross overactivity: A study by direct observation. *Journal of Psychopathology and Behavioral Assessment, 9,* 173–182.

Lyman, R. D. (1984). The effect of private and public goal setting on classroom on-task behavior of emotionally disturbed children. *Behavior Therapy, 15,* 395–402.

Lyon, L. S. (1983). A behavioral treatment of compulsive lip-biting. *Journal of Behavior Therapy and Experimental Psychiatry, 14,* 275–276.

Lyons, D. F., & Powers, V. (1963). Follow-up study of elementary school children exempted from Los Angeles City Schools during 1960–1961. *Exceptional Children, 30,* 155–162.

Maag, J. W., Rutherford, R. B., Wolchik, S. A., & Parks, B. T. (1986). Brief report: Comparison of two short overcorrection procedures on the stereotypic behavior of autistic children. *Journal of Autism and Developmental Disorders, 16,* 83–87.

Maag, J. W., Wolchik, S. A., Rutherford, R. B., & Parks, B. T. (1986). Response covariation on self-stimulatory behaviors during sensory extinction procedures. *Journal of Autism and Developmental Disorders, 16,* 119–132.

MacDonald, W. S., Gallimore, R., & MacDonald, G. (1970). Contingency counseling by school personnel: An economical model of intervention. *Journal of Applied Behavior Analysis, 3,* 175–182.

McAfee, J. K. (1987). Classroom density and the aggressive behavior of handicapped children. *Education and Treatment of Children, 10,* 134–145.

McCarthy, J. M., & Paraskevopoulos, J. (1969). Behavior patterns of learning disabled, emotionally disturbed, and average children. *Exceptional Children, 36,* 69–74.

Mace, F. C., & West, B. J. (1986). Analysis of demand conditions associated with reluctant speech. *Journal of Behavior Therapy and Experimental Psychiatry, 17,* 285–294.

McClure, F. D., & Gordon, M. (1984). Performance of disturbed hyperactive and nonhyperactive children on an objective measure of hyperactivity.

Journal of Abnormal Child Psychology, 12, 651–672.

McConnell, S. R. (1987). Entrapment effects and the generalization and maintenance of social skills training for elementary school students with behavioral disorders. *Behavioral Disorders, 12,* 252–263.

McCord, J. (1986). Instigation and insulation: How families affect antisocial aggression. In D. Olweus, J. Block, & M. Radke-Yarrow (Eds.), *Development of antisocial and prosocial behavior: Research, theories, and issues.* New York: Academic Press.

McDowell, R. L., Adamson, G. W., & Wood, F. H. (Eds.). (1982). *Teaching emotionally disturbed children.* Boston: Little, Brown.

Mace, F. C., & West, B. J. (1986). Unresolved theoretical issues in self-management: Implications for research and practice. *Professional School Psychology, 1,* 149–163.

McEvoy, M. A., & Odom, S. L. (1987). Social interaction training for preschool children with behavioral disorders. *Behavioral Disorders, 12,* 242–251.

Maher, C. A. (1987). Involving behaviorally disordered adolescents in instructional planning: Effectiveness of the GOAL procedure. *Journal of Child and Adolescent Psychotherapy, 4,* 204–210.

McHugh, J. (1987, April 5). Portrait of trouble: Teen's crimes began early. *The Daily Progress,* pp. A1, A6.

McKenzie, T. L. (1986). A behaviorally-oriented residential camping program for obese children and adolescents. *Education and Treatment of Children, 9,* 67–78.

McKinney, J. D., Mason, J., Perkerson, K., & Clifford, M. (1975). Relationship between classroom behavior and academic achievement. *Journal of Educational Psychology, 67,* 198–203.

McMahon, R. J. (1984). Behavioral checklists and rating scales. In T. H. Ollendick & M. Hersen (Eds.), *Child behavioral assessment: Principles and procedures.* New York: Pergamon.

McManus, M. (1985). *Modification of adolescent students' off-task behaviors using self-monitoring procedures.* Unpublished manuscript, University of Virginia, Charlottesville, VA.

Maccoby, E. E. (1986). Social groupings in childhood: Their relationship to prosocial and antisocial behavior in boys and girls. In D. Olweus, J. Block, & M. Radke-Yarrow (Eds.), *Development of antisocial and prosocial behavior: Research, theories, and issues.* New York: Academic Press.

Macfarlane, J., Allen, L., & Honzik, M. (1955). *A developmental study of the behavior problems of normal children between 21 months and 14 years.* Berkeley: University of California Press.

Mackie, R. P., Kvaraceus, W. C., & Williams, H. M. (1957). *Teachers of children who are socially and emotionally maladjusted.* Washington, DC: Office of Education, U. S. Department of Health, Education and Welfare.

MacMillan, D. L., Forness, S. R., & Trumbull, B. M. (1973). The role of punishment in the classroom. *Exceptional Children, 40,* 85–96.

MacMillan, M. B. (1960). Extra-scientific influences in the history of childhood psychopathology. *American Journal of Psychiatry, 116,* 1091–1096.

Magliocca, L. A., & Stephens, T. M. (1980). Child identification or child inventory? A critique of the federal design of child identification systems implemented under P.L. 94–142. *Journal of Special Education, 14,* 23–36.

Mahler, M. S. (1952). On child psychosis and schizophrenia. *Psychoanalytic Study of the Child, 7,* 286–305.

Mahoney, M. J. (1974). *Cognition and behavior modification.* Cambridge, MA: Ballinger.

Maloney, D. M., Fixsen, D. C., & Maloney, K. B. (1978). Antisocial behavior: Behavior modification. In B. B. Wolman (Ed.), *Handbook of treatment of mental disorders in childhood and adolescence.* Englewood Cliffs, NJ: Prentice-Hall.

Maloney, M. J., Pettigrew, H., & Farrell, M. (1983). Treatment sequence for severe weight loss in anorexia nervosa. *International Journal of Eating Disorders, 2*(2), 53–58.

Mann, L. (1979). *On the trail of process: A historical perspective on cognitive processes and their training.* New York: Grune & Stratton.

Marlowe, M., Cossairt, A., Moon, C., Errera, J., MacNeel, A., Peak, R., Ray, J., & Schroeder, C. (1985). Main and interaction effects of metallic toxins on classroom behavior. *Journal of Abnormal Child Psychology, 13,* 185–198.

Marlowe, R. H., Madsen, C. H., Bowen, C. E., Reardon, R. C., & Logue, P. E. (1978). Severe classroom behavior problems: Teachers or counselors. *Journal of Applied Behavior Analysis, 11,* 53–66.

Martin, B. (1975). Parent-child relations. In F. D. Horowitz (Ed.), *Review of Child Development Research* (Vol. 4). Chicago: University of Chicago Press.

Martin, E. W. (1972). Individualism and behaviorism as future trends in educating handicapped children. *Exceptional Children, 38,* 517–525.

Martin, J. A. (1981). A longitudinal study of the consequences of early mother-infant interaction: A microanalytic approach. *Monographs of the Society for Research in Child Development, 43* (3, Serial No. 190).

Martin, R. P., Wisenbaker, J., Matthews-Morgan, J., Holbrook, J., Hooper, S., & Spalding, J. (1986). Stability of teacher temperament ratings over 6 and 12 months. *Journal of Abnormal Child Psychology, 14,* 167–179.

Marushkin-Mott, J. (1986). Portrait of Mark Matthews. *Gifted/Creative/Talented, 9*(6), 53.

Mash, E. J., & Johnston, C. (1983). Parental perceptions of child behavior problems, parenting self-esteem, and mothers' reported stress in younger and older hyperactive and normal children. *Journal of Consulting and Clinical Psychology, 51,* 86–99.

Mash, E. J., & Terdal, E. G. (Eds.). (1981). *Behavioral assessment of childhood disorders.* New York: Guilford.

Maslow, A. (1962). *Toward a psychology of being.* New York: Van Nostrand.

Maslow, A. (1968). Some educational implications of the humanistic psychologies. *Harvard Educational Review, 38,* 385–396.

Maudsley, H. (1880). *The pathology of the mind.* New York: Appleton.

Mayer, G. R., & Butterworth, T. (1981). Evaluating a preventive approach to reducing school vandalism. *Phi Delta Kappan, 62,* 498–499.

Mayer, G. R., Butterworth, T., Nafpaktitis, M., & Sulzer-Azaroff, B. (1983). Preventing school vandalism and improving discipline: A three-year study. *Journal of Applied Behavior Analysis, 16,* 355–369.

Mayer, G. R., Nafpaktitis, M., Butterworth, T., & Hollingsworth, P. (1987). A search for the elusive settings events of school vandalism: A correlational study. *Education and Treatment of Children, 10,* 259–270.

Mayo, T. (1839). *Elements of pathology of the human mind.* Philadelphia: Waldie.

Maypole, D. E., & Anderson, R. B. (1987). Culture-specific substance abuse prevention for blacks. *Community Mental Health Journal, 23,* 135–139.

Mednick, S. A., Moffitt, T., Gabrielli, W., & Hutchings, B. (1986). Genetic factors in criminal behavior: A review. In D. Olweus, J. Block, & M. Radke-Yarrow (Eds.), *Development of antisocial and prosocial behavior: Research, theories, and issues.* New York: Academic Press.

Meichenbaum, D. (1977). *Cognitive-behavior modification: An integrative approach.* New York: Plenum.

Meichenbaum, D. (1979). Teaching children self-control. In B. B. Lahey & A. E. Kazdin (Eds.), *Advances in clinical child psychology* (Vol. 2). New York: Plenum.

Meichenbaum, D. (1980). Cognitive-behavior modification: A promise yet unfulfilled. *Exceptional Education Quarterly, 1*(1), 83–88.

Meichenbaum, D. (1983). Teaching thinking: A cognitive-behavioral approach. In *Interdisciplinary voices in learning disabilities and remedial education.* Austin, TX: Pro-Ed.

Meichenbaum, D., Bowers, K. S., & Ross, R. R. (1969). A behavioral analysis of teacher expectancy effect. *Journal of Personality and Social Psychology, 13,* 306–316.

Meichenbaum, D., & Goodman, J. (1969). Reflection-impulsivity and verbal control of motor behavior. *Child Development, 40,* 785–797.

Meichenbaum, D., & Goodman, J. (1971). Training impulsive children to talk to themselves. *Journal of Abnormal Psychology, 77,* 115–126.

Menninger, K. (1963). *The vital balance.* New York: Viking Press.

Menolascino, F. J. (1972). Primitive, atypical, and abnormal-psychotic behavior in institutionalized mentally retarded children. *Journal of Autism and Childhood Schizophrenia, 3,* 49–64.

Mesinger, J. F. (1986). Alternative education for behaviorally disordered youths: A promise yet unfulfilled. *Behavioral Disorders, 11,* 98–108.

Miksic, S. (1987). Drug abuse management in adolescent special education. In M. M. Kerr, C. M. Nelson, & D. L. Lambert, *Helping adolescents with learning and behavior problems.* Columbus, OH: Merrill.

Milby, J. B., Wendorf, D., & Meredith, R. L. (1983). Obsessive-compulsive disorders. In R. J. Morris & T. R. Kratochwill (Eds.), *The practice of child therapy.* New York: Pergamon.

Milgram, G. G., & Nathan, P. E. (1986). Efforts to prevent alcohol abuse. In B. A. Edelstein & L. Michelson (Eds.), *Handbook of prevention.* New York: Plenum.

Miller, L. C. (1972). School Behavior Checklist: An inventory of deviant behavior for elementary school children. *Journal of Consulting and Clinical Psychology, 38,* 138–144.

Miller, W. B. (1958). Lower class culture as a generating milieu of gang delinquency. *Journal of Social Issues, 14,* 5–19.

Mizes, J. S. (1985). Bulimia: A review of its symptomatology and treatment. *Advances in Behavior Research and Therapy, 7,* 91–142.

Monahan, J. (1984). The prediction of violent behavior: Toward a second generation of theory and policy. *American Journal of Psychiatry, 141,* 10–15.

Moore, D. R., & Arthur, J. L. (1983). Juvenile delinquency. In T. H. Ollendick & M. Hersen (Eds.), *Handbook of child psychopathology.* New York: Plenum.

Moore, D. R., Chamberlain, P., & Mukai, L. H. (1979). Children at risk for delinquency: A follow-up comparison of aggressive children and children who steal. *Journal of Abnormal Child Psychology, 7,* 345–355.

Morena, D. A., & Litrownik, A. J. (1974). Self-concept in educable mentally retarded and emotionally handicapped children: Relationship between behavioral and self-report indices and an attempt at modification. *Journal of Abnormal Child Psychology, 2,* 281–292.

Morgan, D., Young, K. R., & Goldstein, S. (1983). Teaching behaviorally disordered students to increase teacher attention and praise in mainstreamed classrooms. *Behavioral Disorders, 8,* 265–273.

Morris, R. J. (1985). *Behavior modification with exceptional children.* Glenview, IL: Scott, Foresman.

Morris, R. J., & Kratochwill, T. R. (1983a). Childhood fears and phobias. In R. J. Morris & T. R. Kratochwill (Eds.), *The practice of child therapy.* New York: Pergamon.

Morris, R. J., & Kratochwill, T. R. (1983b). *Treating children's fears and phobias.* New York: Pergamon.

Morse, W. C. (1953). The development of a mental hygiene milieu in a camp program for disturbed boys. *American Journal of Orthopsychiatry, 23,* 826–833.

Morse, W. C. (1965a). The crisis teacher. In N. J. Long, W. C. Morse, & R. G. Newman (Eds.), *Conflict in the classroom.* Belmont, CA: Wadsworth.

Morse, W. C. (1965b). Intervention techniques for the classroom teacher. In P. Knoblock (Ed.), *Educational programming for emotionally disturbed children: The decade ahead.* Syracuse, NY: Syracuse University Press.

Morse, W. C. (1971a). Crisis intervention in school mental health and special classes for the disturbed. In N. J. Long, W. C. Morse, & R. G. Newman (Eds.), *Conflict in the classroom* (2nd ed.). Belmont, CA: Wadsworth.

Morse, W. C. (1971b). The crisis or helping teacher. In N. J. Long, W. C. Morse,& R. G. Newman (Eds.), *Conflict in the classroom* (2nd ed.). Belmont, CA: Wadsworth.

Morse, W. C. (1974). William C. Morse. In J. M. Kauffman & C. D. Lewis (Eds.), *Teaching children with behavior disorders: Personal perspectives.* Columbus, OH: Merrill.

Morse, W. C. (1985). *The education and treatment of socioemotionally impaired children and youth.* Syracuse, NY: Syracuse University Press.

Morse, W. C., Ardizzone, J., MacDonald, C., & Pasick, P. (1980). *Affective education for special children and youth.* Reston, VA: Council for Exceptional Children.

Morse, W. C., Cutler, R. L., & Fink, A. H. (1964). *Public school classes for the emotionally handicapped: A research analysis.* Washington, DC: Council for Exceptional Children.

Morse, W. C., & Wineman, D. (1965). Group interviewing in a camp for disturbed boys. In N. J. Long, W. C. Morse, & R. G. Newman (Eds.), *Conflict in the classroom.* Belmont, CA: Wadsworth.

Mosher, L. R., & Gunderson, J. G. (1974). The study of children at risk—A research strategy whose time has come. *Schizophrenia Bulletin, 8,* 13.

Motto, J. J., & Wilkins, G. S. (1968). Educational achievement of institutionalized emotionally disturbed children. *Journal of Educational Research, 61,* 218–221.

Mountjoy, P. T., Ruben, D. H., & Bradford, T. S. (1984). Recent technological advancements in the treatment of enuresis. *Behavior Modification, 8,* 291–315.

Moustakas, C. E. (1953). *Children in play therapy.* New York: McGraw-Hill.

Mulhern, R. K., & Passman, R. H. (1979). The child's behavioral pattern as a determinant of maternal punitiveness. *Child Development, 50,* 815–820.

Murphy, D. M. (Ed.). (1986a). Handicapped juvenile offenders [Special issue]. *Remedial and Special Education, 7*(3). Murphy, D. M. (1986b). The prevalence of handicapping conditions among juvenile delinquents. *Remedial and Special Education, 7*(3), 7–17.

National Institute on Drug Abuse. (1982). *Marijuana and youth* (Publication ADM 82-1186). Washington, DC: Department of Health and Human Services.

National Mental Health Association. (1986). *Severely emotionally disturbed children: Improving services under Education of the Handicapped Act (P.L. 94-142).* Washington, DC: Author.

Neill, A. S. (1960). *Summerhill.* New York: Hart.

Nelson, C. M. (1977). Alternative education for the mildly and moderately handicapped. In R. D. Kneedler & S. G. Tarver (Eds.), *Changing perspectives in special education.* Columbus, OH: Merrill.

Nelson, C. M. (1981). Classroom management. In J. M. Kauffman & D. P. Hallahan (Eds.), *Handbook of special education.* Englewood Cliffs, NJ: Prentice-Hall.

Nelson, C. M. (1985). Who's crazy? II. In S. Braaten, R. B. Rutherford, & C. A. Kardash (Eds.), *Programming for adolescents with behavioral disorders* (Vol. I, pp. 9–15). Reston, VA: Council for Children with Behavioral Disorders.

Nelson, C. M. (1987). Handicapped offenders in the criminal justice system. In C. M. Nelson, R. B. Rutherford, & B. I. Wolford (Eds.), *Special education in the criminal justice system.* Columbus, OH: Merrill.

Nelson, C. M., & Kauffman, J. M. (1977). Educational programming for secondary school age delinquent and maladjusted pupils. *Behavioral Disorders, 2,* 102–113.

Nelson, C. M., & Rutherford, R. B. (1983). Time-out revisited: Guidelines for its use in special education. *Exceptional Education Quarterly, 3*(4), 56–67.

Nelson, C. M., Rutherford, R. G., & Wolford, B. I. (Eds.). (1987). *Special education in the criminal justice system.* Columbus, OH: Merrill.

Neufeld, A., & Fantuzzo, J. W. (1984). Contingent application of a protective device to treat the severe self-biting behavior of a disturbed autistic child. *Journal of Behaviour Therapy and Experimental Psychiatry, 15,* 79–83.

Neufeld, A., & Fantuzzo, J. W. (1987). Treatment of severe self-injurious behavior by the mentally retarded using the bubble helmet and differential reinforcement procedures. *Journal of Behaviour Therapy and Experimental Psychiatry, 18,* 127–136.

Newsom, C., & Lovaas, O. I. (1987). A neurobiological nonalternative: Rejoinder to Lewis, Baumeister, and Mailman. *Journal of Applied Behavior Analysis, 20,* 259–262.

Newsom, C., & Rincover, A. (1981). Autism. In E. J. Mash & L. G. Terdal (Eds.), *Behavioral assessment of childhood disorders.* New York: Guilford.

Nicol, S. E., & Erlenmeyer-Kimling, L. (1986). Genetic factors and psychopathology: Implications for prevention. In B. A. Edelstein & L. Michelson (Eds.), *Handbook of prevention.* New York: Plenum.

Nietzel, M. T., & Himelein, M. J. (1986). Prevention of crime and delinquency. In B. A. Edelstein & L. Michelson (Eds.), *Handbook of prevention.* New York: Plenum.

O'Banion, D., Armstrong, B., Cummings, R. A., & Strange, J. (1978). Disruptive behavior: A dietary approach. *Journal of Autism and Childhood Schizophrenia, 8,* 325–337.

O'Brien, F. (1981). Treating self-stimulatory behavior. In J. L. Matson & J. R. McCartney (Eds.), *Handbook of behavior modification with the mentally retarded.* New York: Plenum.

O'Brien, S., Ross, L. V., & Christophersen, E. R. (1986). Primary encopresis: Evaluation and treatment. *Journal of Applied Behavior Analysis, 19,* 137–145.

Oldenburg, D. (1987, September 22). Child abuse: The emotional side. Some scars aren't found on the body. *The Washington Post,* p. D5.

O'Leary, K. D., & Johnson, S. B. (1986). Assessment and assessment of change. In H. C. Quay & J. S. Werry (Eds.), *Psychopathological disorders of childhood* (3rd ed.). New York: Wiley.

O'Leary, K. D., & Wilson, G. T. (1975). *Behavior therapy: Applications and outcomes.* Englewood Cliffs, NJ: Prentice-Hall.

O'Leary, S. G. (1980). A response to cognitive training. *Exceptional Education Quarterly, 1*(1), 89–94.

Ollendick, T. H., & Hersen, M. (1983). A historical overview of child psychopathology. In T. H. Ollendick & M. Hersen (Eds.), *Handbook of child psychopathology.* New York: Plenum.

Ollendick, T. H., & Hersen, M. (Eds.). (1984). *Child behavioral assessment: Principles and procedures.* New York: Pergamon.

Ollendick, T. H., & Matson, J. L. (1983). Stereotypic behaviors, stuttering, and elective mutism. In T. H. Ollendick & M. Hersen (Eds.), *Handbook of child psychopathology.* New York: Plenum.

Olweus, D. (1979). Stability of aggressive reaction patterns in males: A review. *Psychological Bulletin, 86,* 852–875.

Olweus, D. (1986). Aggression and hormones: Behavioral relationship with testosterone and adrenaline. In D. Olweus, J. Block, & M. Radke-Yarrow (Eds.), *Development of antisocial and prosocial behavior: Research, theories, and issues.* New York: Academic Press.

Olweus, D., Block, J., & Radke-Yarrow, M. (Eds.). (1986). *Development of antisocial and prosocial behavior: Research, theories, and issues.* New York: Academic Press.

Omizo, M. M., Cubberly, W. E., Semands, S. G., & Omizo, S. A. (1986). The effects of biofeedback and relaxation training on memory tasks among hyperactive boys. *The Exceptional Child, 33,* 56–64.

Ornitz, E. M. (1986). Prevention of developmental disorders. In B. A. Edelstein & L. Michelson (Eds.), *Handbook of prevention.* New York: Plenum.

Osborne, S. S., Kiburz, C. S., & Miller, S. R. (1986). Treatment of self-injurious behavior using self-control techniques with a severe behaviorally disordered student. *Behavioral Disorders, 12,* 60–67.

Palkes, H., Stewart, M., & Freedman, J. (1971). Improvement in maze performance of hyperactive boys as a function of verbal training procedures. *Journal of Special Education, 5,* 337–342.

Palkes, H., Stewart, M., & Kahana, M. (1968). Porteus maze performance of hyperactive boys after training in self-directed verbal commands. *Child Development, 39,* 817–826.

Panella, D., & Henggeler, S. W. (1986). Peer interactions of conduct-disordered, anxious-withdrawn, and well-adjusted black adolescents. *Journal of Abnormal Child Psychology, 14,* 1–11.

Paget, K. D., Nagle, R. J., & Martin, R. P. (1984). Interrelations between temperament characteristics and first-grade teacher-student interactions. *Journal of Abnormal Child Psychology, 12,* 547–560.

Park, C. C. (1972). *The seige.* Boston: Little, Brown.

Parke, R. D., & Collmer, C. W. (1975). Child abuse: An interdisciplinary analysis. In E. M. Hetherington (Ed.), *Review of child development research* (Vol. 5). Chicago: University of Chicago Press.

Parker, H., & Parker, S. (1986). Father-daughter sexual abuse: An emerging perspective. *American Journal of Orthopsychiatry, 56,* 531–549.

Parkinson, J. (1963). Observations on the excessive indulgence of children, particularly intended to show its injurious effects on their health, and the difficulties it occasions in their treatment during sickness. London: Symonds et al., 1807. In R. Hunter & I. Macalpine (Eds.), *Three hundred years of psychiatry, 1535–1860.* London: Oxford University Press.

Parsons, J. A. (1972). The reciprocal modification of arithmetic behavior and program development. In G. Semb (Ed.), *Behavior analysis and education—1972.* Lawrence: Kansas University Department of Human Development.

Patterson, G. R. (1965a). An application of conditioning techniques to the control of a hyperactive child. In L. P. Ullmann & L. Krasner (Eds.), *Case studies in behavior modification.* New York: Holt, Rinehart & Winston.

Patterson, G. R. (1965b). A learning theory approach to the treatment of the school phobic child. In L. P. Ullmann & L. Krasner (Eds.), *Case studies in behavior modification.* New York: Holt, Rinehart & Winston.

Patterson, G. R. (1971). *Families.* Champaign, IL: Research Press.

Patterson, G. R. (1973). Reprogramming the families of aggressive boys. In C. Thoresen (Ed.), *Behavior modification in education.* Chicago: University of Chicago Press.

Patterson, G. R. (1975). The aggressive child: Victim or architect of a coercive system? In L. A. Ham-

erlynck, L. C. Handy, & E. J. Mash (Eds.), *Behavior modification and families.* New York: Brunner/Mazel.

Patterson, G. R. (1980). Mothers: The unacknowledged victims. *Monographs of the Society for Research in Child Development, 45* (5, Serial No. 186).

Patterson, G. R. (1982). *Coercive family process.* Eugene, OR: Castalia.

Patterson, G. R. (1986a). The contribution of siblings to training for fighting: A microsocial analysis. In D. Olweus, J. Block, & M. Radke-Yarrow (Eds.), *Development of antisocial and prosocial behavior: Research, theories, and issues.* New York: Academic Press.

Patterson, G. R. (1986b). Performance models for antisocial boys. *American Psychologist, 41,* 432–444.

Patterson, G. R., Cobb, J. A., & Ray, R. S. (1972). Direct intervention in the classroom: A set of procedures for the aggressive child. In F. W. Clark, D. R. Evans, & L. A. Hammerlynck (Eds.), *Implementing behavioral programs in schools and clinics.* Champaign, IL: Research Press.

Patterson, G. R., Reid, J. B., Jones, R. R., & Conger, R. E. (1975). *A social learning approach to family intervention: Vol. 1. Families with aggressive children.* Eugene, OR: Castalia.

Patton, J. R., Payne, J. S., Kauffman, J. M., Brown, G. B., & Payne, R. A. (1987). *Exceptional children in focus* (4th ed.). Columbus, OH: Merrill.

Pearson, G. H. J. (1954). *Psychoanalysis and the education of the child.* New York: Norton.

Peterson, C. C., Peterson, J. L., & Seeto, D. (1983). Developmental changes in ideas about lying. *Child Development, 54,* 1529–1535.

Petti, T. A. (1983). Depression and withdrawal in children. In T. H. Ollendick & M. Hersen (Eds.), *Handbook of child psychopathology.* New York: Plenum.

Petty, L. K., Ornitz, E. M., Michelman, J. D., & Zimmerman, E. G. (1984). Autistic children who become schizophrenic. *Archives of General Psychiatry, 41,* 129–135.

Pfeffer, C. R. (1984). Clinical aspects of childhood suicidal behavior. *Pediatric Annals, 13,* 56–61.

Pfiffner, L. J., & O'Leary, S. G. (1987). The efficacy of all-positive management as a function of the prior use of negative consequences. *Journal of Applied Behavior Analysis, 20,* 265–271.

Pfiffner, L. J., Rosen, L. A., & O'Leary, S. G. (1985). The efficacy of an all-positive approach to classroom management. *Journal of Applied Behavior Analysis, 18,* 257–261.

Phillips, E. L. (1967). Problems in educating emotionally disturbed children. In N. G. Haring & E. L. Phillips (Eds.), *Methods in special education.* New York: McGraw- Hill.

Phillips, E. L., & Haring, N. G. (1959). Results from special techniques for teaching emotionally disturbed children. *Exceptional Children, 26,* 64–67.

Phillips, L., Draguns, J. G., & Bartlett, D. P. (1975). Classification of behavior disorders. In N. Hobbs (Ed.), *Issues in the classification of children* (Vol. 1). San Francisco: Jossey-Bass.

Piaget, J. (1932). *The moral judgment of the child.* New York: Free Press.

Polirstok, S. R. (1986). Training problematic adolescents as peer tutors: Benefits for the tutor and the school at large. *Techniques: A Journal for Remedial Education and Counseling, 2,* 204–210.

Polirstok, S. R. (1987). A specialized peer tutoring program for academically and behaviorally handicapped adolescents. In J. Gottlieb (Ed.), *Advances in special education* (Vol. 6). Greenwich, CT: JAI Press.

Polirstok, S. R., & Greer, R. D. (1977). Remediation of mutually aversive interactions between a problem student and four teachers by training the student in reinforcement techniques. *Journal of Applied Behavior Analysis, 10,* 707–716.

Polirstok, S. R., & Greer, R. D. (1986). A replication of collateral effects and a component analysis of a successful tutoring package for inner-city adolescents. *Education and Treatment of Children, 9,* 101–121.

Pollard, S., Ward, E. M., & Barkley, R. A. (1984). The effects of parent training and Ritalin on the parent-child interactions of hyperactive boys. *Child and Family Behavior Therapy, 5*(4), 51–69.

Polsgrove, L. (1979). Self-control: Methods for child training. *Behavioral Disorders, 4,* 116–130.

Polsgrove, L. (Ed.). (1983). Aversive control in the classroom [Special issue]. *Exceptional Education Quarterly, 3*(4). Polsgrove, L. (1987). Assessment of children's social and behavioral problems. In W. H. Berdine & S. A. Meyer (Eds.), *Assessment in special education.* Boston: Little, Brown.

Potter, H. W. (1933). Schizophrenia in children. *American Journal of Psychiatry, 89,* 1253–1270.

Prescott, D. A. (1954). *Emotions and the education process.* Washington, DC: American Council on Education.

Prior, M., & Werry, J. S. (1986). Autism, schizophrenia, and allied disorders. In H. C. Quay & J. S. Werry (Eds.), *Psychopathological disorders of childhood* (3rd ed.). New York: Wiley.

Pugliese, M. T., Lifshitz, F., Grad, G., Fort, P., & Marks-Katz, M. (1983). Fear of obesity: A cause of short stature and delayed puberty. *New England Journal of Medicine, 309,* 513–518.

Pulkkinen, L. (1986). The role of impulse control in the development of antisocial and prosocial behavior. In D. Olweus, J. Block, & M. Radke-Yarrow (Eds.), *Development of antisocial and prosocial behavior: Research, theories, and issues.* New York: Academic Press.

Pullen, P. L., & Kauffman, J. M. (1987). *What should I know about special education? Answers for classroom teachers.* Austin, TX: Pro-Ed.

Pullis, M., & Cadwell, J. (1982). The influence of children's temperament characteristics on teachers' decision strategies. *American Educational Research Journal, 19,* 165–181.

Pullis, M., & Cadwell, J. (1985). Temperament as a factor in the assessment of children educationally at risk. *Journal of Special Education, 19,* 91–102.

Quay, H. C. (1975). Classification in the treatment of delinquency and antisocial behavior. In N. Hobbs (Ed.), *Issues in the classification of children (Vol. 1). San Francisco: Jossey-Bass.*

Quay, H. C. (1977). Measuring dimensions of deviant behavior: The Behavior Problem Checklist. *Journal of Abnormal Child Psychology, 5,* 277–289.

Quay, H. C. (1986a). Classification. In H. C. Quay & J. S. Werry (Eds.), *Psychopathological disorders of childhood* (3rd ed.). New York: Wiley.

Quay, H. C. (1986b). Conduct disorders. In H. C. Quay & J. S. Werry (Eds.), *Psychopathological disorders of childhood* (3rd ed.). New York: Wiley.

Quay, H. C., & La Greca, A. M. (1986). Disorders of anxiety, withdrawal, and dysphoria. In H. C. Quay & J. S. Werry (Eds.), *Psychopathological disorders of childhood* (3rd ed.). New York: Wiley.

Quay, H. C., Morse, W. C., & Cutler, R. L. (1966). Personality patterns of pupils in special classes for the emotionally disturbed. *Exceptional Children, 32,* 297–301.

Quay, H. C., & Peterson, D. R. (1987). *Manual for the Revised Behavior Problem Checklist*. Coral Gables, FL: Author.

Radke-Yarrow, M., & Zahn-Waxler, C. (1986). The role of familial factors in the development of prosocial behavior: Research findings and questions. In D. Olweus, J. Block, & M. Radke-Yarrow (Eds.), *Development of antisocial and prosocial behavior: Research, theories, and issues*. New York: Academic Press.

Rahim, S. I. A., & Cederblad, M. (1984). Effects of rapid urbanisation on child behavior and health in a part of Khartoum, Sudan. *Journal of Child Psychology and Psychiatry, 25,* 629–641.

Raiser, L., & Van Nagel, C. (1980). The loophole in Public Law 94–142. *Exceptional Children, 46,* 516–520.

Raiten, D. J., & Massaro, T. (1986). Perspectives on the nutritional ecology of autistic children. *Journal of Autism and Developmental Disorders, 16,* 133–143.

Rank, B. (1949). Adaptation of the psychoanalytic techniques for the treatment of young children with atypical development. *American Journal of Orthopsychiatry, 19,* 130–139.

Rapoport, J. L. (1986). Childhood obsessive compulsive disorder. *Journal of Child Psychology and Psychiatry, 27,* 289–295.

Rappaport, M. M., & Rappaport, H. (1975). The other half of the expectancy equation: Pygmalion. *Journal of Educational Psychology, 67,* 531–536.

Rappaport, S. R. (1976). Sheldon R. Rappaport. In J. M. Kauffman & D. P. Hallahan (Eds.), *Teaching children with learning disabilities: Personal perspectives*. Columbus, OH: Merrill.

Rapport, M. D., Stoner, G., DuPaul, G. J., Birmingham, B. K., & Tucker, S. (1985). Methylphenidate in hyperactive children: Differential effects of dose on academic, learning, and social behavior. *Journal of Abnormal Child Psychology, 13,* 227–244.

Ray, I. (1846). Observations of the principal hospitals for the insane, in Great Britain, France, and Germany. *American Journal of Insanity, 2,* 289–390.

Raymer, R., & Poppen, R. (1985). Behavioral relaxation training with hyperactive children. *Journal of Behavior Therapy and Experimental Psychiatry, 16,* 309–316.

Redl, F. (1959a). The concept of a therapeutic milieu. *American Journal of Orthopsychiatry, 29,* 721–734.

Redl, F. (1959b). The concept of the life space interview. *American Journal of Orthopsychiatry, 29,* 1–18.

Redl, F. (1966). Designing a therapeutic classroom environment for disturbed children: The milieu approach. In P. Knoblock (Ed.), *Intervention approaches in educating emotionally disturbed children*. Syracuse, NY: Syracuse University Press.

Redl, F., & Wattenberg, W. W. (1951). *Mental hygiene in teaching*. New York: Harcourt, Brace, & World.

Redl, F., & Wineman, D. (1951). *Children who hate*. New York: Free Press.

Redl, F., & Wineman, D. (1952). *Controls from within*. New York: Free Press.

Reed, E. W. (1975). Genetic anomalies in development. In F. D. Horowitz (Ed.), *Review of child development research* (Vol. 4). Chicago: University of Chicago Press.

Rees, T. P. (1957). Back to moral treatment and community care. *Journal of Mental Science, 103,* 303–313.

Reid, J. B., & Hendricks, A. (1973). Preliminary analysis of the effectiveness of direct home intervention for the treatment of predelinquent boys who steal. In L. A. Hammerlynck, L. C. Handy, & E. J. Mash (Eds.), *Behavior change: Methodology, concepts and practice*. Champaign, IL: Research Press.

Reid, J. B., & Patterson, G. R. (1976). The modification of aggression and stealing behavior of boys in the home setting. In A. Bandura & E. Ribes (Eds.), *Behavior modification: Experimental analyses of aggression and delinquency*. Hillsdale, NJ: Erlbaum.

Rekers, G. A. (1977a). Assessment and treatment of childhood gender problems. In B. B. Lahey & A. E. Kazdin (Eds.), *Advances in clinical child psychology* (Vol. 1). New York: Plenum.

Rekers, G. A. (1977b). A typical gender development and prosocial behavior. *Journal of Applied Behavior Analysis, 10,* 559–571.

Rekers, G. A. (1978). Sexual problems: Behavior modification. In B. B. Wolman (Ed.), *Handbook of treatment of mental disorders in childhood and adolescence*. Englewood Cliffs, NJ: Prentice-Hall.

Rekers, G. A. (1981). Psychosexual and gender problems. In E. J. Mash & L. G. Terdal (Eds.), *Behavioral assessment of childhood disorders*. New York: Guilford.

Rekers, G. A. (1985). Gender identity problems. In P. H. Bornstein & A. E. Kazdin (Eds.), *Handbook of clinical behavior therapy with children*. Homewood, IL: Dorsey Press.

Reynolds, M. C., Wang, M. C., & Walberg, H. J. (1987). The necessary restructuring of special and regular education. *Exceptional Children, 53*, 391–398.

Reynolds, W. M., Anderson, G., & Bartell, N. (1985). Measuring depression in children: A multimethod assessment investigation. *Journal of Abnormal Child Psychology, 13*, 513–526.

Rezmierski, V. E., Knoblock, P., & Bloom, R. B. (1982). The psychoeducational model: Theory and historical perspective. In R. L. McDowell, G. W. Adamson, & F. H. Wood (Eds.), *Teaching emotionally disturbed children*. Boston: Little, Brown.

Rhodes, W. C. (1963). Curriculum and disordered behavior. *Exceptional Children, 30*, 61–66.

Rhodes, W. C. (1965). Institutionalized displacement and the disturbing child. In P. Knoblock (Ed.), *Intervention approaches in educating emotionally disturbed children*. Syracuse, NY: Syracuse University Press.

Rhodes, W. C. (1967). The disturbing child: A problem of ecological management. *Exceptional Children, 33*, 449–455.

Rhodes, W. C. (1970). A community participation analysis of emotional disturbance. *Exceptional Children, 37*, 309–314.

Rhodes, W. C., & Head, S. (Eds.). (1974). *A study of child variance: Vol. 3. Service delivery systems*. Ann Arbor: University of Michigan.

Rhodes, W. C., & Paul, J. L. (1978). *Emotionally disturbed and deviant children: New views and approaches*. Englewood Cliffs, NJ: Prentice-Hall.

Rhodes, W. C., & Tracy, M. L. (Eds.). (1972a). *A study of child variance: Vol. 1. Theories*. Ann Arbor: University of Michigan.

Rhodes, W. C., & Tracy, M. L. (Eds.). (1972b). *A study of child variance: Vol. 2. Interventions*. Ann Arbor: University of Michigan.

Rich, H. L., Beck, M. A., & Coleman, T. W. (1982). Behavior management: The psychoeducational model. In R. L. McDowell, G. W. Adamson, & F. H. Wood (Eds.), *Teaching emotionally disturbed children*. Boston: Little, Brown.

Rie, H. E. (1971). Historical perspective of concepts of child psychopathology. In H. E. Rie (Ed.), *Perspectives in child psychopathology*. Chicago: Aldine Atherton.

Rimland, B. (1964). *Infantile autism*. New York: Appleton-Century-Crofts (Prentice-Hall).

Rincover, A. (1978a). Sensory extinction: A procedure for eliminating self-stimulatory behavior in developmentally disabled children. *Journal of Abnormal Child Psychology, 6*, 299–310.

Rincover, A. (1978b). Variables affecting stimulus fading and discriminative responding in psychotic children. *Journal of Abnormal Psychology, 87*, 541–553.

Rincover, A., Cook, R., Peoples, A., & Packard, D. (1979). Using sensory extinction and sensory reinforcement principles for programming multiple adaptive behavior change. *Journal of Applied Behavior Analysis, 12*, 221–233.

Rincover, A., & Devany, J. (1982). The application of sensory extinction procedures to self-injury. *Analysis and Intervention in Developmental Disabilities, 2*, 67–82.

Rincover, A., Newsom, C. D., Lovaas, O. I., & Koegel, R. L. (1977). Some motivational properties of sensory stimulation in psychotic children. *Journal of Experimental Child Psychology, 24*, 312–323.

Robins, L. N. (1966). *Deviant children grown up*. Baltimore: Williams & Wilkins.

Robins, L. N. (1974). Antisocial behavior disturbances of childhood: Prevalence, prognosis, and prospects. In E. J. Anthony & C. Koupernik (Eds.), *The child in his family: Children at psychiatric risk*. New York: Wiley.

Robins, L. N. (1979). Follow-up studies. In H. C. Quay & J. S. Werry (Eds.), *Psychopathological disorders of childhood* (2nd ed.). New York: Wiley.

Robins, L. N. (1986). The consequences of conduct disorder in girls. In D. Olweus, J. Block, & M. Radke-Yarrow (Eds.), *Development of antisocial and prosocial behavior: Research, theories, and issues*. New York: Academic Press.

Robinson, F. J., & Vitale, L. J. (1954). Children with circumscribed interest patterns. *American Journal of Orthopsychiatry, 24*, 755–766.

Rogers, C. (1969). *Freedom to learn*. Columbus, OH: Merrill.

Rolider, A., & Van Houten, R. (1985). Treatment of

constipation-caused encopresis by a negative re-inforcement procedure. *Journal of Behavior Therapy and Experimental Psychiatry, 16,* 67–70.

Romig, D. A. (1978). *Justice for our children.* Lexington, MA: Lexington Books.

Rooney, K. J., & Hallahan, D. P. (1985). Future directions for cognitive behavior modification research: The quest for cognitive change. *Remedial and Special Education, 6*(2), 46–51.

Rose, T. L. (1978). The functional relationship between artificial food colors and hyperactivity. *Journal of Applied Behavior Analysis, 11,* 439–446.

Rose, T. L. (1983). A survey of corporal punishment of mildly handicapped students. *Exceptional Education Quarterly, 3*(4), 9–19.

Rosen, H. S., & Rosen, L. A. (1983). Eliminating stealing: Use of stimulus control with an elementary student. *Behavior Modification, 7,* 56–63.

Rosen, J. C. (1987). A review of behavioral treatments for bulimia nervosa. *Behavior Modification, 11,* 464–486.

Rosen, L. A., O'Leary, S. G., Joyce, S. A., Conway, G., & Pfiffner, L. J. (1984). The importance of prudent negative consequences for maintaining the appropriate behavior of hyperactive students. *Journal of Abnormal Child Psychology, 12,* 581–604.

Rosenberg, H. E., & Graubard, P. S. (1975). Peer use of behavior modification. *Focus on Exceptional Children, 7*(6), 1–10.

Rosenberg, M. S. (1986). Maximizing the effectiveness of structured classroom management programs: Implementing rule-review procedures with disruptive and distractible students. *Behavioral Disorders, 11,* 239–248.

Rosenthal, P. A., & Rosenthal, S. (1984). Suicidal behavior by preschool children. *American Journal of Psychiatry, 141,* 520–525.

Rosenthal, R., & Jacobson, L. (1968). *Pygmalion in the classroom.* New York: Holt, Rinehart & Winston.

Ross, D. M., & Ross, S. A. (1982). *Hyperactivity: Research, theory, action* (2nd ed.). New York: Wiley.

Rotheram, M. J. (1987). Evaluation of imminent danger for suicide among youth. *American Journal of Orthopsychiatry, 57,* 102–110.

Rothman, D. (1971). *The discovery of the asylum: Social order and disorder in the new republic.* Boston: Little, Brown.

Rothman, E. P. (1967). The Livingston School: A day school for disturbed girls. In P. H. Berkowitz & E. P. Rothman (Eds.), *Public education for disturbed children in New York City.* Springfield, IL: Charles C. Thomas.

Rothman, E. P. (1970). *The angel inside went sour.* New York: David McKay.

Rothman, E. P. (1974). Esther P. Rothman. In J. M. Kauffman & C. D. Lewis (Eds.), *Teaching children with behavior disorders: Personal perspectives.* Columbus, OH: Merrill.

Rothman, E. P., & Berkowitz, P. H. (1967a). The clinical school—A paradigm. In P. H. Berkowitz & E. P. Rothman (Eds.), *Public education for disturbed children in New York City.* Springfield, IL: Charles C. Thomas.

Rothman, E. P., & Berkowitz, P. H. (1967b). The concept of clinical teaching. In P. H. Berkowitz & E. P. Rothman (Eds.), *Public education for disturbed children in New York City.* Springfield, IL: Charles C. Thomas.

Rothman, E. P., & Berkowitz, P. H. (1967c). Some aspects of reading disability. In P. H. Berkowitz & E. P. Rothman (Eds.), *Public education for disturbed children in New York City.* Springfield, IL: Charles C. Thomas.

Rubenstein, E. A. (1948). Childhood mental disease in America. *American Journal of Orthopsychiatry, 18,* 314–321.

Rubin, R. A., & Balow, B. (1971). Learning and behavior disorders: A longitudinal study. *Exceptional Children, 38,* 292–299.

Rubin, R. A., & Balow, B. (1978). Prevalence of teacher identified behavior problems: A longitudinal study. *Exceptional Children, 45,* 102–111.

Rubin, T. I. (1962). *Jordi, Lisa, and David.* New York: Macmillan.

Ruhl, K. L., & Hughes, C. A. (1985). The nature and extent of aggression in special education settings serving behaviorally disordered students. *Behavioral Disorders, 10,* 95–104.

Runco, M. A., Charlop, M. H., & Schreibman, L. (1986). The occurrence of autistic children's self-stimulation as a function of familiar versus unfamiliar stimulus conditions. *Journal of Autism and Developmental Disorders, 16,* 31–44.

Rusch, F. R., & Phelps, L. A. (1987). Secondary special education and transition from school to work: A national priority. *Exceptional Children, 53,* 487–492.

Rutherford, R. B., Nelson, C. M., & Wolford, B. I. (1985). Special education in the most restrictive environment: Correctional/special education. *Journal of Special Education, 19,* 59–71.

Rutherford, R. B., Nelson, C. M., & Wolford, B. I. (1986). Special education programming in juvenile corrections. *Remedial and Special Education, 7*(3), 27–33.

Rutter, M. (1979). Maternal deprivation, 1972–1978. New findings, new concepts, new approaches. *Child Development, 50,* 283–305.

Rutter, M. (1985). Family and school influences on behavioural development. *Journal of Child Psychology and Psychiatry, 26,* 349–368.

Rutter, M., & Bartak, L. (1973). Special educational treatment of autistic children: A comparative study—II. Follow-up findings and implications for services. *Journal of Child Psychology and Psychiatry, 14,* 241–270.

Rutter, M., Maughan, B., Mortimer, P., Ouston, J., & Smith, A. (1979). *Fifteen thousand hours: Secondary schools and their effects on children.* Cambridge, MA: Harvard University Press.

Rutter, M., & Schopler, E. (1987). Autism and pervasive developmental disorders: Concepts and diagnostic issues. *Journal of Autism and Developmental Disorders, 17,* 159–186.

Rutter, M., Tizard, J., Yule, W., Graham, P., & Whitmore, K. (1976). Isle of Wight studies, 1964–1974. *Psychological Medicine, 6,* 313–332.

Sabornie, E. J. (1985). Social mainstreaming of handicapped students: Facing an unpleasant reality. *Remedial and Special Education, 6*(2), 12–16.

Sabornie, E. J. (1987). Bi-directional social status of behaviorally disordered and nonhandicapped elementary school pupils. *Behavioral Disorders, 13,* 45–57.

Sabornie, E. J., & Kauffman, J. M. (1985). Regular classroom sociometric status of emotionally disturbed adolescents. *Behavioral Disorders, 10,* 268–274.

Safer, D. J. (1982a). Dimensions and issues of school programs for disruptive youth. In D. J. Safer (Ed.), *School programs for disruptive adolescents.* Baltimore, MD: University Park Press.

Safer, D. J. (Ed.). (1982b). *School programs for disruptive adolescents.* Baltimore, MD: University Park Press.

Safer, D. J. (1982c). Varieties and levels of intervention with disruptive adolescents. In D. J. Safer (Ed.), *School programs for disruptive adolescents.* Baltimore, MD: University Park Press.

Safer, D. J., & Heaton, R. C. (1982). Characteristics, school patterns, and behavioral outcomes of seriously disruptive junior high school students. In D. J. Safer (Ed.), *School programs for disruptive adolescents.* Baltimore, MD: University Park Press.

Safer, D. J. (1984). Subgrouping conduct disordered adolescents by early risk factors. *American Journal of Orthopsychiatry, 54,* 603–612.

Safran, J. S., & Safran, S. P. (1987). Teachers' judgments of problem behaviors. *Exceptional Children, 54,* 240–244.

Sahley, T. L., & Panksepp, J. (1987). Brain opioids and autism: An updated analysis of possible linkages. *Journal of Autism and Developmental Disorders, 17,* 201–216.

Sainato, D. M., Maheady, L., & Shook, G. L. (1986). The effects of a classroom manager role on the social interaction patterns and social status of withdrawn kindergarten students. *Journal of Applied Behavior Analysis, 19,* 187–195.

Salvia, J., & Ysseldyke, J. E. (1985). *Assessment in special and remedial education* (3rd ed.). Boston: Houghton Mifflin.

Sameroff, A. J., & Chandler, M. J. (1975). Reproductive risk and the continuum of caretaking casualty. In F. D. Horowitz (Ed.), *Review of child development research* (Vol. 4). Chicago: University of Chicago Press.

Sameroff, A. J., & Seifer, R. (1983). Familial risk and child competence. *Child Development, 54,* 1254–1268.

Sameroff, A. J., Seifer, R., & Zax, M. (1982). Early development of children at risk for emotional disorder. *Monographs of the Society for Research in Child Development, 47* (7, Serial No. 199).

Sanok, R. L., & Ascione, F. R. (1979). Behavioral interventions for childhood elective mutism: An evaluative review. *Child Behavior Therapy, 1,* 49–68.

Savage, G. H. (1891). *Insanity and allied neuroses: Practical and clinical.* London: Cassell.

Scarpitti, F. R., Murray, E., Dinitz, S., & Reckless, W. C. (1960). The "good" boy in a high delinquency area: Four years later. *American Sociological Review, 25,* 555–558.

Schachar, R., Sandberg, S., & Rutter, M. (1986). Agreement between teachers' ratings and observations of hyperactivity, inattentiveness, and defiance. *Journal of Abnormal Child Psychology, 14,* 331–345.

Scharfman, M. A. (1978). Psychoanalytic treatment. In B. B. Wolman (Ed.), *Handbook of treatment of mental disorders in childhood and adolescence.* Englewood Cliffs, NJ: Prentice-Hall.

Schleimer, K. (1983). Dieting in teenage schoolgirls: A longitudinal perspective study. *Acta Paediatrica Scandinavica* (Suppl. 312).

Schloss, P. J., Kane, M. S., & Miller, S. (1981). Truancy intervention with behaviorally disordered adolescents. *Behavioral Disorders, 6,* 175–179.

Schloss, P. J., Schloss, C. N., Wood, C. E., & Kiehl, W. S. (1986). A critical review of social skills research with behaviorally disordered students. *Behavioral Disorders, 12,* 1–14.

Schreibman, L., Charlop, M. H., & Britten, K. R. (1983). Childhood autism. In R. J. Morris & T. R. Kratochwill (Eds.), *The practice of child therapy.* New York: Pergamon.

Schreibman, L., Kohlenberg, B. S., & Britten, K. R. (1986). Differential responding to content and intonation components of a complex auditory stimulus by nonverbal and echolalic autistic children. *Analysis and Intervention in Developmental Disabilities, 6,* 109–125.

Schreibman, L., & Mills, J. I. (1983). Infantile autism. In T. H. Ollendick & M. Hersen (Eds.), *Handbook of child psychopathology* (pp. 123–150). New York: Plenum.

Schroeder, S. R., Schroeder, C. S., Rojahn, J., & Mulick, J. A. (1981). Self-injurious behavior: An analysis of behavior management techniques. In J. L. Matson & J. R. McCartney (Eds.), *Handbook of behavior modification with the mentally retarded.* New York: Plenum.

Schulman, J. L., Stevens, T. M., Suran, B. G., Kupst, M. J., & Naughton, M. J. (1978). Modification of activity level through biofeedback and operant conditioning. *Journal of Applied Behavior Analysis, 11,* 145–152.

Schultz, E. W., & Heuchert, C. M. (1983). *Child stress and the school experience.* New York: Human Sciences Press.

Schultz, E. W., Heuchert, C. M., & Stampf, S. W. (1973). *Pain and joy in school.* Champaign, IL: Research Press.

Schultz, E. W., Hirshoren, A., Manton, A. B., & Henderson, R. A. (1971). Special education for the emotionally disturbed. *Exceptional Children, 38,* 313–319.

Schumaker, J. B., & Deshler, D. D. (1988). Implementing the regular education initiative in secondary schools—A different ball game. *Journal of Learning Disabilities, 21,* 36–42.

Seay, M. B., Suppa, R. J., Schoen, S. F., & Roberts, S. R. (1984). Countercontrol: An issue in intervention. *Remedial and Special Education, 5*(1), 38–42.

Seguin, E. (1866). *Idiocy and its treatment by the physiological method.* New York: William Wood.

Seligman, M. E. P. (1975). *Helplessness.* San Francisco: Freeman.

Shapiro, E. S., Albright, T. S., & Ager, C. L. (1986). Group versus individual contingencies in modifying two disruptive adolescents' behavior. *Professional School Psychology, 1,* 105–116.

Sheldon, W. H. (1967). Constitutional psychiatry. In T. Millon (Ed.), *Theories of psychopathology.* Philadelphia: Saunders.

Sheldon, W. H., Hartl, E. M., & McDermott, E. (1949). *Varieties of delinquent youth: An introduction to constitutional psychiatry.* New York: Harper.

Sheras, P. L. (1983). Suicide in adolescence. In C. E. Walker & M. C. Roberts (Eds.), *Handbook of clinical child psychology.* New York: Wiley.

Sherman, H., & Farina, A. (1974). Social inadequacy of parents and children. *Journal of Abnormal Psychology, 83,* 327–330.

Sherman, J. A., & Bushell, D. (1975). Behavior modification as an educational technique. In F. D. Horowitz (Ed.), *Review of child development research* (Vol. 4). Chicago: University of Chicago Press.

Shinn, M. R., & Marston, D. B. (1985). Differentiating mildly handicapped, low-achieving, and regular education students using curriculum-based assessment procedures. *Remedial and Special Education, 6*(2), 31–38.

Shinn, M. R., Ramsey, E., Walker, H. M., Stieber, S., & O'Neill, R. E. (1987). Antisocial behavior in school settings: Initial differences in an at risk and normal population. *Journal of Special Education, 21,* 69–84.

Shores, R. E. (1987). Overview of research on social interaction: A historical and personal perspective. *Behavioral Disorders, 12,* 233–241.

Siegel, L. J. (1983). Psychosomatic and psychophysiological disorders. In R. J. Morris & T. R. Kratochwill (Eds.), *The practice of child therapy.* New York: Pergamon.

Siegel, L. J., & Ridley-Johnson, R. (1985). Anxiety disorders of childhood and adolescence. In P. H. Bornstein & A. E. Kazdin (Eds.), *Handbook of clinical behavior therapy with children.* Homewood, IL: Dorsey Press.

Sigman, M., Ungerer, J. A., & Russell, A. (1983). Moral judgment in relation to behavioral and cognitive disorders in adolescents. *Journal of Abnormal Child Psychology, 11,* 503–512.

Silberberg, N. E., & Silberberg, M. C. (1971). School achievement and delinquency. *Review of Educational Research, 41,* 17–32.

Silberman, C. E. (1978). *Criminal violence, criminal justice.* New York: Random House.

Silver, L. B. (1987). The "magic cure": A review of the current controversial approaches for treating learning disabilities. *Journal of Learning Disabilities, 20,* 498–504, 512.

Simmel, E. C., Hahn, M. E., & Walters, J. K. (1983). Synthesis and new directions. In E. C. Simmel, M. E. Hahn, & J. K. Walters (Eds.), *Aggressive behavior: Genetic and neural approaches.* Hillsdale, NJ: Erlbaum.

Simonds, J. R., & Glenn, T. (1976). Folie à deux in a child. *Journal of Autism and Developmental Disorders, 6,* 61–73.

Simpson, R. L. (1987). Social interactions of behaviorally disordered children and youth: Where are we and where do we need to go? *Behavioral Disorders, 12,* 292–298.

Sinclair, E., Forness, S. R., & Alexson, J. (1985). Psychiatric diagnosis: A study of its relationship to school needs. *Journal of Special Education, 19,* 333–344.

Singh, N. N., & Millichamp, C. J. (1985). Pharmacological treatment of self-injurious behavior in mentally retarded persons. *Journal of Autism and Developmental Disabilities, 15,* 257–267.

Skinner, B. F. (1953). *Science and human behavior.* New York: Free Press.

Slavson, S. R. (1954). *Re-educating the delinquent through group and community participation.* New York: Harper.

Smith, C. R. (1985). Identification of handicapped children and youth: A state agency perspective on behavioral disorders. *Remedial and Special Education, 6*(4), 34–41.

Smith, C. R., Wood, F. H., & Grimes, J. (in press). Issues in the identification and placement of behaviorally disordered students. In M. C. Wang, M. C. Reynolds, & H. J. Walberg (Eds.), *Handbook of special education: Research and practice* (Vol. 2). New York: Pergamon.

Smith, D. D. (1984). *Effective discipline.* Austin, TX: Pro-Ed.

Smith, J. O. (1962). Criminality and mental retardation. *Training School Bulletin, 59,* 74–80.

Smith, M. D., & Belcher, R. (1985). Teaching life skills to adults disabled by autism. *Journal of Autism and Developmental Disorders, 15,* 163–175.

Snarr, R. W. (1987). The criminal justice system. In C. M. Nelson, R. B. Rutherford, & B. I. Wolford (Eds.), *Special education in the criminal justice system.* Columbus, OH: Merrill.

Spence, S. H. (1986). Behavioural treatments of childhood obesity. *Journal of Child Psychology and Psychiatry, 27,* 447–453.

Spitz, R. (1946). Anaclitic depression. *The Psychoanalytic Study of the Child, 2,* 313–342.

Spivack, G., & Shure, M. B. (1982). The cognition of social adjustment: Interpersonal cognitive problem-solving thinking. In B. B. Lahey & A. E. Kazdin (Eds.), *Advances in clinical child psychology* (Vol. 5). New York: Plenum.

Spivack, G., & Swift, M. S. (1966). The Devereux Elementary School Behavior Rating Scales: A study of the nature and organization of achievement related disturbed classroom behavior. *Journal of Special Education, 1,* 71–90.

Spivack, G., & Swift, M. S. (1977). The Hahnemann High School Behavior (HHSB) Rating Scale. *Journal of Abnormal Child Psychology, 5,* 299–307.

Sprafkin, J., & Gadow, K. D. (1986). Television viewing habits of emotionally disturbed, learning disabled, and mentally retarded children. *Journal of Applied Development Psychology, 7,* 45–59.

Sprafkin, J., Gadow, K. D., & Dussault, M. (1986). Reality perceptions of television: A preliminary comparison of emotionally disturbed and non-handicapped children. *American Journal of Orthopsychiatry, 56,* 147–152.

Sprafkin, J., Gadow, K. D., & Kant, G. (1988). Teaching emotionally disturbed children to discriminate reality from fantasy on television. *Journal of Special Education, 21*(4), 99–107.

Sprafkin, J., Kelly, E., & Gadow, K. D. (1987). Reality perceptions of television: A comparison of emotionally disturbed, learning disabled, and nonhandicapped children. *Journal of Developmental and Behavioral Pediatrics, 8,* 149–153.

Sroufe, L. A., Steucher, H. U., & Stutzer, W. (1973). The functional significance of autistic behaviors for the psychotic child. *Journal of Abnormal Child Psychology, 1,* 225–240.

Steinberg, L. (1987). Single parents, stepparents, and the susceptibility of adolescents to antisocial peer pressure. *Child Development, 58,* 269–275.

Stephens, T. M. (1978). *Social skills in the classroom.* Columbus, OH: Merrill.

Steucher, U. (1972). *Tommy: A treatment study of an autistic child.* Reston, VA: Council for Exceptional Children.

Stevens, G. E. (1980). Invasion of student privacy. *Journal of Law and Education, 9,* 343–351.

Stevenson, D. L., & Baker, D. P. (1987). The family-school relation and the child's school performance. *Child Development, 58,* 1348–1357.

Stevenson-Hinde, J., Hinde, R. A., & Simpson, A. E. (1986). Behavior at home and friendly or hostile behavior in preschool. In D. Olweus, J. Block, & M. Radke-Yarrow (Eds.), *Development of antisocial and prosocial behavior: Research, theories, and issues.* New York: Academic Press.

Stone, F., & Rowley, V. N. (1964). Educational disability in emotionally disturbed children. *Exceptional Children, 30,* 423–426.

Stouthamere-Loeber, M., & Loeber, R. (1986). Boys who lie. *Journal of Abnormal Child Psychology, 14,* 551–564.

Strain, P. S. (Ed.). (1981). *The utilization of classroom peers as behavior change agents.* New York: Plenum.

Strain, P. S. (1983). Generalization of autistic children's social behavior change: Effects of developmentally integrated and segregated settings. *Analysis and Intervention in Developmental Disabilities, 3,* 23–34.

Strain, P. S. (1984). Social behavior patterns of non-handicapped and developmentally disabled friend pairs in mainstream schools. *Analysis and Intervention in Developmental Disabilities, 4,* 15–28.

Strain, P. S. (1987). Comprehensive evaluation of young autistic children. *Topics in Early Childhood Special Education, 7*(2), 97–110.

Strain, P. S., Lambert, D. L., Kerr, M. M., Stagg, V., & Lenkner, D. A. (1983). Naturalistic assessment of children's compliance to teachers' requests and consequences for compliance. *Journal of Applied Behavior Analysis, 16,* 243–249.

Strain, P. S., Odom, S. L., & McConnell, S. (1984). Promoting social reciprocity of exceptional children: Identification target behavior selection, and intervention. *Remedial and Special Education, 5*(1), 21–28.

Strain, P. S., Steele, P., Ellis, T., & Timm, M. (1982). Long-term effects of oppositional child treatment with mothers as therapists and therapist trainers. *Journal of Applied Behavior Analysis, 15,* 163–169.

Strauss, A. A., & Kephart, N. C. (1955). *Psychopathology and education of the brain injured child: Vol. 2. Progress in theory and clinic.* New York: Grune & Stratton.

Strauss, A. A., & Lehtinen, L. E. (1947). *Psychopathology and education of the brain injured child.* New York: Grune & Stratton.

Strauss, C. C., Forehand, R., Smith, K., & Frame, C. L. (1986). The association between social withdrawal and internalizing problems of children. *Journal of Abnormal Child Psychology, 14,* 525–535.

Stribling, F. T. (1842). Physician and superintendent's report. In *Annual Reports to the Court of Directors of the Western Lunatic Asylum to the Legislature of Virginia.* Richmond: Shepherd & Conlin.

Stullken, E. H. (1950). Special schools and classes for the socially maladjusted. In N. B. Henry (Ed.), *The education of exceptional children.* Forth-ninth Yearbook of the National Society for the Study of Education, Part II. Chicago: University of Chicago Press.

Stutte, H., & Dauner, I. (1971). Systematized delusions in early life schizophrenia. *Journal of Autism and Childhood Schizophrenia, 1,* 411–420.

Swanson, J. M., & Kinsbourne, M. (1980). Food dyes impair performance of hyperactive children on a laboratory learning test. *Science, 207,* 1485–1487.

Swap, S. (1974). Disturbing classroom behaviors: A developmental and ecological view. *Exceptional Children, 41,* 163–172.

Swap, S. (1978). The ecological model of emotional disturbance in children: A status report and proposed synthesis. *Behavioral Disorders, 3,* 186–196.

Swap, S., Prieto, A. G., & Harth, R. (1982). Ecological perspectives on the emotionally disturbed child. In R. L. McDowell, G. W. Adamson, & F. H. Wood (Eds.), *Teaching emotionally disturbed children.* Boston: Little, Brown.

Swift, M. S., & Swift, G. (1968). The assessment of achievement related classroom behavior: Normative, reliability, and validity data. *Journal of Special Education, 2,* 137–153.

Swift, M. S., & Swift, G. (1969a). Achievement related classroom behavior of secondary school normal and disturbed students. *Exceptional Children, 35,* 677–684.

Swift, M. S., & Swift, G. (1969b). Clarifying the relationship between academic success and overt classroom behavior. *Exceptional Children, 36,* 99–104.

Swift, M. S., & Swift, G. (1973). Academic success and classroom behavior in secondary schools. *Exceptional Children, 39,* 392–399.

Switzer, E. G., Deal, T. E., & Bailey, J. S. (1977). The reduction of stealing in second graders using a group contingency. *Journal of Applied Behavior Analysis, 10,* 267–272.

Szasz, T. S. (1960). The myth of mental illness. *American Psychologist, 15,* 113–118.

Tallmadge, G. K., Gamel, N. N., Munson, R. G., & Hanley, T. V. (1985). *Special study on terminology.* Mountain View, CA: SRA Technologies.

Tamkin, A. S. (1960). A survey of educational disability in emotionally disturbed children. *Journal of Educational Research, 53,* 313–315.

Tansey, M. A., & Bruner, R. L. (1983). EMG and EEG biofeedback training in the treatment of a 10-year-old hyperactive boy with a developmental reading disorder. *Biofeedback and Self-Regulation, 8,* 25–37.

Taylor, P. D., & Turner, R. K. (1975). A clinical trial of continuous, intermittent, and overlearning "bell and pad" treatments for nocturnal enuresis. *Behaviour Research and Therapy, 13,* 281–293.

Tedeschi, J. T., Smith, R. B., & Brown, R. C. (1974). A reinterpretation of research on aggression. *Psychological Bulletin, 81,* 540–562.

Tharp, R. G., & Wetzel, R. J. (1969). *Behavior modification in the natural environment.* New York: Academic Press.

Thomas, A., & Chess, S. (1975). A longitudinal study of three brain damaged children. *Archives of General Psychiatry, 32,* 457–462.

Thomas, A., & Chess, S. (1984). Genesis and evolution of behavioral disorders: From infancy to early adult life. *American Journal of Psychiatry, 141,* 1–9.

Thomas, A., Chess, S., & Birch, H. G. (1968). *Temperament and behavior disorders in children.* New York: New York University Press.

Thomas, A., Chess, S., & Korn, S. J. (1982). The reality of difficult temperament. *Merrill-Palmer Quarterly, 28,* 1–20.

Thomas, M. H., Horton, R. W., Lippincott, E. C., & Drabman, R. S. (1977). Desensitization to portrayals of real-life aggression as a function of exposure to television violence. *Journal of Personality and Social Psychology, 35,* 450–458.

Tiegerman, E., & Primavera, L. H. (1984). Imitating the autistic child: Facilitating communicative gaze behavior. *Journal of Autism and Developmental Disorders, 14,* 27–38.

Tobin, D. D. (1971). Overcoming crude behavior in a "600" school. In N. J. Long, W. C. Morse, & R. G. Newman (Eds.), *Conflict in the classroom* (2nd ed.). Belmont, CA: Wadsworth.

Tolan, P. H. (1987). Implications of age of onset for delinquency risk. *Journal of Abnormal Child Psychology, 15,* 47–65.

Trieschman, A. E., Whittaker, J. K., & Brendtro, L. K. (1969). *The other 23 hours.* Chicago: Aldine.

Trippe, M. J. (1970, April). *Love of life, love of truth, love of others.* Presidential address, Annual meeting of the Council for Children with Behavioral Disorders, Gary, IN.

Trites, R. L., & Tryphonas, H. (1983a). Food additives: The controversy continues. *Topics in Early Childhood Special Education, 3*(2), 43–47.

Trites, R. L., & Tryphonas, H. (1983b). Food intolerance and hyperactivity. *Topics in Early Childhood Special Education, 3*(2), 49–54.

Trosch, L. A., Williams, R. G., & Devore, F. W. (1982). Public school searches and the fourth amendment. *Journal of Law and Education, 11,* 41–63.

Tuma, J. M., & Sobotka, K. R. (1983). Traditional therapies with children. In T. H. Ollendick & M. Hersen (Eds.), *Handbook of child psychopathology.* New York: Plenum.

Turnbull, A. P., Strickland, B. B., & Brantley, J. C. (1982). *Developing and implementing individualized education programs.* Columbus, OH: Merrill.

Turnbull, A. P., & Turnbull, H. R. (1986). *Families, professionals, and exceptionality: A special partnership.* Columbus, OH: Merrill.

Twardosz, S., Nordquist, V. M., Simon, R., & Botkin, D. (1983). The effect of group affection activities on the interaction of socially isolate children. *Analysis and Intervention in Developmental Disabilities, 3,* 311–338.

Ullmann, L., & Krasner, L. (1969). *A psychological approach to abnormal behavior.* Englewood Cliffs, NJ: Prentice-Hall.

Underwood, M. (1987). A matter of life or death. *New Jersey School Boards Association: School Leader, 16,* 32–36.

U.S. Department of Education (1984). *Sixth annual report to Congress on the implementation of Public Law 94-142.* Washington, DC: U.S. Government Printing Office.

U.S. Department of Education (1986). *Eighth annual report to Congress on the implementation of Public Law 94-142.* Washington, DC: U. S. Government Printing Office.

Valcante, G. (1986). Educational implications of current research on the syndrome of autism. *Behavioral Disorders, 11,* 131–139.

Varley, C. K. (1984). Diet and the behavior of children with attention deficit disorder. *Journal of the American Academy of Child Psychiatry, 23,* 182–185.

Varni, J. W., & Henker, B. (1979). A self-regulation approach to the treatment of three hyperactive boys. *Child Behavior Therapy, 1,* 171–192.

Vivian, D., Fischel, J. E., & Liebert, R. M. (1986). Effect of "wet nights" on daytime behavior during concurrent treatment of enuresis and conduct problems. *Journal of Behavior Therapy and Experimental Psychiatry, 17,* 301–303.

Volkmar, F. R., & Cohen, D. J. (1985). The experience of infantile autism: A first-person account by Tony W. *Journal of Autism and Developmental Disorders, 15,* 47–54.

Von Isser, A., Quay, H. C., & Love, C. T. (1980). Interrelationships among three measures of deviant behavior. *Exceptional Children, 46,* 272–276.

Votel, S. M. (1985). Special education in France for the emotionally/behaviorally disordered as it relates to that of the United States. In S. Braaten, R. B. Rutherford, & W. Evans (Eds.), *Programming for adolescents with behavioral disorders* (Vol. 2). Reston, VA: Council for Children with Behavioral Disorders.

Wagner, M. K. (1968). A case of public masturbation treated by operant conditioning. *Journal of Child Psychology and Psychiatry, 9,* 61–65.

Walk, A. (1964). The pre-history of child psychiatry. *British Journal of Psychiatry, 110,* 754–767.

Walker, E., & Emory, E. (1983). Infants at risk for psychopathology: Offspring of schizophrenic parents. *Child Development, 54,* 1269–1285.

Walker, H. M. (1982). Assessment of behavior disorders in school settings: Outcomes, issues, and recommendations. In M. M. Noel & N. G. Haring (Eds.), *Progress or change: Issues in educating the emotionally disturbed: Vol. 1. Identification and program planning* (pp. 11–42). Seattle: University of Washington.

Walker, H. M. (1983). Application of response cost in school settings: Outcomes, issues, and recommendations. *Exceptional Education Quarterly, 3*(4), 47–55.

Walker, H. M. (1986). The Assessment for Integration into Mainstream Settings (AIMS) assessment system: Rationale, instruments, procedures, and outcomes. *Journal of Clinical Child Psychology, 15,* 55–63.

Walker, H. M., Greenwood, C. R., Hops, H., & Todd, N. M. (1979). Differential effects of reinforcing topographic components of social interaction: Analysis and direct replication. *Behavior Modification, 3,* 291–321.

Walker, H. M., Hops, H., & Greenwood, C. R. (1981). RECESS: Research and development of a behavior management package for remediating social aggression in the school. In P. S. Strain (Ed.), *The utilization of classroom peers as behavior change agents.* New York: Plenum.

Walker, H. M., & McConnell, S. (1988). *The Walker-McConnell Scale of Social Competence and School Adjustment: A Social Skills Rating Scale for Teachers.* Austin, TX: Pro-Ed.

Walker, H. M., McConnell, S., Holmes, D., Todis, B., Walker, J., & Golden, N. (1983). *The Walker social skills curriculum: The ACCEPTS program.* Austin, TX: Pro-Ed.

Walker, H. M., & Rankin, R. (1983). Assessing the behavioral expectations and demands of less restrictive settings. *School Psychology Review, 12,* 274–284.

Walker, H. M., Reavis, H. K., Rhode, G., & Jenson, W. R. (1985). A conceptual model for delivery of behavioral services to behavior disordered children in educational settings. In P. H. Bornstein & A. E. Kazdin (Eds.), *Handbook of clinical behavior therapy with children.* Homewood, IL: Dorsey Press.

Walker, H. M., Severson, H., & Haring, N. (1985). *Standardized screening and identification of behavior disordered pupils in the elementary age range: Rationale, procedures, and guidelines.* Eugene: Center on Human Development, University of Oregon.

Walker, H. M., Severson, H., Stiller, B., Williams, G., Haring, N., Shinn, M., & Todis, B. (1988). Systematic screening of pupils in the elementary age range at risk for behavior disorders: Development and trial testing of a multiple gating model. *Remedial and Special Education, 9*(3), 8–14.

Walker, H. M., Shinn, M. R., O'Neill, R. E., & Ramsey, E. (1987). A longitudinal assessment of the development of antisocial behavior in boys: Rationale, methodology, and first year results. *Remedial and Special Education, 8*(4), 7–16.

Walker, L. J., de Vries, B., & Trevethan, S. D. (1987). Moral stages and moral orientations in real-life and hypothetical dilemmas. *Child Development, 58,* 842–858.

Wallace, B. R. (1975). Negativism in verbal and nonverbal responses of autistic children. *Journal of Abnormal Psychology, 84,* 138–143.

Wallace, G., & Kauffman, J. M. (1986). *Teaching students with learning and behavior problems* (3rd ed.). Columbus, OH: Merrill.

Wallerstein, J. S. (1987). Children of divorce: Report of a ten-year follow-up of early latency-age children. *American Journal of Orthopsychiatry, 57,* 199–211.

Wallis, C. (1985, December 9). Children having children. *Time,* pp. 77–90.

Warboys, L. M., & Shauffer, C. B. (1986). Legal issues in providing special education services to handicapped inmates. *Remedial and Special Education, 7*(3), 34–40.

Warren, R. P., Margaretten, N. C., Pace, N. C., & Foster, A. (1986). Immune abnormalities in patients with autism. *Journal of Autism and Developmental Disorders, 16,* 189–197.

Waters, E., Hay, D. F., & Richters, J. E. (1986). Infant-parent attachment and the origins of prosocial and antisocial behavior. In D. Olweus, J. Block, & M. Radke-Yarrow (Eds.), *Development of antisocial and prosocial behavior: Research, theories, and issues.* New York: Academic Press.

Watkins, C. E., & Schatman, M. E. (1986). Using early recollections in child psychotherapy. *Journal of Child and Adolescent Psychotherapy, 3,* 207–213.

Watt, N. F. (1986). Prevention of schizophrenic disorders. In B. A. Edelstein & L. Michelson (Eds.), *Handbook of prevention.* New York: Plenum.

Watt, N. F., Stolorow, R. D., Lubensky, A. W., & McClelland, D. C. (1970). School adjustment and behavior of children hospitalized for schizophrenia as adults. *American Journal of Orthopsychiatry, 40,* 637–657.

Webster-Stratton, C. (1985). Comparison of abusive and nonabusive families with conduct-disordered children. *American Journal of Orthopsychiatry, 55,* 59–69.

Wechsler, J. A. (1972). *In a darkness.* New York: Norton.

Weinstein, L. (1969). Project Re-ED schools for emotionally disturbed children: Effectiveness as viewed by referring agencies, parents, and teachers. *Exceptional Children, 35,* 703–711.

Weinstein, R. S., Marshall, H. H., Sharp, L., & Botkin, M. (1987). Pygmalion and the student: Age and classroom differences in children's awareness of teacher expectations. *Child Development, 58,* 1079–1093.

Weiss, G., Williams, J. H., Margen, S., Abrams, B., Cann, B., Citron, L. J., Cox, C., McKibben, J., Ogar, D., &

Schulz, S. (1980). Behavioral responses to artificial food colors. *Science, 207,* 1487–1489.

Weissberg, R. P., & Allen, J. P. (1986). Promoting children's social skills and adaptive interpersonal behavior. In B. A. Edelstein & L. Michelson (Eds.), *Handbook of prevention.* New York: Plenum.

Wells, K. C., & Forehand, R. (1985). Conduct and oppositional disorders. In P. H. Bornstein & A. E. Kazdin (Eds.), *Handbook of clinical behavior therapy with children.* Homewood, IL: Dorsey Press.

Wells, K. C., Forehand, R., & Hickey, K. (1977). Effects of a verbal warning and overcorrection on stereotyped and appropriate behaviors. *Journal of Abnormal Child Psychology, 5,* 387–403.

Wenar, C., Ruttenberg, B. A., Kalish-Weiss, B., & Wolf, E. G. (1986). The development of normal and autistic children: A comparative study. *Journal of Autism and Developmental Disorders, 16,* 317–333.

Werry, J. S. (1986a). Biological factors. In H. C. Quay & J. S. Werry (Eds.), *Psychopathological disorders of childhood* (3rd ed.). New York: Wiley.

Werry, J. S. (1986b). Organic and substance use disorders. In H. C. Quay & J. S. Werry (Eds.), *Psychopathological disorders of childhood* (3rd ed.). New York: Wiley.

Werry, J. S. (1986c). Physical illness, symptoms and allied disorders. In H. C. Quay & J. S. Werry (Eds.), *Psychopathological disorders of childhood* (3rd ed.). New York: Wiley.

Werry, J. S., Elkind, G. S., & Reeves, J. C. (1987). Attention deficit, conduct, oppositional, and anxiety disorders in children: III. Laboratory differences. *Journal of Abnormal Child Psychology, 15,* 409–428.

Wesolowski, M. D., & Zawlocki, R. J. (1985). Stereotyped movement disorders. In P. H. Bornstein & A. E. Kazdin (Eds.), *Handbook of clinical behavior therapy with children.* Homewood, IL: Dorsey Press.

Wetzel, R. (1966). Use of behavioral techniques in a case of compulsive stealing. *Journal of Consulting Psychology, 30,* 367–374.

Whalen, C. K. (1983). Hyperactivity, learning problems, and the attention deficit disorders. In T. H. Ollendick & M. Hersen (Eds.), *Handbook of child psychopathology.* New York: Plenum.

Whalen, C. K., & Henker, B. (Eds.). (1980a). *Hyperactive children: The social ecology of identification and treatment.* New York: Academic Press.

Whalen, C. K., & Henker, B. (1980b). The social ecology of psychostimulant treatment: A model for conceptual and empirical analysis. In C. K. Whalen & B. Henker (Eds.), *Hyperactive children: The social ecology of identification and treatment.* New York: Academic Press.

Whalen, C. K., Henker, B., Dotemoto, S., & Hinshaw, S. P. (1983). Child and adolescent perceptions of normal and atypical peers. *Child Development, 54,* 1588–1598.

Whelan, R. J. (1963). Educating emotionally disturbed children: Reflections upon educational methods and therapeutic processes. *Forum for Residential Therapy, 1,* 9–14.

Whelan, R. J. (1966). The relevance of behavior modification procedures for teachers of emotionally disturbed children. In P. Knoblock (Ed.), *Intervention approaches in educating emotionally disturbed children.* Syracuse, NY: Syracuse University Press.

Whelan, R. J. (1974). Richard J. Whelan. In J. M. Kauffman & C. D. Lewis (Eds.), *Teaching children with behavior disorders: Personal perspectives.* Columbus, OH: Merrill.

Whelan, R. J., & Gallagher, P. A. (1972). Effective teaching of children with behavior disorders. In N. G. Haring & A. H. Hayden (Eds.), *The improvement of instruction.* Seattle, WA: Special Child Publications.

Whelan, R. J., & Haring, N. G. (1966). Modification and maintenance of behavior through systematic application of consequences. *Exceptional Children, 32,* 281–289.

Wickman, E. K. (1929). *Children's behavior and teachers' attitudes.* New York: The Commonwealth Fund, Division of Publications.

Williams, G. J. (1987). Methods of instruction. In N. G. Haring (Ed.), *Assessing and managing behavior disabilities.* Seattle: University of Washington Press.

Williams, R. L. M. (1985). Children's stealing: A review of theft-control procedures for parents and teachers. *Remedial and Special Education, 6*(2), 17–23.

Willis, D. J., Swanson, B. M., & Walker, C. E. (1983). Etiological factors. In T. H. Ollendick & M. Hersen (Eds.), *Handbook of child psychopathology.* New York: Plenum.

Winterling, V., Dunlap, G., & O'Neill, R. E. (1987). The influence of task variation on the aberrant behaviors of autistic students. *Education and Treatment of Children, 10,* 105–119.

Wolery, M., Kirk, K., & Gast, D. L. (1985). Stereotypic behavior as a reinforcer: Effects and side effects. *Journal of Autism and Developmental Disorders, 15,* 149–161.

Wolf, M. M. (1978). Social validity: The case for subjective measurement or how applied behavior analysis is finding its heart. *Journal of Applied Behavior Analysis, 11,* 203–214.

Wolf, M. M., Braukmann, C. J., & Ramp, K. A. (1987). Serious delinquent behavior as part of a significantly handicapping condition: Cures and supportive environments. *Journal of Applied Behavior Analysis, 20,* 347–359.

Wolf, M. M., Risley, T. R., & Mees, H. (1964). Application of operant conditioning techniques to the behavior problems of an autistic child. *Behavior Research and Therapy, 3,* 305–312.

Wolford, B. I. (1983). Correctional education and special education—an emerging partnership; or "Born to lose." In R. B. Rutherford (Ed.), *Monograph in behavioral disorders.* Reston, VA: Council for Exceptional Children.

Wolford, B. I. (1987). Correctional education: Training and education opportunities for delinquent and criminal offenders. In C. M. Nelson, R. B. Rutherford, & B. I. Wolford (Eds.), *Special education in the criminal justice system.* Columbus, OH: Merrill.

Wolpe, J. (1975). Laboratory-derived clinical methods of deconditioning anxiety. In T. Thompson & W. S. Dockens (Eds.), *Applications of behavior modification.* New York: Academic Press.

Wong, M. R. (1979). Drug abuse and prevention in special education students. In D. Cullinan & M. H. Epstein (Eds.), *Special education for adolescents: Issues and perspectives.* Columbus, OH: Merrill

Wood, F. H. (1987a). Issues in the education of behaviorally disordered students. In R. B. Rutherford, C. M. Nelson, & S. R. Forness (Eds.), *Severe behavior disorders of children and youth* (pp. 15–26). Boston: College Hill.

Wood, F. H. (1987b). Special education law and correctional education. In C. M. Nelson, R. B. Rutherford, & B. I. Wolford (Eds.), *Special education in the criminal justice system.* Columbus, OH: Merrill.

Wood, F. H., & Braaten, S. (1983). Developing guidelines for the use of punishing interventions in the schools. *Exceptional Education Quarterly, 3*(4), 68–75.

Wood, F. H., & Lakin, C. (1979). Defining emotionally disturbed/behavior disordered populations for research purposes. In F. H. Wood & C. Lakin (Eds.), *Disturbing, disordered, or disturbed? Perspectives on the definition of problem behavior in educational settings* (pp. 29–48). Minneapolis: Advanced Training Institute, Department of Psychoeducational Studies, University of Minnesota.

Wood, F. H., Smith, C. R., & Grimes, J. (Eds.). (1985). *The Iowa assessment model in behavioral disorders: A training manual.* Des Moines: Iowa Department of Public Instruction.

Wooden, W. S., & Berkey, M. L. (1984). *Children and arson: America's middle class nightmare.* New York: Plenum.

Worobey, J. (1986). Convergence among assessments of temperament in the first month. *Child Development, 57,* 47–55.

Wright, W. G. (1967). The Bellevue Psychiatric Hospital School. In P. H. Berkowitz & E. P. Rothman (Eds.), *Public education for disturbed children in New York City.* Springfield, IL: Charles C. Thomas.

Wundheiler, L. N. (1976). "Liberty Boy": The play of a schizophrenic child. *Journal of the American Academy of Child Psychiatry, 15,* 475–490.

Yates, A. (1970). *Behavior Therapy.* New York: Wiley.

Younger, A. J., & Boyko, K. A. (1987). Aggression and withdrawal as social schemas underlying children's peer perceptions. *Child Development, 58,* 1094–1100.

Ysseldyke, J. E., & Foster, G. G. (1978). Bias in teachers' observations of emotionally disturbed and learning disabled children. *Exceptional Children, 44,* 613–615.

Zabel, M. K. (1986). Timeout use with behaviorally disordered students. *Behavioral Disorders, 12,* 15–21.

Zentall, S. S. (1975). Optimal stimulation as a theoretical basis of hyperactivity. *American Journal of Orthopsychiatry, 45,* 547–563.

Zentall, S. S. (1979). Effects of environmental stimulation on behavior as a function of type of behavior disorder. *Behavioral Disorders, 5,* 19–29.

Zentall, S. S. (1983a). Effects of psychotropic drugs on the behavior of preacademic children. *Topics in Early Childhood Special Education, 3*(3), 29–39.

Zentall, S. S. (1983b). Learning environments: A review of physical and temporal factors. *Exceptional Education Quarterly, 4*(2), 90–115.

Zentall, S. S., & Zentall, T. R. (1983). Optimal stimulation: A model of disordered activity and performance in normal and deviant children. *Psychological Bulletin, 94,* 446–471.

Zimmerman, D. (1983). Moral education. In A. P. Goldstein (Ed.), *Prevention and control of aggression*. New York: Pergamon.

Zimmerman, J., & Zimmerman, E. (1962). The alteration of behavior in a special class situation. *Journal of the Experimental Analysis of Behavior, 5,* 59–60.

Zionts, P. (1985). *Teaching disturbed and disturbing students*. Austin, TX: Pro-Ed.

Zirpoli, T. J. (1986). Child abuse and children with handicaps. *Remedial and Special Education, 7*(2), 39–48.

Zirpoli, T. J., & Bell, R. Q. (1987). Unresponsiveness in children with severe disabilities: Potential effects on parent-child interactions. *The Exceptional Child, 34,* 31–40.

Zirpoli, T. J., & Lloyd, J. W. (1987). Understanding and managing self-injurious behavior. *Remedial and Special Education, 8*(5), 46–57.

Zucker, K. J., Finegan, J. K., Doering, R. W., & Bradley, S. J. (1984). Two subgroups of gender-problem children. *Archives of Sexual Behavior, 13,* 27–39.

Zuger, B. (1984). Early effeminate behavior in boys: Outcome and significance for homosexuality. *Journal of Nervous and Mental Disease, 172,* 90–97.

Name Index

Beck, M. A., 65, 81
Becker, W. C., 171, 174
Beers, C. W., 58, 73
Belcher, R., 381
Bell, R. Q., 5, 164–66
Bellack, A. S., 335, 336
Bemis, K. M., 347
Bender, L., 61, 73
Bentzen, F., 63, 67, 73, 250
Berg, I., 296
Bergman, P., 61
Berkey, M. L., 295
Berkowitz, L., 13, 268
Berkowitz, P. H., 12, 48, 57, 58,
  61, 62, 65, 73, 81, 261, 268
Bernal, J. J., 66
Besalel, V. A., 395
Beschner, G., 324
Bettelheim, B., 62, 63, 73, 81, 267,
  268
Bettes, B. A., 369
Billings, A. G., 175, 360
Binkoff, J. A., 5, 385, 393
Birch, H. G., 52, 93, 147, 154, 155,
  172, 173, 176, 177, 183, 191,
  193, 194
Bird, B. L., 149
Birmingham, B. K., 239
Birnbrauer, J. S., 277
Bisgay, K., 326, 327
Bissinger, C., 345
Blagg, N. R., 343
Blankenship, C. S., 196
Blanton, S., 59
Blatt, B., 30, 49, 53
Blaylock, M., 350
Blechman, E. A., 350
Block, J., 264
Bloom, R. B., 65, 81
Blouin, A. G., 149, 150, 252
Blouin, J. H., 150
Blumenfeld, P. C., 290
Bockoven, J. S., 53, 56, 57
Bodanis, D., 322
Boland, J., 277
Bornstein, P. H., 104, 244, 349,
  365
Bortner, M., 183
Botkin, D., 336, 337
Botkin, M., 194

Bowen, C. E., 202
Bower, E. M., 14, 22–25, 39, 64,
  73, 92, 98, 183, 185, 188, 189
Bower, K. B., 237, 238
Bowers, K. S., 195
Boyko, K. A., 217
Braaten, B., 41, 70, 94, 115
Braaten, S. R., 41, 46, 70, 94, 115,
  277, 279, 280
Bradford, T. S., 349
Bradley, S. J., 351
Brantley, J. C., 116
Brantner, J. P., 279
Braud, L., 251
Braud, W. G., 251
Braukman, C. J., 306, 310, 312–14,
  318
Breaux, A. M., 230
Breit, M., 349
Bremner, R. H., 47, 48, 50, 53, 56,
  59, 257
Brendtro, L. K., 62
Brigham, A., 49, 53, 56
Bristol, M. M., 173, 174, 380
Britten, K. R., 185, 384, 385
Broden, M., 201, 202
Brody, G. H., 175, 345, 361
Bronfenbrenner, U., 213
Bronner, A. F., 59
Brown, C. S., 66
Brown, G. B., 12, 13, 387
Brown, L. L., 95, 98
Brown, R. C., 264
Brown, R. E., 201, 297
Brown, R. T., 236, 244
Bruner, R. L., 251
Brungardt, T. M., 205, 304–6,
  309–11
Bry, B. H., 326, 327
Bryan, D. P., 152
Bryant, B. K., 218
Buehler, R. E., 264
Burbach, H. J., 17, 21
Burke, D., 66, 81
Burke, J. C., 384
Burke, M., 360, 361
Burns, K., 167
Burns, W. J., 167
Bushell, D., 200
Butler, K. G., 385

Butterworth, T., 192, 193, 200,
  257, 296, 314
Bybee, R. W., 314

Cadwell, J., 156
Cairns, B. D., 174, 216
Cairns, R. B., 174, 216
Camara, K. A., 170, 171
Campbell, M., 150, 239, 252, 362,
  381
Campbell, S. B., 20, 21, 93, 143,
  151, 228, 230–35, 239
Cann, B., 149, 233
Cantor, D. S., 147
Cantwell, D. P., 359, 363
Caplan, R. B., 53, 57, 390
Carlson, C. F., 80
Carlson, E. T., 53
Carlson, P. E., 212
Carr, E. G., 5, 257, 272, 385, 393
Cartledge, G., 338
Cataldo, M. F., 149, 345, 393
Cataldo, M. R., 393
Cederblad, M., 220
Center, D. B., 26, 197
Chadwick, W. L., 13
Chamberlain, P., 174, 291, 293
Chandler, M. J., 147, 164–66
Charlop, M. H., 184, 383, 385, 389
Chasnoff, I. J., 167
Chess, S., 52, 93, 147, 154–56,
  172, 173, 176, 177, 191, 193,
  194
Chessman, F. L., 290
Chiodo, J., 347
Chisum, G., 167
Christie, D. J., 251
Christoff, K. A., 339, 340
Christophersen, E. R., 349, 350
Churchill, D. W., 384
Citron, L. J., 149, 233
Clarke-Stewart, A. K., 164
Clifford, M., 187
Cloward, R., 307
Cobb, J. A., 259
Coffey, O. D., 69
Cohen, A. K., 307
Cohen, D. J., 379
Cohen, I. L., 150
Coie, J. D., 216

Farrington, D. P., 111, 213, 216, 218–21, 264
Fauber, R., 360, 361
Faust, J., 360, 361
Favell, J. E., 395
Feinberg, T. L., 358
Feingold, B. F., 80, 149, 251
Feldman, D., 4, 196
Feldman, P., 318
Fenichel, C., 63, 73, 81
Fenske, E. C., 381
Ferinden, W., 349
Fernald, W. E., 52
Feuerstein, M., 147
Ficula, T., 92, 93, 192, 214, 216, 234
Field, T., 334
Finch, A. J., 236
Finch, M., 216, 217, 334–36, 338
Finegan, J. K., 351
Fink, A. H., 64, 74
Finkelstein, R., 358
Finney, J. W., 391
Firestone, P., 152, 233
Firestone, P. B., 387, 388
Fischel, J. E., 349
Fishbein, D., 149
Fizzell, R. L., 82, 315
Fletcher, D., 233
Flippo, J. R., 172, 257, 259, 281
Folstein, S., 145
Forehand, R., 175, 263, 332, 361, 391
Foreyt, J. P., 347
Forness, S. R., 67, 122, 175, 239, 358, 359, 403
Fort, P., 348
Foster, A., 150, 380
Foster, G. G., 195, 196
Foster, H. L., 12
Fox, J. J., 110, 217, 349
Foxx, R. M., 279, 390, 391
Fraleigh, M. J., 177
Frame, C. L., 259, 275, 281, 332
Francis-Williams, J., 147, 157, 232
Franco, D. P., 339, 340
Fredericks, B., 316
Freedman, A. M., 63
Freedman, J., 247
Freeman, R. D., 147
French, N. H., 360, 369, 370

Freud, A., 62, 65, 81
Friedman, A., 324
Friman, P. C., 391
Fritz, G. K., 154
Frostig, M., 60
Fundis, A. T., 334
Fundudis, T., 347
Furnham, A., 348
Furniss, J. M., 264

Gabrielli, W., 142, 143, 146, 174, 262, 310
Gadow, K. D., 214, 239
Gallagher, P. A., 68
Gallimore, R., 297
Gamel, N. N., 70
Gansneder, B., 4, 70, 196
Garbarino, J., 213
Garmezy, N., 142, 162, 189, 220–22
Garner, D. M., 247
Garrison, W. T., 154–56
Gartner, A. F., 81
Gast, D. L., 151, 390
Gauthier, B., 349
Gee, E. G., 349
Gelfand, D. M., 17, 21, 79, 92, 93, 192, 214, 216, 234, 249, 273, 343
Geller, E., 141
George, C., 166
Gerber, M. M., 26, 30, 203, 244, 247, 248, 277, 403
Germann, G., 113, 114
Gershaw, N. J., 217, 271
Gersten, R., 198, 384
Gesten, E. L., 175, 196
Gibbs, J. C., 290
Gibbs, J. T., 210
Gilliam, J. E., 196, 306
Gittelman, R., 150, 239, 240, 381
Glass, C. R., 228
Glenn, T., 385
Glidewell, J. C., 39, 191–93
Golden, N., 217
Goldman, J. A., 149
Goldstein, A. P., 66, 217, 257, 259, 262–64, 270–72, 275, 281, 290, 318
Goldstein, S., 203
Goldston, S. E., 64

Goodall, K., 68
Goodman, J., 247
Goodman, J. T., 233
Goodwin, S. E., 247
Gordon, M., 236
Gottesman, I., 143–45
Grad, G., 348
Graham, P. J., 39
Graubard, P. S., 67, 183, 185
Green, R., 352
Green, W. H., 150, 239, 252, 362, 381
Greenwood, C. R., 64, 335
Greer, R. D., 203
Grenell, M. M., 228
Gresham, F. M., 271
Griest, D. L., 281
Griffin, B. S., 305
Griffin, C. T., 305
Griffith, E. E., 345
Griffiths, W., 39
Grimes, J., 4, 16, 17, 19, 21, 22, 26, 30, 40, 70, 94, 108
Grimm, L. G., 111, 112
Grob, G. N., 53, 57
Grosenick, J. K., 41, 69
Grossman, H., 66, 268
Grumet, G. W., 383
Guetzloe, E., 366, 369, 371, 374
Guirguis, W. R., 185
Gump, P. V., 66
Gunderson, J. G., 163
Guthrie, J. W., 186
Guthrie, R., 146

Hagen, J. W., 247
Hagenhoff, C., 212, 350
Hahn, M. E., 262
Haines, T. H., 59
Hall, R. J., 243, 244, 245, 400
Hall, R. V., 201, 202, 297
Hallahan, D. P., 13, 20, 21, 38, 40, 41, 49, 60, 69, 70, 148, 151, 187, 189, 232, 236, 243–47, 249, 274, 275, 400
Halle, J. W., 393
Hallinan, M. T., 216
Hamilton, D. I., 342, 343
Hamilton, V. L., 290
Hammill, D. D., 95, 104, 110
Hammond, W. A., 57

Subject Index

Achievement
  antisocial behavior and, 189–91
  family influences on, 175–78
  intelligence and, 109–10, 184–85, 189–91
  later adjustment and, 188–91
  of mildly/moderately disturbed, 185
  of severely/profoundly disturbed, 185
  social problems and, 186–87
  television and, 215
Aggression
  assertiveness and, 273
  assessment of, 266
  causes, 167–70, 171–72, 174, 213–18, 261–65
  counter control and, 280–81
  definition, 256
  family coercion in, 166–70, 174
  intervention and education
    psychodynamic, 276–70
    psychoeducational, 270–71
    social learning, 271–77, 281–82

interventions contrasted, 268–69, 282–83
  prevalence, 256
  prevention, 265–66
  punishment and, 169–70, 264, 272, 277–80
  rates of noxious behavior and, 257–59
  school environment and, 193–94
  television and, 213–16, 263–64
American Association on Mental Deficiency, 30
American Orthopsychiatric Association, 60, 73
American Psychiatric Association, 122–25, 231, 351, 358–59. *See also* DSM-III-R.
Anorexia nervosa, 10, 125, 346–48
Antisocial behavior. *See also* Aggression, Conduct disorder.
  covert conduct disorder and, 288–89

overt conduct disorder and, 256
  school failure and, 189–91
Anxiety-withdrawal
  definition, 332–33
  eating disorders, 153, 345–48
  elimination disorders, 348–50
  fears and phobias, 340–43
  obsessions and compulsions, 343–44
  reluctant speech, 345
  school phobia, 342–43
  sexual problems, 350–52
  social ineptitude and, 338–40
  social isolation and, 333–38
  stereotyped movement disorders, 153, 352
Arlington Project, 67, 73
Assessment. *See also* Classification, Evaluation, Screening.
  intervention and, 87
  of anxiety-withdrawal, 332–33, 334–35
  of conduct disorders, covert, 290

473

James M. Kauffman received his B.S. from Goshen College in 1962 and his M.Ed. from Washburn University in 1966, both in elementary education. He has been a general education teacher of students in grades four through eight and a special education teacher of students with behavioral disorders in public schools and at Southard School, the children's division of the Menninger Clinic. He received his Ed.D. in special education from the University of Kansas in 1969. Since 1970, he has been a member of the faculty of the Curry School of Education at the University of Virginia, where he was chairman of the department of special education for four years and associate dean for research for three years. He has been a frequent speaker at professional conferences, the author or coauthor of numerous professional publications, and codirector (with John W. Lloyd) of a federally funded research project (1987–90) to find more effective ways of integrating students with behavioral disorders into general education. In 1988, he was elected to serve as vice president (1988–89), president-elect (1989–90), and president (1990–91) of the Council for Children with Behavioral Disorders.

WE VALUE YOUR OPINION—PLEASE SHARE IT WITH US

Merrill Publishing and our authors are most interested in your reactions to this textbook. Did it serve you well in the course? If it did, what aspects of the text were most helpful? If not, what didn't you like about it? Your comments will help us to write and develop better textbooks. We value your opinions and thank you for your help.

Text Title _____ Edition _____

Author(s) _____

Your Name (optional) _____

Address _____

City _____ State _____ Zip _____

School _____

Course Title _____

Instructor's Name _____

Your Major _____

Your Class Rank _____ Freshman _____ Sophomore _____ Junior _____ Senior

_____ Graduate Student

Were you required to take this course? _____ Required _____ Elective

Length of Course? _____ Quarter _____ Semester

1. Overall, how does this text compare to other texts you've used?

   _____ Superior _____ Better Than Most _____ Average _____ Poor

2. Please rate the text in the following areas:

	Superior	Better Than Most	Average	Poor
Author's Writing Style	_____	_____	_____	_____
Readability	_____	_____	_____	_____
Organization	_____	_____	_____	_____
Accuracy	_____	_____	_____	_____
Layout and Design	_____	_____	_____	_____
Illustrations/Photos/Tables	_____	_____	_____	_____
Examples	_____	_____	_____	_____
Problems/Exercises	_____	_____	_____	_____
Topic Selection	_____	_____	_____	_____
Currentness of Coverage	_____	_____	_____	_____
Explanation of Difficult Concepts	_____	_____	_____	_____
Match-up with Course Coverage	_____	_____	_____	_____
Applications to Real Life	_____	_____	_____	_____

3. Circle those chapters you especially liked:

   1   2   3   4   5   6   7   8   9   10   11   12   13   14   15   16   17   18   19   20

   What was your favorite chapter? _____

   Comments:

4. Circle those chapters you liked least:

   1   2   3   4   5   6   7   8   9   10   11   12   13   14   15   16   17   18   19   20

   What was your least favorite chapter? _____

   Comments:

5. List any chapters your instructor did not assign. _____

6. What topics did your instructor discuss that were not covered in the text?_____

   _____

7. Were you required to buy this book? _____ Yes _____ No

   Did you buy this book new or used? _____ New _____ Used

   If used, how much did you pay? _____

   Do you plan to keep or sell this book? _____ Keep _____ Sell

   If you plan to sell the book, how much do you expect to receive? _____

   Should the instructor continue to assign this book? _____ Yes _____ No

8. Please list any other learning materials you purchased to help you in this course (e.g., study guide, lab manual).

   _____

9. What did you like most about this text? _____

   _____

10. What did you like least about this text? _____

    _____

11. General comments:

    May we quote you in our advertising? _____ Yes _____ No

    Please mail to: Boyd Lane
                      College Division, Research Department
                      Box 508
                      1300 Alum Creek Drive
                      Columbus, Ohio 43216

    Thank you!